eero saarinen

eero saarinen shaping the future

Edited by
Eeva-Liisa Pelkonen
and
Donald Albrecht

with essays by
Donald Albrecht
Mark Coir
Sandy Isenstadt
Reinhold Martin
Will Miller
Eeva-Liisa Pelkonen
Vincent Scully

Yale University Press, New Haven and London

in association with
The Finnish Cultural Institute in New York
The Museum of Finnish Architecture, Helsinki
and
The National Building Museum, Washington, D.C.
with the support of the
Yale University School of Architecture

This book has been published in conjunction with the exhibition *Eero Saarinen: Shaping the Future,* organized by the Finnish Cultural Institute in New York, the Museum of Finnish Architecture, Helsinki, and the National Building Museum, Washington, D.C., with the support of the Yale University School of Architecture.

Kunsthalle Helsinki
October 7–December 6, 2006
The National Museum of Art, Architecture, and Design, Oslo
January 20–March 18, 2007
CIVA, The International Centre for Urbanism, Architecture, and Landscape, Brussels
April 19–September 16, 2007
Cranbrook Academy of Art, Bloomfield Hills, Michigan
November 17, 2007–March 30, 2008
National Building Museum, Washington, D.C.
May 3–August 23, 2008
The Minneapolis Institute of Art and Walker Arts Center
September 14, 2008–January 4, 2009
Mildred Lane Kemper Art Museum, Washington University in St. Louis
January 31–April 26, 2009
Yale University Art Gallery and Yale University School of Architecture
New Haven, Connecticut
Spring 2010

ASSA ABLOY
ASSA ABLOY is the global sponsor of *Eero Saarinen: Shaping the Future.* This publication has been supported by the National Endowment for the Arts and Furthermore: A Program of the J. M. Kaplan Fund.

Designed by Michael Bierut and Jena Sher, Pentagram.

Set in Miller, Eurostile Extended 2, and Galaxie Polaris.

Printed in Singapore by CS Graphics

Front-matter illustrations
frontispiece: Bell Telephone Corporate Laboratories
p. vi: Trans World Airlines Terminal
p. viii: Knoll advertisement for Pedestal tables, graphic design by Herbert Matter
p. xi: David S. Ingalls Hockey Rink
p. xii: Trans World Airlines Terminal

Library of Congress Cataloging-in-Publication Data
Saarinen, Eero, 1910–1961
Eero Saarinen : shaping the future / edited by Eeva-Liisa Pelkonen and Donald Albrecht.
p. cm.
Published in conjunction with an exhibition held in the Helsinki kunsthalle and other venues in Europe and the U.S. 2006–2010.
Includes bibliographical references and index.
ISBN-13: 978-0-300-11282-5 (hardcover : alk. paper)
ISBN-10: 0-300-11282-3 (hardcover : alk. paper)
ISBN-10: 0-9724881-2-X (pbk. : alk. paper)
ISBN-13: 978-0-300-12237-4 (pbk. : alk. paper)
1. Saarinen, Eero, 1910–1961—Exhibitions. I. Pelkonen, Eeva-Liisa. II. Albrecht, Donald. III. Taidehalli (Helsinki, Finland) IV. Title.
NA737.S28A4 2006
720.973—dc22 2006020557

A catalogue record for this book is available from the British Library.

The paper in this book meets the guidelines for permanence and durability of the Committee on Production Guidelines for Book Longevity of the Council on Library Resources.

10 9 8 7 6 5 4 3 2 1

ASSA ABLOY

ASSA ABLOY is honored to be the global sponsor of *Eero Saarinen: Shaping the Future,* and to partner with its distinguished organizers—the Finnish Cultural Institute in New York, the Museum of Finnish Architecture in Helsinki, Finland, and the National Building Museum in Washington, D.C., with the support of the Yale School of Architecture—in its presentation.

Our decision to sponsor the exhibition and related programs was easy, not only because Eero Saarinen connects with our company's Finnish roots, but mostly because we believe architecture creates the foundation and spirit of a community. Architects have the power to connect people by envisioning building designs that facilitate free and safe interactions. ASSA ABLOY strives to unlock the architect's creative vision by offering life-safety and security solutions that encourage freedom without compromising design.

Eero Saarinen is recognized as a master of twentieth-century architecture, as much for what he envisioned and created as for the undeniable impact his work has had and continues to have on architects and architecture to this day.

We hope you are moved and inspired, as we are, by his life and accomplishments.

Sincerely,

Thanasis Molokotos
President
ASSA ABLOY Americas

contents

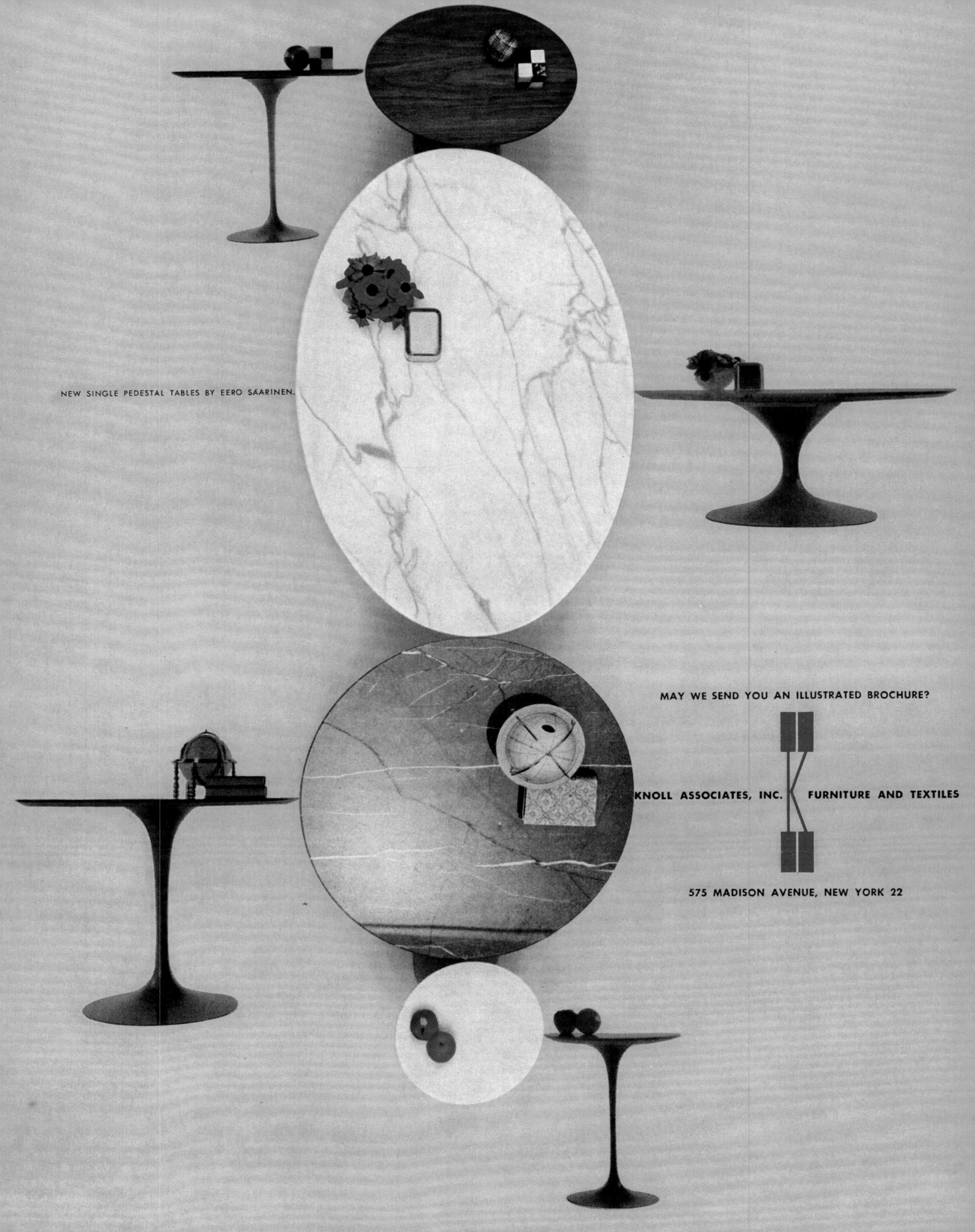

NEW SINGLE PEDESTAL TABLES BY EERO SAARINEN.
MAY WE SEND YOU AN ILLUSTRATED BROCHURE?
KNOLL ASSOCIATES, INC.
FURNITURE AND TEXTILES
575 MADISON AVENUE, NEW YORK 22

foreword

This book and the exhibition it accompanies result from the efforts of four institutions: the Finnish Cultural Institute in New York, the Museum of Finnish Architecture, and the National Building Museum, with the support of the Yale University School of Architecture. When the project was first conceived, there had never been a retrospective of the life and work of Eero Saarinen, one of the most prolific and important architects of the twentieth century. A meeting held in 2000 in New York City established the project's Finnish-American scope. However, Kevin Roche's donation of the Eero Saarinen and Associates office archives in 2002 to the Yale University Library was the project's most important milestone. This donation launched the preliminary phase of the project, which was made possible primarily by two grants from the Getty Foundation: the first was awarded to the Finnish Cultural Institute in New York for research, and the second to Yale University to inventory and conserve the Saarinen collection. For the first time, dozens of scholars and students from Finland and the United States were able to inspect these original drawings, letters, and other rare materials. Seminars devoted to Saarinen were held with Yale undergraduate and graduate students, and previously unpublished and forgotten projects were discovered. A two-day symposium at the Yale School of Architecture in April 2005 offered the public its first encounter with this new research.

The collaborative nature of the project has fostered ties between the two countries that shaped Saarinen's life and work: Finland, where he was born in 1910 and spent his childhood under the guidance of a creative and artistic family, and the United States, to which he and his family emigrated in 1923 and where Saarinen was educated and maintained his professional office.

The launch of the exhibition at the Kunsthalle Helsinki in October 2006 and the publication of this book serve not only to return Saarinen to the center of architectural discourse after more than four decades since his untimely death in 1961, but also to celebrate the fiftieth anniversary of the Museum of Finnish Architecture. The show will travel in Europe and the United States until 2010, the centennial of Saarinen's birth.

The exhibition and publication have greatly benefited from the participation of an honorary committee. We thank Her Excellency Tarja Halonen, President of the Republic of Finland, for acting as the committee's chairwoman. We also want to thank His Excellency Jukka Valtasaari, former Ambassador of Finland to the United States, for his early enthusiasm and continuing support, and the Honorable Earle I. Mack, former Ambassador of the United States to Finland, for his commitment to the Saarinen project. Other members of the honorary committee were Carolyn Schwenker Brody, former chairwoman of the board of the National Building Museum, who also took an active role in the project's progress, as well as Florence Knoll Bassett, Kenneth Frampton, Gloria Jussila Jackson, Markku Komonen, Paavo Lipponen, Riitta Nikula, Terence Riley, Kevin Roche, and Vincent Scully.

We wish to acknowledge the efforts of those who sponsored the project. In addition to the Getty grants, funding for the research was provided by the Finnish Cultural Foundation. The project's generous global sponsor is ASSA ABLOY. Lead funding has been supplied by an anonymous donor, the Finnish Ministry of Education, and Kevin Roche John Dinkeloo and Associates. Additional support has been received from Florence Knoll Bassett, Elise Jaffe and Jeffrey Brown, Agnes Gund, Jeffrey Klein, Earle I. Mack, and Marvin Suomi. The National Endowment for the Arts and Furthermore: A Program of the J. M. Kaplan Fund provided funding for the book.

Exhibitions require artifacts to bring them alive, and we are especially grateful to the many institutions and individuals who agreed to lend to the show and allowed their material to be reproduced in the publication. In addition to the loans from the Museum of Finnish Architecture and the Eero Saarinen Papers at Yale, we acknowledge the Anderson Gallery, Drake University; Archives of American Art, Smithsonian Institution; Centre Canadien d'Architecture/Canadian Centre for Architecture; Cranbrook Archives; Cranbrook Art Museum; Design Museum, Helsinki; Eames Foundation; Robert Galbraith; General Motors and the General Motors Technical Center; Grace Guggenheim; Jefferson National Expansion Memorial, National Park Service; Sean Khorsandi; Knoll International; Library of Congress, Prints and Photographs Division; Oliver Lundquist; Miller Family; Museum of Modern Art, New York; NBC Archives; Ruth Nivola; Ralph Rapson; Susan and Eric Saarinen; Michael Salazar; James Smith; Smithsonian American Art Museum; Ronald Saarinen Swanson; Marko Tandefelt; United States Department of State, OBO Division; Robert Venturi and the University of Pennsylvania Architectural Archives; and the Yale University Art Gallery. Neither the exhibition nor the book would have been complete without the iconic photographs of Balthazar Korab and Ezra Stoller/ESTO.

Last, we wish to acknowledge the efforts of Eeva-Liisa Pelkonen, leader of the research team and publication co-editor, and Donald Albrecht, exhibition curator and publication co-editor. They saw the project through several years of development, ensuring that the resulting superb book and exhibition would do ample justice to Eero Saarinen.

Juulia Kauste Executive Director, Finnish Cultural Institute in New York
Severi Blomstedt Director, Museum of Finnish Architecture
Chase W. Rynd Executive Director, National Building Museum, Washington, D.C.
Robert A. M. Stern Dean, Yale University School of Architecture

YALE VISITOR

acknowledgments

The Eero Saarinen exhibition and research project would not have been possible without two key events: Kevin Roche's donation in 2002 of the Saarinen office archives to Yale University, and the Getty Foundation's award to the Finnish Cultural Institute in New York of a generous grant that allowed Finnish and American scholars and curators led by Eeva-Liisa Pelkonen to dedicate themselves to the project starting in 2004. This team—Sandy Isenstadt, Pekka Korvenmaa, and Reinhold Martin, as well as Donald Albrecht, Mark Coir, Christopher Monkhouse, Jennifer Komar Olivarez, Susanna Santala, and Timo Tuomi—met four times: at Cranbrook in Bloomfield Hills, Michigan; in Hvitträsk, Saarinen's childhood home outside Helsinki; and twice at Yale University. The Getty grant also subsidized an internal research Web site, created by Michael Barbano and containing nearly two thousand images.

We are grateful to the four organizing institutions and their directors, who guided the project and offered unwavering support and advice: Severi Blomstedt, director of the Museum of Finnish Architecture; Juulia Kauste, executive director of the Finnish Cultural Institute in New York; Chase W. Rynd, executive director of the National Building Museum, Washington, D.C.; and Robert A. M. Stern, dean of the Yale University School of Architecture. Juulia Kauste played a crucial role in coordinating the entire project. Administrative assistance was provided by Magdalena Herrgård, Päivi Matala, Essi Rautiola, and Hanna Suihko. Kristiina Nivari, project coordinator at the Museum of Finnish Architecture, adeptly managed the Finnish constituency of the project and organized a memorable meeting in Hvitträsk.

We want to offer special thanks to Dean Stern for his support of the symposium "Eero Saarinen: Formgiver of 'the American Century'" on April 1 and 2, 2005. Attended by 450 people, the event served as the first public forum presenting the new research that underlies the essays in this book. Jean Sielaff, assistant to Dean Stern, and Jennifer Castellon, events coordinator in the dean's office, contributed to the symposium's success. We also gratefully acknowledge the contributions of all the symposium participants: Barry Bergdoll, Mark Coir, Kurt Forster, Sarah Goldhagen, Sandy Isenstadt, Pekka Korvenmaa, Keith A. Krumwiede, Greg Lynn, Reinhold Martin, Detlef Mertens, Will Miller, Cesar Pelli, Alan J. Plattus, Kevin Roche, Harold Roth, Vincent Scully, Timo Tuomi, Robert Venturi, and Sarah Whiting.

Many others have contributed to the project in various capacities. We have been extremely privileged to share the archive and ideas with a number of scholars who also contributed to the book; they are, in addition to those who participated in the Yale symposium, Leslie S. Edwards, Rosamond Fletcher, Sean Khorsandi, Alexandra Lange, Hélène Lipstadt, Brian Lutz, Thomas Mellins, Michael Rey, and Susanna Santala.

Richard Szary, the Carrie S. Beinecke Director of Manuscripts and Archives and university archivist at the Yale University Library, made the archives accessible to researchers and students. The staff at the Yale archives deserves special recognition: Laura Tatum, archivist of the Eero Saarinen Papers, and Diana Kaplan helped our students and researchers navigate the collection; and Christine Connolly, Michael Frost, Dika Goloweiko-Nussberg, Charmaine Jackson, Cynthia Ostroff, Raman Prasad, and Sandra Stanton patiently accommodated our numerous special orders, which sometimes seemed to fill the entire reading room. We thank Helen Chillman at the Visual Resources Collection of Yale's Arts Library for her assistance in retrieving Saarinen's personal and travel slides. Leslie S. Edwards, archivist of the Cranbrook Archives, conducted critical research on Saarinen's early work, assisted by Mira Burack. In addition, Timo Keinänen and Riku Johansson at the Museum of Finnish Architecture aided us in gathering material about Saarinen's work in Finland; Pepita Ehrnrooth-Jokinen shared details about Eero's life at Hvitträsk; and Michelle Ellicott, Christian Larsen, and Jennifer Tobias unearthed resources about Eero's contacts with the Museum of Modern Art, New York. Michael Vitale, consulting archivist of the American Academy in Rome, provided information about the Saarinens' vacations in Rome. Susan Saarinen kindly answered many questions about her parents.

A number of people who worked with Saarinen shared their memories of these experiences with us: Edna Andrade, Florence Knoll Bassett, Gunnar Birkerts, Robert Burley, Patricia Burley, Spero Daltas, Chris Dinkeloo, Carl Feiss, Edgar Rollins Kimball, Balthazar Korab, Anthony Lumsden, Oliver Lundquist, Donal McLaughlin, Cesar Pelli, the late Warren Platner, David Powrie, Ralph Rapson, Frances Rich, Harold Roth, James Smith, the late Allan Temko, Abba Tor, Robert Venturi, and Lewis Wetzel. Will Miller shared his knowledge about the relationship between his father, J. Irwin Miller, and Eero Saarinen. We are especially grateful for the many hours that Kevin Roche spent with us and other members of the team. We consulted with Peter Papademetriou, and Jayne Merkel kindly shared her book manuscript before its publication in 2005.

The research project was aided by two remarkable Yale students who served as the main researchers. Rosamond Fletcher played an important part in selecting images for the book and the exhibition. Her diligence and perfectionism were crucial for the success of this project. Sean Khorsandi helped put together the project inventory and discovered many previously unknown projects. A passionate researcher, he also worked for the archive on the inventory of the collection. Rosamond's and Sean's excitement carried over to the other research assistants, Nathan Elchert, Marc Guberman, and Frida Rosenberg.

Several other Yale graduate and undergraduate students participated in the seminars on Eero Saarinen taught by Eeva-Liisa Pelkonen and Dean Stern and helped uncover new information and provide new interpretations: Abir Ahmad, Ralph Bagley, Jordan Barr, Nora Bergsten, A. Talley Burns, Sung Ik Cho, Daniel Chung, Adrian Coleman, Kevin Conway, Michael Cook, Nathan Elchert, Peter Feigenbaum, Tala Gharagozlou, Michael Grogan, Marc Guberman, Ashley Heeren, Kirk Henderson, Patrick Hyland, Chimaobi

Izeogu, Matthew Jogan, Sean Khorsandi, Brendan Lee, Christian Nakanaro, Alice Phillips, Columba Gonzalez Quintanilla, Michael Rey, Robert Ringemann, Frida Rosenberg, Gregory Sabotka, Robert Selzer, Andrea Sreshta, Leo Stevens, Jeffrey Stone, Mark Unger, Steve Ybarra, and Esin Yurekli. Bess Williamson, a student of Donald Albrecht's in the Cooper-Hewitt Masters Program in the Decorative Arts, undertook important research in the Aline and Eero Saarinen Papers and the Lilian Swann Saarinen Papers at the Smithsonian Institution's Archives of American Art.

Jack Meyers, assistant to the provost at Yale, as well as Adrianne Gallagher and Monica Robinson of Yale's development office, assisted in the initial stages of fund-raising. We also want to thank Iain Boyd Whyte, special visiting program officer for the Getty Grant Program, for his advice and encouragement. Tiffany Eng and especially Fredrick Wodin oversaw the primary fund-raising efforts, which were aided by Virpi Näsänen in Finland. Ileen Gallagher and her assistant Gerrie Bay Hall organized the exhibition's tour, and Andrea Schwan headed the public relations campaign. Richard Anderman provided expert legal advice.

This volume accompanies the first retrospective exhibition of Eero Saarinen's work, a project that required equal dedication from many people in addition to those already acknowledged. The show was curated by Donald Albrecht. Roy Mänttäri created a superb exhibition design, collaborating with graphic designers Michael Bierut and Jena Sher of Pentagram and with Hannu Hellman as exhibition coordinator at the Museum of Finnish Architecture. Bill Ferehawk, Bill Kubota, and Ed Moore, partners of KDN Films, who are producing a documentary about Saarinen, not only generously shared their interview material with us but also made a special film to be included in the show. Janice Carapellucci created elegant graphic representations of Saarinen buildings for the exhibition and the book. Tina D'Auria, Susan Gail Johnson, and Justina Michaels provided valuable research assistance. Donald Albrecht thanks Natalie Shivers for her editorial advice on his catalogue essay and the exhibition's script. Michael Arnold and Tom Eichbaum produced detailed models. Marko Tandefelt assisted in developing the media component and coordinated the audio-visual technology for the exhibition. John Eberhardt, director of digital media at the Yale School of Architecture, is to be thanked for the success of the digital animations that resulted from the seminar co-taught with Eeva-Liisa Pelkonen. Students whose work is included in the show are Marina Dayton, Ayat Fadaifardt, Karl Mascarenhas, Frank Melendez, Timothy Newton, Andrew Steffen, and Kathryn Stutts. Teaching assistant Thom Moran introduced students to the graphic software used to create the animations.

The exhibition took considerable effort to mount and would not have been possible without the assistance of the National Building Museum, specifically Rosemary deRosa, contract registrar; Cathy Frankel, director of exhibitions; Hank Griffith, exhibitions coordinator; Martin Moeller, senior vice-president for special projects; and Dana Twersky, senior registrar.

This book far exceeds a conventional exhibition catalogue in its scope. We want to thank Patricia Fidler and Michelle Komie of Yale University Press for taking on this ambitious project. We would not have been able to bring it to successful completion without our managing editor, Diana Murphy, and her assistant, Claudia De Palma; it is hard to find equals to their dedication and professionalism. We are grateful to manuscript editor Philip King for his keen eye and close attention. Last but certainly not least, we thank Michael Bierut and Jena Sher, who have designed a book that brilliantly captures the optimism and energy of Eero Saarinen's architecture.

Eeva-Liisa Pelkonen
Donald Albrecht

introduction

Fig. 1 Eero Saarinen and Associates, United States Jefferson National Expansion Memorial, St. Louis, Missouri, under construction, 1965

The iconic, landmark buildings of Eero Saarinen (1910–1961) captured the aspirations and values of mid-twentieth-century America. The swooping concrete vaults of Saarinen's TWA Terminal at John F. Kennedy International Airport (known as Idlewild Airport at the time) in New York thrilled travelers with the glamour of international flight when the building opened in 1962, and served as the gateway to the country's cultural and financial capital. The 630-foot-tall stainless-steel Jefferson National Expansion Memorial, better known as the Gateway Arch, in St. Louis, commemorated America's westward expansion at the very moment the nation was emerging as the world's leading economic and political power, while the twenty-four-building aluminum-and-glass General Motors Technical Center, outside Detroit—heralded as a place "where today meets tomorrow"—bore witness to the power of American industry (figs. 1, 2). Potent expressions of national identity, these and other Saarinen-designed structures helped create the international image of the United States in the post–World War II decades of what Henry R. Luce, the founding publisher of *Time, Fortune,* and *Life* magazines, in 1941 called the American Century.[1]

Saarinen belonged to the so-called second generation of the modern movement, which also included Philip Johnson, Minoru Yamasaki, the team of Wallace K. Harrison and Max Abramovitz, Paul Rudolph, and Edward Durell Stone. While advancing modernism's most revered precepts, such as its emphasis on new construction technologies, these architects turned away from its abstraction and formal constraints in search of variety and visual effects. Saarinen's facilities for General Motors (figs. 3, 4), Bell Laboratories, and IBM took Ludwig Mies van der Rohe's simple, rectilinear volumes of muted colors in new and surprising directions by adding vivid hues and exuberant details. In his designs for the David S. Ingalls Hockey Rink at Yale University and the Dulles International Airport terminal outside Washington, D.C. (figs. 5, 6), Saarinen gave structure an expressive dimension, while Yale's concrete-and-

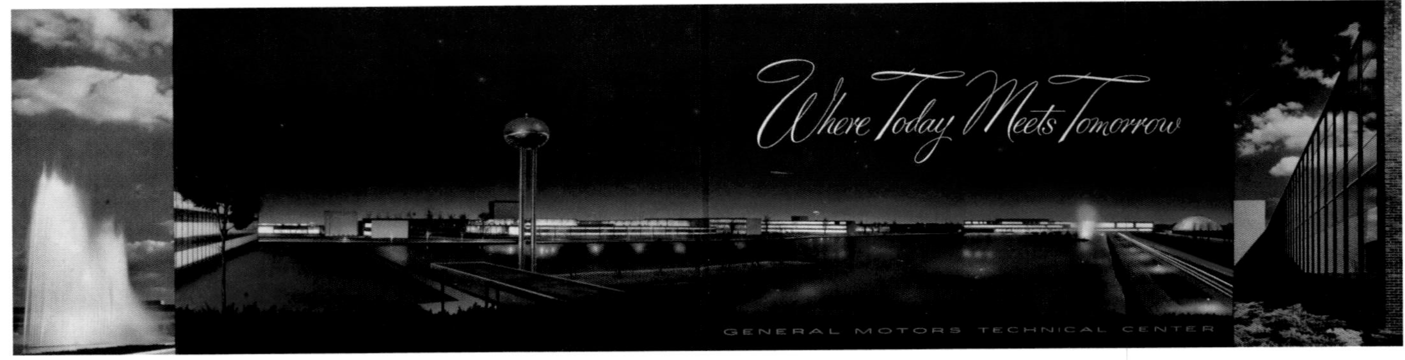

Fig. 2 "Where Today Meets Tomorrow," company brochure for General Motors Technical Center, ca. 1956

stone Morse and Stiles Colleges, which pioneered a new technique for making masonry walls without masons, were frankly historicist and deliberately contextual, drawing on images of medieval Italian hill towns as modern equivalents to the university's neo-Gothic buildings (fig. 7). Searching for a richer and more varied modern architecture, one that he said would expand "our vocabulary beyond the measly ABC," Saarinen never developed a signature style.[2]

From the 1930s onward Saarinen helped introduce modern architecture to the mainstream of American practice through his buildings and, even more important, competition schemes, many of them done in partnership with his father, Eliel (1873–1950). The most prominent of his competition submissions was for the Smithsonian Gallery of Art in Washington, D.C. It featured an elegant composition of low structures grouped around a reflecting pool to be built directly across the Mall from John Russell Pope's classical National Gallery of Art. Eero's individual breakthrough, however, came with the St. Louis competition, which he won in 1948, besting his father with a shining metal arch that was a dramatic pinnacle of the era's search for modern monumental expression.

Working on his own from 1950 until his untimely death in 1961, Saarinen became one of the most prolific practitioners of his time. His office in Bloomfield Hills, Michigan, grew rapidly in the early 1950s and within a decade employed more than a hundred architects from around the world. Throughout this period, Saarinen proved he had an eye for talent; his success can in part be attributed to his brilliant collaborators. John Dinkeloo led the production department and was responsible for many of the firm's technical and material innovations, from curtain walls to glazed bricks, for which the office was famous. Kevin Roche was Saarinen's close collaborator in design, and Joseph N. Lacy managed the business side of the practice, which attracted other talents including Gunnar Birkerts, Glen Paulsen, Cesar Pelli, Warren Platner, Harold Roth, and Robert Venturi.

In the 1950s Eero Saarinen and Associates served clients who made up a who's who of midcentury America, including government officials, university presidents, and business leaders. For corporate clients like Thomas J. Watson, Jr., of IBM, and Frank Stanton of CBS, leaders in the new technologies of computers and television, respectively, the firm deployed equally progressive technologies—zippered-in neoprene gasket windows, mirrored glass, ultra-thin metal walls. William A. Hewitt, CEO of the tractor maker Deere and Company, admired the Cor-Ten steel that Saarinen chose for his company's headquarters because it communicated a rugged midwestern ethos that resonated with the manufacturer's clientele of farmers. Innovative university presidents, such as A. Whitney Griswold of Yale, supported Saarinen's fusion of new forms and historical allusions for their time-honored campuses because they wanted to create an image that blended tradition and innovation. For the midwestern banker and businessman J. Irwin Miller, a man of exceptional vision and broad interests, Saarinen built a bank, a church, a summer retreat, and a private house with a formal garden that *Architectural Forum* heralded as "a contemporary Palladian villa" (fig. 8).[3]

Fig. 3 Eero Saarinen and Associates, General Motors Technical Center, Warren, Michigan, 1948–56

Fig. 4 General Motors Technical Center, base of water tower and, in background, Styling Dome

Saarinen's clients also profited from the fact that the architect was completely conversant with modern media, garnering extensive press coverage and presaging the contemporary phenomenon of the celebrity architect who designs signature buildings and furniture (fig. 9). Eero's second wife, Aline B. Saarinen (formerly Louchheim), was employed as an art critic for the *New York Times* before she married Saarinen and became his close professional confidant and public relations adviser (fig. 10). Throughout the 1950s, Saarinen's buildings were widely covered in the popular and the professional press, even during their construction phases. *Harper's Bazaar, Look,* the *New York Times Magazine, Playboy,* and *Vogue* heralded Saarinen as the most important architect of his era, in terms of both success and artistic genius. Supporters included the Museum of Modern Art, whose exhibitions and publications first brought him critical acclaim.[4]

The extensive praise lavished by the professional press reveals another reason why so many of Saarinen's buildings became so widely appreciated: they lent themselves to literal and metaphoric readings and were more accessible to the layman than most modern architecture. *Architectural Forum* dubbed the Ingalls Rink "Yale's Viking vessel" and the TWA Terminal "the concrete bird." Saarinen further captured the popular imagination by producing the most technologically advanced buildings of the time. The IBM Manufacturing and Training Facility in Rochester, Minnesota, utilized the world's thinnest curtain wall, measuring only five-sixteenths of an inch thick. Deere's administrative center boasted the first architectural use of Cor-Ten steel, while the Milwaukee War Memorial featured the world's longest cantilevers. Saarinen was a man of superlatives. In 1962 *Architectural Forum* praised the Bell Labs for being "the biggest mirror ever."[5]

The press also made much of the fact that Eero was the son of a famous architect: "Now Saarinen the Son," heralded the *New York Times Magazine* in 1953. From then on articles about Saarinen always told the story of the father, his phenomenal career in his native Finland, the critical acclaim of his second-prize-winning entry to the Chicago Tribune competition, the family's immigration to the United States in 1923, and the creation of the artistic colony Cranbrook, in Bloomfield Hills, Michigan, which Eliel designed and presided over from 1924 to 1941.

Although Eero was Finnish-born to Finnish parents, the popular media consistently presented him as a quintessentially American architect forging a quintessentially American modernism. John Anderson's 1961 article "Designs for Living" in *Playboy* typifies the contemporary view: "Exuberance, finesse, and high imagination characterize U.S. furniture design today. For the crusading era of modern is over. . . . Early modern thrived on dogma ('Form Follows Function!,' 'Less is More!,' 'Structure is Beauty!') that rivaled Milton in Puritan passion. . . . Today design is more likely to reflect great good spirits than profound philosophies; to relish shapely contours rather than 'honest' structure; to pride itself more highly on elegance than earnestness."[6]

The postwar embrace of Anderson's "great good spirits" was manifest not only in the furniture designed by the second generation of modern architects, but also in their buildings. The contrast between austerity and luxury is perhaps nowhere as clear as in the way Saarinen and his generation responded to Mies's highly abstract classicism. Saarinen's GM Tech Center and Gordon Bunshaft's Lever House (1952) exemplified this trend: the second generation of American architects turned their attention to fine detailing, color and lighting effects, and even outlandish technological wizardry just for fun, as in the motorized tables and the streamlined wooden cabinetry in the office of GM chief of design Harley Earl. The sensuousness and exuberance of midcentury modernism culminated in the decorative classicism of Johnson, Stone, Harrison and Abramovitz, and Yamasaki, whose delicate tiptoeing arches led critics, including Reyner Banham, to dub it modernism's "Ballet School."[7]

Saarinen's diverse work, from the sculptural TWA Terminal to the historicist Morse and Stiles Colleges, made him a central figure in this search

Fig. 5 Eero Saarinen and Associates, Dulles International Airport, Chantilly, Virginia, 1958–63

for new architectural expressions and one of the most controversial architects of his time. Historians of the modern movement, particularly Europeans, were consistently less kind to Saarinen than the popular press. Bruno Zevi, for example, commenting in 1956 on the newly finished buildings at MIT—the Kresge Chapel and Auditorium—denounced Saarinen as a mannerist architect who contributed to the decline of modern architecture by breaking off from the form-follows-function rule. Indeed, Saarinen's even more overt embrace of historicism in the U.S. Chancellery Building in London and Morse and Stiles Colleges dealt the final blow to his reputation as a modernist. After seeing the Yale colleges under construction in 1962, Banham did not hide his disgust, exclaiming: "Yale is a very sick place!" He later reversed his verdict, viewing Saarinen as the perfect ad-man, able to create a "style for the job," that is, an image to suit each client's needs. Those who believed in the modern project of social change based on the Enlightenment ideal of social and technological progress were hardly convinced. One of Saarinen's harshest critics was Vincent Scully, the eminent American architectural historian, who found the architect's work "curiously lunar and remote" and famously exclaimed that the Yale hockey rink "embodied a good deal that was wrong with American architecture in the mid-1950s: exhibitionism, structural pretension, self-defeating urbanistic arrogance."[8]

Saarinen's death at age fifty-one cut off his career in the middle of its development; clearly, his work could not evolve nor could he respond to his critics, and he soon disappeared from architectural consciousness. Until recently, only two monographs on Saarinen had been published: Allan Temko's *Eero Saarinen* (1962) and Rupert Spade's book of the same title (1972). Indeed, Saarinen may be the least-known famous architect of the twentieth century, as many major surveys of modern architecture mention him only in passing. The index of Kenneth Frampton's *Modern Architecture: A Critical History* (1980) lists the work of the father Eliel and the son Eero under a single heading, "Saarinen, E.," and most of the indicated pages are devoted to the former. Manfredo Tafuri and Francesco Dal Co considered Saarinen's buildings symptomatic of a crisis in modern architecture in general and American modernism in particular. Their *Modern Architecture* (1979) cites his architecture—using the curtain wall as an example—as a prime instance of how American architects of the 1950s first compromised the social and utopian ideals of European modernism by commercializing it, and later tried to correct the situation by introducing formal exuberance into their buildings as a stand-in for meaning.

How best, then, to understand and present the work of this complex and extraordinary figure? To be sure, Saarinen's life provides irresistible material for a biography: the famous son of a famous father, sudden death at the peak of his career, a relentless ambition and passion for work, two wives and many more candidates. His is a life that we all want to take a peek at. A standard monograph would sanctify and celebrate his life as a sequence of meaningful events. His Finnish origins could be used to explain his guts and energy, attributes in which the Finns take pride. His is also the classic American success story: the child of immigrants who makes it big. A psychological reading would locate the source of his success in his strong, artistic mother, Loja, who choreographed Eero's life to the point that she had even a bride, Florence Margaret Schust (later Florence Knoll Bassett), picked out for him.

Yet because Saarinen died when most of his best-known buildings were still in the making, it is difficult to organize his life and work in the conventional chronological order spanning from early to middle to late. Placing the multiple styles in succession is equally difficult because he explored various idioms at once. Indeed, even Saarinen's role in the design and execution of his firm's jobs is complicated in a very modern way. Although clearly in control of all projects, he had to delegate work to others. A conventional emphasis on the individual would undermine the collaborative nature of his practice.

Fig. 6 Dulles International Airport, interior view of an entrance wall

Fig. 7 Eero Saarinen and Associates, Samuel F. B. Morse and Ezra Stiles Colleges, Yale University, New Haven, Connecticut, 1958–62, with Payne Whitney Gymnasium in background

Saarinen and his projects also beg to be considered within larger frameworks than personal biography and monographic chronology. The sheer scale and span of his oeuvre can be understood only against the expansive canvas of post–World War II America, when his clients' efforts and interests were benchmarks of national life and identity, from higher education to automobile culture, air travel, suburbanization, popular forms of entertainment like television, and the newest information technologies. At the same time, Saarinen's stylistic diversity, its much-maligned "style for the job" approach, came to represent the American ideal of an open-ended society of unbounded choice. Saarinen's work was also deeply embedded in the architectural culture of his time. His writings and lectures prove that he chose to engage the era's architectural discourse. Thus, the diversity of his output responded not only to American identity and values, but also to various architectural themes, from the calls for regional modernism to monumental expression to the use of a rich array of historical precedents.

The primary themes of this book and the exhibition it accompanies are framed in the volume's first section, with seven interpretive essays that situate Saarinen and his work in his social, intellectual, and artistic milieu. We begin with an essay by Vincent Scully drawn from the keynote address he delivered at the symposium "Eero Saarinen: Formgiver of 'the American Century,'" held at the Yale School of Architecture on April 1–2, 2005. His goal is to revisit Saarinen's architecture from a more contemporary perspective. "I can certainly neither defend nor disavow my remarks of thirty-some years ago," he writes, noting that he still feels a "twinge of guilt" for his earlier criticisms and striving here for a fresh appraisal.[9] (This publication also includes the transcript of a panel discussion with Saarinen's former colleagues Roche, Roth, Pelli, and Venturi, held during the symposium.)

The next three essays center on Saarinen's social context and are inspired by the ideas that no individual is an island, that architecture is an inherently collaborative process, and that everyone is a product of his or her time. The

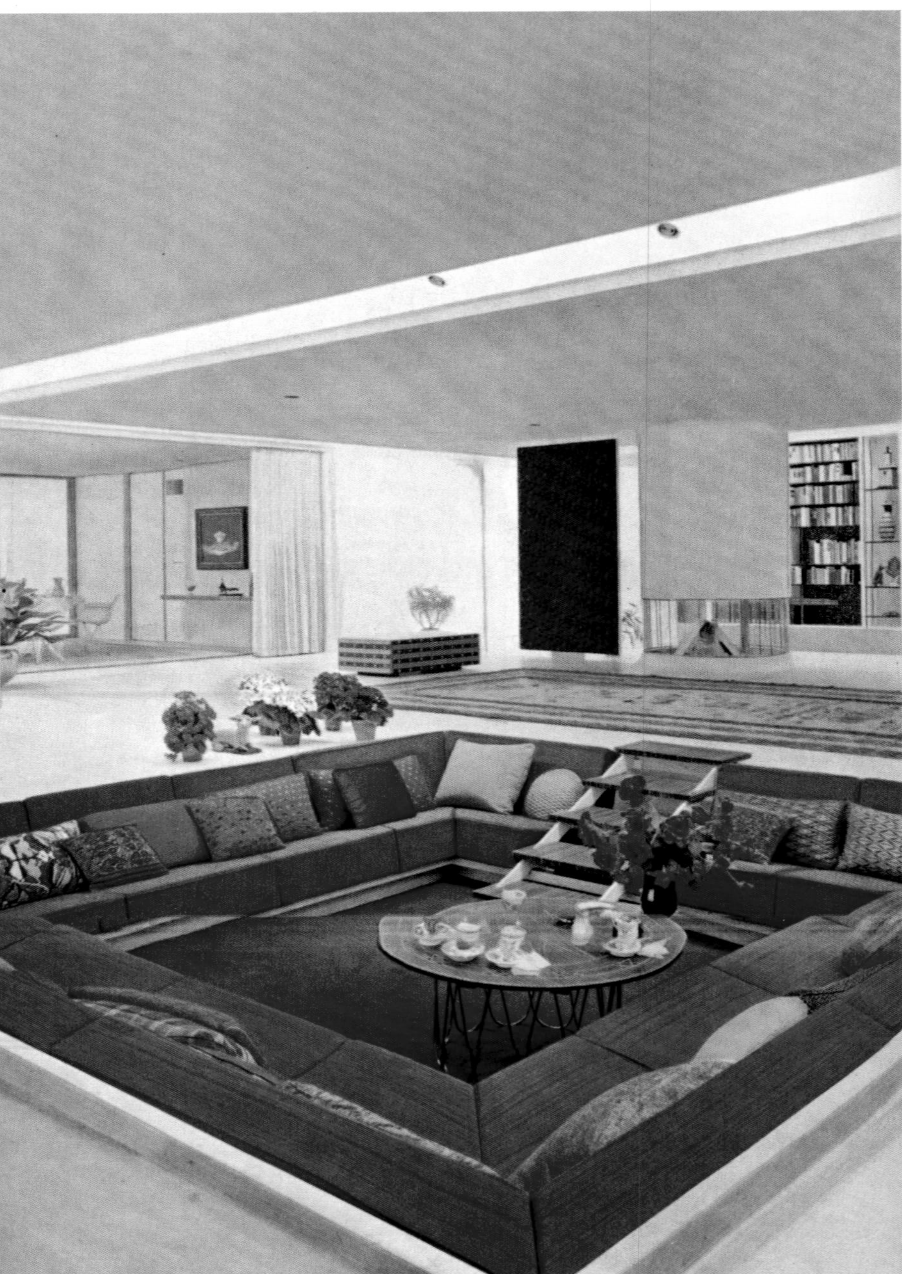

three pieces locate him within a network of clients, friends, family, and colleagues, many of whom belonged to the American cultural and economic elite. Mark Coir's "The Cranbrook Factor" examines Cranbrook's influence on Saarinen's life and career, highlighting Eero's early work with his father and his collaborations and lifelong friendships with Florence Knoll and Charles Eames, who both studied at the Cranbrook Academy of Art. Donald Albrecht's article, "The Clients and Their Architect," focuses on Saarinen's corporate clientele, which included the leading businesses of the nation, and the strategies the architect developed for them. "Eero and Irwin," by Will Miller, the son of one of Saarinen's major clients, J. Irwin Miller, sheds new light on this very particular client-architect relationship, which resulted in five buildings, the first of which was designed by Eliel with Eero as an assistant.

The final three essays in this section single out three themes—materiality, form, and theatricality—that place Saarinen and his work within the intellectual and artistic culture of his era. Reinhold Martin's "What Is a Material?" explores how Saarinen's architecture mediates between nature and culture, material and image. The author shows, for example, that although the buildings have become deeply associated with their materiality, reaching this outcome was

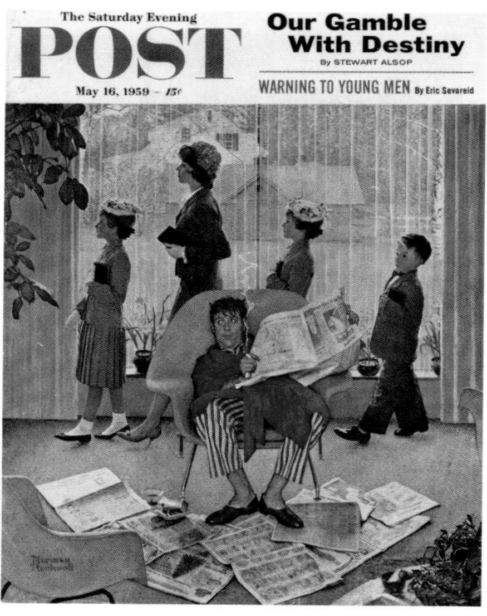

Fig. 8 (left) Eero Saarinen and Associates, Miller House, Columbus, Indiana, 1953–57, conversation pit with textiles by Alexander Girard

Fig. 9 (above) Norman Rockwell, cover of *Saturday Evening Post* featuring Saarinen's Womb chair, May 16, 1959

hardly "natural" but involved negotiation between multiple factors and players, such as unpredictable weathering processes, market forces (the price and availability of the material), and balancing architect's and client's preferences. Structures consisting of curvilinear forms—the Gateway Arch, the Ingalls Hockey Rink, and the TWA Terminal—negotiate between the structural and the formal imperatives. Eeva-Liisa Pelkonen's "The Search for (Communicative) Form" situates Saarinen's projects within the wider discussions about the genesis and meaning of form at the moment when architecture in general and Saarinen's architecture in particular started to distance themselves from the modernist dogma of form following function, structure, and zeitgeist to engage ideas about expression and communication. In his essay "Eero Saarinen's Theater of Form," Sandy Isenstadt uses TWA and GM as examples with which to counter the critics' frequent pejorative claim that Saarinen's buildings looked like stage sets and invited the user to become an actor.

These themes offer a way of approaching the extraordinary material available in Yale University's unparalleled archive and in some twenty other collections, most notably those at Cranbrook. The Yale archive consists of material donated by Saarinen's widow, Aline B. Saarinen, in 1971, as well as Kevin Roche's donation of the Saarinen office archives, now known as the Eero Saarinen Papers, in 2002. It is the largest repository of Saarinen-related material in the world, containing five hundred rolls of drawings and more than a hundred archival boxes of miscellaneous material, from letters to brochures to advertisements. At the beginning of this research project it was still uncatalogued, and it continues to offer a surfeit of surprising finds. The majority of the illustrations in this book are drawn from the archives at Yale and Cranbrook.

The Yale archive also allowed us the opportunity to create the second major section of this book: the most complete portfolio of Saarinen projects to date. Whereas the longer interpretive essays in the first part of the book discuss only a small portion of Saarinen's oeuvre, the Project Portfolio presents a chronological survey of more than one hundred projects, far exceeding those identified and included in previously published monographs. In addition to this survey, the portfolio features eleven short essays that discuss individual projects and building types. These analyze the Gateway Arch, the General Motors Technical Center, the Ingalls Rink, the Miller House, and other structures, as well as the general categories of furniture, domestic architecture, churches, corporate headquarters, chancelleries, airports, and campus plans for American colleges and universities.

The archive at Yale contains as well a large number of Saarinen's published and unpublished articles and lectures, and this book also features a sampling of previously unpublished pieces written by him. These works document Saarinen's engagement in the architectural discourse of his time, which centered on the debate about the current state of modern architecture and its future.

Finally, to dispel persistent myths about Saarinen, we have included a detailed narrative chronology of his life and career. Drawing on a multitude of sources, from interviews to private datebooks and letters, the chronology traces diverse personal and professional aspects of Saarinen's life: family, friends, collaborators, clients, education, travel, and critical reception. We hope that some of the new information, for example the facts about Saarinen's education at Yale, will inspire further research.

This book is published at a moment when, after forty years of near complete neglect, Saarinen's life and work are receiving renewed interest from scholars, the public, and a younger generation of architects. The popularity of "midcentury modernism" in the 1990s, for instance, focused attention on Saarinen's house and furniture designs, which have become widely accepted as icons of the period. These include the Entenza and Miller Houses, and the Womb chair and Pedestal furniture, which are still produced by Knoll, Inc. The activities of the international organization Documentation and Conservation of the Modern Movement (DOCOMOMO) have contributed to

Fig. 10 Aline and Eero Saarinen at a party, ca. 1960

the recent appreciation of postwar corporate modernist architecture and support for its preservation, which has extended to Saarinen's work for IBM, GM, and Bell. Reinhold Martin's *The Organizational Complex: Architecture, Media, and Corporate Space* (2003) gave Saarinen's oeuvre relevance for young architecture students and practitioners whose interests include branding, imaging, and cybernetic theory and who move easily between architecture and product design. Jane Loeffler's *Architecture and Diplomacy: Building America's Embassies* (1998) deepened our understanding of Saarinen's chancelleries in London and Oslo by situating them in the context of a larger national building program during the cold war. Two new monographs have also been published: Antonio Román's *Eero Saarinen: An Architecture of Multiplicity* (2003) and Jayne Merkel's *Eero Saarinen* (2005).

This book and exhibition build upon and contribute to the existing scholarship by painting a heterogeneous picture. Instead of attempting to contain Saarinen within a single identifier—Saarinen the lifestyle modernist, corporate architect, or creator of national symbols—they seek to show that aspects of his work coexisted in an ever changing manner. History writing, even when based on the study of primary materials, can be approached in different ways that highlight diverse facets of Saarinen's life and designs, from their social context to their formal attributes.

We are also interested in speculating on how Saarinen's era, a formative one for American modernism, continues to shape contemporary practice. We have been drawn to themes that resonate with today's architecture culture, such as Saarinen's use of new technologies to create innovative form, his embrace of the media, and the collaborative nature of his office. "A generation of architects liberated by the computer," Scully noted in his symposium address, "finds Eero's work compelling." They are fascinated by how Saarinen achieved his extraordinary forms. Greg Lynn, a symposium panelist and a leading architect of the new generation who is known for the complex geometries of his own work, admitted to having been a longtime student of Saarinen. At the age of twenty-one, he recalled, "I went to see all the Saarinen buildings and tried to figure out how TWA was constructed with the rolled surfaces, how the arch was built as a parabolic ellipsoid defined with segments, and the one thing I could not get was drawings and models."[10]

Scully also reminded us that "Eero [was] clearly . . . concerned with human use and meaning." Thus we find it important to consider both Saarinen's forms and the effects and meanings they produced. Discussed together, the formal, technical, and experiential dimensions of his work teach us how architecture helps shape not only the culture of its time but also the culture of future generations.

Notes

1. Henry R. Luce, "The American Century," *Life,* Feb. 17, 1941, 64. Luce exclaimed: "The world of the 20th century, if it is to come to life in any nobility of health and vigor, must be to a significant degree an American century."

2. Eero Saarinen, "Function, Structure, and Beauty," *Architectural Association Journal* 7-8 (July-Aug. 1957), 49.

3. "A Contemporary Palladian Villa," *Architectural Forum,* Dec. 1958, 126.

4. Aline B. Saarinen, "Four Architects Helping to Change the Look of America," *Vogue,* Aug. 1955, 118-21, 149-52; Aline B. Louchheim, "Now Saarinen the Son," *New York Times Magazine,* Apr. 26, 1953, 26-27; "The Maturing Modern," *Time,* July 2, 1956, 50-58; "Eero Saarinen: Second Generation Genius," *Look*, Sept. 20, 1958, 66-68; Robin Boyd, "The Counter-Revolution in Architecture," *Harper's Magazine,* Sept. 1959, 40-48. Saarinen and Charles Eames's furniture designs won first prizes in the Museum of Modern Art's Organic Design in Home Furnishings competition (1940) and were published in Eliot F. Noyes, ed., *Organic Design in Home Furnishings* (New York: Museum of Modern Art, 1941), 10-17; MoMA's exhibition and catalogue *Built in USA, 1932-1944* (1944) heralded the father-and-son team's winning entry to the Smithsonian Gallery of Art competition as a prime example of new monumentality; *Built in USA: The Post-war Years* (1952) was the first to display the General Motors Technical Center; and *Four Buildings: Architecture and Imagery* (1959) celebrated the formal expression of the TWA Terminal. The Metropolitan Museum of Art's show *Form-Givers at Mid-Century* placed Saarinen's by then significant body of work among that of the modern masters.

5. "Yale's Viking Vessel," *Architectural Forum,* Dec. 1958, 105-11; "The Concrete Bird Stands Free," *Architectural Forum,* Dec. 1960, 114-15; "The Biggest Mirror Ever," *Architectural Forum,* Apr. 1967, 33-38.

6. John Anderson, "Designs for Living," *Playboy,* July 1961, 46-52, 108-9.

7. Reyner Banham used the phrase to describe the U.S. Chancellery Building in London in "Monument with Frills," *New Statesman,* Dec. 10, 1960, 618.

8. Bruno Zevi, "Three Critics Discuss M.I.T.'s New Buildings," *Architectural Forum,* Mar. 1956, 157; Reyner Banham, "Morse and Stiles," *New Statesman,* July 13, 1962, 55; Vincent Scully, "Modern Architecture: Toward a Redefinition of Style," *Perspecta* 4 (1957), 7; Vincent Scully, *American Architecture and Urbanism* (New York: Praeger, 1969), 198.

9. See Vincent Scully's essay "Rethinking Saarinen" in this book. Video recordings of the original lecture are available through Manuscripts and Archives, Yale University.

10. Greg Lynn, comments delivered at panel discussion during the symposium "Eero Saarinen: Formgiver of 'the American Century,'" Yale School of Architecture, Apr. 2, 2005. Transcribed from video recordings available through Manuscripts and Archives, Yale University.

reframing saarinen

Vincent Scully

rethinking saarinen

A recent earnest study of Eero Saarinen characterizes the criticism of some of his buildings that I wrote in the 1960s as "derisive" and "even hostile."[1] I'm sorry for that, if it is so, but it is true that at that time most of us, as evangelical modernists, tended to be more categorical and exclusive in our judgments than I for one would be today, and at that time I earnestly believed that the work of Louis I. Kahn and Robert Venturi offered a much better way toward a reasonable future for architecture than Saarinen's did. I saw Kahn as developing a newly integral kind of design in contrast to what I believed then to be Saarinen's stylish packaging of forms (Manfredo Tafuri called them "corporate advertising"—which is pretty much what I thought as well). I also came to regard Venturi's contextualism as releasing architecture from the crushing weight of that Germanic zeitgeist to which Saarinen referred all too often.

I think I wasn't entirely wrong in much of that, but times have changed, as they always do, and today a good part of the architectural profession, liberated by the computer (or unleashed by it), may well regard Eero's more spectacular shapes as heroically conceived and inadequately appreciated precursors of their own: so more sympathetic and even useful to them than Kahn's massive geometries or Venturi's contextual and semiological concerns. That may or may not be true, but some sense of it has surely played a part in inspiring the exhibition and symposium associated with this book, which Eero richly deserves. He was clearly much more, at once more complex and more deeply serious, and more directly concerned with human use and meaning, than I thought he was so many years ago.

But I have asked myself what I can possibly contribute to his revival now. I can certainly neither defend nor disavow my remarks of thirty-some years ago: a fool in the first instance, a poltroon in the second. (Nor do I wish to fall, all too easily, into the trap of the American good guy who wants to make everybody happy, and to speak nothing but good of the dead.) Still, the twinge of guilt is there, as is clear enough in a paragraph about Saarinen I wrote some five years ago in a book about Yale architecture, published only last year:

So by the mid-fifties, Kahn was gone. It was Eero Saarinen who had Griswold's confidence. He was a graduate of Yale and a truly brilliant architect, loved and trusted by his clients in ways foreign to Kahn. His tragically short career was therefore unique, advancing rapidly from success to success like Marlowe's Tamburlaine. His designs from Kennedy to Dulles [I should have had a broader spread there] exemplified what has been called "the style for the job," and each of them evoked a brand new, knock-your-eye-out form coupled with some equally new and spectacular structural device and functional innovation. At the time I did not like Saarinen's buildings very much but I respect and admire them now. They have rather surprisingly worn very well.[2]

I hope that establishes my bona fides as a wimp.

But then I thought of two photographs together, first Eero and his Womb chair, its sculptural shape reminding me that his mother was a sculptor and that Eero himself had studied sculpture in Paris, but that he had in fact chosen to become an architect, like his father. So it was the other photograph that counted for me, Eero and Eliel, Eero and his father—Eliel posed like Oenomaus on the East Pediment at Olympia, very much in command, Eero the dutiful son, all manly and eager to do well, indeed to do good—and suddenly the issue that had engaged the rapt attention of so many of us in 1950, and about which I hadn't thought very much in more than thirty years, came flooding back to mind (fig. 1). That issue was, What does it mean to be an American? What is an American art? Everything in those years around 1950 seemed to contribute to that concern. Henry Luce's idea of "the American Century" set a nationalist, triumphalist tone to the question, but there was a deeper sense that the power and the responsibility were now with us. And what were we? Hence the sudden emergence of American Studies departments all over the country, conspicuously at Yale. And the contemporaries I most respected were reading D. H. Lawrence's magically perceptive *Studies in Classic American Literature* and asking, How does European become American art?[3] And does American art have special and important qualities of its own? In architecture that question was especially cogent; depression and war had destroyed our memory of our urban traditions. We hardly knew what architecture was anymore. We had to invent it, and America, anew. And out of what? Every one of the young architects working in Saarinen's office whom we think of as outstanding architects today, Cesar Pelli, Kevin Roche, Venturi, were consciously or unconsciously involved with that question—as of course was Lou Kahn as well. Every one of them was an immigrant or the son of an immigrant, and if they, how much more Eero himself, whose father was a famous European architect, one who ranked high in what Henry-Russell Hitchcock in 1929 called "The New Tradition in Modern Architecture" (in his book *Modern Architecture: Romanticism and Reintegration*), and whose work seemed to embody, and indeed strove to reflect, the very soul of Finland, that far northern country of lakes and dark forests, high on the edge of Europe, haunted, as in the house where Eero was brought up, by intense folk traditions and, as in Eliel's formidable railroad station in Helsinki, by a history at once violent, somber, and brave. There Eliel worked with all the certainty and power of a man who, as Lawrence might have written, drew strength from the earth where his fathers were buried.

Fig. 1 Eliel and Eero Saarinen at Hvitträsk, ca. 1920

Fig. 2 (pp. 16–17) Eero Saarinen and Associates, General Motors Technical Center, Warren, Michigan, 1948–56, entrance facade of Styling Building

And what about Eero, the son, uprooted from Finland and set down in America in 1923, soon at Cranbrook, where until he was forty years old he worked, as he often said, "in the forms" of his father? And those forms remained as powerful and essentially traditional as those in Finland had been. Most of all, they built a whole campus, one of the few architectural programs in America where an entire physical environment could be shaped. Here it was a Garden City of campus neighborhoods, the boys' school, the girls' school, and the Academy of Art. Eero's lifelong definition of architecture surely arose from that fact. The *Perspecta* of 1961 indeed published his last word on the subject:

I think of architecture as the total of man's man-made physical surroundings. The only thing I leave out is nature. You might say it is the man-made nature. . . . It is the total of everything we have around us, starting with the largest city plan, includes the streets we drive on and the telephone poles and signs, down to the building and house we work and live in and does not end until we consider the chair we sit in and the ash tray we dump our pipe in. . . . So . . . what is the scope of architecture? I would answer it is man's total physical surroundings, outdoors and indoors.

At Cranbrook that architectural environment survived changes of style, as by 1940 the Stripped Classic of the 1930s had begun to take over from the more indigenous vernacular forms. Its presence could still be felt in Eliel and Eero's first overtly "modern" projects together—which means projects more or less in the idiom of what Hitchcock in 1929 had called "the New Pioneers" and he and Philip Johnson named in 1932 the International Style—such as the Smithsonian of 1939 and the Tabernacle Church of Christ in Columbus, Indiana, of 1942. These tentative beginnings were soon focused in America by the coming of the Bauhaus to Harvard and, even more to the point for perceptive young architects, by the iconic presence of Mies van der Rohe on these shores. Out of this two-pronged German invasion the American architect also absorbed the dominant idea of the zeitgeist, which from that time onward was to qualify Eero's previous definition of architecture, sometimes seeming even to weigh it down. It was still the whole environment he believed in, but along with that, he now solemnly wrote that "each age must create its own architecture out of its own technology, and one which is expressive of its own Zeitgeist—the spirit of the time."

The concept of the zeitgeist is as old as modernism. It surfaced in Voltaire, Herder, and Hegel at the very beginning of the modern age. And from the beginning there was a strong sense of cultural determinism involved (a style could be chosen; the zeitgeist imposed itself), a decided totalitarian slant. Herder seems to have thought of it as a mighty demon controlling us all, and Aldous Huxley in 1933 expressed the English view, crying out, "The Zeitgeist is a dismal animal and I wish to heaven we could escape from its clutches."

Whatever the case, the imperative of the zeitgeist became a canon of modernism, and something that a young architect needed enormous intelligence and originality to question. Who says what the spirit of the time is? Must it be bound to technology? In general it was interpreted in architecture as telling the modern architect what he could not do, which was most things. Paradoxically, it also demanded that he be "original." Certainly for Eero, who had been taught by Eliel to trust his emotions and to express them in his work, it seems to have meant finding a way to do so while satisfying the stern demands of the zeitgeist as well. At his boldest he exploited or transcended them; at his feeblest, they crippled or trivialized his work, but in the larger sense, his entire career may be seen as an instinctive attempt to break their bonds and even to escape from the conceptual grip of style itself.

The tensions arising out of that encounter between instinct and received ideology, or conflicting ideologies, did much to shape Eero's architecture in the short crowded eleven years that remained to him after the death of his father in 1950. It was a decade teeming with shapes, all conceived by Eero at what amounted to the same time, and all in building together. They varied spectacularly in kind and, I think we have to say, in quality, and what Saarinen might have learned from them at last we cannot say. Johnson, Kahn, and the others lived on. But Eero died before most of his buildings were completed. It is a sad story and a rather heroic one. In 1961, at the time of his death, Saarinen, for all his achievement, was only beginning to find his way.

At first it was Mies who was his guide, not the American Frank Lloyd Wright, who was consistently snide about Eliel, nor Le Corbusier either, and not primarily the Mies of the houses, as it was for Johnson—but the Mies of IIT: a campus, a drastically modernized and reduced Cranbrook, but one classically conceived. Its hallucinatory symmetry clearly appealed to Saarinen when he took up the program of the General Motors Technical Center outside Detroit

again in the late 1940s and 1950s and on his own, causing him to jettison a much less elegant, if highly streamlined scheme that he and his father had worked out in the previous decade. Fortunate that Mies was there, since the zeitgeist had, as at Cambridge, forbidden symmetry and the creation of traditional urban spaces to Walter Gropius—but clearly not to Mies. His final scheme for IIT, less bold in scale because of the requirements of the site, still shaped what seemed a beautiful classic volume of urban space at a perfectly pedestrian scale.

And it seemed to reintroduce us to the way that cities had always been formed, by simple repetitive buildings shaping a place. It all seemed a miracle of order to us at that time, used as we were to the obsessively asymmetrical demands of the International Style. Indeed almost immediately, Peter Blake in *Architectural Forum*—I, too, and others—began to compare it to the Renaissance, especially to the very first Renaissance square, Piazza Annunziata in Florence. The scale, of course, is different, but we saw the same quality of permanence and timelessness, of something typical, almost beyond style, creating what Venturi came to call "generic" architecture.

On the other hand, no one could compare the General Motors Technical Center to a Renaissance piazza. It is, it seems to me, Eero's first great leap into typically American space. He takes European pedestrian scale, so important to Mies's meticulous detailing, and blows it up to the scale of the automobile, with which, of course, everyone in America was entranced at that time. We were destroying our cities for its free passage and were hailing the urban sprawl that we so deplore today. The General Motors Technical Center is at that scale, and it demanded a different kind of architecture. Mies's was to be experienced on foot, Saarinen's from an automobile, and sometimes from vast distances. So it required, for example, brighter, broader, flashier colors than Mies had used. And where Mies would design each building so that we perceived its whole frame, Saarinen cut across all that to shape big signboards of bright red brick—or even more typically American, of thin screen walls of glass, which covered over the structure behind them (fig. 2). In doing so he earned—in my view of 1960, when I wrote an article to this effect—a place in what I called "The Precisionist Strain in American Architecture." I cite this piece not for any special value it may have, but because it indicates what we were worried about at the time. It seemed to me then that American architecture from the very earliest days tended to clarify, simplify, and thin out the surfaces of its inherited European forms. So the seventeenth-century house soon shears off the frontal gables, covers over with clapboarding whatever timbering may be underneath, and brings the windows right up to the surface, to create a thin, taut weather seal. That survives changes of style into the eighteenth century. And in masonry, especially in brick, the same things are true. The windows are tight to the frontal plane. All the details could be sliced off with a razor. In the 1920s that tendency was encouraged by the International Style, which underlay the achievements of architects like Albert Kahn in the 1930s, in his factories with their walls of glass.

Now in the 1950s Eero and his close friend Gordon Bunshaft, at Connecticut General Life Insurance Company, far out in the exurbs beyond Hartford, Connecticut, were working together to make a wall that was just as thin as possible. The architectural magazines expressed their delight that Eero's wall at General Motors was only two and a half inches thick. But that was soon to be surpassed, spread thinner, much as American architecture as a whole was being spread out across the landscape. Connecticut General especially intended to get its employees out of the city, onto what had recently been farmland, in that eventually terminal sprawl I mentioned above. And General Motors was in every way that American space, stretched out across the landscape, its forms only reflections in glass, hardly there, dematerialized.

All of that culminated at the IBM building in Yorktown Heights, New York, about which the architectural magazines exulted in the fact that the curtain wall had gotten down to five-sixteenths of an inch in thickness. English critics like Reyner Banham, at that time not always sympathetic to any of us, hailed this as a fundamentally American professional achievement, something that no English architectural office could rival. And Allan Temko credited it all to "a brilliant young Irish architect" who had come to America to work with Mies and soon joined Saarinen's office. That, of course, was Kevin Roche. But IBM is much more than that thin wall. It is a kind of archetype illuminating a fundamental truth. We approach by auto, traversing a wide landscape. We come up behind the building. We park. As we go forward on foot, it is all opening out into an arc. We are enclosed in a courtyard which is all masonry, which continues to enclose the laboratories inside, and which only gives way just a few feet behind the long glass screen that swells out on the other side. There is a corridor behind that whole arc, opening to the void beyond, to which it opposes only a reflecting surface. It is much like what was made to happen at Versailles, about which Louis XIV wrote in his manual, *Manière de Montrer les Jardins de Versailles,* printed twice during his reign. Louis tells us we will come first into the court of his father, Louis XIII, the Cour de Marbre, a tightly enclosed space. We pass through it and come out onto the vast Parterre d'Eau, into that great void of Cartesian space that will go on "indefinitely," and through which Louis's vision of the New France can leap across the horizon. The building is merely a screen between old and new worlds. The American building is much the same, less focused than at Versailles, but opening to a vaster, empty arc, and in the end the building becomes almost nothing, merely a way to confront the void. One of the greatest poets of that time understood it all perfectly. He was Wallace Stevens, and he described what he called "The American Sublime" as, "The spirit and space, / The empty spirit / In vacant space."

Yet, while Europeans hailed IBM's achievement, the young American architects of that period instantly turned away from it to something totally different, the ruins of Rome. And American architects like Johnson, Venturi, and Kahn were especially open to Rome, partly because of the important role played by its American Academy. There architects could come to know the great archaeologist—to me the most important of all modern Roman archaeologists—Frank E. Brown of the American Academy and the department of classics at Yale. He taught that Roman architecture was not basically an affair of crass engineering, as it had been written about by almost everybody before, but a poetry of space, of water, columns, and wind blown canopies. He especially loved Hadrian's Villa for all those things, and that unique complex of buildings had also been brought to American attention in 1950, when Eleanor Clark wrote her beautiful book called *Rome and a Villa,* in which she dedicates the chapter on Hadrian's Villa to Brown.[4]

Fig. 3 (opposite) Eero Saarinen and Associates, Kresge Auditorium (left) and Kresge Chapel (right), Massachusetts Institute of Technology, Cambridge, Massachusetts, both 1950–55

Fig. 4 Eero Saarinen and Associates, David S. Ingalls Hockey Rink, Yale University, New Haven, Connecticut, 1958–62, sketch

What about Eero and Rome? It certainly seems to me that in the Kresge Auditorium at MIT he would not produce a dome but wanted a dome shape, preferably in a building that he could also call Miesian, enclosed within a taut plane of glass. Yet we cannot look at his auditorium without seeing that he was obviously thinking of the profile of the very Roman domes preexisting right next to it at MIT (fig. 3). Of course, he had already built a silvery metal dome at General Motors. But this shape is of concrete, which is in the end a Roman material. But Eero's Kresge Chapel is much more directly Roman. It is of brick construction, arched, and the filmmaker Bill Ferehawk has shown me a letter in which Eero tells a friend that he wants his building to evoke Hadrian's Tomb in Rome, the Castel Sant'Angelo, with its cylindrical shape, relieving arches, and rough brick and concrete surface. His chapel employs the Roman oculus as well, which Eero also mentions in the letter. On the other hand, it seems to me that the building is even more intimately related to Hadrian's Villa (for which, I am happy to say, there is no confirming document; it seems a shame to deprecate perception with documentation). I do not know whether Eero even went to the villa. But the very heart of Hadrian's whole group, the so-called Maritime Theater, a sacred circle surrounded by a moat of water, is much like the chapel. Moreover, the undulations in the plan of its interior immediately suggest what Trajan, in an exasperated letter to Hadrian, called his "pumpkins," which he advised Hadrian to go to the villa and plant. These are clearly Hadrian's pumpkin-shaped vaults as we see them in the antechamber of his Piazza d'Oro at the villa. Eero might even have been making a feeble attempt to suggest the curves of the culminating Nymphaeum there. Similar curves are found at Brandeis, as is the oculus.

But these forms cannot help but seem weak indeed in comparison to those of the ruins themselves, and with what Piranesi was able to do with them at the very beginning of the modern age. Surely the whole doctrine of the Sublime was suggested by the awe and terror of these great arches springing underground, with light streaming down on them from above. It is the very quality which Louis Kahn revived in the 1960s when he was able to draw out of Piranesi and the ruins themselves the whole generating power that was, in a basic sense, the beginning of modern architecture—those "primitive beginnings" about which Kahn was always writing. From that point of view, Eero's essays in these

Fig. 5 Eero Saarinen, rendering of Hewitt Quadrangle, Yale University, New Haven, Connecticut, ca. 1950

forms, if that is what they were, seem toylike in character. On the other hand, it also seems clear that they are not what Eero was basically after, not the cryptoporticus or the Roman vault, not that kind of Sublime. Instead, the Ingalls Rink at Yale suggests that he was inspired more by the common tent, the kind of structure that is erected for the county fair, where you might also play hockey later or hold ad hoc mass meetings of any kind.[5]

It is a building about which it is possible to have strong feelings. When we see Eero's early sketches for it, we immediately thank God that he went on and continued to work on the design. The first view of the exterior looks like a wounded stegosaurus that has been banged over the head and is crumpling to its knees (fig. 4). The final stage is much better. It does not crumple, but comes sailing forward like a whale shark gleaning the whole ocean. Rather wonderful. Inside, I once criticized the two-dimensionality of the arch and the cable and wood construction draped from it. But I now think that those qualities are important. It is they that evoke the circus tent, impermanent, propped up overnight by American roustabouts. I compared the result unfavorably to Kenzo Tange's great stadium for the Tokyo Olympics of 1964, which embodies all the power and primitive sense of imminent force that some of the best Japanese architecture has always had. But Eero was after something else. All the teams that have played in the rink have loved it, saying that it was like playing outside. It surely picks up the swoosh and the movement of hockey. And the wood surface is good too. Though always criticized, it enhances that effect of American impermanence and of adaptability to every kind of use.[6]

Other drawings by Eero for Yale that were not available to me a few years ago have now come to light in the archives (fig. 5).[7] None of these proposals, perhaps fortunately, was ever built. But Morse and Stiles Colleges were, and they are another story. They were designed with the contextual sensitivity and concern that were lacking in the other Yale projects, and which fundamentally determined the character of their design. The whole point was that they were to be built between James Gamble Rogers's Art Deco Graduate School tower and the more than Mayoid mass of John Russell Pope's gym across Tower Parkway. Eero's towers were carefully studied to relate to those (fig. 6). It is Eero who said, "I believe very strongly that the single building must be carefully related to the whole and the outdoor spaces it creates . . . the total environment is more important than the single building." None of that concerned Reyner Banham. The colleges caused him to write as follows:

> I have seen one building in the last month that disgusted me at sight, and it still disgusts me after four weeks. . . . The dormitories, organized as two separate "colleges" exhibit the symptoms of a fairly advanced case of that mania for the picturesque . . . that has affected recent academic architecture on both sides of the Atlantic . . . [and] causes an increasing number of returning Europeans to say "Yale is a very sick place."

There's hostility for you. Whatever Banham's complicated reasons for it, I assume that he did not sympathize with the principle of contextuality or have any idea of what was going on here. He would, of course, have been even more annoyed if he had realized that Eero's composition was related to a picturesque view of Italian hill towns, such as San Gimignano, of which there is a famous watercolor by Louis Kahn. I do not have any drawings of those towers by Saarinen, though he apparently did some. Kahn was basing the final form of the Richards Laboratories at the University of Pennsylvania on exactly the same model at exactly the same time, and I will refer to that again in a moment.

Nor does Banham credit the wonderful plan, with its beautiful classical clarity. Here one might question the Italian model Saarinen has chosen, which has the two colleges joining in the center at the lowest part of the space, which then rises outward in a way that members of Saarinen's office have told me was inspired by the Campo of Siena. But beyond that is the lovely hemicycle, which is approached through a central pedestrian street and opens to the gym. Even more apparent here is the passion with which Eero tried to correct what he regarded as the major fault of Rogers's colleges, which was that they were fortified quadrangles that closed New Haven out. The citizens of the town were strictly excluded. So Saarinen opened up the old quadrangles with his major diagonal and encouraged everyone to walk through it. There were to be no gates. Then he died before it was finished, and the Yale administration demanded that gates be installed. Aline Saarinen, Eero's widow, fought them tooth and nail. Finally they agreed that the gates would never be closed. Now they are locked all the time, itself a tragic comment on the changing relationship between Yale and New Haven over the years.

Still, Morse and Stiles pose real problems. Critics at the time were delighted that they had only single rooms, all of different shapes. Eero had in fact jettisoned an ancient Yale tradition that can be traced to Colonel John Trumbull's first drawings of 1791 for Yale's Old Brick Row. These initiated a system consisting of one study and two bedrooms for each unit, and Rogers continued that arrangement in the colleges. It worked very well when we had to double the occupancy of those colleges in the early 1970s, but we had a terrible time with Eero's single rooms. His system was inflexible. Another more serious defect was Eero's inclusion of what he called a "buttery." All the older colleges had wonderful common rooms adjacent to the dining rooms and flooded with light. Eero would have none of them. I suspect that he did not want another large void in his concrete masses. So he replaced the common rooms with the butteries, which were in fact horrid basements, not adjacent to the dining rooms, hardly lighted, and incapable of sustaining any intelligent use. When I was master at Morse College we employed every conceivable device to make the things work. But they don't. Eero had probably gotten the idea (for this "whammo functional innovation") from an obscure document in the archives.[8]

The other issue that came up in Morse and Stiles is that of their material fabric, which ended up looking a good deal like adobe. Eero intended it to be made up of big, gritty, flinty pieces of sharp-edged rock floating in concrete. Here he was clearly thinking contextually, but not very well. Kahn, at the same time, while building his towers at Penn, apparently did not think about the context at all, so he designed an integral structure of precast concrete members, which has always been admired by critics. But Eero, one might say, had a more generous impulse. He wanted to pay his respects to the preexisting masonry

Fig. 6 Eero Saarinen and Associates, Samuel F. B. Morse and Ezra Stiles Colleges, Yale University, New Haven, Connecticut, 1958–62, walkway to Payne Whitney Gymnasium

Fig. 7 Eero Saarinen and Associates, Columbia Broadcasting System, Inc., Building, New York, 1960–65, sketch of early scheme

Fig. 8 Composite panoramic photograph of Trans World Airlines Terminal by Robert Galbraith

buildings that he was trying to get along with. And he had the idea that you could throw the stone into the concrete mix and then hit the half-dry wall with a powerful hydraulic jet to bring out the edges of the stones. But it did not work out that way. How could it? It remained adobe with rocks in it, somewhat evoking Taliesin West.

Banham had something to say about this as well. He wrote: "It is difficult to imagine a more cheap and nasty way of trying to style up concrete to look like something more romantic."

But again, that's not really what Eero was after. Yet it poses a deeper problem. If Eero felt that the traditional masonry was a good thing and he wanted to evoke it in his own building, then why change it? Why sneak up on it from the rear? Is it really better than the original in that way? Would we rather be in Stiles or Morse than in Branford College, say, Rogers's first great work at Yale? If not, why not do it Branford's way, and leave it at that? Eero, of course, would say that the zeitgeist did not permit it. And he might cite economic reasons, dubious at best. No, people who were close to it have assured me again and again that it was not economics, but "the spirit of the times" that was involved. Eero had to invent something; he had to be modern.[9]

But if we are going to question Eero's relation with the zeitgeist, I think we have to be concerned with CBS. As everyone said at the time, the stylistic background for CBS was Mies's Seagram Building, just across town. Still, they are very different things. Seagram's is designed as a slab, which, though set back from Park Avenue, is inflected to define it. CBS is an almost square, freestanding tower. The subtle verticality of the mullions in Mies's scheme is transformed into the strongly exaggerated verticality of the hard, stiff, granite-faced piers of CBS. Again, we can be happy that Saarinen did not build his first drawing. It resembles a tipsy fellow teetering on rubber legs (fig. 7). Here, as in the first drawing for Ingalls, there seems to be the same curiously biomorphic quality that characterizes so many of Eero's early studies. Was he able to sustain that quality in the final design of CBS? It seems instead to become stiff, static, and abstract. We cannot help but compare it with the entry contributed by his father to the Chicago Tribune competition of 1922. The contrast is startling. Eliel's building lifts and burgeons and sets back as it rises, feathering its edges to the sky, like a work of nature itself; CBS is a dried stick, sterile, which we feel

could be broken off halfway through. In 1922, Louis Sullivan, whose skyscrapers were very different from Eliel's, wrote about Eliel's entry, saying that it rose like the earth itself, like a force of earth. And he went on: "The Finnish master-edifice is not a lonely cry in the wilderness, it is a voice, resonant and rich, ringing amidst the wealth and joy of life. In utterance sublime and melodious, it prophesies a time to come, and not so far away, when the wretched and the yearning, the sordid and the fierce, shall escape the bondage and the mania of fixed ideas."

But none of this touched Eero at CBS; he seems fixed in the zeitgeist, and it would never have occurred to him to build something like Eliel's mountain. But if Eliel's building had been built in New York, even in the 1950s, we can be sure it would be one of the city's icons right now. It would have appeared in Rem Koolhaas's *Delirious New York,* swimming with the other beloved skyscrapers of the period in the waters around Manhattan. Eero could not do it because it was not permitted to employ masonry like that anymore, or setbacks, or sculptural mass of that kind. The Museum of Modern Art had condemned the set-back skyscraper long before. How appalling, too, that Eliel's design was not unconnected with the work of Rogers at Yale. Its colossal figures, appearing high up near the ultimate escarpments, are similar to those on Harkness Tower, much maligned in the 1950s but published to considerable acclaim in 1920. Both buildings step back, feathering their ridges like pine trees, rising to the sky.

In fact, Eliel's entry, though it lost in Chicago, came to dominate New York. Eliel won there over the very rival who had beaten him in Chicago: Raymond Hood, who in that same year, 1922, adapted Saarinen's design for his Radiator Building in New York—and became a close friend of Saarinen's thereafter. In fact, Eliel's design, modified by incremental influences, primarily from the Maya, created the great stepped-back skyscrapers of the 1920s and '30s in New York. Of course, after World War II, none of the modern architects could learn from them, because they were clad in masonry and were heavy and richly adorned.[10]

What about Eero? For a while, when he was at Yale in the early 1930s, he was clearly full of the old excitement about skyscrapers, and they come alive in marvelous drawings for which he won prize after prize at the school. One of them seems to reflect the Harold Lloyd movies of the period, wherein Lloyd crawls around on clocks high up in space and the hand drops down and he almost goes with it. There is another drawing which can make us feel that power of the earth that Sullivan hailed in Eliel's design. It moves: we feel the force. But of course Eero had to give up all that and do something more compatible with the abstraction demanded by the zeitgeist. I wonder if that is a partial explanation for the unevenness of his work. Trying always to do the opposite of what he had been educated to do, he could become trivial, fidgety, as in the University of Chicago Law School, or nervously inventive, as in the blocky women's-dormitory-as-fortification of Hill Hall at Penn, with its grotesque fenestration. Worst of all, perhaps, was the U.S. Chancellery Building in London. It's hard not to agree with what the English architects and critics wrote about it at the time. Peter Smithson called it "frozen and pompous," hardly a convincing expression of the great democratic republic for which it was supposed to stand: with its odious details, some of them imitating fortifications, which are, as Banham pointed out, at once crude and inconsequential. The chancellery has to be contrasted with Eero's beautiful company headquarters for John Deere at Moline, Illinois, similar in parti, but beautifully sited, and elegantly detailed with its American stick-style skeleton of steel members. It has always moved me very much, and, heretically from a contextual point of view, I would rather see it as an embodiment of the United States on Grosvenor Square than the embassy as we see it crouched brutishly behind its fortifications there today. Again, though, symbolic government buildings were not Eero's forte at the time.[11]

But what Eero did understand—had always understood—was American space, America's vacant space, and he understood the airport, which best serves it. Two of Eero's greatest designs clearly come out of that understanding of America's continental scale, TWA first of all (fig. 8). I criticized TWA at the time, reacting to the concrete structure choked with steel and questioning the bird imagery when it was the planes that flew. But what Eero was trying to do with those forced forms is much more important from a human point of view. It is to make those of us who are about to fly move calmly and intelligently from the tin-can containers of our automobiles to those other tin cans out there on the field, in order to be shut up in them and projected into empty space. What an irrational series of actions. Anything could happen at any time, and yet we do it all the time, habituated to it though never entirely free of reasonable anxieties. (I suspect that the bravest hero of the Middle Ages could not have been induced to climb into one of those things.) But everything about Eero's TWA Terminal says, you can do it; it is going to be wonderful up there. The beautiful volutes of the plan sweep us up and forward and into space. Out of that humane and simple movement came, it seems to me, Eero's most beautiful drawings.[12] They are Beaux-Arts drawing at its best: symmetrical, classical, swelling out from the very center of an artist whose very life it was. Just so, it sweeps us through the terminal and shows us the flying field through a great wall of glass and then leads us as gently as may be out to the plane. Everything says go forward, have heart, it's possible; and we go. We see the void and are led out to it through restricted corridors like enclosed tubes. Temko believed that the original idea was to leave those pathways open, but I am told that they were always intended to be enclosed. And I think they have to be because, while our view of the field is the true climax, we then need to be changed a little before we go, die a little and be reborn. It is what Jung would have called a death and resurrection archetype. And I suppose it is. It takes this secular act of faith that so many Americans make so often in their lives, this commitment to flight, and transforms it into a sacrament. The first time I flew out of TWA, which I am sorry to say was long after Eero's death, I thanked his shade, and asked his pardon for my blindness.

The same is true at Dulles. What I said about it long ago rings true enough to me still. There is our knock-your-eye-out shape, with its knock-your-eye-out structural innovation. Again, a tent. Here the whammo functional innovation, the people movers, the mobile lounges that took us out from the terminals to the planes. Admittedly, I should never have called them "Afrika Korps troop

Fig. 9 George Caleb Bingham, *The Jolly Flatboatmen*, 1845

carriers." I probably did so because I had seen a photograph of one of them apparently mangling a little airplane. But how wonderful and easy the whole sequence of movement surely is. If we were designing it we would probably think of approaching the lower side and rising up to the field. Eero did the opposite. This was his true government building. So he leads us from Washington's temples to the higher side, the temple itself, a noble and important facade. Then the tent sweeps down behind it as it lifts again, but now more gently, to the sky, marked by the single great tower Eero set out in the empty space. It is the entrance side that states the temple theme, and the lower side that releases us to the air. I once criticized what seemed to me the tentative visual relationship of the cables to the beams. Now, such is the quality of association that I tend almost to see the points of contact as triglyphs in a frieze. Then the ceiling comes calmly down and carries us forward. I deplored the exposed drain at the time. I still regret it, but I am willing to ignore it because of the simple majesty of the movement that takes us out to the carriers and then to the planes. Once more triumphant, we are soon in the sky.

Eero's ultimate monument to American space, the Jefferson Memorial Arch in St. Louis, seizes a piece of that sky to shape its own triumphal arch. I say ultimate, but the story of its design is a long and rather terrible one. The competition for it was held in 1947–48, and word came to the house in Cranbrook that Eliel had won it. It was not for some time that the family learned that it was not he, but the son. It was Eero. That moment must have been one of wrenching liberation for one and of the closing of a door for the other. Surely, the arch itself became a major image of liberation when it was finally completed after Eero's death. As in a painting from 1845 by George Caleb Bingham, *The Jolly Flatboatmen*, where, above the closed European composition, the American raftsman leaps high into the empty sky over the river, so Eero's arch rises over the water, far above the buildings of the city, in particular over the dome of the grand old courthouse down below (fig. 9). We don't care much if it resembles Adalberto Libera's for Mussolini's EUR, though that is much thicker at the base. Eero's arch is not on the Tiber but on the shore of the Mississippi at St. Louis, at the beginning of the West: seen from the East it frames the city, which itself arcs out in plan toward Jefferson's whole Louisiana Purchase beyond it. St. Louis, where the waters of the Mississippi and the Missouri first flow together, just south of their great bend called Portage des Sioux, with one suburb named Florissant and one called Spanish Lake and another Creve Coeur, so recalling what Stephen Vincent Benét, in his epic poem, *John Brown's Body*, of 1928, called, "The black-robed priests who broke their hearts in vain / To make you God and France or God and Spain." They were supplanted, so Benét wrote, by "The homesick men [who] begot high-cheekboned things."

That, of course, was Jefferson himself, who opened the gate to it all. And that is just the way he wanted the French sculptor Houdon to see him in 1789, as an American frontiersman, tall, lanky, lantern-jawed, with a wry frontier wit and narrowed eyes, squinting against the sun out across a whole new world. Jefferson's vision made the continental United States, and what Benét had to say about that can memorialize Eero, who saw it too—it was the vision for which he had abandoned the forms of his father—Eero and the young immigrants who worked beside him:

The homesick men begot high-cheekboned things
Whose wit was whittled with a different sound
And Thames and all the rivers of the kings
Ran into Mississippi and were drowned.

Notes

I am grateful to all the people who have helped me put this talk together from far away: Helen Chillman, Bob Stern and his office, Catherine Lynn, Kevin Roche, Eeva Pelkonen and her seminar and the Eero Saarinen Papers at Yale, and Saarinen's lifelong friend Shu Bassett, once Florence Knoll. But I also think of people whose intimate knowledge of Saarinen's work far surpasses mine: Cesar Pelli, Kevin Roche (again), Bob Venturi, Peter Papademetriou, and the late Allan Temko, whose book of 1962 is still the best and most measured analysis of Saarinen's career. This is in all likelihood true of Jayne Merkel as well, who has a new book on Saarinen, not to mention Bill Ferehawk and his crew, who are making a movie on Saarinen. I'm not sure that he shouldn't be here as well. Indeed, I can't help but feel that Dean Stern, in ruthlessly manipulating my highly developed sense of guilt in order to induce me to present these reflections, was acting less as my friend than as my executioner. I am clearly cast as the villain of this international melodrama.

1. I wrote about Saarinen in several articles and books during the 1950s and 1960s, including the following: "Archetype and Order in Recent American Architecture," *Art in America*, Dec. 1954; "Modern Architecture: Toward a Redefinition of Style," *Perspecta* 4 (1957); *Modern Architecture: The Architecture of Democracy* (New York: George Braziller, 1961); *American Architecture and Urbanism* (New York: Praeger, 1969); "RIBA Discourse 1969: A Search for Principle Between Two Wars," *RIBA Journal* 76 (June 1969).

2. Vincent Scully, Catherine Lynn, Erik Vogt, and Paul Goldberger, *Yale in New Haven: Architecture and Urbanism* (New Haven: Yale University, 2004), 306.

3. Especially my friend the literary critic Leslie Fiedler, then at Montana, and my colleague John McCoubrey at Yale.

4. Philip Johnson, alert to all these things, came upon the villa in 1952, when he was advised to go there. He saw, for example, the small baths with their oval bay and dark vertical void. We note that this is all the opposite of IBM: no glass, no shine, no skin, just brick and concrete construction and what we had hardly ever seen in modern architecture (the zeitgeist rarely allowed them), vaulted volumes of space. Instantly, Johnson transposed it all into thin-planed American terms. He took the oval and its void and transformed it into the entrance pavilion of his synagogue at Port Chester. Inside, the windblown vaults appear on Johnson's own terms.

5. In this connection, there is a letter that was written in 1956 by the members of Yale's history of art department, of which I was one. We wrote it in response to a request for help from Whitney Griswold, which we were not normally used to receiving. It came about because Charles Gage, the treasurer of the university, had reacted to Saarinen's first proposals by circulating the photograph of a hockey rink that had just been built at Cornell, seating twice as many people and costing half as much. Gage asked, why not this? So, Griswold needed to rally support for Eero's extravagant project. Our department was eager, apparently even avid, to supply it. I will not quote much of our letter—I have cited it before many times, but thought it was forever hidden in the archives. It has since been exhumed by the Pelkonen seminar. Among our comments were the following:

"One of our number felt that it would revivify the essential principles of Gothic construction (real Gothic); another felt something of the grandeur and unity of the best Roman architecture. Still another was struck by the delicacy of exterior scale, achieved by the natural curves of the roof—recalling Oriental qualities, and all the more remarkable considering the vast interior space which had to be enclosed. What impressed us all was the character and integrity of principle as carried out with Twentieth-Century means—quite up to date, but never likely to go out of date."

It reads pretty much as nonsense today and shows how confused we all were about everything. Whitney Griswold thanked us profusely, and after that was as rigorous with us as he had always been.

6. For example, we gathered there for our famous mass meeting, at the time of Yale's most stirring cultural caper, the Panther Trial of 1970. You will notice that we directed our attention across the long axis, like Protestants turning a Catholic church sideways. I remember that the revolutionary enthusiasm of the meeting was considerably dampened when one of the Black Panthers—freed from a punitive contempt-of-court decision in New Haven—advised us to go out and get guns and shoot the police. A chill settled over the place. Quite soon some life-and-death issue which I have completely forgotten came up for a vote, which was counted at something like 2,127 for, 2,127 against, and we all accepted it without question; it was the Yale solution. And nothing was done. But good things did come out of Yale's decision to open the campus to the demonstrators who were converging on us from all over the United States and, we were told, were going to set us afire. Kingman Brewster, in his bravest act, said let them come. And we fed them all a terrible gruel of the time called, I think, Familia. Yale did not know how to cook it properly, so that the revolution broke its teeth on raw corn.

7. I remembered from long ago having seen a proposal of Eero's for a building to be placed across the axis of Hillhouse Avenue on Science Hill. I thought that was a bad idea, and, because I had never seen the relevant document, I credited Paul Schweikher with the decision to move his Gibbs Lab to one side, so opening the summit. But it now turns out that it was Eero who more or less designed Gibbs Lab, and moved it to its present location. Hence Johnson was able to make the right decision too, and kept his tower to the left of the summit, allowing the axis of Hillhouse Avenue to go on uninterrupted and opening to the view of East Rock beyond it. Other proposals for the campus that I dimly remembered have also come to light. The Cross Campus proposal seems to me much less generous, much less sympathetic, than Rogers's wider spaces and more richly articulated forms.

I also feared what the tower was going to look like. The whole thing seemed very tight. Even worse, from my point of view, was a project I had never seen before. It was Eero's proposal to complete Hewitt Quadrangle-Beinecke Plaza. It seemed to me he chose the worst possible way to do so, employing a thick slab with a very banal surface. It was both too wide and too long and pushed too far up against both Commons and the Law School, thereby crowding them, and causing me to say the only good word I have ever said in my life about the Beinecke Library, which is that it stays away from both and allows the natural boundaries of the space to shape themselves, and so remains an object within it.

8. Lesley Baier recently discovered in the archive a university catalogue from 1919–20 that describes how, until 1817, Connecticut Hall contained a kind of sutler's store, called a Buttery, where students could buy commissary items and whatnots. Here Eero revived it, but it never worked for its original purpose or any other.

9. Again, we ask if it was worth it? When I was made master by Kingman Brewster in 1969 he did not tell me which college he was going to appoint me to. I knew that Berkeley was open, and possibly Branford as well, and then there was Morse. So I went around and looked at them and was rather shocked to discover in myself that I would much rather be in Branford. It was clearly a much more agreeable environment and came across as a place, not a stage set. (Rudolph called Morse and Stiles "sets for Ivanhoe.") Of course, there are critics today who say that modern architecture should be tough and hard because life is that way. Again, the zeitgeist demands it. But it's difficult for me to agree with that now. As I get older, it makes less and less sense. It seems to me that hard times ought to call up a very different kind of architecture. But Branford is a good deal like Cranbrook, especially the boys' school there, and Eero could not possibly do what his father had done. He had to change it, to invent something.

Later generations of Yale students did not agree with him. The convincing places that Rogers could make were what struck people like Andrés Duany and Elizabeth Plater-Zyberk about the Yale campus. They and their contemporaries of the early 1970s were much more moved by Rogers than by Saarinen, or Rudolph or Kahn. They were ready to embrace a fundamental contextualism employing basic classic and vernacular traditions and familiar forms. On the other hand, we look at Morse and Stiles and say, but that is almost entirely Eero's idea. Eero wants to be a contextualist in Morse and Stiles, but there is something that will not permit him to go all the way. Then somebody out of his office, Robert Venturi, showed very soon that it was not all that difficult to inflect the forms of your building toward the texture, even the style, of the preexisting place, and that it was possible to be closer to Main Street—Main Street being, as Venturi wrote, "almost alright"—than Eero had allowed. Venturi asked what could prevent the architect from making buildings that were clearly modern in every essential way, but which were not only reflective of the preexisting place, but also took formal suggestions from it, so making not simply an individual building, but a place which was better than it was before on its own terms. That is "the style for the job," or perhaps, better, the style for the place. So, for instance, Venturi's Institute for Scientific Information in Philadelphia is on an International Style street teeming with traffic. And that is the kind of building he puts there, enhancing the vehicular velocity of the place with Le Corbusier's *fenêtre en longueur*—in direct contrast with his Tudorish allusions to the preexisting buildings adjacent to Princeton's Wu Hall. Now the principle is not style but context. And, as in the Sainsbury Wing of the National Gallery in Trafalgar Square, that can lead on to the revival of the classical and vernacular traditions as a whole and toward the continued enhancement of our cities in ways that make sense.

10. Nobody of Eero's people whom I know has been more insistent—and consistently so—than Cesar Pelli on the zeitgeist's demand for thin surfaces in modern skyscrapers. But Pelli learned how to build the mountain out of glass, as in the World Financial Center. And he used it to mediate between the intractable towers of the World Trade Center and the older towers of downtown Manhattan, indeed drawing them into a new pyramidal relationship similar to that which the old skyscrapers had formed. Pelli says, touchingly, "I designed them around a mountain, and now the mountain is gone." But when the towers were gone, the solemn bodies of his buildings shaped the void and allowed Daniel Libeskind to envision buildings that could rear back, and mourn, and gesticulate above the fatal site. All that of course deals much more with a set of emotions suggested by Eliel's work than by anything Eero had so far been able to realize—as do, of course, Pelli's highest mountains, his minarets in Kuala Lumpur.

11. Indeed, none of the determinedly "modern" embassies of that period by him or other architects were really very good—with the possible exception of Gropius's in Athens. The program was one of those things (could the zeitgeist be partly right?) that people somehow could not do right at that time. It was hard to know how to present Luce's Imperial America to the world, and it remains so.

12. Shu Bassett has told me that Eero could draw equally well with both hands, and I can remember Lou Kahn standing in front of a blackboard and simultaneously drawing absolutely symmetrical arabesques like these.

Mark Coir

the cranbrook factor

Fig. 1 Wilho Sjöström, portrait of Eliel and Eero Saarinen at Hvitträsk, 1919

Arriving at Cranbrook's doorstep just as the campus was taking shape, Eero Saarinen grew up with the institution, helping along the way to give it form and to establish the foundations of its venerable artistic legacy. Cranbrook, in turn, provided him with a wealth of opportunity—an extraordinary environment in which to ply his creative gifts, support from one of America's great art patrons, daily interaction with some of the most innovative artists of his age, and the freedom to develop his talents at his own pace and on his own terms. These experiences shaped his life in profound ways, as did the friendships he forged in his years at the Cranbrook Academy of Art. Through them, Cranbrook was never far from Saarinen's thoughts and always remained a significant part of his life.

In many respects, Eero's early years at Cranbrook were an extension of the life he had known growing up in Finland. At Hvitträsk, as was true later at Cranbrook, life in the Saarinen household centered on Eliel's architectural practice, so work and domestic activities were always intertwined. Eero and his older sister, Pipsan, interacted with a steady stream of draftsmen and family guests, among them some of the grandest names in Finnish and European cultural circles, who often stayed for protracted visits. Thus, despite Hvitträsk's remoteness, the Saarinens were never at a loss for cultural pleasures or social interaction; the world came to them. In this rarefied environment Eero and Pipsan learned to appreciate the demands and rewards of an artistic life. Through the process, both children acquired an intimate working knowledge of the architectural and design trades at a very young age.[1]

Although Pipsan and Eero always acknowledged their father's role in shaping their lives (fig. 1), their mother, Loja, an accomplished artist in her own right, also paid close attention to their creative and social growth. Perpetuating the gender roles she had been raised with, however, Loja reminded her daughter through example that she had given up her career for more important duties, namely, to raise her children and support her husband. For Eero, or "Poju" (Sonny), who as a toddler made paper octahedrons and dodecahedrons while

Fig. 2 Eliel Saarinen, Cranbrook Academy of Art, model constructed by Eero and Loja Saarinen, 1925

pestering draftsmen with questions, she had nothing but praise. To all, she extolled him as a genius destined for a glorious career in the arts. Pipsan, certainly just as accomplished as her younger brother in her childhood, never received the same praise. Thus, a bond developed between Eero and his mother that had tremendous ramifications in his life. He later claimed that it was his mother and not his father who had urged him into a creative life, and when he did decide to pursue an artistic career, he first gravitated toward his mother's art, sculpture. His introduction to the plastic arts was as a model maker, assisting his mother as she executed finely detailed models of Eliel's projects (fig. 2).[2]

In spite of their worldliness, the Saarinens struggled with assimilating to American life.[3] One of the first to assist them when they arrived in Ann Arbor in the fall of 1923 was J. Robert F. Swanson, a student enrolled in Eliel's architecture studio at the University of Michigan. A handsome, ambitious young man from northern Michigan, Swanson was raised in a Swedish-speaking home and so was able to serve as an interpreter and English instructor to the entire family. The Saarinens appreciated his services, and he soon became a familiar fixture in their household. His elopement with Pipsan in 1926 angered Loja and Eliel, but they came to accept him as a son-in-law and eventually as a business partner.

Of greater consequence to the family while in Ann Arbor was their introduction to the Booth family. George Gough Booth, Michigan's reigning newspaper magnate, was one of the most active art patrons in the country and the primary supporter of the university's architectural program; his youngest son, Henry (or Harry), a student of Eliel's, was Bob Swanson's closest friend. The elder and younger Booths became enamored of Eliel's architectural talents and, through Swanson's encouragement, engaged him to help transform Cranbrook, the Booths' Bloomfield Hills estate, into a magnificent cultural complex with several institutions. The Saarinens moved to Cranbrook in 1925, living in temporary quarters, including Towerknoll, the Swansons' house (fig. 3), while

Fig. 3 Eero Saarinen, woodblock print Christmas card sent by Mr. and Mrs. J. Robert F. Swanson

Fig. 4 The Saarinens and friends at Cranbrook, ca. 1927. From left: Eliel Saarinen, Loja Saarinen, Géza Maroti, Pipsan Saarinen, Eero Saarinen, Leopoldine Maroti, and Stromberg (the Saarinens' housekeeper from Hvitträsk)

Fig. 5 (right) Eero Saarinen, wrought-iron gates at Cranbrook School for Boys, ca. 1929

awaiting construction of their permanent home on campus. Eero attended high school in nearby Birmingham and graduated in February 1929, some six months before the family took up residence in Saarinen House. A bright and popular student, Eero excelled in the arts at school and even won a national soap-carving contest in his junior year, a feat that garnered him local fame.[4]

Eliel's position at Cranbrook afforded an unusual opportunity, underwritten by George Booth, to establish an artistic colony on campus for the purposes of decorating Cranbrook buildings, educating apprentices, and offering products for sale to the public. Eliel immediately called on old family associates, such as Géza Maroti, a Hungarian sculptor who had lived intermittently with the Saarinens for years (fig. 4), and Tor Berglund, a Swedish cabinetmaker, to set up shops on campus.[5] Not letting the opportunity slip by, Loja established Studio Loja Saarinen for the production of handwoven goods. Eliel also looked for ways to involve his children in the decoration of Cranbrook buildings.

Eero's first opportunity to do so arose in his sophomore year in high school, when his father invited him to create several decorative pieces for the Cranbrook School for Boys. He confidently responded by fabricating sculptural tiles, designs for wrought-iron gates (fig. 5), inserts depicting cranes for chairs in the dining hall, the school seal, and several carved-stone pieces, ranging from support columns for a baldachin to a series of grotesque faces for an exterior facade reminiscent of the ones that embellished Gesellius, Lindgren, Saarinen's Pohjola Building in Helsinki. The pieces are notable for their artistry, range of expression, and, in the case of the faces, their subtle humor. Collectively, they make up Eero's first commissions in the United States.[6]

He next turned his attention to Saarinen House and, at his father's invitation, between 1928 and 1930 designed furniture and other items for his parents' bedroom suite (fig. 6): a sterling silver vanity ensemble for his mother, sculptural tiles, chairs, and a handsome bronze bust of his father that soon found a home in the studio alcove. Other pieces of his were added to the residence later, as it underwent refurbishment.[7] In 1929 he departed for eight months of study at the Académie de la Grande Chaumière in Paris.

Impressed by the Saarinens' collective talents, George Booth asked the entire family to work on Kingswood School for Girls, the most thoroughly designed of all the Cranbrook buildings. Eero was newly returned from his sculptural studies in Paris and barely twenty when he received the commission to design most of the school's furniture—altogether hundreds of tables, chairs, sofas, beds, and other pieces (fig. 7). He also contributed designs for leaded-glass windows and sculpted a playful lion lamp and a plinth for the

Fig. 6 Master bedroom at Saarinen House, Cranbrook, ca. 1930. Eero Saarinen designed the furniture and sterling silver vanity ensemble.

Fig. 7 Kingswood School for Girls, office of the headmistress, ca. 1932, with furniture designed by Eero Saarinen

school's lobby, which were fired at Detroit's Pewabic Pottery. Enamored with Eero's accomplishments, Booth gave him something that his father never received at Cranbrook—the rights to his Kingswood furniture designs, as a show of support for his promising career.[8]

Saarinen left for Yale University to study architecture in the autumn of 1931. Despite the rigors of the program's time-honored Beaux-Arts curriculum (which clashed with his father's contemporary approach to architectural education), Eero thrived at Yale, managing to complete four years of study in three, while building friendships with fellow students and piling up prizes in the process. Awarded the coveted Charles Arthur and Margaret Omrod Matcham Traveling Fellowship in 1934, Eero embarked on a lengthy trip to Europe and the Middle East, touring with the Swedish sculptor Carl Milles and American friends before settling into a position in his uncle Jarl Eklund's architectural practice in Helsinki. There Eero gave the city's famous Swedish Theater a contemporary makeover and developed plans for a mixed-use commercial center in the heart of Helsinki that was never built. At his parents' request, he also finalized the construction of the modest residence at Hvitträsk to replace the imposing Armas Lindgren tower, which was destroyed by fire in 1922.[9]

When Eero returned to Cranbrook in the summer of 1936, he found matters much changed. In his absence, his father and Booth had eliminated the arts and crafts studios and reorganized the Cranbrook Academy of Art to encourage the production of contemporary art and design. To ensure its vibrancy, Booth and Saarinen seized on the idea of developing the academy as a small community of creative artists living and working in constant interplay. With the infusion of prominent artists-in-residence, including Milles, who arrived in 1931, and through scholarship offerings to the best and brightest students that could be found, the academy was just beginning to emerge as a forceful presence in the American art scene.[10]

In fact, Saarinen's homecoming heralded a golden epoch in Cranbrook's history. Marianne Strengell, Eero's childhood friend from Finland, and ceramist Maija Grotell, another Finn, arrived to strengthen the faculty, and soon a steady stream of brilliant students began to appear, including Don Albinson, Ben Baldwin, Harry Bertoia, Charles Eames, Ray Kaiser, Ralph Rapson, and Harry Weese.[11] Also among them was Florence Margaret Schust, home from her architectural studies. As a student at Kingswood, she had shown such extraordinary architectural potential that Eliel personally took her under his wing and tutored her in her junior and senior years. Afterward he enrolled her as the youngest student at the academy. Eliel's devotion to her was in part fatherly, for he and Loja had long since come to dote on the orphaned Schust and dared to dream of her as a potential daughter-in-law.[12] Though this never materialized, Eero and Schust's relationship had settled into a close friendship by the late 1930s. After marrying Hans Knoll, she became one of Eero's most ardent patrons through her work at Knoll Associates (fig. 8).

Although students availed themselves of Detroit's attractions, their social lives largely revolved around the academy. Days spent in studios were frequently followed by evening diversions at the Art Club, where students put on dances, skits, and parties (fig. 9), or in faculty houses, where they were introduced to eminent artists and architects, museum directors, and manufacturers. In warmer weather, students played touch football and tennis, swam at Lake Jonah, and roamed Cranbrook's impressive grounds, which featured fine gardens and a number of architecturally significant buildings filled with works of art. In the winter, they skied and tobogganed. For those so inclined, a bowling alley was also available. Whether the reputation was fair or not, the academy soon became known as the "country club" of art schools.

Acknowledging the adult character of the academy, George Booth was willing to turn a blind eye to much of what transpired in the school's sole dormitory, which featured men and women living informally, separated on two floors. Even the antics of Weese, who frequented the women's dormitory so often that students joked that the ladies had to draw straws to win his affections

Fig. 8 Florence and Hans Knoll visiting the Saarinens at Saarinen House, Bloomfield Hills, Michigan, ca. 1946. Back row from left: Eero Saarinen, Lily Swann Saarinen, Florence Knoll, and Hans Knoll. Foreground: Eliel Saarinen, Eric Saarinen, and Loja Saarinen.

Fig. 9 Pipsan Saarinen Swanson, Eero Saarinen, and Doris Otter at Cranbrook Academy's Mae West Party, February 1934

for the night, seemed to have been taken lightheartedly. Nonetheless, Booth occasionally expelled students whose actions were so blatantly scandalous as to cause "talk" in the otherwise straitlaced Cranbrook community, and he drew the line at married men who transgressed their wedding vows. Inevitably, the situation led to several marriages within the academy, including, in 1939, that of Eero to Lily Swann, a talented sculptor from a prominent Long Island family.[13]

Given the intensity of the program and the small world in which they operated, most students formed lifelong friendships with those around them. Saarinen was no exception. Before his return in 1936, he had been reluctant to befriend students, given his limited time on campus and the realization that most would quickly depart from his life. His outlook changed as he committed more of himself to academy affairs, especially after his appointment to the architecture faculty in 1939. Nearly all the academy colleagues he befriended during this period remained dear to him later, none more than Charlie Eames, his best friend. Saarinen initially dismissed Eames as a conventional artist, but over cocktails in late 1938 he discovered that he and Eames were kindred spirits, and their friendship quickly blossomed.[14]

Eames benefited from his friend's more experienced hand in the fields of art and architecture, particularly in the way Eero followed his father's practice of thoroughly investigating design problems before attempting solutions, while always keeping in mind the next largest element. Saarinen's fondness for sculpture awakened Eames to an appreciation of the plastic arts. Most important, Eero helped Eames embrace a modernist perspective of utilizing research, new materials, and technology to attain desired artistic ends. Although Eames was impressed with Eero, he bristled, Eero observed, at his "smugness" early in their relationship, especially whenever he pointed out that he had accomplished more in his life than Eames had. Such trying moments, however, were rare between the two men. Eero thought the world of Eames and genuinely appreciated him for his talent, quick wit, and charming personality. For his part, Eames served as a foil to his friend, helping him step out of his "solid and somber" persona. The two enjoyed nothing more than tossing ideas back and forth, sparring over positions. People noticed a marked change in Eero whenever Eames was present. It was as though Eames held the power to transform him into a completely different person, if only for the moment. Eero's affection for Charlie carried over to his wife, Ray. To him, they represented the ideal partnership, in which both contributed creatively and mutually to achieve common goals in work and life.[15]

Many encountering Eero for the first time were struck by his serious demeanor and penchant for hard work, which made him seem older than he was. Adult draftsmen working on the Kingswood project, for instance, were shocked and saddened to hear the nineteen-year-old Saarinen claim he had no time to read the Sunday funnies because of his design commitments and workload. To them, adolescence seemed tragically to have passed him by. His uncanny ability at mirror writing—creating documents that could be read only in a mirror—and at drawing different images with both hands simultaneously amazed those who witnessed them. Carl Feiss recalled: "[Eero] would draw on the drawing board with both hands—I have never seen anything like it. . . . [H]e would be drawing a straight architectural detail of something or another with one hand and with the other hand he would be drawing little cartoons."[16]

These faculties, coupled with his wunderkind background, his gifts for working in many media, his slow and methodical speech patterns, intense powers of concentration, and introverted ways set him well apart from his peers. People respected him for his talents and accomplishments, and for the most part they enjoyed his company. Nonetheless, there was a dark side to Eero that could not be overlooked. Academy sculptor Frances Rich, among others, decried his arrogance and the callous way he treated many at the academy to further his own ambition. "[Eero] was clever enough to coordinate what [his architects] had to offer and when they were exhausted they left. . . . [One] said that he left finally, absolutely a shell of himself. . . . Eero would work them up until

Fig. 10 George Gough Booth and Charles Eames with model for *Exhibition of the Work of the Academy Staff*, 1939

dawn every morning. . . . He was deeply ambitious. . . . He was pretty arrogant." Rapson, one of Saarinen's closest friends, admitted that his humor, while frequently expressed and quite witty, was often "very pointed and rather sharp." He could also be confrontational. Weese saw this side of Saarinen soon after he arrived at Cranbrook: "Our relationship got off on a really bad foot. Eero challenged me to a duel when he found me standing in a huge urn with his future wife. . . . He took me out in the woods and said, 'Let's have a duel.' I said, 'Let's do something else.'"[17]

In the absence of formal classes, Eliel encouraged academy students to experiment in a variety of media, to enter national competitions, and to pursue private commissions as a means of furthering their careers. This gave students great freedom to develop their creativity in projects of their own choosing in a collaborative setting. Eames, for instance, a professional architect with years of experience, spent very little time in the architecture studio (fig. 10). Instead he studied weaving, ceramics, and metalworking and took up photography and filmmaking while organizing the academy's design department at the request of the elder Saarinen. There he began to investigate fabrication methods with others involving molded plywood forms, textiles, metal, and other materials. Bertoia, though officially admitted into the painting department, was drawn to the underutilized metals shop and began working in metal forms. Eliel invited him formally to head the metals department, and soon it became one of the most popular venues at the academy. When war conditions forced the closure of the department in 1942, Bertoia moved to the print shop and began exploring block printing, monoprinting, woodcutting, and lithography in addition to teaching graphic arts. Architect Weese, ostensibly coming to study city planning under Eliel, did "everything *but* city planning." Instead, he studied sculpture under Milles and Marshall Fredericks, ceramics under Grotell, and textile design under Strengell, while also executing a landscape design for a Rome Collaborative Project involving Rapson, sculptor Donald Gregory, and painter Clifford West, which would win a prize. Such experiences became the hallmark of a Cranbrook education.[18]

Beginning in the late 1930s, Eero entered several national competitions with his father and other academy artists. The first was the Wheaton College Art Center competition of 1938, in which he placed fifth in a field of more than 240 submissions. Saarinen conceived his scheme in New York in the spring of that year while helping Norman Bel Geddes design the General Motors Futurama Pavilion for the 1939–40 New York World's Fair.[19] His father and Rapson assisted in finalizing his submission for the competition, the first in America to call for modernist forms for academic buildings. Saarinen's entry featured an asymmetrical T-shaped plan with abstract, geometrical elevations.[20] Almost immediately afterward, the same team, this time headed by Eliel, entered a competition for a library and campus development plan for Goucher College. The Saarinens' solution called for a series of low, flat-roofed structures organized along two axes converging on a central plaza. Dominating the plaza was an imposing library, designed in a restrained functional style that featured an arc-shaped reading room lined with tall windows. The submission took second prize.

Eero's third try that year fared even better. Joining with Rapson and Cranbrook Academy painter Fred James, he won first prize in a competition to design a performing and fine arts complex for the College of William and Mary (fig. 11). Saarinen had little interest in the competition until he became intrigued by his colleagues' ideas and insisted that he be included on their team. With Rapson as lead architect, the men envisioned a tightly organized cluster of flat-roofed buildings linked by corridors and bridges spread across a site that featured deep ravines, dense woods, and a pond. The two largest elements were a 1,500-seat festival theater and a wing housing the fine arts department. Eero concentrated mainly on the theater, for which he and Rapson devised a flexible stage that could be aligned in several ways. Though not built, the scheme was exhibited at the Museum of Modern Art and the New York World's

Fig. 11 Eero Saarinen, Ralph Rapson, and Fred James shortly after winning the College of William and Mary competition, February 1939

Fair, among other venues, and attracted a good deal of critical attention. All three competitions helped stimulate public awareness and acceptance of new modernist approaches to campus design. They also contributed to the growing national reputation of Saarinen and the Cranbrook Academy.[21]

Within months of the College of William and Mary competition, the Smithsonian Institution announced a competition for an art museum to be erected on the Mall in Washington, D.C. The Saarinens, in partnership with Bob Swanson, drew on the talents of a number of academy artists in producing their modernist design, which was praised by the jury for "its remarkable clarity of composition in mass and . . . [its] restraint and dignity in expression," and it won first prize. The model featured marble facing, delicate silver railings and window muntins by Bertoia, a small silver fountain portraying Pegasus by Milles, and hundreds of tiny paintings by Baldwin that could be viewed on the gallery walls when the detachable roof was removed.[22] Although Eliel was publicly assumed to have been responsible for the design, Eero later claimed to have "contributed the form as well as all the work." In retrospect, it is easy to see why many believed his father took the leading role in the design, but on closer examination, much about the design suggests a younger, more adventuresome hand. The Smithsonian entry can be seen as a more careful and thoughtful working out of the spatial relationships that were explored in the William and Mary competition. Despite the excitement the proposal elicited in modernist architectural circles, the Smithsonian design met with scorn from many critics. Congress refused to appropriate any construction funds, and the project soon withered and died.[23]

By the time the Museum of Modern Art announced its Organic Design in Home Furnishings competition in 1940, the academy was ready for the challenge. Eero and Eames collaborated to design entries for a side chair, several versions of an armchair and a lounge chair, sectional sofas, and modular case units, two of which won prizes. The chairs, featuring lightweight molded-plywood shells on attenuated legs, were the most significant, for they portended innovative approaches for producing functional and well-designed seating for the contemporary market. Saarinen was the first to suggest their forms, but it took Eames, with considerable help from Albinson, Bertoia, Kaiser, and Jill Mills, to work out the necessary fabricating techniques. The team produced hundreds of models to solve material, design, and production issues. Other academy students also submitted entries, including Weese and Baldwin, who jointly earned a first award in the outdoor living furniture category and shared honorable mentions in two others. Rapson's entry for a rocking chair with a black wood frame and white webbing failed to take a prize, but years later it was put into production by the Knolls, making Rapson the first of many Cranbrook designers to work for their company.[24]

The Wheaton, Goucher, and Smithsonian competitions were carried out by the Saarinens' private architectural practice at the academy. An outgrowth of Eliel's non-Cranbrook work since his arrival in the United States, the firm was the principal source of the Swansons' livelihood as well as an important income stream for Eliel and Eero. Eero entered the practice upon his return to Cranbrook in 1936 and soon joined his father and brother-in-law in designing a modernist home in Grosse Pointe Farms for a wealthy industrialist, Charles Koebel. Eero's role was limited essentially to the parti, the basic conceptual idea for the design. Bob Swanson led the project, and Pipsan was responsible for the interior decoration, which featured Studio Loja Saarinen textiles, Lily Swann sculptures, and extensive use of Eliel's and Bob and Pipsan Swanson's Flexible Home Arrangement furniture, a line of fine modern pieces designed for complete interchangeability.[25]

Beginning in 1937 Eliel and Eero embarked on a number of important commissions as co-architects that came to have tremendous meaning to both men. For Eliel, these projects constituted the last great architectural phase of his long and distinguished career; for Eero, they offered extensive opportunity for developing his architectural prowess, building his reputation, and, perhaps most important, allowing him the pleasure of working with his father as an equal. They also served as a means of transitioning the Saarinens away from Cranbrook, toward greater opportunities outside Michigan.

Most of these commissions were, in part, occasioned by the last spate of building activity at Cranbrook, begun by George Booth in the mid-1930s to complete his vision for the cultural complex. Eliel handled all of this work at Cranbrook, producing with Booth plans for the permanent home of the Cranbrook Institute of Science, additions to Cranbrook School for Boys, and the final development of the Cranbrook Academy of Art. (There is no evidence that Eero participated in any of these initiatives, since he was not at the time employed by Booth's in-house architectural studio, the Cranbrook Architectural Office.) Seizing on Booth's architectural suggestions, Eliel fashioned a functional, stripped-down vocabulary that, though in contrast with the Arts and Crafts sensibilities of his earlier Cranbrook projects, possessed similar elegance, attention to detail, and high-quality craftsmanship. This approach, which reached its culmination at Cranbrook in 1939 with the Art Museum and Library, came to dominate the Saarinens' private architectural practice for the next few years, as clients sought Eliel's expertise to fashion a little bit of Cranbrook in their own backyards.[26]

Employing academy students and professional staff to help them, the firm of Saarinen and Saarinen designed between 1937 and 1942 a community center for nearby Fenton, Michigan; a general plan and opera shed for the Berkshire Music Center at Tanglewood, Massachusetts; the Kleinhans Music Hall in Buffalo; the Crow Island School in Winnetka, Illinois; the Tabernacle Church of

Christ (First Christian Church) in Columbus, Indiana; and the Albert Wermuth House in Fort Wayne, Indiana. Most of these projects show the influence of the forms that Eliel had employed in the Cranbrook Institute of Science (1936–38) and the ones that the Saarinens explored in their competition entries of 1938. With only a couple of exceptions, they were also significant projects calling for substantial detailing of exteriors and interiors and the fabrication of furniture and other appurtenances.

Although Eero collaborated with his father on all aspects of the commissions and frequently served as the firm's representative on the job site, in general he concentrated on the interiors, with the assistance of Charles Eames and others. In two instances, however, he was responsible for the lion's share of the work. At Tanglewood Eero realized Serge Koussevitzky and Eliel's ideas for a four-hundred-seat opera shed in a bold manner, employing bowed laminated-wood arches springing above a sloping roof to lend a striking look to the building. Lily Swann Saarinen confirmed that Eero was commissioned to build the hall. She wrote, "This was one of the first and finest small concert halls that Eero built alone, and the acoustics were perfect."[27] In contrast, Eliel's remarkable plans for a 4,300-seat pavilion at the opposite end of the site became so bastardized through design and structural changes to meet a slim budget that it was built by another architect. Eero also took the clear lead in designing the home for Albert Wermuth, the general contractor of Cranbrook and most of the Saarinens' work during the period. Eero's modernist design, conceived to meet the client's desire to have "the best of the aspects he admired in the various Cranbrook houses on Academy Road," provided a clear and logical plan that separated public and private spaces and took full advantage of the site's topography.[28]

Those witnessing Eliel and Eero's interaction reported that they worked comfortably and well together, relying on procedures that had served them for years. Generally speaking, they began by exploring the nature of the project at hand, coming to terms with the clients' desires as much as the architectural problems that needed to be solved. They then retired to their own tables to sketch out ideas for mutual critique and discussion. The process inevitably led to a great amount of debate, some compromises, and finally the arrival at a scheme that was "in most cases an inseparable combination" of their collective thinking. The two rarely quarreled or failed to see the merit in each other's ideas—a testament to their "rare friendship" and total spiritual and intellectual accord.[29]

Be this as it may, Eero later acknowledged that, as his father's partner, he always felt beholden to follow his forms and to operate within that context to create the finest building possible. Lily Swann Saarinen recalled that the first time Eero disagreed with his father concerning a point in design was the First Christian Church project. "Eero wanted the bell tower to be an open metal structure so that one could see the construction and mechanical workings of the chimes from the ground. Eliel wanted 'closed' chimes. Eero's concept was more progressive and contemporary; however, Eliel won out so the tower was mostly brick, except for the top. It was at this point that Eero started off in a more independent direction and developed more confidence in his contemporary inventiveness."[30] Even so, the ease with which the pair collaborated and the range of their finished products naturally gave rise to speculation as to who was influencing whom. Friends of the architects were always insistent that the matter was easily explained: each benefited from the expertise, inspiration, and talent of the other. Virginia Christ-Janer, the wife of Eliel's biographer Albert Christ-Janer, noted:

> I think today's architectural critics tend to dwell too emphatically on Eero's influence on his father. I would prefer to say that they influenced each other, and leave it there. They were both strong individuals, of two different generations, influenced by customs and mores of two eras and two quite different countries. Albert never ceased to be amazed that during the first half of Eliel's professional life he lived in such a formal atmosphere that if ladies were to be present at the table he dressed for dinner in

Fig. 12 Staff members of Saarinen, Saarinen, and Associates with Detroit Civic Center model. Back row from left: Ted Luderowski, James Conn, Earl Moursund, Alice Warren, Ed Elliott, James Smith, Dan Kiley, and unidentified man. Seated: Joseph N. Lacy, Eliel Saarinen, Eero Saarinen, and Lily Swann Saarinen.

Fig. 13 (opposite) Eero Saarinen and Associates party at Eero's house on Vaughn Road, Bloomfield Hills. Saarinen stands near doorway at right; Alexander Girard is to his right and Charles Eames, in bow tie, to his left.

white-tie regalia. The adjustment to the comparative informality of his later life was simply immense. It was a flexible man who managed it so gracefully, and a wise father who permitted his son to influence his work.[31]

The artist Zoltan Sepeshy, who later became the director of the academy, offered another view of their relationship: "While Eliel loved his daughter, in his son he had not only a son but a fellow architect. A tough old despot and cussed in some ways, Eliel adored his boy and 'surrendered' to him architecturally. He was never dominated by Eero, but 'allowed' him to do his thing in their partnership. There's a great deal of difference."

The Saarinens found other professional opportunities in the 1940s as well. With Bob Swanson, they played off Eliel's extensive city and campus planning experience to position themselves in the campus planning market and take advantage of the government funding being directed toward defense housing and higher education programs. They won a number of contracts, ranging from "Bomber City," the town center and housing units associated with Henry Ford's famous bomber plant in Ypsilanti, Michigan, to development plans for Antioch College, Drake University, Stephens College, and the Detroit Civic Center (fig. 12). Eero shepherded some of his work during World War II in a small branch of the Saarinen office he had opened in 1943 while serving as a civilian consultant to the Office of Strategic Services (OSS) in Washington, D.C.[32] In 1945 he returned to Bloomfield Hills to help his father and brother-in-law prepare plans for a new engineering and design complex in Warren, Michigan, for the General Motors Corporation, the firm's largest client. Eero garnered extensive experience as a planner through all these projects, expertise that served him well in the coming years as his office took on many comparable commissions. The General Motors Technical Center, which he eventually inherited from his father, would become his breakaway architectural statement and provide his entrée into corporate America.

These jobs also redefined the relationship between him and his father. As the decade unfolded, Eero steadily assumed greater control over most of the projects on the firm's boards, leaving Eliel to concentrate on a handful of pet commissions while continuing his teaching duties at the academy.[33] Eero's increased authority allowed him to introduce new technologies, materials, and stylistic changes into the work, positioning the office as a forward-looking practice. Certainly his sculptor's sensibilities, nurtured by his mother, caused him to approach modernity quite differently than his father did. The Womb chair and the Gateway Arch, designed in the Saarinens' office in the mid- to late 1940s, made that very clear.

For all his talents, however, Saarinen had difficulty realizing his architectural aspirations. Unlike his father, who had a genius to fully conceptualize projects in his mind and could effortlessly produce detailed presentation drawings in a single sitting, Eero struggled in his father's shadow to achieve acceptable solutions to the challenges that confronted him. He wrote, "My life has been a fanatical concentration on architecture at the expenses [*sic*] of all other phases of life—This has probably been due to the fact that I largely pattern my life upon my fathers [*sic*] and since competition is very keen today and my talents are not as freeflowing as my fathers such a concentration has been necessary to succeed."[34] He worked methodically and intensely, churning out hundreds of sketches and models in order to find approaches that appealed to him. In his zeal, he expected and often demanded long working hours from his office mates, regardless of outside obligations. Invariably, many departed rather than put up with his workaholic ways, which consumed and at times disrupted the office. Those who endured did so out of personal fondness for Eero and out of professional admiration for his prodigious design capabilities (fig. 13). They understood that his brilliance depended on the process he put them through, as difficult and convoluted as it may have been.

One person who refused to tolerate Saarinen's behavior was Bob Swanson, who left the family partnership in 1947, exasperated by Eero's consistent refusals to meet design deadlines, which significantly eroded the firm's profits. The break caused lasting repercussions in the family. Pipsan and Eero continued to see each other socially, but their relationship naturally suffered. Swanson must have been pleased to hear of continuing grumblings from Eero's staff concerning his penchant for last-minute design changes and his lack of business sense. As one old-timer put it, "We'll make money on Eliel's job and lose it on Eero's." For his part, Eero thereafter despised Swanson and always sought to minimize his contributions to the firm. Needing a publicity photograph to promote the Saarinen office after Swanson's departure, he took an old negative shot at

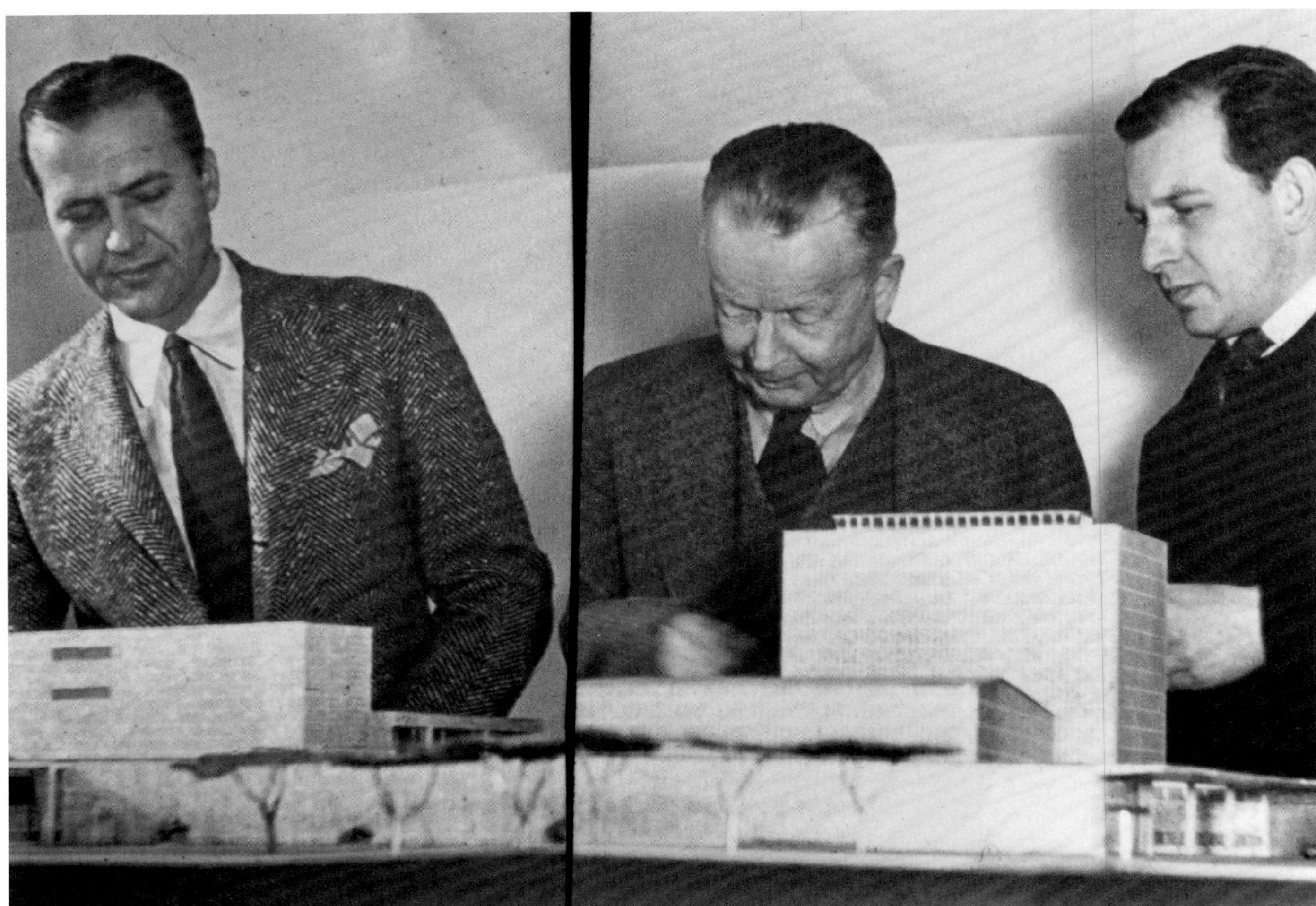

Fig. 14 J. Robert F. Swanson, Eliel Saarinen, and Eero Saarinen with Smithsonian Gallery of Art model, 1939; print made from restored negative

the time of the Smithsonian competition, cut out Swanson's figure, and had new images printed of himself and his father (fig. 14).[35]

The dissolution of the family partnership occurred against the backdrop of several earlier events that had been just as jarring to the Saarinens—the closing of Studio Loja Saarinen, the termination of Eero's appointment at the academy, and the removal of the Saarinens' professional practice from Cranbrook.[36] George Booth had authorized these measures in late 1941, ostensibly to protect the academy's tax-exempt status. The Saarinens, however, viewed Booth's actions in much starker terms. To them it foreshadowed a purposeful effort on the part of the Booth family to downplay their contributions to Cranbrook, especially their role in making the academy world-renowned. These feelings intensified in 1946, when Booth replaced Eliel as director of the academy with Sepeshy, who the Saarinens felt had no interest in sustaining the family's legacy. Perhaps surprisingly, Booth's death in 1949 further troubled the Saarinens. Believing that Harry Booth, the new executive officer of Cranbrook, and his siblings were chiefly interested in promoting their parents' legacy above all else, Eero began contemptuously referring to the Booths as "the Medicis." For this reason, after Eliel died in 1950, Saarinen dissuaded his mother from donating his father's architectural drawings to Cranbrook.[37] Whether maliciously intended or not, the ensuing events culminated in severing the Saarinens' formal ties to Cranbrook. Loja was given a year to settle her affairs on campus, then she had to relocate. She moved to a new home that her son designed for her behind his Victorian residence on nearby Vaughn Road. There she lived out her days, surrounded by the trappings of her life at Hvitträsk and Saarinen House.

In the years following Saarinen's departure from Cranbrook, his contact with the institution lessened, though he still kept in touch with his former academy cohorts and helped them professionally. He was pleased that so many became prominent in their fields. He especially enjoyed the success that came to Eames

Fig. 15 Loja Saarinen, Eero Saarinen, and Marianne Strengell

and Bertoia, both of whom he continued to see regularly. He collaborated with Eames to design the Case Study House #9, the John Entenza House, and he commissioned Bertoia to produce a metal screen for the cafeteria of the General Motors Technical Center as well as the altar screen for the Kresge Chapel at MIT. Like so many others in the design field, Saarinen debated the relative merits of Eames's and Bertoia's chair designs—and squarely came down on the side of the former. His admiration for Bertoia's sculptural abilities, however, remained undiminished. His relationship with Florence Schust Knoll remained as close as ever through her widowhood, his affairs, his divorce from Lily, and both of their remarriages. At Cranbrook, he continued to see Strengell, one of his oldest friends (fig. 15), and Grotell, whom he commissioned to produce textiles and ceramic wares, respectively, for the General Motors project.[38]

Saarinen was not entirely generous to all of his former Cranbrook colleagues, however. He disliked Marshall Fredericks's sculptural work and fought unsuccessfully to keep his pieces from being installed in the Detroit Civic Center.[39] More egregiously, he failed to credit Milles for his significant help on the Gateway Arch. Milles strongly advised Saarinen to drop his initial plans to fashion the arch with a quadrilateral section in favor of a more sculpturally pleasing triangular section. Eero's failure publicly to recognize Milles's contribution to the monument angered the Swedish sculptor, who thereafter severed contact with Saarinen.[40]

As his marriage to Lily dissolved, Eero leaned heavily on his Cranbrook friends for emotional support. But apart from exhibition openings and formal gatherings, he kept his distance from the institution. His busy career had carried him well beyond the community, and with a new wife, Aline Louchheim, at his side, a rising reputation, and prospects for a fresh start on the East Coast, Saarinen could look confidently to the future. From his vantage point at the northern fringe of campus, however, he could not help but consider all that Cranbrook had given him through the years and, in turn, recall with pride the many contributions that he and his family had made to the institution.
His father, with George Booth's financing and support, had not only fashioned one of America's great campuses but had helped establish one of the world's most eminent and innovative art schools, with an enviable record for turning out first-rate artists, designers, and architects despite its young age. In an environment brimming with choice works of art and design, the Saarinens' own production stood out distinctively, perfecting Cranbrook's overall character. Eero could proudly claim credit for much of this heritage, knowing that his contributions as an artist, designer, architect, and educator were a critical part of his family's artistic legacy, at Cranbrook and beyond.

Notes

1. Albert Christ-Janer, *Eliel Saarinen: Finnish-American Architect and Educator*, rev. ed. (Chicago: University of Chicago Press, 1979), 18–21.

2. Marika Hausen et al., *Eliel Saarinen: Projects, 1896–1923* (Cambridge: MIT Press, 1990), 52, 53. Mark Jaroszewicz heard about Loja Saarinen's comments on her son's genius from Pipsan Swanson and related them to me on Aug. 12, 1995. Eero told Harry Booth about his mother's role in shaping his career. According to Booth, Eero began assisting Loja on Eliel's models at Hvitträsk and helped construct the models for his father's 1924 Detroit Riverfront scheme and his 1925 project for an academy of art at Cranbrook.

3. Saarinen wrote: "[My parents] never really acclimated themselves—never really became a part of USA. My mother was 45 when she came over and it took her 10 years before she could feel at home." Eero Saarinen, letter to Astrid Sampe, n.d., frame nos. 273–74, Aline and Eero Saarinen Papers (microfilmed), Archives of American Art, Smithsonian Institution (hereafter AAA).

4. "Younger Saarinen Follows in His Father's Footstep," n.d., *Detroit News*, Eero Saarinen biography file, Cranbrook Archives, Bloomfield Hills, Mich.

5. Davira S. Taragin, "The History of the Cranbrook Community," in Robert Judson Clark et al., *Design in America: The Cranbrook Vision, 1925–1950* (New York: Abrams in association with Detroit Institute of Arts and Metropolitan Museum of Art, [1983]), 40–41.

6. Drawings for most of these objects are held in the Cranbrook Archives and the Cranbrook Art Museum.

7. A comprehensive listing of Eero's contributions to Saarinen House is published in Gregory Wittkopp, ed., *Saarinen House and Garden: A Total Work of Art* (New York: Abrams, 1995).

8. "Memorandum of an understanding reached with Eero Saarinen February, 1931," folder 31, box 19, George Gough Booth Papers, Cranbrook Archives. Eero was paid six hundred dollars for designing the furniture for Kingswood School at Cranbrook; Helen L. McIlroy, "Inventory of Equipment and Supplies," 2, Kingswood School Cranbrook file, Cranbrook Archives.

9. Jayne Merkel, *Eero Saarinen* (New York: Phaidon, 2005), 35–36. The Saarinens had been working on the Hvitträsk residence project since 1929; Koti Taideteoksena, *Hvitträsk: The Home as a Work of Art* (Helsinki: Otava, 1988), 67.

10. Taragin, "The History of the Cranbrook Community," 41–44.

11. Other talented students were already enrolled at the academy. One was Edmund Norwood Bacon, who had come to study urban planning under Eliel in 1935. In 1937 Eero assisted Bacon in his studies of Flint, Michigan, undertaken for the Institute of Research and Planning, Flint.

12. Florence Margaret Schust, application for admission to the Cranbrook Academy of Art, Sept. 14, 1934, Cranbrook Archives. Eero and Florence Schust were for a time romantically linked; Florence Knoll Bassett in conversation with the author, Apr. 21, 1998.

13. Ralph Rapson, on-camera interview, KDN Films, Aug. 23 and 24, 2004, transcript, 14, Eero Saarinen Papers, Manuscripts and Archives, Yale University. Additional dormitories at the academy were later added, including one designated solely for single women. Albinson, Bertoia, Wallace Mitchell, Rapson, and Strengell, among others, selected academy mates. Charles Eames, burdened by a troubled marriage when he came to Cranbrook, found happiness with Kaiser, one of his students.

14. Eero Saarinen, letter to Aline Louchheim, May 29, 1953, frame nos. 402–3, Aline and Eero Saarinen Papers, AAA.

15. Pat Kirkham, *Charles and Ray Eames: Designers of the Twentieth Century* (Cambridge: MIT Press, 1995), 48–49; Eero Saarinen, letter to Aline Louchheim, July 7, 1953, frame no. 496, Aline and Eero Saarinen Papers, AAA; Eric Larrabee et al., *Knoll Design* (New York: Abrams, 1990), 56; Eero Saarinen, letter to Aline Louchheim, n.d., frame no. 513, Aline and Eero Saarinen Papers, AAA. Despite his friendship with Eames, Eero was mindful of the fact that they were competitors. He gave instructions to his staff to hide his furniture prototypes whenever Eames paid a visit to his office; Anthony Lumsden, interview with Wes Janz, Aug. 3, 1992, 12, Wesley R. Janz Collection of Oral History Transcripts, Bentley Historical Collections, University of Michigan, Ann Arbor.

16. Lewis "Mac" Wetzel, interview with the author, May 1, 1990, tape recording, Cranbrook Archives; Carl Feiss, interview with Roy Slade, Oct. 25, 1982, transcript, 8, Design in America Collection, Cranbrook Archives.

17. Frances Rich, interview with Roy Slade, Feb. 24, 1981, transcript, 18, 62, Design in America Collection, Cranbrook Archives; Rapson interview, 11; Harry Weese, quoted in John Brunetti, *Baldwin Kingrey: Midcentury Modern in Chicago, 1947–1957* (Chicago: Wright, 2004), 77.

18. Rapson interview, 5; Nancy N. Schiffer and Val O. Bertoia, *The World of Bertoia* (Atglen, Pa.: Schiffer, 2003), 17–19; Bruce N. Wright, "The Furniture Designs of Harry Weese," *Inland Architect* 38 (Nov.–Dec. 1994), 14; "Academy Members Win Major Prizes," *Academy News*, May 1939, 4.

19. Another Yale graduate, Worthen Paxton, was instrumental in bringing Eero into Bel Geddes's office to work on the Futurama project; Merkel, *Eero Saarinen*, 43, 45.

20. Jane King Hession et al., *Ralph Rapson: Sixty Years of Modern Design* (Afton, Minn.: Afton Historical Society Press, 1999), 24.

21. Ibid., 23–26.

22. Ibid., 28; Benjamin Baldwin, *Benjamin Baldwin: An Autobiography in Design* (New York: Norton, 1995), 22, 194. Baldwin managed the construction of the model.

23. Eero Saarinen, letter to Aline Louchheim, Feb. 2, 1953, frame nos. 305–6, Aline and Eero Saarinen Papers, AAA; Hession, *Ralph Rapson*, 28.

24. R. Craig Miller, "Interior Design and Furniture," in Clark et al., *Design in America*, 110–12; Jayne Merkel, "American Moderns: Eero Saarinen and His Circle," *Architectural Design*, July 2002, 28–29.

25. The Koebel House is well documented in the Swanson Family Papers, Cranbrook Archives.

26. George Booth was a talented amateur architect who routinely offered architects ideas and sketches of his own to begin discussions of buildings he wished to erect. This practice continued throughout the years he and Eliel Saarinen worked together on the Cranbrook campus. The best published account of Booth's involvement with Cranbrook buildings is in Lee A. White et al., *Cranbrook Institute of Science: A History of Its Founding and First Twenty-five Years* (Bloomfield Hills: Cranbrook Institute of Science, 1959). Booth was clearly pushing Saarinen to design crisp-looking, functional buildings at Cranbrook as early as 1935.

27. Lily Swann Saarinen, letter to Nancy Rivard Shaw, Apr. 5, 1973, quoted in Shaw, "Eliel Saarinen in America," master's thesis, Wayne State University, 1973, 99. For plans and a description, see "Opera Shed," *Progressive Architecture*, Mar. 1947, 53–58.

28. Shaw, "Eliel Saarinen in America," 104; Christ-Janer, *Eliel Saarinen*, 103–4.

29. Christ-Janer, *Eliel Saarinen*, 103.

30. Ibid., 117; Lily Swann Saarinen, letter to Nancy Rivard Shaw, Mar. 17, 1973, quoted in Shaw, "Eliel Saarinen in America," 103.

31. Mrs. Albert Christ-Janer to Harold Nelson, Sept. 1, 1980, "Correspondence—Nelson, Harold," box 8, Albert Christ-Janer Papers, AAA; Zoltan Sepeshy, letter to Nancy Rivard Shaw, Jan. 19, 1973, quoted in Shaw, "Eliel Saarinen in America," 111.

32. Merkel, *Eero Saarinen*, 50. Saarinen's former Yale classmate Donal McLaughlin enlisted him to work for the OSS, the precursor of the CIA, at the time Eero received his draft notice. He served under McLaughlin in the Presentation Division for roughly three years, turning out graphics for bomb defusing and other projects. McLaughlin recalled that Saarinen developed his own chair designs at his Georgetown residence during his off hours; Bill Kubota and Ed Moore, notes on Donal McLaughlin and Susan Alexander, interview with Bill Kubota and Ed Moore, May 24, 2004, Eero Saarinen Papers, Yale University, 3, 7.

33. Joseph N. Lacy, letter to Albert Christ-Janer, Mar. 17, 1971, "Correspondence—Lacy, Joseph N.," box 8, Albert Christ-Janer Papers, AAA.

34. Eero Saarinen, undated document, frame no. 251, Aline and Eero Saarinen Papers, AAA.

35. James Smith, the Saarinens' model maker since the mid-1940s, made the comment on Eliel and Eero; James Smith, interview with John Gerard, Apr. 8, 1982, transcript, 4, Design in America Collection, Cranbrook Archives. The negatives are in the Cranbrook Archives.

36. George G. Booth, letter to Eliel Saarinen, Dec. 29, 1941, folder 33, box 19, George Gough Booth Papers, Cranbrook Archives. Comparable letters announcing these decisions were sent to Eero and Loja Saarinen. Although supplanted as the president of the academy, Eliel continued as director of the department of architecture and urban design until his death.

37. "The Booth boys are interested in making G. G. [Booth] look like Lorenzo il Magnifico—so that Harry will look like Cosimo I and Warren [like] Giovanni di Medici, etc. This is why Cranbrook will never, in the end, be able to look after Dad's things well." Eero Saarinen, letter to Loja Saarinen, n.d., folder 9, box 3, Saarinen Family Papers, Cranbrook Archives, translated from the Swedish by Ann Gheorghiade.

38. Eero Saarinen, letter to Aline Louchheim, n.d., frame no. 711, Aline and Eero Saarinen Papers, AAA.

39. Eero Saarinen, letter to Aline Louchheim, Sept. 16, 1953, frame no. 610, and Eero Saarinen, letter to Aline Louchheim, n.d., frame no. 685, Aline and Eero Saarinen Papers, AAA.

40. Carl Milles, letter to Virginia and Albert Christ-Janer, Feb. 24, 1950, "Correspondence—Milles, Carl, c. 1945–1955," box 1, Albert Christ-Janer Papers, AAA; Lilian Swann Saarinen, interview with Robert Brown, Feb. 2, 1981, transcript, 31, AAA.

Donald Albrecht

the clients and their architect

The 1950s saw a near perfect meshing of Eero Saarinen's form-making abilities and his clients' financial and cultural capabilities to realize those forms on a major public scale. In the boom era that followed the Great Depression and World War II, Saarinen and his clients collaborated on a vision of America's future—a vision that gave architectural expression to the country's new financial, political, and cultural might. The war's expansive military economy had produced extraordinary prosperity that ended the depression and sparked a postwar economic miracle, giving rise to a national middle class and irrevocably altering the course of architectural and urban development. For returning veterans and their families, the GI Bill of Rights offered the chance for a college education and a new house, spurring a wave of new campus building and vast suburban developments that were constructed using wartime mass-production techniques and new materials like plywood and plastic. The work environment changed as well, as business and industry developed suburban office parks and urban steel-and-glass towers. Military victory and the rise of multinational corporations thrust the United States into a global position of unprecedented power and prestige, fostering construction overseas of new embassies, offices, and international chains of hotels, or "little Americas," as they were dubbed by Conrad Hilton.[1]

Ranking among the era's leaders, Eero Saarinen's clients constituted a veritable who's who of the most prominent industries and institutions that defined postwar America. Their range of influence extended from the expansion of higher education to the promotion of automobile culture and air travel, suburbanization, popular forms of entertainment like television, and the newest information technologies. Signifying their key roles as shapers of a postwar United States, at least five of Saarinen's clients—as well as Saarinen himself (fig. 1)—were featured on the cover of *Time* magazine, while *Esquire* and *Fortune* heralded many others. Significantly, in the early 1950s the publisher of *Time* and *Fortune*, Henry R. Luce, had approached Saarinen to design a

Fig. 1 *Time* magazine cover featuring Eero Saarinen with site plan of General Motors Technical Center, July 2, 1956

new corporate campus for the company in the suburbs outside New York City. A decade earlier, Luce had coined the term "the American Century" to define the country's future role as world leader.[2]

For all of these clients, modern architecture and design were important tools to achieve their goals of fostering and representing the new America. A. Whitney Griswold (fig. 2), the president of Yale University, Saarinen's alma mater, spoke for many of Eero's clients when he said that "a great university should look at architecture as a way of expressing itself." Another key client, IBM's Thomas J. Watson, Jr. (fig. 3), upheld the credo that "good design is good business." Their commitment to architecture and their understanding of design's power to communicate progressive and egalitarian values would be shared by Saarinen's business, institutional, and government clients.[3]

Saarinen, in fact, considered his clients and their culture "co-creators" in making his buildings and believed that this synergy moved him into an arena beyond the exchange of funds for architectural services into one that had larger social ramifications. "Architecture," Saarinen told *Time* magazine, "is not just to fulfill man's need for shelter, but also to fulfill man's belief in the nobility of his existence on earth. Our architecture . . . should be prouder, more aggressive, much richer and larger than we see today. I would like to do my part in expanding that richness." To achieve this nobler goal for architecture, Saarinen nurtured the relationship between architect, client, and the country's changing society. He noted in 1953, for example, that painting and sculpture were adrift because "they had lost their traditional client, the baron, and have not yet found their new client, society as a whole." It was the contemporary architect, Saarinen said, who best understood that society *was* the new client. The architect, he wrote, "must recognize that this is a new kind of civilization in which the artist will be used in a new and different way. . . . He must be sensitive and adaptable to trends and needs; he must be part of and understand our civilization. At the same time, he is not just a mirror; he is also a co-creator and must have the strength and urge to produce form, not compromise."[4]

The former "baron" client had been replaced in Saarinen's era by a new kind of socially beneficent one, who may be dubbed not an "autocrat" but a "popucrat." Popucrats advanced a postwar ideal of a United States that was both egalitarian and democratic, on one hand, and a rich global power on the other. With their architect, Eero Saarinen, they hoped to fulfill what many contemporary thinkers sought for the country's expanding mass culture: a place for high culture within the popular sphere. Alan Valentine, the former president of the University of Rochester and chief of the Marshall Plan in the Netherlands, wrote about a class he called "custodians of culture" in his book *The Age of Conformity,* one of many works published at the time that dealt with the subject of the individual in mass culture. He observed: "Those who create new ideas for submission to the popular jury are relatively small in number. Without their creative stimulus democratic society would be intellectually inert, and their vigor and quality is therefore essential to culture. But even the finest creative spirits cannot elevate culture unless they are esteemed by the average man, whose values and standards therefore become the crucial issue."[5]

The media — newspapers, magazines, radio, television, exhibitions — provided the broadest means for transmitting new ideas and persuading Valentine's "popular jury" of their worth. Throughout the 1950s and early 1960s Saarinen's buildings and furnishings were widely publicized in an international network of popular and professional publications, advertisements, radio and television programs, and corporate communications like press releases, in-house newsletters, dedication brochures, and annual reports. Saarinen's first major commission, the $100-million General Motors Technical Center in suburban Detroit, merited his appearance on the cover of *Time* magazine, marking the beginning of a mutually beneficial relationship between Saarinen and the press that would continue throughout his career. Heralded as a "Technopolis" in GM's brochure titled "Where Today Meets Tomorrow," the twenty-five-building center clad in glass and brightly colored brick was officially dedicated on

Fig. 2 *Time* magazine cover featuring Yale University president A. Whitney Griswold, June 11, 1951

Fig. 3 *Time* magazine cover featuring IBM chairman Thomas J. Watson, Jr., March 28, 1955

May 16, 1956, with huge fanfare. Both the popular and the professional press offered accolades. *Architectural Forum* wrote that the center was a "historic symbol of today's industrial progress, also of tomorrow's ambition." In its cover story on Saarinen, *Time*, which played a major role after World War II in reporting on and promoting modern American art and architecture, stated that "of the whole U.S. cast of modern architects, none has a better proportioned combination of imagination, versatility and good sense than Eero Saarinen."[6]

The design and public relations strategies that Saarinen developed so successfully for the General Motors project became his template for future commissions. This template generally comprised several important components: the creation of iconic architectural forms for each client, the commission of site-specific artworks, and the development of technological and planning innovations. This stylistic and technical range not only suggested a national ethos of individual choice, but also may be viewed as a strategy of giving each client a distinctive building that became a major component of the company's branding and publicity. Saarinen's design process, which involved the use of large-scale models and full-scale mock-ups to test new materials and systems, also received a great deal of press; they demonstrated a flair for the dramatic that made his projects popular with the media.

General Motors' combination of employee-friendly environments with planning strategies that reinforced the company's power and authority also set the pattern for future Saarinen buildings. Features that benefited Valentine's "average man," such as sunlit cafeterias and air-conditioned offices, were contained within formally imposing settings that represented his clients' wealth and power. The Tech Center, for instance, had been heralded by *Life* magazine as "a Versailles of Industry," connecting GM to royal patrons of an earlier age. Saarinen himself reinforced the link between his own clients and commissions and great historic landmarks, telling *Time:* "When you do a job like this, your mind goes back to Versailles, the Tivoli Gardens, San Marco. . . . And you think, Boy! Let's do that!"[7]

Although Saarinen often claimed that his buildings were inevitable solutions to his clients' unique needs, his continuing use of architectural strategies developed for General Motors suggests a fundamental appreciation of their potential for media and branding opportunities that made him one of postwar corporate and institutional America's favorite architects. So close was Saarinen's association with his clients that a backlash arose from some critics who complained that his designs were overtly media-driven. "When you see client-orientation of this kind," architecture critic Reyner Banham wrote, "you realize there is no irony in [Saarinen's] work for GM at all—it was the building Harley Earl wanted. Like a good advertising agency, Eero really serviced his clients, and in finding for them the 'unique solution' he did, fairly painlessly and without short-calling anybody's cultural standards, exactly what David Ogilvy has to knock himself out to do in advertising—he bestowed status, improved the image."[8]

For Saarinen, however, servicing his clients was hardly a cause for shame—representing their needs and values in architectural form was the goal of his profession. Saarinen's relationship with Watson, the head of IBM, offers a fascinating case study in the architect's commitment to this goal. Like so many of his clients, IBM was in the vanguard of a major postwar development—computers—and was also a highly prestigious company that served as a business ambassador of America overseas. IBM was the only corporate client for whom Saarinen worked more than once, so their relationship can be studied over time. IBM, under Watson, was also an organization that valued modern architecture and design as a way to communicate its prestige and progressiveness and that did so as part of a long-standing, determined, and very well documented campaign of corporate patronage.[9]

In 1956, after working at IBM for almost two decades, Watson took over the company from his father, who died a few months later. The younger Watson wanted to define his regime as forward-looking in contrast to the elder Watson's more conservative business strategy and design taste. He deployed vanguard design in the form of newly styled machines and bold graphics, showrooms in bright colors, and modernist buildings to symbolize IBM's transformation from a national company headquartered on the eastern seaboard of the United States to a corporation with facilities and customers all over the world. Watson wanted visually to express the company's exponential growth as well as its groundbreaking move away from paper punch cards, the technology his father had championed, toward his own vision for IBM as global leader in electronic calculating technologies.

Watson owed the inspiration for IBM's new machines, graphics, and buildings to the Italian business machines manufacturer Olivetti, whose products he had seen in its Fifth Avenue showroom. Unlike Olivetti, whose products, graphics, and showrooms were visually cohesive, fitting "together like a beautiful picture puzzle," IBM under Watson, Sr., presented an incoherent array of different images. "We wanted to improve IBM design," Watson, Jr., said, "not only in architecture and typography, but color, interiors—the whole spectrum."[10]

To help implement his new agenda, Watson hired the architect and industrial designer Eliot Noyes, who had studied with Bauhaus-founder Walter Gropius at Harvard and worked as curator of industrial design at the Museum of Modern Art in New York. (Noyes initiated the Organic Design in Home Furnishings competition, in which Saarinen and Charles Eames won first prizes.) When Watson decided to change IBM's design direction, he invited Noyes, whom he had met when both served in the air force during World War II and who was the only designer Watson said he knew, to attend an IBM meeting in the Pocono Mountains to brainstorm about the new design program. "At the end of three days," according to Watson, "he convinced us to do an about face in our design trends." Noyes advised Watson not to create a strict IBM look that had to be followed slavishly and would soon become dated. Instead, Noyes suggested that IBM's theme be "simply the best in modern design." Whenever the company needed a new building or product, it would commission the best architects and designers and give them a relatively free hand within the constraints of time, budget, and function.[11]

Under the direction of Noyes, who started as consultant director to the company in February 1956, IBM hired graphic designer Paul Rand to create a new logo, Charles and Ray Eames to make films and exhibitions, and such leading architects as Ludwig Mies van der Rohe and Marcel Breuer to design buildings for its expanding real estate holdings. Noyes himself designed IBM's typewriters, its pavilion at the 1958 World's Fair in Brussels, and several of the company's buildings.

In 1955, just before Noyes's arrival, IBM's factories in Endicott and Poughkeepsie, New York, were overflowing with almost ten thousand employees each, and IBM was building huge satellite plants nearby to accommodate another ten thousand employees for military work. More manufacturing plants were needed, and Watson was concerned about turning the factories' existing locations into company towns and driving other employers out. "So," he declared, "we began a great movement west."[12]

For the design of IBM's first new building outside the East Coast, a manufacturing and training plant in Rochester, Minnesota, Noyes recommended Saarinen. Saarinen was also given the commission for IBM's research center in Yorktown Heights, New York. Noyes felt Saarinen could be trusted to meet Watson's requirement for ever-changing modernity. "When I recommended Saarinen for the job, I was not thinking about what appearance his building would have. I was thinking that if he does the job, I will not have to worry about its integrity or its modernity. And these are certainly the qualities IBM should represent."[13]

IBM's charge to Saarinen was to create structures that responded to four of the company's needs (figs. 4–6). First, the buildings had to be designed for future expansion. Second, they needed to be seen as "good neighbors" in their communities, and, third, to contain spaces that fostered the company's

Fig. 4 Eero Saarinen and Associates, International Business Machines Manufacturing and Training Facility, Rochester, Minnesota, 1956–58, mock-up of curtain wall

own community of loyal employees. Finally, they were visually to express the character of the new IBM. Watson situated his company's modern identity in contexts both populist and aristocratic, contemporary and historic. According to Watson, the company's new facilities must create "some imaginative surroundings to make the attitude of our people who work in them lifted and more rapid and more efficient." At the same time, "history alone is the ultimate judge of what good design is. . . . The Egyptian pyramids survived because of sound engineering. But I think one reason we go to see them is their design—very simple, very attractive, very pleasing to the eye." Leading critics heralded Watson's intentions for his buildings' historical significance. "It used to be Church and State," Peter Blake wrote about IBM's efforts, "but today, Industry is the new and practical patron of art in architecture."[14]

Saarinen responded to IBM's requirements with different architectural solutions, following the non–cookie-cutter approach defined by Noyes. The

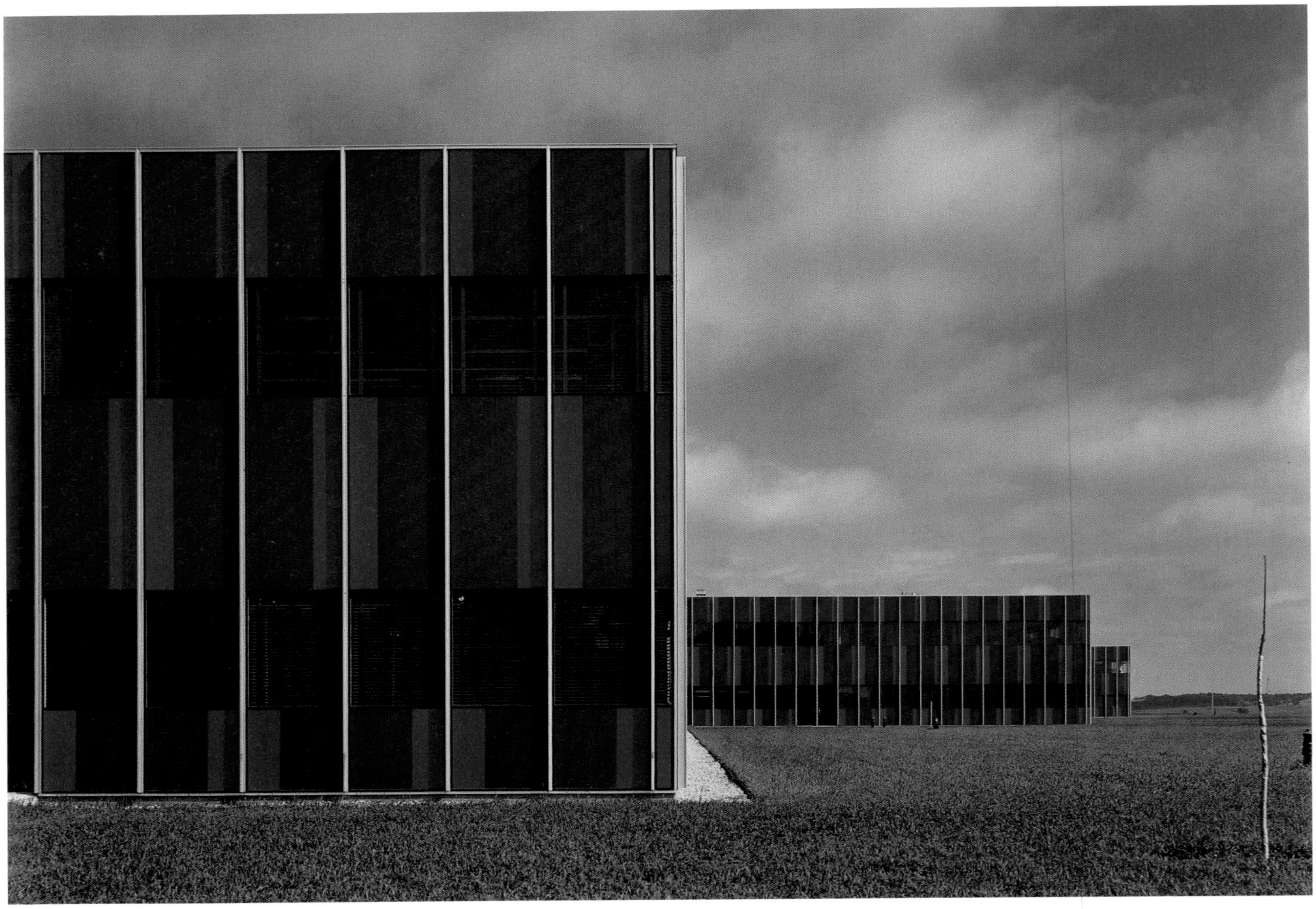

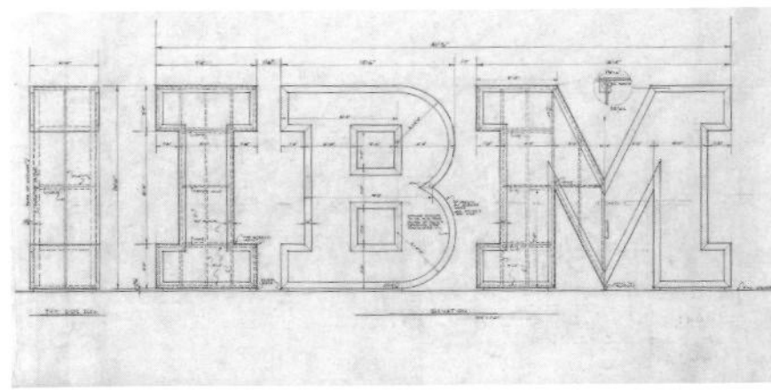

Fig. 5 IBM Manufacturing and Training Facility, Rochester, Minnesota

Fig. 6 Eero Saarinen and Associates, measured drawing for IBM Manufacturing and Training Facility signage, based on Paul Rand's corporate logo, ca. 1956

Rochester facility was conceived as a family of spatial modules that could be endlessly repeated across the flatlands of Minnesota. There were three different modules, based on function: large squarish blocks (one story in height) for manufacturing; a medium-size unit for the staff cafeteria; and thin two-story rectangles that housed offices, labs, and classrooms. Seen from the air, IBM Rochester was a checkerboard of blocks linked into one vast entity and bounded by parking lots that served as buffers between the building and its rural setting.

Saarinen clad the entire complex of interconnected modules in the structure's most distinctive—and publicized—feature: a newly invented factory-produced aluminum spandrel panel, just five-sixteenths of an inch thick. The spandrel panels were set flush with the glass window panes and separated from each other by shiny aluminum mullions that extended the full height of the building. The panels featured a special asbestos-cement insulating core, and their interior and exterior surfaces were coated with a porcelain enamel finish. The exterior surfaces of the panels were striped in a lively syncopated pattern in two shades of blue. The thin wall boldly affirmed human control over the harsh midwestern winters and, as the building was air-conditioned, its hot summers. The wall's image of technological progressiveness was also valuable to DuPont, which boasted of its porcelain enamel finish in its company magazine, while Kaiser Steel trumpeted its role in the manufacture of the panel in advertisements in architectural magazines.

Aesthetically, Saarinen's crisp, straight-edge, colorful wall evoked the modernity of IBM's new product lines, most notably Noyes's redesign of its 705 computer. "The IBM designers in Endicott and myself were working over an early version of its design. It was completely covered with grey panels, and the more panels we stripped, the more beautiful it became. We found blues and oranges and wonderful reds, and wound up exposing the entire unit behind glass." Saarinen used the bright blue colors of the machine's apparatus for the palette of his new building's skin. The palette was also tailored to the landscape:

Fig. 7 Promotional photograph showing IBM's Rochester facility viewed from the neighboring farm of Lincoln Schroeder, 1960

"The vibrancy of the two blues," Saarinen said, "which helps avoid monotony at close view, changes when seen from the distance. Then the total effect is a dark blue band making a transition from the tawny-green, rolling landscape to the sky. In winter, the blue vibrates with greater intensity across the snowscape." Thus, the building harmonized with its surroundings, which was important to IBM. To prove the perfect fit of company and community, IBM issued a promotional photograph in 1960 in which neighboring farmer Lincoln Schroeder gazes admiringly at the distant structure on the horizon, its long and low machine-made facades a modern counterpart to the horizontal slats of his weathered wooden fence (fig. 7).[15]

Dubbed the "world's thinnest wall," the Rochester spandrel panel was one of many highly publicized building components that the Saarinen office developed for its clients. This strategy had been launched with the windows of the General Motors Technical Center, which were zippered in with neoprene gaskets like automobile windshields (similar gaskets would be used in both IBM facilities). Other technical innovations developed by Saarinen's office include the first architectural use of Cor-Ten steel at the John Deere administration building in Moline, Illinois, and the pioneering utilization of mirrored glass for Bell Labs in Holmdel, New Jersey. All generated considerable press for Saarinen and his clients, and the corporations used them to brand their new buildings in public relations campaigns. Bell's mirrored facade became the company's signature, its application as a logo extending to staff cafeteria placemats.

Beyond its ability to project the image of a new and modern IBM, the Rochester structure's bright and cheerful appearance counteracted the negative impression of the company as an ever expanding behemoth that was turning humans into faceless automatons in the service of computers. Watson referred to this concern in his dedication speech for the new Rochester facility on September 30, 1958. "People think we build electronic brains," he noted. "But nobody, of course, can build a brain. We build tools to lighten the burden on men's brains and enable them to do greater things with their brains. . . . But we do think that better tools make better individuals and we want to continue to build good tools to lift drudgerous, boresome, and difficult tasks from the brain and let the brain soar on to greater things." Saarinen's dazzling building performed the necessary lift, impressing the public and the press alike.[16]

In addition to the symbolism of the exterior facades, it was Saarinen's design of communal spaces that created a sense of inspiration and camaraderie for workers at the Rochester facility. These features included glass-walled corridors where employees could meet and talk, as well as a cafeteria and landscaped outdoor dining patios. Such public spaces fostered IBM's "community character" and social cohesiveness, which were important values for the company and were responsible for making this branch of the corporation so appealing.

IBM's desire to have communal spaces for its employees built not only on the company's ethos of a corporate family—seen in its celebrated "Two Generations" clubs of father and son employees—but also the growing importance of the field of human relations in American business. Interest in worker relations had steadily increased since the post–Civil War era, when the rise of the "company," a term derived from military language, brought about a new level of bureaucracy—"middle" management. Employees were hired to implement marketing strategies, coordinate long-distance distribution networks, and perform myriad other managerial tasks. By the turn of the century, a paternalistic work culture had begun to emerge in the office. Frank Lloyd Wright's Larkin Administration Building in Buffalo, New York (1906), built for a soap company's mail-order business, embodied a progressive ideal of uplifting work. Boasting the most advanced architectural design and mechanical systems, it also provided opportunities for employees' self-improvement: a YWCA, a library, and a music lounge in a light-filled atrium that was adorned with carved inspirational sayings and furnished with an organ for lunchtime performances. In subsequent decades the field of human relations would take shape, propelled by studies that suggested good relationships with co-workers and supervisors resulted in higher productivity. IBM's interest in spaces that fostered such accord was a contemporary manifestation of this idea.

Saarinen's second job for IBM was the Thomas J. Watson Research Center, located in Yorktown Heights in Westchester County, about forty miles north of New York City. Commissioned in 1957 and dedicated in 1961, the building was erected in an elegant suburb in IBM's traditional East Coast base. Intended to house fifteen hundred scientists working on advanced computer science, the elite of the company's brain trust, it would also serve as a crossroads for what Dr. Emmanuel Priore, IBM's head of research and engineering, described as a new mobility between academia, government, and industry. This confluence was an outgrowth of developments during World War II, when such efforts as the Manhattan Project joined the talents of government and academia to produce the atomic bomb. This military-industrial-academic complex would be a major catalyst for the construction of new laboratories on college campuses as well as corporate facilities like IBM's in Yorktown Heights.

Although in the Yorktown project Saarinen had to address the same corporate requirements as in the Rochester facility—expandability, good community relations, communal spaces, and progressive design—his strategy for Yorktown varied from that employed in the midwestern locale. Unlike the flat plains of Minnesota, the 240-acre Westchester site had rolling hills, which inspired a different architectural response. Like Rochester, the first Yorktown design called for a series of buildings located around landscaped courtyards that stepped up the hilly terrain. Sketches illustrate a scheme with hipped-roofed pavilions topped by decorative finials—a radical change from the unsentimental modernism of Rochester. But as the design for the Yorktown Heights facility developed it became simpler and bolder: a series of masonry-and-glass boxes separated by courtyards. Fusing architecture and promotion, Saarinen's office created a graphic logo of this plan for the cover of the presentation brochure for IBM (figs. 8, 9).

Fig. 8 Eero Saarinen and Associates, "IBM Research Center," presentation brochure for first scheme

Fig. 9 (opposite, top) Eero Saarinen and Associates, International Business Machines Thomas J. Watson Research Center, Yorktown Heights, New York, 1957–61, plan of first scheme (from presentation brochure)

Fig. 10 (opposite, bottom) IBM Thomas J. Watson Research Center, Yorktown Heights, New York, view from entrance road

But after extensive research into the work habits of the scientists who would use the building—another well-publicized aspect of the Saarinen process that included interviews with staff and the construction of a full-scale office mock-up to test planning innovations—the courtyard parti was abandoned and replaced by a single, dramatically curving building, clad in local fieldstone and dark glass with metal mullions (fig. 10). Saarinen had noticed that most researchers sat with their backs to windows and kept venetian blinds drawn. This observation led him to design the interior as a curving row of windowless offices and laboratories, like beads on a necklace. These spaces were separated by radial aisles that led to two curving corridors running the full length of the building's convex and concave facades. The crescent-shaped plan could be easily extended, simply by adding new modules of aisles and offices.

This unusual plan, the project's principal innovation, was Yorktown's answer to Rochester's ultra-thin wall. The curving corridor running along the 1,090-foot convex side of the structure would serve as a promenade where IBM employees could walk, converse, and even work at Saarinen-designed tables while enjoying the landscape through full-height windows.

Materials as well as views related building and site. As the promenade's windows extended to the floor, its wall-to-wall carpeting seemed to merge with the lawn's manicured grass. The fieldstone clad the building's end walls and interior partitions in rooms like the cafeteria, which featured other natural materials such as slate and teak. IBM's publicity photographs self-consciously made the connection to the site and its history. One shows a historic wood-and-stone shed, seemingly on the new building's site or in the vicinity. "The wooded, rolling hills and fieldstone walls," the photograph's caption begins, "play a large part in shaping the character of the building."[17] Another image depicted the new structure barely visible behind a suburban tract house, reinforcing IBM's expressed goal to build facilities that served as "good neighbors" and did not overwhelm their communities.

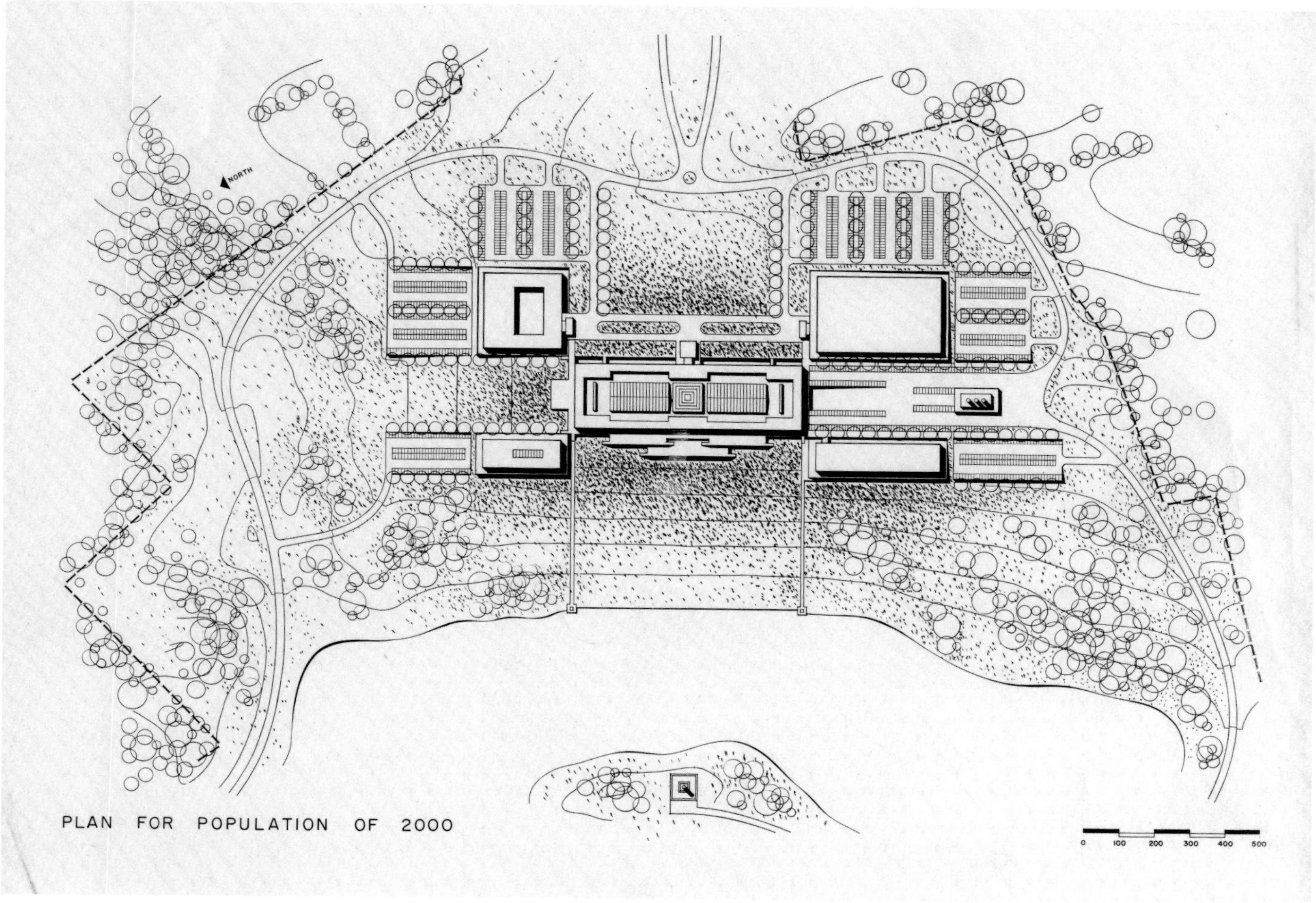

NORTH

PLAN FOR POPULATION OF 2000

0 100 200 300 400 500

Fig. 11 Eero Saarinen and Associates, Columbia Broadcasting System, Inc., Building, New York, 1960–65, model with corporate logo on roof

Nestled into the top of the site's crescent-shaped hill, IBM Yorktown was a commanding presence in the landscape that advanced a new postwar typology of corporate estates erected by companies moving from central cities to the suburbs. With its sweeping front lawn, the building dominated its setting like a grand English country house. Akin to Saarinen's design for GM's industrial Versailles, IBM Yorktown elevated the image of corporate America by successfully trading on aristocratic associations. And, like GM, the project included commissioned artwork, most notably Seymour Lipton's matching sculptures that flanked the facility's canopied entrance.

Upon its opening in the spring of 1961, IBM Yorktown was greeted with considerable press coverage extolling the design's innovative features. *Architectural Record* praised the "spectacular setting" and "unique cross-curve plan." *Architectural Forum* heralded the building as "a sweeping departure in laboratory planning." Manufacturers of the building's hinges, floor tiles, and folding partitions sponsored advertisements and even special postcards mailed to architects that boasted of their companies' collaborations with IBM and the Saarinen office.[18]

A key aide to Saarinen and his office in client and media relations was his second wife, Aline B. Louchheim, whom he had married in 1954. Previously, in a letter to his psychiatrist, Saarinen had expressed his ambitions to be not only an architect "who contributes to culture" but also a "person of culture," and mused as well on the qualifications of the ideal wife.[19] Louchheim would prove a perfect candidate to help Saarinen meet this goal. She was an associate art critic for the *New York Times* from 1947 to 1959, often examining in her articles the relation between art and society. She was also the author of the popular book *The Proud Possessors* (1958), which explored the kinship between wealthy collectors and dealers in the creation of taste, and after Saarinen's death she would become a pioneering television talk show host. Throughout their marriage, Aline served Eero as a valuable cultural adviser. With her extensive contacts in the New York–based media, she also assisted Saarinen and his office on press relations (later listing her tenure at the office as "Head of Information Services") and, from her art-historical perspective, provided the broader social and cultural framework Saarinen sought for his practice.[20]

Aline and Eero had met in 1953, when she interviewed him for a *New York Times Magazine* article titled "Now Saarinen the Son." In all her efforts on behalf of Saarinen's career, she used the media to reach the broadest possible audience. After visiting the GM Tech Center, Aline wrote that Eero had professionally come of age; his contribution to American society was "in giving form or visual order to the industrial civilization in which he belongs." In subsequent years she continued to garner coverage for Saarinen in the popular and professional press—she herself wrote about him in *Vogue*. She also forcefully controlled access to his projects, urging both writers and clients to publicize them when they were completed; only then could the buildings be fully experienced and their value accurately presented to the popular jury. By 1958, writing in a letter to her mentor, Bernard Berenson, Aline admitted, "Now I observe myself ardently promulgating the Eero-myth."[21]

Among the many clients who worked closely with Aline was CBS; its granite-clad midtown Manhattan tower would be Saarinen's last commission. As a leader in the postwar era's most popular form of entertainment, television, CBS clearly understood the building's media potential. At one point in the new headquarters' development, CBS considered placing its corporate logo on the structure's roof (fig. 11), and it later turned the building's construction into popular entertainment by erecting a 300-foot-long Plexiglas wall along the site that offered pedestrians the chance to watch the structure going up as they listened to ongoing commentary about its progress on loudspeakers. Whereas Saarinen's projects had long involved a synergistic process between client, architect, and media, here, finally, the building itself became a media event, viewed, assessed, and judged every day by America's popular jury.

Notes

1. Conrad Hilton, quoted in Annabel Jane Wharton, *Building the Cold War: Hilton International Hotels and Modern Architecture* (Chicago: University of Chicago Press, 2001).

2. "The American Century" was the title of an article Luce wrote in the Feb. 17, 1941, issue of *Life*.

3. A. Whitney Griswold, transcript of interview with Jonathan Barnett, *Architectural Record*, Jan. 23, 1962, "Records of A. Whitney Griswold as President," RU22, YRG 2-A, box 249, folder 2315, Manuscripts and Archives, Yale University. "Good Design Is Good Business" is the title of a Tiffany/Wharton lecture on corporate design management that Watson delivered, although he had long used the expression to describe IBM's design program. The lecture was published in *The Art of Design Management* (New York: Tiffany, 1975).

4. Eero Saarinen, "The Challenge to the Arts Today," in *Seventy-Five* (New Haven: Yale University Press, 1953), 191; "The Maturing Modern," *Time*, July 2, 1956, 57; Saarinen, "The Challenge to the Arts Today," 113, 191.

5. Alan Valentine, *The Age of Conformity* (Chicago: Henry Regnery, 1954), 113.

6. "Where Today Meets Tomorrow," promotional brochure (Detroit: General Motors, ca. 1956), Eero Saarinen Papers, Manuscripts and Archives, Yale University; "GM's Industrial Versailles: A Color Portfolio on the Completed Technical Center," *Architectural Forum*, May 1956, 123; "The Maturing Modern," 50.

7. "Architecture for the Future: GM Constructs a 'Versailles of Industry,'" *Life*, May 21, 1956, 102; "The Maturing Modern," 52.

8. Reyner Banham, "The Fear of Eero's Mana," *Arts Magazine*, Feb. 1962, 73.

9. There also were affinities between the two men's personal biographies. Watson and Saarinen studied at Ivy League schools and served in the government during World War II. Both also had successful fathers from whose shadows they emerged in the 1950s.

10. Watson, "Good Design Is Good Business," 58.

11. Ibid.; Thomas J. Watson, Jr., and Peter Petre, *Father, Son & Co.: My Life at IBM and Beyond* (New York: Bantam, 1990), 260.

12. Watson and Petre, *Father, Son & Co.*, 261.

13. Hugh B. Johnston. "From Old IBM to New IBM," *Industrial Design*, Mar. 1957, 51.

14. Thomas J. Watson, Jr., Sept. 30, 1958, dedication speech, "Rochester—Box 19—Dedication," IBM Archive, Somers, N.Y.; Watson, "Good Design Is Good Business," 79; Peter Blake, "Buildings that Speak for Themselves," *Think*, May–June 1977, 17.

15. Johnston, "From Old IBM to New IBM," 48; Eero Saarinen, quoted in Martin, *The Organizational Complex: Architecture, Media, and Corporate Space* (Cambridge: MIT Press, 2003), 163.

16. Watson, dedication speech, Sept. 30, 1958.

17. The photograph is located in the file "Yorktown—Box 59—Site Models—circa 1959," IBM Archive, Somers, N.Y.

18. "Unique Cross-curve Plan for IBM Research Center," *Architectural Record*, June 1961, 137, and "Research in the Round," *Architectural Forum*, June 1961, 81.

19. Eero Saarinen, unaddressed letter, Apr. 1952, Aline Saarinen Papers, Archives of American Art, Washington, D.C.

20. "Resume/Biographical Information," Aline Saarinen Papers, Archives of American Art.

21. Aline B. Louchheim, "Now Saarinen the Son," *New York Times Magazine*, Apr. 26, 1953, 26; Aline Saarinen, letter to Bernard Berenson, May 24, 1958, Aline Saarinen Papers, Archives of American Art.

Will Miller

eero and irwin
praiseworthy competition with one's ancestors

Great architecture is, therefore, a triple achievement. It is the solving of a concrete problem. It is the free expression of the architect himself. And it is an inspired and intuitive expression of his client. The greatest architecture accomplishes all this with no appearance of strain or awkwardness, but rather with an evident conviction that these simultaneous goals have enriched the whole enterprise and have not simply watered it down by compromise.

J. Irwin Miller, preface, *Kevin Roche John Dinkeloo and Associates, 1962–1975*

One of the important relationships in Eero Saarinen's life, professionally and personally, was with J. Irwin Miller (fig. 1). For Saarinen and his colleagues, Miller was "the perfect client."[1] For Miller, who worked with many of the most celebrated postwar architects, Saarinen was his favorite. Together they completed four projects, three of which have been designated National Historic Landmarks.

Miller's business career centered primarily on the Cummins Engine Company, which he ran from 1934 until his retirement as its CEO in 1977. In those forty-three years he built it from a job shop that had not made a profit in its fifteen years of existence into a Fortune 500 company with global operations. It remains today the world's leading independent manufacturer of diesel engines. Miller was also well known for his philanthropy in his hometown of Columbus, Indiana, and for his role nationally in the ecumenical and civil rights movements in the 1960s.

Eero and Irwin's relationship flowered in the decade before Saarinen's premature death. The 1950s was the apex of the American Century. The war was over. The American economy was exploding, propelled by a baby boom and the dominance of American industry in the expansion of global trade. Both men felt the stimulation and excitement of a whole new attitude about what the future could and ought to be. As each came into the prime of his life, in an era unencumbered by the limitations on American ambition that would follow in the latter half of the century, he perceived an opportunity to make a difference in society and (to use the term most often favored by Saarinen) a meaningful contribution to civilization.[2]

It is not hard to understand why Eero and Irwin became close friends. Both were heirs to powerful traditions embodied by accomplished and influential men—Eliel Saarinen and Miller's great-uncle, William G. Irwin, one of the most successful bankers and venture capitalists in Indiana in the first half of the twentieth century. Each took his received traditions in his

Fig. 1 J. Irwin Miller in a Womb chair at his house in Columbus, Indiana, ca. 1947. Also pictured are Xenia Miller and their daughter Catherine.

Fig. 2 (below) Eero Saarinen and Associates, Miller Cottage, Ontario, Canada, 1950–52, view from west

own direction, building on them, neither rejecting their major tenets nor merely repeating them.

Eero and Irwin shared an approach to their work that was grounded in a strong moral framework. In 1959 Saarinen remarked, "I would say that the common denominator of my work is the constant philosophy—the constant respect for the principles in which I believe."[3] For Miller, the necessity of a moral framework was rooted in his Christian faith, which he understood as applying to every aspect of his life and behavior. In the 1930s, when other businessmen in the United States were calling in police forces to crush unionization movements, Miller actively supported the formation of a union at his company. Miller was the first layperson to be elected president of the National Council of Churches in the United States. In this capacity, he helped organize the historic civil rights march on Washington in 1963, leading Rev. Martin Luther King, Jr., to call him "the most progressive businessman in America." In the 1970s, when the South African government under apartheid would not let his company run its factories and offices in a racially integrated manner, Miller chose to pull Cummins out altogether, abandoning a 20 percent share of the South African market for diesel engines.

For both men, seeking to do the best they could in every endeavor was an imperative. When they worked together, each viewed the design process as a search for the best solution to the particular problem involved. Every project was an opportunity to start with a clean sheet of paper and seek to create a new model that would express the modern age but could also serve to improve the efforts of others.

They were also both Yale graduates, and thus members of a community known for loyalty to its alma mater. Contrary to a story often published, Saarinen and Miller did not meet as undergraduates at Yale. Born in 1909, Miller was one year older than Saarinen. When Saarinen first came to Yale to study in the department of architecture in 1931, Miller had already graduated. They met in 1939 when Saarinen accompanied his father to Columbus for meetings with the building committee of the First Christian Church. As neither Eero nor Irwin was permitted in these meetings, Irwin was assigned the duty of playing host to Eero and Charles Eames, two young men about his age. The three of them made a habit of going to a local Victorian soda fountain where, over ice cream and long discussions of design and the political situation in Finland, they struck up a friendship.

The parallels in Eero's and Irwin's lives set the groundwork for their deep friendship. The intersection of their work gave it expression. Miller was Saarinen's most consistent client: from 1950 until Saarinen's death, his office never lacked a project for Miller.

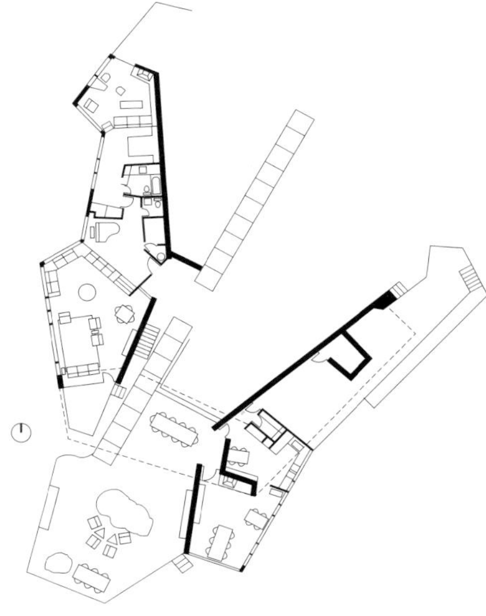

Fig. 3 Miller Cottage, as-built plan, drawn by Will Miller, 2006

Fig. 4 (above right) Miller Cottage, living room

The buildings Saarinen did for Miller are among his best, in no small part because they work beautifully in addition to being beautiful. Their functionality reflects the fact that Miller was, as Kevin Roche notes, "a good judge of what was appropriate and what was not appropriate. . . . He followed the evolution of the [architectural] profession so he knew what was going on, he knew what was being considered, he knew what was being written about and he was informed about it."[4] Miller enjoyed the entire range of expression in Saarinen's work. Of the four buildings Eero designed for Irwin, each had its own vocabulary.

THE MILLER COTTAGE (1952)

Saarinen's first commission from Miller came in 1950, the year Eliel died, for a summer cottage on property in the Muskoka District of Ontario, Canada, where Miller's family had been summering since 1886. In both the cottage and the Miller House that followed, Irwin's wife, Xenia, played as active a role in the design process as he did. Xenia Simons Miller grew up in Columbus and surrounding towns, the daughter of the owner of a furniture manufacturing business that failed in the Great Depression. After high school, she went to work as a purchasing agent at Cummins, where she became a skillful negotiator and reader of blueprints. She planned on attending college in the late 1930s, but a supervisor convinced her she would make more money pursuing her career in manufacturing. Irwin and Xenia began dating in the early 1940s. They were married in Washington, D.C., in February 1943, while he was in naval officer training.

In sharp contrast to the Miesian formal language of the General Motors Technical Center, which Saarinen was working on at the same time, the design of the Miller Cottage shows an interest in regional modernism (fig. 2). It is best understood as a physical interpretation of the family's needs, growing directly out of the site and employing a palette of indigenous materials, rearranged into a totally fresh and radical expression. This approach was consistent with Saarinen's philosophy: "I see architecture not as the building alone, but the building in relation to its surroundings, whether nature or man-made surroundings."[5] The particularities of the topography on the long rocky peninsula led him to abandon any repetition of a building module, instead arranging the rooms so that almost no wall intersects another at a right angle (fig. 3). He reinterpreted the indigenous architectural traditions of the Muskoka District "cottage country"—board-and-batten siding, fine stonework, open-air porches, and simple uninsulated construction techniques—in a manner as shocking locally as Frank Gehry's use of chain-link fence in his house in Santa Monica would be twenty-five years later.

Fig. 5 Miller Cottage, terrace

Among the constraints the Millers placed on the design for the cottage was a desire to remove as few of the mature trees as possible and to avoid blasting any of the rock. The changes in level necessitated by a large boulder on the west side of the site were used to organize the functions of the master bedroom (private sitting area and desk below; sleeping area above) and living room (raised platform for a piano; fireplace, seating areas, and card table on a lower level [fig. 4]), which flow from north to south over the boulder and down the other side. The exceptional stonework of local masons was used both for the walls that define the courtyard and for the large terrace that created an outdoor living room. The simplicity of local cottage construction was expressed in the open-joist ceilings. The simplicity is deceptive, however, particularly in the living room: as the walls diverge, the span of the joists increases, which meant they had to be placed progressively closer together. While the ceiling's structure was meticulously engineered, the visual effect of this changing rhythm of the joists creates an almost musical counterpoint to the space.

Everywhere the spaces, indoors and out, are arranged to connect function to the patterns of nature. On the east, where the family could enjoy the morning sun, Saarinen placed the kitchen and eating porch. To the south, in a position that would provide a windbreak for the terrace, he placed the dining room. On the west, with views of the lake and the setting sun, he put the living room and master bedroom. Between these two wings, he fashioned a large open terrace divided into areas for sitting and open-air dining by a pair of fifty-foot pine trees (fig. 5).

In an early scheme, the children were to be housed in a separate building to the north on a high point of the peninsula. As architect and clients gathered around the model, Xenia expressed reservations about being so disconnected from the children. Saarinen suddenly tore the children's wing off the hill and placed it on top of the other two sections to act as a bridge between them. Thus was born the dramatic horseshoe shape of the house, which solved the practical requirement of keeping the bedrooms of the young children close at hand while covering the rear portion of the terrace to create a protected outdoor eating area directly off the kitchen. The move integrated the interior and exterior spaces formed by the house.

The other great integrative element was the copper roof, which covers the entire house except the dining room in a single tilted plane. The slope of the roof interacts with the changing levels inside the west wing to vary the scale of the rooms, from the intimacy of the master bedroom to the grandness of the two-story living room. The angles of the exterior walls are arranged both to accommodate function and to pull the best views of the lake, the islands, and the sky into each room. As there is no link between the two wings on the first floor, and as there are no corridors connecting the second-floor rooms, most of the circulation takes place outdoors under the protection of the overhang of the roof.

One of Saarinen's collaborators was Alexander Girard, an architect and interior designer who also lived in Michigan at the time. Saarinen had been impressed with the design and decoration of Girard's home in Grosse Pointe.[6] He engaged Girard to work as a color consultant on both the General Motors Technical Center (1948–56) and the Miller Cottage. Girard's love of folk art and his skill with color particularly appealed to Xenia. Together they selected a palette of dark brown wood siding, gray plywood panels, and white wood sashes, with vivid splashes of red, yellow, and orange on the doors of the cottage.

In the early 1950s the contemporaneous design in different parts of Saarinen's office of the GM Tech Center and the Miller Cottage represented the first flowering of his interest in the simultaneous exploration of multiple design approaches, each uniquely suited to the programs of very different clients. Upstairs he strove in the GM project to harness and humanize the industrial styles that preoccupied many American architects working for corporate clients, while extending the possibilities of these idioms with new technologies. Downstairs he pursued a totally different strategy based on

Fig. 6 Eero Saarinen and Associates, Irwin Union Trust Company, Columbus, Indiana, 1950–54

Fig. 7 (right) Irwin Union Trust Company, view of lobby showing teller line and ceiling

the particularities of the site, abandoning repetitive modules and orthogonal relationships. Neither he nor his clients saw a contradiction in this method. Each design was true to the problem it was solving.

IRWIN UNION TRUST COMPANY (1954)

In 1950 Miller decided it was time to build a new headquarters for the Irwin Union Bank and Trust Company, his family's bank. Once again he turned to Saarinen. The site, irregularly shaped and slightly larger than a quarter block, is located at one of the most significant intersections in downtown Columbus. Surrounding it are two- and three-story Victorian commercial buildings. The existing bank headquarters, immediately across the street, offered a traditional image of wealth, power, and security through its barred teller cages and heavy limestone-clad exterior.

Miller desired a radical departure, given his belief that the bank was too stuffy and unfriendly. He wanted everything about the bank to make it comfortable and easy for customers from all walks of life to do business there, and at the same time he wanted the new building to be a good neighbor to the existing fabric of the town. In particular, barred teller windows with signs that said "closed" when not in use struck Miller as aggressively inhospitable. He also asked that the office of the bank's president be placed in the middle of the lobby, forcing daily interaction with a full range of customers. The boardroom was to double as a conference room available for use by community groups.

Saarinen often repeated his father's dictum that called for seeking the solution in terms of the next larger thing. This approach is evident in the Irwin Union Bank (fig. 6). The main level contains a core housing the president's office and two small conference rooms surrounded by a glass pavilion of freely flowing open space. The lobby ceiling (fig. 7) is lifted and given visual interest by the placement of nine shallow domes with upward-facing light fixtures that are strongly reminiscent of his father's and his work at Cranbrook. To harmonize this glass-walled structure with its Victorian context, Saarinen set the pavilion back from the street and surrounded it with a single band of trees. He further integrated it with the town by placing most back-office functions in a connected building on the irregular portion of the site, restoring the orthogonal grid of the town and creating a solid three-story backdrop on the north that echoed a neighboring building on the west.

Saarinen designed every detail of the lobby to convey friendliness and accessibility. Customers enter at grade through an airlock of floor-to-ceiling glass. The floor is a basket-weave of brick, reflecting Miller's concern that a factory worker with oil on his boots should not feel uncomfortable walking in

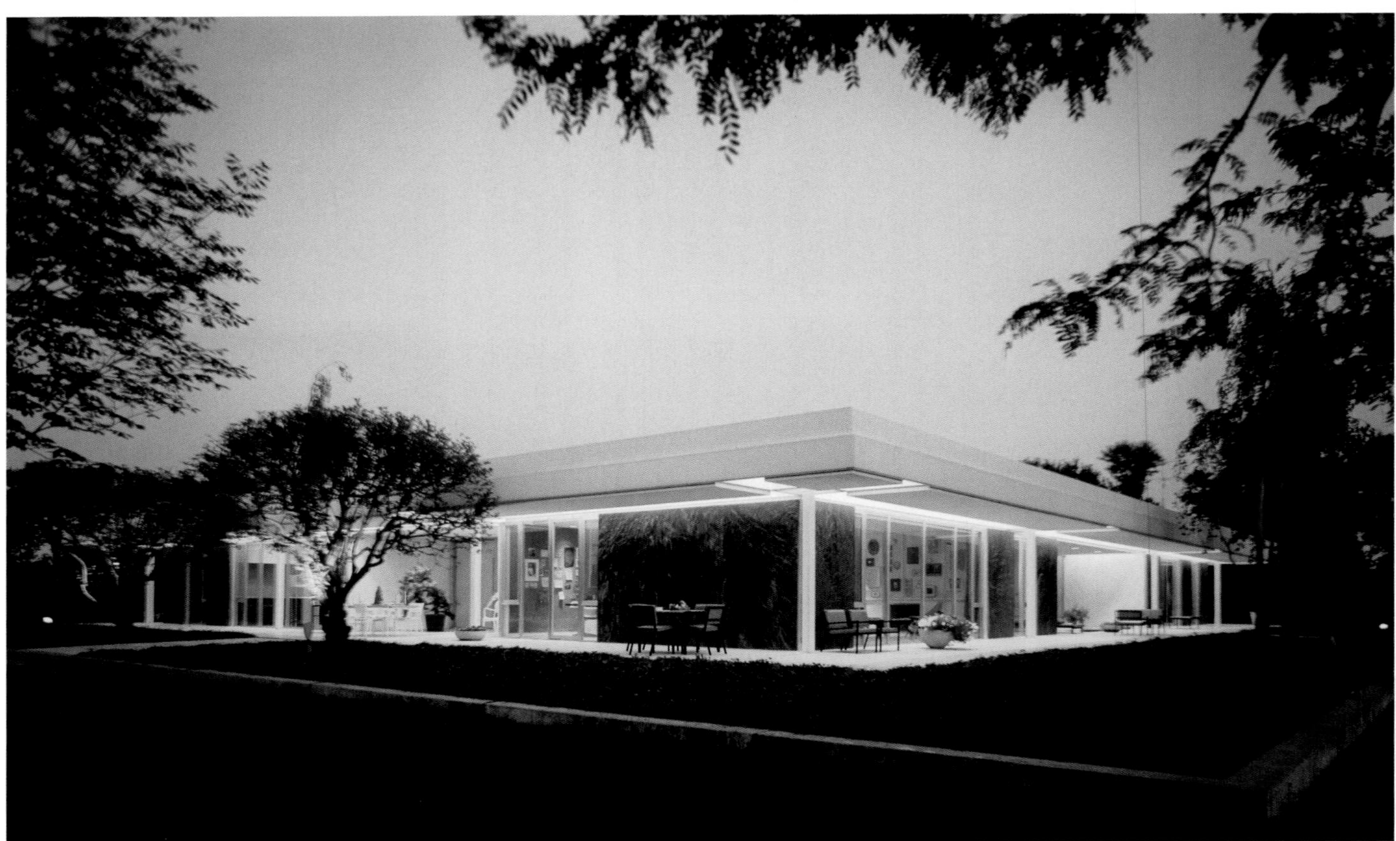

Fig. 8 Eero Saarinen and Associates, Miller House, Columbus, Indiana, 1953–57

to do business. Loan officers and deposit personnel sit at Knoll desks, available to discuss a mortgage or set up an account without forcing customers to go into an office. A drive-up teller window, an innovation at the time, is provided. A large open stairway is positioned at the center of the lobby leading downstairs to the boardroom/community room and safe-deposit area, placed on the lower level to provide more privacy. To eliminate the unfriendly "closed" signs at the teller windows, Saarinen invented a new kind of teller line. Open above counter height, it has a band of fiberglass hoods that are removed when a teller window is open, to indicate clearly where service is available, but when in place form a continuous band that causes a closed position to disappear. The inviting and comfortable spirit of the architecture has a timeless quality thanks to the skillful blend of Miesian formality and warm Cranbrook touches.

THE MILLER HOUSE (1957)

Nearly as soon as the cottage in Canada was complete, Irwin and Xenia Miller asked Saarinen to design a year-round home for them in Columbus, Indiana (fig. 8). Given his role as the CEO of a rapidly growing international company located in a small town without good hotels or restaurants, Miller and his wife wanted a place to entertain business guests from around the world without sacrificing a good environment in which to raise their children. Kevin Roche took a lead role on the Miller House as the associate architect in the firm. Girard was engaged, as he had been on the cottage, to design the interiors.

On the thirteen-acre rectangular site stretching between a busy street and a river, architect and clients chose the edge of a thirty-foot drop in grade about a third of the way back from the street as the best location. The plan of the house is organized as a rectangle divided into nine sections. Four distinct elements in the corners are dedicated to the master bedroom suite, the children's area, the kitchen/laundry, and a zone encompassing the guest room, servant's quarters, and a carport. The children's suite borrowed its layout from what Saarinen described to the Millers as a typical arrangement of children's rooms in Finland. The private bedroom of each child was made relatively small and functional. A common playroom of generous proportions was intended to encourage

Fig. 9 Miller House, entry hall with X-column and skylight

Fig. 10 Miller House, detail of conversation pit, skylight, and X-column

social interaction in the family. The four corner elements were arranged to create spaces between them that are finely tuned to their respective functions of entryway, living room, dining room, and den.

Aesthetically the house represents a continuation of the dialogue between Saarinen and the predominant contemporary architectural thinking as represented in Ludwig Mies van der Rohe's German Pavilion in Barcelona (1929) and Farnsworth House in Plano, Illinois (1951). From the Barcelona pavilion, Saarinen and Roche drew the ideas of creating the main walls of the public areas out of floor-to-ceiling slabs of marble cut several inches thick and mounted with exposed edges; eliminating a sense of separation between the interior and the natural surroundings through the use of huge panes of glass; and using the structural system of X-columns without load-bearing walls to provide great flexibility in the arrangement of the rooms (fig. 9).

The principal problem to be solved in this approach was how to enliven the interior spaces, especially those farthest from the windows. The solution was found in the network of skylights that defines the nine-square grid of the plan. The skylights are brilliantly integrated with the structural system and X-columns and bathe the interior of the house in natural light (fig. 10). Every linear foot of skylight is used to maximum advantage. In the living room, the skylights run along the interior walls, casting natural light on the artwork and causing the ceiling to appear to float. Skylights cross the vanity in both the master bathroom and that of the Millers' three daughters. A line of skylights runs immediately outside each exterior wall, mitigating the darkening effect on the outer rooms of the deep soffit that surrounds the house. However, a skylight never crosses a sleeping area.

The interior details are spare. The white marble walls and travertine floors in the public spaces were intended to create a neutral environment that the family would personalize by displaying its own collection of art, objects, and books, which would change over time. The interiors incorporate a number of Girard's signature elements: the conversation pit, the storage wall, and a number of curtains, fabrics, and rugs designed specifically for the home. Girard was a great match for Xenia, who brought considerable knowledge of practical function, a love of detail, and a color sense that rivaled Girard's to the client side of the table. The embodiment of the collaboration between interior designer and client is the storage wall running fifty feet through the living room and den, a series of vertical dividers of white Formica that hold adjustable glass shelving and rosewood cabinets (fig. 11). The storage wall incorporates a concealed stereo system, TV, bar, sheet-music cabinet, bookshelves, and numerous well-lit opportunities to display paintings and art objects in front of small patches of colorful wallpaper, all assembled by Girard and Xenia into a harmonious composition.

Surrounding the house and beautifully integrated with it stands the Miller Garden (fig. 12), a masterwork of Dan Kiley, one of the greatest landscape architects of the twentieth century. Joining the project after the plans for the house were well developed, Kiley used them as one touchstone for his design. The other was Irwin Miller's love of European landscapes, developed on travels through France and Spain as a student at Oxford, in particular the idea of approaching the house through an allée of horse chestnut trees.

While the Millers wanted a home of the best quality, they also wished to avoid creating an ostentatious image in a small community where they were among the wealthiest residents. They asked that the house be set back from the street, screened from public view, and no larger than their functional needs required. The approach was to be through the residential neighborhood to the south, not directly off the main street. The principal issue was how to achieve privacy without seeming unneighborly. Kiley solved the problem with two rows of short hedges of arborvitae, staggered with openings to eliminate the sense of exclusion yet arranged to provide visual privacy. Within this perimeter, Kiley used the same hedges to enclose a series of outdoor rooms, extending the house's grid onto the landscape and echoing Saarinen's strategy of fashioning

Fig. 11 Alexander Girard, Miller House, storage wall

Fig. 12 Dan Kiley, Miller Garden, 1956–57

Fig. 13 (opposite) Eero Saarinen and Associates, North Christian Church, Columbus, Indiana, 1959–64

important moments as much *between* the indoor rooms as within them. In four distinct zones, one on each side of the house, Kiley blended the groves and allées he admired in the works of André Le Nôtre with the crushed gravel and precisely trimmed plants of a Japanese garden, enlivened by occasional informal groupings of locust, beech, and willow trees. The entire site was reshaped to reflect the Cartesian nature of the house. Dramatically, Kiley scraped the undulating slope leading down to the floodplain, transforming it into a flat plane placed orthogonally to the house. Only at the farthest western reaches in the woods at the edge of the river did he leave the natural patterns intact. Kiley's boldest move was to place a grand allée of honey locust trees parallel to the house and running its full length along the upper edge of the slope.

The designs of the house and garden were not without their flaws. Over the years, the family came to view the conversation pit as a mistake. As they aged, the Millers and their guests had trouble getting in and out of it. Perhaps the most significant interior design flaw was the inability to move between private areas without going through the open public space at the center, which could be awkward for family members when Irwin and Xenia were entertaining. Kiley proved to be a great aesthetic visionary but something less of an arborist. Several of his original species choices were poorly suited to the local climate, and more appropriate selections had to be substituted. His design specifications apparently lacked some sophistication as well. The regrading of the slope down to the floodplain compacted the soil at the top so densely that the allée of locust trees along the summit had to be replaced less than twenty years later. Not a single tree had been able to grow its roots outside its original root ball.

The ultimate triumph of the design of Saarinen's Miller House, however, rests in its integration with the artworks contained inside and with the art of the garden created outside. Space and light flow freely, unifying a collection of disparate objects and uniting interior with landscape in a manner reminiscent of the Imperial Villa of Katsura in Kyoto. The end result fashions what would otherwise be cool, elegant materials into a warm and comfortable domestic environment.

NORTH CHRISTIAN CHURCH (1964)

Of the four projects Saarinen and Miller built, North Christian Church was the only one where Miller shared the role of client with a committee, which he chaired. The congregation had been formed in 1956 when Miller and several other ecumenically minded members of the First Christian Church were forced out by a conservative senior minister. By 1958 the new church had grown large enough to contemplate constructing its own building. Saarinen was one of a number of young, first-rate architects with national reputations—including Eduardo Catalano, Victor Lundy, Walter Netsch, Paul Rudolph, Edward Durell Stone, John Carl Warnecke, Harry Weese, and Minoru Yamasaki—invited to apply for the job. He was interviewed in January 1959 and was ultimately the unanimous choice of the committee, even though he could not begin work on the commission until the fall.

The design process stretched out over two years. Saarinen saw this commission as an opportunity to create a new model of church design, and he clearly wanted it to be one of his major works. In characteristic fashion, he kept rethinking the design long after the client wanted to get on with building it. In April 1961 Miller wrote to warn Saarinen that the length of the design process was straining the patience of the congregation. Eero responded:

> It would be so easy to say—as you would like me to—"Let's go ahead with it as it is." But against that I have perhaps a greater conscience, because I would know in my heart that it would not really be the best I can do. We have finally to solve this church so that it can become a great building. I feel I have this obligation to the congregation, and as architect I have that obligation to my profession and my ideals. I want to solve it so that as an architect when I face St. Peter I am able to say that out of the buildings I did in my lifetime, one of the best was this little church, because it has in it a real spirit that speaks forth to all Christians as a witness to their faith.[7]

This was exactly the kind of appeal to principle that resonated with Miller, who argued successfully with the building committee to give him more time. Tragically, no one could know that Saarinen would die unexpectedly within five months, although not before he felt he had achieved his objective. In July he wrote to Irwin, "I think we have finally solved the Columbus church."[8]

The flat site in a residential district at the northern entrance to the community led Saarinen to conclude that the church must be elevated "so that it stands proudly above the parked cars and the surrounding little ranch-type houses and can be seen." Bothered by the prominence in contemporary church design given to secondary functions, Saarinen wished to restore the primacy of the sanctuary seen in European cathedrals of the eleventh and twelfth centuries. In considering the form of the church, Saarinen concentrated on how the primary symbol of Christian buildings, the tower or spire, had been handled historically. He concluded that the new opportunity was "to make the church really all one form: all the tower" (fig. 13).[9]

Reflecting the era's interest in abstract art, Saarinen incorporated the congregation's desire for symbolism directly into the design of the building without resorting to ornamentation. In plan, the church is an elongated hexagon, symbolically linking the structure to the Star of David. Here the Christian form of the spire literally grows out of its roots in Judaism. The sanctuary has a bowl shape, making it seem as if the congregation sits in the hands of God (fig. 14). Saarinen interpreted the central importance of weekly communion in the denomination's tradition by placing the communion table at the center of the sanctuary. The table is broken down into twelve small tables, each representing a disciple, with a taller Christ Table at the end. Reflecting the congregation's decidedly democratic flavor, the preacher speaks from a pulpit on the same level as that of the congregation, not from above. Pews are arranged in the round, so that worshipers look one another in the eye rather than at the back of each other's heads. Given the importance placed by the congregation on the quality of their worship music, Saarinen used the organ pipes as the primary sculptural element in the sanctuary. The church's symbols are also expressed directly through tapestry, candelabra, and color; these were the contributions of Girard.

Saarinen understood, however, that the most important element in creating the spiritual atmosphere he sought was light. The sanctuary is on the whole a dark, inward-focused space, in contrast to the light-filled sanctuary of the First Christian Church (1942), just two miles away. Natural light comes from two sources, the oculus at the apex of the ceiling and a horizontal band of clerestory windows around the upper rim of the sanctuary carrying reflected natural light up the plates of the ceiling, creating a sensation that the roof is floating. The

Fig. 14 North Christian Church, sanctuary

Fig. 15 North Christian Church, sanctuary entrance

scheme is similar to that of his Kresge Chapel at MIT (1950–55) and comes directly from Saarinen's personal experience. In 1959 he wrote, "I have always remembered one night on my travels as a student when I stayed in a mountain village in Sparta. There was bright moonlight overhead and then there was soft, hushed secondary light around the horizon. That sort of bilateral lighting seemed best to achieve this other-worldly sense."[10]

As Saarinen noted in a discussion of the North Christian design, a central idea was that religion should not be easy: "I think you should have to work for it and it should be a special thing." The entire entry sequence was carefully planned as a metaphor for the spiritual journey. First you climb a set of steps from the parking lot on axis with the spire of the church. Reaching the brow of the berm that surrounds the church, you descend a few steps to the front doors with the massive slate roof looming above you, almost forcing you to bow your head as you enter the narthex. Saarinen conceived of this space as a "decompression chamber" buffering the spiritual concerns appropriate to the sanctuary from the cares of the outside world. Lest you think your journey is over, the sanctuary lies above you, up a set of steeper steps than those you ascended from the parking lot. As you climb these steps, you are drawn upward to the oculus—the eye of God—floating at the center of the tentlike ceiling (fig. 15).[11]

One of the most innovative features of the church was the movable dais at its center. In its normal position it served to elevate the communion tables as the central element of the Sunday worship service. These tables, however, could be removed and the dais rotated ninety degrees to become a platform for weddings, funerals, or music and arts performances.

In his desire to invent a new prototype for a worship space, Saarinen deliberately broke with the European hall-church form chosen by his father for the nearby First Christian Church. In his "theater in the round"—where the preacher is literally on the same level as the congregation and the faces of the other worshipers form the backdrop for the service—Saarinen found a true expression for a church rooted in the confluence of Christian piety and American democratic ideals.

THE ARCHITECTURE PROGRAM AT COLUMBUS

Miller is perhaps best remembered for the program that transformed his small town of Columbus, Indiana, into one of the most significant concentrations of postwar architecture in America. Although Saarinen never built a building under the Architecture Program, Miller could not have gotten it started without the active support and involvement of his friend.

In the manufacturing boom after World War II, Columbus nearly doubled in size within a few short years, driven in no small part by the success of Miller's Cummins Engine Company. The associated baby boom increased pressure on the local school system for new classrooms to handle the surge in school-age children. A negative view of the local public school facilities was beginning to affect Miller's ability to recruit talented managers and engineers to the community.

In this context, Miller had an idea. He thought the best way to change the quality of school construction was to engage the most talented architects to drive the design process from the beginning. In late 1954 his company formed the Cummins Engine Foundation, for "religious, educational, and charitable purposes." At the time it was one of only 250 company-sponsored foundations in the United States. One of its first actions was to make an offer to the local school system: if the school board would select an architect from a list provided by the foundation, it would pay the architect's fees. The grants served Miller's philanthropic purposes by improving schools for everyone in the community, but they were also an act of enlightened self-interest, as better schools would make recruiting easier for his local business interests.

Two practical issues had to be resolved: how to identify architects of the right caliber and how to interest them in accepting commissions in a small town in southern Indiana. Miller turned to Saarinen for the answers. The strategy they devised was to identify the most promising young architects without established reputations, for whom a school commission would be a great opportunity no matter how remotely located. Saarinen consulted with Pietro Belluschi, dean of the School of Architecture at MIT, to put together the initial list of five young architects. Eero contacted each one to explain the intent behind the program and encourage him to respond to the opportunity. Harry Weese was chosen, and his design was so popular that the school board took the initiative to ask the foundation if it could have the same incentive for its next building. What was initially conceived as a one-time solution to a specific community problem evolved over time into the Architecture Program, with eligibility being extended to all public buildings in the county.

Over the course of nearly fifty-five years, either directly or by inspiring nonpublic entities to strive for excellence in design, the Architecture Program has transformed the built environment of the community. Of the more than sixty notable modern structures that resulted from this effort, half received a subsidy from the Cummins Foundation. In a national survey of eight hundred American architects in 1991, Columbus was ranked in the top six American cities for architectural quality and innovation, behind only Chicago, New York, San Francisco, Boston, and Washington, D.C. The significance of the modern architecture in Columbus led to the designation of the community as a whole, and four specific Saarinen buildings in it, as National Historic Landmarks in 2000.[12]

Reflecting his enduring love of the classics, Miller often summed up his approach to life by borrowing a notion from the Roman historian Tacitus, defining a good life as one led in praiseworthy competition with one's ancestors. He believed that the best response to the gifts we receive from previous generations is to create something of lasting value in our own time and in our own way for future generations.

In April 1956, Saarinen gave a speech in which he said, "You young architects will find the twin qualities necessary for an architect are humility and 'crust.' Humility for the problem and the realities, 'crust' for solving the problem and sticking with the essentials of the solution."[13] This humane combination of personal humility and unshakable devotion to principle bound Saarinen and Miller together. They shared an intense commitment to solving problems, whether of a particular architectural program or of society as a whole, based on the contextual application of core principles rather than inflexible rules of style or tradition. Both men developed and reinforced in each other an ability to embrace a wide variety of approaches to challenges, within a consistent framework of deeply held personal values. This ability to embrace diversity without compromising the self offers a powerful example for the present day, when Americans are struggling to make multiculturalism work while learning to live and function as a coherent nation in an increasingly interdependent world.

Notes

1. Kevin Roche, interview with the author, Feb. 14, 2005.

2. Ibid.

3. Eero Saarinen, *Eero Saarinen on His Work: A Selection of Buildings Dating from 1947 to 1964*, with statements by the architect, ed. Aline B. Saarinen (New Haven: Yale University Press, 1962), 6–8.

4. Roche interview.

5. Saarinen, *Eero Saarinen on His Work*, 7.

6. Roche interview.

7. Eero Saarinen, letter to J. Irwin Miller, Apr. 18, 1961, J. Irwin Miller Estate, Columbus, Ind.

8. Eero Saarinen, letter to J. Irwin Miller, July 28, 1961, J. Irwin Miller Estate.

9. Saarinen, *Eero Saarinen on His Work*, 88.

10. Ibid., 36.

11. Ibid., 88.

12. "Architects Select the Best of American Architecture in AIA Survey," American Institute of Architects press release, Sept. 6, 1991, 5–6.

13. Saarinen, *Eero Saarinen on His Work*, 8.

Reinhold Martin

what is a material?

Fig. 1 Eero Saarinen and Associates, Deere and Company Administrative Center, Moline, Illinois, 1957–63, facade detail

We need only think of modern architecture's long-standing (if often rhetorical) identification with steel and glass, as well as with concrete, to recall that entire categories of architectural production and their attendant ideologies have frequently been defined in relation to the use of materials. From 1950 to 1966, Eero Saarinen and Associates contributed more than its share of innovations to this realm. Therefore, as we reconsider the career of Eero Saarinen in historical perspective, it seems important to ask a simple question: What is a material?

This question can be answered straight off. What is commonly called a material in architecture is nothing more and nothing less than what the philosopher of science Bruno Latour has called a "nature-culture hybrid."[1] On the face of it, this seems self-evident. For what is a material if not an impure combination of natural objects (say, iron oxide or rust) and cultural objects (say, farm machinery or the image of the "rust belt")? And yet with Saarinen, the hybrid materiality of architecture in general turns out to be a particularly complex matter.

Saarinen is often thought of as a proto-postmodern—or what Charles Jencks once called a "late modern"—architect. To be sure, Saarinen makes various appearances in Jencks's catalogue of "late modernism," all of which are at the level of image, something for which the Saarinen office was well known. But the firm's many innovations in the use of new materials or groundbreaking techniques in constructing these images—often under the guiding hand of John Dinkeloo—have been less widely acknowledged.

Though replacing image with materiality as the centerpiece of Saarinen's contribution would still leave behind the utopianism that characterized the modernist turn toward glass, steel, and concrete, it might at least complicate our understanding of Saarinen as a precursor to postmodernism. Yet in doing so, it would also risk flattening our historical understanding in a different way, by recruiting him into the service of another, equally dubious historical trajectory —that of an officially sanctioned, anti-utopian (and in that sense, postmodern) neomodernism currently in vogue. In order to sidestep all of this, I want to emphasize the enigmatic character of the work, not only with respect to the relation of materiality to image, but also concerning the relation of the modern to the postmodern, since Saarinen's case is also a kind of hybrid, in which such polarities as modern versus postmodern and material versus image intermingle and overlap.

STEEL

Think of the infamous accusation leveled at Saarinen's architecture for providing a "style for the job."[2] In the case of the John Deere headquarters in Moline, Illinois, we get a renovated corporate image for a farm equipment company on the cusp of the postindustrial age, located at the edge of what would soon become known as the rust belt. This slightly perverse set of associations is materialized most dramatically in the building's rusty, exposed ASTM A-242 Cor-Ten steel frame (fig. 1). But there is much more to it than that. In undertaking the project, Deere made the decision to reinforce its status as a major multinational corporation by—somewhat counterintuitively—building its new administrative headquarters in northwestern Illinois rather than in a metropolitan center, although off-site from the nearby factory where the company was founded in 1837. The selection of a new location, which ran parallel with the selection of an architect, reflected this decision by emphasizing scenery over convenience. Saarinen reinforced it by suggesting that Deere choose a site with built-in scenery, rather than rely solely on distant panoramic views (fig. 2).[3] In the end the corporation settled on a 680-acre piece of land made up of a number of separate parcels.

Fig. 2 Saarinen studying Deere site from truck lift

Fig. 3 (opposite, top) Eero Saarinen and Associates, Deere and Company Administrative Center, working drawing sheet 10, showing existing tree survey by Sasaki, Walker, and Associates

Fig. 4 (opposite, bottom) Eero Saarinen and Associates, Deere and Company Administrative Center, working drawing sheet 50, showing new tree plan by Sasaki, Walker, and Associates

Thus began the process of acquiring the built-in scenery, as nature and culture collided in the form of rolling landscapes and real estate. Here is an excerpt from Progress Report No. 1, issued to Deere chairman William A. Hewitt on January 31, 1957, by Nathan Lesser of the Deere engineering department:

1. Option money has been deposited with Mr. Howard Connell, realtor, who has been given the go ahead in acquiring real estate.
2. Mr. Connell has already contacted approximately a dozen people. He expects to close John and Hagstrom promptly. He will push the closing with White, which is the next key piece.
3. As soon as White is closed Gooch is next in line. It is understood that he will be approached by Mr. Hewitt personally.[4]

And so on. What Saarinen's official statement described as a site "studded with trees and . . . intimately connected to nature" was also, like so many building sites, an elaborate construction enabled by subtle financial and social maneuvering.[5]

This maneuvering extended to the trees, which like the ravine where the structures were eventually nestled must be understood as among the project's many construction materials, working in visual, rhythmic sympathy with the building's exposed steel. By contrast, the Cor-Ten appeared only after a substantially different design—an inverted concrete pyramid—had been tried out on Hewitt, who failed to react with enthusiasm. Three weeks later he was shown a model of a new scheme, the one eventually to be built, which was later described by Saarinen's colleague Paul Kennon as "absolutely sympathetic with the trees."[6] At the time, however, many of these trees (which were apparently fewer than Saarinen had imagined) were dying of Dutch elm disease. And so the landscape architects Sasaki, Walker, and Associates, who were hired after the preliminary design had been approved, were obliged to reconstruct the site in sympathy with a building that had been designed in sympathy with another, somewhat idealized version of the actual site. This circularity is documented by sheet 10 of the working drawings (fig. 3), which records the results of a survey of the existing trees in the area around the proposed structures (which included many oaks), while sheet 50 documents the same area with a portion of

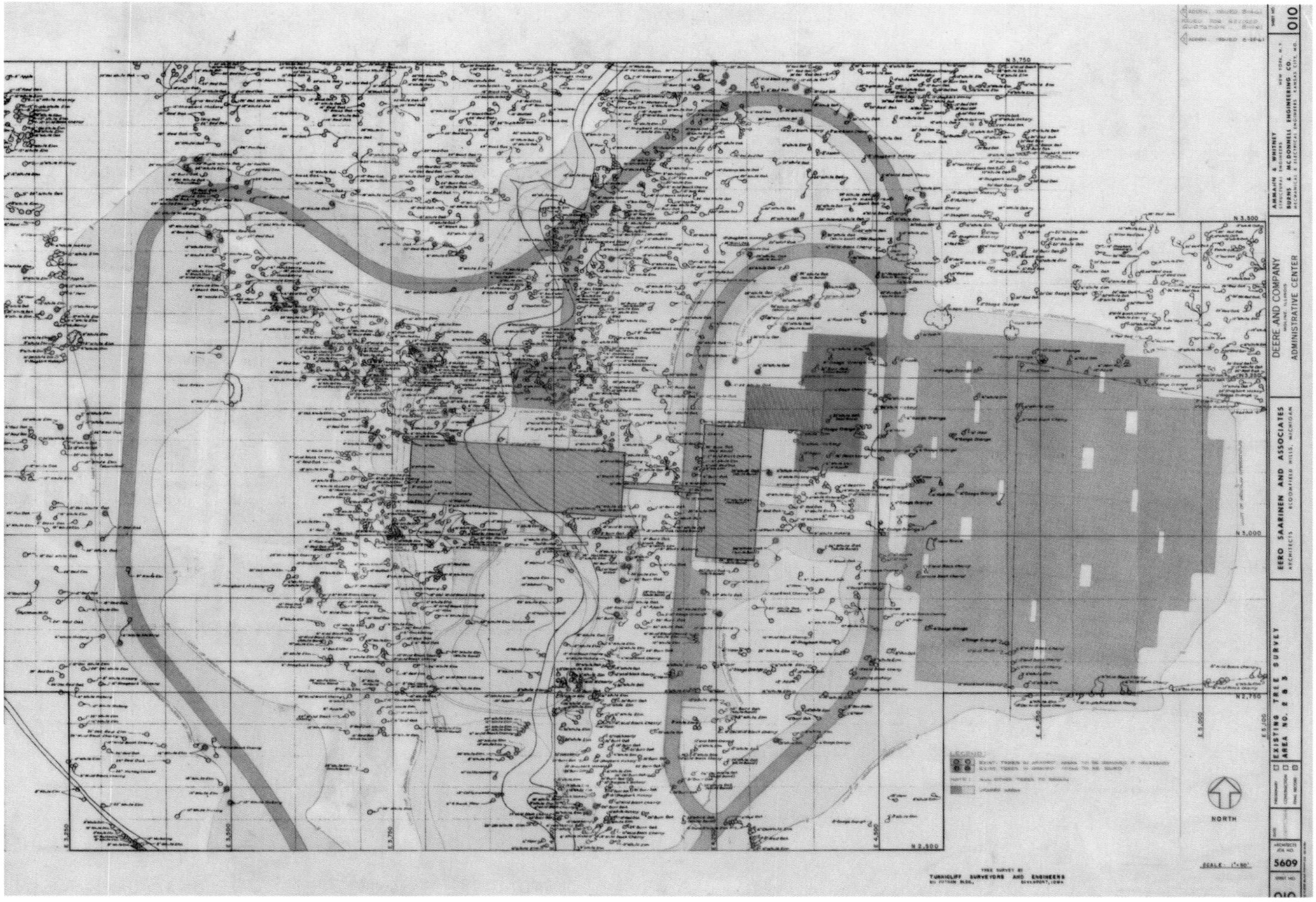

NORTH

SCALE: 1" = 50'

TREE SURVEY BY
TUNNICLIFF SURVEYORS AND ENGINEERS
DAVENPORT, IOWA

EXISTING TREE SURVEY
AREA NO. 2 & 3

EERO SAARINEN AND ASSOCIATES
ARCHITECTS BLOOMFIELD HILLS, MICHIGAN

DEERE AND COMPANY
MOLINE, ILLINOIS
ADMINISTRATIVE CENTER

AMMANN & WHITNEY
STRUCTURAL ENGINEERS NEW YORK, N.Y.
BURNS & McDONNELL ENGINEERING CO.
MECHANICAL & ELECTRICAL ENGINEERS KANSAS CITY, MO.

5609

010

NOTES

PLANT LIST

NORTH

SCALE: 1" = 50'

SASAKI, WALKER AND ASSOCIATES INC.
SITE CONSULTANTS AND LANDSCAPE ARCHITECTS

SITE PLANTING PLAN
AREA 2

EERO SAARINEN AND ASSOCIATES
ARCHITECTS BLOOMFIELD HILLS, MICHIGAN

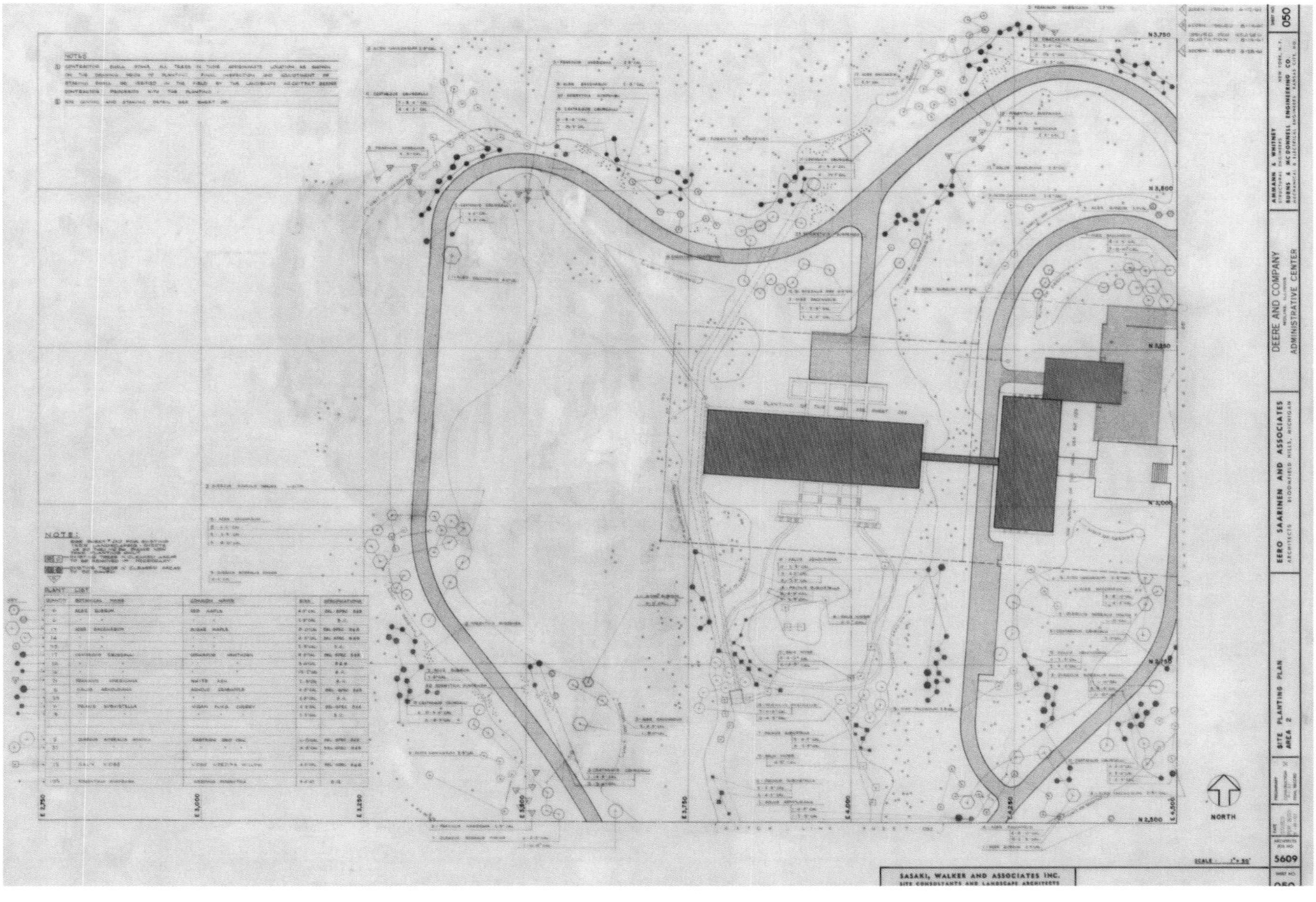

DEERE AND COMPANY
ADMINISTRATIVE CENTER

AMMANN & WHITNEY
BURNS & McDONNELL ENGINEERING CO.

5609

050

the 1,148 new trees and 4,861 new shrubs laid out by Sasaki, Walker on a seventy-acre portion of the site, along with fifteen acres of sod (fig. 4).[7]

Also shown on sheet 50 is the relation between new planting immediately in front of the office building and the two new bodies of water that the Saarinen-Sasaki team added to the site. Here, in addition to further articulating the landscape, water operates as a construction material in at least two ways. The upper pond sits at eye level of the executives relaxing in their dining room and forms a horizontal surface that both reflects and opposes the transparency of the facade; the lower pond operates technically, as a receptacle for the creek and associated drainage, whose flows were interrupted by the building, and as a heat-exchange medium for the facility's air-conditioning system. Natural or artificial? Material or image? Such questions cease to be meaningful when asked of these objects or elements.

Still, both Saarinen and the Deere leadership encouraged the impression that the building's Cor-Ten steel exterior was designed to harmonize with a nature that was, in a sense, a priori—already there, original, authentic. As the Deere press kit put it: "As this steel weathers, it develops a deep hue, similar to that of the trunks of oak trees." But there is ample evidence that the reverse is also the case: that the supposedly natural setting (including the trees) was designed to harmonize with the steel facade. At the level of corporate identity, Hewitt set the stage for a renaturalization of the resulting oscillation in an early letter to Saarinen (written before the building had been designed). This renaturalization, which seeped into subsequent discourse around the building, was accomplished via the company's identification with an agricultural working class, even as the company moved its administrative headquarters away from the actual site of manual labor at its main plant: "The men who built this company and caused it to grow and flourish were men of strength—rugged, honest, close to the soil. Since the company's early days, quality of product and integrity in relationships with farmers, dealers, suppliers,

Fig. 5 Deere and Company Administrative Center, Cor-Ten sample on site

Fig. 6 (right) Deere and Company Administrative Center, mock-up of steel frame

and the public in general have been Deere's guiding factors. In thinking of our traditions and our future, and in thinking of the people who will work in or visit our new headquarters, I believe it should be thoroughly modern in concept, but at the same time be down to earth and rugged."[8]

It would seem, then, that the choice of Cor-Ten steel for the exterior satisfied this requirement, and thus qualifies as an instance of a "style for the job." Indeed, Saarinen's own words did not discourage this reading: "John Deere and Company is a secure, well-established, successful farm machinery company, proud of its Midwestern farm-belt location. Farm machinery consists not of slick, shiney [*sic*] metal but of forged iron and steel in big, forceful shapes. The proper character for its headquarter's [*sic*] architecture should likewise not be a slick, precise, glittering glass and spindly metal building but a building which is bold and direct, using metal in a strong basic way." Toward that end, Saarinen went on to describe the Cor-Ten as making a "beautiful dark surface on the steel" as it oxidizes to form a protective coating.[9]

But there is a chicken-and-egg game going on here, in which image (in the form of the equation: exposed steel frame = "rugged character") is tested against nature and vice versa. Once Cor-Ten was floated as a possible material for the exterior frame—by Dinkeloo, according to an early Deere memo—it was necessary to study what effect the Moline weather would have on this sensitive alloy, as well as how the exposed steel might also act as a *brise-soleil,* and how the mirrored glazing would be "zipped" into its subframe with a neoprene gasket (a technique first developed at the General Motors Technical Center). Cor-Ten samples were installed on-site in various configurations, and a full-scale two-story mock-up was constructed two miles away (figs. 5, 6). Among the questions asked of these tests were, according to Dinkeloo, "How would horizontal and vertical surfaces vary in wetting? How would wetting affect rivet and bolt fastenings? What would happen in our detailing if puddling occurred in certain sections? . . . What would be the welding techniques and the problems that might come with welding?" The results were later incorporated into a brochure for U.S. Steel (the manufacturer of Cor-Ten), which also displayed a kind of color chart that illustrated the gradual formation of the oxidized coating.[10]

Though all this research appears to be in the service of obtaining an effect that, as Dinkeloo put it, "only nature can give" (thereby reinforcing the naturalization of the cultural meanings projected onto the "rugged" steel frame), it also worked to reproduce an aesthetically contrived *image* of nature. This was a piece of architectural mimesis that could only be achieved by subjecting a quintessentially human invention—steel—to the ravages of a nature from which the machine-made abstractions of steel and glass associated with modernism seemed already to have freed themselves. Likewise for the mirrored glazing, which reproduced a modulated image of Sasaki's modulated, aesthetically enhanced landscape on the building's exterior. Further, the modular enclosure was supported by a fully modular interior, reflected in a patterned ceiling that was itself studied carefully in the prototypical mock-up as well as in models. Again the question arises: Which comes first—nature or image-oriented culture? If the answer is nature, then we remain in the realm of classical mimesis. If it is culture, we are effectively in full-fledged postmodernism, in the form of a "style for the job." But if the answer is neither, or both, then we are someplace slightly different.

STONE

Witness CBS. Like Deere, very early on the CBS headquarters in New York was given a rather more dramatic form in reinforced concrete than the monolith that was eventually realized, though in this case the basic structural material remained the same (figs. 7, 8). Having rapidly passed through this initial formal experiment, the structural framing was ultimately transformed into a ring of concrete piers at the exterior wall. These piers hollowed out as they rose to thirty-eight stories—higher than concrete had ever gone before—and left the interior column-free, with a solid concrete core.

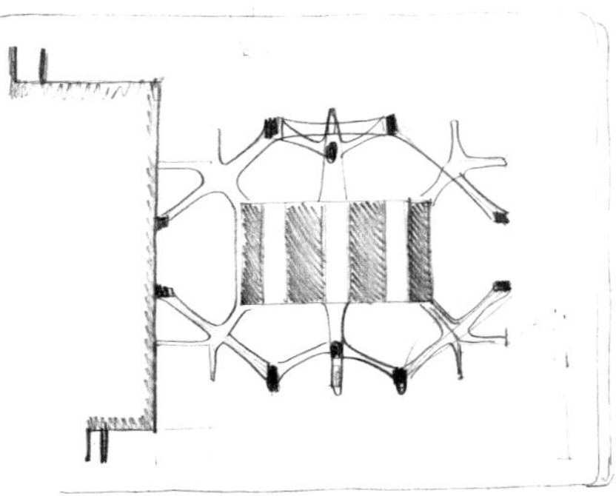

Fig. 7 Eero Saarinen and Associates, Columbia Broadcasting System, Inc., Building, New York, 1960–65, early plan sketch

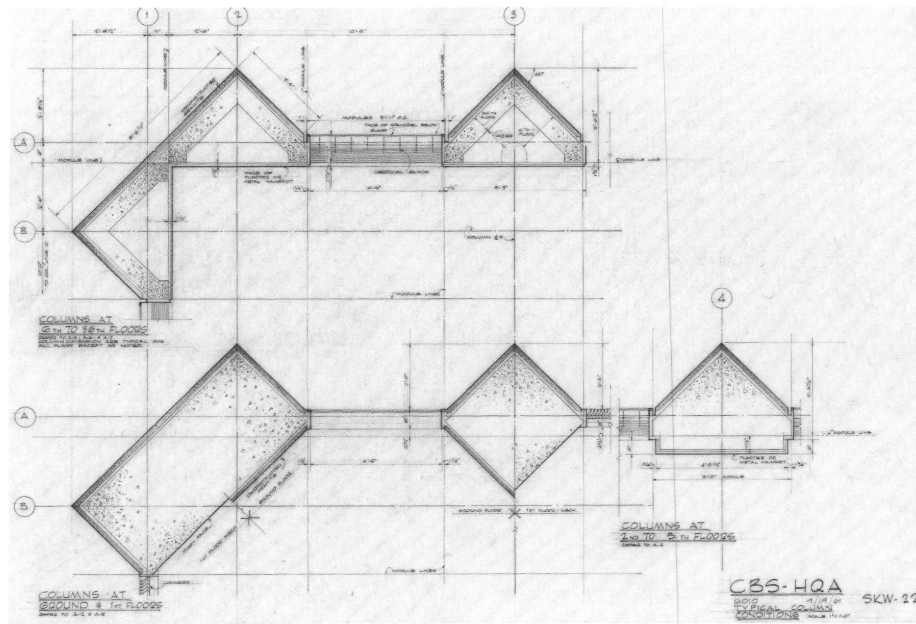

Fig. 8 (right) CBS Building, column sections

"Dark," "somber," "formal." Such were the adjectives used in headlines to describe the CBS headquarters. Some authors seemed to allow funereal, memorial connotations to attach to the building, which one writer called "the last Saarinen," and which was unveiled shortly after Saarinen's untimely death in 1961 and finished in 1965. Indeed, compared by many to its less distinguished steel-and-glass neighbors (which Peter Blake accused of collectively perpetrating a "slaughter on Sixth Avenue"), this weighty skyscraper does occupy a space somewhere between the monument and the tomb reserved by Adolf Loos for architecture as an art form. Or at least it qualifies as what Louis Sullivan once called a "tall office building artistically considered." Either way, it has shown itself capable of eliciting a certain affect, a stream of foreboding melancholy.[11]

This enigmatic object, which is also a node in the communications network called CBS and bears the entertainment industry nickname Black Rock, can be compared to the enigmatic space-slab in Stanley Kubrick's *2001: A Space Odyssey*—another of the many black boxes yielded by the 1960s.[12] But how was its affect—its blackness, its dull, melancholic opacity—produced? The concrete skeleton of the CBS building is clad in a uniformly dark matte granite. Various participants and observers report that this was largely the result of a desire, on the part of CBS president Frank Stanton, for a building that would contrast with the perceived slickness of steel and glass—including that of the Seagram Building and Lever House, as well as of Sixth Avenue. Saarinen, who died before the stone was chosen, seems only to have indicated that it ought to resemble the composite panels on the recently completed United States Chancellery Building in Oslo (fig. 9). Stanton, in a recent interview, takes a good deal of the credit, noting that "before we [he and Saarinen] talked seriously I had concluded I wanted a dark building in granite." He reports dispatching a CBS colleague to South Africa in search of the right stone. And he further reports that during a lunch with Saarinen at the Four Seasons restaurant in the Seagram Building (of all places), to which, it seems, the CBS president wore a tweed jacket, Stanton told his architect that he would "like the surface as rough as the coat." Saarinen sent him to Oslo, but Stanton returned unconvinced.[13]

Eventually, an appropriate black granite was located in Canada in sufficient quantity. It hardly matters who was ultimately responsible for the choice, since this is a matter of complex circuits and feedback loops, rather than simple questions of authorship. And in the same sense, the stone that was chosen and quarried was not the actual material that would elicit the complex affect when hung on a concrete frame. Nor was it the same

Fig. 9 Kevin Roche and CBS chairman William S. Paley observing mock-up of CBS facade with different stone samples

Fig. 10 CBS Building, facade mock-up

material that Stanton would later have cut into three-inch square pieces, placed in aluminum frames, and distributed to his fellow CBS executives as mementos. Like the steel at John Deere, it had to be modified further—in effect, "finished"—though not, this time, by way of a process so "natural" as oxidation. To avoid the slickness of polished granite, the stone was roughened via thermal stippling, which involved flaking off the surface with an extremely hot flame. However, upon seeing the results (which turned the stone light gray) Stanton was, as he put it, "brokenhearted." Further mediation was required. The solution was to subject the stone to a process borrowed from the aircraft industry called liquid honing, in which the stippled slabs of granite were sprayed with a high-pressure slurry made of water and glass beads, thus restoring the stone to its muted blackness while preserving the dullness of the thermally stippled surface.

Shortly after Saarinen's death, a mock-up of a stone facade was built (fig. 10). But different from the Deere tests, all that was really prototyped was the exterior of the exterior wall—a crenellated granite-and-glass surface. Variously finished stone was hung on a matter-of-fact frame, at a scale just large enough to measure its impact as a soaring expanse. Here again, what we are calling a "material" is inseparable from the many tests and other mediations to which it was subjected, all of which effectively repositioned it with respect to the laws of both nature and culture—in this case, both the laws of glare and sunlight, and those of the anti-slick and, in a sense, anti-image image called CBS. Somewhere in between these lay the somber, dark affect elicited by an igneous rock that had been quarried, cut, burned, and honed, and then hung on a faceted concrete frame with the help of metal clips and caulk. Neither structural nor superficial, this skin and its effect can be described in terms of an essential hybridity, an irreducible multiplicity on which are left the traces of all of the various techniques, devices, individuals, and images required to produce a thing called a material.

CONCRETE

The original sketches for CBS exploring an "organic" concrete base, as well as the first, concrete scheme for Deere also index another dimension of Saarinen's production that possesses a materiality of its own. This is the so-called expressive form to which he often had recourse—in these two cases as a preliminary instance, while in others as an end result. Notable among the latter is the terminal for Trans World Airlines completed in 1962 at New York (later John F. Kennedy) International Airport in New York. Though the strikingly literal image of a bird in flight evoked by TWA's sweeping concrete roofs distinguishes the building as the most figurative of Saarinen's works, it also belongs, at a technical level, to a line of research carried out on a series of projects into the technical and expressive potential of the structural concrete shell.

This series is enumerated by Saarinen himself, in an unfinished dictation titled "General Statement about the sculptural, curved/shapes that we have been involved with, beginning with St. Louis, the water tower and dome at General Motors, MIT, Yale, TWA, and now the Washington International Airport." As the document's title indicates, this research began in a combination of steel and concrete (the Gateway Arch in St. Louis), transitioned into steel alone (General Motors Technical Center), then into concrete (the Kresge Auditorium at MIT), into a combination of wood and concrete with steel cables (the David S. Ingalls Hockey Rink at Yale), back to concrete (the TWA Terminal), and finally to a more complex hybrid (Dulles International Airport). It would therefore be a mistake to evaluate TWA in isolation as a unique experiment in concrete.[14]

In St. Louis, as with the quasi-ornamental Cor-Ten steel at Deere, concrete gives equivocal expression to what the biologist D'Arcy Wentworth Thompson had long ago called a "diagram of forces." In the arch, which was designed in 1947 but not completed until 1965, that diagram is drawn by a concrete shell triangular in cross-section and extruded into what Saarinen called (in the crossed-out opening paragraph of his "General Statement") "an absolutely pure

Fig. 11 Eero Saarinen and Associates, Trans World Airlines Terminal, New York International Airport, New York, 1956–62, concrete pour

shape where the compression lines goes [*sic*] right through the center line of the structure" to the ground—a "perfect catenary." This center is voided to maximize the moment of inertia. But rather than expose the concrete shell through which this is achieved, the "pure shape" is clad entirely in stainless steel, giving the impression of an enormous metallic extrusion that captures the glint of the sun rising and setting on the national myth of manifest destiny to which the monument is dedicated. It is this myth, in the form of the internal horizons captured and regulated in the Jeffersonian planning grid stretching across the midwestern plains, that the arch finally diagrams. In St. Louis, the structurally "perfect catenary" is, like the grid, as much an object of the cultural imaginary—a dream—that enables the finite-infinite horizon to be "seen" at the level of national fantasy, as it is a mathematically rational figure framing an abstract space.[15]

Saarinen pursued this "departure from the completely rational" in the next section of his statement on curved shapes with respect to the water tower at the GM Tech Center. Here, as in St. Louis, the apparent structural integrity of the outer form is deceptive, since what he called the "flat sphere" of the tank is reinforced internally to accommodate a transfer of load to its three supporting columns. Saarinen described the object as "a piece of sculpture as well as a piece of structure" that had undergone twenty different variations before the final "beautiful shape" arrived. The entire assembly is of welded stainless-steel plates, formed into compound curves in the tank atop its cylindrical supports. In reflecting on the result, Saarinen was at his most philosophical: "Just as one thought of and learned a great deal about stainless steel as a cladding material in St. Louis, so one learned a great deal about its actual application at the water tank, but one also learned that the structural and rational cannot always take precedent when another form proves more beautiful. This is dangerous but I believe true."[16]

That the departure from structural rationalism can be described as "dangerous"—not in the sense that the structure might collapse, but that it might be overwhelmed by its own aesthetic excesses—is an indication of just how ingrained the ideological moralism of modernist "rationality" still was in the thought and practice of a postwar architect like Saarinen. Thus his deliberate departures from what he considered to be "rational" must be understood as proto-postmodern reactions to the modernist myth of structural purity. But to whom were they "dangerous"? To the modernist architect who still believes in metaphysical truths made available through technical calculation, if any such monster ever really existed? Perhaps, but only because departing from the inner necessities of structurally efficient form meant tipping the precarious balance of form and function irreversibly in favor of the former, thereby risking a spiral of self-referential image-making devoid of utilitarian purpose and ungrounded in the firmament of reason.

And yet, forms function. Not merely in the sense of enclosing a useful space no matter what their sculptural qualities, as was the case in the one-eighth of a sphere executed in concrete and used to enclose a thoroughly functional auditorium at MIT. More important in Saarinen's case, forms function as images circulating in a cultural economy that by this time was beginning to shape the flows and fluxes of history itself. This cultural economy has since been called "postmodernism."[17] And ultimately, what made Saarinen postmodern was not his stylistic excess but rather his attentiveness to the realities of an image-based economy in which entire material assemblies like a 630-foot arch circulate.

So too—though to a much lesser extent—at MIT, which Saarinen in his "General Statement" on curved shapes lamented as resembling a "half-inflated balloon," adding that "I do sympathize with [Sigfried] Giedion's statement that this building looks earthbound." The MIT dome is a reinforced-concrete shell, which, along with its edge beams, Saarinen insisted was kept "as small as possible." Still, in his estimation "one has to criticize this building," though not so much for its didactic adherence to a structurally efficient geometry as for both its details and its materials. Saarinen regretted the omission of something like an "intentional flare" at the base, "to counteract the earthbound quality of the dome." And yet he confessed that much was learned at MIT, including the surprising fact that "glass is opaque" and therefore the interior of the concrete shell (the hollowness of which would presumably lighten the overall effect) is invisible on the exterior, despite the extensive glazing.[18]

Fig. 12 Trans World Airlines Terminal, "keystone"

The Saarinen office was not the only one experimenting with domed shapes at this time. Among others, there was Saarinen's friend and Detroit colleague Minoru Yamasaki, whose St. Louis airport combined a series of shell-like domes. In his characteristically even-handed "General Statement," Saarinen criticized this combination of domes while also acknowledging its advantages. He compared it to the (slightly later) combination of steel dome and brick walls at General Motors, which in his estimation "worked much better."[19] The General Motors Styling Dome, which housed an auditorium for the display of new cars under an uplit simulated "sky," utilized some of the same techniques and materials as the water tower the office had previously designed for the Technical Center campus. Structurally, its 186-foot diameter was spanned by a welded steel shell three-eighths of an inch thick, clad on its exterior with reflective aluminum shingles. On the interior, a second shell composed of perforated stainless-steel plates was suspended from it, producing a surface onto which a variety of lighting effects could be projected to achieve the desired ambience for the display of the steel-shelled General Motors automobiles. A solid brick base darkened the perimeter, concealing the interior while offering a visual podium on which the squat dome could rest. Inside, during one of GM's automobile fashion shows, the physical substance of the dome disappeared in a flood of artificial light, the primary material out of which this particular image was constructed.[20]

Although its title also lists Yale, TWA, and Dulles, Saarinen's dictated statement on curved shapes ends with the General Motors dome. But we can speculate that were he to have continued, Saarinen would surely have celebrated the upturned "flare" at the base of the Ingalls Hockey Rink (next on the list), which was already hinted at in his critique of the MIT Auditorium. And whether or not he was satisfied with the way the Yale building met the ground, this problem was at the very core of the TWA Terminal. Indeed, the paradoxical gesture of constructing a giant "bird" out of so earthbound a material as concrete was enabled only by a specific technical effect. This effect gave the impression that the TWA Terminal utilized primarily "thin shell" construction, and thus partook of the capacity of double-curved shapes to optimize structural performance with minimum thickness, while offering a definitive solution to the visual problem of the light shell turned downward.

But the sweeping roofs of TWA were only nominally thin. In fact, these four shells, cast in four separate pours that lasted thirty hours each, combined with much heftier elements to carry their forces to the ground (fig. 11). At the building's center they were connected by a massive horizontal "keystone"—a forty-four-inch deep pentagon of solid concrete (fig. 12). Abba Tor, the project engineer for the structural engineering firm of Ammann and Whitney, describes the pattern of steel reinforcing embedded in this concrete plate as a "path of forces" necessary to keep the shells suspended without a central column. At their edges, the shells flared upward to produce quasi-arches, between which the concrete roofs spanned. Indeed, the technical performance of the shells themselves, like all such constructions, depends on a very precise combination of steel and concrete. Likewise for the four supporting columns, which assist in preserving the lightness of the concrete volume as it meets the ground by capturing both the horizontal and vertical forces in dynamic bundles of steel embedded in concrete buttresses with—as Tor puts it—"slimmed waistlines."[21]

Indeed, Tor testifies that in these columnar buttresses "the major formal concern was to minimize the waistline." In other words, from a formal point of view TWA followed Ingalls in absorbing the lessons of the MIT dome: the concrete shell must "flare" up as it meets the ground. It is these flared buttresses, together with the flared, upturned edge beams running around the giant bird's "wings," that impart to the TWA Terminal something like a sense of liftoff. Frontally, each of the two "feet" on either side of the main entrance forms a "Y" that accepts the thrust of two adjacent shells, leaving a skylit gap between them to accentuate the geometrical and technical transition. The bird's "beak" (also a rain spout) appears to carry those same forces forward and downward, in a sleight of hand that mockingly suspends the corner of the central shell—the same corner that at MIT would have been "rationally" (and dogmatically) grounded—above the heads of entering passengers.[22]

The other branch of Saarinen's experiments in concrete stemming from the problem posed by the "earthbound" MIT dome—again by way of Ingalls—culminates in the hybrid structure of the Dulles International Airport. At Ingalls, the use of concrete was restricted to the central arch and its pair of edge beams, which together describe the outlines of a three-dimensional surface that is filled in with suspension cables on which visibly rest wooden planks. At Dulles, a similar assembly was achieved entirely in concrete, save for the now-invisible steel cables.

Both formally and structurally, the terminal building at Dulles can be described as nothing more than a giant flare—a willful manipulation of the "inherent" properties of reinforced concrete to achieve a counterintuitive effect: liftoff, again. But where the entire TWA structure was cast in place, Dulles combined a cast-in-place framework of canted columns joined by a curvilinear upturned edge beam, through which the vertical elements pass only to curl back downward (fig. 13). Rather than columns, however, these vertical elements are more properly understood as cantilevered beams, since their bulk is dedicated less to carrying downward forces than to absorbing the lateral thrust of the roof structure.[23] Each of the larger verticals consists of approximately fourteen tons of steel embedded in one hundred tons of concrete. That is, nearly 15 percent of the material used in these sculptural

Fig. 13 Eero Saarinen and Associates, Dulles International Airport, Chantilly, Virginia, 1958–63, construction photograph showing canted columns

concrete solids is steel. The roof itself is made up of one-inch-thick precast-concrete planks with eight-inch-deep stiffeners, which are suspended on one-inch-diameter steel cables hung in a catenary (that is, an upside-down Gateway Arch) and joined together horizontally by cast-in-place curved concrete beams. These beams act as inverted arches that both stiffen the roof and translate its substantial lateral loads to the perimeter supports.

In other words, in the series of "curved shapes" enumerated by Saarinen in his unfinished dictation, the line of development ran contrary to anything like the "natural" tendencies of thin-shell concrete. At TWA in particular, the materially efficient thin shells—seven inches at their minimum dimension—were offset by thickened elements like the forty-four-inch-deep horizontal concrete "keystone" suspended invisibly above the terminal's main lounge, the flared buttresses, and the upturned edge beams, all of which were used to maximum formal effect to reinforce the image of flight. At Dulles, by comparison, the MIT dome and the St. Louis arch were effectively turned on their heads. Further, where both MIT's thin shell and the arch's extruded triangle took advantage of reinforced concrete's compressive strength, the roof at Dulles turned the tables with its recourse to structural tensile steel, reducing the concrete shell to—essentially—cladding.

WOOD

With this reversal we find architecture at something like an inner—rather than an outer—limit. The technical research of the Saarinen office into the production of "curved shapes" led ultimately to the monumental effort at Dulles to overturn the "earthbound" materiality of concrete in order to open up the building to the outside—in effect, to turn the closed steel/concrete forms of the MIT and GM domes inside out. At TWA, the concrete roof, sprayed with asbestos and mineral wool inside and covered in silicone outside, could still map a virtual diagram of structural forces onto the sweeping arcs of circulation described by the building's baroque interior. At Dulles, concrete joined the stone at CBS to become cladding. But unlike CBS, where the cladding was to be seen from the urban street surrounded by steel and glass—Sixth Avenue having been newly converted into what Peter Blake memorably called a "sample case for the curtain wall salesman"—at Dulles the semi-structural concrete cladding was to be seen only from the inside. This massive concrete building was, literally, an inverted tent providing temporary shelter to the nomads of the jet age: the business executives and their colleagues who, in the cultural imaginary constructed by Saarinen's architecture, were always in some sense both his clients and his audience.[24]

Saarinen's trajectory of "curved shapes" mediated by the virtualities of image building evidenced at Deere and CBS might therefore seem to encapsulate a microcosm of architectural history running from Filippo Brunelleschi to Gottfried Semper. But it does so—as Saarinen noted—only at great risk since the inner limit of architecture represented by this trajectory is the limit that marks architecture's irreducible materiality as image.

Returning briefly to Deere, we see that this limit marked the moment the outside comes in—in the sunlight streaming through tinted windows, in the water coursing through the air-conditioning system, and, most visibly, in the many desks and tables designed (under the direction of Warren Platner) for executives, secretaries, and receptionists (figs. 14, 15). Much of this furniture, which was executed in teak (some with leather tops) had built-in telephone boxes hardwired through built-in conduits to what the company claimed was the "fastest, most flexible and efficient telephone system yet designed for modern business communications." This was the agitated, virtual infrastructure of business that connected Deere to a multinational economy. But like the building itself, the furniture accomplished this in sympathy with its supposedly natural surroundings, in a warm, sedate shell of natural wood and leather.[25]

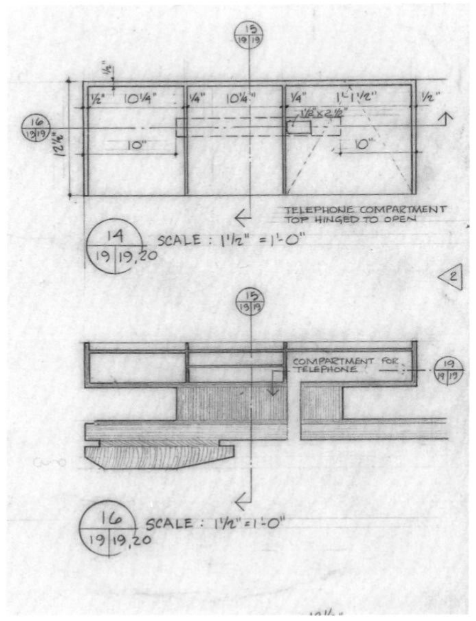

Fig. 14 Deere and Company Administrative Center, desks with built-in telephone equipment

Fig. 15 Deere and Company Administrative Center, construction drawing of telephone compartment in desk

More than a century ago, a political economist described a very stable, very functional wooden table that became animated—or, some have said, haunted—as it began to communicate its value as a commodity.[26] Perhaps we can say that something similar happens here, as architecture attempts to communicate, both symbolically and technologically, its own role in the business of business. Again and again, at a variety of scales, the details of Saarinen's buildings give this communication material form. But even as they do so, they dissolve into a penumbra of cultural resonance opened up by that very materiality. This cultural dissolve, which thereby reveals the nature of materials rather than obscures it in a haze of postmodernist spectacle, is evidence of architecture's internal hybridity, made visible by a new, animated, and ungrounded form of historical materialism.

Material, materiality, materialism: a string of associations that might otherwise lead us to conclude that architecture's interior, its natural essence, its soul, lies in its utility and its construction. This in turn may lead us to conclude, for example, that the technical drawings and processes we have been referring to are somehow more real or more authentic than objects and images that offer mere "style." But as we have seen, deep inside, in the very grain of the wood drawn with such delicacy and care in the Saarinen office, lies something that we might dare to call the truth about architecture.
This is the moment when virtuality—image, style, but also cultural meaning—reappears in architecture's irreducibly material core, as ghostly and disembodied as the voice at the other end of a telephone. Such ghosts must be reckoned with. They must remain—as it were—on the table, as we observe the inseparable interpenetration of the modern and the postmodern, of substance and image, and consider the new realities that this state of affairs may conjure.

Notes

I am grateful to Eeva-Liisa Pelkonen and Detlef Mertins for their responses to earlier versions of this essay, and to Rosamond Fletcher and Frida Rosenberg for their assistance with the research.

1. Bruno Latour, *We Have Never Been Modern,* trans. Catherine Porter (Cambridge: Harvard University Press, 1993), 96–97.

2. See, for example, Reyner Banham, "The Fear of Eero's Mana," *Arts Magazine,* Feb. 1962, 72.

3. An internal Deere memorandum states that numerous sites were chosen for consideration "in accordance with a suggestion made by Mr. Saarinen that we seek an area which contained within itself its own scenic appeal. This resulted in looking at sites containing vallies [*sic*] and rolling ridges as opposed to the previous search which was for flat area containing a view looking south over the Rock River Valley." Nathan Lesser, "Memorandum: Office Building Site," Sept. 7, 1956, doc. no. 130533, Deere & Company Archives, Moline, Ill. (hereafter Deere Archives). For a detailed analysis of the process of designing the Deere landscape, see Louise A. Mozingo, "The Corporate Estate in the USA, 1954–64: 'Thoroughly Modern in Concept, but . . . Down to Earth and Rugged,'" *Studies in the History of Gardens and Designed Landscapes* 20 (Jan.–Mar. 2000), 25–56.

4. Nathan Lesser, report to William A. Hewitt, "Office Building Project: Progress Report No. 1," Jan. 31, 1957, doc. no. 130535, Deere Archives.

5. Eero Saarinen, "John Deere and Company Administration Center, Moline, Illinois," June 17, 1960, Eero Saarinen Papers, Manuscripts and Archives, Yale University.

6. Paul Kennon, interviewed in "Eero Saarinen and His Works," *Architecture and Urbanism (A+U),* extra edition, Apr. 1984, 235.

7. The quantities of planting are given in "Press Information: Deere & Company Administrative Center (Landscaping)," 1, n.d., doc. no. 43768, Deere Archives.

8. Ibid.; William A. Hewitt, letter to Eero Saarinen, Aug. 23, 1957, doc. no. 130536, Deere Archives.

9. Eero Saarinen, "John Deere and Company Administration Center, Moline, Illinois," n.d., Eero Saarinen Papers, Yale University.

10. G. F. Neiley, letter to William A. Hewitt, Aug. 4, 1958, doc. no. 130537, Deere Archives; John Dinkeloo, "The Steel Will Weather Naturally," *Architectural Record,* Aug. 1962, 150; U.S. Steel Corporation, "Cor-Ten Steel for Exposed Architectural Applications," brochure, n.d., no. 1995-46, folder 2, box 1, Jack M. Goldman Collection of Eero Saarinen and Associates Material, Cranbrook Archives, Bloomfield Hills, Mich.

11. Eric Larrabee, "Saarinen's Dark Tower: The CBS Building and How It Grew," *Harper's Magazine,* Dec. 1964, 55–61; "CBS: Somber Power on Sixth Avenue," *Progressive Architecture,* July 1965, 187–92; "For Formal Dining: Black Granite?" *Progressive Architecture,* Mar. 1966, 180–83; "The Last Saarinen," *Architectural Review,* Dec. 1961, 370; Peter Blake, "Slaughter on Sixth Avenue," *Architectural Forum,* June 1965, 13–19; Adolf Loos, "Architecture," trans. Wilfred Wang, in *The Architecture of Adolf Loos: An Arts Council Exhibition* (London: Arts Council of Great Britain, 1985), 104–9; Louis Sullivan, "The Tall Office Building Artistically Considered," *Lippincott's,* Mar. 1896, 204–6.

12. For more on this topic, see Reinhold Martin, *The Organizational Complex: Architecture, Media, and Corporate Space* (Cambridge: MIT Press, 2003), 223–30.

13. Frank Stanton, in an unpublished interview by Bill Kubota and Ed Moore, July 31, 2004.

14. Eero Saarinen, "General Statement about the sculptural, curved/shapes that we have been involved with, beginning with St. Louis, the water tower and dome at General Motors, MIT, Yale, TWA, and now the Washington International Airport," undated manuscript, Eero Saarinen Papers, Yale University, published in this volume.

15. Ibid., 1. D'Arcy Wentworth Thompson revised and reissued his classic *On Growth and Form* (1917) in 1942. The book became an important touchstone in many postwar architectural debates over form and structure. D'Arcy Wentworth Thompson, *On Growth and Form* (Cambridge, England: Cambridge University Press, 1942).

16. Saarinen, "General Statement," 1.

17. See, for example, Andreas Huyssen, *After the Great Divide: Modernism, Mass Culture, Postmodernism* (Bloomington: Indiana University Press, 1986), and Fredric Jameson, *Postmodernism: Or, the Cultural Logic of Late Capitalism* (Durham: Duke University Press, 1991).

18. Saarinen, "General Statement," 2.

19. Ibid., 3.

20. See Martin, *The Organizational Complex,* 153–55.

21. Abba Tor, "TWA Flight Center Presentation," unpublished typescript, Oct. 4, 2004, 7, Abba Tor Collection.

22. Ibid., 6.

23. James B. Lyttle, "Unique Roof Construction at Dulles Airport," *Journal of the American Concrete Institute,* July 1963, 836.

24. Blake, "Slaughter on Sixth Avenue," 18.

25. "Press Information: Deere & Company Administrative Center (Telephones)," 1, n.d., doc. no. 43768, Deere Archives.

26. The political economist was Karl Marx, who used the example of a simple wooden table turning on its head (i.e., becoming fetishized) as it enters the market to illustrate the "mystical" character of commodities in the opening chapter of *Capital.* Jacques Derrida revisited Marx's example as a "haunting" in *Specters of Marx: The State of the Debt, the Work of Mourning, and the New International,* trans. Peggy Kamuf (New York: Routledge, 1994), 149–52.

Eeva-Liisa Pelkonen

the search for (communicative) form

By the mid-1950s Eero Saarinen had become not only one of the most successful but also one of the most controversial architects of his time, whose buildings were criticized for a seeming formal willfulness and inconsistency because of their lack of a fixed style. The line of criticism was directed at Saarinen as well as a number of other second-generation modernists, who were seen as wandering too far from modernist aesthetics and principles. While Saarinen's General Motors Technical Center (1948–56) gained universal praise, his apparent embrace of historicism in the U.S. Chancellery Building in London (1955–60) dealt the final blow to his reputation as a solid modernist. Moreover, there was a growing sense that architects like Saarinen had lost control of the architecture they created. Writing about the London Chancellery in 1960, the influential London-based critic Reyner Banham complained that the building couldn't decide whether to be "monumental" or "frilly."[1]

Troubled by the state of affairs, Thomas H. Creighton, editor of *Progressive Architecture,* circulated a questionnaire among fifty leading architectural practitioners and academics sometime between late 1960 and early 1961, and published the results in three parts in the March, April, and May issues under the heading "The Sixties: A P/A Symposium on the State of Architecture" (fig. 1). The first part, titled "The Period of Chaoticism," launched the debate with a quotation from Norbert Wiener's book *The Human Use of Human Beings: Cybernetics and Society,* published in 1950, that read, "We are immersed in a life in which the world as a whole obeys the second law of thermodynamics: confusion increases and order decreases."[2]

All the participants agreed that architecture was in a state of unprecedented formal plurality bordering on confusion. Yet, as Creighton pointed out in his introduction, there were questions regarding the acceptance and duration of this "chaos." Followers of Ludwig Mies van der Rohe and members of the so-called Ballet School represented the opposite ends of the opinion poll. The first group condemned stylistic plurality. As Mies himself put it when answering

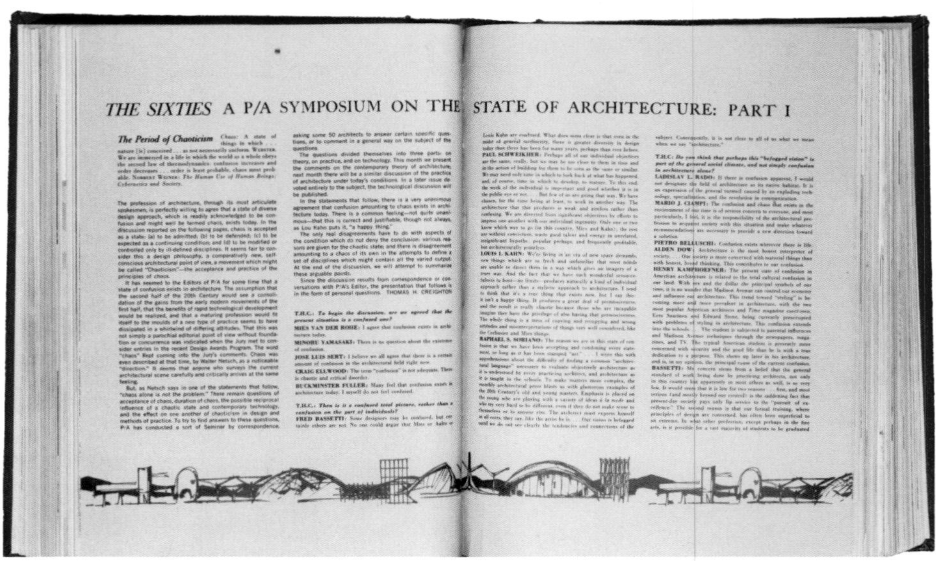
THE SIXTIES A P/A SYMPOSIUM ON THE STATE OF ARCHITECTURE: PART I

the *Progressive Architecture* questionnaire: "Certainly it is not necessary or possible to invent a new kind of architecture every Monday morning." The latter group, which included Philip Johnson and Edward Durell Stone, celebrated formal diversity as a symptom of "youthful" energy and enthusiasm. Johnson, who was fifty-five at the time, mused: "Can't we just wander aimlessly? The world is so full of a number of things. . . . Let us enjoy the multiplicity of it all. Let the students have a different hero every year. Maybe it is good for them."[3]

Oscar Nitzchke's reasoning that architecture culture was simply going through a transitory phase before settling into a straight course revealed a hidden dimension to the debate: an anxiety about the loss of the conventional idea of stylistic change, according to which every period has its own style. In other words, those who disapproved of stylistic plurality feared that architecture around 1960 was hopelessly out of sync with its time. Crisis of meaning followed: forms, in such a condition, were at large. They could mean anything or nothing.[4]

We can only speculate on whether Saarinen received the questionnaire, or whether he undertook to respond to it. He certainly could have used the opportunity to explain the stylistic plurality of his own work. Saarinen was, in fact, one of the few architects whom colleagues singled out as confused in the *Progressive Architecture* debate; Henry Kamphoefner, the respected dean of the School of Architecture at North Carolina State University, issued the same verdict regarding Saarinen and Stone: both were too interested in styling and fashion.

Nowhere else was the link between Saarinen's stylistic diversity and loss of linear temporal narrative more apparent than in the two buildings he completed on the MIT campus in 1955, the Kresge Auditorium and Chapel. The auditorium was a billowing reinforced-concrete thin-shell structure, one of the first of its kind, and the chapel a brick cylinder reminiscent of Roman architecture—the Pantheon and Hadrian's Tomb come to mind. These buildings challenged the linear narrative of architectural history in two ways: the auditorium by applying new technologies, and the chapel by appropriating historical precedents. The idea that each period had its own style thus dissolved simultaneously into the past and the future.[5]

The genesis of architectural form and its meaning was the central theme when *Architectural Forum* summoned three critics, Bruno Zevi, J. M. Richards, and Sigfried Giedion, to discuss Saarinen's buildings at MIT. Using the auditorium as an example, Zevi condemned the use of "universally valid 'form[s]' separate from functional and technical requirements." He considered this a sign of a wider societal decline:

> Saarinen has chosen to dissociate form from function, construction from technological needs. He appears to embrace the philosophy of Mannerism, typical

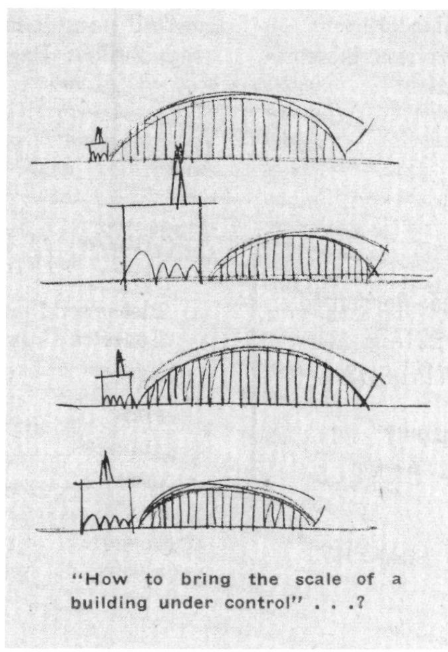
"How to bring the scale of a
building under control" . . .?

Fig. 1 (opposite) Thomas H. Creighton, "The Sixties: A P/A Symposium on the State of Architecture," *Progressive Architecture*, April 1961

Fig. 2 J. M. Richards, illustration from "Three Critics Discuss M.I.T.'s New Buildings," *Architectural Forum*, March 1956

of the production that followed Michelangelo's genius, in the late sixteenth century. Mannerism did not prevent artistic creation, but was the expression of an escape from reality, of an architectural nervous breakdown, of an evasion from the rational and organic approaches to architecture. Mannerist architects were unhappy and bored, so were their clients, so was their society.[6]

Richards, however, had a different interpretation. He admired the "structural conception of the buildings," but he called for more attention to how the buildings were experienced. He was particularly concerned about the lack of scale, which he illustrated with diagrams showing various alternative relations between the two buildings (fig. 2). According to Richards, "to bring the scale of a building under control without inhibiting the free and inspiring use of modern technical possibilities is one of the esthetic problems that modern architecture has yet to solve." He linked the scale problem to the debate on New Monumentality and subsequently to the broader issue of the psychology of architectural experience: "We are supposed to be searching for a new monumentality in architecture, which will enable it to create viable social symbols. This means thinking in terms of psychology as well as technology, because what is required is to recreate the spectator's sense of himself in relation to the monument."[7]

Richards's comments were emblematic of a larger shift in architectural modernism wherein functional and technological imperatives were replaced by an emphasis on the perception and experience of buildings. Sigfried Giedion's enormously popular book *Space, Time, and Architecture: The Growth of a New Tradition* (1941) led the way by calling for architecture that would correspond with the structure of the mind. Such architecture, like the mind, was based on what he called "constituent factors," which transcended the concern for a particular program and place. In subsequent editions of the book, Giedion cited the curvilinear wall found in baroque architecture as well as in Alvar Aalto's Baker Dormitory at MIT as an example. Similarly, he was sympathetic to the fact that the Kresge Auditorium simply aimed to "find a solution to the problem of vaulted interior space," also a recurring theme throughout architectural history. According to this idea Saarinen's mistakes and successes were to be evaluated in relation to architecture's perennial problems rather than to the particular functional and structural problem at hand.[8]

Facing criticism about formal plurality, fashion mongering, and mixed messages, Saarinen emphasized that all of his buildings were based on the same principles, which he called the "six pillars of architecture."[9] The first three—functional integrity, honest expression of structure, and awareness of our time—corresponded to the modernist orthodoxy—form follows function, structure, and zeitgeist—and the notion that architecture should respond to the particular problem at hand. Saarinen called them the "timeless principles of architecture."[10] The latter three—the expression of the building, the concern for total environment, and the principle of carrying a concept to the ultimate conclusion—responded to the new interest in the perception and experience of architecture. The question was how to balance these two sets of concerns. To illustrate his approach to form he called the water tower at General Motors both "a piece of sculpture as well as a piece of structure." Conscious that structural engineers like Pier Luigi Nervi criticized his buildings for a lack of structural rigor, he elaborated on the design process as follows:

After twenty different alternate designs we finally narrowed this down to this[,] which seemed like the most beautiful shape. It would have been easy to find a more rational shape of [*sic*] a purer structural shape because the flat sphere that rests on the three tubes has to be reinforced by an inside structure at the joints between tube and sphere, but after satisfying ourselves that the beauty of this shape was greater than any one which was made by a more visible structure, we had to decide on this. In other words, the water tower at General Motors is a departure from the completely rational.[11]

Saarinen addressed the issue of chaoticism in an essay published in *Perspecta* about half a year after his death, in fall 1961. He began the essay, which was conducted in the form of a self-interview, by stating matter-of-factly: "Today there must seem a great confusion in architecture to a layman—different architects seem to be going off in different directions." Without expressing his opinion about this state of affairs, he traced the events that led to it. The 1920s and '30s were dominated by the principle "form follows function." In the 1940s architects became interested in technological and scientific developments. According to Saarinen things went awry in the late 1940s and early '50s, when American architects compromised this organic development of modern architecture by codifying Mies's language into stylistic dogma. Freeing themselves from the Miesian straitjacket was the first task: "There was more to architecture than that. A startling thing happened. The leaders of the generation to follow refused to stop. We, I shall say, because it was my generation, felt that there must still be time for search." For Saarinen, this "search" meant most of all filtering through an unprecedented amount of new technical and formal choices:

> There were new and significant things to be done in structure. The whole science of concrete thin shell construction was developing exciting new possibilities. There were new and unexplored materials. . . . There were new things coming out of Europe from Corbu and his followers . . . and, above all, the challenges of the great variety of problems to be solved seems to indicate a greater variety of answers than [modern] style tolerated.[12]

Saarinen suggested that by the late 1950s architects had become information processors and that the architectural object had become part of the information flow. Increased information led to a greater number of available formal choices. Form was thus no longer considered as an outcome of an ultimate structural and functional solution, but as a choice of the architect.

The generational shift was obvious: the first generation of modern architects saw architecture as a project able to solve functional, structural, and societal problems, while the second generation treated architecture as information flow, whose main value was based on its impact on the viewer. Saarinen exemplified this view by stating that the idea of "structural honesty" had given way to the quest for the "expression of structure," which at times led to "structural expressionism."[13]

This was of course no minor change. The exhibition *Architecture and Imagery: Four New Buildings,* co-curated by Arthur Drexler and Wilder Green and presented at the Museum of Modern Art, was symptomatic of the radical paradigm shift that took place during the late 1950s. As the title suggests, the four buildings were chosen as examples of modern architects' ability to create compelling imagery. Jørn Utzon's Sydney Opera House (1956–73), Guillaume Gillet's Notre Dame de Royan in France (1958), Harrison and Abramovitz's First Presbyterian Church in Stamford, Connecticut (1958), and Saarinen's TWA Terminal in New York (1956–62) demonstrated what this meant in practice: idiosyncratic formal language limited to a few moves. Drexler and Green addressed the communicative aspect of the buildings as follows: "It is increasingly desirable that a building's shape expresses some particular aspect of its purpose. An apartment house, they [contemporary architects] believe, should not look like an office building and a church should not look like a gymnasium." Quoting Saarinen, the authors celebrated how the TWA Terminal "expresses the excitement of travel." The forms were "evocative" of function and "suggested" a moving subject.[14]

The architectural magazines joined in, attempting to provide a broad theoretical umbrella for this new architectural trend. Referring to the MoMA exhibition, Creighton of *Progressive Architecture* saw it as expressing an interest in "imagery addressing the senses as the chief element of beauty." He labeled the movement "new sensualism" and published a two-part article under this title in the September and October 1959 issues of the magazine, cataloguing the different formal strategies that enable "sensuous" encounters with buildings: "sensuous plasticity," "sensual delight," "sculptural concept," "stereo-structural sensualism," "romantic expressionism," and "neo-liberty." This departure from modernism's alliance with technological-rationalist thinking is most apparent where Creighton defined the fourth category by quoting Nervi: "It is the capacity to feel a structure in an intuitive way, as one feels a ratio of volumes or a color relation, which represents the indispensable basis for structural design." Even structure eluded mathematical formulas.[15]

In Creighton's essays on sensualism, Saarinen's work appears in two categories. The University of Chicago Law School (1955–60) is cited as an example of buildings that provide "sensual delight" via the ornamental and tactile qualities of their facades. The TWA Terminal and Concordia Senior College (1953–58) appear under "romantic expressionism." The key concept describing this category is the "symbol." The TWA Terminal, for example, "symbolizes aerodynamics" and Concordia "echoes a Scandinavian village."[16]

Creighton's interpretations did not appeal to Saarinen, who wrote him a letter after reading the first part of the article: "I have read your 'New Sensualism' article—it is good—you always write well—but, personally, I would not have mixed certain sheep with certain goats—and I think you have made too large an umbrella encompassed by one name. (Egocentrically I prefer the division Robin Boyd made in HARPER's)."[17]

Saarinen was referring to an article by the Australian architect and critic Robin Boyd titled "Counter Revolution in Architecture," published in the September 1959 issue of *Harper's Magazine*. Contrasting the new developments with Miesianism, Boyd called for "affluence" and "austerity" and proposed two formal strategies to achieve them: "a search for new richness on the surface and a search for new excitement in form." The first category was represented by Stone, the second one by Saarinen, whom Boyd celebrated as the leader of the pack: "The simplest way to study the galloping development of the excitement—the new search for form—is, as I have said, to follow the second of the two leaders of second-generation modern: Eero Saarinen." For Boyd, three buildings—the Kresge Auditorium, the Ingalls Hockey Rink, and the TWA Terminal, listed in that order—exemplified Saarinen's "search for new form." According to the author, Saarinen had found the ultimate sensuous forms and thus the ultimate architectural experience in the Ingalls Rink and the TWA Terminal, where "the initial stimulus was not functional or structural; nor was it intellectual as at MIT. It was emotional. . . . Thus Saarinen, under the gaze of a lost, impressionable generation of younger architects, developed in a few years from reasoned rectangles to felt space."[18]

Saarinen's preference for Boyd's interpretation was a nod to his version of how forms communicate to the onlooker. The difference between Creighton's and Boyd's theories is most apparent in their treatment of TWA. While Creighton emphasized the communication of explicit meaning—the form "symbolizes aerodynamics"—Boyd's notion of "felt space" suggested that, rather than communicating particular meanings, forms were simply "felt" through psycho-physical spatial immersion.

Boyd's reading alluded to a wider interest in the art and architecture culture of the 1950s in how and what forms communicate. Susanne Langer's book *Feeling and Form* (1953) laid the theoretical foundation for the shift of emphasis from principles of form-giving to how forms were experienced. The key word was "expressiveness." Langer considered art a "symbol," that is, "a highly articulated sensuous object, which by virtue of its dynamic structure can express the forms of vital experience which language is peculiarly unfit to convey." In other words, art did not communicate feelings or any other type of information from the artist to the onlooker, but instead "imported" "feeling, life, motion, and emotion" directly from the object to the subject.[19] She believed in a complete homology between aesthetic experience and life:

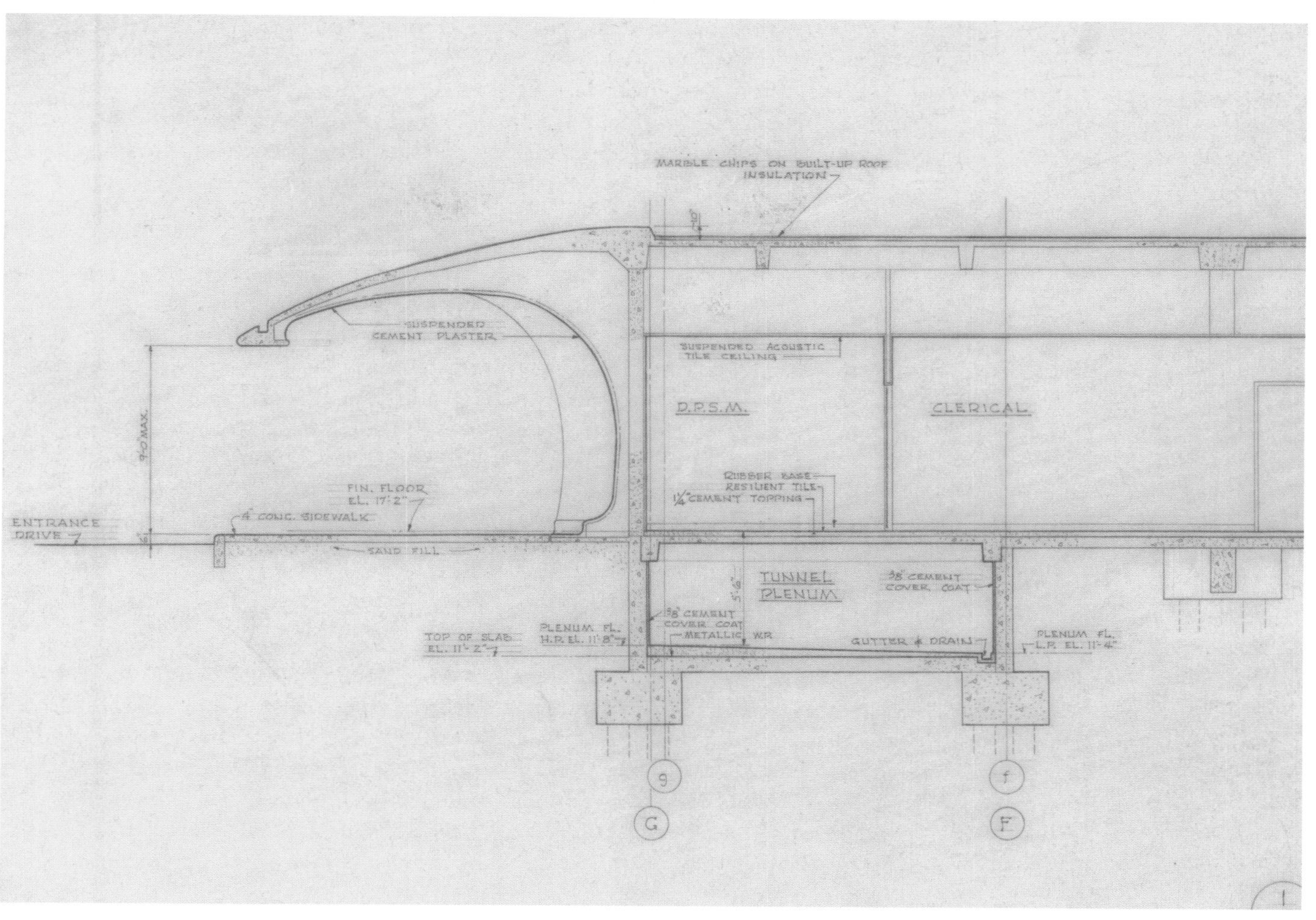

Fig. 3 (opposite) Eero Saarinen and Associates, Trans World Airlines Terminal, New York International Airport, New York, 1956–62, base of information billboard

Fig. 4 Trans World Airlines Terminal, section through entrance canopy

> Symbolic expression is something miles removed from provident planning or good arrangement. It does not suggest things to do, but embodies the feeling, the rhythm, the passion or sobriety, frivolity or fear with which any things at all are done. That is the image of life which is created in buildings; it is the visible semblance of an "ethnic domain," the symbol of humanity to be found in the strength and interplay of forms.

Although Langer acknowledged that forms had power over the onlooker, she insisted that "since art symbol is not a discourse, the word 'message' is misleading. A message is something communicated." Langer replaced the word "message" with "symbol," a concept she inherited from her teacher Ernst Cassirer, the famed Yale professor, whose 1931 book *The Philosophy of the Symbolic Forms* was published in English in 1953. He defined the symbolic dimension as the dimension of forms, which, while still "wholly sensory . . . disclose a formed sensibility . . . governed by the spirit," invested in the form "by some form of free creation." True art was always symbolic. It did not state itself as a fact but required creative investment on the part of the onlooker. In Langer's words, "An art lover who views, hears, or reads a work from 'the audience standpoint' enters into a direct relation not with the artist, but with the work. He responds to it as he would to a 'natural' symbol, simply finding its significance, which he is likely to think of as 'the feeling' in it. This 'feeling' . . . is not 'communicated,' but revealed; the created form 'has' it."[20]

In most instances Saarinen, like Langer, called for architecture that engaged the viewer emotionally and by total immersion. He talked about architecture that had the "fullest impact and expression" on the viewer. This, he believed, was achieved by formal consistency leading to the creation of a "total environment." Saarinen cited the TWA Terminal and the Morse and Stiles Colleges at Yale (1958–62) as successful demonstrations of this approach, writing that he had "come to the conviction that once one embarks on a concept for a building, this concept has to be exaggerated and overstated and repeated in every part of its interior, so that wherever you are, inside or outside, the building sings with the same message. That is why, for instance, the interior of the TWA had to be the way it is; that is why the interior of the new Yale colleges have to be just so."[21]

In the case of TWA this translated into curvilinear forms, which twist and turn endlessly without settling into a single figural object (fig. 3). The working drawings demonstrate that this "totalizing" effect required at times a blurring of the distinction between structural and expressive form, as can be seen, for example, by looking at a vertical section through the entrance canopy where the structural skeleton is covered by bent sheetrock (fig. 4). In the case of the four Y-shaped columns supporting the four barrel vaults, which create the large-span space, similar forms are made of poured concrete (fig. 5). Saarinen's discussion of the vaulted roof demonstrates his thinking: while structurally sound, the "shapes of these vaults were deliberately chosen in order to emphasize an upward-soaring quality of line, rather than the downward gravitational one common to many domed structures."[22] Charles Eames's photograph of a child climbing on a warped surface inside the building demonstrates how the ideal user acted out the structure's formal dynamism (fig. 6). The close-up view of the nearby adults makes the point that such "totalizing" architecture could never be contemplated from a distance and analyzed; people merged with the buildings.

On certain occasions Saarinen tolerated more explicit communication of meanings. He singled out the Ingalls Rink as one of his favorite buildings because players felt the building kept telling them: "Go Yale Go!" Here, the way forms translated into action bordered on behavioralism. In the case of TWA he was aware that for the building to communicate its function some people needed to give the form literal interpretation—the building was often referred to as "a bird." Saarinen wrote that, although the bird analogy was unintentional, "that doesn't mean that one doesn't have the right to see it that way or to explain it to laymen in those terms, especially because laymen are usually more literally than visually inclined."[23]

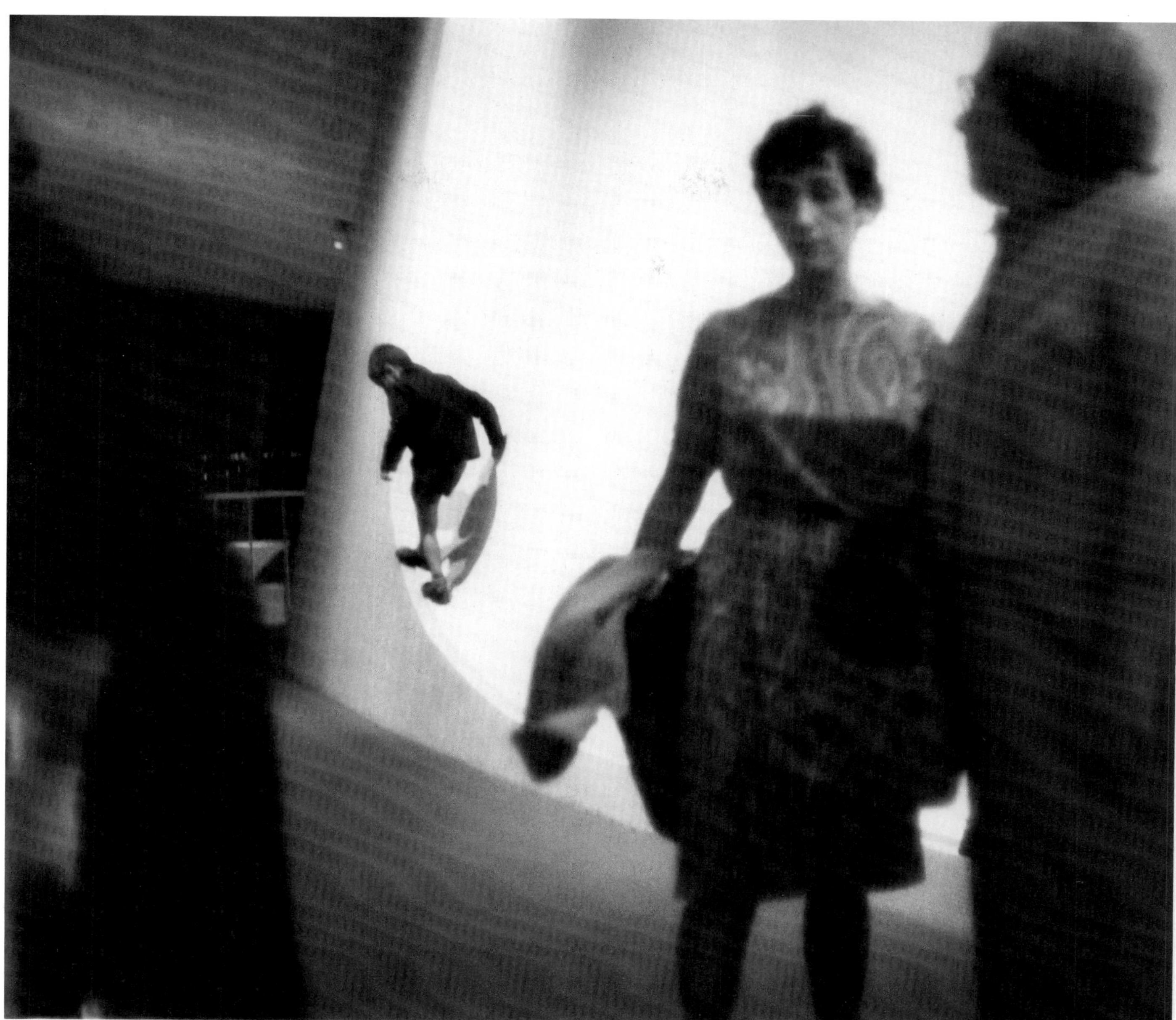

Fig. 5 (opposite) Trans World Airlines Terminal, close-up of column showing formwork

Fig. 6 Trans World Airlines Terminal, photographed by Charles Eames.

The quest for communicative form was also pursued in buildings that have seemingly abstract patterns—arrangements that, while distancing themselves from the intrinsic material, structural, or functional qualities of the buildings, communicate these ideas to the onlooker as pure visual structure. The precast facade of the U.S. Chancellery Building in Oslo (1955–59) serves as an example of this approach (figs. 7, 8). Saarinen described how functional and structural qualities translate into surface patterns as follows: "The precast façade is the most interesting and successful part of this building. Our attempt was to integrate the module, on which the offices are all based, with the structural system, so that one could conceive, all in one, a precast modular structural system with an integrated facade material."[24]

The goal in the Oslo project was also to trigger engagement with the viewer. Saarinen described the visual effect of the surface: "The material has a rich, dark green color and an inherent luster. It gives the facade a changing sheen and a vitality which are uncommon in precast walls. The three-dimensional quality of the wall, which is derived from its basic structural shape, enhances these qualities. As one walks along Drammensveien, these structural units seem to become a changing checkerboard of mat and shiny, light and dark surfaces." It is important to note that Saarinen does not say the Oslo facade was a checkerboard. The pattern was created by the passer-by, who, seduced by the flickering surface, would start to look for such regularity.[25]

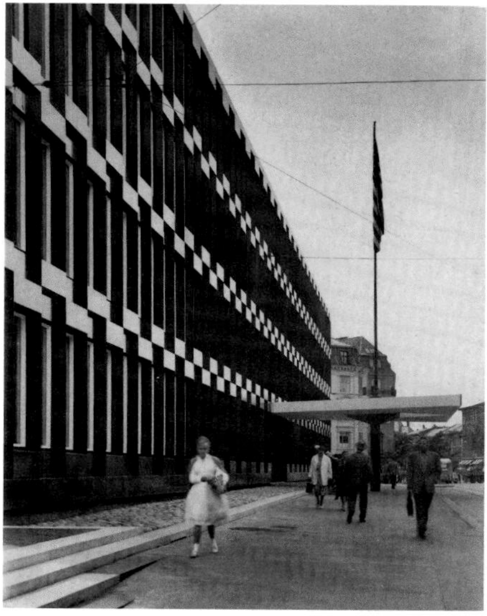

Fig. 7 (opposite) Eero Saarinen and Associates, United States Chancellery Building, Oslo, Norway, 1955–59, facade detail

Fig. 8 United States Chancellery Building, Oslo, oblique view of entrance along Drammensveien

Fig. 9 Gyorgy Kepes, cover of *Form Givers at Mid-Century*, 1959

In *The Language of Vision* (1944), the Hungarian-born American artist and designer Gyorgy Kepes set out to explain how pure optical effects communicate. What Kepes called "optical communication" was based on the idea that "visual language is capable of disseminating knowledge more effectively than almost any other vehicle of communication." Kepes believed that "visual communication is universal and international: it knows no limits of tongue, vocabulary, or grammar, and it can be perceived by the illiterate as well as by the literate." In the book Kepes used predominantly early-twentieth-century art and photography as examples, and language familiar from discussions of early-twentieth-century abstraction, including such terms as "compression," "interpenetration," "transparency," and "rhythm." The goal was to fight passive contemplation and engage the viewer in an active process of form creation.[26]

Critics celebrated architects whose work reached the level of pure formal expression without any external referents as the great "form givers." Saarinen was frequently accorded this distinction in the late 1950s. The term was popularized by the exhibition *Form Givers at Mid-Century*, which took place at the Metropolitan Museum of Art, New York, in 1959. The show was organized by Cranston Jones for the American Federation of Arts and sponsored by *Time* magazine. It featured most of the major American practitioners of Saarinen's era, among them Wallace K. Harrison, Philip Johnson, and Minoru Yamasaki; the European émigrés Marcel Breuer, Walter Gropius, and Mies; and, of those who remained in Europe, only Le Corbusier and Aalto. Kepes designed the catalogue.

The concept of the primacy of form can be traced to the English scholar, poet, and self-taught historian of architecture Geoffrey Scott, who had insisted in his book *The Architecture of Humanism* (1914) that Renaissance architecture had reached the level of excellence it did because its formal sensibility was free of material constraints. In the 1950s, Vincent Scully was among those reading Scott, whom he quoted in his article "Modern Architecture: Toward a Redefinition of Style" as having written of architectural humanism: "'The centre of that architecture was the human body; its method, to transcribe in stone the body's favorable states, and the moods of the spirit took visible shape along its borders, power and laughter, strength and terror and calm.'" The link between humanism and certain types of form or shape was made also by Pietro Belluschi, dean of the School of Architecture at MIT, who in the introduction to the show's catalogue, *Form Givers*, states that the new genius architect at midcentury does not settle into rationalizations but is searching for certain kinds of form, color, and texture. "We may feel that ornament and richness of space may again return as a part of man's long heritage. The architect is in effect the humanizer of society, the artist with the will to make the era a fitting place in which to live."[27]

Kepes's cover for the catalogue bears an illustration of the gradual transformation of a circle into an oval and of a square into a line, thus expressing the phenomenon that allowed such transhistorical leaps to be made: forms can create forms (fig. 9). Significantly, Jones made no attempt to categorize the different formal strategies employed by the architects in the show; each project represented a unique case in the endless chain of formal possibilities that stemmed from the work and philosophies of the modern masters. Belluschi made no secret of the exhibition's, and implicitly the museum's and *Time* magazine's, political agenda, declaring that the stylistic diversity of American architecture bore witness to the "freedom and vitality of American institutions."[28] The "form givers" played an important role in the organization of society as protectors of freedom conceived as something perpetually new.

The idea that new architecture could be based on preexisting forms was most explicit in buildings based on historical precedents. According to this generative process, preexisting meanings could change or be completely lost. Saarinen's Miller House in Columbus, Indiana (1953–57), serves as an example.

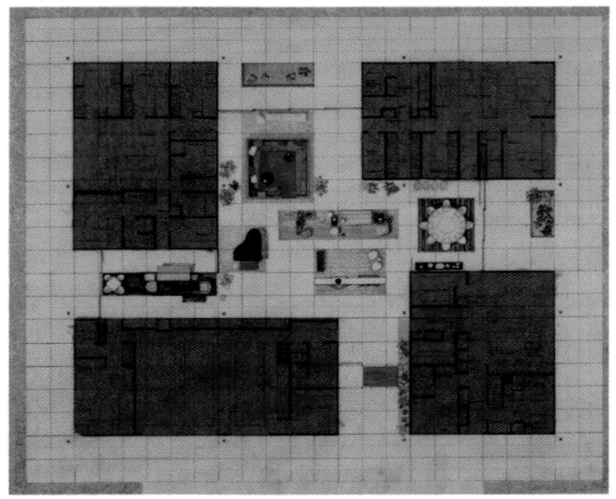

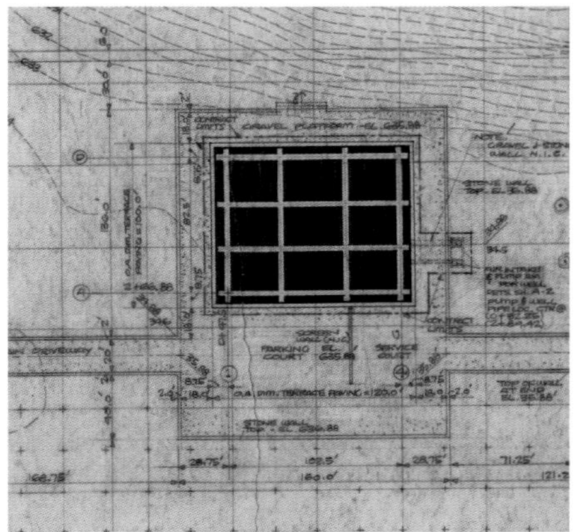

Fig. 10 Eero Saarinen and Associates, Miller House, Columbus, Indiana, 1953–57, floor plan, not final

Fig. 11 Miller House, roof plan

Fig. 12 Miller House, detail of X-column and skylight

The house is based on a nine-square grid, which was commonly used in Italian Renaissance villas. Saarinen took the grid through several modifications, one of which is clearly visible: the plan is neither square nor fully centralized (fig. 10). The living room, located off-center, flows into the outdoors. Light, instead of entering in a concentrated manner through a central cupola, is spread evenly along the grid lines by skylights (fig. 11). Even the stability of the grid is challenged. The bedrooms and service spaces, located in each corner according to their internal programmatic needs, break out of the grid. So do the double beams, which are located off-axis to give way to the skylights (fig. 12). When one moves about the house, the space dissolves into a dynamic flow of vistas through different sequences both within and extending outside the building. Consequently, two alternate readings coexist: that of the symmetrical static order represented by the white cube, and that of the fluid secondary order, where both body and eye are guided by plush materials—marble, travertine, rosewood, and textiles designed by Alexander Girard—and shifting light (fig. 13).

Saarinen was frank about his interest in using and studying historical precedents, including those from the recent past. In the *Perspecta* article, while condemning the codification of Mies's formal vocabulary, he endorsed borrowing from the modern masters in a fluid and creative way. He chose a culinary metaphor to describe the circulation and reappropriation of forms that characterized midcentury architecture, writing of Le Corbusier, Mies van der Rohe, and Frank Lloyd Wright:

> These three made the great principles which together form our architecture. Mixed together, they make the broth which is modern architecture. In different parts of the world, the ingredients of the broth have different proportions. For instance, architecture in South America and Italy is primarily made up out of the fundamental principles plus Corbu. This forms a different product than that of the U.S.[,] which has primarily Mies, comparatively little Corbu, and FLW as a spice.[29]

Saarinen's ideas about the circulation of forms, artistic influence, and the notion that people in different parts of the world understand similar forms differently automatically dismantled the view of stylistic change as an organic process in which each period and place had its own style, and with it the idea that forms possess fixed meanings. Credit for this perception goes to his father, Eliel Saarinen, who had addressed the issue of intellectual influence among individuals and cultures in his book *Search for Form: A Fundamental Approach to Art* (1948). Eliel's ideas about how forms migrate and are appropriated was based on the simple realization that neither individuals nor cultures exist in isolation but come into contact with other people and other cultures. The elder Saarinen talked about "form migration" and asked whether the appropriation of forms leads to direct copying or whether forms can be invested with new meanings when they are adopted by different cultures.[30]

The influential art historian George Kubler, who taught at Yale, further developed the idea of "form migration," breaking away from the conventional art historical approach, which tied forms to the particular time and place of their creation. In his book *The Shape of Time* (1962), Kubler argued that art history, when reduced to the study of coherent styles, is unable to explain how forms circulate through time and gain meaning in new contexts. To describe stylistic change he replaced the biological metaphor that linked forms to a single author, time, and place, with one drawn from the language of electrodynamics, referring to "impulses, generating centers, and relay points; with increments and losses in transit; with resistances and transformers in the circuit." He believed that works of art function as signals, which trigger other individuals to repeat them. As Kubler's teacher Henri Focillon observed, forms have lives of their own. Focillon explained the process as follows: "The sign itself becomes form and, in the world of forms, it gives rise to a whole series of shapes that subsequently bear no relation whatsoever to their origin."[31]

Saarinen's work and words suggest that he thought about forms along

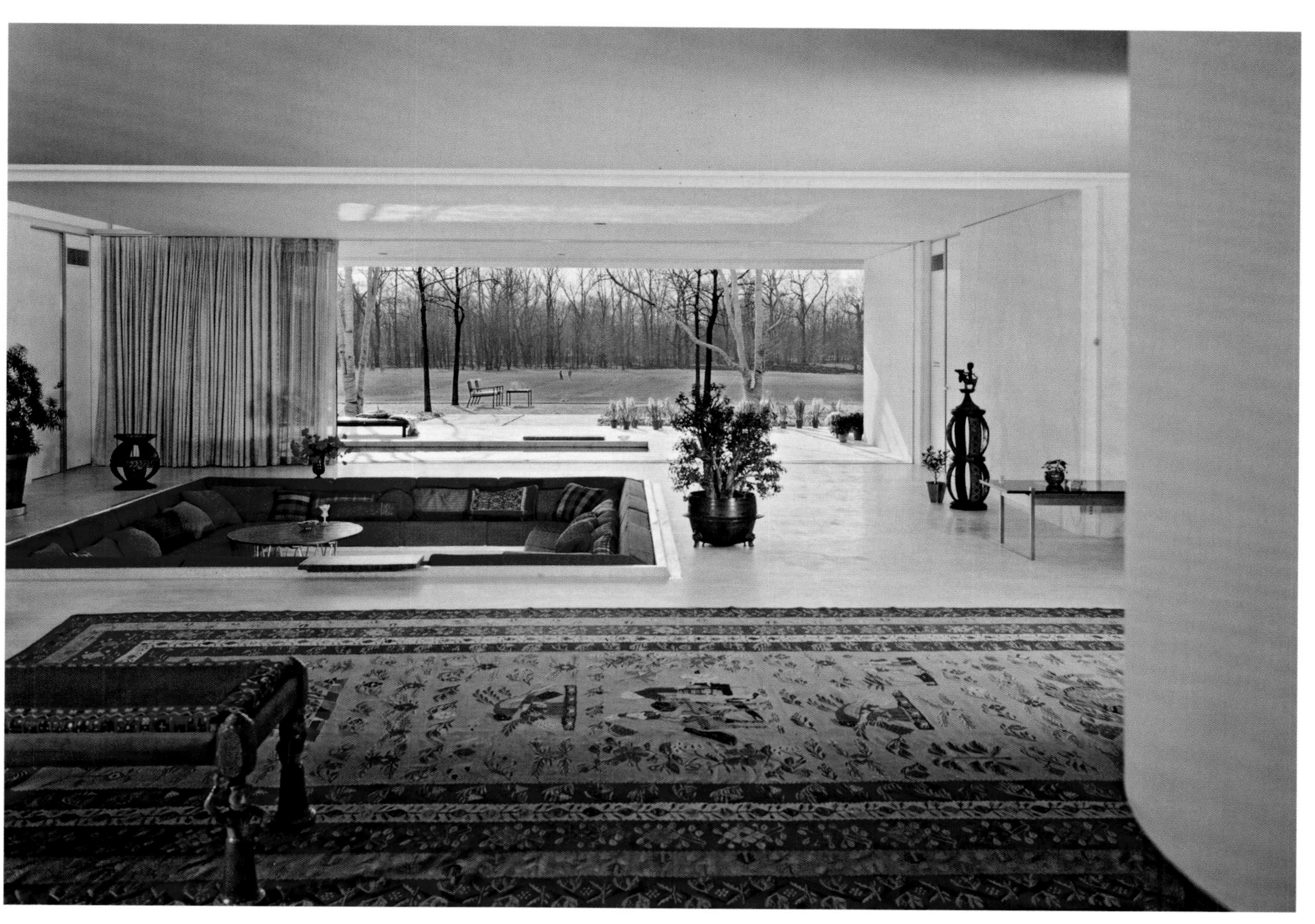

Fig. 13 Miller House, living room with conversation pit

similar lines as his father and Kubler. On the one hand he realized that while meanings cannot be conveyed without forms, forms themselves go through evolutions with no relation to their original or intended meanings. This is where "chaoticism" comes in: forms render the author unable to control their effect. In fact, Saarinen often shifted his role from that of author to that of viewer to test whether the forms had the desired impact. At times he talked about his buildings with unusual detachment. He said of the Kresge Auditorium: "In retrospect one has to criticize this building. It looks like a half-inflated balloon. The windows bulging out, the round base, the narrow edge beam, and the complete spherical shape, I believe all contribute to that, and I do sympathize with Gideon's [*sic*] statement that this building looks earthbound" (fig. 14).[32] Saarinen seems to have considered himself and his buildings as "relay points" and accepted the fact that in some cases his attempts to solve a transhistorical problem—in the case of the auditorium, that of a vaulted space—were not satisfactory. It remained for future projects and generations to get it right.

How does one evaluate the body of work of an architect who did not make claims to perfection and whose approach to architecture at times did not seem to amount to much more than individual creative search? It certainly makes no sense to argue endlessly about whether Saarinen was a good or bad architect, since he was the first one to acknowledge that some of his buildings worked better than others. Therefore, instead of singling out the ones that communicate to us—TWA, for example—it is worth looking at the less successful projects, such as Concordia Senior College in Fort Wayne, Indiana. Here Saarinen's goal was to communicate with the college's Lutheran and predominantly Scandinavian constituency by creating a quasi-vernacular "Northern European village" of dormitories with broad gables (more reminiscent of alpine ski lodges than Scandinavian houses), which lined the roads leading to an A-frame church (fig. 15). Despite Saarinen's attempt to communicate specific cultural associations through form, the A-frame church was subsequently copied by

Fig. 14 Eero Saarinen and Associates, Kresge Auditorium, Massachusetts Institute of Technology, Cambridge, Massachusetts, 1950–55, with Kresge Chapel in foreground

Fig. 15 (right) Eero Saarinen and Associates, Concordia Senior College, Fort Wayne, Indiana, 1953–58, aerial view

architects all around the world, divorced from the intended reference. Concordia and its copies thus demonstrate that once architecture culture let go of modernist dogma, forms gained meaning only through and in relation to other forms.[33]

One could then conclude that the random pluralism that Saarinen and his contemporaries were blamed for was a function of a new conception of architectural form that broke loose from classical modernism and its insistence that architectural form can be tied to a particular meaning. What seemed to have come as a surprise to them was that unleashing the communicative potential of form disabled them as authors. Forms, as Langer well knew, did not communicate and could not communicate in any real sense. Forms had lives of their own.

Notes

I thank Reinhold Martin, Detlef Mertins, Robert A. M. Stern, and Christopher Wood for reading and commenting on earlier versions of this essay.

1. Reyner Banham, "Monument with Frills," *New Statesman*, Dec. 10, 1960, 618.

2. Norbert Wiener, quoted in Thomas H. Creighton, "The Sixties: A P/A Symposium on the State of Architecture," *Progressive Architecture*, Mar. 1961, 122.

3. Creighton, "The Sixties," 123, 125, 127. "Ballet School" was a derogatory term that critics such as Reyner Banham and William Jordy used to refer to the modernist classicism of architects like Philip Johnson, whose New York State Theater at Lincoln Center was intended to showcase ballet.

4. Oscar Nitzchke was a French-born architect who worked with George Nelson as well as with Harrison and Abramovitz. He taught at Yale in the 1940s.

5. My discussion of temporality is informed by Pamela M. Lee's article "'Ultramoderne': Or, How George Kubler Stole the Time in Sixties Art," *October*, spring 2001, 46–77.

6. Bruno Zevi, in "Three Critics Discuss MIT's New Buildings," *Architectural Forum*, Mar. 1956, 157.

7. J. M. Richards, in "Three Critics Discuss MIT's New Buildings," 174.

8. Sigfried Giedion, *Space, Time, and Architecture: The Growth of a New Tradition* (Cambridge: Harvard University Press, 1941). Giedion added a chapter on Aalto to the 1949 edition, and his comment about Saarinen first appeared in the 1959 edition. See 1959 edition, 18 and 178.

9. Saarinen discussed the six principles in several articles and lectures, sometimes in the same words, including "The Six Broad Currents of Modern Architecture," *Architectural Forum*, July 1953, 110–15; Dickinson College Arts Award Address, Dec. 1, 1959, Eero Saarinen Papers, Manuscripts and Archives, Yale University, manuscript published in this volume; "Problems Facing Architecture," a lecture given at the University of Pennsylvania, Dec. 8, 1960, unpublished manuscript, Eero Saarinen Papers, Yale University; and "Function, Structure, Beauty," *Architectural Association Journal*, July–Aug. 1957, 40–51.

10. Eero Saarinen, "Saarinen," *Perspecta* 7 (1961), 32.

11. Eero Saarinen, "General Statement about the sculptural, curved/shapes that we have been involved with, beginning with St. Louis, the water tower and dome at General Motors, MIT, Yale,

TWA, and now the Washington International Airport," undated manuscript, Eero Saarinen Papers, Yale University, published in this volume.

12. Saarinen, "Saarinen," 30.

13. Ibid.

14. Arthur Drexler and Wilder Green, "Architecture and Imagery: Four Buildings," *Museum of Modern Art Bulletin* 26, no. 2 (1959), 1, 17.

15. Thomas H. Creighton, "The New Sensualism II," *Progressive Architecture,* Oct. 1959, 180.

16. Ibid., 183.

17. Eero Saarinen, letter to Thomas H. Creighton, Sept. 8, 1959, Eero Saarinen Papers, Yale University.

18. Robin Boyd, "The Counter Revolution in Architecture," *Harper's,* Sept. 1959, 44, 46, 47.

19. Susanne K. Langer, *Feeling and Form: A Theory of Art* (New York: Charles Scribner's Sons, 1953), 32.

20. Ibid., 99, 393, 394; Ernst Cassirer, *The Philosophy of Symbolic Forms* (New Haven: Yale University Press, 1953), 87.

21. Eero Saarinen in an interview regarding TWA from January 1959, excerpted in Eero Saarinen, *Eero Saarinen on His Work: A Selection of Buildings Dating from 1947 to 1964,* with statements by the architect, ed. Aline B. Saarinen (New Haven: Yale University Press, 1962), 60; Saarinen, "Saarinen," 32.

22. Saarinen interview regarding TWA, 60.

23. Eero Saarinen, interview in *Horizon Magazine,* June 19, 1959, 76–82, 123, quoted in *Eero Saarinen on His Work,* 60.

24. Saarinen discussing the Oslo Chancellery Building in March 1959, in *Eero Saarinen on His Work,* 52.

25. Ibid.

26. Gyorgy Kepes, *The Language of Vision* (New York: Paul Theobald, 1944), 13. Kepes taught visual design at MIT between 1946 and 1974.

27. Geoffrey Scott, *The Architecture of Humanism: A Study in the History of Taste* (ca. 1914; Gloucester, Mass: Peter Smith, 1965); Vincent Scully, "Modern Architecture: Toward a Redefinition of Style," *Perspecta* 4 (1957), 7; Pietro Belluschi, introduction, in *Form Givers at Mid-Century* (New York: Time, 1959), 7.

28. Belluschi, introduction, 7.

29. Saarinen, "Saarinen," 30. The same statement appears in his Dickinson College Arts Award Address.

30. Eliel Saarinen, *Search for Form: A Fundamental Approach to Art* (New York: Reinhold, 1948), 174–75. He wrote: "By form-migration—or why not 'form-immigration' or 'form-intermigration'—we mean form-influence between various ramifications of human civilization. . . . Before we go further into this simple matter we must first pause to deliberate upon what the implication of the word influence really is. Does it mean creative inspiration derived from contacts with alien forms or is it to be understood as a direct adoption of these alien forms—meaning that the commandment forbidding us to take things belonging to others can be violated?"

31. George Kubler, *The Shape of Time: Remarks on the History of Things* (New Haven: Yale University Press, 1962), 9; Henri Focillon, *The Life of Forms in Art* (New York: Zone Books, 1992), 38 (originally titled *Vie des Formes,* Paris, 1934).

32. Saarinen, "General Statement," 2.

33. Saarinen, *Eero Saarinen on His Work,* 44. Edward Saad, one of Saarinen's employees at the time, recalls that Concordia was one of Saarinen's least favorite projects. Coming around one night when people were charretting on the project, Saarinen said: "This looks like a Detroit Free Press design for a house"; Edward Saad, interview with Bill Ferehawk, KDN Films, Dec. 16, 2004.

Sandy Isenstadt

eero saarinen's theater of form

Fig. 1 Eero Saarinen and Associates, Samuel F. B. Morse and Ezra Stiles Colleges, Yale University, New Haven, Connecticut, 1958–62, sketch

One observation contemporaries made frequently regarding the work of Eero Saarinen is that it was theatrical. Critics disdained what they called "structural acrobatics" and distrusted Saarinen's serial virtuosity, thinking he aimed more for spectacular effect than, say, technical candor. Reyner Banham, for example, said that the Morse and Stiles Colleges at Yale University (1958–62) displayed "Caligari lighting effects," alluding to the 1919 German Expressionist film directed by Robert Wiene, and "Gordon Craig–type scenic effects," referring to the English theater designer and director who advocated abstract and evocative sets rather than naturalistic ones (fig. 1). But admirers, too, felt compelled to account for Saarinen's theatrics. *Progressive Architecture* said that, yes, Morse and Stiles were "histrionic," but they were also well planned, whereas *Architectural Forum* thought Saarinen, given the circumstances of context, had shown courage: "Inserting two brand-new building groups into the determinedly ancient environs of Yale University was . . . as dangerous as introducing a pair of young 'method' actors into a group of retired Shakespeareans." Even Saarinen's wife, Aline, remarked after the buildings were complete: "He thought of college architecture, in its relation to students, as stage scenery." Allegations of theatricality posed a problem for both critic and admirer because they situated the design as a performance: an architect turning the spotlight on his own skills, or construction used only as an armature for scenographic effects, or institutional imagery costumed in three dimensions. All of these approaches subordinated other, allegedly more essential aspects of architecture and, in doing so, descended from artifice to deceit, or, as Ada Louise Huxtable wrote, Saarinen tempted the "dangerous transition from freedom to license."[1]

In contrast, Saarinen's earlier projects, most famously the General Motors Technical Center (1948–56), explicitly thematized rationalized, unaffected construction and a modernist conception of continuous space. Its five-foot module organized otherwise disparate building systems into a single uniform grid and allowed indoors to flow outward through the wide intervals between. It was an architecture about architecture—construction and space—and in this regard Saarinen gladly acknowledged the influence of Ludwig Mies van der Rohe, whose designs for the Illinois Institute of Technology were by the late 1940s a touchstone for postwar American architects. IIT's influence is evident at GM in its palette of materials and its site plan of low steel, glass, and brick boxes sliding one past the other in an otherwise uninterrupted field. Saarinen's later work would depart from this crisp articulation of core modernist principles, which were embraced by client as well as architect. Saarinen's short solo career was characterized, as Robin Boyd put it in 1959, by a shift from "reasoned rectangles to felt space," from an intellectual inquiry into truth to an emotional impulse for expression.[2]

A consideration of Saarinen's work through the lens of theater is warranted by the views of his contemporaries, although, it must be noted, Saarinen himself seems to have ignored the issue altogether in any written statement. Nonetheless, looking at Saarinen from this vantage point addresses several issues. First, in relation to his own career, it demonstrates a lifelong engagement with theater as a building type. Second, since theatricality implies a self-awareness of the actor and the conditions of his self-display, it calls attention to Saarinen's evident awareness that he was playing a leading role in modernism's second act. Third, and more generally, by examining a term common to both his admirers and his detractors, we can also begin to account for the popular warmth and critical chill that simultaneously greeted his work. Reviewing his popular reception can help clarify how his designs resonated within their social context, and help situate the success of his practice in terms other than individual artistic invention. Finally, examining how theatricality was considered a critical term in the first place reveals perhaps even more about the postwar understanding of modernism than about Saarinen himself. The profile of anxieties regarding the work of a leading proponent of modernism may be a more reliable indicator of contemporary beliefs than any explicit statement about him.

MODERN THEATER

Before a charge of theatricality became a term of disapproval for postwar critics, theater was a focus of modernist energies. Responding to developments in other fine arts, a number of figures sought to create an explicitly modern theater, one that addressed the urban life of its time or sought to portray new psychic conditions, recently excavated by depth psychology, or that took advantage of new technologies like electric lighting, stage lifts, moving platforms, and revolving stages. As Manfredo Tafuri wrote regarding the role of such innovators as Adolphe Appia and Georg Fuchs, theater promised to be the means "for the recovery of a portion of unalienated space."[3] Playwrights, directors, and actors were all affected. Gordon Craig, whom Banham referred to in his critique of Morse and Stiles Colleges, had a galvanizing effect on set design, for example. Reacting against the naturalism of contemporary theater, Craig emphasized the possibilities of dramatic lighting and produced abstract sets that established moods to reinforce a play's emotional directions rather than conform to ideas of verisimilitude. Craig also argued that all aspects of artistic production should be harmonized under the unitary vision of a single designer, a position that led architects like Henry van de Velde and Josef Hoffmann to embrace him as a like-minded reformer. Craig predicted as well a new and vastly more flexible theater to accommodate the unified spectacles of sound, form, and narrative he called for. A number of directors furthered these views, most notably Max Reinhardt, who directed the Volksbühne in Berlin from 1915 to 1918 and the following year opened the Grosses Schauspielhaus there, renovated by Hans Poelzig to incorporate innovative stage machinery, a transformable stage, and the newly invented cyclorama, a sheer plaster dome that could become a canvas for transient lighting effects and forestall spectators' judgments of depth. Later pioneers of such "total theater," like Erwin Piscator, for whom Walter Gropius designed a theater in 1927, drew upon the earlier ferment and were typically free in their praise of such figures as Craig.[4]

In the United States these ideals were stripped of the socialist ambitions that many of them carried, infused with a penchant for effect, and introduced as part of the "New Stagecraft," led by dramatists and set designers like Robert Edmond Jones, Lee Simonson, Aline Bernstein, Joseph Urban, Norman Bel Geddes, and Claude Bragdon, the latter three also involved in architecture. Bel Geddes was particularly influential in adapting Craig's work, especially with his "massively sculptural" sets, the best known of which was his thoroughgoing 1924 conversion of New York's Century Theater into a medieval cathedral for an epoch-making presentation of Reinhardt's *The Miracle.* Historicist in form, the vast spectacle was nonetheless a breakthrough in modern American theater, thrilling audiences with its coordination of elements, including odors, its melding of actors and audience with singers scattered throughout the theater such that "spectators themselves seem to participate in the play," and its overall immersive quality—an "unimaginably atmospheric" total environment, in the words of one reviewer. In lectures Bel Geddes gave shortly afterward, he stressed the need, drawing directly from Craig and Appia, to correlate all aspects of a theatrical production under a single idea: "Each part must be an essential element of this basic concept rather than something appended. The value of the design lies in its homogenous integrity in giving significance to an idea and fulfilling it." Or, as one critic wrote of *The Miracle,* all parts of the performance were, "algebraically speaking, functions of the space." Such was the rapid success of the New Stagecraft that an international exposition of modernist theater opened in New York in 1926 with a statement by Frederick Kiesler, a Viennese émigré architect and stage designer, that European architects were looking to such Americans as Bel Geddes, Donald Oenslager, and Jo Mielziner, all young set designers whose work was represented at the show.[5]

In a sense, Saarinen was raised in a theater set, fashioned by his father with partners Herman Gesellius and Armas Lindgren at Hvitträsk, Finland. There they created a fantastic world apart from modern Helsinki, with medievalizing elements that harkened to the Finnish folk epic the *Kalevala.* Later, as a young man at Cranbrook, itself a self-consciously isolated arts community, Saarinen would lead a life punctuated by the school's masque balls and elaborate exhibitions. His various early decorative arts designs at Cranbrook exhibit an animated, at times animist quality, endowing material with a sense of vitality and movement, with forms expressive of life and self-determination, in keeping with the Arts and Crafts ethos that prevailed at both Hvitträsk and Cranbrook. One of his graphic designs, for example, relies on a framed setting; his mother's dressing table is complete with uplights and a curtained proscenium; theatrical masks inspired stone carvings. Even Saarinen's lifelong admiration of the Swedish sculptor Carl Milles, a student of Rodin and an artist enamored of allegory, might be taken as a weakness for the dramatic gesture.

When Saarinen went to study for his professional degree, he enrolled in Yale University's School of Fine Arts, which in 1931 was best known nationally for its drama department. It was still a new department then, having been founded only six years before, when Yale hired away from Harvard George Pierce Baker, the country's leading playwriting teacher, and built for him one of the finest university theaters of its time—an event described at the time by Heywood Broun, a journalist and Harvard alumnus, as "Harvard fumbles; Yale recovers." Baker swiftly hired a number of emerging talents, such as Oenslager, who became professor of scenic design. Almost overnight, Yale's drama department became a center of the New Stagecraft or, more simply, the "New Movement" in theater. For his last elective at Yale, Saarinen took a class in set design taught by Oenslager, who, for his part, always included architecture as part of his lectures.[6]

Baker also appointed, as professor of stage lighting, Stanley McCandless, who, along with George Izenour, would become a leading lighting engineer and

Fig. 2 Eliel and Eero Saarinen, Kleinhans Music Hall, Buffalo, New York, 1938–40, stair

make Yale the first school to offer such courses. McCandless lectured regularly in the architecture department, presumably on his work for architects like John Russell Pope and Delano and Aldrich. McCandless was himself an architect, with a degree from Harvard and experience in the office of McKim, Mead, and White. He considered Bel Geddes's staging of *The Miracle* to be "a new high in elaborate architectural production with important lighting effects," and made it a goal of his own work to bring architecture and dramatic lighting into greater harmony, as he felt Bel Geddes had done. At Radio City Music Hall, for instance, McCandless wrote that he had aimed specifically at "combining architecture and lighting in a unified expression." In addition, McCandless offered at Yale a class on lighting, specifically for architects. Architectural lighting involved many practical considerations but was also, he said, an important opportunity to consolidate a building's formal themes. Lighting provided a clarifying and "contributing mood," as he had learned from his work in theater.[7] Although Saarinen did not take a class with him, he soon came to rely professionally on McCandless for advice on architectural lighting.

SAARINEN'S MODERN THEATERS

Saarinen's direct involvement with theater building began shortly after he completed his professional training at Yale University. In the summer of 1935 he worked in Helsinki with Finnish architect Jarl Eklund on renovations to the Swedish Theater, built in the nineteenth century. Saarinen sketched designs for furniture, interior spaces, and a streamlined exterior that recalled the designs of Erich Mendelsohn from the previous decade. Beginning in 1938 Saarinen worked with his father, Eliel, on the Kleinhans Music Hall in Buffalo, which was completed in 1940 (fig. 2). It was an important commission for the office, coming during the Great Depression and extending the Saarinen practice beyond Cranbrook to a city noted for innovative architecture. The project bears signs of its streamlined age, breaking functions out into separate

Fig. 3 Saarinen and Swanson, first scheme for General Motors Technical Center, Warren, Michigan, ca. 1945, rendering by Hugh Ferris

volumes and rejoining them with curving lines echoed in both building and landscape, and continuing inside to harmonize assorted details. It was also the first of many projects for which Saarinen hired McCandless. Indeed, Saarinen believed McCandless's contribution to that project had been particularly significant: he wrote to McCandless to say that "the lighting is one of the most interesting things on the building." McCandless, for his part, was glad about the collaboration. He wrote to a colleague in Buffalo, "I am particularly thankful to be working with the Saarinens. . . . [They] cooperat[ed] more than any architects I have ever worked with."[8] Saarinen continued to employ McCandless afterward on a number of projects, including the Kresge Auditorium and Chapel at MIT (1950–55) and the United States Chancellery Building in London (1955–60).

Subsequent theaters and performance spaces in the Saarinen family practice included the auditorium for the Crow Island School and an open-air stage for the Berkshire Music Center, both begun in 1938, a theater for Oberlin College in 1941, and the Ford Theater, as part of the Detroit Civic Center, from 1946 to 1949, as well as an auditorium and opera house for Los Angeles that Eero worked on in 1948 as part of a team of noted architects.

Certainly Eero's best-known theater project of this period, and his first commission independent of his father, came in 1939, with the American National Theater at the College of William and Mary, in Williamsburg, Virginia, which, along with closely watched competitions for Wheaton College in Norton, Massachusetts, Goucher College in Towson, Maryland, and the Smithsonian Institution in Washington, D.C., were evidence of rising American interest in modernism: the winning entries all proposed modern forms in otherwise traditional contexts. Saarinen is the only architect to have been recognized in all four competitions. At William and Mary, he collaborated with Cranbrook friends Ralph Rapson and Fred James, with Charles Eames helping to visualize different stage configurations. The design was praised by Lee Simonson, an author of the program and a juror for the competition, in *Theatre Arts* for a well-conceived flexibility that would allow manifold relations between actors and audience. Simonson considered the design an advance in the possibilities of theater as well as a sensible piece of architecture.[9]

A number of Saarinen's friends at Yale had been deeply interested in theater, even as they studied architecture. One of his roommates, for example, was Harold "Hecky" Rome, who left with his degree in architecture for a successful career writing songs for Broadway. Leslie Cheek was another classmate and would remain a lifelong friend and admirer. Cheek went on to direct the department of fine arts at the College of William and Mary; he not only lobbied successfully to locate the American National Theater there but also served on the jury of the competition for the new building. Along with his fellow judges, Cheek passed up entries by such established architects as Richard Neutra, Marcel Breuer, Gropius, and Wallace K. Harrison to select a scheme by the unseasoned Saarinen. Cheek continued to follow the new currents in theater and in his subsequent role as director of the Virginia Museum of Fine Arts, from 1948 to 1968, he made use of numerous theatrical devices in a continuing effort to popularize art, becoming a "master-builder of audiences" by designing engaging environments for viewing art, incorporating odors—tar and salt water in a show of seascapes—sounds, dramatic lighting, and a narrative circulation into "sensurround" installations. He also used actual artworks in dramatic performances, at times having the cast assemble in tableaux of paintings that were concurrently onstage. In 1961, just before Saarinen's death, Cheek made a simultaneous award to Saarinen and the late Carl Milles for their contributions to the arts.[10]

As suggestive as such relationships may be, the most important theatrical influence on Saarinen resulted from an invitation in spring 1938 to work with Bel Geddes—not an architect but a set designer—to develop the facade of the General Motors Pavilion for the World's Fair to be held in New York the following year.[11] The finished project was a sensation, easily the fair's most popular exhibit. It contained a spectacular and expensive model, with changing moods created by lighting and music, and projecting balconies and a conveyer belt that allowed viewers to look down on the scene, a utopian American city, as if from an airplane, while channeling them along a narrative path to the future, for which Bel Geddes named the exhibit: Futurama. The overview was both panoramic and intimate, with all faces focused inward on the model, and so viewed in collective isolation as in a theater.[12] The whole ensemble was gathered together in a building that recapitulated the interior movement: widely curving walkways vined along the facade and then disappeared into a great vertical slash that contrasted sharply with the winding horizontal ramps. As much as the interior experience was cinematic in its continuously changing scenery, the building itself was a set piece in keeping with such recent feature films as Alexander Korda's production of *Things to Come* (1936), which borrowed freely from streamlined industrial designs proposed by figures like Raymond Loewy and Bel Geddes himself. Indeed, with GM as the client, highways of the future as one of the subjects, the "people mover" balconies as the technology, and the animated facade of architectural form and human figures, the design insisted on movement at all levels and scales as much as it seemed also to replicate the very mobility of the movie camera.

Early designs for the General Motors Technical Center by Saarinen and Swanson, from 1945–46, clearly show the formal influence of Bel Geddes (fig. 3). The Research Building, as Allan Temko put it, "was given an expressionistic air-foil shape, reminiscent of a 'streamlined' car."[13] In the next designs that Eero executed for GM, beginning in 1948—after Mies's completion of several buildings on the IIT campus—he abandoned such overt attempts at futurist styling in favor of apparently more rationalized construction and programming.

As his career expanded in other directions in the 1940s and 1950s, Saarinen nonetheless returned to the theater type, although usually not as an independent building. Indeed, his evident attention to performance spaces

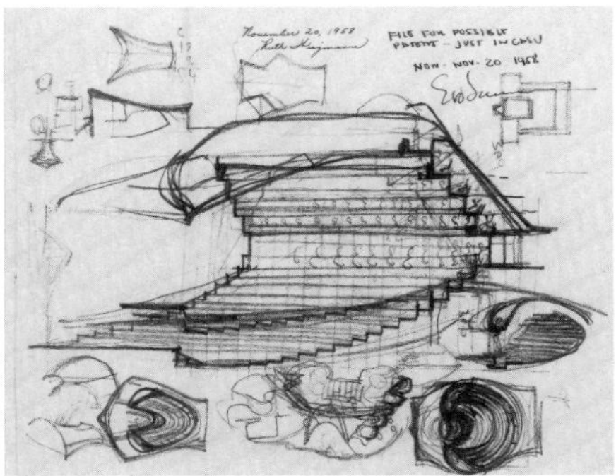

Fig. 4 (opposite) Eero Saarinen and Associates, Deere and Company Administrative Center, Moline, Illinois, 1957–63, auditorium

Fig. 5 Eero Saarinen and Associates, Vivian Beaumont Repertory Theater, Lincoln Center for the Performing Arts, New York, 1958–65, sketch of auditorium

in the context of other, larger programs seems only to have substantiated his interest in their possibilities. The headquarters for Deere and Company, in Moline, Illinois, begun in 1957, for example, required an auditorium in which to display tractors and other farm equipment to potential buyers (fig. 4). Saarinen made the space not simply accessible but almost mandatory, part of the entry sequence for visitors. He also preserved in the section of the theater his initial scheme for the entire site, an inverted pyramid whose upper floors would reach farther out into the landscape at each additional level. In the theater, this diagram becomes a "reverse balcony arrangement" that allows spectators to look not just forward but down onto the displayed objects, as if from an airplane. The most conspicuous precedent for this arrangement is Bel Geddes's Futurama. John Jacobus paid special attention to the theater in his review of the project, completed in 1963, after Saarinen's death, finding it one of the "most delightful small theatres" anywhere in contemporary architecture. The "actors," he wrote, are "self-propelled" tractors and the "'skied' spectators" were afloat in the reversed balconies. Moreover, the stage itself includes a turntable and is bounded at the rear by a glass wall to allow the courtyard outside to become yet another stage, a novel attempt to fuse a by-then iconic element of modern architecture with the flexible space needs of modern theater. Although the theater is small relative to the rest of the building, its innovations make Saarinen's attention evident here and, with its section recalling the initial pyramid, suggests that his attitude toward landscape more generally was one of spectatorship.[14] Similarly, to take another example, the main dining halls at Morse and Stiles Colleges feature raised seating areas that can become performance stages, just as the colleges' courtyards become bowl-shaped as they approach the dining-hall windows, as if the collective act of dining were in itself a drama inviting contemplation.

One of Saarinen's last designs was for the Vivian Beaumont Repertory Theater at Lincoln Center, in New York City (1958–65). It was developed in close collaboration with Mielziner (who was a roommate of Saarinen's when he worked at the OSS in Washington, D.C.) as a steeply sloping arena to maintain sight lines for an audience of more than a thousand (fig. 5). The stage could remain within a wide proscenium or could grow to ten thousand square feet with a series of aprons and thrust stages capable of reaching into the audience when the first several rows of seats were lowered into the basement. It featured hidden entrances, an elaborate lighting system, a revolving center stage, and a host of mechanical contrivances for maximum flexibility. The ambitiousness of the design was both condemned and praised. Its flexibility allowed for surprising intimacy, argued Mielziner, while Robert Brustein, then dean of the Yale University drama school, thought the design tempted directors to "overproduce" shows to better fit the interior space.[15] In any case, Saarinen revisited for this late design a number of elements he had explored in earlier schemes, including a "people wall," a further development of the reverse balcony design at Deere and innovative enough for Saarinen to consider filing a patent, and a glass wall that makes the Beaumont's lobby into a drama of circulation visible from the outside.

THEATRICALITY AT THE TWA TERMINAL

Saarinen's evident interest in theater as a building type does not, however, address the critical charge of theatricality, which had to do with the appropriation of theatrical techniques to create dramatic effects, which, in turn, masked an otherwise affectless construction generally thought to be more authentically architectural. The meaning of the word "theatricality," of course, is fluid, denoting anything from the use of expressive forms to an overt sentimentality to dissimulation. Most often, in relation to Saarinen, it seems to have implied an emotional indulgence, which ran counter to reigning principles of rationalist architecture. For a number of observers, such lapses in an otherwise self-disciplined mind were the product of his professional upbringing, at the foot of Eliel Saarinen. The elder Saarinen, according

to Jacobus, never lost a "post–Art Nouveau sentimentalism" that, in the final analysis, was at odds with the "American utilitarianism" as codified by Mies. Aline Saarinen, too, noted that both father and son had a taste for the picturesque, while Eero himself thought that the greatest deviation from his "long-term allegiance" to Mies was, precisely, his sympathy with the views of his father.[16]

A number of Saarinen's designs reveal a fondness for theatrical gestures: the structural lyricism of Yale's David S. Ingalls Hockey Rink (1956–58), the carefully staged lighting at MIT's ecumenical Kresge Chapel, or the village of theology at Concordia Senior College in Fort Wayne, Indiana (1953–58). Wolf Von Eckardt called the chapel "sculptured emotion" and regarding Concordia said it could have been a scene by Lyonel Feininger. The chapel, although foreshadowed in some of Saarinen's earlier unbuilt designs, directly evokes elements used by Bel Geddes in 1938, for example, the round plan, raking reflected lighting, and toplit altarlike table at the entry to the Elbow Room restaurant in New York City, or the shimmering atmosphere on the set of *Dead End* (1935), which Bel Geddes created by focusing spotlights on mirrors submerged in trays of water. McCandless especially appreciated the chapel, which, along with the auditorium, he thought remarkable to find anywhere "outside of a World's Fair."[17]

Saarinen's expressionism would reach full flower in the TWA Terminal (1956–62), the most visibly dramatic of his designs (figs. 6, 7). Numerous accounts describe the building as a grand pageant and do not fail to hint at the sense of virtual flight. The popular press was typically breathless. The *St. Louis Post-Dispatch* characterized TWA's vaults as "the proscenium over a ballet of stairways, balustrades, [and] promenades . . . that perform arabesques of flowing and leaping lines." *McCall's* magazine compared the building to motion pictures: "The sight of people promenading over the rise seemed like a scene from *Here Comes Mr. Jordan*, that old Robert Montgomery film about heaven," which is the story of a man who dies before his time and, after refusing to board the airplane to heaven, returns to earth transformed to achieve, first, wealth, then fame, and finally, true love; it is an unprecedented roundtrip ticket, where paradise is the trip itself. Footage of the terminal shot for a film commissioned by NBC features a thriller score, with portentous brass notes and off-key piano highs that lend a sense of tense anticipation. A series of long tracking shots and slow pans leads at the end to the heroic proportions of a swelling score and camera turned skyward to follow a jet soaring off to points unknown. Such responses register the building's resonance and sympathy with American movie fantasies.[18]

Professional journals were more restrained but used the same metaphor of participatory theater, an architecture animated equally by emotive form and physical movement. *Architectural Forum* wrote that the first impression of the terminal is a "dramatic and symbolic form" but that, upon entry, visitors "will become part of the drama themselves as they mount the central stairs to the waiting area." The waiting lounge was described as "theater-like," with the glass walls turning the tarmac into a kind of nomadic scenery.[19] The building is both stage and protagonist in a play whose plot is motion. Indeed, the terminal's evocation of flight is far more fulfilling than the actual experience of sitting for hours in a cramped airplane cabin.

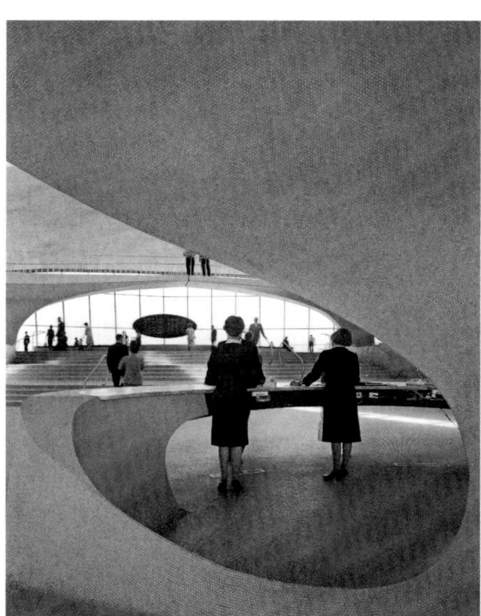

Fig. 6 (opposite) Eero Saarinen and Associates, Trans World Airlines Terminal, New York International Airport, New York, 1956–62; photographed by Charles Eames

Fig. 7 Trans World Airlines Terminal, information booth

Although the terminal was published widely, the primary audience for this project was limited to a certain audience of ticketholders. Airfares had declined significantly in the postwar period, particularly in relation to disposable income, while the number of passengers flying rose rapidly, which meant that although it was still expensive to fly, it was becoming less so. The American middle class had begun to appropriate the freedom of movement formerly enjoyed by a wealthier class.[20] Thus, the "excitement of the trip" that Saarinen hoped to convey was available to those who could distinguish themselves not so much by income but in terms of a new class definition based on a volitional mobility on a global stage. The idiosyncratic curves of the TWA Terminal were in this way a counterpart to the standardized spaces of international hotel chains that were then being built around the world to welcome jet-age travelers recently launched from the likes of that facility. Just as the hotels were designed with pools, lawns, and lounges, and served burgers and soda to comfort Americans once they were abroad, the TWA Terminal evoked an exotic destination before anyone had left the ground. TWA was a lobby to the world that reflected to travelers an image of their own journeys to come. Indeed, as *McCall's* suggested, with the terminal's Lisbon Lounge, London Club, Paris Café, and Italian snack bar, "a couple of hours in the terminal is almost as good as a trip abroad. And cheaper, too."[21] Terminal and international hotel were spatial bookends, a familiar setting upon arrival and an alien place for departure (fig. 8).

The terminal was experientially compelling not because it mimicked the forms of aircraft but because it scripted a visual fiction that was actualized by the physical movement of travelers. Balconies, bridges, and wide platforms encourage multiple paths toward the same portals while wayfaring interior lines resist collapse into a single geometry. Forgoing reference to some other time or place, the terminal's flowing forms thematize circulation, continually reasserting the present space and the precise moment of occupation. In this sense, its expressionism lay less in its plastic biomorphism than in its union of actor and audience in a choreography of motion, or, as a New York cabdriver put it more colloquially: "That's not just a building, Mac. It's a feeling. You get inside and you feel like you're floating."[22]

In developing many of its designs, Saarinen's firm was noted for its use of models, which, as *Architectural Forum* wrote, proved that TWA, in particular, "is not just a shallow stunt." Working models were introduced into the office beginning with the Ingalls Rink, but Saarinen had been convinced of their usefulness long before. One classmate at Yale recalled that Saarinen regularly worked with plastilene, a nonhardening modeling clay familiar to sculpture students.[23] Bel Geddes, too, had been famous for his use of models to develop scenery;

Fig. 8 Trans World Airlines Terminal, Ambassador Club

Fig. 9 (opposite) Trans World Airlines Terminal, model

they helped him avoid the pictorialism he felt was inherent in most theatrical productions. For Bel Geddes, models were the "best way of rendering a plastic, architectonic or sculpturesque stage." In his own work, Saarinen felt the models facilitated the visualization of spatially complex forms or, as he said regarding TWA, they made possible "marvelous-looking things that could never have been arrived at on paper."[24] Models were a pivotal means of reaching one of Saarinen's most desired goals, a complete unity of design, a harmony of form encompassing the building and everything in it, a "homogenous integrity," as Gordon Craig had said of the same ambition in regard to theater (fig. 9).

As constantly changing objects in the office, models became the focus of gradual unfolding of form. They manifested the "slow progression" of design and, with the iterative process thus made visible, invited collaboration far more than could the introspection of drawing and intermittent presentation. As Kevin Roche put it, the model was "an instrument for keeping people involved," while photographic records, made periodically, refreshed the designers' vision by reinstating perceptual distance and so "[brought] out the best in the models, emphasizing dramatic form by skilful lighting and viewpoint." While the design's complex geometries required models, and models helped the designers integrate forms at all levels of scale, the models also took on a performative role themselves, as the design would develop in the real time of the workday and the physical space of the office. Indeed, Saarinen had memorably likened building design to "orchestrating the architecture."[25] In this way, the use of models for the TWA Terminal combined with the building's forms—along with the mobility of passengers through the structure and, once airborne, across borders—to achieve an integration of design intentions and process, built form and use, structure and significance, all composed under the marquee of a new kind of mobility (fig. 10).

There were many potential sources for Saarinen's symphony of curves at

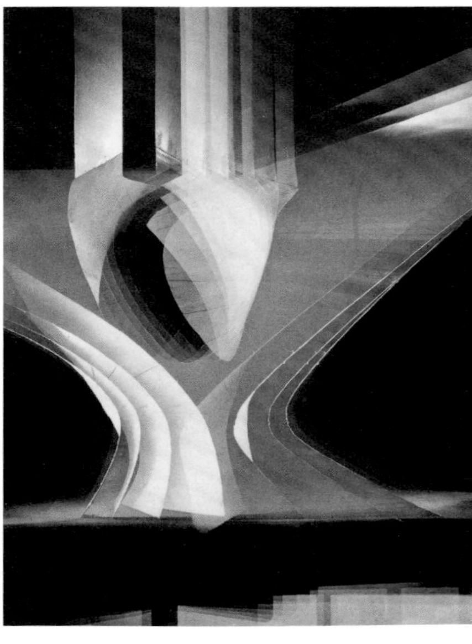

Fig. 10 Trans World Airlines Terminal, multiple-exposure photograph of model of column

Fig. 11 (opposite) Eero Saarinen and Associates, General Motors Technical Center, Warren, Michigan, 1948–56, model of Styling Dome

TWA: Art Nouveau and Expressionist designs such as those of Mendelsohn or Rudolf Steiner, Alvar Aalto's architecture or Isamu Noguchi's furniture, or even Saarinen's own organic furniture designs from the 1940s. The use of curves to exemplify and celebrate movement was already evident in such works as Henri Sauvage's Dance Pavilion for Loie Fuller at the 1900 World's Fair, in Paris, and was ubiquitous with streamlining. An environmental evocation of flight, specifically, seems most clearly presaged in the literal drama of flight at the Futurama exhibit, while the closest formal analogue to the conflation of curved forms and travel would have to be another Bel Geddes project, Copa City, an entertainment complex and tourist destination that opened in Miami in 1948 and was immediately hailed for both its evocative swooping forms and its technically advanced structure.[26]

But curves were for Saarinen more than just a formal approach. They signified a new phase of modernism entrusted to a second generation of designers. Like others, Saarinen reckoned the first generation's merit to have been a brave refusal of past conventions and a disciplined housecleaning of fossilized notions of style. Then, with building practices newly relevant to its own time, the next generation's role was to develop an architecture commensurate with its expanded cultural role. Rather than merely codify the work of the pioneers, the "leaders of the generation to follow refused to stop."[27] For Saarinen, the self-consciousness of second-generation modernism was only doubled by his evident emulation of Mies, especially at GM, and was doubled yet again by having followed in his famous father's footsteps, whose alleged sentimentality someone like Mies had rendered obsolete. Thus, as perhaps the most overdetermined of second-generation modernists, Saarinen was especially sensitive to his prominent position as both inheritor of modernism's *sachlich* dimensions, and a leading purveyor of projects that, with their intimations of theatricality, undermined sachlich claims to legitimacy. He took the diversity of his designs, for instance—the serial virtuosity distrusted by critics—as a measure of his modernist empiricism: unique functions required unique forms. This was equally a tenet of the New Stagecraft, as Oenslager wrote just after Saarinen left Yale: "Scenery is never designed twice in the same way. Every play must be its own designer." Had Mies himself turned his attention to thin-shell concrete vaults, Saarinen wrote, he would surely have seen their expressive potential and, in effect, reasoned his way to emotion. Not content standing in the wings, Saarinen took his place under the same light cast upon the pioneers, and explained his own performance in terms of this canonical first act. Curves did not simply describe the "new sensualism" or the new "counter-revolution in architecture," they validated it in terms of an ongoing narrative of modernist evolution.[28]

THEATRICALITY AT GM

In contrast with the TWA Terminal, the GM Technical Center does seem sober and unaffected. Nonetheless, it, too, can be understood as a kind of theater partly in terms of its inclusion of spaces explicitly intended for performance and, more generally, as a dramatized encounter between opposing forces. The most explicit stage on the site is found in the Styling Dome (fig. 11). Underneath its 186-foot-wide clear span, automobile designers and executives gathered to develop and applaud the coming year's car models. For bright and uniform lighting, Saarinen sheathed the inside of the dome with perforated metal, which scatters reflected light evenly across its surface. The device is an updated version of the cyclorama of early-twentieth-century theater, the *Kuppelhorizont,* as it was first called. It was most famously used in the United States in the 1924 production at the Provincetown Playhouse of *The Emperor Jones,* the Expressionist play written by Eugene O'Neill, who studied under George Pierce Baker. The set, designed by Oenslager just before Baker brought him to Yale, was a whitewashed hemisphere. As Oenslager wrote of the design, variously veiled "behind folds of dark gauze, there is no scenery whatever. All is changing light." Scene changes were effected simply by altering the lighting. Oenslager's later use of a cyclorama, for a 1933 production of *Salomé* at the Metropolitan Opera House in New York, was reviewed independently of the play: its "vistas of suggestion" were taken to be indicative of the modern spirit, "as free of gewgaws and extraneous bedizening as the Empire State Building."[29] Although Saarinen studied with Oenslager the following year, he hinted only that the GM cyclorama was inspired by "a silk tent" he had seen in a restaurant in Cannes. But its usefulness for theater was in any case recognized by Oenslager himself, who said at the first retrospective of his work—held in Detroit, just as GM was completed—that the "pleasure dome of Saarinen" was one of several examples from the contemporary arts that would be an inspiration for stage designers.[30]

Within the larger GM site, the dome turns out to be only one of a number of elements that are conspicuously alien to the predominant modular fabric. Taken together, they set up a dialogue between opposites: unique, often curved

forms episodically qualify the field of rectilinear, machined volumes. Many contemporary accounts of the project characterize it in terms of such dualities: *Fortune* magazine, for instance, said it was "modern but not freakish, functional but not barren, imposing but not overblown"; Russell Lynes wrote, "Here is unity with variation; . . . consistency without boredom; seriousness without pedantry, function with playfulness."[31] To cognoscenti reading between the lines, "freakish" and "barren" or "consistency" and "seriousness" described Mies's designs for IIT. Saarinen clearly took that work in another direction, and the result was seen by some as a much needed dose of delight, and by others as a cavalier disregard of Mies's rigorous honesty. While fans liked the note struck by the vibrant colors of the glazed brick end walls, for example, critics said they were logically external to the system of steel construction; the most prominent features, like the Styling Dome and the water tower, could not be deduced from the low boxes and modular curtain wall.[32]

Such contrasts at GM are entirely consistent in their own way. The brightly colored brick walls that end the extruded volumes are a synopsis of Saarinen's method. Carefully glazed in the Cranbrook tradition, they are a visually lush and crafted terminus to the efficiency of the industrial system. Alongside the modular buildings they "contribute an element of surprise: the rhythm is stopped abruptly by end walls of brick."[33] In an otherwise ordered analytical space, the end walls function as planes of emotional discharge, which makes their trespass of color and craft an earned one. At GM, Saarinen evinced a theatrical sensibility from the repeated dramatic encounter of unlike elements that forthrightly declaim their dissimilarity.

This sort of implied theatricality also occurs at several striking stairways. The stair in the Research Building seems to burst through the precisely rectilinear box that would contain it (fig. 12). Its spiral form is foreshadowed by the circles on the pressed ceiling panels overhead until the stair itself springs upward through a round opening. The stair is a study in tension and restraint,

Fig. 12 General Motors Technical Center, Research Building, lobby stair model

with its granite treads suspended by thin cables; it foregrounds the strength of the materials and so seems like a lesson in modern technology. But walking onto the floating slabs is a different matter altogether. Unlike the solid earth from which they were cut, these rectilinear rocks move subtly in response to each footfall. A faint physical echo of one's own steps returns to elicit a sense of the self-consciousness of performance. When one pauses on the stairs, sensations of others enter one's body through soles sensitive to slight vibrations. Whether a friend, stranger, or sworn enemy is passing, his weight and gait register physically—immediately and involuntarily—and, as a result, with an unanticipated intimacy.[34] The experience is dramatic in terms of the visitor's unwitting participation in a dynamic encounter of otherwise divergent elements—steel and stone, lightness and gravity, the visual and the somatic, restraint and release—that are rejoined by the almost self-willed animation of this sudden stair.

The stair in the Styling Building lobby, enclosed on three sides as if on a stage, is no less a performance (fig. 13). The landing is level with the floor, but as it is over water, before proceeding, one pauses to test the surface's stability. The treads are broad and slow one's steps; the overhead down lights reflect off the treads and illuminate one's face from below, like footlights; experience becomes increasingly somatic as the space, freely flowing elsewhere, is contained by colored brick and thinned mortar joints on one side and glimmering steel tendrils on the other. Color and reflected light, arrested motion, even the faint smell of chlorinated water and a sonic resonance subtly shifted by the heterogeneous adjaceny of brick, steel, stone, and water: all press in upon the senses. The breadth of the first landing comes as a relief. Moving up the second flight, one sees that only the first flight is lit directly. Others who follow, still adjusting to the wide treads, are therefore unknowingly onstage, seen through the scrim of steel cables and encased in light as if performing some minor miracle of ascension. The visitor then sees himself as both spectator and

As Tom dreams at his desk, Iby appears as a phantom on the steel-suspended marble staircase in GM's styling building.

46

Fig. 13 General Motors Technical Center, Styling Building, lobby stair

Fig. 14 First page of George Koether, "Boy and His Dream," *Look*, May 1956, photographs by Phil Harrington. The protagonist of the story, Tom Green, an aspiring automotive engineer, has a dream structured by a car, to his right, and an emergent fashion model, to his left; they are brought together at the stairway in the Styling Building at the General Motors Technical Center.

performer in the routine chore of climbing stairs. IIT has nothing to equal this mise-en-scène.

The dialogue between realms of reason and emotion at GM is evoked by calculated exaggeration, each element intentionally enlarged and made conspicuous. Besides being an approach common to set designers like Oenslager, the method is explicit in Saarinen's own writings. In a note from the time he was working on GM, for instance, Saarinen claimed to often use the terms "male and female . . . the convex and the concave" to discuss architecture. Because Americans had become in his time increasingly aware of "basic psychological reactions," he said, "therefore we deal in big contrasts," to amplify the architectural message. Later, regarding his professional agenda, Saarinen suggested that the question of how a building can "convey emotionally" its purpose was the source of architecture's "real significance" and the core of his contribution as part of the second generation of modernists. For a building to express emotion, he wrote, its central "concept has to be exaggerated and overstated and repeated in every part of its interior, so that wherever you are, inside or outside, the building sings with the same message."[35] At GM, a compound rather than a single building, two distinct orders are articulated one against the other, and aligned with allegedly male and female traits: a rigorous rectilinear rationality is set in opposition to curvaceous and seemingly capricious forms.

Saarinen's duet of a constant spatial matrix counterposed with vividly physical, almost transgressive episodes not only served GM's symbolic needs. It strikes a playfully erotic note most closely paralleled in American automobile culture. The country's most ubiquitous machine, the car, was typically presented as the product of both precision engineering and imaginative styling as a means of appealing simultaneously to reason and desire (fig. 14). In contemporary advertisements, for instance, female models were frequently contrasted with machined forms—"Filmy evening dresses shimmer against stainless steel," as proposed in the title of a *Vogue* shoot on location at GM—to make it apparent that the purpose of advanced automobile technology was to heighten the pleasure of driving, which was made visually manifest by suggesting intimate bodily relations with machinery.

Saarinen repeatedly set up a system at GM only to stop it with a flourish; consistency was there to be broken. What appears at first as a lapse within a larger system can thus be seen as kind of tango: sustained cerebral restraint that is suddenly and somatically snapped. The visual dynamics of GM enact this fundamental heterogeneity and a familiar cultural plot of technology in service to gratification, rather than recite a moral monologue of constructional truth.

Saarinen did not so much relinquish his early flair for theatricality as sublimate it, and herein lay the menace to the postwar defenders of modernism. He made masterful use of techniques of modernist abstraction to refine and advance construction, but he also employed them to bring to the same plane of expression otherwise incommensurate factors of symbolic use and cultural narrative. Function was abstracted and visually and often lyrically expressed, not just accommodated in a minimal steel cage. The dramatic dialogue of form and meaning that resulted resonated with the public as much as it unnerved the critics. Saarinen clearly understood that the formal unity guaranteed by the exaggeration and overstatement of a design theme came at the risk of hyperbolizing function. But without attending to these second-generation pillars of overdrawn expression, "our architecture will stay an empty dance," he wrote, a formal exercise without emotional meaning.[36] The threat Saarinen posed to contemporaries, as well as the source of the ambiguous judgments regarding his work, may be seen in the denouement he achieved between an architecture based on the conditions of its making and one based on the performance of its meaning.

Notes

I am grateful to the following individuals for their substantial contributions to this essay: Donald Albrecht, Mark Coir, Leslie Edwards, Rosamond Fletcher, Pekka Korvenmaa, Reinhold Martin, Christopher Monkhouse, Diana Murphy, Eeva-Liisa Pelkonen, Robert A. M. Stern, and Richard Szary.

1. Walter McQuade, "The New Yale Colleges," *Architectural Forum*, Dec. 1962, 105, 110; "Saarinen Colleges *In Situ* at Yale," *Progressive Architecture*, Nov. 1962, 57; "Morse and Stiles," *New Yorker*, Dec. 22, 1962, 27; Ada Louise Huxtable, "Eero Saarinen, 1910–1961," *New York Times*, Sept. 10, 1961.

2. Robin Boyd, "The Counter-Revolution in Architecture," *Harper's*, Sept. 1959, 47.

3. Manfredo Tafuri, *The Sphere and the Labyrinth* (Cambridge: MIT Press, 1987), 96.

4. Denis Bablet, *Edward Gordon Craig*, trans. Daphne Woodward (New York: Theatre Arts Books, 1966), 69–70, 180.

5. Mary C. Henderson, *Theater in America* (New York: Abrams, 1996), 206; Michael Monahan, "The Miracle," *New York Times*, Feb. 17, 1924; John Corbin, "'The Miracle,' Fine Spectacle Shown," *New York Times*, Jan. 16, 1924; Norman Bel Geddes, *Miracle in the Evening* (Garden City, N.Y.: Doubleday, 1960), 258–62; Orville Larson, *Scene Design in the American Theatre from 1915 to 1960* (Fayetteville: University of Arkansas Press, 1989), 170; Rudolph Kommer, "The Genesis of 'The Miracle,'" *New York Times*, Dec. 30, 1923; "Exposition Reveals New Theatre Ideas," *New York Times*, Feb. 28, 1926.

6. J. Anthony Lukas, "Harvard Theater: Puritans in Greasepaint," *Harvard Crimson*, Dec. 10, 1953, reprinted at www.thecrimson.com/article.aspx?ref=212305, retrieved Jan. 6, 2006; Donald Oenslager Papers, Yale University Archives, box 1, folder "Drama 12."

7. Stanley McCandless, "Stage Lighting—A Survey Since 1906," typescript, n.d., Stanley McCandless Papers, Yale University Archives, box 7; McCandless, "Lighting and Design," School of Drama Papers, Yale University Archives, series 2, box 32, folder "History of the Drama School"; McCandless, "1931," Stanley McCandless Papers, Yale University Archives, box 4; Stanley McCandless, "An Outline of a Course in Lighting for Architects" (1930), 2–3, from a paper presented to the Illuminating Engineering Society, Richmond, Va., Oct. 1930. McCandless addresses the "Psychology of Vision" in *A Syllabus of Stage Lighting* (New Haven, Conn.: Whitlock's, 1931), 42–44.

8. Eero Saarinen, letter to Stanley McCandless, May 1, 1941, Stanley McCandless Papers, Yale University Archives, box 4, folder "1939"; Stanley McCandless, letter to Stewart King, Mar. 20, 1939, ibid., box 4, folder "1939."

9. Lee Simonson, "Prize-Winning Theatres," *Theatre Arts* 23 (summer 1939), 436. See also "Biographical Sketch," *Theatre Arts* 23 (Apr. 1939), 238.

10. Donal McLaughlin Papers, Yale University Archives, box 1, folder "McLaughlin, Donal"; James Kornwolf, ed., *Modernism in America, 1937–1941* (Williamsburg, Va.: College of William and Mary, 1985), 1–19, 125–75; Jane King Hession, *Ralph Rapson: Sixty Years of Modern Design* (Afton, Minn.: Afton Historical Society Press, 1999), 24–26; K. Richmond Temple, *Designing for the Arts: Environments by Leslie Cheek* (Williamsburg, Va.: College of William and Mary, 1990), 14; Parke Rouse, Jr., *Living by Design: Leslie Cheek and the Arts* (Williamsburg, Va.: Society of Alumni of the College of William and Mary, 1985), 148. In 1947 Saarinen and Cheek served together on a Yale Council subcommittee to upgrade the university's visual and performing arts.

11. Jeffrey Meikle, *Twentieth Century Limited: Industrial Design in America, 1925–1939* (Philadelphia: Temple University Press, 1979), 230n.32; Donal McLaughlin, interview with Bill Kubota and Ed Moore, Garrett Park, Md., May 24, 2004. It is possible Bel Geddes first met Saarinen when he visited Yale as a critic; Rouse, *Living by Design*, 53.

12. See Adnan Morshed, "The Aesthetics of Ascension in Norman Bel Geddes's Futurama," *Journal of the Society of Architectural Historians* 63 (Mar. 2004), 74–99.

13. Allan Temko, *Eero Saarinen* (New York: Braziller, 1962), 23.

14. John Jacobus, "John Deere Office Building, Moline, Illinois, USA," *Architectural Review*, May 1965, 366; "Theater for Tractors," *Architectural Record*, Dec. 1964, 142, and discussed in *Steel Facts* 197 (June–July 1967), 6. Jacobus thought the project's ubiquitous outrigging had likewise perfected the "spectacle of nature" from the building; Jacobus, "John Deere Office Building," 366.

15. Robert Brustein, *The Third Theatre* (New York: Knopf, 1969), 179; Sam Zolotow, "Mielziner Views Beaumont Design," *New York Times*, Sept. 14, 1965; Mary C. Henderson, *Mielziner: Master of Modern Stage Design* (New York: Back Stage Books, 2001), 239–43.

16. John Jacobus, review of Eero Saarinen, *Eero Saarinen on His Work: A Selection of Buildings Dating from 1947 to 1964, with statements by the architect*, ed. Aline B. Saarinen (New Haven: Yale University Press, 1962), in *Journal of the Society of Architectural Historians* 22 (Dec. 1963), 238; Aline B. Louchheim, "Now Saarinen the Son," *New York Times Magazine*, Apr. 26, 1953, 26; "Became Aware of Mies," undated manuscript, 3, Eero Saarinen Papers, Manuscripts and Archives, Yale University.

17. Wolf Von Eckardt, "Father and Son," *New Republic*, Feb. 15, 1964, 33; "The Elbow Room," *Architectural Forum*, Sept. 1938, 172–74; McCandless, "Auditorium and Chapel MIT Lighting," 1, 3.

18. George McCue, "Sculptured Space for Air Travelers," *St. Louis Post-Dispatch*, June 17, 1962; Horace Sutton, "Travel Notes," *McCall's*, Sept. 1962, 145; "Saarinen Theme and Variations," directed by Scott Berner, score composed and conducted by Jacques Belasco, aired on *Chet Huntley Reporting*, NBC, July 20, 1962, NBC Archive, New York.

19. "TWA's Graceful New Terminal," *Architectural Forum*, Jan. 1958, 79.

20. "Facts and Figures About Air Transportation," *ATA Annual Report* (Washington, D.C.: Air Transport Association of America, 1960), 2–4, and reckoned from Nawal Taneja, *The Commercial Airline Industry* (Lexington, Mass.: D. C. Heath, 1976), 189–95; Frank A. Smith, *Transportation in America: A Statistical Analysis* (Westport, Conn.: Eno Foundation for Transportation, 1989), 37; William Fruhan, Jr., *The Fight for Competitive Advantage* (Boston: Harvard University Graduate School of Business Administration, 1972), 81; U.S. Census Bureau, "Historical Income Tables: Families," last revised July 4, 2004, http://www.census.gov/hhes/income/histinc/f01.html.

21. "I Want to Catch the Excitement of the Trip," *Architectural Forum*, July 1962, 72; Sutton, "Travel Notes," 145. Variations of the "excitement of the trip" phrase were common in reviews of the building.

22. Cited in Jack Hunter, "Blinds for a Brilliant Building," *DuPont Magazine*, Jan–Feb. 1963, 2–3.

23. "TWA's Graceful New Terminal," 79; Kevin Roche, interview with author, Feb. 23, 2005. Donal McLaughlin thought that Saarinen had introduced plastilene to architectural students, although shortly after, in 1937, Dean Everett Meeks reported that its use was "plentiful" in studios. Plastilene may already have been used by professional architects, including Raymond Hood, who taught at Yale while Saarinen was there, and by architectural sculptors such as René Chambellan. See Donal McLaughlin, videotaped interview, Yale University Archives, box 2; and Everett Meeks, "Foreign Influences on Architectural Education in America," *Octagon*, July 1937, 39.

24. Norris Houghton, "The Designer Sets the Stage: Norman Bel Geddes and Vincente Minnelli," *Theatre Arts* 20 (Oct. 1936), 782; "TWA's Graceful New Terminal," 79. See also Glen Paulsen, interview no. 2, Mar. 12, 1992, and Cesar Pelli statement, Saarinen/Swanson Reunion Papers, box 1, folder 33, Cranbrook Archives.

25. Gilbert Courdier, "An Introduction to the Study of Architecture by Means of the Model," typescript, Birmingham, Mich., 1960, Eero Saarinen Papers, Yale University; Roche interview; Courdier, "Introduction to the Study of Architecture"; Maurice Allen, cited in Brian Carter, "Workflow in the Saarinen Office," Saarinen/Swanson Reunion Papers, 2001–14, box 1, folder 10, Cranbrook Archives.

26. See Christopher Innes, *Designing Modern America: Broadway to Main Street* (New Haven: Yale University Press, 2005), 94–96.

27. Eero Saarinen, "Saarinen," *Perspecta* 7 (1961), 29–32.

28. Donald Oenslager, *Scenery Then and Now* (New York: Norton, 1936), xiii; Eero Saarinen, "General Statement about the sculptural, curved/shapes that we have been involved with, beginning with St. Louis, the water tower and dome at General Motors, MIT, Yale, TWA, and now the Washington International Airport," undated manuscript, Eero Saarinen Papers, Yale University, published in this volume; "Became Aware of Mies"; Thomas Creighton, "The New Sensualism," *Progressive Architecture*, Sept. 1959, 141–47.

29. See "Mariano Fortuny" and "Mehr Licht!—Die Lichtbühne," in Nora Eckert, *Das Bühnenbild im 20. Jahrhundert* (Berlin: Henschel Verlag, 1998), 23–25, 106–7; Oenslager, *Scenery Then and Now*, 252–53; "New 'Salome' Setting," *New York Times*, Dec. 31, 1933. McCandless had inquired about buying cyclorama equipment for Yale's theater; McCandless Papers, box 4, folder "1931."

30. Eero Saarinen, letter to Astrid Sampe, Mar. 12, 1953; Astrid Sampe Collection, Cranbrook Archives, box 1, folder 4; Donald Oenslager, "Design in the Theatre Today," in *Donald Oenslager: Stage Designer and Teacher—A Retrospective Exhibition* (Detroit: Detroit Institute of Arts, 1956), 9.

31. "G.M. Technical Center," *Fortune*, Dec. 1951, 82; Russell Lynes, "After Hours: The Erosion of Detroit," *Harper's*, Jan. 1960, 22.

32. In a similar vein, Allan Temko wrote that Mies studied chess while Saarinen played checkers, in "American Architecture: Down to Skin and Bones," *Journal of the AIA* 30 (Nov. 1958), 22.

33. Arthur Drexler, *Buildings for Business and Government* (New York: Museum of Modern Art, Feb.–Apr. 1957), 22.

34. Regarding this stair, George Wagner suggests it is a "calculated eruption" of the body into rationalized space, and "actually in open confrontation with the deterministic rationalism of the center's architecture"; George Wagner, *Thom Mayne Sixth Street House* (Cambridge: Harvard University Graduate School of Design, 1989). I am grateful to Gabriel Feld for alerting me to Wagner's essay.

35. Eero Saarinen, "Random undigested thoughts on gravity and architecture," ca. 1953, frame no. 557, Aline and Eero Saarinen Papers, Archives of American Art, Smithsonian Institution; Saarinen, "Saarinen," 29–32. The validation of exaggeration to achieve formal integrity that reveals an idea's significance recalls the advice of Bel Geddes, cited above. Saarinen's performance metaphor, again, was a common one, according to Aline Saarinen in Joy Hakanson, "A Walk in the Shadow of Genius," *Detroit News Pictorial Magazine*, June 26, 1966.

36. Saarinen, "Saarinen," 29–32.

project portfolio

Edited by Donald Albrecht and Thomas Mellins

project portfolio

Kevin Roche's donation of the Eero Saarinen and Associates office archive, known as the Eero Saarinen Papers, to Yale University in 2002 provided an unprecedented opportunity: the creation of the first comprehensive illustrated portfolio documenting the work of Eero Saarinen, one of the twentieth century's most important architects.

This portfolio is divided into two sections: a project inventory and short essays. More extensive than any previously published record on Saarinen, the chronologically arranged inventory presents 103 descriptions of buildings, building complexes, planning schemes, furnishings, and competition entries, many of which are accompanied by illustrations. To the greatest extent possible, each entry includes information on the project's client, program, site, structure, design, and materials, as well as collaborators both inside and outside the Saarinen office. The eleven essays that follow expand upon the descriptions.

In compiling the inventory, a simple criterion for deciding whether to feature a particular project was established: there had to be some visual evidence demonstrating Saarinen's design intent. Unexpected treasures were found in the Eero Saarinen Papers: newspaper clippings with renderings of a scheme for a Los Angeles Auditorium and Opera House from 1948; original drawings of a corporate headquarters for Time Inc. in suburban New York City; renderings of an entry in the Chicago Tribune's Sixth Annual Better Rooms competition of 1952; and a House of Tomorrow for General Motors, 1955, among others. Visual materials for eight projects, attributed to Saarinen by written records in the archives (or by the recollections of former colleagues) have not yet been found: the American Gas Association Small House competition, 1926; the Norrmalm competition for Stockholm, 1934; the Negro Community House in Michigan, 1937; the People's Bank and Trust Company, Fort Wayne, Indiana, 1947; the Scottish Rite Lodge in Fort Wayne, Indiana, 1954, the first project that Cesar Pelli was asked to run after joining the firm that year; the Butler University School of Religion, Indianapolis, Indiana, 1956; a stadium in Indonesia, 1957; and the Christian Theological Seminary, Indianapolis, Indiana, 1950s. The Eero Saarinen Papers, which are still being inventoried at the time of this writing, may yield information about these and other projects. In addition to Roche's donation, a smaller archive given to Yale in 1971 by Saarinen's second wife, Aline Louchheim Saarinen, containing sketches, photographs, and other office materials, has also proven very valuable in our research.

The Cranbrook Archives were also important in developing this inventory. Cranbrook houses drawings, photographs, and correspondence related to Saarinen's work with his father, Eliel Saarinen, and his brother-in-law, J. Robert F. Swanson, as well as drawings and other materials donated to its archive after a Saarinen-Swanson reunion held at Cranbrook in August 1995. Additionally, we benefited from drawings in the collection of the Museum of Finnish Architecture in Helsinki and from interviews with colleagues and friends of Eero's, some of whom possess additional material.

In the inventory descriptions, projects are identified by the name most commonly used today. In cases where the Saarinen office employed a different name, it is provided parenthetically; for example: "Samuel F. B. Morse and Ezra Stiles Colleges (New Colleges), Yale University." In instances where a building has since become known by another name, that name is given as well; for example, "Tabernacle Church of Christ, later First Christian Church." Numbers assigned to a project by the Saarinen office were found in the Eero Saarinen Papers and are provided. From 1925, when Saarinen began to work with his family at Cranbrook, until 1950, with the official establishment of Eero Saarinen and Associates, Saarinen designed buildings and projects either under his own name or, depending on the commission, under the name of three different firms involving his father and brother-in-law. These identifications have been made with the assistance of the Cranbrook Archives and are provided within the project descriptions. The inventory also features new drawings created by Janice Carapellucci for this book.

The inventory entries were written by Donald Albrecht (DA), Leslie S. Edwards (LSE), Rosamond Fletcher (RF), Sean Khorsandi (SK), Pekka Korvenmaa (PK), Alexandra Lange (AL), Hélène Lipstadt (HL), Brian Lutz (BL), Thomas Mellins (TM), Jennifer Komar Olivarez (JO), Eeva-Liisa Pelkonen (ELP), and Timo Tuomi (TT). Entries are cross-referenced to relevant essays in the book, and bibliographical citations, focused on period sources, suggest further readings. For more comprehensive bibliographies, including profiles, obituaries, and surveys, readers may refer to William Bainter O'Neal, *Eero Saarinen: A Bibliography* (Charlottesville: American Association of Architectural Bibliographers, 1963); Robert A. Kuhner, *Eero Saarinen: His Life and Work* (Monticello, Ill.: Vance Bibliographies, 1975); and Lamia Doumato, *The Work of Eero Saarinen: A Selected Bibliography* (Monticello, Ill.: Vance Bibliographies, 1980). Additionally, a bibliography, organized by project, was compiled by Rosamond Fletcher in the course of research for this publication and is now part of the Eero Saarinen Papers.

The eleven essays that follow the inventory focus on two themes. Four of the pieces place individual projects within the context of larger issues in Saarinen's practice: Hélène Lipstadt examines the United States Jefferson National Expansion Memorial in St. Louis as an exemplar of the pivotal role design competitions played in Saarinen's career; Rosamond Fletcher looks at Saarinen's work at the General Motors Technical Center in Warren, Michigan, as a model of collaboration; Christopher Monkhouse examines the Miller House in Columbus, Indiana, with an eye to its reception in the media; and Michael Rey explores the David S. Ingalls Hockey Rink at Yale University, focusing on Saarinen's relationship with his client, A. Whitney Griswold, the university's president. The seven other essays are typological in nature: Alexandra Lange writes about three corporate suburban campuses; she also collaborated with Sean Khorsandi on a piece about Saarinen's early houses; Brian Lutz writes about Saarinen's furniture; Jennifer Komar Olivarez about his churches and chapels; Timo Tuomi about an embassy and two chancelleries; Susanna Santala about airports; and Alan Plattus about campus plans.

inventory of buildings and projects

Cranbrook School for Boys, baldachin with carvings

Cranbrook School for Boys, baldachin carving

1925

Cranbrook School for Boys
furnishings and decorative elements
Bloomfield Hills, Michigan
1925–31

Saarinen's earliest architectural experience was working with his family in 1925. At the Cranbrook Architectural Office in 1926, he created decorative elements for the boys' school, including five Pewabic tiles for the south lobby fireplace, the crane insert for chairs in the dining hall, curvilinear designs for iron gates, and pedestals for the niches in the lobby walls. He also designed stone caricatures for the exterior walls of Page Hall and the column supports of a baldachin under a pergola designed by his father. [LSE]

"Cranbrook School, Bloomfield Hills, Michigan," *Architectural Record,* Dec. 1928, 452–60, 475–506, 525–28

Florence Davies, "Cranbrook Foundation," *Country Life,* June 1935, 11–15, 74

Saarinen House furnishings, master bedroom

1928

Saarinen House furnishings
Bloomfield Hills, Michigan
1928–30

The suite of painted wooden furniture for the house's master bedroom marked Saarinen's debut as a furniture designer. The dressing table, with an upholstered bench, was curtained and accompanied by a sterling silver vanity set, three-part freestanding mirror, and torchères. A light-colored wood table featured cantilevered shelves. Saarinen also designed tubular-steel lounge chairs for the porch. [LSE]

"Cranbrook Academy of Art, Bloomfield Hills, Mich.," *Architectural Record,* Dec. 1930, 444–51

Henry P. Macomber, "The Michigan Home of Eliel Saarinen," *House Beautiful,* Oct. 1933, 133–36

1929

Kingswood School for Girls furnishings
Bloomfield Hills, Michigan
1929–31

Saarinen received this commission shortly after returning from his studies in Paris in spring 1960, following George Gough Booth's invitation to the family to design the school. Saarinen designed the majority of the furniture for the school: cantilevered tubular-steel auditorium chairs, furniture for the study hall, dormitories, corridors (including the Green Lobby), and the headmistress's living room. He also designed chairs, tables, and buffet stations for the dining room made of natural-colored wood with trim painted pink. Each chair's horizontal backrest was punctuated by a grid of five rectangular openings, which echoed the patterns in the ceiling and window vents. Saarinen, who was paid $600 for his work, also sculpted the lion torchère for the stairway in the Green Lobby, as well as the pedestal above the lobby's fireplace. [LSE]

"The Kingswood School for Girls, Cranbrook, Michigan," *Architectural Forum,* Jan. 1932, 37–60

Bertel Jung, "Eliel Saarinen," *Arkkitehti,* Mar. 1932, 33–43

"Kingswood School," *Suomen Kuvalehti* 16 (May 7, 1932), 692–93

Florence Davies, "Cranbrook Foundation," *Country Life,* June 1935, 11–15, 74

Hvitträsk Studio and Home alteration
Kirkkonummi, Finland
1929–37

Saarinen designed a replacement of the north, "Lindgren" wing of the Hvitträsk studio and home complex, which had burned down in 1922. The original complex had been designed by Eliel Saarinen, Armas Lindgren, and Herman Gesellius in 1901–3. Eero's new stuccoed brick wing followed the original's plan but was lower, simpler in detail, and did not include a tower. [PK]

Marika Hausen, "Hvitträsk: Koti Taideteoksena" (Hvitträsk: The Home as a Work of Art), in *Hvitträsk: Koti Taideteoksena,* ed. Juhani Pallasmaa (Helsinki: Suomen rakennustaiteen museo/Museum of Finnish Architecture, 1987), 10–69

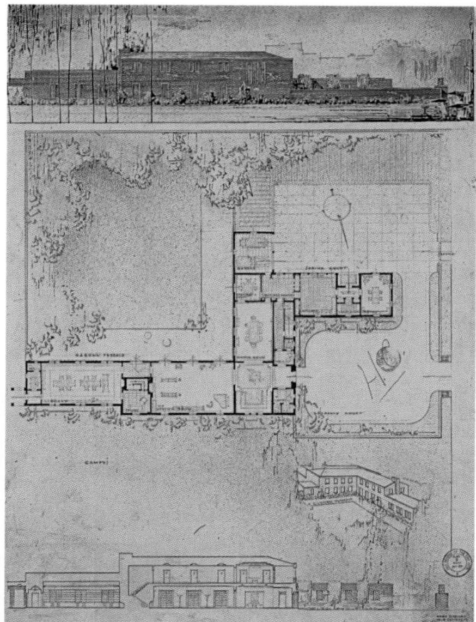

Student project for Yale University School of Fine Arts, Department of Architecture, elevation, plan, perspective, and section of "A Residence for a College Dean," 1932

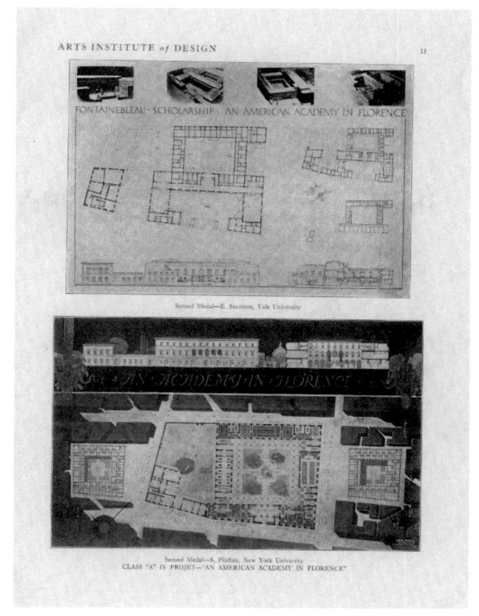

Student project for Yale University School of Fine Arts, Department of Architecture, model, plans, and elevation of "An American Academy in Florence," published in *Beaux-Arts Institute of Design Bulletin*, 1933

1931

Student projects for Yale University School of Fine Arts, Department of Architecture New Haven, Connecticut 1931–34

Following the Beaux-Arts curriculum taught at Yale, Saarinen's design projects ranged from residences to large civic buildings to monuments. According to his school records, his design projects as a student included a bus and streetcar terminal, an end wing for an embassy, a mountain studio, a monumental stair, two pylons at the entrance to a bridge, a dovecote, a workers' community, a state hospital for nervous diseases, a textile museum, a commemorative plaza, a circular salon, a water tower, a highway filling station, a police station, an airport, a memorial tunnel entrance, a residence for a college dean, a palace for an exiled monarch, a garden-club building, a synagogue, a cemetery chapel, a monumental clock, a winter sports club, a fine city residence, a theater lobby, a monumental bandstand, a college of a university, a general waiting room for a railroad station, a memorial chamber in a municipal building, an American academy in Florence, an entrance to a zoological garden, a municipal market, a world's fair building for textile manufacturing, a sculptor's studio, a country courthouse, a marina, a new $1,000 bill, an industrial city, the interior of a church, an immigration station, a Catholic chapel, a baroque fountain, and monuments to Daniel Boone, Thomas A. Edison, and Johann Sebastian Bach. [SK]

1934

Helsinki Central Post Office and Telegraph competition Helsinki, Finland 1934, unbuilt

Saarinen's entry, titled Sanansaattaja (Messenger), won third prize in a national competition for the headquarters of the Finnish postal administration in the city's center. Saarinen proposed a six-story concrete building housing offices, spaces for handling mail, and a large hall for public services. The most prominent feature of the building's stucco-coated facades was an asymmetrically placed, full-height entrance colonnade. [PK]

"Tävlan om Posthus I Helsingfors," *Arkkitehti*, Nov. 1934, 164–71

Swedish Theater alteration and expansion, perspective

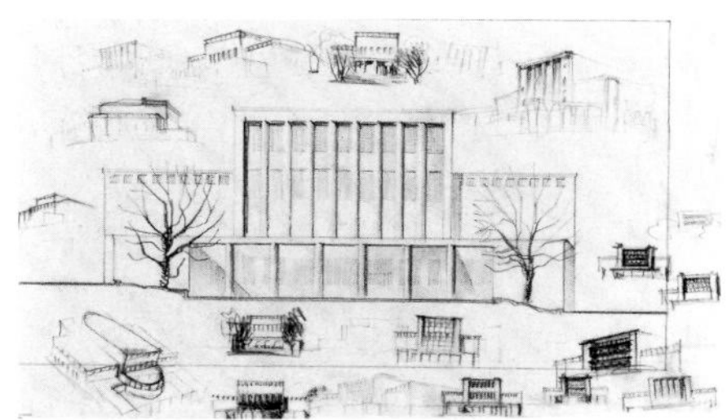

Swedish Theater alteration and expansion, elevation and perspectives

Forum project, perspective

1935

Swedish Theater alteration and expansion
Helsinki, Finland
1935–36

Saarinen's role in his father's alteration and expansion of this theater, designed by Nicholas Benois and completed in 1866, began in 1935 when he started attending design presentations in Helsinki in Eliel's place. The presentations were made with Jarl Eklund, to whom Eliel had entrusted responsibility for the design. Eero's many sketches of 1936 show a variety of schemes for the renovation and addition. Located at the crossroads of the city's two main arteries, the renovated building, which included theaters and a restaurant, featured two stacked semicircular volumes that were coated in smooth white stucco and devoid of applied ornamentation. Arched doorways and rows of arched windows punctuated the lower volume. [TM]

Forum project
Helsinki, Finland
1935–37, unbuilt

Saarinen made sketches for this project, which had been conceived in 1928 by the Konstsamfundet (Swedish Art Foundation). The foundation wanted a commercial building with a restaurant and shops for a prominent site that it owned in the center of Helsinki. Sketches Eero produced on his own, both while working in Helsinki with Jarl Eklund on the Swedish Theater and when he returned to the United States in 1936, show a glass-walled building with floors externally expressed as thin slabs. Saarinen marked the two-story building's corner location with a semicircular volume that was alternately two and three stories. [PK]

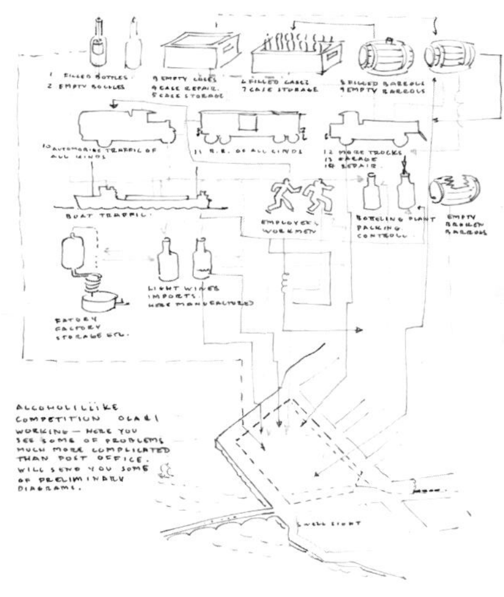

Alko competition, diagrams

Flint Cultural and Civic Center project, perspective

1936

Alko competition
Helsinki, Finland
1936, unbuilt

This competition, announced in 1935 and sponsored by Oy Alkoholiliike Ab (Alko), the Finnish alcohol monopoly, was for a factory and warehouse complex on a full-block site in the Ruoholahti area, ten miles west of downtown Helsinki. Eero helped his father by creating programmatic planning diagrams of the factory's bottling and handling functions. The entry, which was officially submitted by Eliel from Cranbrook in March 1936, proposed an asymmetrical grouping of structures, centered on a six-story building surrounded by one-, two-, and three-story buildings. All were flat-roofed and featured horizontal strip windows and cantilevered canopies. Väinö Vähäkallio won the competition and executed the building. [TT]

Flint Cultural and Civic Center project
Flint, Michigan
1936–42, unbuilt

In July 1935, representatives from General Motors, the University of Michigan, the Mott and Rackham foundations, and the city of Flint met with Eliel Saarinen at Cranbrook to "replan" the city of Flint. Cranbrook Academy of Art students Edmund Bacon and William Comstock subsequently went to Flint to work on the plan. Eero, who was employed by the Flint Institute of Research and Planning (one of the agencies under the umbrella organization of the Flint Community Fund), designed a cultural center for the plan, proposing an L-shaped complex with a bow tie–shaped double auditorium (seating for 500 and 1,500), an allied arts building, a museum of transportation, and an art school running along Kearsley Street. A large mall rounded out the plan. The buildings were to be long two-story structures whose simple, boxlike volumes would be faced with unadorned masonry and stucco walls. The entrance of the allied arts building was to be glass-walled with overhangs. Eero and Eliel were asked to draw up a second plan for the Flint Art Center (at Church and Traverse streets). In 1942 financial difficulties due to World War II put the Flint project on hold indefinitely. Although Eero's scheme was never realized, his preliminary studies assisted architects in conceptualizing the plans for the center as built in 1958. [LSE]

A Combined Living-Dining Room-Study project, model

A Combined Living-Dining Room-Study project
1937

Saarinen designed this project at the request of *Architectural Forum*, which published it in October as a way to introduce him and his ideas to its readers. "Such a room," the magazine's editors explained, "might be part of a small house or an apartment with a roof terrace." Saarinen designed the rectangular space for maximum flexibility. It could be either one large room or subdivided into three separate spaces: a living room, a dining room, and a study. A folding partition or drapery could be used to enclose the areas. An exterior wall of floor-to-ceiling folding glass doors opened onto a landscaped yard. The interior featured adjustable light fixtures, nesting tables, a bar on wheels, a built-in desk, bookcase, and entertainment center with a radio and phonograph, and was to contain bentwood armchairs and plywood dining chairs designed by Alvar Aalto. [SK]

See also Lange and Khorsandi, "Houses and Housing," in this volume.

"A Combined Living-Dining Room-Study," *Architectural Forum*, Oct. 1937, 303–5

Fenton Community Center

Koebel House, garden elevation

Fenton Community Center
Fenton, Michigan
1937–38

Saarinen and Saarinen designed this flat-roofed, asymmetrically composed building with a prominent chimney for a sloping site in a residential area. The two-story structure incorporated variegated brick walls punctuated by vertical strip windows and topped by wafer-thin cantilevered coping. The entrance was decorated with a perforated screen wall. Inside, a large multipurpose room contained a stage at one end and a fireplace at the other. [TM]

N. L. Engelhardt, "What Can School Designers Expect?" *Pencil Points*, Nov. 1942, 46–60

Spencer House
Huntington Woods, Michigan
1937–38

This three-bedroom house constructed in suburban Detroit for J. F. Spencer was a two-story brick-clad structure with a hipped tile roof and attached garage. The house had a large picture window on the ground floor and horizontal windows on the second floor. It was Eero Saarinen's first built, freestanding project developed independently of his father. [DA]

Koebel House
Grosse Pointe Farms, Michigan
1937–40

Saarinen, Swanson, and Saarinen designed this two-story brick house on a flat corner lot in a wealthy suburb of Detroit, but after Eero and Eliel Saarinen's participation in its initial design the project was carried through to completion by J. Robert F. Swanson. Pipsan Swanson orchestrated the interior design, which incorporated draperies and carpets designed by Loja Saarinen, sculptures by Lily Swann, and furniture designed by Eliel Saarinen, Robert Swanson, and Pipsan Swanson. The clients, Charles and Ingrid Koebel, had met Eliel on a boat to Finland; Charles owned the Diamond Tool Company. The house's plan was rectangular with curving walls in the entrance hall and dining room; most notably, it had a semicircular wing that served as a sun porch. On the first floor, the living and dining rooms—separated by floor-to-ceiling drapery—looked out onto a walled garden through large south-facing aluminum-framed windows. The second floor contained four bedrooms, a maid's bedroom, and four bathrooms. [SK]

See also Lange and Khorsandi, "Houses and Housing," in this volume.

"The Swansons Design and Furnish a House," *Interiors*, July 1941, 12–17

"Four Bedrooms, Maid's Room," *Architectural Forum*, Aug. 1941, 112–13

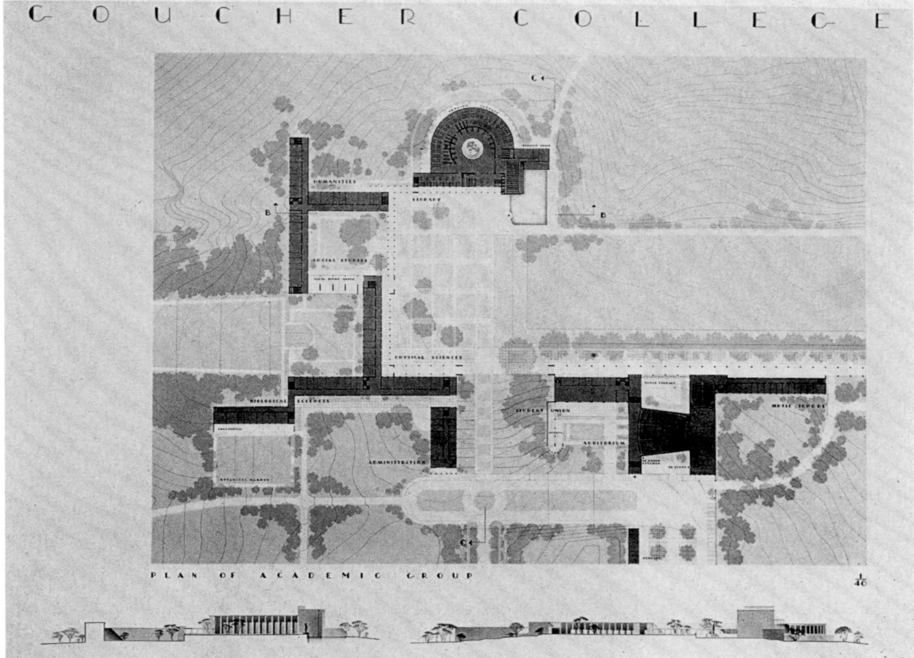

Goucher College Campus Plan and Library competition, site plan and elevations

1938

Goucher College Campus Plan and Library competition
Towson, Maryland
1938

Goucher College, located outside Baltimore, invited Eliel and Eero Saarinen to participate in a competition for a master plan and library. Collaborating with Ralph Rapson and other members of the Cranbrook community, the Saarinens submitted an entry calling for an asymmetrical arrangement of low buildings surrounding a rectangular landscaped plaza that opened onto a lawn. The library, which was located on the plaza, was to feature a cylindrical landscaped glass-enclosed atrium. The atrium was flanked on one side by a three-story rectilinear volume that contained offices and book stacks and fronted the plaza with a full-height colonnade, through which visitors entered the building. On the other side of the atrium, a U-shaped fully glazed reading room overlooked an undeveloped section of the campus. Other entrants included Walter Gropius, Wallace K. Harrison, George Howe, Richard Neutra, and the firm of McKim, Mead, and White. In addition to two representatives of the college, the jury consisted of Gilmore D. Clarke, chairman of the Commission of Fine Arts in Washington, D.C.; the architect John Holabird; and Everett V. Meeks, dean of the Yale School of Fine Arts and chairman of its department of architecture. Charging that the jury lacked a progressive point of view, Gropius withdrew, urging others to do the same. Howe was the only other competitor to withdraw. The Saarinens placed second to Moore and Hutchins's winning scheme. [TM]

Eleanor Patterson Spencer, "A College Builds a College: The Goucher Competition," *Magazine of Art*, Dec. 1938, 705–7

Wheaton College Art Center competition
Norton, Massachusetts
1938, unbuilt

The Museum of Modern Art, New York, and *Architectural Forum* jointly sponsored this competition for a fine arts center at a women's liberal arts college. The proposed center was to be the first academic building in the United States to adopt a modernist idiom. The competition was also the first one Eero entered without working in collaboration with his father. Saarinen's submission called for a one- and two-story structure built into a shallow hill. Four wings, one of which contained a pair of auditoriums, were arranged asymmetrically around a long narrow spine containing a foyer and art gallery. The horizontality of the exterior, which was accentuated by bands of glass and masonry, contrasted with the verticality of the tall stage house. Writing in *Pencil Points*, the architecture critic Talbot Hamlin praised the design overall, but criticized the building's siting, with the windowless walls of the auditoriums facing the lake.

Kleinhans Music Hall

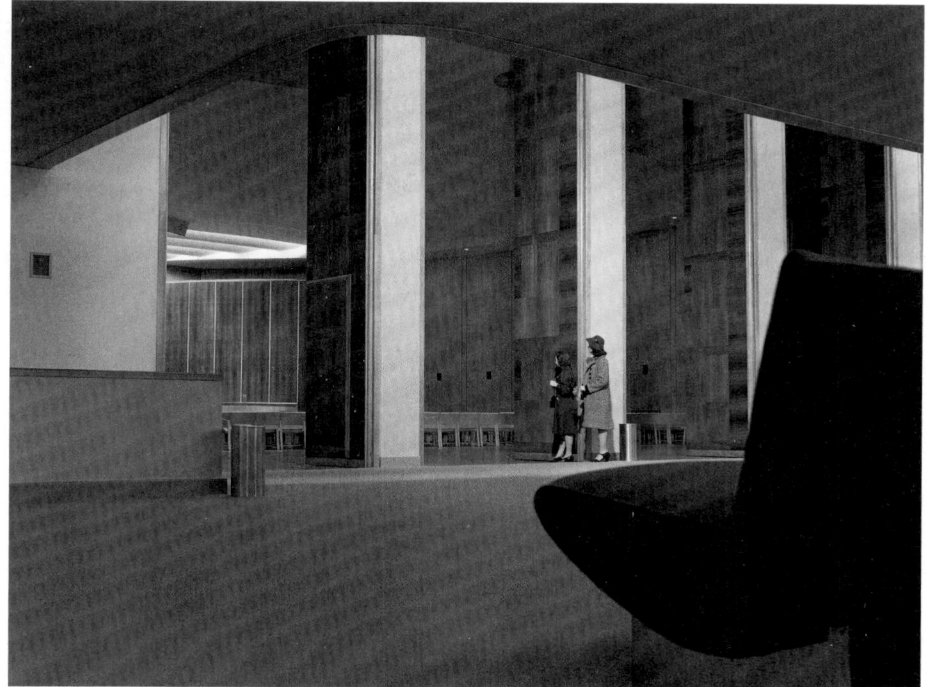

Kleinhans Music Hall, view from lobby toward chamber music hall

The submission shared fifth prize with entries by Percival Goodman and Lyndon and Smith. Richard M. Bennett and Caleb Hornbostel won first prize; Walter Gropius and Marcel Breuer, previously colleagues at the Bauhaus, placed second; John W. Steadman, Jr., and Paul Lester Wiener placed third; Alexis Dukelski placed fourth. The jury consisted of Esther Isabel Seaver, a Wheaton College professor of art who may have been responsible for organizing the competition; John McAndrew (competition chairman), a curator of architecture at the Museum of Modern Art; the architect and historian Walter Curt Behrendt; Stanley R. McCandless, a lighting designer and a member of the Yale School of Drama faculty; Roland A. Wank, the Tennessee Valley Authority's first chief architect; and the architects John Welborn Root and Edward Durell Stone. The winning entries were exhibited at the Museum of Modern Art, and Saarinen received a fifty-dollar prize. [TM]

"Wheaton College Art Center," *Architectural Forum*, Aug. 1938, 154

Kleinhans Music Hall
Buffalo, New York
1938–40

project number 154

Buffalo merchant Edward Kleinhans and the Works Progress Administration commissioned and paid for this music hall located at The Circle, a public park designed by Frederick Law Olmsted and Calvert Vaux. The architects of record for the project were F. J. and W. A. Kidd, Architects; Eliel and Eero Saarinen were consulting architects and were hired after the client became disenchanted with the work of the Kidd office. Collaborating with Charles Eames and Ralph Rapson, the Saarinens designed a building incorporating a tripartite curvilinear plan. The flat-roofed red- and tan-dappled brick and sandstone building was composed of two semi-elliptical structures, one housing a 3,000-seat auditorium suitable for orchestral music and a smaller one containing an 800-seat theater, intended for chamber music, with flexible seating designed by Eero Saarinen and Eames. A promenade, flanked by a horseshoe-shaped reflecting pool, bordered the chamber-music theater's curving exterior wall. Both performing spaces utilized wood paneling and ridged ceilings to ensure the even distribution of sound. Charles J. Potwin served as acoustical consultant. [TM]

Joseph Hudnut, "Kleinhans Music Hall," *Architectural Forum*, July 1941, 35–42

"Kleinhans Konserthall," *Arkkitehti*, July–Aug. 1948, 79–81

Crow Island School, auditorium

(opposite, top) Crow Island School, activity room

(opposite, bottom) Crow Island School, play area with sculptures by Lilian Swann Saarinen

Crow Island School, classroom

Crow Island School, under construction

Crow Island School
Winnetka, Illinois
1938–42

In 1938, the newly established Chicago-based firm Perkins, Wheeler, and Will, which later specialized in school buildings, invited Eliel and Eero Saarinen to work with them on the design of the Crow Island School in Winnetka, Illinois. Carleton Washburne, Winnetka's superintendent of schools from 1919 to 1943, pursued an activity-oriented pedagogical approach based on the ideas of the pioneering educational philosopher John Dewey, and he wanted the new school's architecture to express that progressive stance.

Occupying a corner site in a wealthy Chicago suburb, the brick building, of masonry-bearing-wall construction, contained twelve rectangular classrooms that were each augmented by an "L" extension housing a workroom and bathrooms. Between the units, modestly scaled fieldstone courtyards provided children with outdoor play space, while window walls allowed teachers to keep their students always in sight. In its self-sufficiency, each classroom unit resembled the one-room schoolhouse that had once been a standard feature of education in rural America. Emanating from a central core containing a library and an auditorium, a double-loaded corridor (with rooms on both sides) served eight classroom units, while a single-loaded hallway, placed off axis and oriented in the opposite direction, led to four more. A simplified version of the pinwheel floor plan, rendered in raised brick, served as a decorative motif on the building's exterior. Despite the plan's similarity to other schemes by the Saarinens, Larry Perkins of Perkins, Wheeler, and Will repeatedly claimed that the plan was devised by his partner Philip Will, and that it was heavily dependent on the classrooms' L-shapes, a feature for which he said he and his colleagues were responsible. Inside the school, some of the concrete block walls were faced with oak or Ponderosa pine paneling. Reinforced concrete slabs were covered with asphalt tiles, with the exception of the library, which had an elm floor. To create a child-friendly sense of scale, classroom ceiling heights were lowered from the school district's standard twelve feet to nine. Rendering the building a visually cohesive environment, Eero designed children's chairs and benches and, with Perkins, the school's desks and tables. Additionally, Eero's wife, Lilian Swann Saarinen, sculpted ceramic plaques, some illustrating Bible stories, which were used to decorate both interior and exterior walls. In 1955, thirteen years after the building's completion, the editors of *Architectural Forum* called it the nation's most architecturally influential contemporary school. [TM]

"Crow Island School, Winnetka, Ill.," *Architectural Forum*, Aug. 1941, 72–92

"School at Winnetka, Illinois," *Architectural Review*, Jan. 1942, 3–4

Elizabeth Mock, ed., *Built in USA, 1932–1944* (New York: Museum of Modern Art, 1944), 74–75

"Schools: A Look Backward and Forward," *Architectural Forum*, Oct. 1955, 129–38

"1940: Winnetka: Crow Island School," *Casabella*, Nov. 1960, 24

Jane Clarke, "Philosophy in Brick," *Inland Architect*, Nov.–Dec. 1989, 54–59

What Is Modern Architecture? (New York: Museum of Modern Art, 1942)

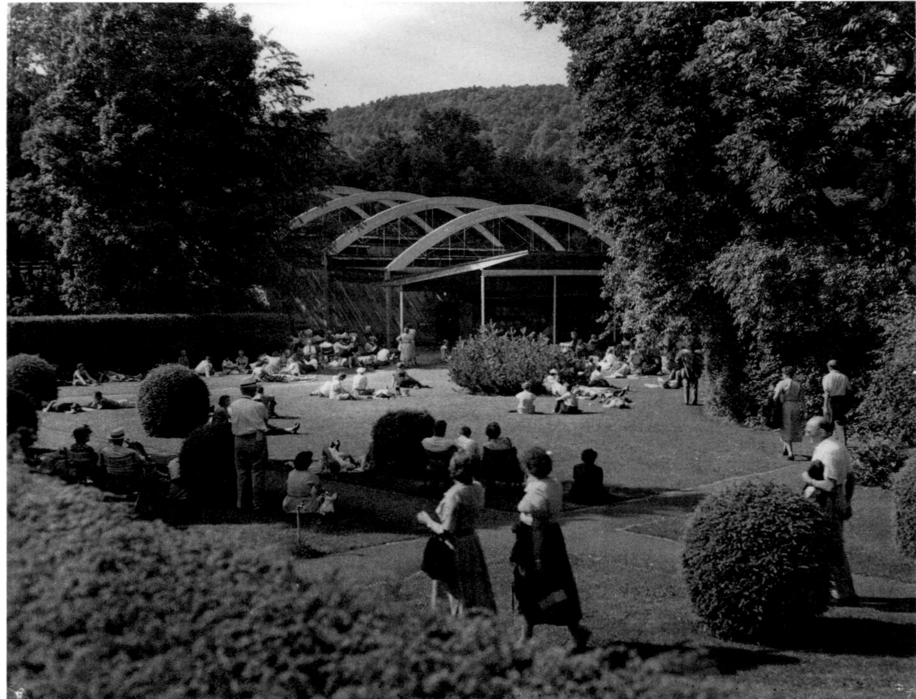

Berkshire Music Center, Edmund Hawes Talbot Orchestra Canopy, Tanglewood Shed

Berkshire Music Center, Chamber Music Shed

Berkshire Music Center
Lenox, Massachusetts
project number 4101

Tanglewood Shed, later Koussevitzky Shed, 1938
Chamber Music Shed, 1947
Edmund Hawes Talbot Orchestra Canopy, 1959

Serge Koussevitzky, the Russian-born conductor of the Boston Symphony Orchestra, hired the Saarinen firm to prepare a master plan for an extensive music center to include a music pavilion, an open-air theater, a school, and an inn. The Saarinens' design for the pavilion, known as the Tanglewood Shed, called for a fan-shaped structure, clad in wood, with a flat roof and a clear span in the interior. Before construction began, the symphony, seeking to save money, decided to incorporate interior columns, which caused the firm to quit the job. The symphony later hired a local architect, Joseph Franz, who followed the symphony's request. In most other respects, the pavilion reflected the Saarinens' scheme. The firm also designed a building intended for chamber music and opera, which nestled at the edge of the main field. The wood structure incorporated a roof, stepped to break up and distribute sound waves, suspended from exterior laminated-wood arches. In 1959, Eero Saarinen, working with the acoustical engineering firm Bolt, Beranek, and Newman, added an internal canopy of suspended triangular panels to the Tanglewood Shed, now called the Koussevitzky Shed. [TM]

"Proposed Pavilion Designed for Summer Symphonic Festivals," *Architectural Record,* Jan. 1939, 44-45

"Opera Shed," *Progressive Architecture,* Mar. 1947, 53-58

"Tanglewood Opera House," *Architectural Review,* May 1947, 163-64

"Théâtre Lyrique du Centre Musical de Berkshire," *L'Architecture d'Aujourd'hui,* May 1949, 19-21

American National Theater and Academy competition, perspective by Ralph Rapson

Exhibition of the Work of the Academy Staff, installation view

American National Theater and Academy competition, model

1939

Exhibition of the Work of the Academy Staff installation design
Cranbrook Academy of Art
Bloomfield Hills, Michigan
December 1–31, 1939

Eero Saarinen and Charles Eames, in their first collaboration, designed this installation in the Cranbrook Pavilion on the Cranbrook campus. Photographs, drawings, and models were displayed in an environment of partitions that were either solid multicolored panels or latticelike frames. The partitions were kept upright by an overhead plane of tautly stretched wires and were placed perpendicular to one another, creating an overlapping asymmetrical series of flowing spaces. The installation also included freestanding model bases and plants. [DA]

"Exhibition of the Work of the Academy Staff," *Cranbrook Academy News*, 1940

American National Theater and Academy competition
College of William and Mary
Williamsburg, Virginia
1939, unbuilt

The American National Theater and Academy, chartered by Congress in 1935 to bolster the dramatic arts, sponsored this competition for a theater and fine arts building intended for a sloping lakefront site. Joseph Hudnut, dean of the Harvard Graduate School of Design, wrote the competition program, which called for a theater, exhibition space, and classrooms for the drama, music, sculpture, and architecture departments. Eero Saarinen, Ralph Rapson, and Frederic James began to work on a scheme in 1938 and early in 1939 won first prize out of a pool of 122 entries. Their proposal, for which Rapson drew the principal renderings, called for four interconnected volumes, ranging in height from two to four stories. Three of the volumes, including one spanning the lake, were to incorporate horizontal strip windows, while the fourth was to contain a wedge-shaped theater and a brick stage-house tower. Terraces were to descend from the theater, which occupied the site's highest point, to the lakefront. Other architects to enter the competition were Marcel Breuer and Philip L. Goodwin, who placed second; Richard Neutra and Hugh Stubbins, who each received an honorable mention; and the firm of Harrison and Fouilhoux. The jury was composed of Lawrence B. Anderson, a professor at MIT; Leslie Cheek, a professor at the College of William and Mary who had been a friend of Saarinen's at Yale; the architect Antonin Raymond; Lee Simonson, a scenic designer; and Roland Wank of the Tennessee Valley Authority. [TM]

"Winners of National Theater Competition Are Announced," *Architectural Record*, Apr. 1939, 61–64

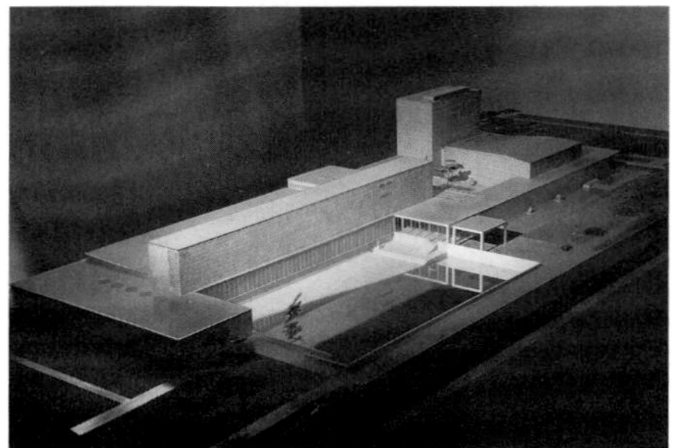

Smithsonian Gallery of Art competition, model

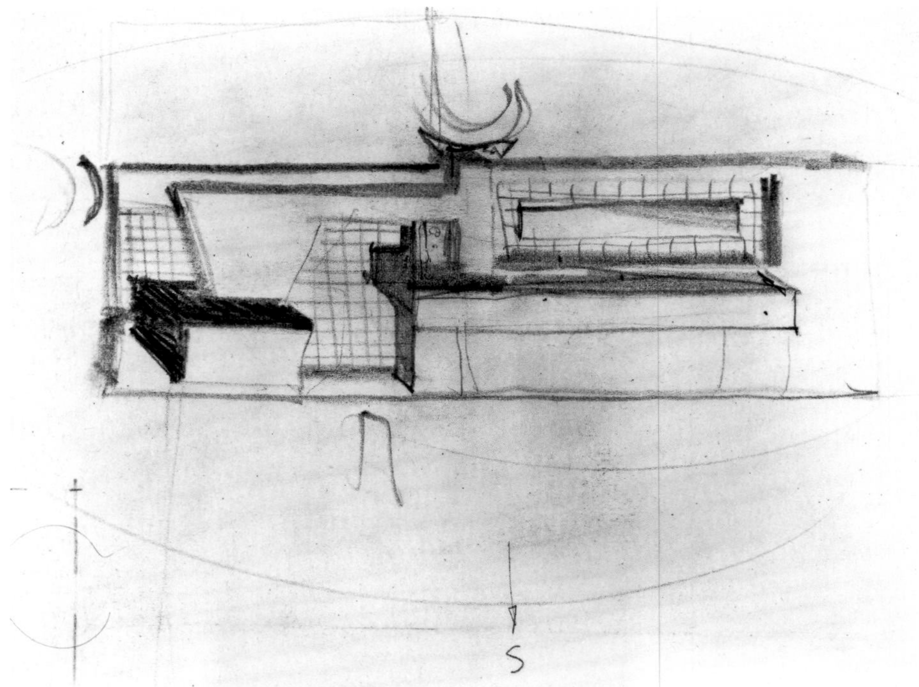

Smithsonian Gallery of Art competition, sketch

Smithsonian Gallery of Art competition
Washington, D.C.
1939, unbuilt

Eero Saarinen, assisted by a team including Charles Eames and Ralph Rapson, took the lead in designing Saarinen, Swanson, and Saarinen's entry in this two-part competition, sponsored by the Smithsonian Gallery of Art Commission, for a building on the Mall. The new building was to sit directly opposite John Russell Pope's classical National Gallery of Art, then under construction. The firm won first place, out of a field of 408 entrants, with a scheme calling for an asymmetrical composition of one- to four-story volumes clad in marble with metal trim. Horizontal strip windows and window walls contrasted with a windowless stage-house tower serving the building's auditorium, which formed the principal vertical element. The gallery's main entrance was reached from the Mall by means of a walkway bordered by a sunken court containing a curving patio and a reflecting pool with a fountain sculpture depicting Pegasus by Cranbrook artist Carl Milles. On the second floor, a library was flanked by terraces, one overlooking the reflecting pool, the other overlooking a sculpture garden. The commission was chaired by city planner Frederic A. Delano and composed of architects Walter Gropius, John A. Holabird, George Howe, and Henry R. Shepley, with Joseph Hudnut serving as professional adviser and Thomas D. Mabry, executive director of the Museum of Modern Art, New York, as technical adviser. [TM]

"The Smithsonian Gallery of Art Competition," *Architectural Forum*, July 1939, i–xvi

Joseph Hudnut, "Smithsonian Gallery of Art Competition," *Magazine of Art*, Aug. 1939, 456–59, 488–89

"Winners of Smithsonian Gallery of Art Competition," *Architectural Record*, Aug. 1939, 50–52

Lorimer Rich, "A Study in Contrasts," *Pencil Points*, Aug. 1941, 497–516

Elizabeth Mock, ed., *Built in USA, 1932–1944* (New York: Museum of Modern Art, 1944), 24–25

Tabernacle Church of Christ

Tabernacle Church of Christ, nave

Tabernacle Church of Christ,
later First Christian Church
Columbus, Indiana
1939–42

project number 4001

The Tabernacle Church of Christ marked the beginning of a close relationship between the Saarinens and the J. Irwin Miller family that would result in the Saarinens completing five buildings for the family. The church was distinguished by simple geometric forms rendered primarily in buff brick and limestone, asymmetrical composition, complex circulation paths, and careful manipulation of natural light. In collaboration with Charles Eames, Eero designed furniture, screens, railings, and light fixtures for the church's interiors. Eliel and Loja Saarinen designed a figurative tapestry, *The Sermon on the Mount,* for the sanctuary. E. D. Pierre and George Wright served as associate architects. [TM]

See also Olivarez, "Churches and Chapels," in this volume.

"Piety in Brick," *Time,* Jan. 27, 1941, 39–40

"Tabernacle Church of Christ," *Architectural Forum,* Oct. 1942, 35–44

"Tabernacle of Christ," *Architects' Journal,* Sept. 9, 1943, 183–86

Demountable Space project, model

Organic Design in Home Furnishings competition, armchair prototype

Organic Design in Home Furnishings competition, desk, side chair, and credenza

(opposite) Organic Design in Home Furnishings competition, relaxation chair prototype

1940

Demountable Space project
1940, unbuilt

When the United States Gypsum Company asked Saarinen to develop a building system fostering new uses for its materials, he proposed a Demountable Space that was planned as a flexible community center adaptable to different residential areas in a typical American city. (Cranbrook colleague Ralph Rapson collaborated on the project, for which he produced a series of sketches.) Designed to be easily and quickly erected, the building featured a central mast with cables that were used to hoist the building's large wall panels during construction, and also supported the roof. The square building housed a two-story auditorium, which doubled as a gymnasium, as well as an entry foyer, a nursery, and offices located beneath mezzanine-level conference and meeting rooms. [SK]

See also Lange and Khorsandi, "Houses and Housing," in this volume.

"Demountable Space" (U.S. Gypsum advertisement), *Architectural Forum,* Mar. 1942, 50–53

Organic Design in Home Furnishings competition
1940, not mass produced

This competition, sponsored by the Museum of Modern Art, New York, was intended to encourage collaborations between designers, manufacturers, and merchants in an effort to create mass-produced furniture for the American family of moderate income. Saarinen and Charles Eames won first prizes for their upholstered molded-plywood living room chairs and for their simple straight-lined wood benches, cabinets, desks, and tables. Twelve department stores planned to market the winning pieces. Handmade examples of the furniture were exhibited at the Museum of Modern Art. The Heywood-Wakefield Company and the Haskelite Corporation were set to mass produce the chairs, and the Red Lion Table Company, the storage cabinets, but the outbreak of war canceled the program. [DA]

See also Lutz, "Furniture," in this volume.

Eliot Noyes, *Organic Design in Home Furnishings* (New York: Museum of Modern Art, 1941)

"To Show Furniture in 'Organic Design,'" *New York Times,* Sept. 21, 1941

"Organic Design," *Arts and Architecture,* Dec. 1941, 16–17

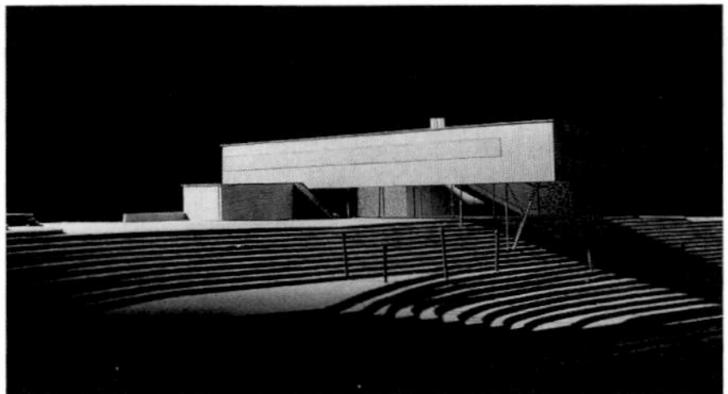

Bell House project, model

Bell House project, sketch by Ralph Rapson

Hall Auditorium, Theater, and Inn competition, Oberlin College, model

1941

Bell House project
New Hope, Pennsylvania
1941, unbuilt
project number 4102

Saarinen designed this five-bedroom residence for General Mills heir Samuel Bell. Intended to be located atop a hill, the house featured a first floor that formed an irregularly shaped L, crossed by a long, rectangular second floor raised on thin columns. Saarinen proposed that the structure be faced in stone and wood and that thermal plate-glass windows be used. The open-plan ground level contained the living area and kitchen. The upper level was designed with a single-loaded corridor along one facade and housed the servants' quarters and the master bedroom suite, with its own seating area, bathroom, and closets. [SK]

See also Lange and Khorsandi, "Houses and Housing," in this volume

Hall Auditorium, Theater, and Inn competition
Oberlin College
Oberlin, Ohio
1941, unbuilt

Around the time of World War I, Charles Martin Hall willed Oberlin College the funds to construct an auditorium, to be named after his mother, Sophronia Brooks Hall, and to be shared by the college and the town. Cass Gilbert, the architect of numerous buildings on the Oberlin campus, prepared designs for the auditorium, which was never built. In 1941, the college hired Eliel and Eero Saarinen to design a building housing both an auditorium and a theater.
The structure they proposed was to consist of two wedge-shaped wings of different sizes, placed apex to apex, with a rectangular element positioned as a crossbar through the point of intersection. The large wing housed the auditorium, and the small wing contained the theater. A shared lobby and a conference room occupied the crossbar element, one end of which terminated in an outdoor amphitheater. Study models of the project depict different schemes for linking the building to others, including a hotel to be designed by the Saarinen office. In one scheme, the outdoor amphitheater was backed by a freestanding arcade. The building was never realized, having been deemed by the college too radical a contrast to Gilbert's historicist architecture. [TM]

Center Line Defense Housing, school

Center Line Defense Housing, housing development, model

Center Line Defense Housing, later Kramer Homes Co-operative
Center Line, Michigan
1941–42, altered incrementally starting in the 1960s

The client for this project, the federal government's Division of Defense Housing, hired Saarinen, Swanson, and Saarinen to design a development on a flat, approximately twenty-five-acre site outside Detroit. The goal was to build 10,000 housing units for aircraft workers; 477 units were constructed. The development contained a looping road that encircled a six-acre "village green" and provided access to four residential neighborhoods, which were separated by tenants' parking lots. One- and two-story wood-frame houses, each accommodating between two and eight families, were sheathed in redwood. Roofs were either flat or gabled, with generous overhangs functioning as brise-soleils. Board-and-batten cladding was arranged in both vertical and horizontal patterns. In an effort to build quickly and inexpensively, the office employed prefabricated modular elements. In keeping with wartime restrictions, the architects minimized the use of metal in the buildings' construction, specifying steel only for the window sashes. Wood girders and columns, as well as wood roof framing and trusses, were employed throughout. Asphalt tile floors were applied directly to a concrete slab resting on precast concrete joists. In 1949, the development's tenants, over 90 percent of whom were members of the United Auto Workers union, assumed ownership from the federal government and incorporated as Kramer Homes Co-operative, which exists today.

The project was part of a government initiative that embraced modern architecture for defense housing. To meet this goal, the government hired Marcel Breuer, Walter Gropius, George Howe, Louis Kahn, Antonin Raymond, Oscar Stonorov, Frank Lloyd Wright, and William Wurster, among other architects. The division's previously completed projects included Gropius and Breuer's Aluminum City Terrace in New Kensington, Pennsylvania, and Howe, Stonorov, and Kahn's Carver Court in Coatesville, Pennsylvania. [TM]

"Center Line Defense Houses," *Architectural Forum*, Oct. 1941, 229–31
"Center Line: 476 Permanent Units," *Architectural Forum*, May 1942, 281–84
"Center Line School Community Center," *Pencil Points*, Nov. 1942, 56–60

Wermuth House

Wermuth House

Wermuth House
Fort Wayne, Indiana
1941-42

The two-story residence of Albert and Muriel Wermuth—Wermuth's firm was the contractor that built Cranbrook and the Tabernacle Church of Christ in Columbus, Indiana—was located outside the city center of Fort Wayne on an open landscaped site atop a hill commanding elevated views of a wooded ravine. The design consisted of two rectangular volumes. The first floor contained a living room, dining room, kitchen, and a screened-in porch. The second-floor volume partially overlapped the one below but extended beyond it on thin columns to create a covered ground-level terrace. The second floor housed bedrooms. The two volumes intersected at a slight angle. The garden facade, which overlooked the ravine, had large windows, whereas the entrance facade was more enclosed, facing a curving driveway and freestanding garage that was connected to the house by a covered walkway. The house featured flat roofs with overhangs, exposed exterior stairways, walls of clapboard and fieldstone, and ribbon windows set flush with the walls. A brick chimney rose twenty feet above the low-lying structure. Inside, an open-plan living room incorporated a sitting area placed on a slightly lower level. In addition to built-in shelves and cabinetry, the house was furnished with chairs designed by Alvar Aalto. [DA]

See also Lange and Khorsandi, "Houses and Housing," in this volume.

Albert Christ-Janer, *Eliel Saarinen* (Chicago: University of Chicago Press, 1948), 90–93

1942

American Museum of Natural History alteration project
New York, New York
1942, unbuilt

The City of New York hired Eliel Saarinen, working with Eero, to serve as design adviser for a remodeling and expansion of the American Museum of Natural History, to be executed by Aymar Embury II, who had long worked in close collaboration with the city's parks commissioner, Robert Moses. The Saarinens were critical of Embury's proposal to replace the existing museum's facades with unornamented walls, punctuated by vertical strip windows, and suggested constructing an entirely new building. They refused a request to submit a formal proposal but produced drawings depicting brick facades adorned by entrance colonnades to the north and south and reflecting pools and fountains on the museum's grounds. Neither Embury's nor the Saarinens' proposal was realized. [TM]

Unfolding House project, model

Willow Run Town Center and Willow Lodge, Tap Room, perspective by Ralph Rapson

Willow Run Town Center and Willow Lodge, second scheme dormitories, model

Unfolding House project
1942, unbuilt

Saarinen designed this project to meet the needs of World War II defense housing. Model photographs demonstrated the phases of on-site assembly. The house was to be made of metal and composed of two sections that, when placed together, formed a trailer, which could be shipped anywhere. On delivery at the site, the unit was "unfolded," the two sections forming the end walls of a full-size house. In between, and underneath an arched metal roof, builders were to insert a modular system of pivoting windows and doors set in metal frames. [DA]

See also Lange and Khorsandi, "Houses and Housing," in this volume.

"Eero Saarinen and Associates," *Michigan Society of Architects Monthly Bulletin* 27 (July 1953), 34

Willow Run Town Center
and Willow Lodge
Near Ypsilanti, Michigan
1942–43, town center unbuilt,
Willow Lodge demolished

The Federal Housing Authority and the United Auto Workers proposed to develop this new town located within commuting distance of a bomber plant run by the Ford Motor Company, and hired Saarinen and Swanson to design a town center containing a shopping center, city hall, school, post office, police station, fire station, bus station, and hotel. The proposal, which Eero worked on, called for long and narrow one- and two-story civic and commercial buildings fronting on landscaped courtyards with parking lots behind. The shopping center was to be accessible from the nearest residential neighborhood by means of an underpass beneath a major looping road. The town center was never realized, but in an effort to meet the immediate demand for 2,500 units of workers' housing, the firm was hired to design Willow Lodge, a temporary development offering dormitories and community buildings, including a tavern. This wood-frame structure had an interior with exposed roof trusses, wood-paneled walls, and a brick fireplace. The development's residential component was built in two phases. In the first, groups of four simply articulated, two-story wood dormitories were placed parallel or perpendicular to each other. The complex's use of steam heat determined layouts in which long runs of dormitory rooms were joined by a centrally located structure containing lavatories and a boiler room. In the second phase, smaller units were each equipped with a hot-air heating plant and arranged in a looser, non-orthogonal pattern. [TM]

"FPHA Dormitories to Serve Midwestern Bomber Plant," *Architectural Record*, July 1942, 47

"The Town of Willow Run," *Architectural Forum*, Mar. 1943, 37–54

"A Dormitory Plan in Two Versions," *Architectural Record*, Oct. 1943, 54–60

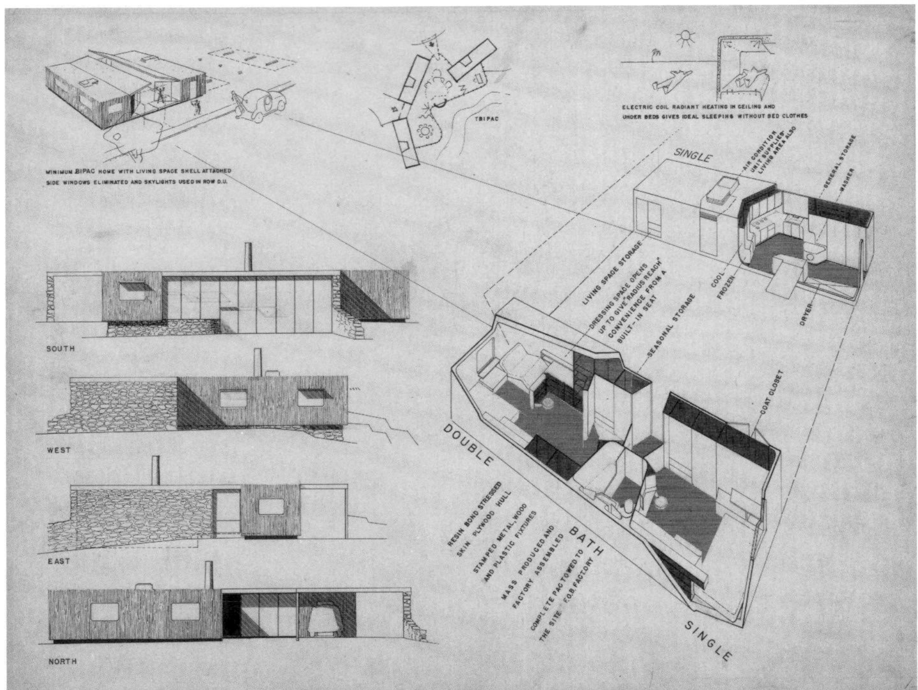

PAC (Pre-Assembled Components) for Designs for Postwar Living competition, competition board

Grasshopper chair

1943

PAC (Pre-Assembled Components) for Designs for Postwar Living competition 1943, unbuilt

Twenty-three building-materials manufacturers sponsored this design competition, limited to Americans, which was organized by the journal *Arts and Architecture*. The jury members—architect and designer Charles Eames, and architects Gregory Ain, Richard Neutra, John Leon Rex, and Sumner Spaulding—culled through the 512 submissions and unanimously selected Eero Saarinen and Oliver Lundquist's design, called PAC (pre-assembled components), which received the $1,000 first prize. (Second prize was awarded to I. M. Pei and E. H. Duhart; third prize went to Raphael Soriano.) The PACs were intended as workers' housing. Saarinen and Lundquist, who were both at the time employed by the Office of Strategic Services in Washington, D.C., proposed two PACs, identified as "A" and "B." The "A" component contained a kitchen, a bath, a laundry area, and a single bedroom; the "B" component contained a double bedroom, a single bedroom, and a bath. The components could be arranged on site in a variety of combinations including "A," "AB," and "ABB"; they could be used to produce single-family freestanding houses or collected to build row houses. Units also could be joined together by irregularly shaped glass-enclosed living spaces. Stamped plastic, metal, and wood fixtures were to be mass produced and, on factory assembly lines, integrated into hulls, approximately ten by thirty feet, made of stressed plywood. A fully assembled PAC could be towed from the factory to the site. The architects claimed that electric radiant-heat coils installed in the ceiling as well as under beds would eliminate the need for bed linens. They also anticipated that if standardized units were created to suit different climates and income levels, PACs could meet 80 percent of the nation's postwar housing needs. [TM]

See also Lange and Khorsandi, "Houses and Housing," in this volume.

"Designs for Postwar Living Competition," *Arts and Architecture*, Aug. 1943, 28–31

"Designs for Postwar Living Competition," *Architectural Forum*, Sept. 1943, 88–89

Grasshopper Chair 1943–46, discontinued 1965

The Grasshopper chair was the result of experiments in sculptural forms for chairs that Saarinen undertook during World War II. Called Model 61 by its manufacturer, Knoll Associates, the chair featured a pair of identical laminated-wood frames that were bent to form its legs and armrests and gave the chair its name because they resembled the hind legs of a grasshopper. A single molded-plywood frame was wrapped in surplus parachute webbing and shaped to form the chair's seat and back. Connected to the leg-and-armrest units at only four points, this seat-and-back form seemed to hover above the floor. Knoll also offered a companion footstool. [DA]

See also Lutz, "Furniture," in this volume.

Detroit Civic Center, perspective

Detroit Civic Center, model

Detroit Civic Center
Detroit, Michigan
1943–51, unbuilt

project number 4627

The city of Detroit hired Saarinen, Swanson, and Saarinen to serve as consultants on this project for a forty-three-acre site along the Detroit River, for which they developed many schemes. (Eliel Saarinen had created concepts in 1924 and 1937–38, which were not realized. Eero Saarinen worked with his father on the latter design.) All the new schemes called for the creation of a large landscaped riverfront plaza containing the Veterans' Memorial Building, flanked by a convention center and an auditorium, and separated from the rest of the city by a "wall" of new government office buildings. In some schemes, this wall was composed of a single four-block-long slab building, fifteen stories tall and raised on columns to allow vehicular traffic to reach a broad tree-lined thoroughfare bordering the plaza and give pedestrians access to the riverfront park. As shown in the final master plan, publicly released in March 1949 and published in *Architectural Forum* that April, the center, estimated to cost $50 million, included thirteen buildings and a band shell. (This iteration was published under the Saarinens' name only, as Swanson left the firm in 1947.) The wall of government office buildings had been broken into seven separate structures, the tallest of which was eighteen stories and clad in horizontal bands of windows and opaque spandrels. A circular convention hall seated 17,500 and a civic auditorium seated 3,500. This version also included two parking garages, one serviced by an access road tunneled beneath the plaza. Paul S. Calkins was the project's structural engineer. Despite receiving approval from the city's planning commission, the design was not realized. [TM]

"Fifty Million Dollar Civic Center Is Created for Detroit," *Architectural Forum*, Apr. 1949, 12–13

Quito Government Palace competition, main hall, perspective

Quito Government Palace competition, model

Serving Suzy Restaurant project, exterior, perspective

1944

Quito Government Palace competition
Quito, Ecuador
1944, unbuilt

The design competition for a new government complex to occupy a hilltop site in the northern section of Quito, Ecuador, was the first competition that Eliel and Eero Saarinen entered separately. Eero proposed a fourteen-story T-shaped building raised on pilotis and flanked on three sides by four-story structures with curving walls. The complex sat on a paved plaza that was separated from the surrounding hilly landscape by low retaining walls. The crossbar of the T terminated a road with a wide median strip. The building's elevations combined blank walls, rectangular grids of windows, and large expanses of open grillwork. The complex's most prominent interior, called the Salon de Pasos Perdidos, was a double-height space in which a broad stairway rose to a mezzanine. A curvilinear cutout in the ceiling offered visitors a view of a multistory figurative mural. [TM]

"Eero Saarinen and Associates," *Michigan Society of Architects Monthly Bulletin* 27 (July 1953), 35

Serving Suzy Restaurant and Gift Shop projects
1944, unbuilt

Looking forward to the needs of post-World War II veterans and their families, Pittsburgh Plate Glass sponsored a visionary project calling for the design of a residential community with a civic center and shopping center. Saarinen and Swanson (with Eero's involvement) was selected to design the shopping center; their innovative proposal called for the complex to be housed under a single roof and air-conditioned. The design included schemes for the Serving Suzy Restaurant and a gift shop. The firm's most novel idea for the restaurant was a small electric-powered kitchen on wheels called the "Serving Suzy," which brought chef and food to diners' tables. The gift shop was designed as an open multilevel space where merchandise could be displayed in various ways—on tables, in vitrines, and via a revolving turntable on which craftspeople and their wares could be viewed by the public. [DA]

"Restaurant," and "Gift Shop," *Pencil Points*, Aug. 1944, 42–44, 48

Lincoln Heights Housing, aerial perspective

Antioch College, dormitory room with Grasshopper chair

Antioch College, dormitory

Antioch College, master plan study, aerial perspective

Lincoln Heights Housing
Washington, D.C.
1944–46

The National Capital Housing Authority commissioned Saarinen and Swanson to design this housing project for returning veterans. Eero Saarinen was involved because in 1943 he had opened a small branch office in Washington, D.C. The firm's scheme called for a system of curving roads that provided access to more than fifty freestanding buildings, which were arranged at various angles, creating courtyards and open green spaces on the flat site. Clad in red brick, the rectangular structures ranged from single-family town houses to low-rise apartment buildings and offered one-, two-, three-, and four-bedroom dwellings. [LSE]

Albert Christ-Janer, *Eliel Saarinen* (Chicago: University of Chicago, 1948), 140

Antioch College
Yellow Springs, Ohio
1944–47

Master Plan, 1944–45
project number 4409
Hugh Taylor Birch Hall, 1944–47; altered, 2005
project number 4409

Saarinen, Swanson, and Saarinen's master plan for this college expansion called for the closure of some streets leading to the campus, as well as for the construction of a new library, a theater, and a fine arts building to the south of Antioch Hall, the campus's most imposing structure, and a dining hall and two residential quadrangles to the north. As depicted in perspective renderings, the new buildings were composed of interlocking rectangular blocks built of brick and glass. Though the college had engaged the Saarinen, Swanson, and Saarinen firm, Eero headed up the project, and minutes from the college's board of trustees meetings indicate that he, not his father, attended.

The only building proposed in the master plan to be completed was HughTaylor Birch Hall, which had been intended to form one side of a residential quadrangle marking the main campus's northern boundary. The reinforced concrete flat-roofed dormitory was clad in brick and had horizontal strip windows. Arranged in two long narrow wings offset from each other by approximately ten feet, it housed 110 dormitory rooms, as well as social and game rooms, storage units, and three apartments for faculty members and their families. The south wing was sunk three feet below grade to allow first-floor public rooms higher-than-standard ceiling heights. Birch-paneled bedrooms contained space-saving built-in furniture designed by Eero. Max G. Mercer served as the associate architect, Arton E. Yokon was the structural engineer, and Dan Kiley was the landscape architect. [TM]

"Antioch College Dormitory for Women," *Progressive Architecture*, Aug. 1949, 49–53

Eero Saarinen, "Campus Planning and the Unique World of the University," *Architectural Record*, Nov. 1960, 123–38

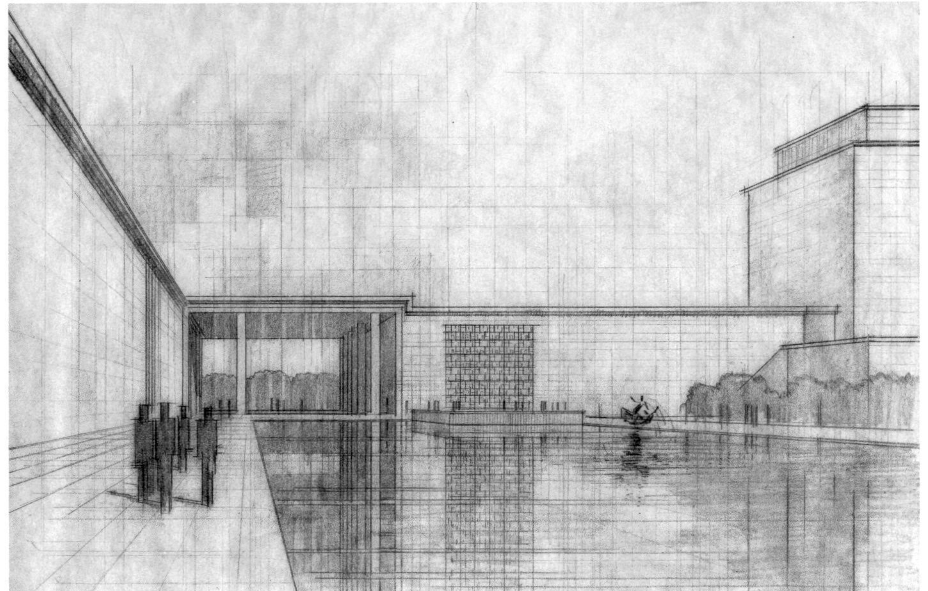

Des Moines Art Center, courtyard perspective

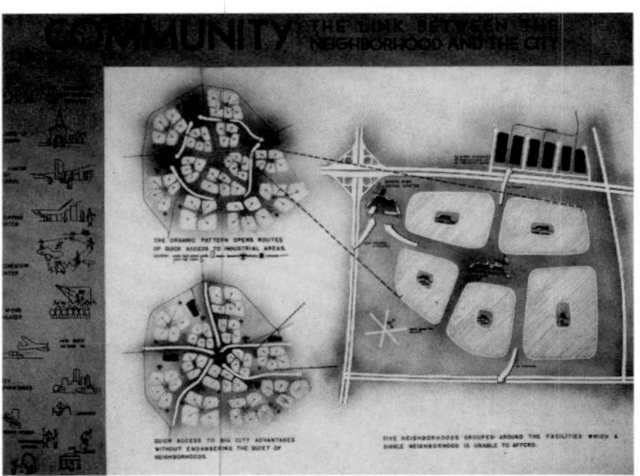

Chicago City Plan, community plan diagrams

Des Moines Art Center
Des Moines, Iowa
1944–48

project number 4404

In March 1945, Saarinen, Swanson, and Saarinen's design for this art center was approved by the Edmundson Memorial Foundation board of trustees. The building, which opened in June 1948, was U-shaped, clad in Lannon limestone, and had overhanging flat roofs. The low-slung structure, effectively integrated into the landscape of Greenwood Park, enclosed a courtyard with a reflecting pool and contained a foyer, galleries, library, and auditorium. A two-story education wing, housing classrooms and studios, featured interiors with coved plaster ceilings and wide-plank oak floors. [LSE]

"Art Center in Des Moines," *Architectural Forum*, July 1949, 65–69

P. Parker, "Des Moines Opens Community Art Center," *Art Digest*, July 1948, 9–10

"Centre des Arts, Cité Des Moines," *L'Architecture d'Aujourd'hui*, Apr. 1950, 55–56

1945

Chicago City Plan
Chicago, Illinois
1945, unbuilt

Saarinen, Swanson, and Saarinen proposed this plan for approximately thirty communities, which were to be spread over the Chicago metropolitan area. The firm advocated the development of clearly articulated residential and commercial areas separated by greenbelts. Arguing that such an arrangement fostered a healthy civic spirit, the architects noted that in contrast to the city's traditional street grid, a system incorporating winding roads and cul-de-sacs required 25 percent less paving and would thus be more economical to build and maintain. A metropolitan-wide network of limited-access highways was to link the communities. [TM]

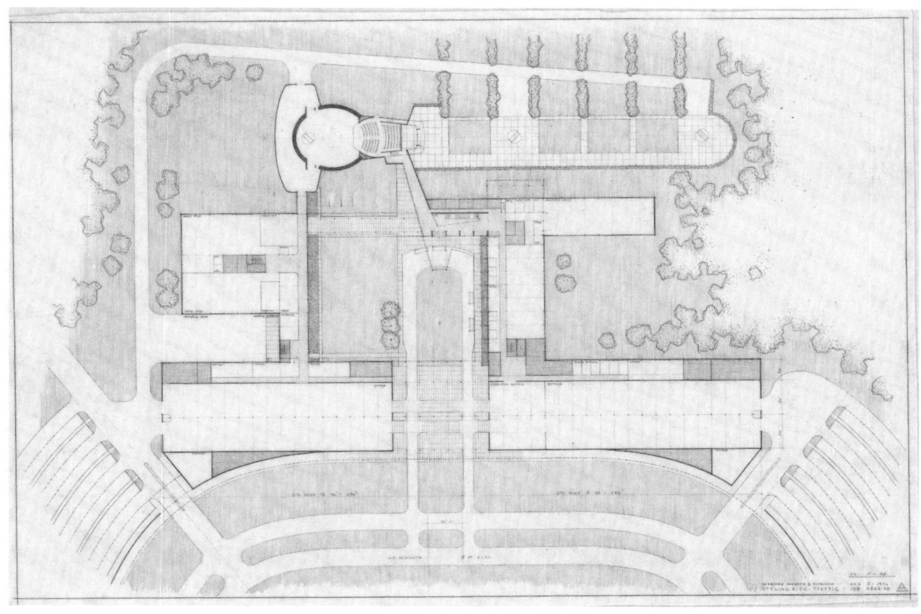

General Motors Technical Center, Styling Building group, ground-floor plan

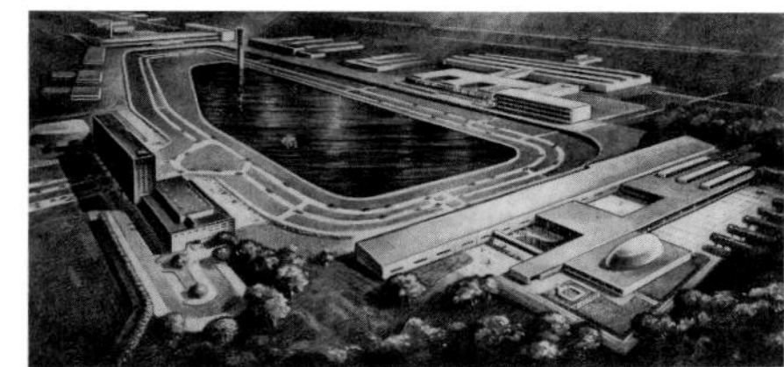

General Motors Technical Center, aerial perspective

Lapeer Veterans Memorial project, perspective

Lapeer Veterans Memorial project
Lapeer, Michigan
1945, unbuilt

This project, initiated by local veterans' groups, primarily the American Legion, called for a memorial to war dead and a civic facility. Designed by Saarinen, Swanson, and Saarinen, the two-story masonry-clad structure featured prominent horizontal windows, glass walls, and a cantilevered entrance canopy. At the rear of the building, two levels of terraces for dining and recreation descended to a river. Inside, folding partitions were to foster multiple uses in the assembly hall and lounge balcony areas. The building was to include bowling alleys, a canteen, and rooms for reading, card playing, and billiards. [LSE]

"Lapeer, Michigan: Veterans Memorial Building," *Pencil Points*, June 1946, 72–73

General Motors Technical Center
Warren, Michigan
1945–46, unbuilt; see 1948 for later scheme

General Motors chairman of the board Alfred P. Sloan, Jr., hired Saarinen and Swanson to design this corporate campus on a flat 320-acre site north of Detroit. Eero later commented that the client had been looking "for another Cranbrook." Eliel Saarinen and Robert Swanson were principally responsible for the scheme, although Eero contributed drawings to the project. In one iteration, an irregularly shaped reflecting pool was encircled by a roadway around which were deployed five groups of buildings. In renderings by Hugh Ferris, some of the structures were depicted as having curved, streamlined roof profiles and canopies. The proposal, which came in over its $20-million budget, was approved, but progress was stymied by a strike and postwar shortages of requisite building materials. [TM]

"General Motors City of Science and Art," *Pencil Points*, Sept. 1945, 16
"General Motors Technical Center," *Architectural Record*, Nov. 1945, 98–103
"General Motors Technical Center," *Architectural Forum*, July 1949, 70–78

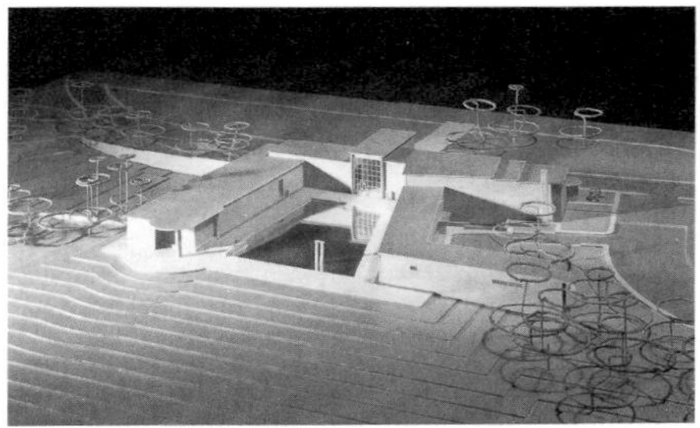

Fort Wayne Art School and Museum project, model

Case Study House #9

Fort Wayne Art School and Museum project
Fort Wayne, Indiana
1945–47, unbuilt

Lawrence Coleman of the American Association of Museums recommended Eliel Saarinen for this project, and the Fort Wayne Art School and Museum's board of trustees chose Saarinen, Swanson, and Saarinen to draw up plans for a site in Foster Park. The design called for an asymmetrically composed building with angled wings defining an open courtyard and a large reflecting pool. The masonry-clad structure featured an entrance lobby with glass walls on both ends. Inside, there were to be classrooms, a library, student lounge, cafeteria, auditorium, lecture hall, and three galleries. By 1949, funding had not materialized for the Foster Park site. In lieu of new construction, the board of trustees accepted the donation of two houses and purchased additional ones to accommodate the museum and school. [LSE]

Case Study Houses #8 and #9
Pacific Palisades, California
1945–49, #8 not built according to the original design, #9 expanded in 1997

Saarinen and Charles Eames designed these two steel-frame houses as part of the Case Study House program launched by *Arts and Architecture* magazine in 1945. The houses are adjacent to each other on a site overlooking the Pacific Ocean. The design of House #8, the residence of Charles and his wife, Ray, originally featured a glass-walled volume raised on thin metal columns, but this scheme was later modified by the Eameses into a house with two double-height volumes separated by a courtyard and nestled into the site's hillside. Saarinen and Eames designed House #9 for John Entenza, the magazine's publisher and the program's director. The 1,600-square-foot, seven-room house was a single story tall and featured a multilevel open-plan living space. [DA]

Case Study House #9, living area, rendering

See also Lange and Khorsandi, "Houses and Housing," in this volume.

"Case Study Houses No. 8 and 9," *Arts and Architecture,* Dec. 1945, 43–51

"Case Study Houses 8–9," *Arts and Architecture*, Mar. 1948, 40–41

"House at Santa Monica for J. Entenza," *Architectural Review,* Oct. 1951, 230–31

Model 71, 72, and 73 Chairs
1945–50, partially realized

Saarinen's Model 72 armless side chair was conceived in model form about 1945 and introduced by Knoll Associates in 1948. It featured molded-shell seating manufactured of fiberglass-reinforced plastic. Saarinen also designed an armchair, to be called Model 73, which, although patented with the Model 72 chair, was never produced because its curved fiberglass-reinforced plastic armrests were not strong enough for office use. Saarinen, however, continued to experiment with the idea of a molded-shell armchair. Working with Florence Knoll's consent and adapting a wood-frame chair she had designed in 1945, he created the Model 71 armchair, which was introduced by Knoll in 1950. [BL]

See also Lutz, "Furniture," in this volume.

"Chemistry Builds a Chair," *Rohm and Haas Reporter,* Nov.–Dec. 1951, 2–4

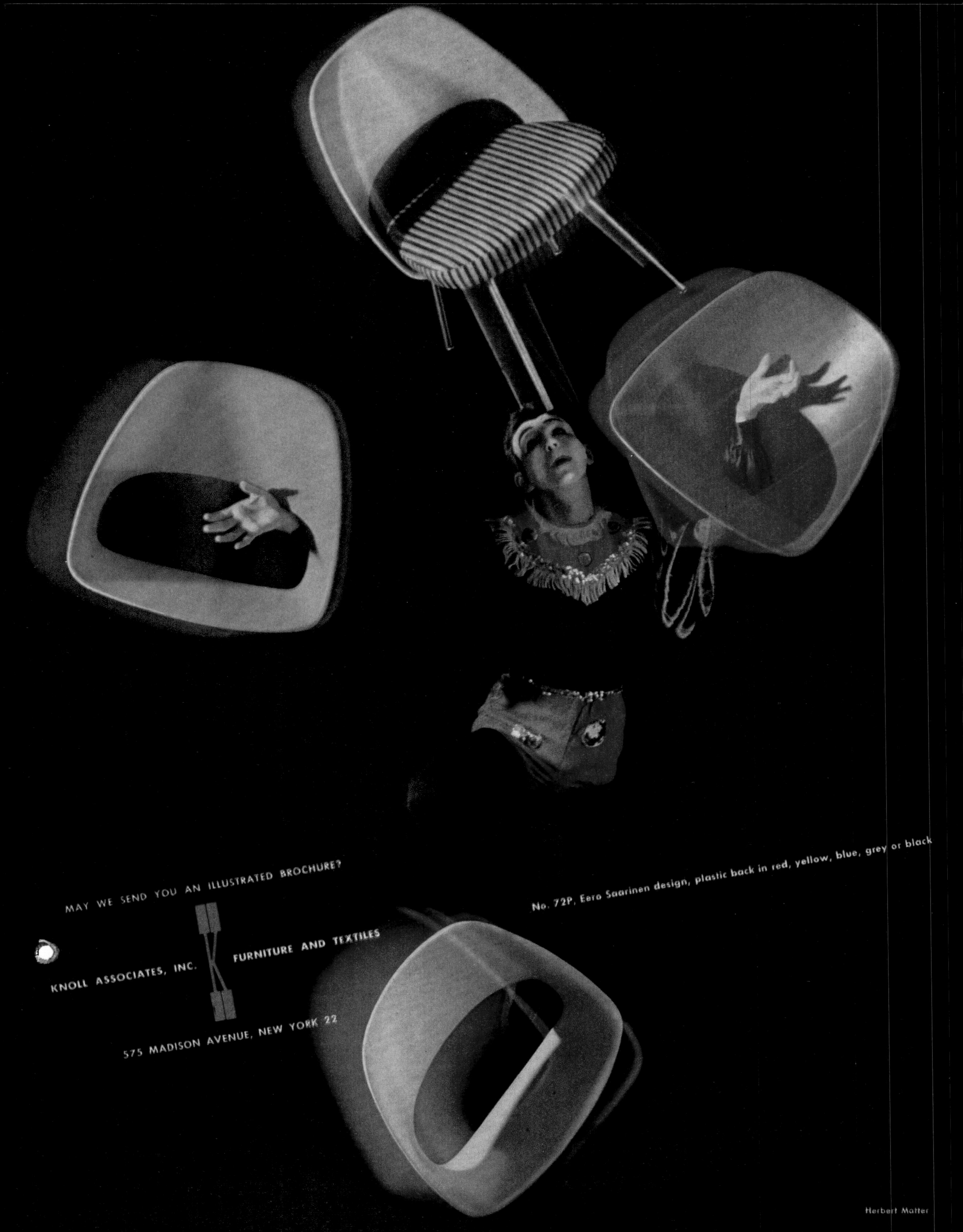
MAY WE SEND YOU AN ILLUSTRATED BROCHURE?
KNOLL ASSOCIATES, INC.
FURNITURE AND TEXTILES
575 MADISON AVENUE, NEW YORK 22
No. 72P, Eero Saarinen design, plastic back in red, yellow, blue, grey or black
Herbert Matter

Birmingham High School, perspective

(opposite) Knoll Associates advertisement for Model 72 series chairs, graphic design by Herbert Matter

Stephens College
Columbia, Missouri
1945–50

Master Plan, 1945–47
project number 5603
Chapel, 1946–50, unbuilt;
see 1953 for later scheme
project number 4612-A

This Baptist-sponsored junior college for women hired the Saarinen firm to devise a master plan, including a quadrangle, a separate row of buildings, and a chapel. Shortly before his death in 1950, Eliel Saarinen made sketches for a proposed chapel; after Eliel's death, Eero Saarinen and Associates produced working drawings, but the project went unrealized. [TM]

"Chapel for a Women's College," *Progressive Architecture*, June 1951, 15–16

Birmingham High School,
later Seaholm School
Birmingham, Michigan
1945–52

Saarinen, Swanson, and Saarinen's design for this high school on a forty-six-acre site in suburban Detroit called for a series of one-, two-, and three-story volumes in an asymmetrical arrangement around a landscaped courtyard. The steel-frame structure with steel joists was clad in pastel-colored brick and sprayed-on concrete. The building, with expansive glass walls, housed classrooms that faced south and east for maximum sunlight, a library, conference room, theater, cafeteria, and gymnasium. The interior incorporated long light-filled hallways and wall surfaces of glazed tile, plaster, or painted concrete. In 1947, the project was taken over by Swanson Associates, which later completed it. [LSE]

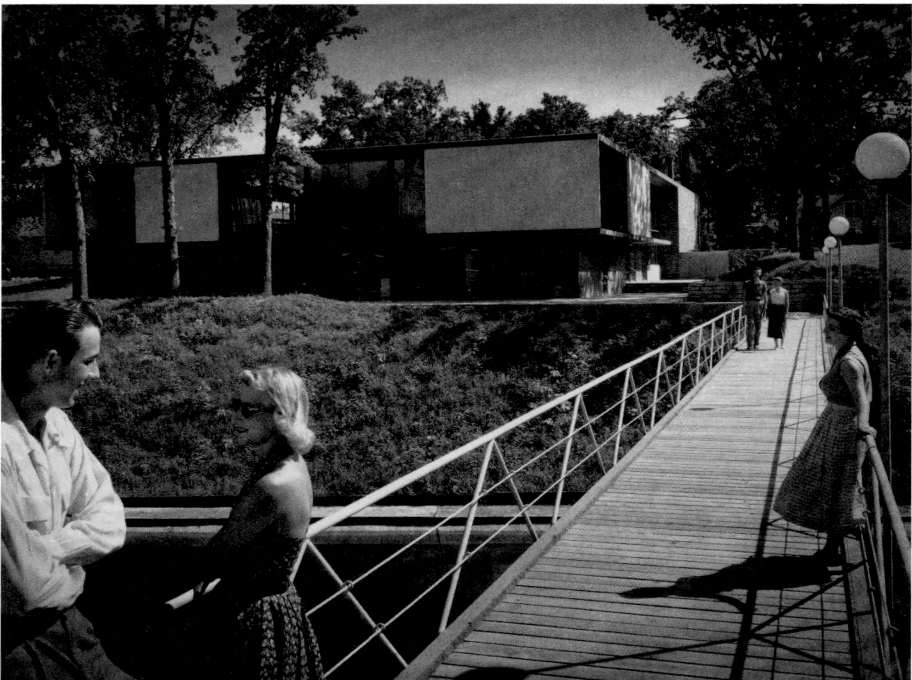

Drake University, dining hall

Drake University, chapel

Drake University
Des Moines, Iowa
1945–57

Campus Plan, 1945–47
project number 4506
Harvey Ingham Hall of Science and Fitch Hall of Pharmacy (Science and Pharmacy Buildings), 1945–50
project number 4506-B
Women's Dormitories and Dining Hall, 1945–55
project number 4506-C
Bible School and Prayer Chapel, 1952–56
project number 5207
Women's Residence: Dormitory #4, 1957
project number 5515
Jewett Union addition, 1957
project number 5516

In 1945, Saarinen, Swanson, and Saarinen prepared a master plan for Drake University and designed a pair of buildings dedicated to the departments of science and pharmacy, as well as a women's dormitory complex. Over a period of more than a decade, Eero further developed the campus plan and designed a Bible school and prayer chapel, another women's dormitory, and a three-story masonry-clad addition to Jewett Union. The master plan called for expanding the campus to the northwest with a collection of loosely defined quadrangles. In 1950, Harvey Ingham Hall of Science and Fitch Hall of Pharmacy, designed primarily by Eero Saarinen, were the first completed of the new buildings. They were flat-roofed and constructed with load-bearing walls of red brick, matching the university's older buildings, as well as structural steel and reinforced concrete. Saarinen collaborated with the Chrysler Corporation to develop prefabricated steel spandrels with baked-on finishes. Separating pedestrian and vehicular traffic, a glazed passageway spanned a street to connect the two structures.

Drake University, dormitory common room, model

Drake University, dormitory

Inside the buildings, utility pipes ran along the ceilings and were left exposed; ductwork was hidden in closets. Brooks-Borg Architects served as associate architects on the project.

The women's residential complex, which included a freestanding dining hall, occupied a hilly site and was designed to maintain many of its existing natural features, including a large number of mature trees. The structures were linked by multilevel pedestrian bridges and elevated walkways, some of which crossed a centrally located, irregularly shaped manmade pool. The buildings varied in height up to five stories and incorporated glazed ground floors. Inside, window embrasures were splayed to diffuse natural light entering the single- and double-occupancy rooms, where most of the furniture was built-in and designed by the Saarinen office. Stuart Davis was commissioned to create a thirty-three-foot-long mural, *Allée,* for the dining hall. Severud, Elstad, Krueger Associates were the complex's structural engineers and Hyde and Bobbio its mechanical engineers.

The Drake Bible School featured exterior walls of glass and aluminum panels arranged in a grid articulated at a smaller module than those of Fitch Hall. In striking contrast, the Prayer Chapel, connected to the Bible School and completed the same year, was a windowless brick drum. Inside, the wood-paneled chapel contained a circular altar placed directly below an oculus. [TM]

See also Olivarez, "Churches and Chapels," in this volume.

"Des Moines, Iowa: A University Campus Plan Under Way for Drake University," *Architectural Record,* Dec. 1947, 71–83

"Science and Pharmacy Buildings for Drake University, Des Moines," *Progressive Architecture,* Nov. 1950, 65–89

"Drake University: Dormitories and Dining Hall," *Progressive Architecture,* Apr. 1955, 96–105

"Un altra cappella a celindor, Drake University," *Architettura,* June 1957, 108–9

Christ Church, perspective

1946

Christ Church
Cincinnati, Ohio
1946, unbuilt

A committee representing Christ Church hired Saarinen and Saarinen to design a new house of worship to replace one built in 1835. Elaborating on the Tabernacle Church of Christ, completed in Columbus, Indiana, five years earlier, the Saarinens' design for the Cincinnati church called for a masonry bearing-wall structure with an asymmetrically placed tower incorporating a crucifix flanked by open grillwork. Inside, a generously scaled entrance hall was to provide a place for members of the congregation to gather. In 1950, following Eliel's death, Eero, presumably out of loyalty to his father, refused to accommodate changes requested by new church leadership in an effort to keep costs down. The church fired him and in 1951 hired the architectural firm David Briggs Maxwell, based in Oxford, Ohio, to devise new plans, which, realized in 1957, were strongly influenced by the Saarinens' design. [TM]

"Christ Church, Cincinnati, Ohio," *Architectural Forum*, Dec. 1949, 60

Milwaukee War Memorial Center
Milwaukee, Wisconsin
1946, unbuilt; see 1952 for later scheme

Saarinen, Swanson, and Saarinen's proposal for this complex, to be built by a citizens' group called the Metropolitan Milwaukee Memorial, Inc., on a six-block site downtown, called for three connected buildings surrounding a two-level courtyard. The lower, street-level plaza was to contain a reflecting pool, while the upper-level plaza was to be landscaped. The complex's central building was itself to be divided into four elements: three fan-shaped theaters (seating 3,500, 1,500, and 500) joined by a rectangular stage house, approximately twice their height. The Veterans Memorial Hall, an arcaded two-story building sited at one side of the pool, was to contain a sheltered exterior wall inscribed with the names of Milwaukee's war dead. The upper-level plaza was to serve as a forecourt for the complex's third structure: a community art gallery composed of one- and two-story volumes and housing exhibition space and classrooms. The two plazas were connected by a flight of steps ornamented with a freestanding sculpture. The project did not go forward, as the public favored addressing the city's postwar housing shortage instead of building an art center. [TM]

"Milwaukee's Proposed Memorial Center," *Architectural Record*, Nov. 1947, 74–77

Washtenaw County Master Plan
Washtenaw County, Michigan
1946

This planning study for Washtenaw County, approximately forty miles west of Detroit, called for the development of neighborhood clusters centered on a business district. Each cluster was composed of three to six residential areas surrounding a community center. The clusters were separated by greenbelts. [TM]

Knoll advertisement for Womb chair, graphic design by Herbert Matter

Womb chair and ottoman

Womb Chair and Ottoman
1946–48

project number E-4601

The Womb chair, manufactured by Knoll Associates, consisted of a single reinforced-fiberglass shell covered with foam, upholstered, and supported on a bent tubular-steel frame. The elongated form of the chair's back seamlessly curved into the seat and, on each side, formed cantilevered armrests. Separate upholstered foam cushions for the seat and back sat inside the shell. The accompanying ottoman consisted of a curving upholstered shell, a separate upholstered foot cushion, and four tubular-steel legs. Early models of the chair were made by a shipbuilder in New Jersey who worked in fiberglass. [TM]

See also Lutz, "Furniture," in this volume.

"Modern Doesn't Pay, or Does It?" *Interiors,* Mar. 1946, 66–74

Mary Roche, "New Chair Offers More Relaxation," *New York Times,* May 19, 1948

"Experts Pick Best-Designed Products of Modern Times," *New York Times,* Mar. 31, 1959

Rita Reif, "Pioneer in Modern Furniture Is Charting Expansion Course," *New York Times,* June 17, 1959

1947

Bloomfield Hills
General Development Plan
Bloomfield Hills, Michigan
1947, unbuilt

This plan, developed by Saarinen, Swanson, and Saarinen, included growth forecasts and called for the rezoning of the intersection of Long Lake Road and Woodward Avenue, near Cranbrook. The scheme proposed a city-hall green, a shopping plaza with courtyards, a high school, and clusters of terraced housing. The buildings were to be one or two stories tall. Bypass roads were intended to facilitate traffic flow. [LSE]

Louisiana State University, campus development plan

Christ Church Lutheran

Christ Church Lutheran, nave, rendering by Eliel Saarinen

Louisiana State University Plan
Baton Rouge, Louisiana
1947, built, modified from original design

In May 1947 Louisiana State University's board of supervisors employed Saarinen, Swanson, and Saarinen to direct its campus planning program, including research and design of its general site plan. The firm completed an interim proposal incorporating traffic, housing, and student enrollment studies, as well as a site plan. The plan proposed a major expansion of the university eastward from its historic core campus, a series of buildings creating a cruciform-shaped open space. While maintaining this original area, the plan added a larger mall defined by new structures that individually incorporated smaller courtyards. Later in 1947, the project went to Swanson Associates, who completed the plan. [LSE]

Christ Church Lutheran
Minneapolis, Minnesota
1947–49, addition 1962
project numbers 5647 (church), 5901 (addition)

Designed by Saarinen and Saarinen, this rectangular steel-frame building occupied a corner site in a residential neighborhood. The long street-facing facade of the tall sanctuary was clad in brick and had a ground-level arcade of glass and stone; its short facade was finished in a slightly recessed wall of rectangular stone panels containing an asymmetrically placed window and a vertical row of four cantilevered sculptures. A narrow glass-fronted passageway connected the sanctuary to a campanile, which marked the building's corner and was surmounted by an asymmetrically placed crucifix. An arcaded courtyard was located on the other side of the sanctuary, which had exposed brick walls—some featuring decorative and sound-absorbing perforations—wooden pews, and uplights; an altar was naturally illuminated by means of a sidelight. Eero Saarinen and Associates designed a brick-clad addition with floor-to-ceiling windows, which was completed in 1962. It housed a Sunday school and lounge on the first level, and a gymnasium, a kitchen, and a library on the basement level. Kraus-Anderson, Inc., was the general contractor. [JO]

See also Olivarez, "Churches and Chapels," in this volume.

"Minneapolis, Christ Church," *Architectural Forum*, July 1950, 80–85
"Église à Minneapolis: Christ Church," *L'Architecture d'Aujourd'hui*, Dec. 1950, 79–83

United States Jefferson National Expansion Memorial

Eero Saarinen House renovation
Bloomfield Hills, Michigan
1947–59

Saarinen remodeled this two-story Victorian house on Vaughn Road, near Cranbrook, twice during the 1950s, converting the two-car garage into a workroom and removing porches. Inside, he renovated the stairway, added built-in furniture, eliminated moldings, and replaced lighting fixtures and appliances. [SK]

"A Modern Architect's Own House," *Vogue*, Apr. 1, 1960, 172–78

United States Jefferson
National Expansion Memorial
St. Louis, Missouri
1947–65

In 1947–48, a local nonprofit corporation sponsored an open national design competition in two stages for the United States Jefferson National Expansion Memorial, to be located on the banks of the Mississippi River in St. Louis. The winning design was to be recommended to the United States Department of the Interior. Saarinen, who entered independently of his father, won the competition. The event brought Eero national renown and launched his career as an independent architect. The main feature of the eighty-acre site he designed was the Gateway Arch. Issues arising from a railway line on the site delayed its realization for a decade. Saarinen oversaw preparations for construction, which did not begin until 1963, two years after his death, and was completed on October 28, 1965. The arch was a weighted, rather than a pure or perfect, catenary, 630 feet tall and 630 feet wide at the base. Constructed of concrete shells clad in stainless

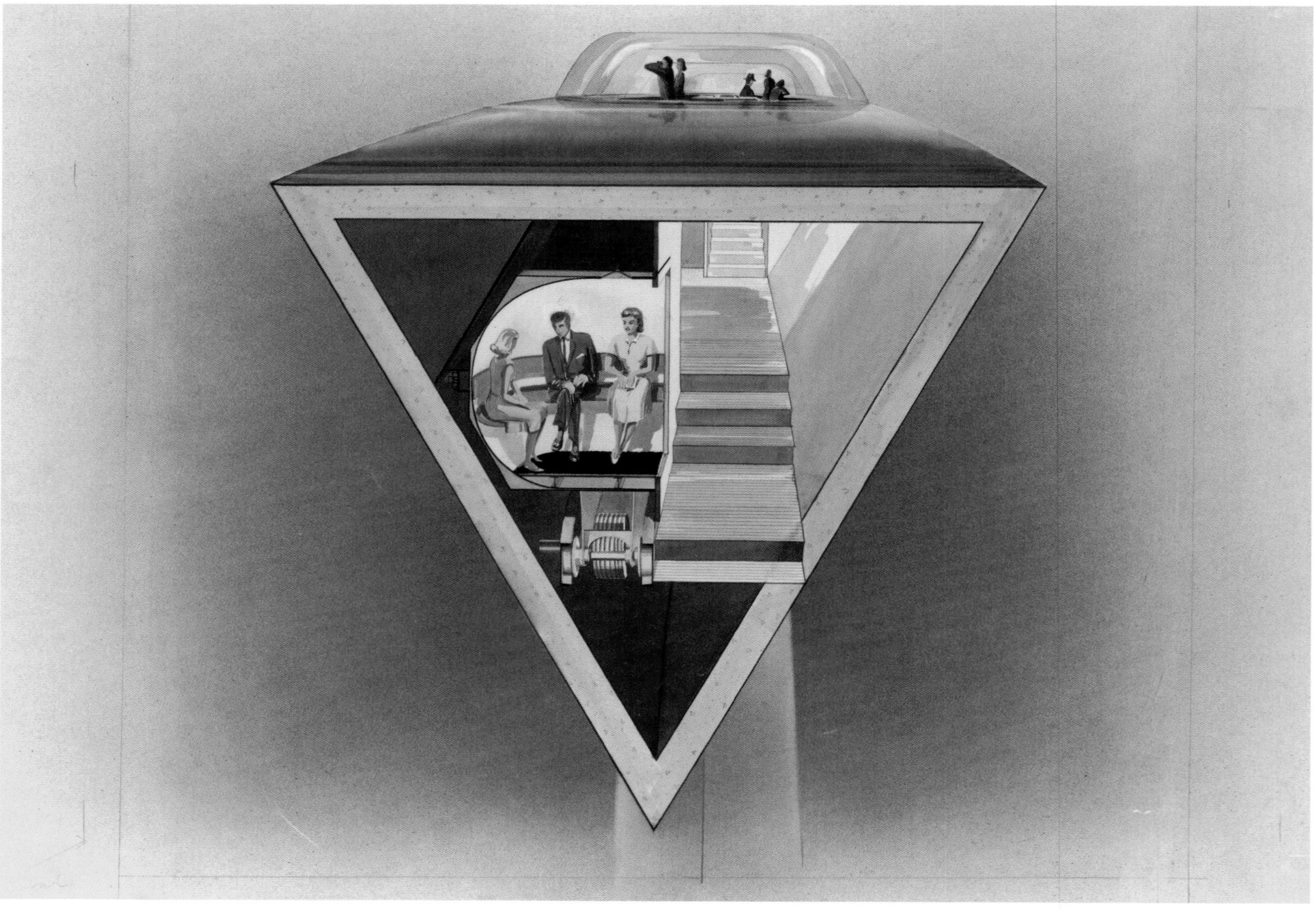

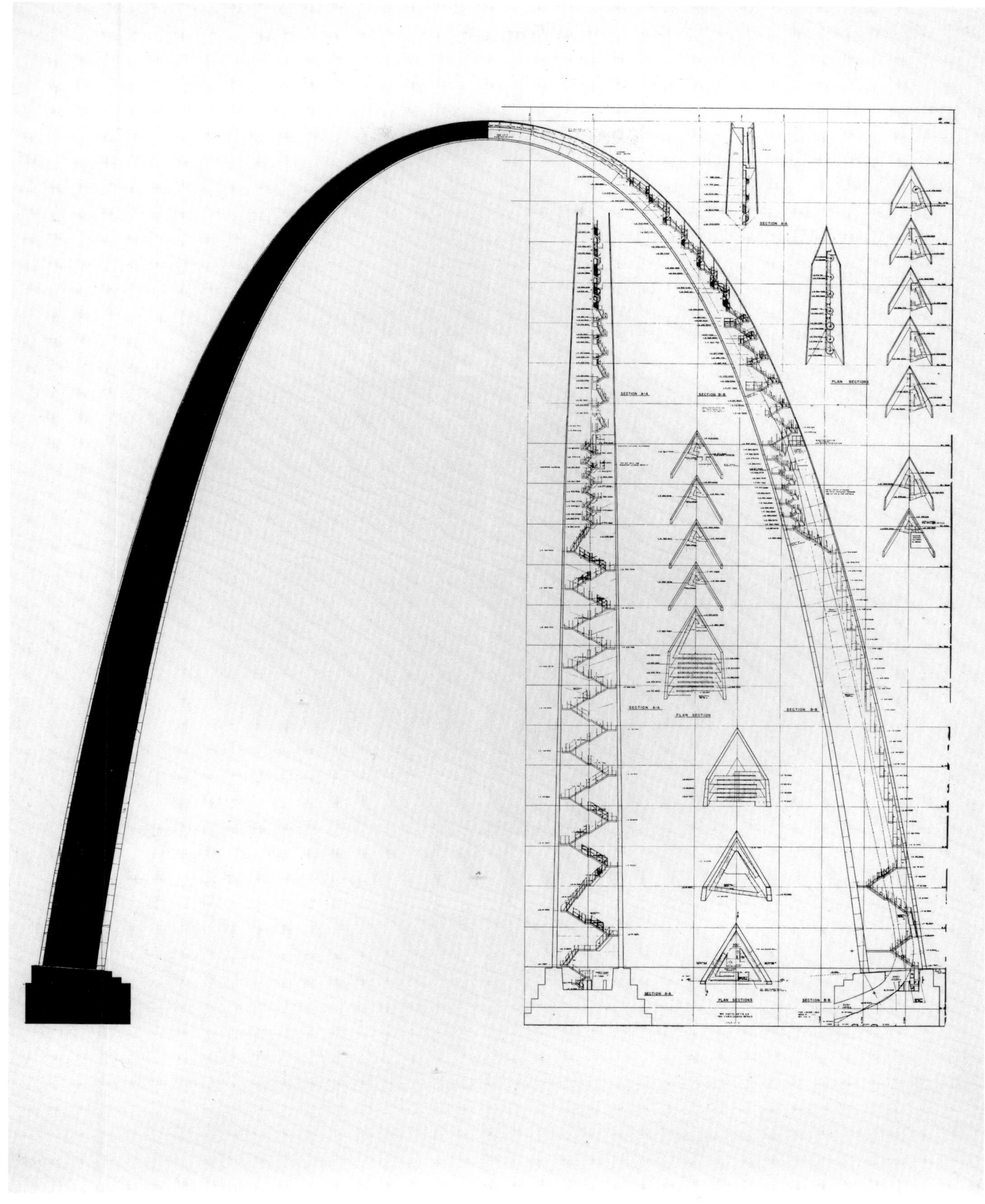

(opposite, top) United States Jefferson National Expansion Memorial, proposed observation platform, rendering

(opposite, bottom) United States Jefferson National Expansion Memorial, passenger transportation system and observation platform, cross-sectional perspective

United States Jefferson National Expansion Memorial, vertical section showing circulation and structure

United States Jefferson National Expansion Memorial, arch under construction scaffolding

steel that formed equilateral triangles in cross-section, each of its legs tapered from 54 feet at the base to 17 feet at the top. The fuselage-shaped Observation Platform held up to 140 people and was reached by two trams specially devised for the structure. Severud, Elstad, Krueger Associates was the structural engineering firm. The landscape was designed by Dan Kiley. [HL]

See also Lipstadt, "The Gateway Arch," in this volume.

Aline B. Louchheim, "For a Modern Monument: An Audacious Design," *New York Times*, Feb. 29, 1948

"Jefferson Memorial Competition," *Architectural Forum*, Mar. 1948, 14–18

"Jefferson Memorial Competition Winners," *Architectural Record*, Apr. 1948, 92–95

"Competition: Jefferson National Expansion Memorial," *Progressive Architecture*, May 1948, 54–59

"Résultats d'un grand cours public aux États-Unis: Jefferson Memorial," *L'Architecture d'Aujourd'hui*, Oct. 1948, ix

Fred N. Severud, "Structural Study: Jefferson Memorial Arch," *Architectural Record*, July 1951, 151–53

"Revised Scheme, Revived Hope, for Saarinen St. Louis Arch," *Architectural Record*, Nov. 1957, 11

J. Jensen, "Steel Arch: Symbol of Spirit of Pioneers," *Civil Engineering*, Oct. 1965, 64–69

"The Gateway Arch—A Comparative View," *St. Louis Post-Dispatch*, Jan. 9, 1966

"The Gateway Arch," *Architectural Forum*, June 1968, 33–37

Leonard Adams, "Saarinen's Gateway Arch," *Inland Architect*, May 1969, 14–21

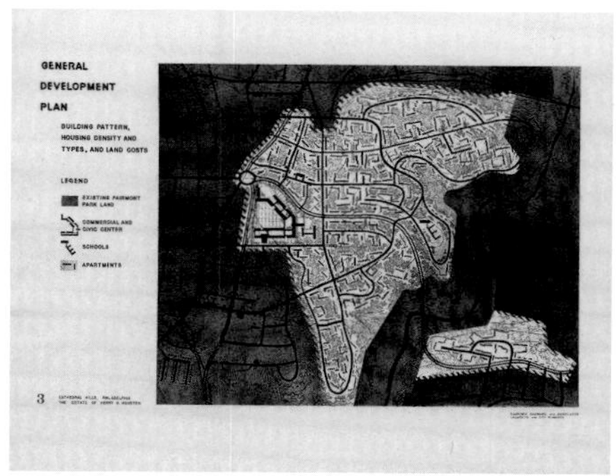

Houston Estate project, development plan

Los Angeles Herald-Express

A VIEW OF THE MAMMOTH 20,000-SEAT AUDITORIUM FOR LOS ANGELES
Shown Are Walkways, Gardens and Traffic Channels With Proposed Veterans' Building in the Background

ENTRANCE TO THE LOS ANGELES OPERA HOUSE FROM WEST LOWER LEVEL
Board of Directors of Greater Los Angeles Plans, Inc., Approves Plans for Two Spectacular Projects

Plan Huge Theatrical Center in Downtown L. A.

HENRY O. DUQUE
Reveals Plans for New L. A. Projects

ANOTHER VIEW OF AUDITORIUM TO BE BUILT IN DOWNTOWN L. A.
In Left Background Is Proposed Veterans' Building; Opera House Will Seat

Los Angeles Auditorium and Opera House project, perspective, as reproduced in the *Los Angeles Herald Express*, June 29, 1948

1948

Houston Estate project
Cathedral Hills, Pennsylvania
1948, unbuilt

project number C-4519

Saarinen, Swanson, and Saarinen created this scheme for a heavily landscaped four-square-mile site on the suburban Philadelphia estate of nineteenth-century industrialist and philanthropist Henry H. Houston, who had developed the nearby suburb of Chestnut Hill. The proposed development for 15,000 people contained garden-type apartment houses, commercial and civic buildings, schools, and a cathedral, all accessed by winding roads. [SK]

Los Angeles Auditorium and Opera House project
1948, unbuilt

The nonprofit organization Greater Los Angeles Plans, Inc., sponsored this project for a new auditorium and opera house, which was presented in the press through renderings produced by a team of eight architects and designers including Henry Dreyfuss, Gordon B. Kaufmann, William Pereira, Eero Saarinen, William Wurster, and Wallace K. Harrison, who also served as the sponsor's chairman of the board of architecture and design. The proposed 20,000-seat glass-enclosed circular auditorium was to be situated downtown, while the 4,500-seat opera house, which had a dramatically ramped entrance, was to be in the Wilshire district. The auditorium was to incorporate an underground railway spur and parking facilities for 5,000 cars. [RF]

"Plans for a Great Auditorium and Opera House Drawn," *Los Angeles Herald Express*, June 29, 1948

Gladwin Hill, "Plans for a Modern Opera Center," *New York Times*, Aug. 15, 1948

UAW-CIO Cooperative
Flint, Michigan
1948, demolished

By the summer of 1948, members of the United Auto Workers had raised $45,000 to build a cooperative warehouse in which to sell staples including groceries, work clothing, hardware, and electrical appliances. After purchasing a small lot and a prefabricated steel building with a bowstring truss roof, they hired Eero Saarinen, who designed, for no fee, a front wall of glass and a freestanding sign made of four tall posts each supporting a disk with letters that spelled out the word "Co-op." According to Saarinen, the facade symbolized the "spirit of cooperation in the world." The warehouse opened in September, but the co-op was unsuccessful and the building was eventually demolished. [LSE]

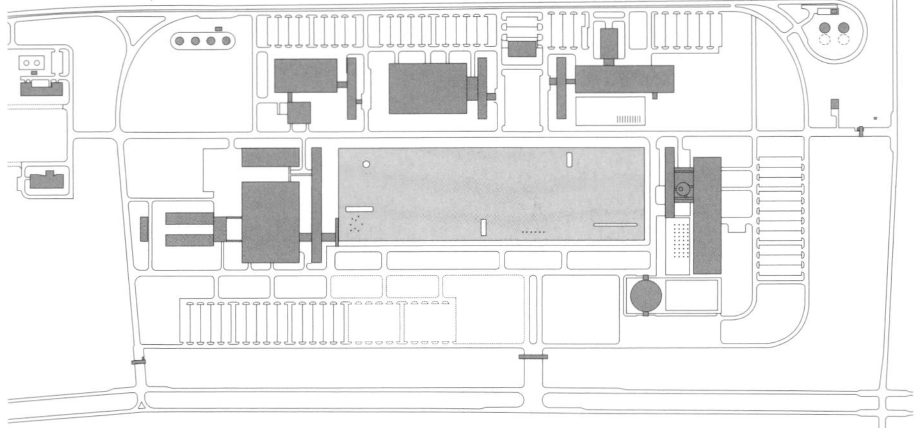

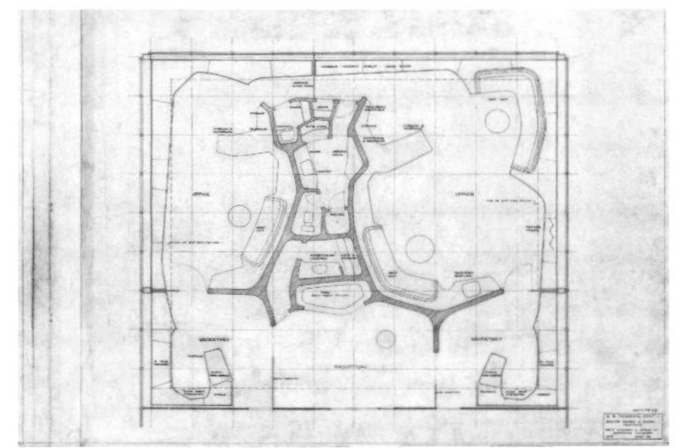

General Motors Technical Center

(opposite) General Motors Technical Center, view from beneath water tower

General Motors Technical Center, site plan, 2006

General Motors Technical Center, office of chief of design Harley Earl, plan

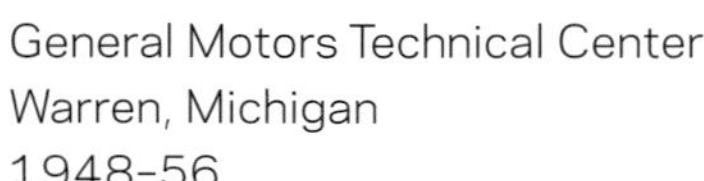

General Motors Technical Center
Warren, Michigan
1948–56

project numbers 4807, 4807 E1, 4807-EB, 4807-EE, 4807-EC, 4807-FC I XI, 4807-FA, 4807-FBX5, 4807-GAX (GA-I-XI, -CB), 5610, 5707, 5710, 6016

This 320-acre industrial research campus outside Detroit contained twenty-five buildings arranged around a rectangular pool. There were five building groups: Engineering, Research, Service, Process Development, and Styling. Each group included a long, narrow three-story structure housing administrative offices, laboratories, and libraries. Although the complex was officially dedicated on May 16, 1956, the groups were constructed and occupied sequentially in the following order: Engineering (construction began in 1949, occupation in 1950); Research (construction began 1950, occupation in stages, 1951–55); Service (construction began 1949, occupation in stages, 1952–54); Process Development (construction began 1953, occupation 1954); and Styling (construction began 1953, occupation 1955).

The buildings were arranged parallel to each other and crosswise in relation to the axis established by the pool. Long north- and south-facing facades of glass and steel contrasted with short east- and west-facing facades of colored glazed brick. Office buildings were flanked by lower, bulkier structures housing research facilities. The buildings were based on a five-foot module (except for the Engineering Building group, where the module was five feet two inches), and many had curtain walls consisting of green-tinted glass and gray enamel panels set in aluminum frames. The three-ply, 2½-inch-thick panels, with insulation sandwiched between layers of porcelain, were developed for this project and were fitted into aluminum frames with a neoprene gasket, similar to the rubber ones used for automobile windshields. The glazed bricks, first tested in a special kiln built by GM and later produced commercially, came in a variety of colors, including yellow, orange, two shades of red, two shades of blue, olive green, gray, and black. Expanses of a single color were by intention not entirely uniform owing to the use of bricks from different kiln lots.

The Styling Building group included a dome 186 feet in diameter and 65 feet high. Three-eighths-inch-thick welded steel plates formed an outer shell that was surfaced in aluminum. Acoustical fill was placed between the dome and an inner, one-eighth-inch shell of perforated metal. Relative to its size, the dome was one-thirteenth the thickness of an eggshell. The enclosed column-free space was used to display cars for research and product-development purposes, as well as serving as a venue for receptions and meetings. The inside of the dome was illuminated with 140 fifty-watt mercury-vapor lamps, 140 thousand-watt incandescent bulbs, and four 3,000-watt cannon spots, all of which could be used to simulate a variety of artificial and natural lighting conditions under which the cars would be seen.

Inside the GM Tech Center's office buildings, ceiling grids, aligned with the buildings' structural grids, could support movable partitions as well as incorporating air-conditioning ducts, sprinkler heads, electrical outlets, and lighting pans. Much of the furniture was

General Motors Technical Center, facade detail

General Motors Technical Center, view of lake, fountain, and Styling Dome

General Motors Technical Center

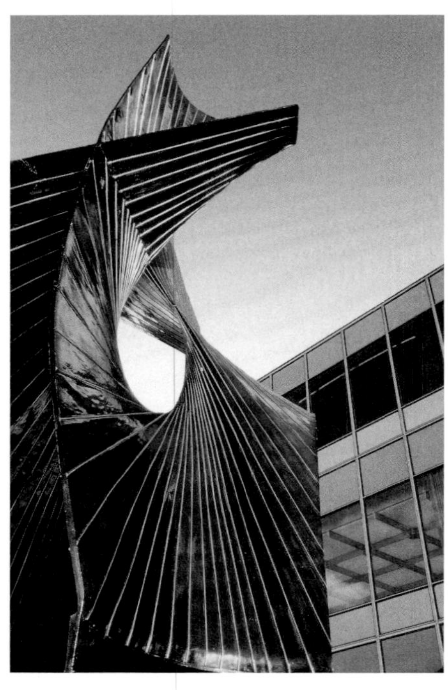

General Motors Technical Center, sculpture by Antoine Pevsner in front of Styling Building

designed by Saarinen, as well as by Florence Knoll and Ludwig Mies van der Rohe, and several interiors contained carpeting designed and woven by Marianne Strengell. The restaurant featured a thirty-six-foot-long screen of bronze and gold openwork designed by Harry Bertoia. In three of the structures, staircases were emphasized as principal architectural features. The main Service Building staircase was composed of metal pans containing travertine treads and supported by a continuous steel spine painted white. In the Research Building, two intersecting cones of stainless-steel tension rods supported the green Norwegian granite treads of a spiral staircase. (Charles Sheeler's oil painting *GM,* an interpretation of the staircase, hung nearby in the lobby.) The circular shape of the staircase functioned as a compression ring providing lateral stability. In the Styling Building lobby, treads of white terrazzo were suspended between rows of vertical stainless-steel rods that rose from a travertine-lined reflecting pool.

The site was ornamented with 13,000 trees and three reflecting pools. The principal pool measured 1,780 by 560 feet (about 22 acres) and contained four islands planted with willow trees, as well as a spherical stainless-steel water tower 132 feet high and a "water wall" 50 feet high and 115 feet wide. Alexander Calder designed additional fountains. Antoine Pevsner's bronze sculpture *Bird in Flight* was placed in front of the Styling Building.

Saarinen worked with a team that included Smith, Hinchman, and Grylls, architects and engineers; Paul S. Calkins, structural engineer; Bolt, Beranek, and Newman, acoustic consultants; Richard Kelly, exterior lighting consultant; Bryant and Detwiler, general contractor; and Thomas D. Church and Edward A. Eichstedt, landscape architects. [TM]

See also Albrecht, "The Clients and Their Architect"; Fletcher, "The General Motors Technical Center"; and Isenstadt, "Eero Saarinen's Theater of Form," in this volume.

"GM Technical Center," *Architectural Forum,* Nov. 1951, 111–23

"Centre Technique de la General Motors, Warren, Mich.," *L'Architecture d'Aujourd'hui,* Dec. 1953, 49–55

John McAndrew, "First Look at the General Motors Technical Center," *Art in America,* spring 1956, 26–33

"Architecture for the Future: GM Constructs a Versailles for Industry," *Life,* May 21, 1956, 102–7

"GM's Industrial Versailles," *Architectural Forum,* May 1956, 122–29

"Tour of the GM Technical Center Interiors," *Architectural Record,* May 1956, 151–58

"Centre Technique de la General Motors, Warren, Mich.," *L'Architecture d'Aujourd'hui,* Dec. 1956, 88–95

"General Motors Technical Center bei Detroit, USA," *Werk,* Feb. 1957, 58–64

"Municipal Machine Aesthetic," *Architectural Review,* Mar. 1957, 151

Ian McCallum, "All-in-One-Wall," *Architectural Review,* May 1957, 316

Charles Eames, "General Motors Revisited," *Architectural Forum,* June 1971, 21–28

Aspen Music Center

Aspen Music Center, interior with seating

1949

Aspen Music Center
Aspen, Colorado
1949, demolished 1963
project number 4901

The Goethe Bicentennial Convocation and Music Festival hired the firm of Saarinen and Saarinen, but Eero was largely responsible for the design of the Aspen Music Center, a fireproof canvas tent 147 feet long on its four sides and 45 feet high. The 2,000-person seating area was set into an eight-foot-deep depression dug out of a sloping site surrounded by mountains and formerly used as a cow pasture. The excavated earth was used to create a four-foot-high berm around the tent's perimeter, which muted sounds from the outside. The tent's white canvas top, supported by naturally finished wooden poles, contrasted with the tangerine-colored side walls. To balance the canvas's sound-absorbing tendencies, a freestanding accordion-pleated plywood wall bordered the rear of the triangular stage, which could accommodate a full symphony orchestra, and pipe scaffolding supported a multifaceted plywood canopy. The tent's four principal masts extended outside and supported light fixtures; at night, light penetrating the canvas from above provided soft illumination inside and made the tent highly visible from a distance. Constructed at a modest cost of $15,000, the tent was connected by a covered walkway to a 23-by-100-foot wood-frame building housing dressing rooms and a storage area, where the disassembled tent could be stored in the off-season. Smith, Hegner, and Moore were the project's associate architects; Bolt and Beranek, acoustical consultants; Stanley McCandless, lighting consultant; Herbert Bayer, color consultant; and Maurice Hoopingarner, general contractor. U.S. Tent and Awning Company manufactured the tent. [TM]

"Goethe in Colorado," *Newsweek*, July 11, 1949, 65

"Music Tent for Goethe Bicentennial Convocation and Music Festival at Aspen, Colorado," *Architectural Forum*, Sept. 1949, 88–89

"Tent to House a Summer Music Festival, Aspen, Colorado," *Arts and Architecture*, Oct. 1950, 32–33

Brandeis University, student union, interior perspective by Matthew Nowicki

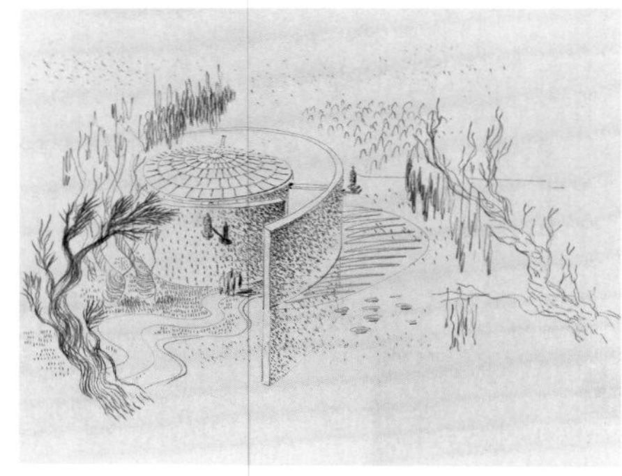

Brandeis University, chapel scheme, perspective by Matthew Nowicki

Brandeis University, chapel scheme, rendering by Matthew Nowicki

Brandeis University
Waltham, Massachusetts
1949–52

Master Plan, 1949–52
project number 5101
Ridgewood Quadrangle Dormitories, 1949–50; renovated 1979
project number 4912
Hamilton Quadrangle Dormitory and Student Center, later Shapiro Hall and Sherman Student Center, 1949–52; Sherman Student Center, expanded 1968 and renovated 1979
project number 5103

Shortly after Brandeis opened its doors in 1948 as the nation's first Jewish-sponsored, nonsectarian university, its president, Abram Sachar, and board of trustees selected Eero Saarinen and Associates to devise a master plan for a ninety-acre campus of rolling hills and wetlands outside Boston. Expected to be realized over ten years, the plan, developed by Saarinen and Matthew Nowicki, who had just joined the Cranbrook faculty, called for the demolition of approximately ten existing buildings on the site, saving only a castlelike structure that had formerly housed Middlesex Medical College. A central open area was to be bordered on two sides by low rectangular buildings housing academic departments, and on a third side by a student center and library. A proposed arts center was distinguished by a dome enclosing an auditorium. Three groupings of dormitories were to be reached by means of a looping peripheral road. The university's program also called for a gymnasium and a nonsectarian chapel. As drawn by Nowicki, the chapel initially took the form of a cylindrical brick building with undulating walls; in one iteration, access to the sanctuary was through a subterranean passageway. Saarinen and Nowicki subsequently altered the scheme, placing the sanctuary in a Y-shaped structure with curving convex walls, although they later returned to the original concept.

The university officially adopted Saarinen and Nowicki's plan, but Saarinen completed only seven structures: the five-building Ridgewood Quadrangle and two buildings in the Hamilton Quadrangle. (Nowicki died in a plane crash in 1950.) The Ridgewood Quadrangle, a residential complex initially intended to house faculty and married students, was located on the periphery of the campus. It consisted of two-story brick-and-concrete volumes with floor-to-ceiling windows, some of which were equipped with brise-soleils. Archie Riskin, a Boston-area architect, produced the working drawings, supervised construction, and was responsible for the selection of the building materials. The quadrangle was rushed to completion in 1950 to meet the demand for undergraduate student housing. A Boston-area firm, Richmond

Yale University, Physics Building, perspective

Yale University Master Plan, perspective

and Goldberg, served as associate architects; Hubbard, Lawless, and Blakely were the consulting engineers. Saarinen's other buildings for Brandeis were the Sherman Student Center and Shapiro Hall, both part of Hamilton Quadrangle. The student center was a rectangular two-story structure built into a hill with a prominent exterior staircase along one of its short, brick-clad walls. In contrast to these opaque facades, one of the long elevations, which faced a pond, featured a curtain wall of glass panels set into metal frames. The principal facade of the four-story Shapiro Hall was clad in alternating vertical bands of brick and glass. Both buildings were designed in collaboration with Richmond and Goldberg, though Riskin completed them. Hyde and Bobbio were the mechanical and electrical engineers, and Paul S. Calkins the structural engineer. [TM]

"Saarinen Campus for Brandeis," *Interiors,* May 1951, 8

"Education: College Buildings," *Progressive Architecture,* Jan. 1951, 74

Yale University Master Plan and Physics Building
New Haven, Connecticut
1949–53, unbuilt

project number 4903

Yale president A. Whitney Griswold asked Eero Saarinen to assist the university in expanding its campus. Saarinen and his associate, Douglas Orr, worked on three areas: a sloping site (now called Science Hill) to the northeast of the main campus, Hewitt Quadrangle, and Cross Campus. For Cross Campus, they proposed a freestanding administrative tower, on axis with the main entrance of the Sterling Memorial Library. The tower, with a square footprint, was to be placed on a plaza enclosed by four new low-rise buildings flanked by existing structures. Six buildings were to be demolished to make way for this group, which nonetheless retained the street walls that were characteristic of the Yale campus. For Hewitt Quadrangle, Saarinen proposed a rectangular, seven-story, flat-roofed administrative building opposite Woodbridge Hall, which housed the offices of the university president. The new structure would have been raised on columns, with glazed long facades and solid short elevations.

The Physics Building, proposed for a site atop Science Hill, was the most developed of the three master-plan projects, calling for a six-story flat-roofed slab structure with glazed long facades. The building was positioned with its short, windowless elevation on axis with Hillhouse Avenue, which led north from the main campus. The building was to sit on a plaza bounded by a two-story wing built into the hill. In one iteration this wing had a curving wall, behind which was an auditorium, while in another scheme it was rectangular. [DA]

See also Plattus, "Campus Plans," in this volume.

"Proposed Physics Building for Yale University," *Architectural Record,* Sept. 1953, 141–47

Loja Saarinen House, rear elevation

Miller Cottage, aerial view

1950

Loja Saarinen House (Guest House for Mr. Eero Saarinen) Bloomfield Hills, Michigan 1950

project number 5005

Saarinen designed this guesthouse, where his mother lived after her husband's death in 1950, next to his own house on Vaughn Road. The house's rectangular plan was symmetrical and divided into three zones: an open-plan living and dining room flanked by two wings, one containing two bedrooms and a bathroom, the other the kitchen and a bathroom. On the nearly identical long facades, the living and dining area was enclosed by floor-to-ceiling glass walls, while the wings had opaque walls. The house's glass side walls opened onto patios. [DA]

Miller Cottage (Miller House) Muskoka District, Ontario, Canada 1950–52

project number 5004

Saarinen designed this lakefront summer cottage, on a long rocky peninsula, for the family of J. Irwin and Xenia Miller. Two one-story units were separated by a stone-paved terrace that was partially roofed by the house's second-floor volume. The ground floor of one unit contained a two-level open-plan living room, with a built-in sofa and freestanding fireplace, and a master bedroom suite. The ground floor of the second unit housed a dining room and a kitchen with an eat-in area. The second floor contained five bedrooms and two bathrooms. The uninsulated house featured interior and exterior walls of wood and stone. [DA]

See also Miller, "Eero and Irwin," in this volume.

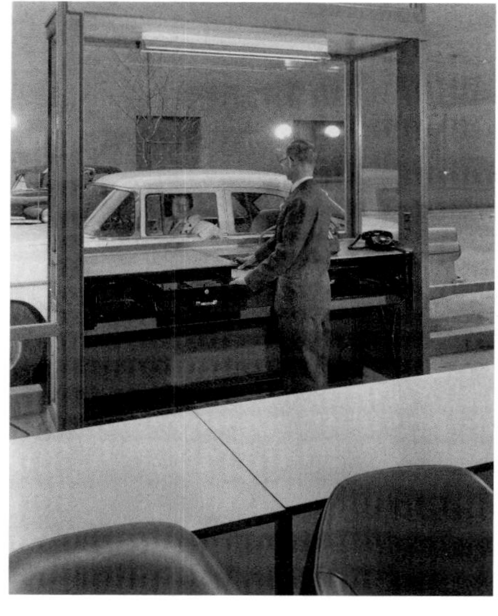

Irwin Union Trust Company, drive-through teller window

Irwin Union Trust Company, perspective rendering by Chuck Bassett

Irwin Union Trust Company
Columbus, Indiana
1950-54

project numbers 5001, 6012, 6606, 8201

This building was the first of three in Columbus designed by Eero Saarinen for the J. Irwin Miller family. The one-story square glass pavilion (with a basement) was set back from its property line on three sides, with the fourth side bordering a tree-shaded parking lot and a driveway featuring an early example of a drive-through banking window. In front of the building's entrance facade on the town's main commercial thoroughfare, Washington Street, a row of sycamore trees helped maintain the street wall. In the back of the building, two glass passageways connected to the brick-clad structure next door, where the bank maintained office space. The bank's flat roof overhung its glass walls by four feet six inches and featured a grid of nine thin-shell concrete domes that motivated some observers to dub the bank "the brassiere factory." Inside the eleven-and-a-half-foot-high main banking hall, the textured acoustic-plaster surfaces of the domes, illuminated by custom-designed hemispherical uplights, contrasted with the smooth plaster ceiling punctuated by a grid of recessed downlights. Every desk was equipped with chairs designed by Saarinen. Cash and safe-deposit vaults were placed in the basement, accessible by means of a staircase with treads suspended between steel rods. Saarinen developed the bank's design after a trip to the Great Mosque in Cordoba, Spain, which, along with San Marco in Venice, he later cited as a design source. Severud, Elstad, Krueger Associates were structural engineers on the project; Hyde and Bobbio, the mechanical and electrical engineers; Bolt, Beranek, and Newman, the acoustical consultants; Stanley McCandless, the lighting consultant; and Dan Kiley, the landscape architect. [TM]

See also Miller, "Eero and Irwin," in this volume.

"Bank Rooms for an Existing Institution," *Progressive Architecture,* Sept. 1954, 12

"Columbus, Indiana: A Study in Small Town Progress," *Architectural Forum,* Oct. 1955, 158-66

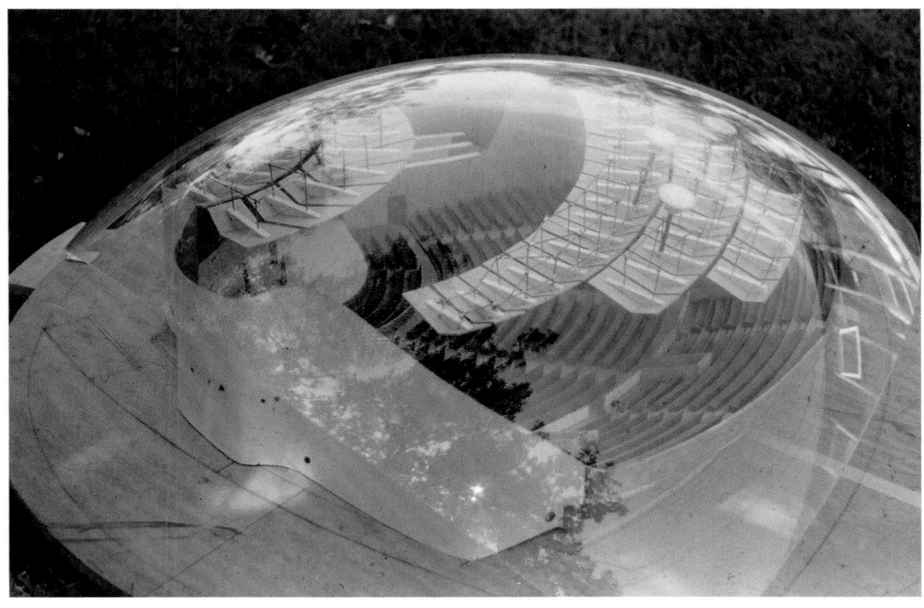

Kresge Auditorium, model

(opposite) Kresge Chapel, interior

Massachusetts Institute of Technology, site model with rectangular chapel

(below) Kresge Auditorium, section, 2006

(overleaf) View of Kresge Chapel from Kresge Auditorium

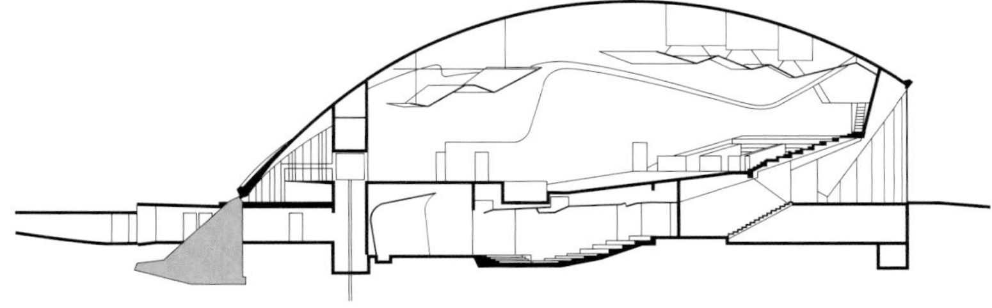

MIT
Cambridge, Massachusetts
1950–55

Kresge Auditorium (MIT Auditorium), 1950–55
project number 5007
Kresge Chapel (MIT Chapel), 1950–55
project number 5303
Student Union project, 1953, unbuilt

The architect William Wurster, dean of the Massachusetts Institute of Technology's School of Architecture and Planning, invited Eero Saarinen and Associates to design an auditorium, a nondenominational chapel, a student union, and a plaza connecting the three buildings on a flat site across Massachusetts Avenue from the institute's domed classical building complex (1912–38) by William Welles Bosworth.

The Kresge Auditorium, designed with Anderson and Beckwith (Lawrence B. Anderson and Herbert L. Beckwith were professors at MIT), was the nation's first large-scale concrete-shell building. The structure constituted one-eighth of a sphere, configured triangularly and placed on a red-brick podium. It was supported on three bases largely concealed below grade and placed approximately 160 feet apart from each other. The resulting arc-shaped spaces between the roof and the ground were filled in with glass walls. The interior space was a sweeping half acre, fifty feet high at the center. An eighteen-inch raised edge outlining the roof stabilized the structure while serving as a gutter directing water to drains at the footings. The concrete shell, eighteen inches thick at its base and three and a half inches at its apex, was poured in three installments, beginning at the footings and progressing toward the top. Upon completion, the dome deflected more than anticipated; to compensate for this effect, some of the curtain walls' metal mullions were widened to be load-bearing. To provide sound insulation and weatherproofing, the dome was covered with an eight-inch-thick surface consisting of felt, glass wool, cinder concrete, asphalt, and an acrylic mixture containing sand and fiberglass. The surface was applied hastily under poor weather conditions and subsequently had to be reapplied. Inside, the raked seating of the column-free oak-paneled main auditorium accommodated 1,238 people. The seating area, which took the shape of a concave shell, mirrored the enclosure above and was visible through the building's glass facades. The auditorium's curved ceiling presented acoustical problems; Saarinen, wanting the ceiling to remain exposed, worked with the acoustical engineers Bolt, Beranek, and Newman to design sound-enhancing white-painted panels that were suspended from above. The panels also contained ventilating shafts and lighting. Below grade, another theater seated 200. Two air-conditioning units did double duty, serving as ice makers for an outdoor skating rink in winter.

Saarinen's other completed building for MIT, the 128-seat Kresge Chapel, was a windowless flat-roofed cylinder fifty feet in diameter, clad in rough-surfaced brick and supported on brick arches springing from a twelve-foot-wide water-filled moat. (The final design

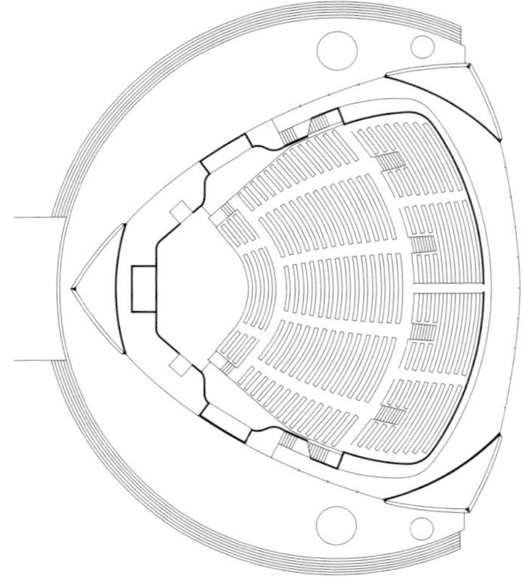

Kresge Auditorium, plan, 2006

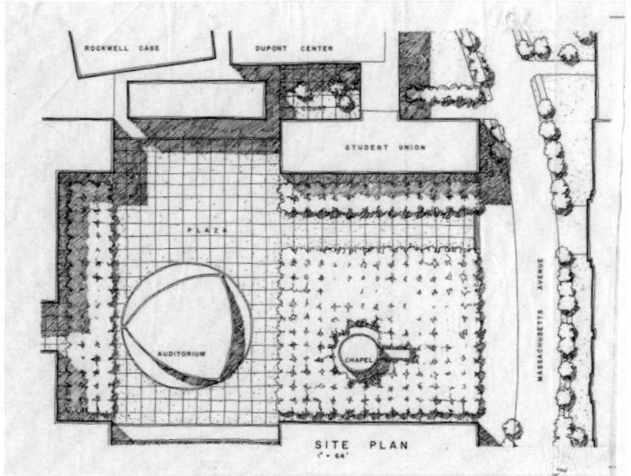

Massachusetts Institute of Technology, student union, perspective

Massachusetts Institute of Technology, site plan with student union

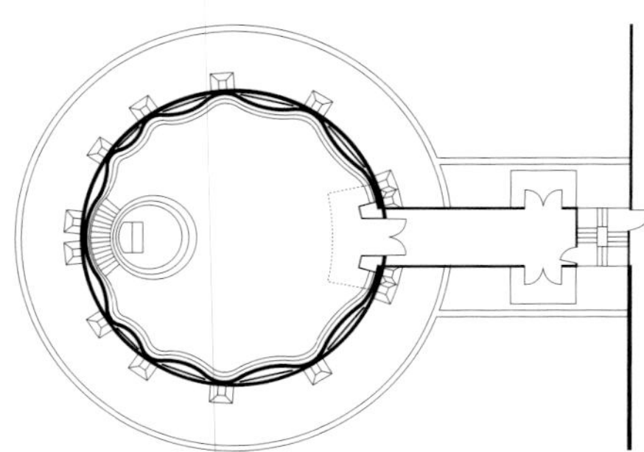

Kresge Chapel, plan, 2006

was a radical departure from an earlier proposal—a flat-roofed rectangular pavilion enclosed in glass.) A glazed rectangular passage bridging the moat formed the entrance to the chapel. Sculptor Theodore Roszak's spire incorporating a bell stood on the chapel's flat roof. Inside, a second undulating brick wall fit within the exterior shell and was separated from a low spandrel wall by a horizontal glass infill panel. Natural light reflected in the water of the moat softly illuminated the chapel's undulating walls. Light also entered the chapel through an oculus directly above a white stone altar raised on a circular dais, producing ever-changing patterns on a curved screen designed by Harry Bertoia. This sculptural element was composed of many small metal rectangles attached to wires stretched between the floor and ceiling. Like the auditorium, the chapel was designed with Anderson and Beckwith. Bruce Adams of the Saarinen office was a principal collaborator on the project.

A third building Saarinen designed for MIT—a student union—was not realized. This long narrow five-story structure was to have facades composed of exposed columns, vertical bands of windows, and stone panels. Sited perpendicular to Massachusetts Avenue, it would have created a wall at the edge of an open plaza on which stood the auditorium and chapel, functioning as an orthogonal foil to their sculptural forms. It was also positioned to reinforce an axis terminating in Bosworth's temple-fronted building complex. The plaza was intended to be surfaced in triangles of grass and paving and to serve as the roof of a below-grade parking garage. The plaza and garage were rejected in favor of a lawn. [TM]

See also Olivarez, "Churches and Chapels," and Pelkonen, "The Search for (Communicative) Form," in this volume.

"Challenge to the Rectangle: MIT Campus Center with Auditorium and Chapel," *Time*, June 29, 1953, 64

"Auditorium, Cambridge, Massachusetts," *Progressive Architecture*, June 1954, 120–25, 130–31

"Auditorium du MIT, Cambridge," *L'Architecture d'Aujourd'hui*, Mar. 1956, 50–53

N. K. Scott, "Eero Saarinen's New Auditorium for MIT," *Journal of the Royal Institute of British Architects* 62 (Feb. 1955), 168–69

"Old Hand at Odd Shapes," *Life*, Mar. 14, 1955, 82

E. Weeks, "Opal on the Charles: MIT Auditorium," *Architectural Record*, July 1955, 131–37

"La Cappella e l'Auditorium de M.I.T.," *Casabella*, Nov.–Dec. 1955, 16–29

"Puddled Spire: Chapel for MIT," *Time*, Dec. 5, 1955, 88

"Buildings in the Round: MIT's Cylindrical Chapel and a Domed Auditorium," *Architectural Forum*, Jan. 1956, 116–21

"MIT's Kresge Chapel," *Architectural Record*, Jan. 1956, 154–57

"New Chapel at MIT," *Progressive Architecture*, Jan. 1956, 65–67

"Three Critics Discuss MIT's New Buildings," *Architectural Forum*, Mar. 1956, 157

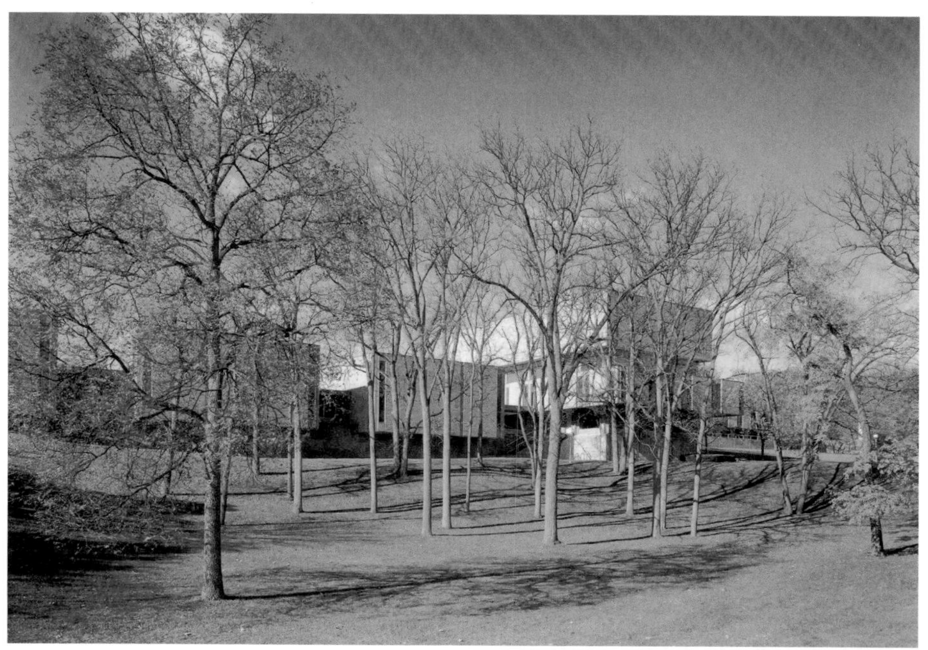

University of Michigan, School of Music

1951

University of Michigan
Ann Arbor, Michigan
1951–56

North Campus Development, 1951–56
project number 5105-N
Engineering Lab Group, 1951, 1955
project numbers 5105-F, 5506
School of Music, 1952–56
project number 5205
Dexter Housing Development, 1953, unbuilt
project number 5301
Continuation Center, 1953, unbuilt
project number 5301
Fletch Park Extension, 1953, unbuilt
project number 5309
Cooley Memorial, 1953, unbuilt
project number 5311
Undergraduate Library, 1954, unbuilt
project number 5404
Phoenix Building, 1954, unbuilt
project number 5405
Central Service Stack Building, 1954, unbuilt
project number 5406
Aeronautical Engineering Building, 1954, unbuilt
project number 5409
Printing Building, 1954, unbuilt
project number 5412
Highway project, 1954, unbuilt
project number 5505
Children's Hospital, 1955, unbuilt

The University of Michigan hired Saarinen to serve as design consultant for a new satellite campus occupying a hilly 376-acre farmland site a mile north of its historic campus in Ann Arbor. Eero Saarinen and Associates proposed a series of loosely linked courtyards located on different levels and surrounding an approximately 15-acre centrally situated court known as "the forum," which would be bordered by four buildings, including a library and student union. The square court would contain five levels progressively stepping down to a decorative pool and fountain. Saarinen hoped that the new campus would be relatively self-sufficient, featuring entire colleges complete with student housing, so that only professors would need to commute and there would always be a lively pedestrian presence. As built, the North Campus contained a wide variety of

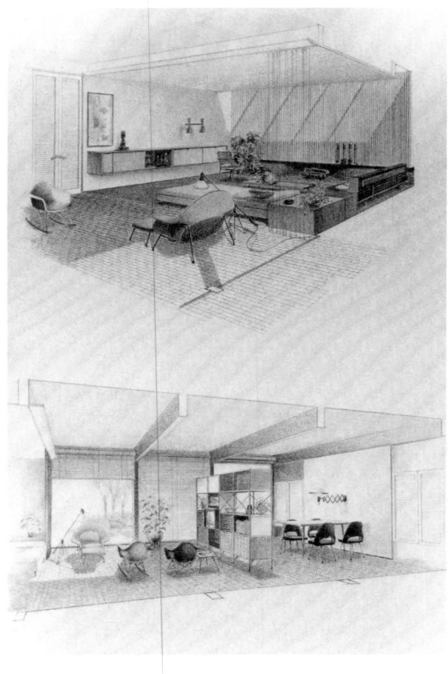

Chicago Tribune Sixth Annual Better Rooms competition, living room

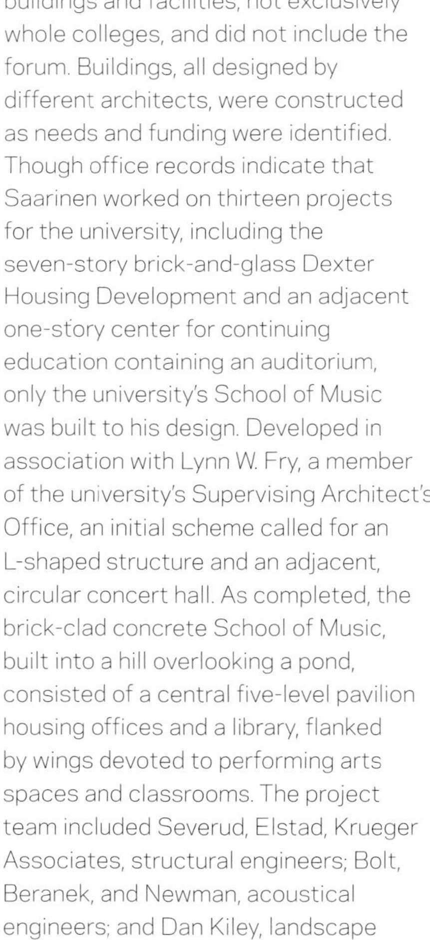

buildings and facilities, not exclusively whole colleges, and did not include the forum. Buildings, all designed by different architects, were constructed as needs and funding were identified. Though office records indicate that Saarinen worked on thirteen projects for the university, including the seven-story brick-and-glass Dexter Housing Development and an adjacent one-story center for continuing education containing an auditorium, only the university's School of Music was built to his design. Developed in association with Lynn W. Fry, a member of the university's Supervising Architect's Office, an initial scheme called for an L-shaped structure and an adjacent, circular concert hall. As completed, the brick-clad concrete School of Music, built into a hill overlooking a pond, consisted of a central five-level pavilion housing offices and a library, flanked by wings devoted to performing arts spaces and classrooms. The project team included Severud, Elstad, Krueger Associates, structural engineers; Bolt, Beranek, and Newman, acoustical engineers; and Dan Kiley, landscape

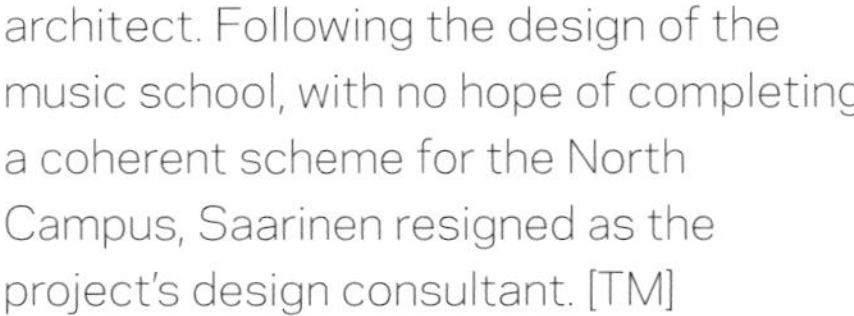

architect. Following the design of the music school, with no hope of completing a coherent scheme for the North Campus, Saarinen resigned as the project's design consultant. [TM]

"At the University of Michigan, An Answer to Expansion: Don't Expand the Old Campus; Add Another One," *Architectural Forum*, June 1953, 118–22

"Proposed School of Music, University of Michigan," *Architectural Record*, Jan. 1955, 134–35

1952

Chicago Tribune Sixth Annual Better Rooms competition
1952, unbuilt

Saarinen's entry in this newspaper-sponsored competition proposed an open-plan house with exposed beams and floor-to-ceiling glass walls overlooking a wooded site. Saarinen used curtains and the 1950 Eames Storage Unit, designed by Charles and Ray Eames, as spatial dividers. Chairs by Saarinen and the Eameses were to furnish the house. [DA]

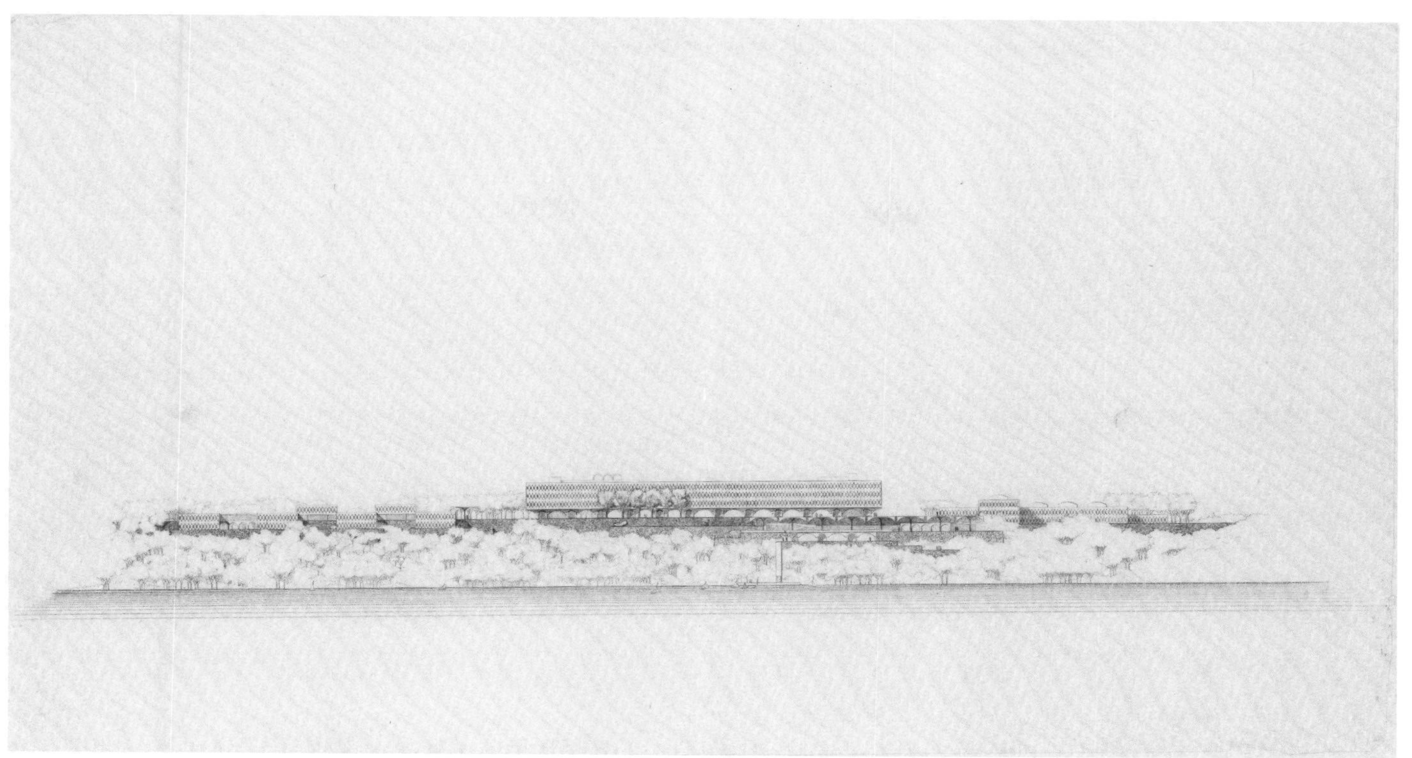

Time Inc. Headquarters project, rendered elevation

Time Inc. Headquarters project
Rye, New York
1952, 1954, unbuilt

Following the publication of the first phase of the General Motors Technical Center, Time Inc. editor-in-chief Henry Luce hired Eero Saarinen and Associates to design a suburban headquarters, with editorial offices for each of the company's magazines, on a fifty-five-acre site in Rye, an affluent suburb of New York City. Saarinen based his plan on the organizational structure of the company, creating a campuslike arrangement. In one scheme, four low concrete buildings were placed in an L across a bluff, with a reflecting pool in the crux of the L. The executive offices were the centerpiece, lofted on an open, arched base. In another scheme, four low pinwheel-shaped buildings were joined by a centrally located square volume and separated from each other by four square courtyards with central reflecting pools surrounding by trees. Two years later, Saarinen, in collaboration with the architect Paul Rudolph, created a third scheme, possibly for a site in Pennsylvania, that retained a campus arrangement of different buildings devoted to the company's various magazines, while shaping these structures into staggered rows of rectangular modules each measuring 54 feet by 81 feet. Luce's employees refused to leave the city, and Time Inc. instead built a skyscraper, designed by Harrison and Abramovitz, on Sixth Avenue in 1959. [AL]

See also Lange, "Corporate Headquarters," in this volume.

American Embassy addition project
Helsinki, Finland
1952–53, unbuilt
project number 5208

Saarinen developed two schemes for an addition to the existing neo-Georgian American Embassy in Helsinki, which was designed by Harrie T. Lindeberg in 1938 and located in Kaivopuisto, a residential neighborhood with views of the city's harbor and the Gulf of Finland. His first scheme called for a five-story freestanding tower with cantilevered floors set at an oblique angle to the existing building. In his second proposal, a three-story structure was to be placed at the same angle as the existing embassy and clad in the same white marble as the embassy's entrance. Saarinen's addition was not built because of personnel changes in the U.S. State Department's Office of Foreign Buildings Operations. [DA]

See also Tuomi, "Embassies and Chancelleries," in this volume.

"U.S. Architecture Abroad: Modern Design at Its Best Now Represents This Country in Foreign Lands," *Architectural Forum*, Mar. 1953, 101–15

Milwaukee War Memorial

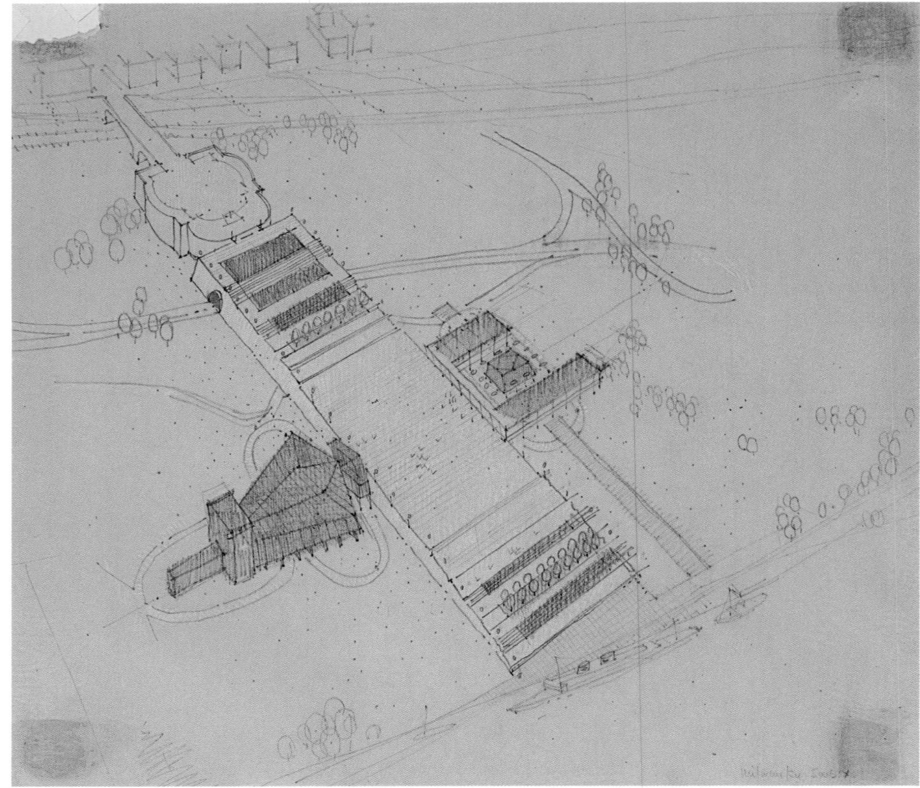

Milwaukee War Memorial Center, site plan, aerial perspective rendering by Robert Venturi

Milwaukee War Memorial
Milwaukee, Wisconsin
1952–57; see 1946 for previous scheme
project number 5203

This cruciform-shaped reinforced concrete building contained an art gallery, community meeting rooms, and a memorial to the city's war dead, which by 1952 included those who had served in the Korean War. The previously proposed downtown site had been rejected, and the completed structure was built into a forty-foot-high bluff in Juneau Park that rose from the shoreline of Lake Michigan to the city's streets above. An ashlar-stone-clad base terminated at street level, where a bridge led to the structure's glazed lobby, through which a courtyard and the lake beyond could be seen. In the courtyard, which contained two freestanding staircases, a reflecting pool was bordered by granite coping inscribed with the names of the war dead. Concrete wedges framed the courtyard and supported wings cantilevered 29½ feet to the north, south, and east. To express visually the cantilevered structure of these wings, Saarinen designed their facades as grids of concrete fins, two units high by three units long, and infilled with deeply recessed glass walls. The west-facing wing was supported on columns and functioned as a canopy over the main entrance. Shortly after the building's completion, a mosaic mural by Edwin Lewandowski depicting in Roman numerals the first and last years of World War II and the Korean War was installed on the upper level of this facade.

The cantilevered wings were constructed of lightweight concrete, then a relatively new building material. The north and south wings counterbalanced each other and created a tensile force that was taken up by reinforcing rods extending across the top of the structure. At the base of each wing, to counteract the tendency of tensile forces to push inward, a series of parallel walls, known as diaphragm walls, punctuated the interior space between the volumes' outer facades and the courtyard. The roof and floor slabs functioned as beams maintaining the walls' verticality. Saarinen worked with a team including Ammann and Whitney, structural engineers; Maynard W. Meyer and Associates, associate architects; Samuel R. Lewis and Associates, consulting engineers; and Richard Klees and Associates, electrical engineers. The James McHugh Construction Company served as general contractor. [TM]

"Museum with a View," *Time*, Nov. 4, 1957, 82

"Milwaukee's Living Memorial: War Memorial Building," *Architectural Forum*, Dec. 1957, 90–95, 144

"Mémorial de Milwaukee, Wisconsin, États-Unis," *L'Architecture d'Aujourd'hui*, Sept. 1959, 26–29

Eero Saarinen and Associates Office, rendered elevation by Glen Paulsen

Eero Saarinen and Associates Office

1953

Eero Saarinen and Associates Office
Bloomfield Hills, Michigan
1953

Built into a hill near a major intersection just a few blocks from Cranbrook, this two-story rectangular flat-roofed structure, approximately fifty feet long and thirty feet wide, was sited behind a parking lot on Long Lake Road. The building faced the street with a one-story entrance facade incorporating clerestory basement windows. The rear facade, which revealed the building's full two-story height, overlooked a wooded area. Both of these facades were grids of awnings and fixed windows set in wood frames with plywood spandrels; the short end walls were solid buff brick. The upper level contained a reception area, two private offices, and an open drafting room; on the lower level were another drafting room, a model shop, a printing room, a sample room, and lavatories. Fluorescent light fixtures were placed so that exposed twelve-inch-deep wood ceiling beams served as partial baffles, preventing excessive glare. Alex Gow served as the general contractor for the project, which cost only $12 per square foot. [TM]

"Saarinen Architecture for Saarinen: Office in Bloomfield Hills," *Architectural Forum*, June 1953, 142–45

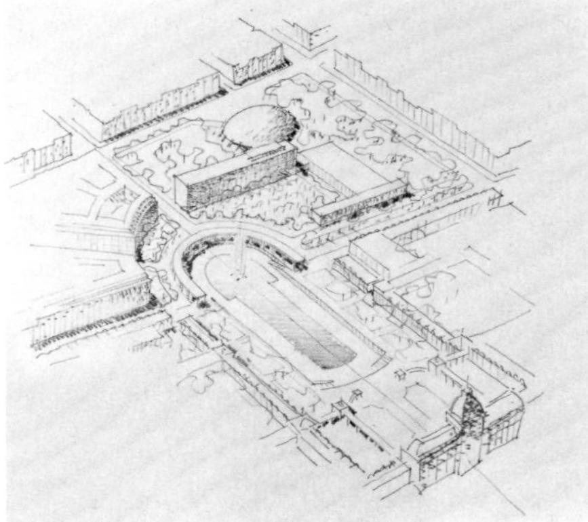

UNESCO competition, perspective study

Stephens College Chapel

(opposite) Stephens College Chapel, ambulatory with view into central space

UNESCO competition
Paris, France
1953, unbuilt

UNESCO, the United Nations Educational, Scientific, and Cultural Organization, founded in 1945, held an international competition in fall 1952 to select a design for its first purpose-built headquarters. The five-member jury consisted of architects Lucio Costa, Walter Gropius, Le Corbusier, Sven Markelius, and Ernesto Rogers. Sketches prepared by Eero Saarinen and Associates for the project show six different schemes for an ensemble of low structures, including one identified as a "French government building." In most of the designs, buildings occupied the perimeter of the site on the Left Bank facing the Place de Fontenoy. In one proposal, however, Saarinen placed the buildings largely away from the streets, leaving much of the site open. The jury eventually selected a scheme by Marcel Breuer, Pier Luigi Nervi, and Bernard Zehrfuss, and as the design of the building developed in 1953, Saarinen served as consultant to this team. [TM]

Stephens College Chapel
Columbia, Missouri
1953–56

project number 5306

In response to a request by this women's college for a chapel at the geographic center of its campus, Eero Saarinen and Associates designed a square building with four nearly identical facades. On each side, a blank wall, composed of the same simple brick used throughout the campus, was punctuated by a small vestibule embellished with stained-glass panels designed by the artist Robert Sowers. At the corners, the brick walls stopped short to reveal steel columns, which connected to exposed steel beams that sloped upward to form a pyramidal roof and spire. Inside, the sanctuary, which stepped down on all four sides toward a central altar, was surrounded by perforated brick walls and an ambulatory. The ceiling incorporated beams intersecting at a central skylight and deep, square coffers, some containing downlights. [TM]

See also Olivarez, "Churches and Chapels," in this volume.

"Central Plan for a College Chapel, Stephens College, Columbia, Mo.," *Progressive Architecture*, June 1958, 132–37

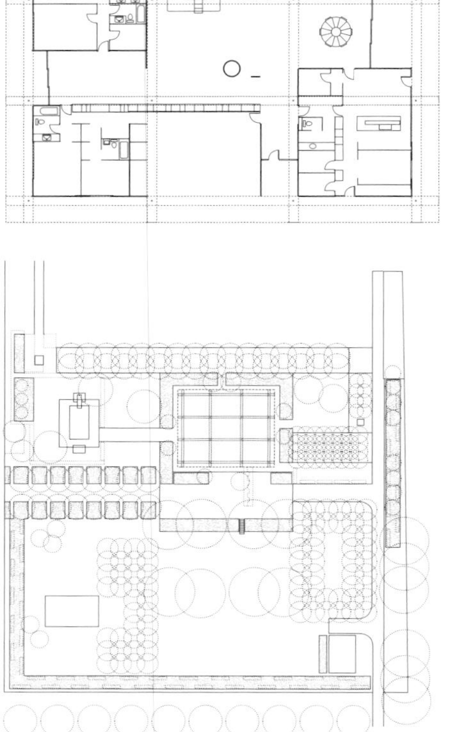

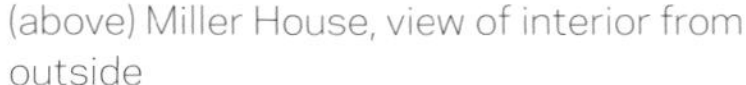

(above) Miller House, view of interior from outside

(top right) Miller House, plan, 2006

(right) Miller House, site plan, 2006

Miller House
Columbus, Indiana
1953–57

The Saarinen office designed this one-story residence for businessman J. Irwin Miller and his family. It occupied a large suburban site close to a busy street but screened from it by tall hedges. The eighty-by-one-hundred-foot house was clad in glass and panels of blue-gray slate and white marble, and sat on a paved plinth that extended beyond its exterior walls to form terraces and a parking court. Its rear garden facade ran parallel to an allée of trees, overlooking a hill that led down to a river flood plain approximately 800 feet away. The house was supported by sixteen cruciform steel columns set free from the walls and painted white. The plan was functionally zoned, with one each devoted to spaces for the parents, children, guests, and service facilities. At the center of the house was a ten-foot-high, thirty-by-forty-foot skylit living space, with a distinctive freestanding fireplace suspended from the ceiling and developed in the office by Balthazar Korab; a fifty-foot long storage wall; and a conversation pit—a space recessed into the floor incorporating built-in seating. Kevin Roche was the senior designer on the project. Alexander Girard designed fabrics, carpets, and other furnishings; he also helped Xenia Miller select decorative objects. Dan Kiley created the landscape. [DA]

See also Miller, "Eero and Irwin," and Monkhouse, "The Miller House," in this volume.

"A Contemporary Palladian Villa," *Architectural Forum*, Sept. 1958, 126–31

"H & G's Hallmark House No. 3: A New Concept of Beauty," *House and Garden*, Feb. 1959, 58–77

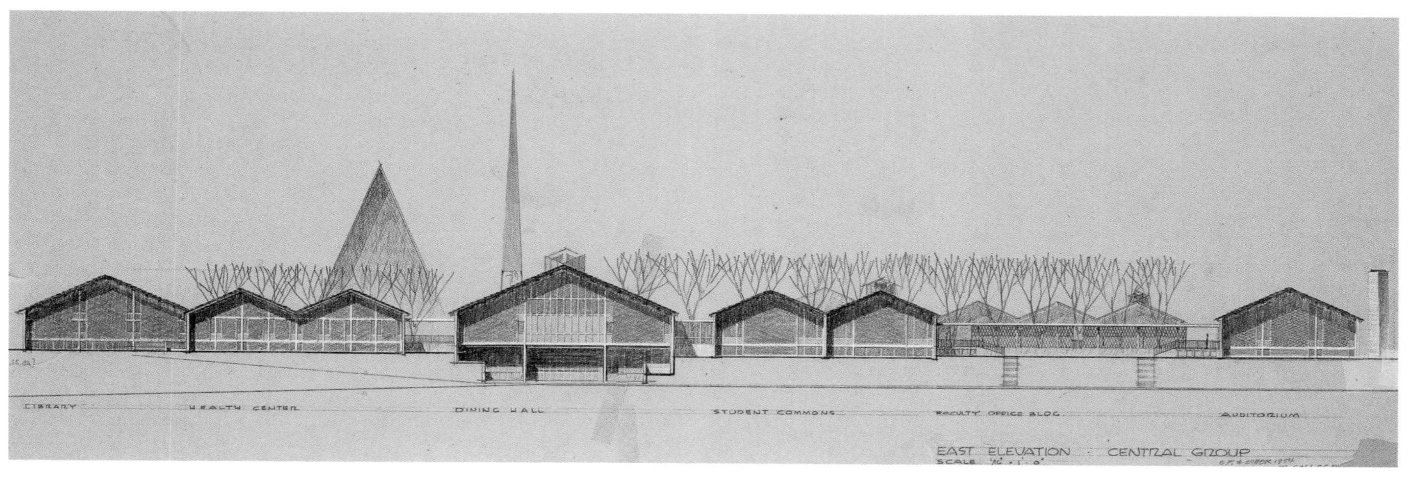

Concordia Senior College, rendered elevation by Glen Paulsen

Concordia Senior College
Fort Wayne, Indiana
1953–58
project number 5302

The Lutheran Church–Missouri Synod hired Eero Saarinen and Associates to design a campus for its new college, founded to prepare students for the ministry. Occupying a 191-acre site on the banks of the St. Joseph River five miles from town, the college comprised approximately forty structures, with the principal academic buildings bordering a plaza dominated by an A-frame chapel and three ranges of dormitories radiating outward along diagonal axes. All of them incorporated steeply pitched gray-tile roofs with the ridges oriented east–west; long buildings running north–south featured series of gable roofs. Roofs, except that of the chapel, were pitched at 23.5 degrees off the horizon line, the same angle at which the earth's axis relates to the sun. Saarinen stated that one of his inspirations for the campus's overall silhouette had been northern European villages. All the buildings conformed to a structural system based on a module of five feet four inches. For the exteriors, Saarinen experimented with different materials, including precast concrete, terra-cotta, and wood, but chose brick. He designed a roof tile that was developed over the course of two years with the Ludowici-Celadon Company, which ultimately introduced the product to the mass market as Concordia Tile. In an effort to avoid cutting the bricks where they abutted the pitched roofs, Saarinen worked with the project's structural engineers, Severud, Elstad, Krueger Associates, and contractor, A. C. Wermuth, to design and produce diamond-shaped bricks. Saarinen had favored whitewashed gray brick but was overruled by the college's building committee, which selected buff brick. He also failed in his effort to decorate interiors with black-and-white photo-murals commissioned from leading contemporary artists; instead, the building committee used far more conventional liturgical art, some of it by Cranbrook artists. Saarinen did, however, successfully replace the program's call for three dormitory halls, each accommodating approximately 150 students, with a grouping of thirteen dormitories, each serving 36 students on staggered floors. The dormitories did not exceed the size of the largest houses found in the vicinity. The dining hall, which seated 450 people, was constructed of box columns and steel bents; the building's wood roof deck was supported by wood purlins.

From its position on a small ridge that constituted the site's highest point, the chapel overlooked a man-made lake, which had formerly been a meadow. Inside, the chapel was illuminated with natural light through a row of small windows at the base of each sloping wall, a skylight running along the roof ridge, and a vertical glass band on one side of the altar. Hubbard, Lawless, and Blakely served as the mechanical and electrical engineers; Richard Kelly as lighting designer; and Dan Kiley as landscape architect. [TM]

Concordia Senior College, view from lake

Concordia Senior College, nave

Callahan House project, client meeting with site model, Eero Saarinen (right), Aline Saarinen (with arms folded), and probably Callahan family members

See also Olivarez, "Churches and Chapels," Pelkonen, "The Search for (Communicative) Form," and Plattus, "Campus Plans."

"An Old Village Silhouette for a New College: Concordia Senior College, Fort Wayne," *Architectural Forum,* Dec. 1954, 132–37

"A 'Village' Design for a College Campus," *Progressive Architecture,* Dec. 1958, 88–101

"Concordia Senior College," *Deutsche Bauzeitschrift,* Sept. 1960, 1090–93

1954

Callahan House project
Birmingham, Alabama
1954, unbuilt

Dr. Alston Callahan, a noted eye surgeon, commissioned Saarinen to design a home on a secluded site in Birmingham. Saarinen proposed a house cantilevered over a wooded bluff. Photographs of a model show a rectangular flat-roofed one-story structure with glass walls. Saarinen assembled complex notes about the family's needs, desires, and habits, including a concept for a home theater. Olav Hammarström, an architect in Saarinen's office, worked on the project. [SK]

Pedestal furniture series, sketches of chairs

Knoll Associates poster for Pedestal furniture series

Pedestal furniture series, drawing of chairs with four-legged table

(overleaf) Pedestal furniture series

Pedestal furniture series
1954–57

The Pedestal series for Knoll Associates consisted of chairs and tables characterized by one-piece cast-metal bases that tapered, then flared as they rose to meet molded-fiberglass chair shells or tabletops. Saarinen originally intended the chairs to be made of a single plastic material, but this proved to be technically impossible at the time. Instead, the chairs' metal bases and fiberglass seats were the same color (either black or white), so that, coupled with their continuous curving lines, each piece appeared to be a single form. Both armchairs and side chairs could be fully upholstered or provided with upholstered seat pads. Dining, coffee, and side tables came with circular or oval tops in wood veneer, plastic laminate, or marble. Stools with upholstered seats were also available, as was an ashtray, manufactured between 1962, a year after Saarinen's death, and 1976. [TM]

See also Lutz, "Furniture," in this volume.

"New Furniture by Saarinen," *Arts and Architecture*, July 1957, 23

"Saarinen Places Furniture on a Pedestal," *Architectural Record*, July 1957, 284

"If I Could Tell a Woman One Thing About Furnishing a Home," *Family Circle*, Mar. 1958, 27–33

"Sièges et tables d'Eero Saarinen," *L'Aujourd'hui: Art et Architecture*, Dec. 1960, 90–91

June 7, 1960 E. SAARINEN 2,939,517

ARTICLES OF FURNITURE AND SUPPORTS THEREFOR

Filed March 27, 1957 2 Sheets-Sheet 1

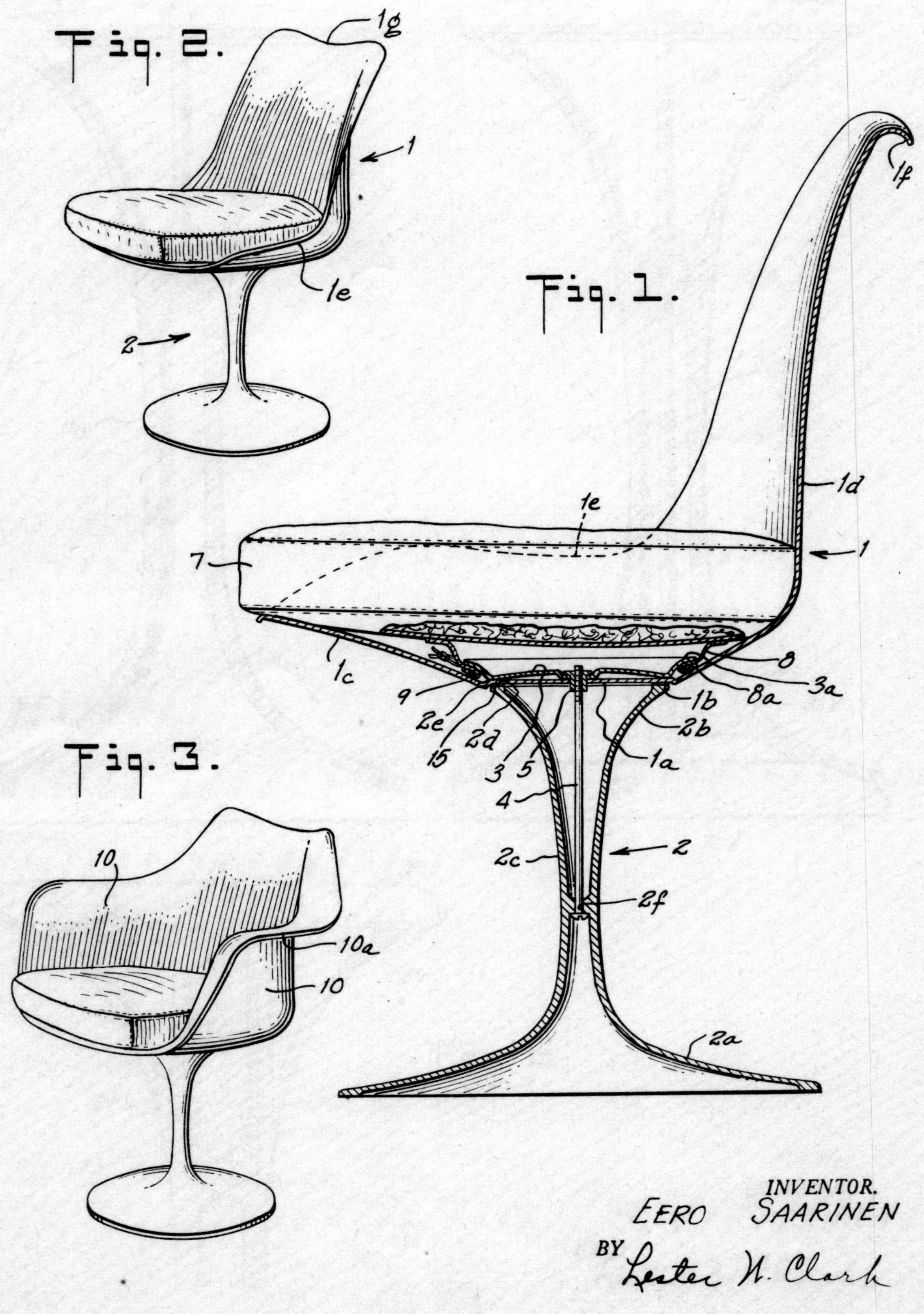

INVENTOR.
EERO SAARINEN
BY Lester W. Clark
ATTORNEY

Pedestal furniture series,
drawing of "Snifter" chair

(opposite) Pedestal furniture series,
patent drawing

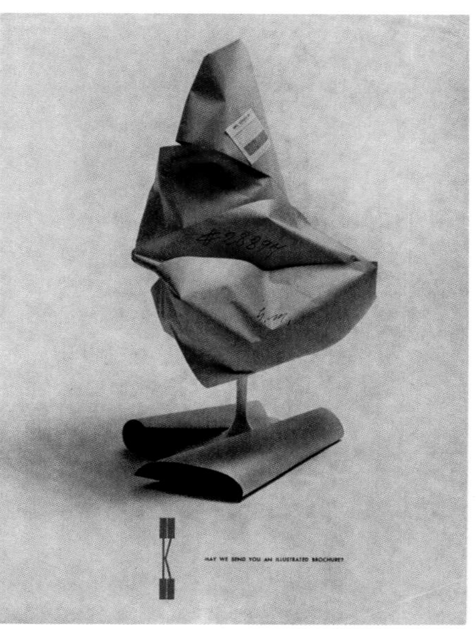

Knoll advertisement for Pedestal chair,
graphic design by Herbert Matter

Knoll advertisement for Pedestal chair,
graphic design by Herbert Matter

Emma Hartman Noyes House,
Vassar College, model

Emma Hartman Noyes House

Emma Hartman Noyes House, conversation pit

Emma Hartman Noyes House (Residence Hall)
Vassar College
Poughkeepsie, New York
1954–58

project number 5408 B

The curving footprint of this four-story, 156-student women's dormitory conformed to the circular open area it faced. Saarinen's original design called for two connected buildings that together bordered half of the circle; as built, Noyes House defined only a quarter of it. The building, with structural engineering by Severud, Elstad, Krueger Associates, consisted of poured-in-place reinforced roof and floor slabs and precast, tilt-up, load-bearing exterior panels faced in rough-surfaced brick set in black mortar. The dormitory's 150-foot-long facade featured twenty-eight bay windows in aluminum frames extending above the roof line to terminate in triangular, finial-like forms, visually connecting the dormitory to the Gothic buildings on campus. At each of the four entrances, an oval-shaped canopy was supported by a single column. Inside, a ground-floor student lounge contained a "conversation pit," which was soon dubbed the "passion pit." On the upper floors, a curving double-loaded corridor was flanked by single-occupancy rooms facing the front, and double-occupancy rooms facing the back. All rooms contained simply detailed built-in furniture designed by the Saarinen office. [TM]

"College Buildings: Vassar, Emma Hartman Noyes House," *Architectural Record*, Sept. 1959, 168–70

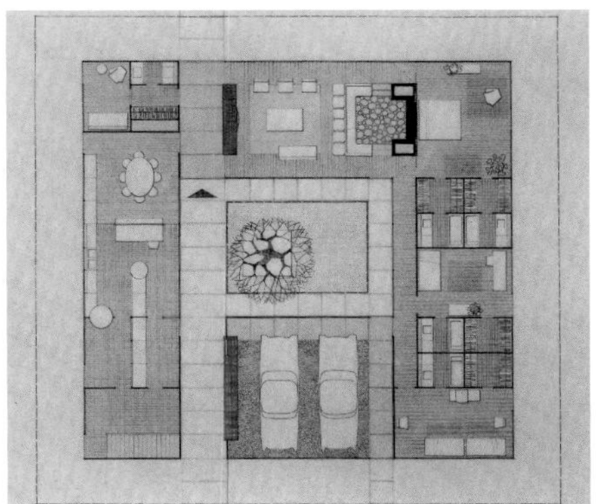

General Motors House of Tomorrow, perspective

General Motors House of Tomorrow, plan

Greenwich Station project, platform, perspective rendering

1955

General Motors House of Tomorrow
Warren, Michigan
1955, unbuilt

General Motors commissioned Eero Saarinen and Associates to design a prototypical house, which was to be built on the site of the General Motors Technical Center in Warren, Michigan. The one-story residence featured a flat roof with overhangs on all four sides. The house had a U-shaped plan; one leg contained three bedrooms with bathrooms and walk-in closets, and the other included a dining room, kitchen, and maid's room. These wings were connected by a glassed-in living room with a stone-paved conversation pit. The house's central area featured an open, landscaped courtyard and a carport. [SK]

Greenwich Station project
Greenwich, Connecticut
1955, unbuilt
project number 5512

In this project for the New Haven Railroad, Saarinen, seeking to maximize a relatively small site, proposed to elevate and expand the existing railroad platform over a street, leaving room for surface parking, multistory parking garages, and improved access roads. The station was to include two structures, one on either side of the tracks, each consisting of an arcade of white-painted metal columns supporting a cantilevered roof of folded planes. The project was part of an effort by Patrick B. McGinnis, president of the railroad, to restore the confidence of commuters who were increasingly dissatisfied with the railroad's poor service, the limited supply and high cost of parking space, and the unattractive appearance of the railroad's stations and trains. To overhaul the railroad visually, McGinnis assembled a design team that included Marcel Breuer, Saarinen, and Minoru Yamasaki, as well as graphic designer Herbert Matter and designer Florence Knoll. The combination of extensive hurricane damage in the fall of 1955 and the railroad's mounting fiscal troubles doomed McGinnis's efforts, and little of the undertaking was completed. [TM]

"New Operations, New Face," *Architectural Forum*, June 1956, 107–12

United States Chancellery Building, Oslo

United States Chancellery Building, London

United States Chancellery Building, Oslo, plan, 2006

United States Chancellery Building
Oslo, Norway
1955–59

Located on a triangular site in the center of Oslo, opposite Slottsparken, or Royal Palace Park, the U.S. Chancellery Building filled the lot to the surrounding streets. Facades comprised precast concrete panels containing a 90 percent aggregate of Norwegian emerald pearl granite, punctuated by teak-framed windows. The main facade, on Drammensveien, was 190 feet long and had a centrally located entrance marked by a cantilevered trapezoidal canopy with a flagpole. Inside, offices wrapped around a four-story, skylit, diamond-shaped atrium flanked by two triangular staircases. The atrium had a beige Roman travertine floor and was centered on a pool next to which were teak benches. Two of its walls contained two-story-high screens made of honey-colored teak louvers with metal spacers; the other two walls were light-toned brick grilles. Office colleagues who worked on the building included Gene Festa, Cesar Pelli, and David Powrie. Engh, Quam, and Kaier were the associate architects, and Nils S. Stiansen, the general contractor. [DA]

See also Pelkonen,"The Search for (Communicative) Form," and Tuomi, "Embassies and Chancelleries," in this volume.

"The American Embassy in Oslo," *Byggekunst*, Oct. 2, 1959, 112–29

"Exciting Embassy by Saarinen Opens Under Fire in Oslo," *Progressive Architecture*, Nov. 1959, 90–91

"New US Embassy in Oslo," *Architectural Record*, Dec. 1959, 107–13

"Norway's Precast Palazzo," *Architectural Forum*, Dec. 1959, 130–33

"Ambassade des États-Unis, Oslo, Norvège," *L'Architecture d'Aujourd'hui*, Apr. 1960, 64–67

"Oslo Completed: Saarinen's Other Embassy," *Architectural Review*, May 1960, 293

"U.S.A. Ambassaden: Oslo," *Arkitektur*, June 1960, 81–91

United States Chancellery Building
London, England
1955–60

At the invitation of the Department of State's Office of Foreign Buildings Operations, eight architects participated in the competition for a new chancellery to be built in London, on Grosvenor Square. In addition to Saarinen, the architects were Anderson, Beckwith, and Haible; Ernest J. Kump; José Luis Sert with Huson Jackson and Joseph Zalewski; Edward Durell Stone; Hugh Stubbins; Wurster, Bernardi, and Emmons; and Yamasaki, Leinweber and Associates. Saarinen's winning design responded to the neo-Georgian buildings that were to be erected on the other three sides of the square in accordance with a master plan commissioned by the Grosvenor Estate. The U-shaped chancellery contained six stories and a recessed attic story. Clad in Portland stone, glass, and gold-anodized aluminum trim, the building employed a stacked, precast-concrete floor system and load-bearing exterior walls. The glazed entrance floor was raised five

Saarinen in front of the United States Chancellery Building, London

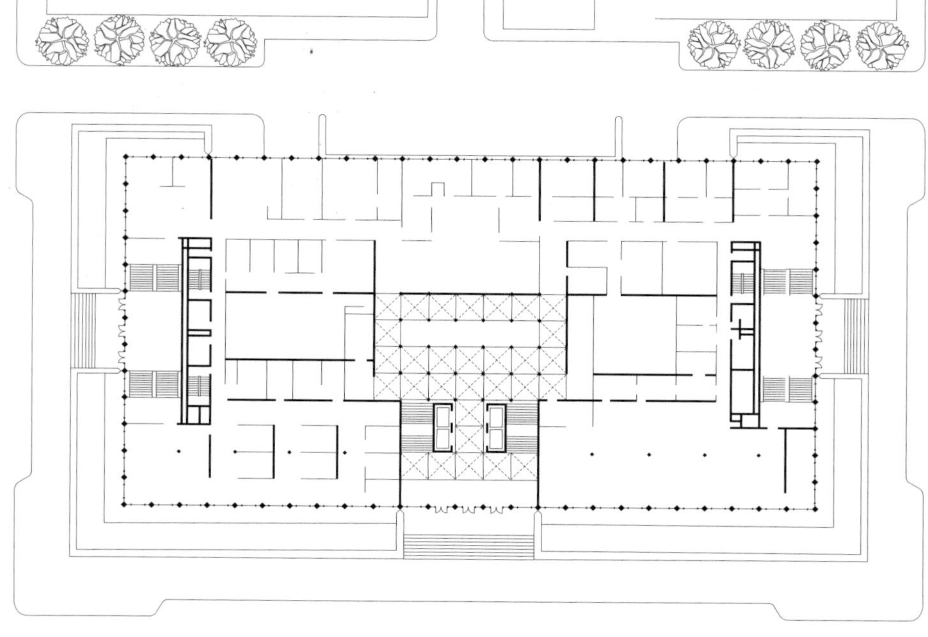

United States Chancellery Building, London, plan, 2006

feet on a Portland-stone-clad battered podium. Above, the building's facades contained an interlocking grid of operable and fixed windows. A 35-foot-wide gilded aluminum eagle by sculptor Theodore Roszak was centered on the 278-foot-long primary facade and mounted on the roof parapet, aligned with the centrally located recessed entrance. The entrance floor featured a lobby, a consular section where foreigners applied for visas, and an information area for American citizens. Visible from the street, the ceilings of this floor's public spaces had exposed beams arranged in criss-cross patterns in which each intersection was marked by four downlights. A lower level housed an auditorium, a gallery, and a cafeteria, below which was an underground parking garage. The design was developed with office colleagues Robert Burley, Spero Daltas, Olav Hammarström, Glen Paulsen, and Edward Saad. The English associate architects were Yorke, Rosenberg, and Mardall. Felix Samuels and Partners were the project's structural engineers, and A. F. Meyers and Partners the mechanical engineers. [DA]

See also Tuomi, "Embassies and Chancelleries," in this volume.

Drew Middleton, "New American Embassy for London's 'Little America,'" *New York Times Magazine,* Mar. 18, 1956, 66

"Home in Eisenhowerplatz: Winning Design for New Embassy in London," *Time,* Mar. 19, 1956, 78

"Saarinen to Design Embassy," *Progressive Architecture,* Mar. 1956, 89

John Knox Shear, "Competition for U.S. Chancery Building, London," *Architectural Record,* Apr. 1956, 220

"New US Embassy for London," *Architectural Forum,* Apr. 1956, 138–39

"'New Look': Diplomatischer Missionen der USA," *Baukunst und Werkform,* June 1959, 313

"U.S. Embassy, Grosvenor Square, London," *Architectural Design,* July 1960, 270–75

Toni Howard, "The Case of the Impudent Bird," *Saturday Evening Post,* Sept. 24, 1960, 43, 46–47, 49

Ada Louise Huxtable, "Sharp Debate: What Should an Embassy Be?" *New York Times Magazine,* Sept. 18, 1960, 36

"U.S.A. Embassy, London," *Architect and Building News* 218 (Dec. 7, 1960), 731–44

Reyner Banham, "Monument with Frills," *New Statesman,* Dec. 10, 1960, 918, 920

Peter Smithson et al., "Controversial Building in London: Saarinen's U.S. Embassy," *Architectural Record,* Mar. 1961, 80–85

F. Atkinson, "U.S. Embassy Building, Grosvenor Square, London," *Architectural Review,* Apr. 1961, 252–58

Lewis Mumford, "The Sky Line: False Front or Cold-War Concept," *New Yorker,* Oct. 20, 1962, 174, 176, 178, 180–85

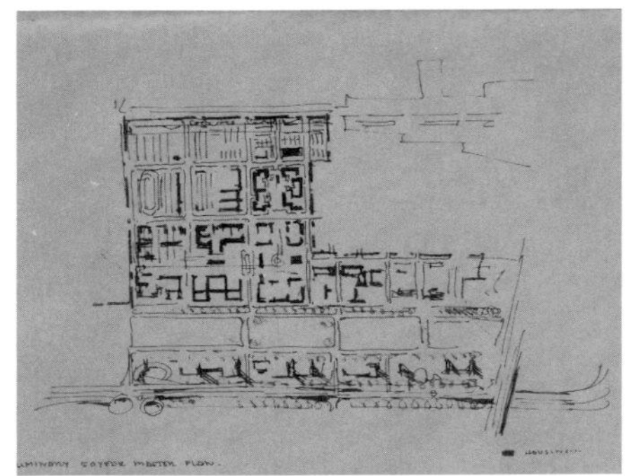

University of Chicago, master plan, sketch

University of Chicago, law school

University of Chicago, women's dormitory

(opposite) University of Chicago, law school, sketch

University of Chicago
Chicago, Illinois
1955–60

Master Plan, 1955
project number 5504
Women's Dormitory and Dining Hall, 1955–58, demolished 2001
project number 5504-A
Law School, 1955–60
project number 5504

Based on a master plan commissioned by the University of Chicago, Eero Saarinen and Associates designed a women's dormitory and law school on opposite sides of the Midway, the campus's centrally located grassy spine. On the Midway's north side, the four-story dormitory adopted a modified U shape. Constructed of reinforced-concrete frames, the dormitory was clad in panels of shot-sawn limestone ashlar, separated by vertical bands of casement windows and dark-toned spandrels. The windows' verticality echoed the neo-Gothic lines of the surrounding campus buildings. The open side of the complex was punctuated by a two-story cruciform dining hall. Above a glass-enclosed ground floor featuring lobby, lounges, and offices was an upper floor housing dining rooms, kitchens, and service areas. Dan Kiley served as landscape architect for the courtyard and surrounding open areas. J. Lee Jones was associate architect; Samuel R. Lewis and Associates, mechanical engineer; and Severud, Elstad, Krueger Associates, structural engineer. The general contractor was the George Sollitt Construction Company.

Saarinen's six-story law school library occupied a raised platform on the Midway's south side, but was separated from it by a reflecting pool. The building was flanked by a two-story administrative wing, which connected to an existing dormitory complex in a neo-Gothic style, and an arcaded classroom wing, which terminated in a new hexagonal-shaped structure; the latter housed a 475-seat auditorium and a moot court. The central library building was concrete-framed and clad in "pleated" dark-glass curtain walls (with thin metal trim) that gave the roof line a serrated appearance. [TM]

"Two Sparkling Stones in Different Settings," *Architectural Forum*, Aug. 1956, 112–16

"Law School Center and Women's Dormitory, University of Chicago," *Architectural Record*, Nov. 1960, 132–37

ERO SAARINEN AND ASSOCIATE
RCHITECTS - BLOOMFIELD HILLS, MICHIGA

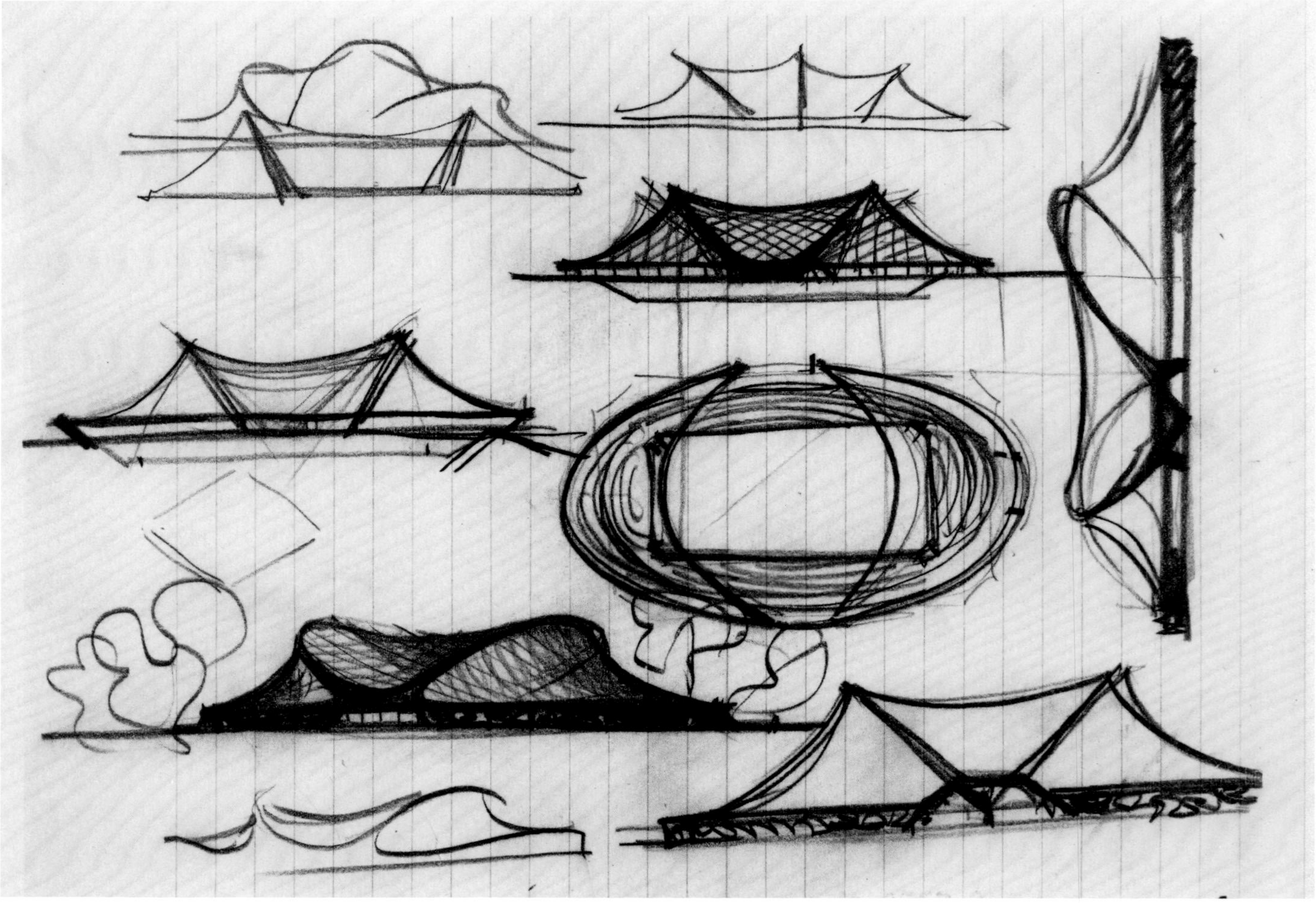

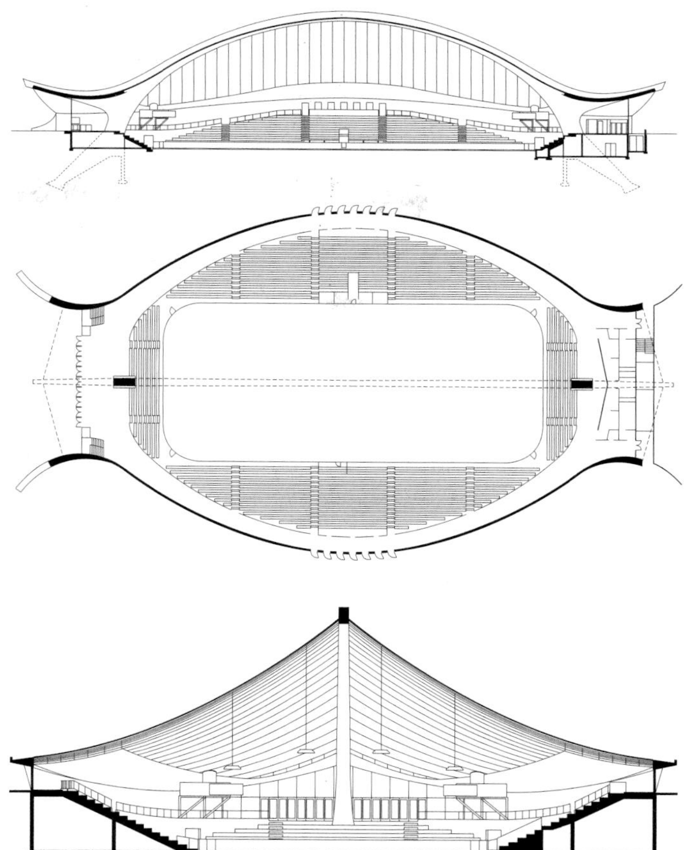

David S. Ingalls Hockey Rink, interior showing concrete spine

(opposite, top) David S. Ingalls Hockey Rink, exterior

(opposite, bottom) David S. Ingalls Hockey Rink, preliminary sketches

(right) David S. Ingalls Hockey Rink, sections and plan, 2006

1956

David S. Ingalls Hockey Rink
Yale University
New Haven, Connecticut
1956–58

Located in a residential area north of Yale's historic campus, this building housed a 2,800-seat hockey rink that could be expanded to accommodate 5,000 people when used for other functions, such as graduation. The dominant feature of the building was a roof suspended on cables from a 333-foot spinelike reinforced-concrete arch, which provided a 288-foot-long and 183-foot-wide column-free area underneath. The arch was braced laterally by three 1¾-inch steel cables on each side. These were anchored to the exterior concrete walls, which, in plan, followed the curves of the arch's profile; this curvature was also adopted for the outdoor parking areas and lawns. The arch featured upward-curved cantilevers at each end.

The roof was constructed of exposed tongue-and-groove wood planks supported by transverse steel cables. It rose to a height of 29 feet above the ice at the arch's center, with the exterior shape expressed on the interior. To better fit the building into the residential neighborhood, the rink was sunk about 15 feet below the entrance level. Spectators entered the building through glass doors under the campus-side cantilever. Ramps ascending and descending along the external walls provided access to seating. New Haven–based architect Douglas W. Orr served as associate architect on the project, and Severud, Elstad, Krueger Associates as the structural engineer. [ELP]

See also Rey, "The David S. Ingalls Hockey Rink," in this volume.

"Hockey Rink: Spines and Catenaries Form New Shape," *Architectural Record*, Aug. 1957, 186–89

Fred Severud, "Cable Suspended Roof for Yale Hockey Rink," *Civil Engineering*, Sept. 1958, 60–63

"Yale Hockey Rink," *Architectural Record*, Oct. 1958, 151–58

"Yale's Viking Vessel," *Architectural Forum*, Dec. 1958, 105–11

"Eisenhockeystadion der Yale Universität in New Haven," *Baukunst und Werkform*, Jan. 1960, 20–22

International Business Machines Manufacturing and Training Facility, aerial perspective rendering

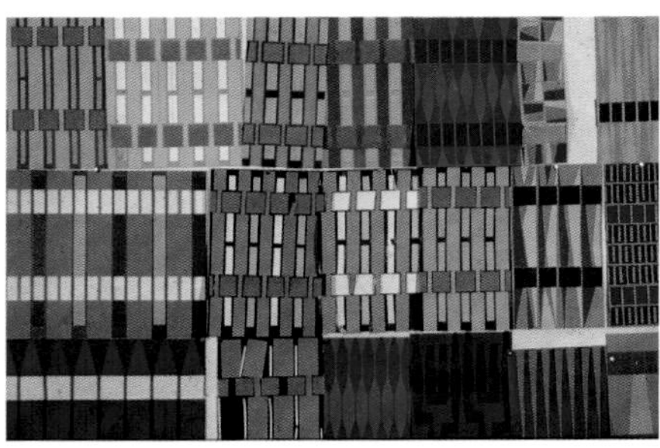

International Business Machines Manufacturing and Training Facility, facade studies

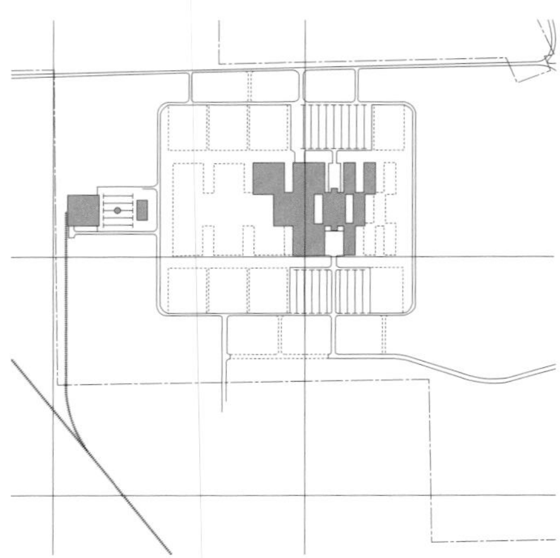

International Business Machines Manufacturing and Training Facility, site plan, 2006

International Business Machines Manufacturing and Training Facility
Rochester, Minnesota
1956–58; continuously expanded

project number 5604

Located on a flat 397-acre site that was formerly farmland, this sprawling 100,000-square-foot building, based on a four-foot module, was composed of a series of one- and two-story volumes surrounding two fully bounded courtyards and two entrance courts that opened onto parking lots set in extensive lawns. The one-story volume located at the core of the facility contained a cafeteria and employee lounges. The other one-story volumes, most of which were 250 by 250 feet in plan, contained 60,000 square feet of manufacturing facilities, while the two-story blocks, each 80 by 250 feet, housed 40,000 square feet of office space. This distribution was based on the findings of IBM researchers that manufacturing required one and a half times the amount of space as administration. The building was clad in porcelain-enameled aluminum panels developed by Saarinen's partner John Dinkeloo. The mass-produced three-ply panels, 5⁄16 inch thick and 4 feet wide, incorporated insulating asbestos-cement cores. Extending to a height of eight feet, the panels were stabilized laterally by aluminum mullions; there were no muntins. Neoprene gaskets sealed the panels, which were striped in two tones of blue. The cost of the curtain wall, including glass, aluminum mullions, neoprene gaskets, panels (fully finished on both interior and exterior sides), and installation, was $4 per square foot. Saarinen's modular plan anticipated the corporation's growth and could be expanded without changing its basic spatial and programmatic organization. [TM]

See also Albrecht, "The Clients and Their Architect," and Lange, "Corporate Headquarters," in this volume

"Saarinen Uses Curtain Wall 5⁄16" Thick," *Progressive Architecture*, June 1957, 57

John Dinkeloo, letter to the editor ("Saarinen Uses Curtain Wall 5⁄16" Thick"), *Progressive Architecture*, Sept. 1957, 14

"In Rochester, Minn.: IBM's Protected Country Surroundings," *Architectural Forum*, Oct. 1958, 140–43

"Usine et bureaux de l'IBM, Rochester, Minnesota, États-Unis," *L'Architecture d'Aujourd'hui*, Sept. 1959, 24

International Business Machines Manufacturing and Training Facility

Trans World Airlines Terminal

Trans World Airlines Terminal
New York International
(now John F. Kennedy International)
Airport
New York, New York
1956–62

project numbers 5603, 6301

Trans World Airlines president Ralph S. Damon commissioned Eero Saarinen and Associates to design a new terminal building for a prominent site on axis with New York International (Idlewild) Airport's main entrance road. The terminal was dominated by a 51-foot-high, 322-by-222-foot vaulted central structure housing an entrance area, waiting rooms, and restaurants. This structure was composed of four reinforced lightweight concrete shells, each varying in thickness from seven inches at the center to eleven inches at the base. The shells were supported by edge beams, which were in turn supported by massive Y-shaped piers containing steel reinforcements. Canted glass walls filled in the arched space beneath the curving edge of each shell. A horizontal plate bound the shells together and stabilized the entire structure. The shells

Trans World Airlines Terminal, model

(below) Trans World Airlines Terminal, elevation, 2006

Trans World Airlines Terminal, construction of formwork

(opposite, top) Trans World Airlines Terminal, construction drawing for shell pouring lines

(opposite, bottom) Trans World Airlines Terminal, exterior detail

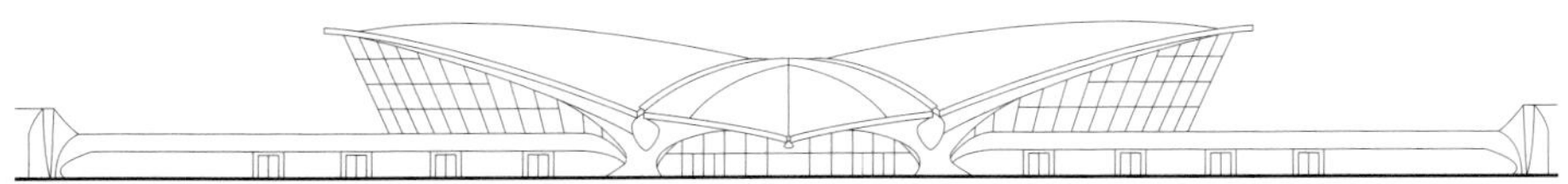

on either side were identical, while the one in front, containing the terminal's main entrance, was narrower than the one in back, commanding views of the landing field. (The terminal was the first to offer waiting passengers a view of the tarmac.) Between the shells were three-foot-wide skylights. Saarinen felt that this arrangement, as well as the decision to make the edge beams larger than structurally necessary, enhanced the view of the building when seen from the air.

The central vaulted structure was flanked by two wings, one dedicated to check-in facilities and the other serving as the baggage claim area. The terminal pioneered the deposit of departing passengers' baggage at the check-in counter and the retrieval of arriving passengers' baggage from revolving carousels located near ground transportation. Two 125-foot-long tubular passageways led from the main terminal complex to podlike boarding areas, referred to as "departure stations," which constituted another innovation in airport design. The boarding areas' remote locations increased the terminal's perimeter and allowed fourteen jets to dock simultaneously.

The terminal's interior was characterized by multilevel spaces, curving stairways, and bridges, with floors and low walls surfaced in small white circular tiles specially manufactured in Japan. Broad shallow steps led under a pedestrian bridge to a sunken lounge, with red carpeting and built-in seating upholstered in red fabric. Directly inside the entrance was a complexly curved flight board and information desk. The building program called for five dining facilities, but the Saarinen firm was commissioned to design only the Ambassador Club, which it furnished with Pedestal tables and molded seating.

Grove, Shepherd, Wilson, and Kruge, contractors, oversaw the building's construction. Forms consisting of both straight wooden boards and boards that were treated and bent could not be re-used, and their cost accounted for nearly half of the total budget for constructing the roof. The concrete for each shell was poured in a single uninterrupted session; the side shells each required thirty hours. A scaffolding system consisting of 2,200 steel frames, placed at two- to four-foot intervals, supported the shells during the several weeks required for the concrete to completely solidify. The project team included the structural engineering firm of Ammann and Whitney, with the firm's Abba Tor playing a key role; Jaros, Baum, and Bolles, mechanical engineers; Bolt, Beranek, and Newman, acoustic consultants; and Stanley McCandless, lighting consultant. From the Saarinen office, Kevin Roche, Norman Pettula, Cesar Pelli, and Edward Saad were key collaborators on the design; Warren Platner was largely responsible for the interiors. [TM]

See also Isenstadt, "Eero Saarinen's Theater of Form," Pelkonen, "The Search for (Communicative) Form," and Santala, "Airports," in this volume.

"Trans-World Airlines Terminal, Idlewild Airport, New York," *Bulletin of the Museum of Modern Art* 26 (winter 1959), 16–21

B. Huber, "Projekt für den TWA Terminal in Idlewild, New York," *Werk*, Feb. 1960, 53–54

Helmut Borcherdt, "Planning des TWA-flughafengebaudes in New York," *Baukunst und Werkform*, May 1960, 256–63

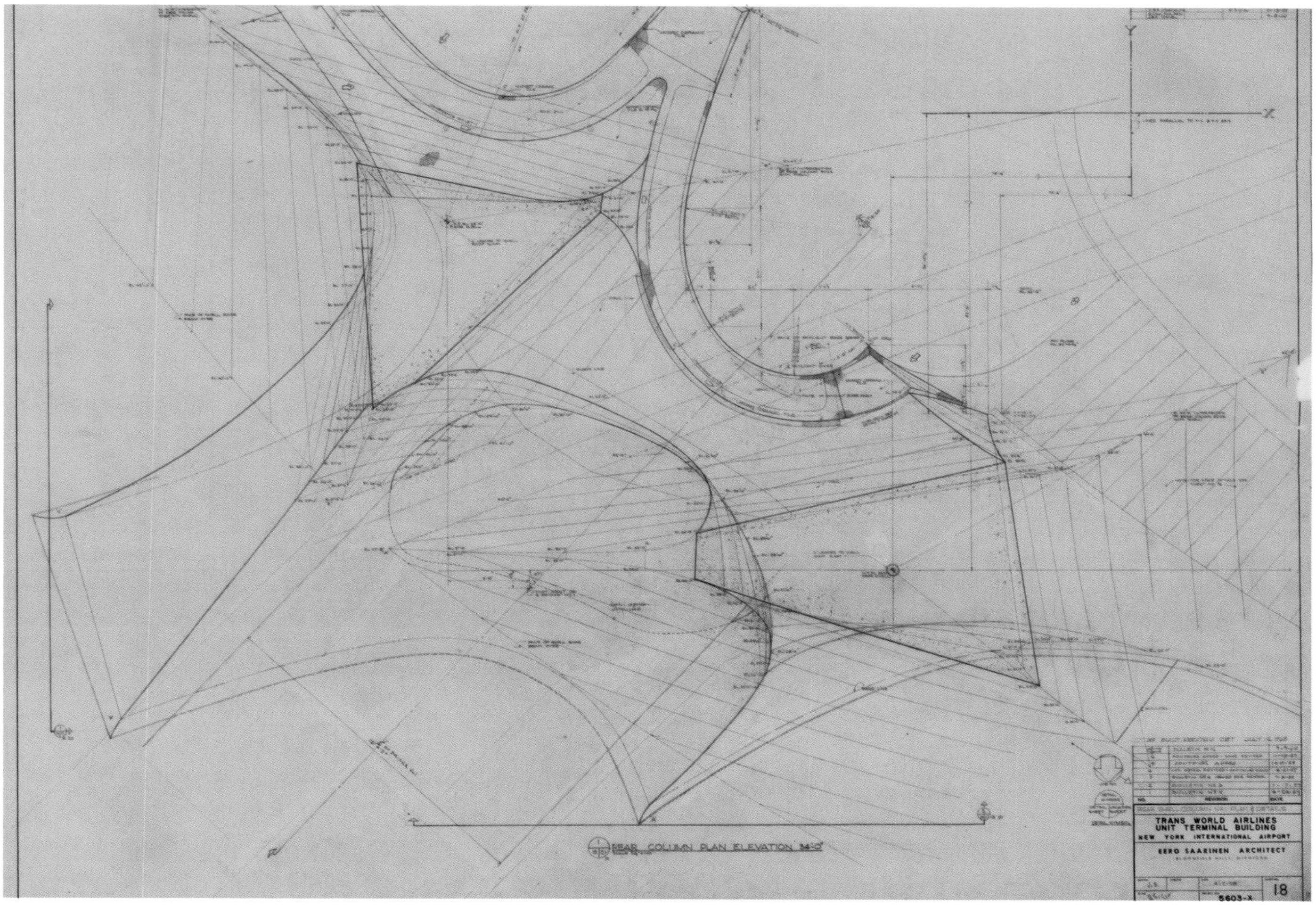

REAR COLUMN PLAN ELEVATION
TRANS WORLD AIRLINES
UNIT TERMINAL BUILDING
NEW YORK INTERNATIONAL AIRPORT
EERO SAARINEN ARCHITECT
5603-X
18

Trans World Airlines Terminal, lounge, rendering of the Ambassador Club

(overleaf) Trans World Airlines Terminal, rear elevation viewed from tarmac

Trans World Airlines Terminal, passenger bridge

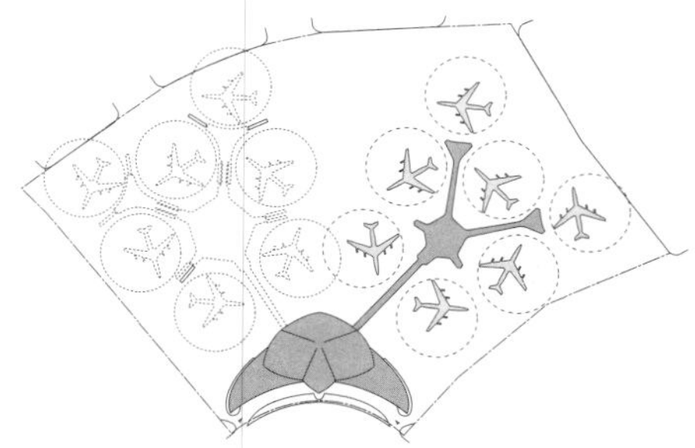

Trans World Airlines Terminal, site plan, 2006

"Shaping a Two-Acre Sculpture: Saarinen's New Terminal for TWA at Idlewild Airport," *Architectural Forum,* Aug. 1960, 118–23

"Il 'Terminal' della TWA alla'aeroporto di Idlewild, New York," *Architettura,* Apr. 1961, 836

Edgar Kaufmann, Jr., "Inside Eero Saarinen's TWA Building," *Interiors,* July 1962, 86–93

"Saarinen's TWA Flight Center," *Architectural Record,* July 1962, 129–34

"Saarinen's TWA Terminal at Idlewild, New York," *Architectural Forum,* July 1962, 72–75

"Bâtiments de la T.W.A. à l'Aéroport de New York Idlewild," *L'Architecture d'Aujourd'hui,* Sept. 1962, 74–81

"TWA's Flight Center," *Kenchiku Bunka,* Sept. 1962, 72–77

"Architecture of Interiors: TWA Terminal, New York International Airport," *Progressive Architecture,* Oct. 1962, 158–65

"Forget the Bird: TWA Appraised," *Architectural Review,* Nov. 1962, 306–7

Udo Kultermann, "Flughafengebaude der TWA, New York-Idlewild," *Deutsche Bauzeitung,* Apr. 1963, 271–78

Hill Hall, University of Pennsylvania

Hill Hall, atrium

1957

Hill Hall (University of Pennsylvania Women's Residence Hall)
University of Pennsylvania
Philadelphia, Pennsylvania
1957–60

project number 5702

The University of Pennsylvania hired Eero Saarinen and Associates to design this five-story dormitory for approximately 650 women on a site sloping down from Walnut Street. The site's topography led Saarinen to locate the dorm's main entrance on the second story, accessible via a pedestrian bridge. The 262-foot-long and 143-foot-wide building was clad in hand-molded red brick whose surface texture was rougher than that of the brick used for neighboring university buildings. The dorm sat on a curved brick base. Each facade was symmetrically divided by a full-height notch clad in vertically oriented metal strips. Deep slots with chamfered brick edges, arranged in a pattern of alternating verticals and horizontals, contained casement windows. Inside the building, a five-story, multilevel atrium and two sundecks were surrounded by the dorm rooms, and thus invisible from the street. Reasoning that an outdoor central space would be unusable for much of the academic year, Saarinen roofed the atrium, spanning its expanse with inexpensive exposed metal trusses. Natural light entered the space through clerestories and two-story-high window walls dividing the atrium from the sundecks. The dorm rooms were clustered into suites housing between sixteen and twenty-four women, with each suite served by a common kitchen and a communal living room. For those rooms overlooking the atrium, operable shutters provided privacy. The editors of *Architectural Forum* felt that this feature suggested "scenes from the Arabian Nights," and added, "If this does not bring romance back to co-education, then nothing can." Ammann and Whitney were the project's structural engineers; Jaros, Baum, and Bolles the mechanical engineers; Stanley McCandless the lighting consultant; and Joseph R. Farrell, Inc., the contractor. [TM]

"Living Space Around a Court," *New York Times Magazine*, Dec. 11, 1960, 7
"Court for Coeds," *Architectural Forum*, Feb. 1961, 120–21

(top) International Business Machines Thomas J. Watson Research Center, exterior view at night

International Business Machines Thomas J. Watson Research Center, interior of glass-walled corridor

International Business Machines Thomas J. Watson Research Center, split corridor

International Business Machines Thomas J. Watson Research Center, fieldstone exterior wall

International Business Machines Thomas J. Watson Research Center, site plan, 2006

International Business Machines Thomas J. Watson Research Center Yorktown Heights, New York 1957–61

The Thomas J. Watson Research Center, Saarinen's second IBM commission, was located on a generously sized property about a one-hour drive north of New York City. Approached by a long, curving road, the building described a 1,090-foot arc along a ridge, its front facade glazed in reflective glass with a cantilevered concrete canopy marking the entrance, which was also called out by Seymour Lipton's abstract sculptures. The rear of the building was faced in local stone, which was carried inside. Concrete bridges connected the building to its raised parking lot, spanning a Japanese-inspired garden designed by Sasaki, Walker, and Associates. Inside, Saarinen devised three stories of double-loaded corridors, windowless labs on one side, windowless offices on the other, which fanned out along the curve. Views were reserved for the front hall, which extended the length of the entire arc like a promenade. [AL]

See also Albrecht, "The Clients and Their Architect," and Lange, "Corporate Headquarters," in this volume.

"Research in the Round: IBM's Research Center in Westchester County, NY," *Architectural Forum*, June 1961, 80–85

"Unique Cross-curve Plan for IBM Research Center," *Architectural Record*, June 1961, 137–46

"Centre de Recherches I.B.M., Yorktown Heights, États-Unis," *L'Architecture d'Aujourd'hui*, Feb. 1962, 48–53

"Centro Recerche della IBM, presso New York," *Architettura*, Feb. 1962, 693

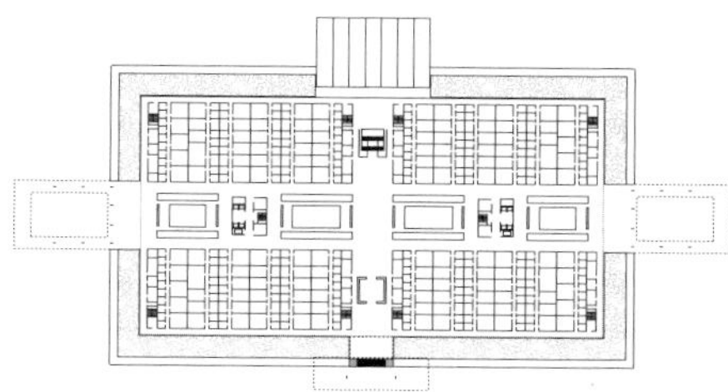

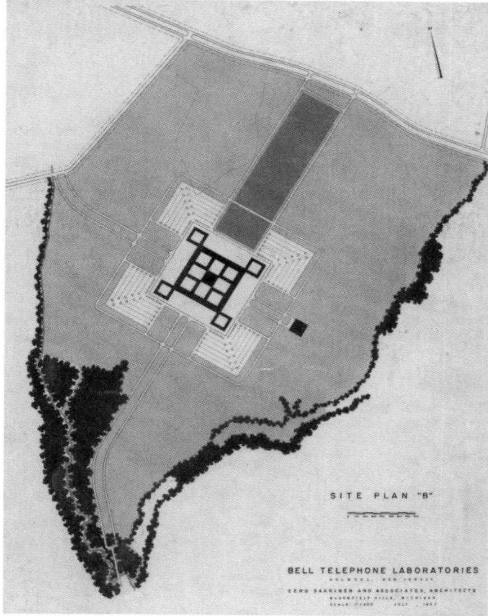

Bell Telephone Corporate Laboratories, hallway, model

Bell Telephone Corporate Laboratories, site plan, 2006

(opposite) Bell Telephone Corporate Laboratories, atrium

Bell Telephone Corporate Laboratories, early site plan

Bell Telephone Corporate Laboratories, exterior viewed across lake

Bell Telephone Corporate Laboratories, facade

Bell Telephone Corporate Laboratories (WECO, Holmdel Laboratory)
Holmdel, New Jersey
1957–62

project numbers 5703, 6301, 7708

Saarinen designed this corporate campus for Bell Telephone when the company decided to move its laboratory facilities in lower Manhattan to a 460-acre site about fifty miles from New York City. A five-story building (with basement), containing 715,000 gross square feet, was composed of four discrete and nearly identical rectangular structures, each incorporating corridors surrounding windowless offices and labs organized on a six-by-six-foot modular grid. The building appeared not to touch the ground; its walls were slightly cantilevered over a base that sat within a shallow recess in the land. Two overlapping canopies, one cantilevered from the building and the other freestanding, marked the main entrance. The building was clad in mirrored glass, a material developed for the project. The production of this glass lagged behind the building's construction, and it initially was used only on the principal facade; when sufficient mirror glass was available, it replaced the clear glass that had been used in the interim. The mirrored glass allowed 25 percent of the available sunlight to pass through, while blocking 70 percent of the sun's heat. A glass-covered space frame of heat-absorbent, self-oxidizing steel enclosed the spaces between the blocks to create a 100-by-700-foot atrium 70 feet high. The lobby contained a large rectangular seating area recessed three steps below the entrance level.

Sited on gently rolling terrain, Bell Labs was approached axially. A 127-foot-high, 300,000-gallon-capacity water tower announced the entrance to the corporate campus. A six-acre artificial lake served both aesthetic and practical purposes, such as fire-fighting and the absorption of water vapor generated by the building's air-conditioning system. Anthony J. Lumsden, an associate in Saarinen's office, served as project architect, with Severud, Elstad, Krueger Associates as the project's structural engineers; Jaros, Baum, and Bolles its electrical and mechanical engineers; and Bolt, Beranek, and Newman its acoustical consultants. The building was constructed by the Frank Briscoe Construction Company and the grounds landscaped by Sasaki, Walker, and Associates. [TM]

"Bell Lab's Mirrored Superblock at Holmdel, N.J.," *Architectural Record*, Oct. 1962, 145–52

Walter McQuade, "Telephone Company Dials the Moon," *Architectural Forum*, Oct. 1962, 88–97

"Saarinen's Telephone Center Opens in New Jersey," *Progressive Architecture*, Oct. 1962, 77

"Biggest Mirror Ever," *Architectural Forum*, Apr. 1967, 33–41

Anthony Vidler, "Bell Telephone Laboratories, Holmdel," *Architectural Design*, Aug. 1967, 355–59

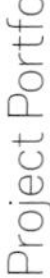

Deere and Company Administrative Center, interior with movable partitions

Deere and Company Administrative Center

Deere and Company Administrative Center, dining room

Deere and Company Administrative Center, facade detail

(opposite) Deere and Company Administrative Center, facade construction system, sectional perspective

Deere and Company Administrative Center
Moline, Illinois
1957–63

Occupying a hilly site of approximately 700 acres outside downtown Moline that had been consolidated from four farms, this 350,000-square-foot headquarters for a manufacturer of farm, construction, and lawn equipment was approached along a curving road that led to a double-height display pavilion. The space, 210 feet long by 35 feet high, showcased a 100-foot-long three-dimensional mural by Alexander Girard made of 2,000 Deere artifacts. A glass-enclosed bridge connected this pavilion to the fourth floor of the seven-story glass-walled main administration building, which spanned a ravine. Cor-Ten steel, in its first architectural use, was employed for columns, beams, sunscreens, and railings. A lower floor, partially below the level of the lake, contained an executive dining room with windows providing water-level views across two man-made lakes. Furniture designed by the Saarinen office was used throughout the interiors. Sasaki, Walker, and Associates were the project's landscape architects. [AL]

See also Lange, "Corporate Headquarters," and Martin, "What Is a Material?" in this volume.

John Dinkeloo, "Steel Will Weather Naturally," *Architectural Record,* Aug. 1962, 147–50

"Bold and Direct: Using Metal in a Strong Basic Way, Eero Saarinen's Design for the Deere and Co. Administrative Center," *Architectural Record,* July 1964, 135–42

"John Deere's Sticks of Steel," *Architectural Forum,* July 1964, 76–85

"Deere and Company Administrative Center," *Kenchiku Bunka,* Jan. 1965, 63–72

Forrest Wilson, "Pavilion in an Industrial Xanadu," *Interiors,* Jan. 1965, 77–91

"Offices—Moline, Illinois," *Architect and Building News* 227 (May 26, 1965), 979–84

John Jacobus, "John Deere Office Building, Moline, Illinois, USA," *Architectural Review,* May 1965, 364–71

"Deere and Co., U.S.A.," *Architectural Design,* Aug. 1965, 404–9

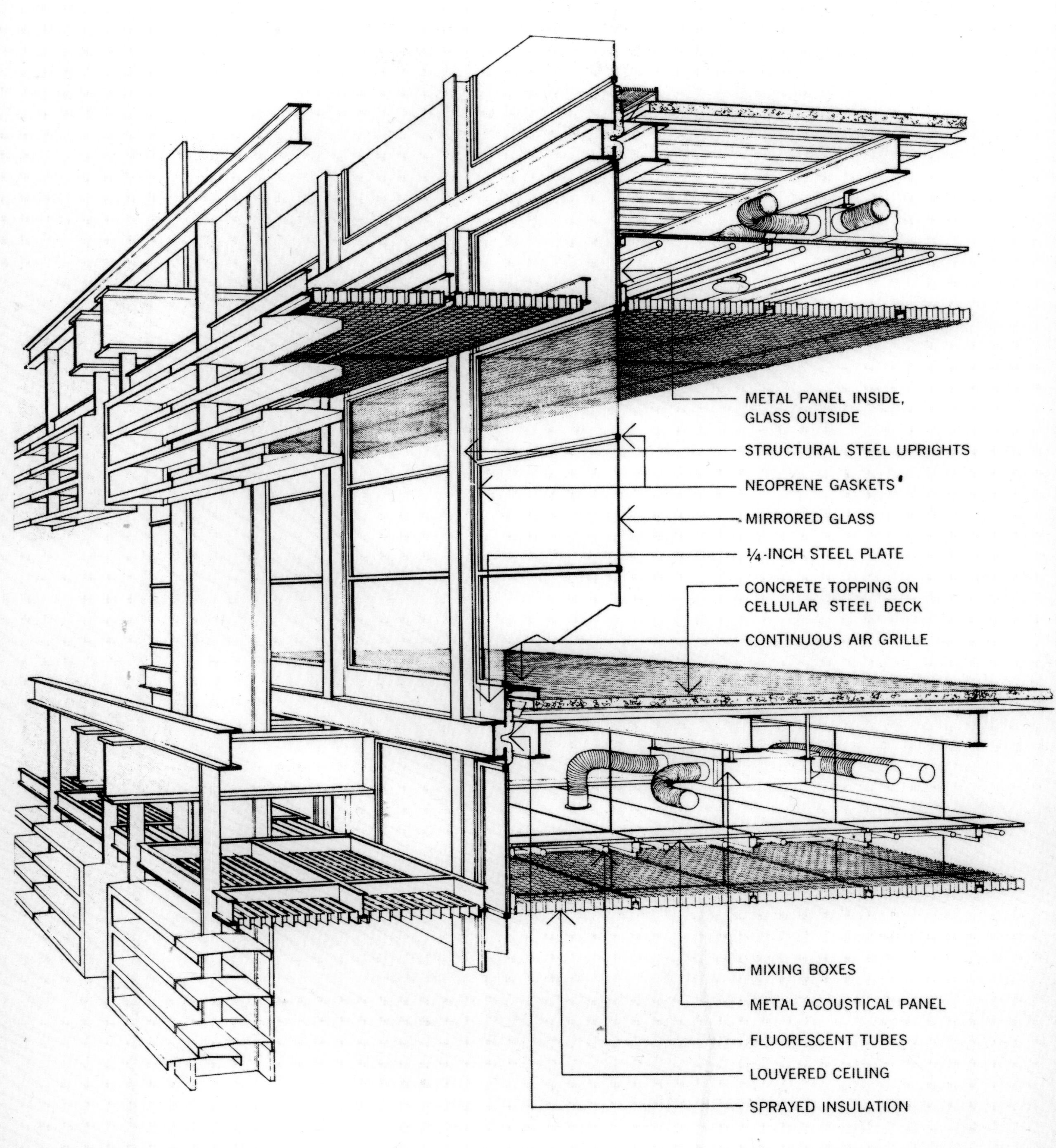

METAL PANEL INSIDE,
GLASS OUTSIDE
STRUCTURAL STEEL UPRIGHTS
NEOPRENE GASKETS
MIRRORED GLASS
¼-INCH STEEL PLATE
CONCRETE TOPPING ON
CELLULAR STEEL DECK
CONTINUOUS AIR GRILLE
MIXING BOXES
METAL ACOUSTICAL PANEL
FLUORESCENT TUBES
LOUVERED CEILING
SPRAYED INSULATION

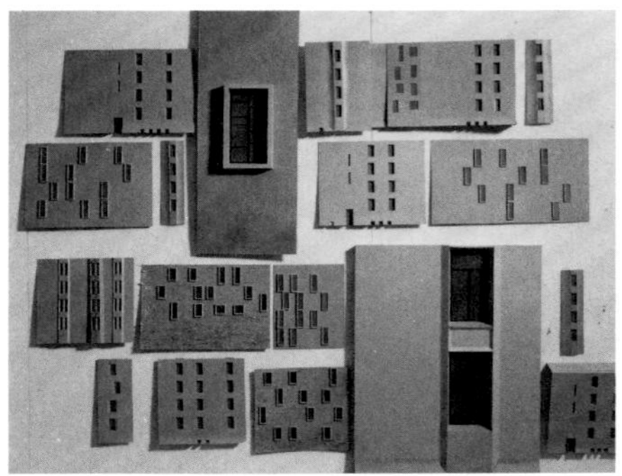

Samuel F. B. Morse and Ezra Stiles Colleges, Yale University, facade study models

Samuel F. B. Morse and Ezra Stiles Colleges, concrete facade detail

Samuel F. B. Morse and Ezra Stiles Colleges, aerial view. Morse is to the left of the central pedestrian walkway, Stiles to the right, with Tower Parkway in foreground.

Samuel F. B. Morse and Ezra Stiles Colleges (New Colleges)
Yale University
New Haven, Connecticut
1958–62
project number 5805

To accommodate 250 students in each of two residential colleges on the northwest edge of the Yale University campus, Eero Saarinen and Associates formed courtyards defined with low-rise polygonal buildings punctuated by two high-rise towers. The colleges were separated by an open pedestrian walk leading to the massively scaled neo-Gothic Payne Whitney Gymnasium, which together with the colleges' curving building wall formed a plaza. The colleges' varied silhouette resulted less from programmatic requirement than design intuition; during the design process, Saarinen reputedly used balloons raised to different heights to help envision the building profile. The facades of the flat-roofed buildings contrasted opaque planes with vertical strips of windows and smaller windows, many of which were placed high. Because the colleges' budget precluded the use of traditional masonry, which had been employed for Yale's older dormitories, Saarinen pioneered a method of concrete construction, aiming to produce what he described as "masonry walls made without masons." The Prepakt Concrete Company of Cleveland, Ohio, which had been identified by John Dinkeloo, built walls through which concrete was poured to surround rough-cut stones three to eight inches in length. An expanding agent was used to maintain the walls' intended width through the drying process. After the formwork was removed, the walls were subjected to high-pressure water blasting to remove some of the concrete and further reveal the stones. Abstract free-standing and relief sculptures by Costantino Nivola were placed throughout the complex. Pedestrian pathways weaving through the residential colleges incorporated shifts in grade and offered varied and changing vistas. Inside, the buildings' complex footprints resulted in irregularly shaped rooms that Saarinen hoped would be "as individual as possible, as random as those in an old inn." Two double-height dining halls had floor-to-ceiling windows and flagstone floors. They shared a kitchen that was located under the exterior passageway separating the two colleges. [TM]

See also Isenstadt, "Eero Saarinen's Theater of Form," Plattus, "Campus Plans," and Scully, "Rethinking Saarinen," in this volume.

"Due nuovi colleges alla Yale University, New Haven," *Casabella*, Jan. 1960, 14–17

"Saarinen Designs Two New Colleges for Yale," *Progressive Architecture*, Jan. 1960, 45

"Polygonal Architecture for the Samuel F. B. Morse and Ezra Stiles Colleges, Yale University," *Architectural Record*, Feb. 1960, 159–64

U. Roth, "Projekt für Studentenhäuser der Yale-Universität, New Haven, USA," *Werk*, Sept. 1961, 303–6

Aline B. Saarinen, "Master Builder at Yale: New Haven's Newest Colleges, the Architect's Own Words, His Ideas Behind a Last Major Work," *Portfolio and Art News Annual* 6 (autumn 1962), 36–39, 109–10

"Saarinen Colleges in Situ at Yale," *Progressive Architecture*, Nov. 1962, 57–60

Reyner Banham and Walter McQuade, "New Yale Colleges," *Architectural Forum*, Dec. 1962, 105–11

"Immagini dei due 'colleges' di Saarinen a Yale, con le scultore di Nivola," *Domus*, Feb. 1963, 17–26

Dulles International Airport, design sketches

Dulles International Airport, section, 2006

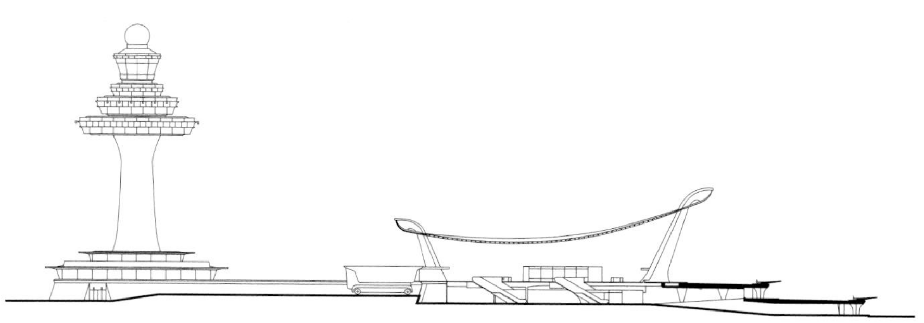

"Colleges Ezra e Morse a Yale," *Architettura*, Apr. 1963, 830–31

"Nouveaux collèges de l'Université de Yale," *L'Architecture d'Aujourd'hui*, Apr. 1963, 20–21

"Master House at Stiles College, Yale," *Interiors*, Dec. 1964, 56–58

"Ezra Stiles College, Morse College, Yale University," *Byggekunst*, Sept. 1965, 163–68

Dulles International Airport
Chantilly, Virginia
1958–63; expanded 1996

The engineering firm Ammann and Whitney was hired by the U.S. government as the prime contractor for a second airport to serve Washington, D.C., which would be the first civilian airport built specially for jets. Ammann and Whitney hired Eero Saarinen and Associates to design a two-level terminal and control tower. The undeveloped 9,800-acre site was reached via a new highway from the capital, twenty-three miles away. At 600 feet long by 150 feet wide, Saarinen's terminal was the nation's largest. The building's upper-level interior space, a single column-free room housing a waiting area and ticket counters, was enclosed by a steel-cable, tensioned roof suspended between rows of sixteen outward-curving concrete pylons. These supports were spaced 40 feet apart from each other, counteracting the cables' pull. Reinforced concrete was placed around the cables to stiffen them. Curving glass curtain walls were set between the pylons.

In designing the terminal, Saarinen pioneered the concept of mobile lounges, which carried passengers from the concourse to their planes. On the landing-field side of the terminal, a wing containing a restaurant and observation deck led to a fourteen-story control tower—a tapered concrete shaft topped by cantilevered control stations. Charles and Ray Eames created a film, *The Expanding Airport* (1958), to present the mobile lounge concept to the government; they also designed leather-and-aluminum Tandem Sling seating for the airport's interior. In the Saarinen office, the design team included Kent Cooper, David Jacob, Paul Kennon, Norman Pettula, Kevin Roche, and Warren Platner. In addition to its role as prime contractor, Ammann and Whitney acted as the associate architect-engineers of the terminal; Burns and McDonnell served as the mechanical engineers, and Dan Kiley was the landscape architect. [DA]

Dulles International Airport, with air traffic control tower

Dulles International Airport, construction of columns

See also Santala, "Airports," in this volume.

Frederick Gutheim, "D.C. Airport to Be Jet-Age Prototype," *Progressive Architecture*, May 1959, 100

"Saarinen Designs Lounge-Bus for Chantilly Airport," *Architectural Forum*, May 1959, 9

"New Airport for Jets, Dulles International Airport," *Architectural Record*, Mar. 1960, 175–82

"Washington to Get a Swooping Saarinen Air Terminal: Dulles Airport Designs Revealed," *Progressive Architecture*, Mar. 1960, 59

"Washington's New Jet Age International Airport," *Journal of the American Institute of Architects* 33 (Mar. 1960), 33

Ada Louise Huxtable, "Jet Age Triumph: Saarinen's New Airport for Washington Is a Superb Monument to Our Time," *New York Times*, Apr. 8, 1962

"Dulles International Airport," *Architectural Record*, July 1963, 101–10

"Portico to the Jet Age," *Architectural Forum*, July 1963, 72–83

"Aéroport International Dulles," *L'Architecture d'Aujourd'hui*, Oct. 1963, 80–83

"Dulles, le salle di attesa mobili di Eero Saarinen," *Architettura*, Mar. 1964, 836–37

Vivian Beaumont Repertory Theater (Lincoln Center Repertory Theater) and Lincoln Center Performing Arts Library and Museum
Lincoln Center for the Performing Arts
New York, New York
1958–65

project number 5807

In 1956, John D. Rockefeller III, who was president of the newly formed Lincoln Center, Inc., and responsible for overseeing the design and construction of the cultural arts complex on Manhattan's Upper West Side, received a preliminary list of international architects recommended by Wallace K. Harrison, but the center's board of trustees insisted that only American architects participate. Two years later, with all of the architects still not chosen, Harrison suggested that Eero Saarinen design the center's repertory theater. Gordon Bunshaft, partner and chief designer at Skidmore, Owings, and Merrill, was selected to design an adjacent structure housing a library and museum. Responding to the site, which faced a plaza containing a 125-foot-by-80-foot reflecting pool with a bronze sculpture

Vivian Beaumont Repertory Theater and Lincoln Center Performing Arts Library and Museum, perspective rendering

by Henry Moore, the architects joined forces to design a single building. The principal facade of the theater was a glazed wall recessed beneath a massive travertine-clad attic, behind which was a roof structure composed of twenty-foot-deep Vierendeel trusses and exposed concrete soffits. This attic was deep enough to house the library's stacks and reading rooms, which encircled the theater's stage house. The exposed concrete columns, set 153 feet apart, each terminated in a capital composed of two bronze-finished pyramids arranged point to point. Throughout the three-year design process, the columns proved the only point of disagreement between Saarinen and Bunshaft, who reached a compromise: Saarinen won authorship of the lucrative working drawings but lost his bid to use clusters of three columns in favor of Bunshaft's single-column design.

Inside, the building featured a sunken lobby leading to the theater's main level, and a cantilevered walkway opening onto the loge. Set in a steeply raked semicircle, none of the 1,100 seats—770 orchestra and 330 loge—were farther than 65 feet from the 10,000-square-foot stage. The stage contained a 46-foot-diameter turntable surrounded by a second, independently moving platform. The proscenium stage could be extended into an apron-thrust arrangement when the first seven rows of seating were lowered into the theater's basement and the proscenium arch, composed of seven panels, was removed or reconfigured. In addition to its principal performing space, the Beaumont contained a 299-seat amphitheater, initially called the Forum and later known as the Mitzi Newhouse Theater, located below the main theater's entrance level. Saarinen designed the Beaumont Theater in collaboration with his associate Cesar Pelli and the theater designer Jo Mielziner; Ammann and Whitney acted as the project's structural engineers, and Syska and Hennessy its mechanical engineers. [TM]

"Lincoln Center's Strong Team," *Architectural Forum*, Jan. 1959, 37

"Saarinen Design for Lincoln Center Repertory Theater," *Architectural Record*, Dec. 1961, 13

"Vivian Beaumont Repertory Theater, Lincoln Center, New York," *Architectural Record*, Sept. 1962, 142–45

"Lincoln Center, New York," *L'Architecture d'Aujourd'hui*, Sept. 1965, 24–26

"Thrust Forward for the Theatre: Vivian Beaumont Theatre and Library Museum," *Progressive Architecture*, Nov. 1965, 189–94

"Lincoln Center's Masterpiece," *Interiors*, Dec. 1965, 84–91

"Library-Museum at Lincoln Center," *Progressive Architecture*, Apr. 1966, 176–83

North Christian Church

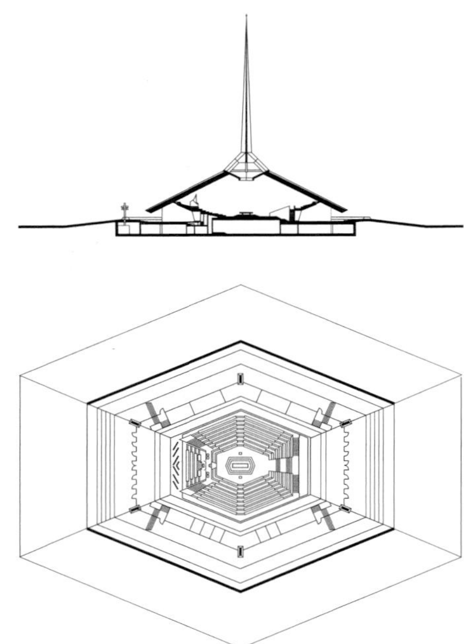

North Christian Church, section, 2006

North Christian Church, plan, 2006

1959

North Christian Church
Columbus, Indiana
1959–64

This project was commissioned by a group of congregants who left First Christian Church and, in affiliation with the Disciples of Christ, founded a new church. The two-story building, located on a flat five-and-a-half-acre site in a residential neighborhood on the northern edge of Columbus, was an elongated hexagon in plan and had an adjacent landscaped parking lot. The upper level housed the main sanctuary and a smaller chapel, both surrounded by an ambulatory. An auditorium and classrooms were located on the lower level. The hexagon's short sides contained banks of glass doors; on the long sides, landscaped berms stopped short of the building to create moatlike light wells, bringing natural illumination into the lower level via clerestory windows. Steel supports, one at each of the hexagon's corners, were sheathed in lead-coated copper and rose to frame the slate-clad roof, above which was a 192-foot spire and a five-foot-tall gold-leafed cross. This massive roof appeared to hover above the ground, an illusion created by the deep recession of the glass walls beneath it. Inside, the bowl-shaped main sanctuary was centered on a communion table. Natural light entered the sanctuary both directly, through a centrally located oculus, and indirectly, through the ambulatory's windows. Light from these windows was reflected onto the sanctuary's angled ceiling planes. Alexander Girard designed a tapestry, candelabra, and plant stands. Repp and Mundt of Columbus worked as the general contractor. [JO]

See also Miller, "Eero and Irwin," and Olivarez, "Churches and Chapels," in this volume.

"Saarinen's Church: The North Christian Church in Columbus, Indiana," *Architectural Record*, Sept. 1964, 185–90

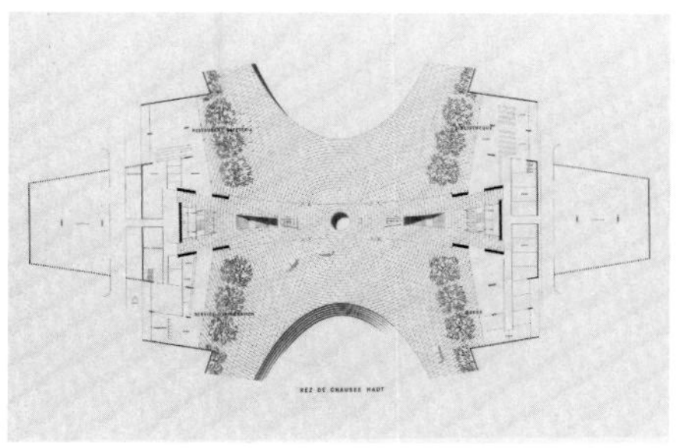

World Health Organization competition, plan

World Health Organization competition, perspective

1960

World Health Organization competition
Geneva, Switzerland
1960

project number 6001

Saarinen took second place in this competition to design an office building for the World Health Organization, the United Nations' health agency, intended for a hilly site outside Geneva. He proposed a concrete structure suspended over a narrow, shallow valley and supported only at the ends on curved piers. The nine-story building's two primary facades were to be gently concave and clad in gray-tinted glass. Saarinen took advantage of the site's natural depression to form a two-level plaza. The upper level would lead to lobbies and public reception rooms, while the lower plaza would be divided into two sections, each defined by sweeping arc-shaped walls and leading to meeting rooms. The Swiss architect Jean Tschumi won the competition, and his design was realized posthumously in 1966 by Pierre Bonnard, his former associate. [TM]

"W.H.O. Competition: Second Place Goes to Saarinen," *Progressive Architecture*, July 1960, 50

Hamden Office
Hamden, Connecticut
1960–61

The building into which Eero Saarinen and Associates moved after leaving Bloomfield Hills, Michigan, was a three-story brick neo-Tudor house on a three-acre site a short drive from New Haven. Saarinen died while the office was relocating. The house, known as Lucerne, was designed in 1905 by Brown and Von Beren for Fred Graves, a local banker and cigar manufacturer. The Saarinen firm renovated the house's interior and added a 6,000-square-foot two-level brick studio off the back. The building remains in use today, as the office of Kevin Roche John Dinkeloo and Associates. [SK]

Saarinen House renovation
New Haven, Connecticut
1960–61

Saarinen's death in September 1961 prevented him from occupying this two-story Tudor-style house at 10 St. Ronan Terrace, although his widow, Aline, and son, Eames, did move there. As late as July 1961, Saarinen was still writing elaborate room-by-room notes about his ideas for renovating the house. He sought to simplify the interiors by eliminating many of the existing decorative moldings, as well as by painting rooms white. His plans also called for converting a sleeping porch into a dressing room and outfitting one of the second-floor rooms as a workspace for himself and Aline. [SK]

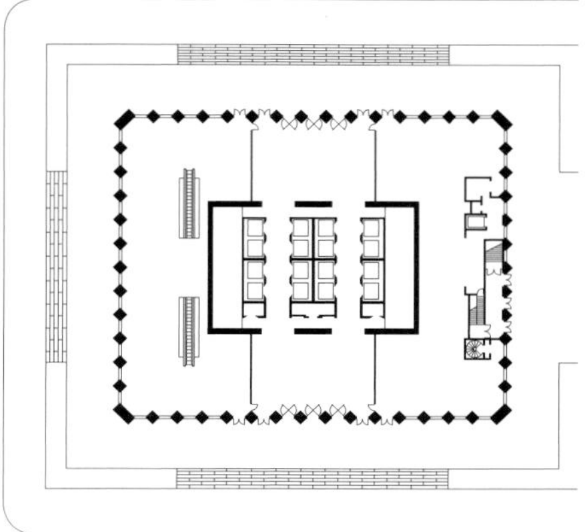

Columbia Broadcasting System, Inc., Building, plan, 2006

Columbia Broadcasting System, Inc., Building

Columbia Broadcasting System, Inc., Building, under construction

Columbia Broadcasting System, Inc., Building
New York, New York
1960–65
project number 6010

The Columbia Broadcasting System, with William Paley serving as chairman of the board and Frank Stanton as president, hired Eero Saarinen and Associates to design this headquarters for a 47,696-square-foot site stretching the full-block front on Sixth Avenue between Fifty-second and Fifty-third streets in midtown Manhattan. Saarinen's design for what would become his only completed tall building anticipated changes to New York City's zoning laws that, when ratified in 1961, encouraged sheer towers rising from plazas rather than traditional set-back buildings that filled their sites. After studying various massing models developed for the 715,440-square-foot building, including a fifteen-story structure fully covering the site, Saarinen decided on a flat-topped thirty-eight-story tower occupying 60 percent of the site. As constructed, the CBS Building, with a 135-by-160-foot plan and a height of 490 feet, was recessed 25 feet behind the building line on all of the site's three street frontages, as well as by an equal distance from a two-story service building to the east, and sunk approximately two feet below sidewalk grade. (Sketches show that an early scheme had proposed lifting the building on angled columns, leaving a sunken plaza fully accessible beneath it.)

The building was the first skyscraper in New York City to be constructed in reinforced concrete. Five-foot-wide V-shaped columns, clad in black Canadian granite and spaced ten feet apart center to center, wrapped the perimeter—thirteen on each short side and sixteen on each long side—interspersed with five-foot-wide expanses of gray-tinted glass. (The building's overall dark and solid appearance garnered it the nickname Black Rock.) After Saarinen's death, the final proportions of the piers and windows were determined under the supervision of Kevin Roche, who, along with colleagues John Dinkeloo and Joseph N. Lacy, assumed responsibility for the project. Stanton rejected fifty varieties of granite and marble before approving one, but even then he and Paley were concerned that the granite would appear too reflective when polished and too light in color when roughened. The Saarinen firm pioneered a method for attaining the desired dark, matte surface: thermal stippling, in which exposure to extreme heat creates an uneven texture, was combined with liquid honing, in which the high-pressure application of a glass-based abrasive restores the granite's dark tonalities.

Utilizing a structural system designed by Paul Weidlinger, an early proponent of computer-assisted design and engineering, the perimeter columns supported floor beams that tied back to the building's 55-by-85-foot concrete core housing elevators, fire stairs, and lavatories. A continuous L-shaped haunch beam set against the interior side of the columns provided additional support. Floors were made of a lightweight concrete weighing 25 percent less than conventional concrete. Although externally the columns remained the same width from top to bottom—Saarinen rejected the

Columbia Broadcasting System, Inc., Building, perspective of proposed base

use of entasis and refused to alter the columnar screen in order to accommodate a prominent entrance—as the columns rose the space within the V widened to allow for larger ducts. The columns did not bear the load evenly and, because the corners required only minimal columnar support, the corner columns served visual purposes more than structural ones.

Inside the building, 35-foot-deep office spaces, measured from exterior wall to service core, were column free and based on a five-foot module. The office interiors were designed by Florence Knoll Bassett and the Knoll Planning Unit, whom Saarinen had recommended. Warren Platner, who had previously worked for Saarinen, designed a street-level restaurant named the Ground Floor. Only the lobby, which had travertine walls, was designed by the Saarinen office. [TM]

See also Martin, "What Is a Material?" in this volume.

"Saarinen's Sophisticated Skyscraper for CBS," *Progressive Architecture*, Oct. 1961, 53–54

"Last Saarinen: CBS Building, New York," *Architectural Review*, Dec. 1961, 30

"Saarinen's CBS Design, New York," *Architectural Record*, Apr. 1962, 149–50

"Skyscraper," *Arts and Architecture*, Aug. 1962, 20

"C.B.S. Headquarters," *Engineering News Record* 172 (May 21, 1964), 64–67

P. Pragnell, "Saarinen's CBS Building, New York," *Architecture Association Journal* 80 (Feb. 1965), 210–12

Peter Blake, "Slaughter on Sixth Avenue," *Architectural Forum*, June 1965, 13–19

"Saarinen's Skyscraper," *Architectural Record*, July 1965, 111–18

Bethami Probst, "CBS Somber Power on Sixth Avenue," *Progressive Architecture*, July 1965, 187–92

"Ground Floor Restaurant of the C.B.S. Building," *Interiors*, Jan. 1966, 66–95

Ada Louise Huxtable, "Eero Saarinen's Somber Skyscraper," *New York Times*, Mar. 13, 1966

"For Formal Dining: Black Granite," *Progressive Architecture*, Mar. 1966, 180–83

"Tale of Two Towers: Saarinen's CBS Building in Manhattan and SOM's Building in Chicago," *Architectural Forum*, Apr. 1966, 28–37

Athens Airport, design sketches

Athens Airport, sketch of exterior

Athens Airport
Athens, Greece
1960–69, airport use discontinued 2001
project number 6005

This new airport and the terminal Saarinen designed for it were located ten miles south of Athens on a site at the base of Mount Hymettus overlooking the Bay of Saronikos. It was built by the Greek government and largely funded with loans from the United States government. The need for a new airport had been determined after President Dwight D. Eisenhower's trip to Athens in 1959 necessitated the destruction of existing buildings to allow his Boeing 707 to land. The antiquated airport then launched an extensive renovation, a project executed by the engineering firm Ammann and Whitney, which had worked with Saarinen on numerous projects and suggested his office to design the new terminal. Though Saarinen was hired in 1960, the project was not completed until 1969. Constructed of concrete containing aggregate made from Pentelic marble, the white stone of the Parthenon, the four-story building was set into a sloping site, so that visitors entered on the second floor, where they could ascend to a mezzanine lounge providing views of the arrival and departure hall below. This double-height area looked out over the airfield through a glazed colonnade, whose cruciform columns contained air-conditioning ducts. The third floor featured a terrace with seaside views and a stairway to the fourth floor, which measured 250 feet long, 120 feet deep, and 10 feet tall. The building's most dramatic feature, this floor was cantilevered 22 feet on each of three sides and carried on cruciform columns and slender, tapering beams. It housed a restaurant and government offices. [TM]

See also Santala, "Airports," in this volume.

"Saarinen's Athens Airport, a Classic Pavilion," *Progressive Architecture*, Aug. 1962, 51

"Saarinen's Athens Air Terminal," *Architectural Record*, Aug. 1962, 111–14

Hélène Lipstadt

the gateway arch
designing america's first modern monument

Fig. 1 Eero Saarinen and J. Henderson Barr studying a competition drawing for the United States Jefferson National Expansion Memorial, 1947

Eero Saarinen's career as an independent architect began with his victory in the two-stage design competition for the Jefferson National Expansion Memorial in St. Louis, Missouri, which was held between September 1947 and February 1948. The monument commemorates President Thomas Jefferson's role as author of the Louisiana Purchase, along with other agents of western expansion. It is one of Saarinen's most visually prominent designs, though the millions who know it as a symbol of St. Louis from its frequent appearance in media and advertising do not know it as his—that is, as the work of Eero Saarinen and Associates, architects, in cooperation with the engineers Severud, Elstad, Krueger Associates. The arch was designed for an eighty-acre United States Historic Site that had been created in the late 1930s by clearing the site of colonial St. Louis, which then consisted mostly of dilapidated late-nineteenth-century warehouses. These were perceived as depressing reminders that St. Louis was no longer the "Gateway to the West" and as threats to the still-vibrant but ailing downtown. All that remained of the nineteenth-century past was the Catholic cathedral and a domed courthouse just across from the historic site. The competition program was written by the traditionalist-turned-modernist architect George Howe for the Jefferson National Expansion Memorial Association, a local nonprofit organization and the sponsor of both the monument and the competition. The client, the federal government's National Park Service, accepted the association's proposed memorial, designed by Saarinen, in June 1948. Saarinen, who was responsible for all the major design decisions during the decade it took to overcome the political, physical, and financial obstacles, made the final choices, but he did not live to see construction, which began in February 1963 and was completed in October 1965.

Although Saarinen later changed the arch's height from 580 to 630 feet, and the client modified the programming of the site, the steel monument one sees today—carbon steel on the interior, stainless steel on the exterior, and concrete in-filling, with an equilateral-triangle-shaped section that tapers from 54 to 17 feet at the top, and the concept of a skin that is also structure—is in essence his competition design.[1] The group responsible for the scheme was made up of Eero Saarinen, designer; J. Henderson Barr, associate designer; Dan Kiley, landscape architect; Lily Swann Saarinen, sculptor; and the designer Alexander Girard, who served as the team's painter (fig. 1).

The design is the result of a collaboration with Saarinen's milieu as well. All competition projects are inherently co-made because they are designed in dialogue with the program and in anticipation of the judgment of jurors and of the imagined solutions and strategies of other competitors, who thus co-make the project artistically and formally. Saarinen was exceptionally well prepared to be a co-maker, for he was able to draw not only on his collaborators and the members of his milieu, but also on the fact that he had learned about architecture crawling under his father's drafting table, as he often said.[2]

THE FIRST STAGE

In the first stage of the two-stage open competition, each designer was required to provide several program components, of which three were specially significant for the modernist debates of the day about "New Monumentality" and the urbanism it advocated. These were the "architectural memorial," which consisted of a main monument, museum facilities, and painted and sculpted representations of western expansion; the "living memorial," an institution for scientific and artistic research and the dissemination of information, whose activities maintained the spirit of the multitalented Jefferson; and areas to accommodate large assemblages of people.

Saarinen's project consisted of a living memorial that was a branch of the United Nations housed in two interlocking slabs placed at the southern edge of the site. A long open arcade and series of courts adorned with sculpture and murals extended behind the parabolic arch, which was 556 feet tall and about 700 feet wide at the base, and stood on the levee of the Mississippi River. The museum was placed underground. The rest of the program requirements that would be retained in the second stage of the competition were dispersed in the densely forested landscape of the historic site.

Saarinen and Kiley, the modernist landscape architect, each independently came up with the idea of collaborating with the other, as they had in the past.[3] But before Kiley could contribute, and even "before any drawings were made," the concepts of "a gateway arch on the bank of a river and a forest covering as much as possible of the site" were devised. These two concepts and that of the intersecting slab plan for the living memorial originated with Saarinen's reading of the program, as his annotated copy suggests (fig. 2). As Kiley wrote, the arch, the "underground solution," which left a very open park, and the confining of motor access "to the extremities of the levee" and the most "obvious buildings" to the boundaries of the site were basic decisions made "before [he] was even connected" with the project in August 1947.[4]

In fact, many more of the basic decisions were made in the margins of the program. Saarinen there resolved all the main siting problems, established the plan forms of the two major buildings and the geometry and shape of the memorial in elevation, and projected the organization of the two required competition entry boards, all the while experimenting with the arch's siting, but maintaining its position on the levee (fig. 3). At some point, he must have worked very late on the program, for he wrote on its cover: "Bang very hard on my door at 8:00 a.m."[5]

As Saarinen sketched, even working on a family vacation taken to allow him to confer with Kiley in New England, office staff, supervised by J. Henderson Barr, prepared rendered plans, a contoured clay model of the site, and finished line drawings at the scale of the competition boards. Throughout, they maintained a "continuous search" for a "free flow" of the many program elements.[6] Simultaneously, Eero oversaw the production of his father's design for the same competition, reporting to him on its progress by mail.

road on the eastern shore; the provision of ferries and footbridges between the banks, and so forth and so on.

ACCESS to the Historic Site is to be provided by road, rail, river, and air. Competitors may offer suggestions for the approaches by road involving changes in the street and traffic systems in the neighborhood of the development, provided the changes fit in with the general Traffic Plan as now proposed and partially shown on the accompanying aerial view of St. Louis (Appendix A). Their Submissions will not be unfavorably considered because their suggestions are impractical for jurisdictional, economic, or other reasons of which they can have no knowledge. They will be judged only by their inventive ingenuity in suggesting an easy flow of traffic to the Historic Site and into the parking facilities described under "The Parking of Vehicles" below. It is proposed to convey visitors arriving by air at the Municipal Airport to the Historic Site by helicopters. *A platform 150′ x 600′ is to be provided for receiving them.* The type of helicopter now in contemplation will carry twenty-four passengers and will require a space 150′ x 150′ to receive it. The platform called for provides temporary storage space for three helicopters in addition to the receiving area. Appropriate facilities for passengers must be provided. It is proposed to convey visitors arriving by air at the new Municipal Airport, being considered for construction on the western bank of the River to the north of the City, to the Memorial by speedboats. *A Municipal Landing reserved for them must be provided.*

THE PARKING OF VEHICLES on the Historic Site is to be provided for underground. Accommodation for 200 buses and 4000 to 6000 motor cars is the goal. Competitors need not study the complex problem of providing such accommodation in detail, but they must indicate in general how they propose to approach the questions of access to the parking space, the handling and disposition of cars, and so forth. As previously stated, Competitors are given a free hand in suggesting any changes in the surrounding street and traffic systems which they feel to be desirable to achieve satisfactory access conditions and their Submissions will not be adversely judged if their suggestions prove to be impossible to carry out provided they show inventive ingenuity. It is suggested that the garage be so arranged that shuttle buses serving the business and shopping area may pick up passengers from the motor car garage underground.

THE RELOCATION OF RAILROAD TRACKS AND THE INTERSTATE HIGHWAY have been discussed above under "Appendix B".

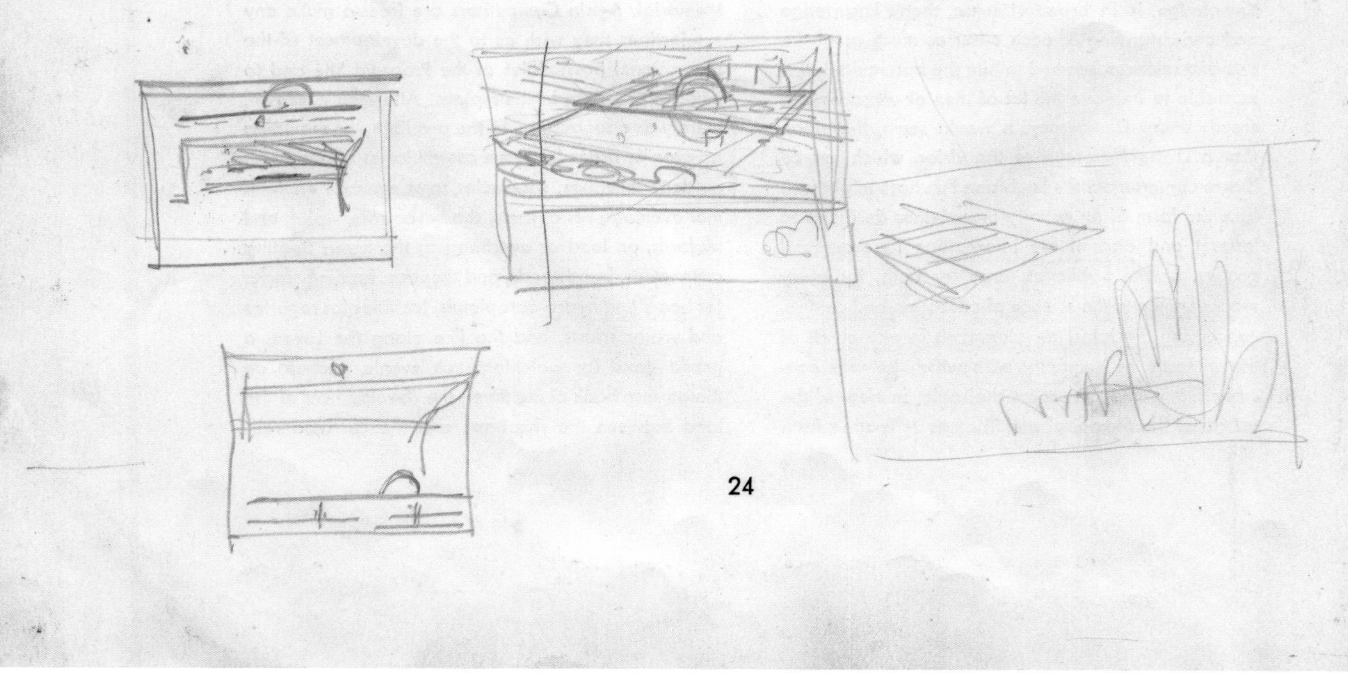

24

Fig. 2 United States Jefferson National Expansion Memorial competition program with Saarinen's sketches, 1947

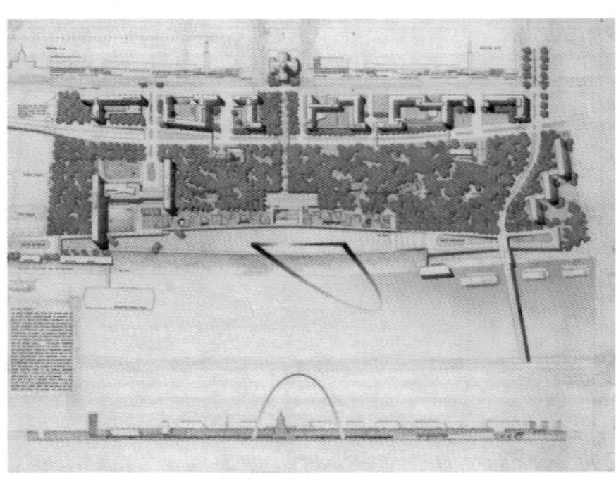

Fig. 3 Saarinen, Saarinen, and Associates, United States Jefferson National Expansion Memorial, first-stage competition rendering, 1947

Fig. 4 (opposite) United States Jefferson National Expansion Memorial, preparatory rendering for second stage of competition by J. Henderson Barr, 1947–48

Saarinen also received help from members of his milieu. He polled his fellow modernists about who was entering the competition and the direction they thought it would take. His close friend Charles Eames, a native of St. Louis and a rival competitor, provided "philosophical talk in the Jeffersonian department"—that is, advice about the living memorial and instruction on the meaning of the site. The writer and planner Frederick Gutheim, who wrote for the *New York Herald Tribune,* reported on rumors about the jury's deliberations. Carl Milles, a sculptor at Cranbrook, was said at the time to have suggested the change from a square to a triangular section.[7]

THE SECOND STAGE

Five finalists were chosen in late September 1947. In addition to Eero Saarinen, they were T. Marshall Rainey; Berger, Hornbostel, and Lewis; Phillips and Eng; and Harris Armstrong.[8] Each team received $10,000 and new instructions for a "problem . . . largely of landscape design" that required "a tree-shaded park, sloping or terraced down to the river, leaving a clear view from the . . . Courthouse to the Levee" and a "non-functional . . . architectural memorial," conceived as a "striking element." The living memorial and spaces for large assemblages were no longer required.[9]

In Saarinen, Saarinen, and Associates' entry, the museum was moved to the south end of the site and raised to ground level, and the historic arcade with its required painting and sculpture was shortened. The monument was moved farther south of the axis of the courthouse and west of the levee, and its span and cross-section modified. The parabolic arch became a weighted catenary, somewhat like a bicycle chain if its links are graded in the same proportion as the arch, and the section was changed to an equilateral triangle. On the drawings submitted to the competition, the arch was 590 feet tall and 592 feet wide at the base, measured from center to center of the triangle.

Kiley was given a major role in all decision making after settling a protracted quarrel with Saarinen about his earlier failure to respect Kiley's "design philosophy of complete collaboration" as well as issues of compensation. The engineer Fred Severud consulted on structure, but it was aesthetics and not his very minimal input that dictated the change in the profile of the arch. Steel was chosen as the material because it was permanent and symbolized that quality. Symbolism, however, seems to have come second to problem solving, as suggested by the tone of Saarinen's description of the "great arch" as "symbolizing the gateway to the West, the national expansion, and whatnot." Aesthetics governed the transformation of the mathematically calculated parabola of the first stage into the weighted catenary of the second, for they had "worked at first with mathematical shapes, but finally adjusted [the arch] according to the eye."[10]

The strategy of using a traditional presentation without betraying the project's modernism led to an emphasis on the required perspective, for which Barr drew ninety-eight preparatory views, and which Saarinen believed won the competition for them (fig. 4). To prepare a "modern looking plan" that still had a "wonderful sculptural quality," site contour lines were incised with engraver's tools onto a plastic sheet, and Saarinen himself did the airbrushing.[11]

Like the arch's form, its symbolism was the fruit of a collaboration. Saarinen relied on Eames for advice about symbolism and commemoration, which Eames believed was so compelling that on the eve of the final judgment he predicted Saarinen had a "75% chance" of winning because that "arch should . . . be enough to swing it." Louis Kahn, speaking from rumored descriptions of the first-stage design, encouraged Saarinen to remain fully engaged with "physical monumentality" and to avoid getting "snarled up with traffic and parking," as he himself had in the first stage. In fact, Saarinen gave equal attention to both.[12]

The finalists had received instructions to prepare their new drawings in secret, but soon "architects all over the U.S. . . . [were] buzzing," thanks in part to Saarinen and Kiley's appeals to members of their milieu. Saarinen's

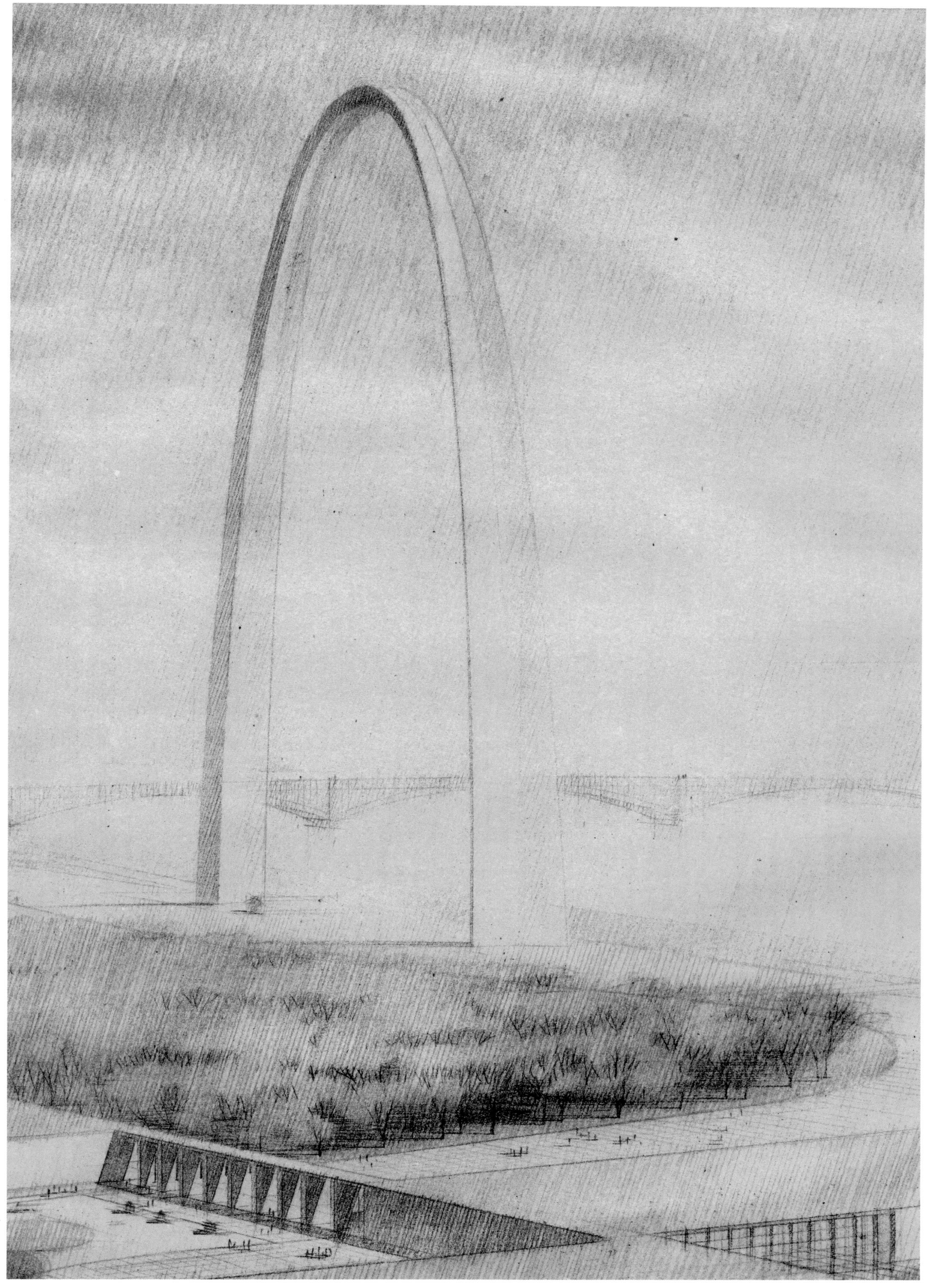

Fig. 5 United States Jefferson National Expansion Memorial, photomontage of post-competition model of Saarinen's winning entry, 1948

strategy was to tell as few people as possible about his entry and to find out as much as he could about others', using the "grapevine" to compensate for the fact that he "lived in the sticks." Kahn and other modernist competitors helped him establish who the other finalists were and gather intelligence on the nature of their projects, showing him or sending descriptions of their unsuccessful entries. When the Saarinen team won the $40,000 prize, they and other modernists showered him with joyful congratulatory messages. Edward Durell Stone, however, was not surprised by yet another Saarinen victory in a competition: "Ho hum again," he telegraphed.[13]

CO-MAKING

Saarinen's entry amalgamated the large-scale, light metallic structures (or the appearance of one such structure) and the mobile forms that partisans of the New Monumentality had called for with an arch, a commemorative building type favored by the old monumentality (fig. 5). Both his arch and the presentation of Saarinen's second-stage entry were exquisitely poised between traditionalism and modernism, and they achieved just the right balance between the current concerns of modernist architects and the sponsor's desire for a striking monument and a reinvigorated city center. Saarinen was also well served by his family's experiences participating in competitions, which gave him an almost sociological understanding of architecture competitions as "a struggle and a fiesta within a small clique" as an occasion of both conflict and cooperation. He was also buoyed by his father's understanding of monumentality, which made it likely that he heard the program's demand for monumentality as a summons meant especially for someone like himself, who had the entire shared heritage of architecture—the traditional and the modern—at his disposal and was thus alert to the potential for radical innovation inherent in it. Working with but also against modernists in his milieu, with a predisposition for competing inherited from his father, and with his collaborators, named and unnamed, Saarinen co-made the Gateway Arch.[14]

Notes

1. Sharon A. Brown, "Jefferson National Expansion Memorial, Administrative History, 1935–1981," National Park Service, 1984, http://www.nps.gov/jeff/adhi%20Folder/adhi.htm, and J. E. N. Jensen, "The Construction of the Arch," National Park Service, http://www.nps.gov/jeff/materials_techniques.html.

2. See Hélène Lipstadt, "Co-Making the Modern Monument: The Jefferson National Expansion Memorial Competition and Saarinen's Gateway Arch," in *Modern Architecture in St. Louis: Washington University and Postwar American Architecture, 1948–1973*, ed. Eric Mumford (St. Louis: School of Architecture, Washington University in St. Louis, 2004), 5–25, for the history of the competition and a fuller discussion of co-making. Rumiko Handa, *Design Through Drawing: Eero Saarinen's Design in the Jefferson National Expansion Memorial Competition* (Ann Arbor: University Microfilms, 1992) interprets the design as Saarinen's effort alone.

3. Gregg Bleam, "Dan Kiley: Planting on the Grid," in *Preserving Modern Landscape Architecture II: Making Postwar Landscapes Visible*, ed. Charles A. Birnbaum, assisted by Jane Brown Gillette and Nancy Slade (Washington, D.C.: Spacemaker Press, 2004), 72.

4. Eero Saarinen, letter to Dan Kiley, Apr. 28, 1947; Dan Kiley, letter to Eero Saarinen, May 2, 1947; Saarinen, Saarinen, and Associates, Comments on Earlier Sketches of the Jefferson National Expansion Memorial Competition, Feb. 26, 1948 (erroneously dated 1947); Dan Kiley, letter to Eero Saarinen, Oct. 29, 1947. Saarinen's annotated copy of the program printed by the Jefferson National Expansion Memorial Association (hereafter JNEMA), *Architectural Competition for the Jefferson National Expansion Memorial—Program* (St. Louis: Jefferson National Expansion Memorial Association, 1947), was recently discovered by the author among the clippings files of the Eero Saarinen Papers at Yale University; it is hereafter referred to as Annotated Program. All correspondence cited in this essay is from box 26 and the drawings are from Jefferson National Expansion Memorial History Tubes, Original Competition Drawings, in the Eero Saarinen Papers, Manuscripts and Archives, Yale University.

5. Annotated Program, front cover, 11, 24, 26, and back cover, verso. In Eero Saarinen, "Saarinen Tells How 'Gateway' Was Conceived," *St. Louis Post-Dispatch*, Mar. 7, 1948, the domed Thomas Jefferson Memorial is said to have been the model, but this account may have been tailored to deflect the accusation that the arch was insufficiently Jeffersonian that was made at precisely the time of its writing, as is suggested by a later statement in Eero Saarinen, letter to Dr. Benjamin Alan Russell, June 6, 1951: "[The] Jefferson Memorial . . . being round and being based on a round dome, [is] too inward an expression for

[Jefferson]." Gilmore D. Clarke, chairman of the federal Commission of Fine Arts, charged that the arch was unworthy of Jefferson because it had been copied from an unexecuted arch design by Adalberto Libera for the Italian Fascist Fair, EUR '42, but Saarinen wrote in a letter to William W. Wurster, Mar. 1, 1948, that neither he nor any of his associates had seen or known of it.

6. Eero Saarinen, letter to Jay [J. Henderson Barr], undated; drawings titled "Gateway to the West" and "The Jefferson Monument" (overlaid scheme); "Competition: Jefferson National Expansion Memorial," *Progressive Architecture,* May 1948, 56.

7. Charles Eames, letters to Eero Saarinen, July 23, 1947, Aug. 8, 1947, and Feb. 18, 1948; Saarinen, "Saarinen Tells How 'Gateway' Was Conceived," describes Eames's advice; Dan Kiley, letter to Eero Saarinen, Sept. 18, 1947 (received); for Milles, see Frederick Gutheim, "Jefferson and Mussolini," *New York Herald Tribune,* Feb. 27, 1948; for square section, see "The Jefferson Monument" (overlaid scheme).

8. Both Eero and Eliel had submitted their designs under the firm name of Saarinen, Saarinen, and Associates, and the resulting confusion has become the stuff of an oft-repeated story that can now be confirmed and corrected. After Eliel was informed by telegram of his selection for the second round, the families celebrated his victory, only to learn later that in fact Eero had won. In an oral history in the Archives of American Art, Eero's first wife, Lilian Swann Saarinen, recalled how, after receiving the telegram and after the families had celebrated, Eero received a call from "George Howell" [*sic*]. "He felt simply terrible, that he'd made an awful mistake. It was Eero who had won it. . . . Eero called that up to his father, and his father said, 'Well, congratulations, come on over and have another bottle of champagne.' . . . Eliel was happy in two ways. He'd come that close and his son had come first." Lilian Swann Saarinen and Robert Brown, "Interview with Lilian Swann Saarinen," Archives of American Art, Smithsonian Institution, Washington, D.C., http://www.aaa.si.edu/collections/oralhistories/transcripts/saarin79.htm.

Eliel did receive a telegram on September 26 informing him of his selection for the second stage. If George Howe had indeed called on September 26, he also confirmed the correction in a letter dated three days later, writing to Eero that his secretary had mistakenly sent the telegram to the first name on the firm's letterhead. Howe laconically concluded, "Please take this to be a correction." A form letter of rejection was sent to Eliel the next day. Howe's handwritten postscript read: "So you wanted two prizes. The parabola got me anyway." George Howe, telegram to Eliel Saarinen, Sept. 26, box 17, 1947 Competition Entry Drawings, JNEMA Records, JEFF-9107, National Park Service, Jefferson National Expansion Memorial. (This reference is to the records before their reorganization as JEFF-9107 in 1997.) George Howe, letter to Eero Saarinen, Sept. 29, 1947, and George Howe, letter to Eliel Saarinen, Sept. 30, 1947, Eero Saarinen Papers, Yale University.

9. Lipstadt, "Co-Making the Modern Monument," 20.

10. Eero Saarinen, letter to Dan Kiley, Oct. 25, 1947; Dan Kiley, letter to Eero Saarinen, Nov. 2, 1947; Eero Saarinen, letter to Frank Severud, Nov. 1947; Eero Saarinen, letter to H. E. Grant, Head, Department of Engineering Drawing, Washington University, Mar. 24, 1948.

11. Eero Saarinen, letter to Philip Johnson, Feb. 23, 1948; Eero Saarinen, letter to Dan Kiley, Nov. 25, 1947.

12. Eames to Saarinen, Feb. 18, 1948; Louis Kahn, letter to Eero Saarinen, Oct. 21, 1947.

13. "St. Louis Competition," *Architectural Forum,* Oct. 15, 1947, 11; Eero Saarinen, letter to Dan Kiley, Oct. 8, 1947; Eero Saarinen, letter to Louis Kahn, Oct. 15, 1947, on "grapevine" and "sticks"; Kahn to Saarinen, Oct. 21, 1947; Dan Kiley, letter to Eero Saarinen, Sept. 24, 1947; Saarinen to Kiley, Nov. 25, 1947; Edward Durell Stone, letter to Eero Saarinen, Feb. 20, 1948.

14. Lipstadt, "Co-Making the Modern Monument," 17, 20, 23; Eero Saarinen, letter to Louis Kahn, Feb. 22, 1947. On the notion of the "space of possibles" and its role in competitions, see Hélène Lipstadt, "Can 'Art Professions' Be Bourdieuian Fields of Cultural Production? The Case of the Architecture Competition," *Cultural Studies* 17 (May 2003), 400–401.

Rosamond Fletcher

the general motors technical center

a collaborative enterprise

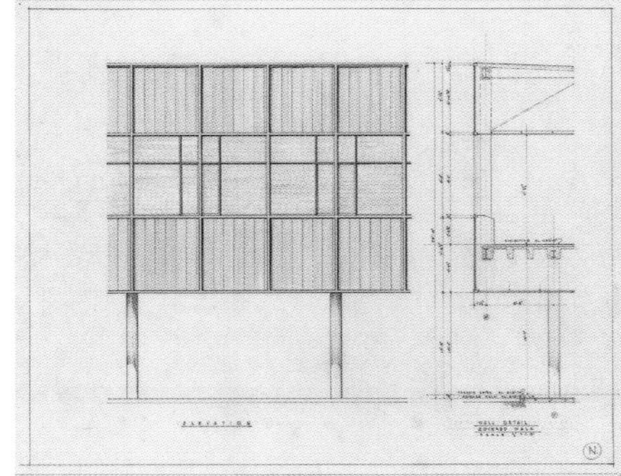

Fig. 1 Saarinen and Swanson, General Motors Technical Center, Warren, Michigan, first scheme, 1946, curtain-wall section and elevation

The extensive press coverage that the General Motors Technical Center received when it opened in the spring of 1956 frames Eero Saarinen as a master collaborator, citing his relationships with participating artists Alexander Calder, Harry Bertoia, and Antoine Pevsner as evidence. Yet despite Saarinen's subsequent reputation for working with artists, research into these partnerships reveals that the dialogue was limited to the specification of dimensions for their pieces.[1] It was in the realm of engineering that Saarinen learned to collaborate, establishing reciprocal lines of communication and developing a new working method. More than by-products of architecture, these exchanges of expertise can be considered the prototype for the research-driven design methodology that became characteristic of Eero Saarinen and Associates.

The role that innovative building technologies would play in architectural expression at GM was already apparent in curtain-wall sections, drawn in 1946, for an initial scheme for the Tech Center, credited to the firm of Saarinen and Swanson (fig. 1). These sections established the office's ambition of creating an ultra-thin glass-and-metal curtain wall. Working with a porcelain-enamel manufacturer, Saarinen realized this vision in gray steel panels measuring just two inches thick. The exterior metal facing was bonded to a resin-impregnated paper honeycomb core filled with perlite, a granular insulation material.[2] This product, heterogeneous in its makeup, represented the height of innovation and ended the quest, first articulated a decade earlier by the engineer Albert Bemis, for a "utopian" material that would provide "adequate strength, durability, satisfactory surfaces for both outside and inside finish, and sufficient insulation value to reduce the flow of heat." The porcelain-enamel panels became a standard product in the building industry, and Saarinen would use and refine them in later projects, including IBM Rochester.[3]

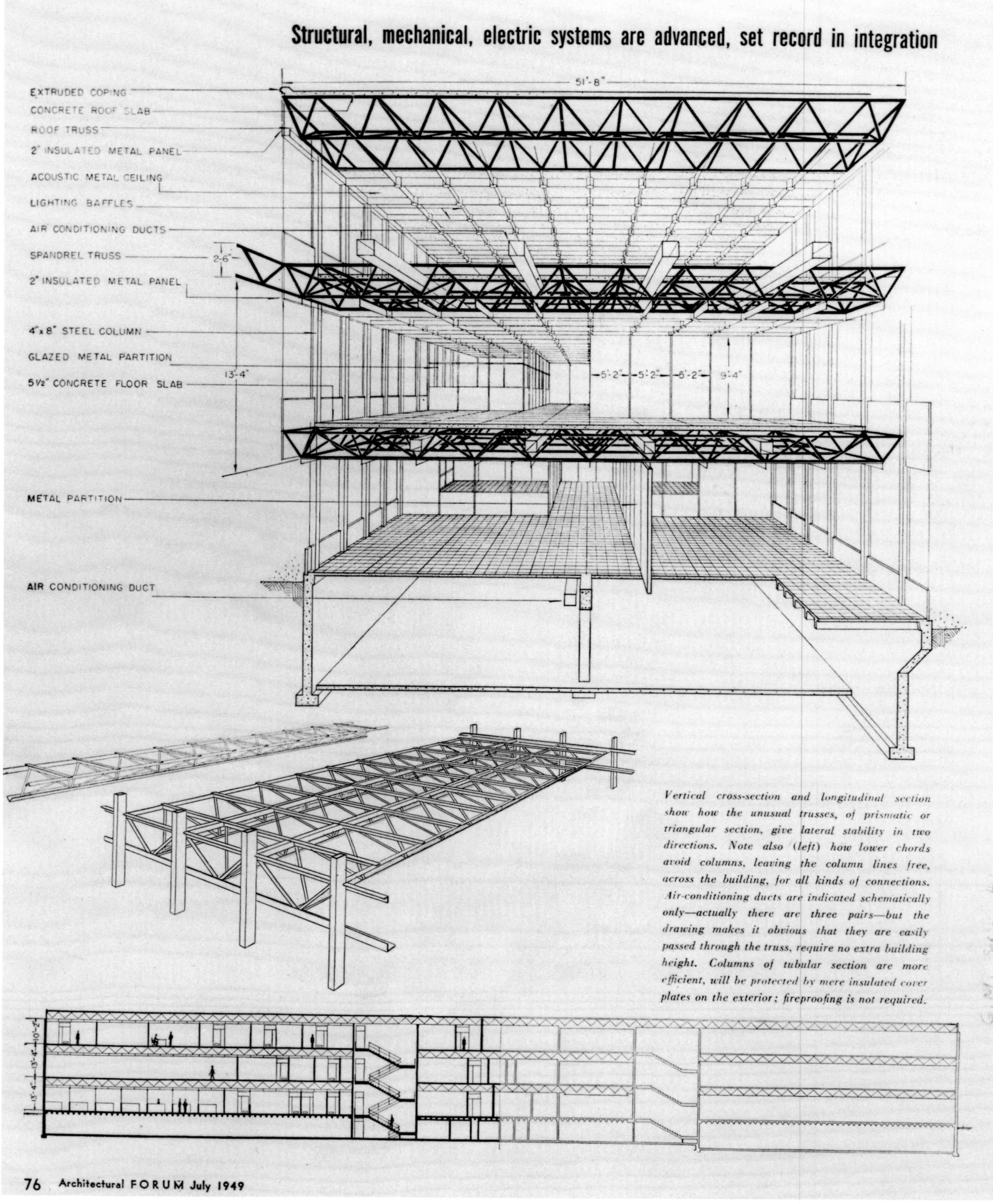

Structural, mechanical, electric systems are advanced, set record in integration

Vertical cross-section and longitudinal section show how the unusual trusses, of prismatic or triangular section, give lateral stability in two directions. Note also (left) how lower chords avoid columns, leaving the column lines free, across the building, for all kinds of connections. Air-conditioning ducts are indicated schematically only—actually there are three pairs—but the drawing makes it obvious that they are easily passed through the truss, require no extra building height. Columns of tubular section are more efficient, will be protected by mere insulated cover plates on the exterior; fireproofing is not required.

76 Architectural FORUM July 1949

Fig. 2 Eero Saarinen and Associates, General Motors Technical Center, 1948–56, sectional perspectives and section showing structural and environmental systems

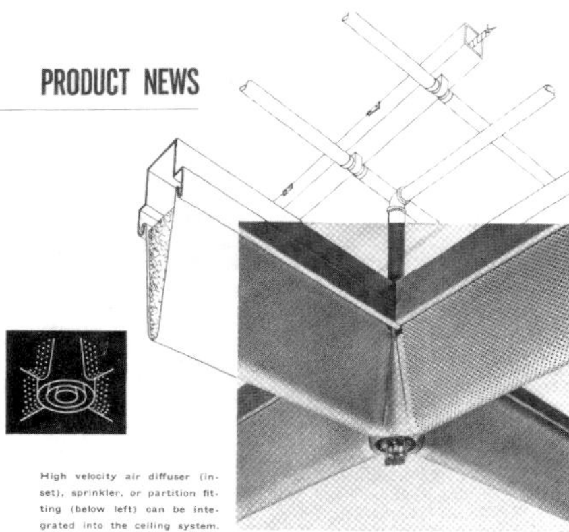

PRODUCT NEWS
High velocity air diffuser (inset), sprinkler, or partition fitting (below left) can be integrated into the ceiling system.

Fig. 3 General Motors Technical Center, curtain-wall mock-up, 1949

Fig. 4 General Motors Technical Center, product profile for air-conditioning diffuser with modular ceiling

The significance of the panels, however, extends beyond their advance in the integration of materials. The panels at GM were also the exposed aspect of a three-dimensional modular grid that integrated many of the building's systems. The five-foot-two-inch module used for the Engineering Building group, which was constructed first, was applied to structural framing, lighting, HVAC, and sprinklers and also prescribed the relation of these systems to lab furniture and partitions, storage, windows, and doors.[4] A section from 1949 shows how the panelized glass-and-metal skin transitions into a modular structure containing three-dimensional trusses (or space frames), the air-conditioning ductwork, and the electrical grid of the ceiling (fig. 2).

The integration of structural, mechanical, and electrical systems within the building module made input from multiple experts a prerequisite for any architectural decision. The interdependence of decision making was demonstrated in a curtain-wall mock-up made circa 1949 that simultaneously tested two proportional variations and the feasibility of the curtain-wall glazing (fig. 3). The crudeness of the construction, with its wood sides and cable stays, differentiates it from subsequent, more sophisticated mock-ups made by Saarinen's office, yet the principle was the same. The mock-up was a means to elicit feedback from materials manufacturers, mechanical and electrical engineers, and other participating parties. Saarinen was interested in engineering and wrote in *Architectural Forum:* "From the miraculous potentials of engineering and science will come new possibilities, new materials and new problems. These will have to be absorbed."[5]

Critics hailed the use of mock-ups, calling it "a procedure as distant as the moon from customary building techniques," but at the same time product testing (and the reliability of manufacturers' information) was often a concern as architectural standards were implemented in the late 1940s and 1950s. Proposed solutions included the A62 Data Service, which was intended to disseminate information on standardized building technologies incorporating results from field testing. For Saarinen, who constantly strove to push building technologies beyond their current limits, testing products and systems in full scale for himself became critical. At GM, he studied and documented the step-by-step method by which automobile prototypes were subjected to cycles of research and input, learning from the design process of engineers and stylists.[6]

One of the first demands on the integrated building was the successful design of the air-conditioning system. After an extensive interview process, GM chose W. J. Caldwell, an inventor, engineer, and manufacturer who was said to be able to control air to such an extent that it "behaves like a liquid instead of a gas." One of the main attractions of Caldwell was that his system used relatively small ducts, slim enough to pass through the buildings' ceiling trusses. Immediately after being hired to work on GM's first three buildings, Caldwell, GM representatives, Eliel and Eero Saarinen, and numerous engineers worked on the development of a mock-up that would meet the detailed design specifications. This list included the following stipulations: all ducts were to pass through openings in the trusses; no window units were to be used; independent controls for private offices and open areas were to be provided; and all air-conditioning outlets were to be contained in the nodes of the five-foot modular system (fig. 4). The development and fine-tuning of the mock-up took nearly fifteen months but resulted in improvements to almost every aspect of the system: "Modifications were made in expanders, dampers, nozzles, the way ducts were fastened together and other features. Considerable progress was made in noise reduction. From the experimental work came such new conceptions as a booster system, operated by a wall switch that can pump from 50 to 100 percent more air into a conference room that is ordinarily needed. This gives a fast purging of stale air and smoke." Rather than simply enabling the system to meet the architectural specifications, the process of modeling it at full scale led to improvements in Caldwell's invention. The modifications were not enough, however, and by 1952 Caldwell's system was proving difficult to balance and operate. GM then hired the Scottish firm

Fig. 5 General Motors Technical Center, lighting mock-up, 1949

Fig. 6 General Motors Technical Center, colored brick mock-up, ca. 1951

of Thermotank Inc. as HVAC designers and contractors for the Research Building group.[7]

While GM explored Caldwell's system, Saarinen and the other participating experts constructed a separate mock-up to test the integration of the lighting into a versatile ceiling grid that also included sound-absorbent material, high-velocity air diffusers, sprinklers, and partition fittings for movable wall panels (fig. 5). The lighting was developed in collaboration with three companies: Rohm and Haas, which manufactured the Plexiglas acrylic sheet; Cadillac Plastics, which fabricated the diffusers; and the Wakefield Company, which made the Sigma-Plex ceiling system. Wakefield also worked independently with Grinnell Company to integrate the sprinkler system, with Thermotank to create the air-conditioning diffusers, and with E. F. Hauserman to fine-tune the partition fittings. Though Robert Smith, an engineer in GM's Styling Division, initially conceived the system, Saarinen modified the details during its many months in development. Two full-scale rooms were set up to test options including exposed fluorescent lights with deep baffles for the drafting areas, and the addition of small louvers to each lighting unit. According to *Rohm and Haas Reporter*, "The problems and frustrations which were encountered in working out the design of the lighting units were persistent and troublesome at times, but this is only history now." By the time the Tech Center opened, Wakefield had manufactured for commercial use more than double the seven acres of Plexiglas that GM required—a testament to the success of this highly researched product.[8]

For Saarinen, these full-scale modeling exercises proved to be studies in the art of communication. As Charles Eames wrote, "By the time the center was completed, Eero had become a master of the feedback principle; he had found confirmation of his natural commitment to systems, but he did not narrow it to technical applications. He retained from then on the capacity to sit down and really communicate with engineers and businessmen." Rather than isolating these communicative practices to technical situations, Saarinen extended what he learned to other aspects of design. In the words of information theorist Norbert Wiener, "Learning is a most complicated form of feedback, and influences not merely the individual action, but the pattern of action." The pattern of action stemming from Saarinen's interest in control and communication can be traced through numerous additional mock-ups. The Saarinen office's slide collection reveals more of these full-scale constructions for GM and makes it clear that even subjective decisions about color, for instance, warranted the same scrutiny and pseudo-scientific methodology.[9]

This was the case for the patchwork wall of brightly glazed bricks built to demonstrate the color options for the end walls of the buildings (fig. 6). The sand-molded Ohio shale bricks, which GM produced and eventually marketed as a product of its own, were intended to be the most distinctive feature of the Tech Center.[10] Although Maija Grotell, a ceramist at Cranbrook, created the glazes for the bricks, the methods employed during the design demonstrate a departure from the Arts and Crafts tradition in which Eero was raised. By constructing a mock-up Saarinen took craft out of the hands of the maker and placed it in a larger network of ideas and expertise. The sharing of information took prominence over any one-to-one relation between an individual and a material product. The brick construction confirmed Saarinen's commitment to design methods where anything could be decided through thorough research, testing, and discussion.

The GM Tech Center was a defining project for Eero Saarinen and Associates, for its magnitude and technological firsts, as well as for the impact that collaborative practices developed during the design phase had on the office's methodology as a whole. The built structures were inseparable from the innovative working methods that contributed to their realization. One could presume that practices generated on the GM project found a lasting place not only in Saarinen's work but also in that of the many individuals who participated in its creation.

Notes

1. Aline Saarinen described the process of artistic "collaboration" when reflecting on the Pevsner sculpture during a visit to the GM Tech Center ten years after its opening: "[Eero and I] saw the Pevsner work first as a small bronze in a Paris gallery. . . . We both felt that in heroic size it would express something of the precision and imagination represented by the automotive industry." Aline B. Saarinen quoted in Joy Hakanson, "A Walk in the Shadow of a Genius: The Widow of Eero Saarinen Casts an Eye on the Tech Center 10 Years Later," *Detroit News Pictorial Magazine,* June 26, 1966, 17. The forty-one-inch-tall sculpture, titled *La Colonne Développable de la Victoire,* which made no direct references to the automobile industry and which Pevsner had completed in 1946, was chosen, scaled up approximately 350 percent, and manufactured by Suses Frères of Paris with only minor modifications. A publication on Pevsner in the artist files for the Tech Center lists the dimensions of the bronze as 105 centimeters high, 70 centimeters long, and 80 centimeters wide without the base; Eero Saarinen Papers, Manuscripts and Archives, Yale University. A similar process of dimensional adaptation was followed with the Charles Sheeler painting for the Research Building group. The Saarinen office's artist files, now part of the Eero Saarinen Papers, Yale University, also include letters in the later years from such artists as the sculptor Norbert Kricke, who was encouraged by Sigfried Giedion to ask Saarinen about collaborating in a more integral way from the beginning of a project.

2. "Designed to Meet Tomorrow's Challenge," *Engineering News-Record,* May 17, 1956, 54.

3. Albert Bemis, *The Evolving House: Rational Design* (Cambridge: The Technology Press, MIT, 1936), 114. Bemis pioneered the dimensional and modular coordination of building materials in the United States. His work was the basis for Project A62, an organization sponsored by the American Institute of Architects and the Producers' Council and implemented by a committee of the American Standards Association. Project A62 proposed the A62 Data Service and established the first national standard for building materials for the United States in 1945. Previously, dimensional coordination among material industries was voluntary and inconsistent. After 1945 numerous heterogeneous products, such as Saarinen's porcelain-enamel panels, demonstrated the potential of the newly coordinated industries.

4. The module was modified to five feet for the rest of the complex.

5. Eero Saarinen, "Six Broad Currents of Modern Architecture," *Architectural Forum,* July 1953, 115. The window system initially used caulk; only later, when GM engineers and Saarinen realized the potential of neoprene, were "zipper" gaskets utilized. Subsequent mock-ups, such as the one undertaken for the Deere and Company Administrative Center in Moline, Illinois, expanded the parameters to test not only the architectural possibilities of Saarinen's designs and new material technologies but also the client's corporate image in the neighboring community. By erecting the Deere mock-up in the building's intended surroundings, it was possible to test the architectural use of rusting Cor-Ten steel, the effects of daylight on the interiors, and the relation of the building to its site. Indeed, after the GM Tech Center, mock-ups grew from simple thickened facades into full-fledged buildings. The Deere mock-up even had its own set of detailed working drawings; see the Eero Saarinen Papers, Yale University, for drawings and photos.

6. "The GM Technical Center," *Architectural Forum,* Nov. 1951, 112; "An A62 Data Service," *Modular Grid Lines: For the Advancement of ASA Project A62,* Sept. 1947, 1–5; photographs of car mock-ups, Eero Saarinen Papers, Yale University.

7. "Caldwell Air Conditioning: Controversial New System Uses Many Special Devices to Get Hurricane Speeds and 'Kinetic Energy Diffusion,'" *Architectural Forum,* July 1950, 114; "High-Velocity Air Conditioning," *Architectural Forum,* Apr. 1955, 163.

8. "Product News: Complete Ceiling Integrated on 4' and 5' Modules," *Architectural Forum,* Mar. 1953, 162; "Investment in Tomorrow," *Rohm and Haas Reporter,* May–June 1956, 6.

9. Charles Eames, "General Motors Revisited," *Architectural Forum,* June 1971, 26; Norbert Weiner, *The Human Use of Human Beings: Cybernetics and Society* (Boston: Houghton Mifflin and Riverside Press, 1950), 69. See the Saarinen office slides, Eero Saarinen Papers, Yale University.

10. "General Motors Technical Center," *Architectural Forum,* Nov. 1951, 115. GM purchased a manufacturing facility and kiln specifically for the production of the bricks. The colored bricks may also be an homage to the vivid hues of masonry and tile at Willem Dudok's Town Hall in Hilversum, the Netherlands. Saarinen visited and admired the architecture of Hilversum, whose Town Hall, built in 1931, established Dudok's reputation. In a letter Saarinen wrote in 1936 to Everett Victor Meeks, dean of the Yale School of Fine Arts and chair of the department of architecture, he noted, "Hilversum was especially interesting from both a sociological as well as an architectural viewpoint." Alumni Files, Yale University School of Architecture.

Christopher Monkhouse

the miller house
a private residence in the public realm

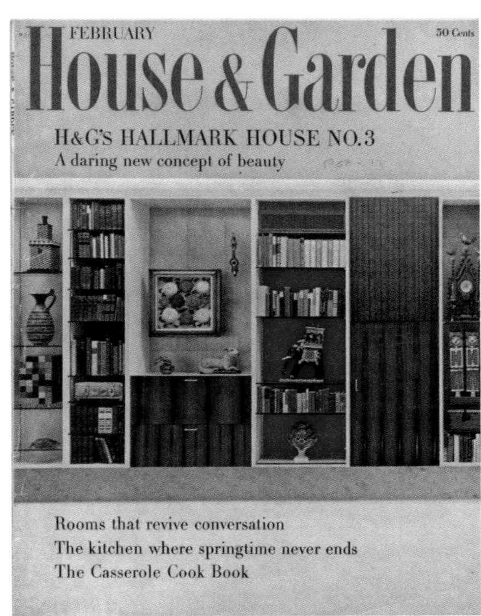

Fig. 1 Interior view of Miller House on cover of *House and Garden*, February 1959

After the Jefferson National Expansion Memorial competition in St. Louis in 1947–48, Eero Saarinen's projects tended to be media events. And after his marriage to *New York Times* critic Aline B. Louchheim in 1954, Saarinen had an in-house publicist. Much of his domestic work of the 1940s was expressly designed for display—in competition, as experiment, or, in the case of the Entenza House, as an example of the possibilities for new, inexpensive materials in the home. But for the Miller House, client and architect went out of their way to avoid attention. Despite (or perhaps because of) J. Irwin Miller's public role in business and banking, religion, education, politics, and the arts, he actively guarded his and his family's privacy. Saarinen and the interior designer Alexander Girard proved sensitive to Miller's concerns when collaborating on the family's Canadian retreat between 1950 and 1952. But that project was on a remote site in Ontario. Privacy was a more pressing issue in Columbus, where Miller was a leading citizen. Miller intended to maintain the low profile of his single-story, flat-roofed house by severely restricting the building's appearance in publications and forbidding any mention of his name, the house's specific location, or its cost.[1]

In 1953 Miller selected a thirteen-acre site on the edge of town, far less conspicuous than the prominently situated brick house of his childhood. The extensive landscape served as a buffer. One side of the house overlooks a floodplain of the Flatrock River, and on the other, landscape architect Dan Kiley created a series of outdoor rooms, enclosed by staggered hedges of tall arborvitae, and locust-lined allées that echo the house's five-foot modular grid. The floor-to-ceiling windows that Saarinen inserted on three sides filled the living room, sitting room, and dining room with Kiley's landscape.

Like the Irwin Union Trust Company (1950–54) in downtown Columbus, designed simultaneously for Miller, the house is subdivided into nine parts. At the bank, nine uplit domes highlight the equal division of the plan, and the custom-designed Knoll furniture mirrors that module; outside, Kiley planted trees on the same grid. At the house, the grid overhead and the grid below diverge. A five-foot-square grid is laid down across the house's footprint, and all the walls, doors, windows, and cabinets follow its lines. But overhead those squares are stretched, creating a grid of nine equal rectangles across the eighty-by-one-hundred-foot space. Their presence is inscribed from above, via linear skylights that bring indirect light into the recesses of the house. These skylights cut across walls, turn up over the mirrors in the bathrooms, follow a logic of their own. The roof, as at Saarinen's Entenza House (1945–49), is a superstructure, a steel-truss umbrella that touches down on sixteen X-shaped steel columns.

At the bank, all the walls are glass, with the floor plan being left as open as possible. At the house, the glass is restricted to the center of each side. The public, open-plan spaces are protected by four slate-sided pavilions, one at each corner, containing private quarters—a master suite, children's bedrooms, the kitchen-laundry, and an area containing a guest room, servants' quarters, and a carport. The bank featured one of the country's first drive-up teller windows; at the house there was a drive-in garage with the same travertine floors as the living areas. Those private pavilions, each slightly different in size, spiral around the voided center of the house, functionally opposing the tidy equality of the skylights.

Fig. 2 Eero Saarinen, Case Study House #9 (Entenza House), Pacific Palisades, California, 1945–49

Fig. 3 (opposite) Alexander Girard, dining-room table at Miller House as depicted in *House and Garden*

The professional architecture community was treated to its first look at the house in the September 1958 issue of *Architectural Forum*. According to Kevin Roche, the senior designer for the project, everything in the article, including the title—"A Contemporary Palladian Villa"—was wrong. Roche had been expecting critics to zero in on a more acceptably modern source—Ludwig Mies van der Rohe's Barcelona Pavilion of 1929.[2] The unidentified author instead drew parallels between the Miller House and Palladio's nine-square Villa Rotonda. Thumbnail sketches illustrated the author's thesis that both structures utilized four loosely connected "houses" performing separate functions, arranged around a dominant space, which in turn reached out into the surrounding landscape on all four sides. Today this analysis seems unobjectionable, and prescient. By the late 1960s, the third generation of modernist architects turned explicitly to Palladio as a base for houses that include spiraling plans and shifted grids. Their ideas developed out of the historical reassessment taking place in the 1950s, of which Saarinen was well aware and which was fueled by the publication of Rudolf Wittkower's *Architectural Principles in the Age of Humanism* and Colin Rowe's article "The Mathematics of the Ideal Villa," which compared plans of Palladio and Le Corbusier.[3]

The public encountered the Miller House on the cover of *House and Garden*'s February 1959 issue (fig. 1). It served as the magazine's "Hallmark House" for the year, the third in a series selected for "the value of the house in human terms—a measure that comprises exhilarating space to move about in, visual richness to delight the eye, a total environment to nurture the spirits of the people who live in it."[4] The "visual richness" provided by Saarinen's palette of materials and Alexander Girard's interior design was shown to full advantage in the cover image, and the eighteen pages of Ezra Stoller photographs within (six in full color). The cover featured a close-up of Girard's rosewood storage wall, which ran the length of the entrance hall and held books, sculpture, folk art, and paintings, set against gold silk and red tea paper. Hidden behind doors were a television, bar, stereo system, and storage for camera equipment. Such built-ins were relatively commonplace in modernist houses, making frequent appearances in the domestic landscapes of Girard, Saarinen, and Charles and Ray Eames. George Nelson developed a mass-produced version for Herman Miller in 1946, after dubbing it the "storagewall" in his book *Tomorrow's House*.[5] The net effect is of a massive art object, a "three-dimensional mural" similar to those Girard would create for corporate clients like Hallmark and John Deere. Perhaps

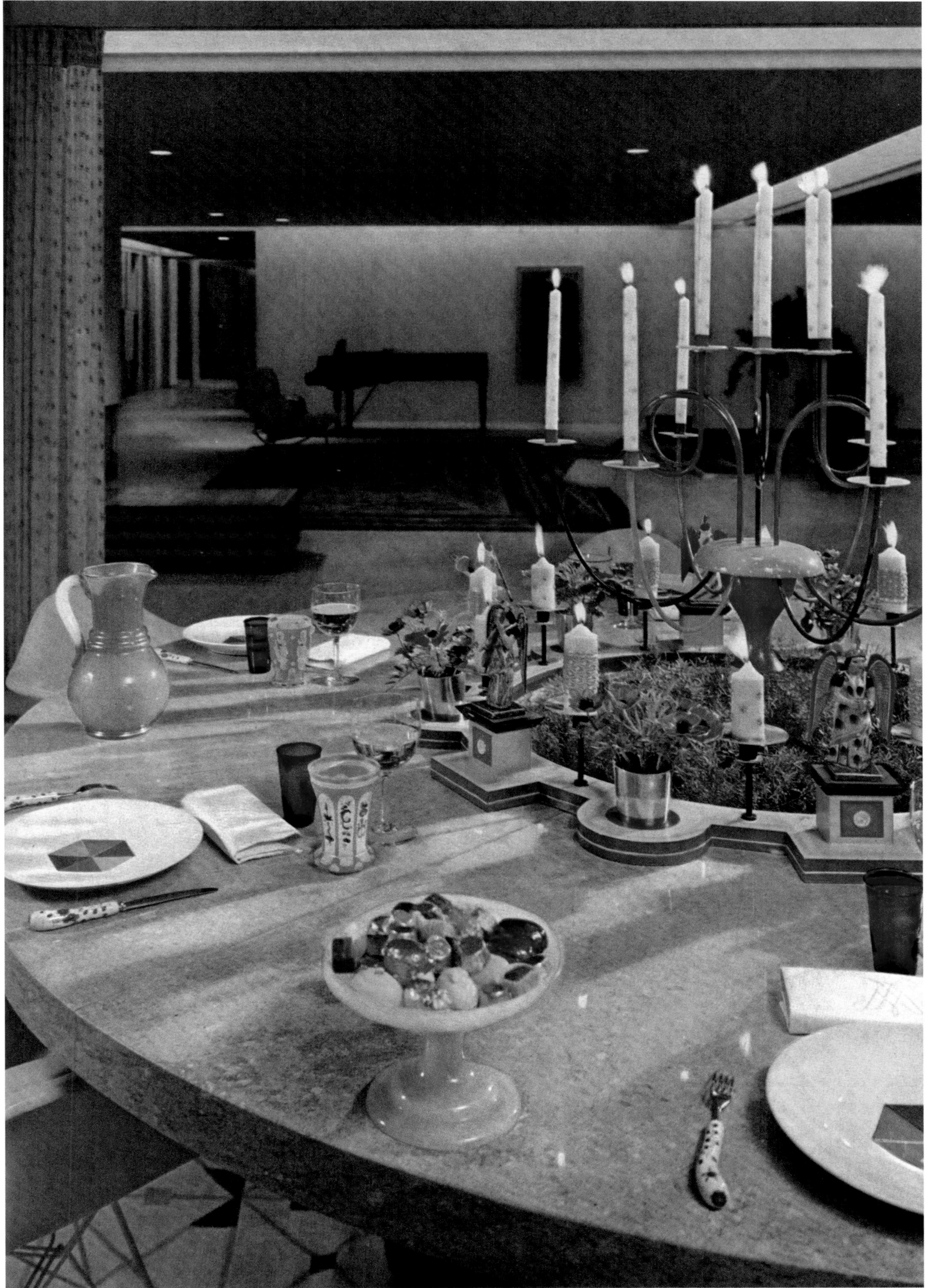

influenced by the unpretentious gaiety of Girard's choices (he and Xenia Miller, Irwin's wife, both collected folk art), the article skipped Palladio and Mies, referencing the vernacular instead. "The great center area is a big, handsome, festive meeting room for activities and entertainment. Inspired by old Mid-West farmhouses where all rooms opened on a common room, it has the same magnetic effect, expresses the common unity of the family."[6]

That center area had two foci, one traditional in function, if not style, the other wholly contemporary. The first was a plaster fireplace, a smooth round form extending from the ceiling to a few feet above the floor, where folding glass panels screened the family from the flames. Such sculptural versions of the classic hearth were known as "feature fireplaces" in the home design magazines of the era. Philip Johnson's Glass House of 1949 (which he compared to the ruins of a burned-out farmhouse, with stone chimneys intact) also had a free plan anchored by a fireplace embedded in a rounded volume. In Johnson's house, the brick cylinder held the bathroom. Saarinen designed a round flue with a built-in brick base in the Entenza House. There, the fireplace screened the intimate sunken sofa from the open views and floor of the main living area (fig. 2). At the Miller House, a fabric panel screened the entrance from the living room and helped anchor the fireplace. The panel functioned as a theater curtain, hiding the action on the other side and serving as a backdrop for a modern painting.[7] Although this area looks awkward and abandoned in published photos, in reality seating was close at hand—Stoller removed the furniture to emphasize the uninterrupted flow of space.

Further accentuating that open center is the house's most memorable element: the conversation pit. Upholstered in red and lined with silk cushions (the cushion covers were changed seasonally, twice a year), the Girard-designed pit provided a counterpoint to the travertine floors, and an analogue in richness to the long storage wall. The recessed pit is also roughly equivalent to the shallow pool placed just outside the living room window, both allowing a western view of Kiley's grounds without distraction. Saarinen and Girard had both been moving toward the conversation pit in their respective work for some time. Girard's living room in Grosse Pointe, Michigan, included a built-in banquette, which created a similar lounge-like effect.[8] Saarinen also used a circular version as the central feature at the Emma Hartman Noyes House (1954–58) at Vassar College. By 1960, he feared they were cliché.

The third custom element in the house's open center was the dining room, set off in a precinct of its own (fig. 3). The dominating circular dining table allowed Saarinen to revisit the ensemble his father had designed for the Saarinen House at Cranbrook in 1930. But unlike Eliel's table, with its four console-like supports rising from an octagonal base to carry a fifty-three-inch inlaid wooden top, Eero's pedestal and ninety-six-inch surface are made entirely of marble. The flared cone support held a brass pump that supplied water to a recessed bowl at the center of the table, which could function as a fountain, a lily pond, or a tiny lawn. Although the Stoller photographs show fiberglass Eames chairs with Eiffel bases, these were soon replaced by Saarinen's Pedestal chairs when they went into production. The conversation pit played the same role, allowing a few elements—the fireplace, the piano, a caryatid bench—to stand out as sculpture.

The Miller House is literally and figuratively the ultimate Saarinen house. It might be the closest he came to the vision he described in the speech he gave at a conference called the "Schöner Wohnen" (beautiful living) congress, held in Munich in 1960, of a retreat with little furniture, a few sculptures, indirect lighting, and a facade subordinate to the roof. But Saarinen's vision sounds more modest—more like a cabin, less like a villa. The Millers seemed comfortable, in Canada, to live light on the land. But despite their desire for a low-key, private home, the Miller House ends up being an essay in modernist inconspicuous consumption. Fiberglass Knoll furniture turns to stone. A metal flue is encased in plaster. The storage wall is not an Eames Storage Unit in molded plywood, but an elegant expanse made of rosewood. The elements are the same, but the materials give the house a glamour rarely part of Saarinen's (or Girard's) vocabulary. Was invention driven within by the need for privacy? Did Saarinen choose a style for the job he thought would suit the town's leading citizen? In Columbus, Saarinen confronted the problem of the house as total design, but he hadn't solved it yet.

Notes

Alexandra Lange provided valuable research and insights in the preparation of this text. I am grateful for the assistance and advice offered by my colleagues Jennifer Carlquist and Jennifer Komar Olivarez. Elizabeth G. Miller, who first introduced me to her family's houses, along with her brother, Will Miller, have also been most helpful.

1. Eric Pace, "J. Irwin Miller, 95, Patron of Modern Architecture, Dies," *New York Times*, Aug. 19, 2004; Aline Saarinen, letter to Rosamond Bernier of *L'Oeil*, Sept. 7, 1962, Eero Saarinen Papers, Manuscripts and Archives, Yale University, in which she refers to the Miller House as "the one job in the office which carries stringent restrictions concerning publications," one of many such citations.

2. "A Contemporary Palladian Villa," *Architectural Forum*, Sept. 1958, 126–27; Kevin Roche, letter to Edgar Kaufmann, Jr., Jan. 27, 1959, Eero Saarinen Papers, Yale University; Will Miller, "Eero and Irwin: Praiseworthy Competition with One's Ancestors," in this volume. Roche, in his letter to Kaufmann, wrote, "We think H & G did an excellent job and while there were obvious shortcomings, it was still very much better treatment than FORUM's."

3. Rudolf Wittkower, *Architectural Principles in the Age of Humanism* (1949; London: A. Tiranti, 1952); Colin Rowe, "The Mathematics of the Ideal Villa: Palladio and Le Corbusier Compared," *Architectural Review*, Mar. 1947, 101–4, repr. in Colin Rowe, *The Mathematics of the Ideal Villa and Other Essays* (Cambridge: MIT Press, 1976). See also *Five Architects: Eisenman, Graves, Gwathmey, Hejduk, Meier* (New York: Wittenborn, 1972), which is based on a Museum of Modern Art conference held in 1968. In the book, Peter Eisenman, Michael Graves, and Richard Meier all play on the nine-square grid.

4. "H and G's Hallmark House Home for 1961: A Total Environment that Fosters a New Pattern for Living," *House and Garden*, Jan. 1961, 64. For Hallmark houses preceding the Miller House, see "Hallmark House Number 1," *House and Garden*, Feb. 1957, 34–49, and, for House Number 2, "We Live as We Like," *House and Garden*, Oct. 1957, 90–99, 131. The first two houses were designed by architects for themselves: Number 1 by Cliff May in Santa Monica, California, and Number 2 by Tony Hiss in Sarasota, Florida.

5. George Nelson and Henry Wright, *Tomorrow's House: A Complete Guide for the Home Builder* (New York: Simon and Schuster, 1945), 132–33; United States Department of the Interior, National Park Service, *National Register of Historic Places Registration Form: Miller House* (Aug. 1986), 8.

6. "A New Concept of Beauty: H and G's Hallmark House No. 3," *House and Garden*, Feb. 1959, 100.

7. Hilary Lewis and John O'Connor, eds., *Philip Johnson: The Architect in His Own Words* (New York: Rizzoli, 1994), 33; Balthazar Korab, conversation with the author, Nov. 12, 2004. Korab worked on the design of the fireplace while in the Saarinen office.

8. "Girard's Clever Corners," *Interiors*, Sept. 1949, 102–9; Donald Albrecht, conversation with the author, May 27, 2005.

Michael Rey

the david s. ingalls hockey rink

eero saarinen and a. whitney griswold at yale

New Haven Journal-Courier

NEW HAVEN, CONN., TUESDAY MORNING, OCTOBER 14, 1958

YALE'S NEW SKATING RINK

DAVID S. INGALLS RINK
YALE UNIVERSITY

Architect — Eero Saarinen
Associate Architect — Douglas W. Orr

★ ★ ★ ★ ★ ★ ★ ★ ★ ★ ★

Structural Engineers — Severud, Elstad & Krueger
Mechanical & Electrical Engineers — Jaros, Baum & Bolles

★ ★ ★ ★ ★ ★ ★ ★ ★ ★ ★

Builder — George B. H. Macomber Company

Fig. 1 "Yale's New Skating Rink," cover of *New Haven Journal-Courier* featuring David S. Ingalls, Sr., and David S. Ingalls, Jr., October 14, 1958

Eero Saarinen had many prominent clients who were adventurous and worked closely with him in producing some of his most important buildings. His relationships with these clients were as unique as the projects themselves. In many cases it was through the client's commitment to Saarinen and his design that the project advanced. This was clearly the case in the development of the David S. Ingalls Hockey Rink at Yale University. Saarinen developed a relationship with Yale's president, A. Whitney Griswold, that would help realize the unusual design despite all the criticism heaped on it during the design process.

Griswold was president of Yale University from 1950 to 1963. Beyond admiring Saarinen's previous work, Griswold had made a commitment "to insure that [Yale's] building program [is] shaped according to [the] best advice" by leading architects of the time. With this objective in mind, Griswold asked Saarinen to assist the university on its campus plan, concentrating on upgrading Yale's science facilities, its central academic core, and its undergraduate and graduate residence halls. Saarinen and his New Haven–based associate, Douglas W. Orr, worked on these three areas, which were intended to expand the existing campus. After a preliminary proposal to construct a new building on Hewitt Quadrangle, Saarinen turned his attention to Science Hill, where he and Orr not only sited the Josiah Willard Gibbs Research Laboratory and Bingham Oceanographic Laboratory, but also determined the location of the David S. Ingalls Hockey Rink. In an interview with Jonathan Barnett in *Architectural Record* Griswold stated that Saarinen was "the most influential spirit and voice in [Yale's] site planning, and one of the most influential in [the university's] building program."[1]

Around 1956 the Yale Hockey Association recognized that the university's freshman and varsity teams were allotted inadequate practice time at their current home, the New Haven Arena, and that additional facilities for recreational skating would also be desirable. That same year the association submitted a formal proposal to the Yale Corporation, asking that an ice rink be built on campus. The proposal outlined the parameters of the facility and fund-raising. It also recommended the architectural practice of Rogers and Butler of New York City, the successor firm to James Gamble Rogers, the architect of Yale's collegiate Gothic campus. The corporation swiftly approved the measure, with the stipulation that the selection of the architect would be left solely to President Griswold.[2]

Griswold again turned to Saarinen, offering him and Orr the opportunity to design the rink. Resistance to Griswold's selection of Saarinen was quickly voiced by alumni and even by Yale's director of athletics, DeLaney Kiphuth, who expressed his concerns regarding Saarinen's lack of experience in designing athletic facilities.[3] Griswold would become the project's staunchest defender throughout its troubles with alumni opposition, construction snags, and an escalating budget. President Griswold's correspondence documents these efforts specifically in addressing the concerns of David S. Ingalls and his wife, Louise Harkness Ingalls, the project's main sponsor. At her request, the rink was named after her husband (class of 1920) and their son, David Jr. (class of 1956), who had each served as captain of the freshman and varsity hockey teams in their respective years at Yale (fig. 1).[4]

Fig. 2 Eero Saarinen and Associates, David S. Ingalls Hockey Rink, Yale University, New Haven, Connecticut, 1956–58, construction photograph

The concept for the rink, according to Saarinen, "was arrived at as a completely logical consequence of the problem." The site, at the northwest corner of Prospect and Sachem streets, close to the center of campus, demanded both a "proud building" and one that would "look well with its neighbors." Saarinen also felt the entrance to the rink should face south, toward the core of the campus. The design's general oval shape came directly from Saarinen's interpretations of the functional requirements. A standard college hockey rink is 200 by 85 feet with seating for approximately 2,800, but Yale also requested that the facility have the flexibility to seat 5,000 when it was used for nonskating purposes. For Saarinen this indicated a "stadium-like plan with access corridors or ramps outside and around the seating area," an arrangement offering more of what he called "seats on the fifty-yard line" than other standard hockey rinks being built at the time. The facilities also included bright lighting on the ice—sixty foot-candles of fluorescent lighting—a one-hundred-ton rink refrigeration system, locker rooms, and showers, as well as office space and storage areas, all located underneath the seating, level with the ice.[5]

In describing in correspondence how the rink's roof was designed, Saarinen made it clear that "the donors and the various committees involved (including the Yale Hockey Association), wanted this to be one of the finest skating rinks in the world." For him this meant creating a facility that was not only functional but also "beautiful." The design of the "spine-like" concrete arch spanning the rink has been criticized as a perverse solution to the problem—conventional rinks are spanned in the short direction. But for Saarinen it was precisely the central structural vertebra that made the design a "graceful" and "dynamic building" (fig. 2). The arch soars up and over the rink's long dimension, swooping down and capping the ends of the rink only to sweep up again through cantilevered extensions marking the entrances to the facility. The cables are attached to the arch at regular increments, hanging down and connecting to the arc-shaped walls on the sides to support the wood plank roof and the flexible neoprene covering. In his explanations for the design Saarinen described why the rink was not roofed spanning the short direction (which would have been less expensive): "We have tried to design a building, which would lend itself to other uses than hockey. The standard barrel-vaulted roof would have been more economical, but besides being less beautiful, it gives ugly, booming echoes. This interior is so shaped that its acoustical properties will be excellent and the building, which can take as many as 5,000 seats, can be used for commencement exercises, lectures, concerts, or for dances."[6]

Saarinen's spanning strategy inspired early opposition to the project, which began in 1956 with the release of the initial design proposal for a dramatic suspended roof structure. Many alumni immediately expressed concern that the

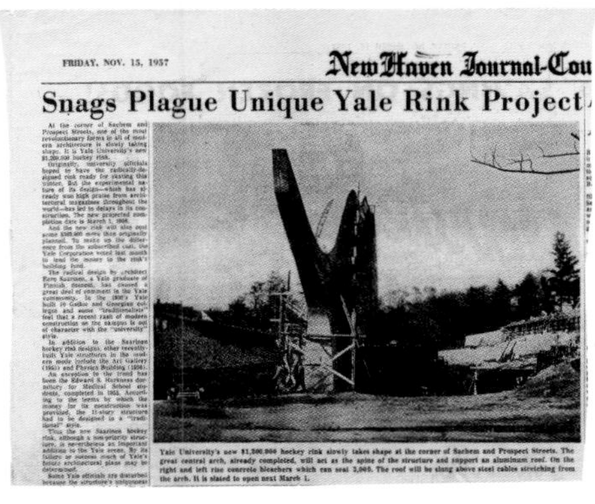
FRIDAY, NOV. 15, 1957 New Haven Journal-Cou

Snags Plague Unique Yale Rink Project

Fig. 3 "Snags Plague Unique Yale Rink Project," *New Haven Journal-Courier*, November 15, 1957

building's unusual form would be out of sync with the traditional Gothic and Colonial Revival styles that characterized the Yale College campus. Additional concerns about the appropriateness of a modern building plagued the construction process as technical complexity led to scheduling delays and severe cost overruns that totaled nearly twice the initially approved budget (fig. 3).[7]

Griswold energetically addressed these concerns and upheld the belief that "a great university should look at architecture as a way of expressing itself." Saarinen stated that he hoped "the architectural character, growing out of [the rink's] structure, will be both expressive and appropriate to our time." For Griswold this expression was guided by the leading architects of the time whose ideas were consistent with his own regarding the projection of Yale University's contemporary academic pursuits. Perhaps this is why Griswold championed Saarinen as a designer and adamantly defended his solution for the rink. Griswold was also supported in his fight by scholars from Yale's art history department, among them Vincent Scully and George Hersey, and ultimately through letters from appreciative users throughout the Yale and New Haven communities.[8]

The David S. Ingalls Hockey Rink opened in the fall of 1958, sparking controversy and debate throughout the Yale academic community. The project was widely published in both major architectural periodicals and popular newspapers in the United States and abroad. In 1962 Griswold recalled the struggle that he and Saarinen endured through the process, noting, "Together we won the Purple Heart and have scars that turn blue in damp weather to prove it." The rink remains a testament to Saarinen's and his client A. Whitney Griswold's determination and commitment to lift architecture above the level of mere problem solving to that of architectural expression.[9]

Notes

1. A. Whitney Griswold, transcript of interview with Jonathan Barnett, *Architectural Record*, Jan. 23, 1962, Records of A. Whitney Griswold as President, RU22, YRG 2-A, box 249, folder 2315, Manuscripts and Archives, Yale University; Douglas Orr's letter with attached sketch to President Griswold dated July 11, 1956, locating the site for David S. Ingalls Rink, Records of A. Whitney Griswold as President, RU22, YRG 2-A, box 36, folder 332; Griswold, interview with Barnett.

2. The Yale Hockey Association's proposal for a new ice rink addressed to the Yale Corporation outlines their needs, fund-raising strategies, and recommendation of the firm Rogers and Butler of New York City for the job, Apr. 2, 1956, Records of A. Whitney Griswold as President, RU22, YRG 2-A, box 36, folder 332; Yale Corporation Meeting Minutes marking the results of the vote on the Hockey Association's proposal for a new ice rink, Apr. 14, 1956, Records of A. Whitney Griswold as President, RU22, YRG 2-A, box 36, folder 332.

3. DeLaney Kiphuth, director of athletics at Yale, visited Saarinen's office during the summer of 1956. After his visit Kiphuth wrote to Griswold regarding his concerns that Saarinen was to lead the design of Yale's new rink; Records of A. Whitney Griswold as President, RU22, YRG 2-A, box 36, folder 332.

4. Griswold's response to Ingalls's concerns regarding the rink, Dec. 28, 1956, Records of A. Whitney Griswold as President, RU22, YRG 2-A, box 36, folder 332; "Yale's New Skating Rink," *New Haven Journal-Courier* (featuring both Ingalls Sr. and Jr. on the cover), Oct. 14, 1958, Records of A. Whitney Griswold as President, RU22, YRG 2-A, box 36, folder 333.

5. Project descriptions written by Eero Saarinen on David S. Ingalls Hockey Rink, Eero Saarinen Papers, Manuscripts and Archives, Yale University.

6. Ibid.

7. "Snags Plague Unique Yale Rink Project," *New Haven Journal-Courier*, Nov. 15, 1957, Records of A. Whitney Griswold as President, RU22, YRG 2-A, box 36, folder 333. The *Yale Daily News*, Dec. 17, 1956, offered preliminary commentary on the project's design and showed images of models and drawings of the interior; Records of A. Whitney Griswold as President, RU22, YRG 2-A, box 36, folder 332. Paul F. Switz (Yale, class of 1929) wrote to Griswold expressing his distaste for the rink and attached an image of the model for the project recently printed in the *New York Times*, Dec. 18, 1956; Records of A. Whitney Griswold as President, RU22, YRG 2-A, box 36, folder 332.

8. Griswold, interview with Barnett; project description by Saarinen; Griswold, interview with Barnett; letter addressed to Griswold from the Yale department of art history advocating the design of Eero Saarinen's new rink, Records of A. Whitney Griswold as President, RU22, YRG 2-A, box 36, folder 332.

9. Griswold, interview with Barnett.

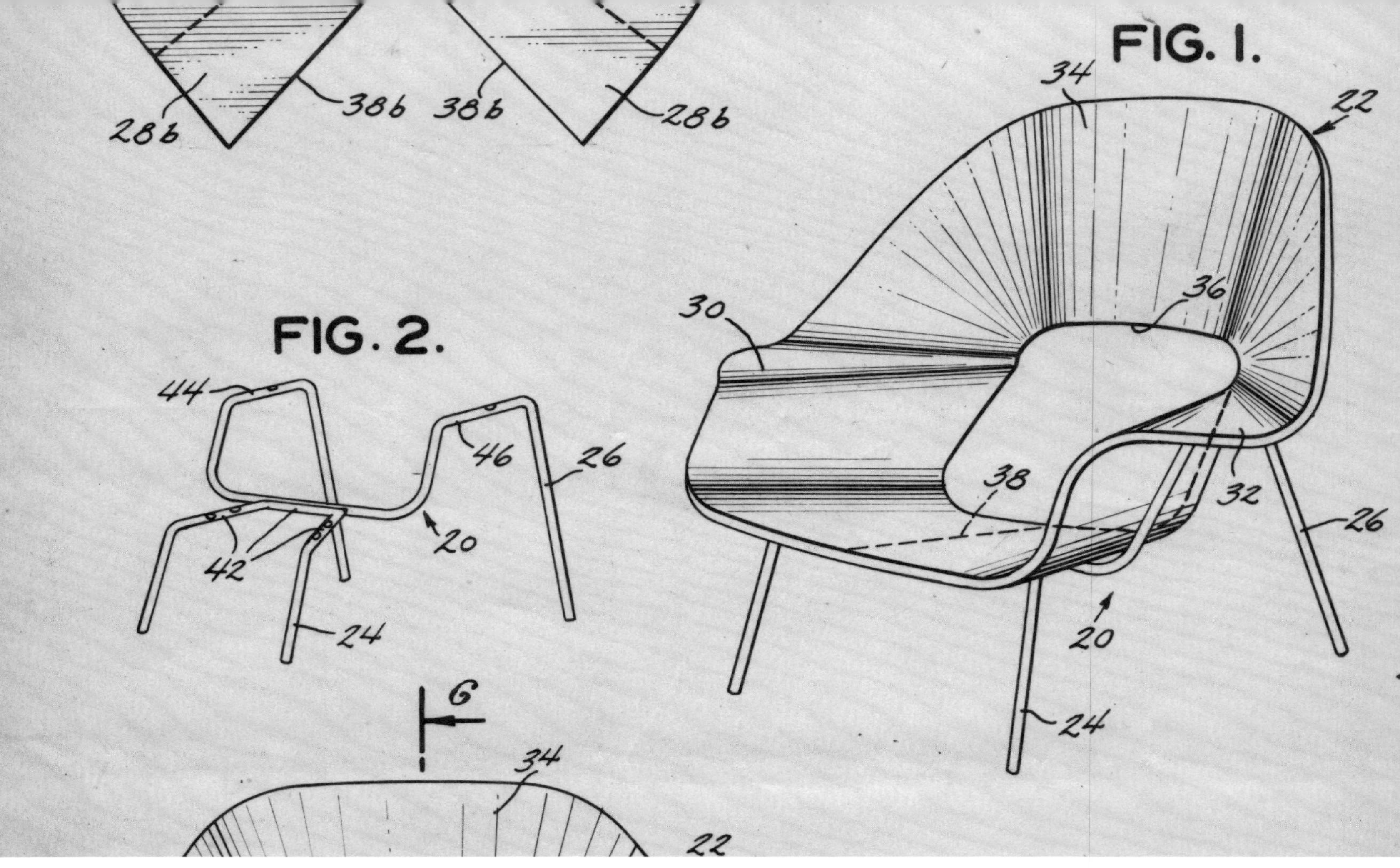

Brian Lutz

furniture form and innovation

Organic Design in Home Furnishings competition, 1940
Grasshopper Chair, 1943–46
Womb Chair, 1946–48
Pedestal furniture series, 1954–57

Fig. 1 Eero Saarinen, Kingswood School for Girls, chairs, 1931

In 1955, around the time he began developing his Pedestal series of chairs and tables for Knoll Associates, Eero Saarinen announced to his colleagues in his office: "We have four-legged chairs, we have three-legged chairs and we have two-legged chairs, but no one has done one-legged chairs, so we are going to do this."[1]

This is perhaps the best summary of Saarinen and his approach to furniture design. Implicit in his statement are Saarinen's understanding of existing designs as a set of solutions, his sense of challenge in the face of what he perceived as an empty category in this composite analysis, and his resolute certainty that there would be a one-legged Saarinen chair. The only thing missing from Saarinen's confident prediction was the timeless popularity his Pedestal chairs and tables would achieve.

Saarinen approached the design of his furniture in the mode of a modernist, balancing art and technology, matching his particular gift as an artist with his insatiable technical curiosity. His innovative use of compound molded plywood and his first use of plastic in a mass-produced chair qualify Saarinen as a leader in twentieth-century furniture design. The forms of Saarinen's furniture designs retain their sculptural appeal to this day.

EARLY DESIGNS

Saarinen created his first furniture designs for the master bedroom of the Saarinen home at Cranbrook, designed and built in the late 1920s when he was still a teenager, and for the Kingswood School for Girls. The

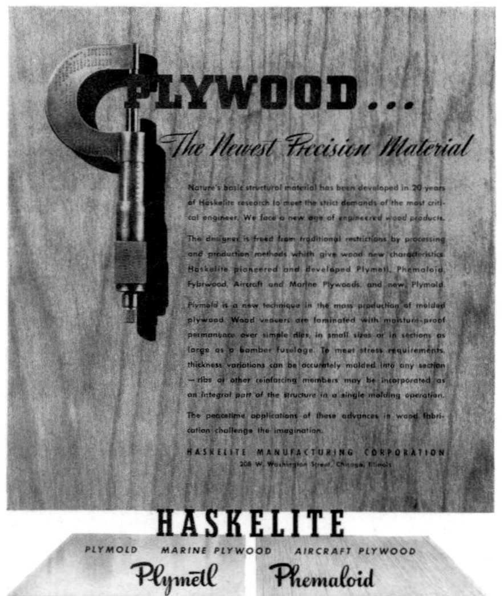

Fig. 2 Eero Saarinen with Charles Eames, Kleinhans Music Hall, chair prototype for chamber music hall, 1938

Fig. 3 Haskelite advertisement, 1942

Kingswood project was begun in 1929, and by the spring of 1931 Saarinen had completed drawings for nearly thirty-five pieces of furniture for the school.

Saarinen referred to himself as "a child of my period," and his designs for Kingswood give clear evidence of this.[2] During the academic year 1929–30, Saarinen studied sculpture in Paris, and his Kingswood designs demonstrate an awareness of furniture design trends emerging in Europe at the time. The most dramatic of these was his incorporation of metal tubing in his Kingswood auditorium chair, cantilevered in the manner of works by Marcel Breuer and Ludwig Mies van der Rohe, designers who validated metal tubing as the symbolic modern furniture material in the 1927 Weissenhof Exhibition in Stuttgart. Saarinen's Kingswood dining chair was designed very much in the style of the Klismos chair, which had become a design standard in Europe and Scandinavia at the time (fig. 1).[3]

After graduating with a degree in architecture from Yale in 1934, Saarinen spent a year traveling through Europe and the Middle East. In the summer of 1935 he returned to Hvitträsk, the Saarinen family home in Finland. Alvar Aalto was a Saarinen family friend and an occasional guest at Hvitträsk. Eero became aware of the work Aalto had been doing with Otto Korhonen, the owner of a small woodworking factory, developing the industrial application of molded plywood in Aalto's chair designs. After his travels Saarinen spent the next year living and working in Helsinki, and by this time Aalto's molded plywood furniture had received widespread international acclaim.[4]

Aalto's designs from this period can be seen as part of the fabric of Saarinen's evolving approach to furniture design. In a telling homage to Aalto, one of the first pieces of furniture Saarinen designed after his return from Finland to Cranbrook drew inspiration from a molded-plywood stacking chair Aalto had designed for the lobby of the Paimio Sanatorium. Saarinen's father's office had been hired as consulting architects by the Buffalo, New York, firm of Kidd and Kidd to complete the Kleinhans Music Hall. Eero, working with a new researcher at Cranbrook named Charles Eames, did a series of seating designs for the project, including an upholstered chair. The form of the Kleinhans chair they created combined Saarinen's softer sculptural shape with Eames's experiments in ergonomic support (fig. 2).[5]

THE ORGANIC DESIGN IN HOME FURNISHINGS COMPETITION

In October 1940 the Museum of Modern Art in New York announced its Organic Design in Home Furnishings competition. In his brief for the competition, Eliot Noyes, head of the museum's department of industrial design and the competition's creator, wrote: "In the field of home furnishings there have been no outstanding design developments in recent years. A new way of living is developing, however, and this requires a fresh approach to the design problems and a new expression." For Saarinen and Eames, this new expression would be a more innovative form of molded plywood. They paired their talents once again and entered the competition.[6]

Aalto is widely credited with advancing the use of molded plywood in furniture design; less well known, however, is his work with Korhonen to produce the first compound-molded plywood chair with a seat shell made from a single sheet of plywood molded in two planes. Saarinen and Eames set out to successfully complete Aalto's experiments, using compound-molded plywood for their Organic Design seating entries.[7]

Don Albinson, an industrial designer who completed his high school education at the Cranbrook School for Boys in 1940, worked with Saarinen and Eames on their Organic Design entries. He recalls: "In Germany, in 1914 or 1915, they were molding three-dimensional curved plywood fuselages for *Albatross* fighters. The molds were not 'deep draws' but tapered over long areas. But they were bias ply and they were being stretched in three dimensions. By 1940 there was a lot of three-dimensional formed plywood out there. Eero discovered that the patent for three-dimensional formed plywood belonged to a man

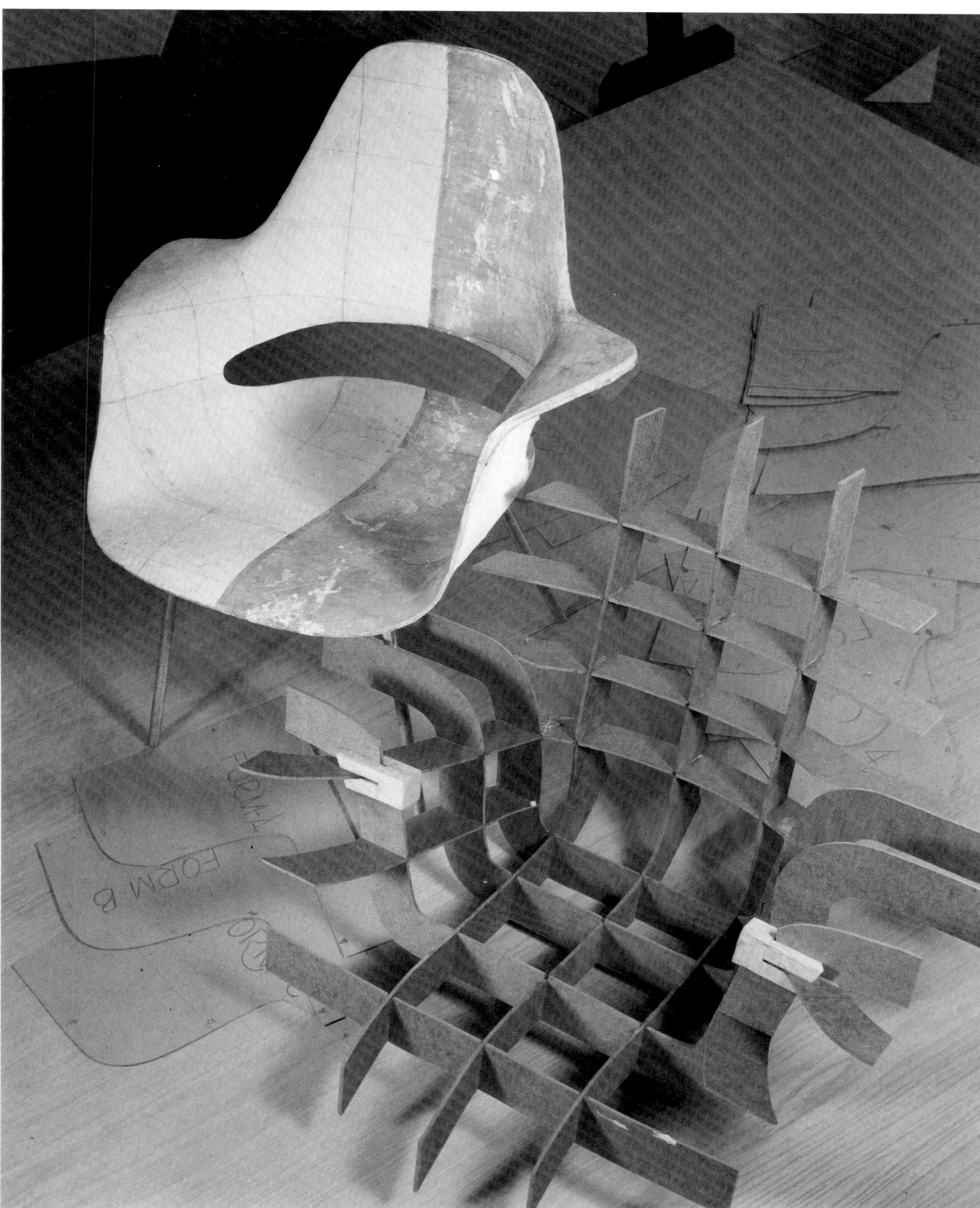

Fig. 4 Eero Saarinen and Charles Eames, Organic Design in Home Furnishings competition, armchair prototype, 1940

named Haskell in Grand Rapids, Michigan." Eames and Saarinen visited the Haskelite Corporation and found the production capabilities they were looking for; they completed preliminary drawings for their Organic Design seating entries based on the use of compound-molded plywood (fig. 3).[8]

The competition required entries to be made in sketch or drawn form. Saarinen and Eames submitted three chair designs: an armless side chair, a low-back armchair, labeled "Conversation," and a high-back armchair, for "Relaxation" (figs. 4, 5). Albinson was part of the group that produced the competition entries. "We made models of the seating and case goods. We had these quarter-scale chair models that [had seat shells] Harry Bertoia pounded out of copper. Charlie made photographs of all the models that went along with the competition entries. The models were so good that the judges thought they were full-size chairs and cabinets!"[9]

Fig. 5 Charles Eames superimposed sitting in an armchair prototype for the Organic Design in Home Furnishings competition

The competition judges included Alfred H. Barr, Jr., the first director of the Museum of Modern Art; Marcel Breuer, the architect and furniture designer; and Noyes. Noyes reviewed Saarinen and Eames's seating entries; his notes read, in part: "Conceived more for comfort than for looks; forms dictated by use, not decorative effect; blunt honesty," and "New structure marks change of style, not a new decoration formula . . . you simply don't arrive at a Saarinen chair by thinking of shapes." Of the hundreds of entries to the competition, the first prize for seating went to Saarinen and Eames.[10]

Full-size plaster prototypes of the chairs were made at Cranbrook by Albinson, but fewer than two dozen chairs were actually produced, and these were done mostly for the exhibition the Modern mounted after the competition (fig. 6).[11] World War II made Noyes's original ambitious plans to bring the winning entries into mass production impossible. Albinson concludes: "[The manufacturers] couldn't get wood because of the war effort; they couldn't get aluminum for the cast-aluminum legs because of the war effort; they couldn't use the cyclebond process because of the war effort. The whole thing came tumbling down because of the war."[12] However, the significance of the Saarinen-Eames Organic Design chairs was uncompromised by wartime production difficulties. The technical and aesthetic innovations in the designs changed the way people thought about furniture and design. As Peter Blake, the architect and critic, put it in a 1994 article: "Just as the Abstract Expressionists moved the center of gravity of modern art from Paris to New York, so Eero Saarinen and Charles Eames, at almost the same moment, shifted the center of gravity of modern design from western Europe to North America."[13]

The Second World War was to interrupt more than chair production for Saarinen and Eames. In 1941, not long after the competition and the exhibition concluded, Charles Eames and his new bride, Ray, left Michigan for California, and in 1942 Saarinen went to work in Washington, D.C., for the Office of Strategic Services (OSS). In the coming years, however, both Saarinen and Eames were to return to their innovative approach to compound molding.

THE GRASSHOPPER CHAIR

During the war years, while Saarinen worked in Washington for the OSS, he continued his experiments in seating forms, making models of sculptural, compound-molded chairs. Wartime restrictions on materials and production technologies continued to limit his creative efforts, however, so that his first design produced by Knoll, the Grasshopper chair, used the only available materials: plywood and surplus parachute webbing (fig. 7).

At Cranbrook the Saarinens had become close friends with a young student named Florence Schust. Schust left Cranbrook in 1939 to pursue her studies in architecture and by 1941 she had moved to New York, where she worked as a freelance interior architect and designer. One of her clients was Hans Knoll, a young German immigrant who had opened a small furniture-importing company. Schust did a few interior design projects for Knoll and in 1943 she joined his company full time. In 1946 Schust and Knoll married and

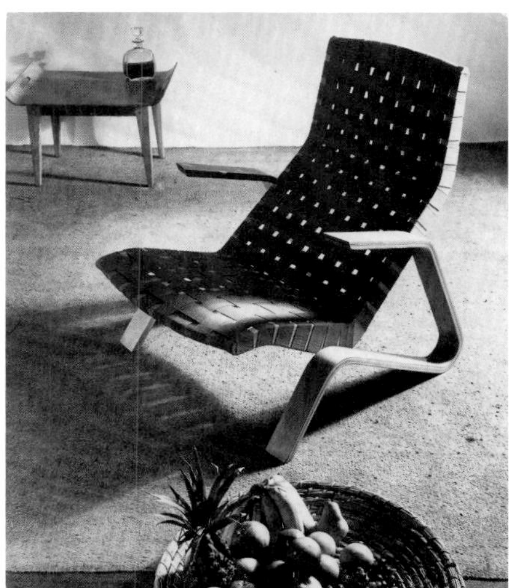

Fig. 6 Organic Design in Home Furnishings, exhibition installation view, Museum of Modern Art, New York, 1941

Fig. 7 Eero Saarinen, Grasshopper chair, Model 61W, 1946

the company was renamed Knoll Associates. Functioning as design director, Florence Knoll wasted no time in bringing the best of her Cranbrook designer colleagues and their designs to Knoll.[14]

A review of the Knoll collection prior to 1945 shows that while numerous small side or pull-up chairs and a few larger upholstered chairs were offered, there was no lounge chair. Saarinen created a chair for Knoll that was more reclined, more relaxed, but still true to his idea of comfort as a function of form, first seen in his Organic Design chairs. As he explained, referring to the Grasshopper chair: "People sit differently today. . . . They want to sit lower and they like to slouch. I [have] attempted to shape the slouch in an organized way, giving support for the back as well as for the seat, shoulders and head." Saarinen, reaching in his mind for the organic form, referred to this as creating three planes of support.[15]

Florence Knoll describes the Grasshopper chair in a similar way: "If you look at the side elevation of the chair, there's a seat and then a back that angles up from it and then another angle that goes for the head. Eero worked on that form to make it generally accessible and comfortable for different types of people. He did the seat in the form of the body—for comfort—and then also for that form to connect to the base."[16]

The Grasshopper chair's base was actually two identical one-piece laminated wood arm-leg constructions that were bent in such a manner that they reminded Saarinen, at least, of the hind legs of a grasshopper. But the shape of the Grasshopper legs was more a matter of efficiency and support than of caricature. As Florence Knoll points out, the seat frame and the arm-leg assemblies, when joined by their clever concealed connections, form a triangle and, as such, give the chair greater strength than would have been possible using the conventional separate boxlike base structure.[17]

Knoll introduced the Grasshopper chair—Model 61—in 1946. An upholstered version was offered, a footstool was added as an optional accessory,

Fig. 8 Eero Saarinen, Knoll 70 series chair development models, 1945

and the Grasshopper chair was marketed as a lounge chair. But the chair was always an interim solution. It was quickly eclipsed by Saarinen's next designs for Knoll and dropped from the company's line in 1965.

THE WOMB CHAIR AND THE 70 SERIES

Even as Knoll completed development of the Grasshopper chair, Saarinen and Florence Knoll were discussing the idea of producing the model chairs Saarinen had done in Washington, D.C. (fig. 8). Although Saarinen was known to consider hundreds or even thousands of possible solutions to a design problem, in this case he proposed only three. Florence Knoll recalls: "He brought three different designs in model form and we talked about them, as we always did. There was an office-type chair and a middle-size chair and then the biggest one. And I said to Eero, 'Why don't we go for the biggest one?' and that's what we did" (fig. 9).[18]

The "biggest one" was the Model 70 Womb chair. Florence Knoll explains: "I told Eero I was sick and tired of the 'one-dimensional' lounge chair . . . long and narrow. . . . 'I want a chair I can sit in sideways or any other way I want to sit in it.'" It would seem Saarinen had this design brief in mind when he explained the chair in the following way: "The 'womb' chair . . . attempts to achieve a psychological comfort by providing a great big cup-like shell into which you can curl up and pull up your legs (something women especially like to do)" (fig. 10).[19]

There are as many explanations for the choice of the name "Womb chair" as there are individuals who were close to Saarinen when the chair was

Fig. 9 Trio of Saarinen's Knoll chair prototypes, 1948

Fig. 10 Eero Saarinen, Knoll Womb chair prototype, 1946

Fig. 11 Womb chair prototype, rear view, 1947

designed. It is perhaps best to accept Saarinen's own explanation, with a side comment from Eames. Saarinen explained that "its unofficial name is the Womb chair because it was designed on the theory that a great number of people have never really felt comfortable and secure since they left the womb." Eames added: "The name is very typical of Eero—to take a word that doesn't particularly sound like a designer's vocabulary." Eames offered an additional comment that fits Saarinen and fits the chair: "Eero was a concept man. The Womb chair was an idea and a concept." The concept has been accepted as the chair's size and shape in relation to its solution for comfort. But on closer examination, a brilliant, more technical aspect of the Womb chair concept becomes apparent: it is a two-dimensional solution to a three-dimensional problem.[20]

Saarinen realized that the simple geometric form of a cone could provide a curved surface that would completely encircle its occupant, a full wraparound curved surface that had only single-plane curves. Every point on a cone is part of a straight line connected to a common vertex, the pointed end of the cone, so there are in fact no compound curves. By folding the cone inward on two opposing sides, Saarinen created two arms and a seat; by chopping off the pointed end of the folded cone, covering the hole with foam and upholstery and adding a small pillow, a very comfortable cup-shaped chair could be made (fig. 11). Saarinen applied for a patent on the "truncated cone" method of construction of his chair in 1948, the year the Womb chair was introduced by Knoll. His patent drawings clearly show this concept (fig. 12).[21]

The original patent describes how the chair could be made, cutting its form from flat sheet materials, such as "plastic or plywood or metal or any other bendable material." Early photographs of prototypes show a chair made of what appears to be a wood-grained material. Drawings of the sister chair, the Model 72, done in Saarinen's office and dated March 27, 1952, reference earlier drawings for a molded plywood back.[22]

But Saarinen was eager to move beyond plywood. The size of the Womb chair meant that a plywood shell would require two halves to be joined. Also, given the size of the chair, a plywood version would have been very heavy. Finally, a two-piece plywood shell construction for the back and arms would have had to have been attached to a separate seat, and this assembly would have required a base.

Reinforced polyester resin was a new material developed during the war years for the hulls of Navy boats. This material and the method used to make boat hulls from it offered the solution Saarinen needed: the hulls were strong and light and could be mass-produced in a single piece. He decided to look for a boat builder to make his chair, and found Winner Manufacturing Company in Trenton, New Jersey. Established in the late 1930s by Hudson Winner, the business had been involved in the production of naval equipment during the war. By 1946 Winner was making reinforced plastic boats for the public. Saarinen and Florence Knoll went to visit Winner and took along Saarinen's model of the Womb chair. The boat builder was intrigued by the somewhat radical idea of producing a chair and accepted the challenge.

Working together with Winner, Saarinen developed what were then called resin-bonded fiber shells. For the Womb chair, fiber reinforcing material was impregnated with a low-pressure bonding resin and placed in a mold that utilized a vacuum bag for forming the shell. The fiber in use at that time was sisal. Glass fiber in loose and, later, woven-mat form was subsequently employed.

The resulting shells were a success: strong and light, they were easily mass-produced at a fairly low cost. In addition, the plastic material offered a degree of flex beyond that of plywood, providing additional comfort in the chair.

Winner also developed a production method for the back shell of the Model 72 armless side chair, using hot-press molding with male and female

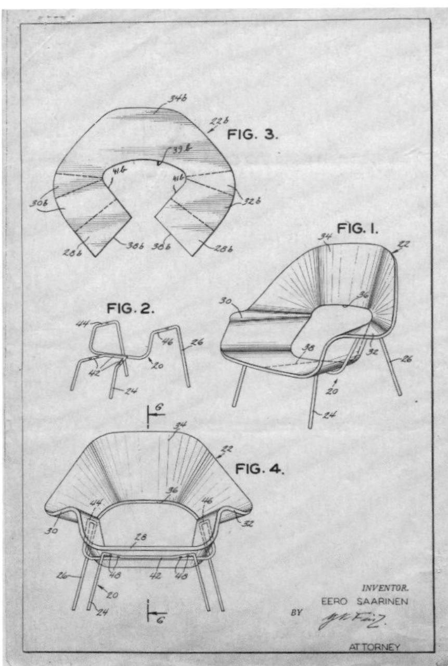

dies. The 72 chair was introduced by Knoll Associates in 1948 along with the Model 70 Womb chair.

The team encountered difficulties developing the Model 73 armchair, however. In an undated letter to Astrid Sampe, the Swedish textile designer, Saarinen referred to work he was completing on the design of the "little sister" to the Womb chair, saying: "I have bothered a lot, made about 15 models, but I am now satisfied with it. They are funny things, almost impossible to draw."[23]

Saarinen's difficulty in drawing the 73 chair foretold the problems that were experienced in molding the complex shape of this smaller compound-curved chair. Even after the form had been successfully molded, its flexible nature meant that the armrests, curved outward in this smaller shell, were not strong enough for heavy use in an office, the primary application intended for the chair. Although the 73 armchair was patented together with the 72 chair, it was never produced.[24]

Saarinen continued his search for a solution to making a molded shell armchair. He found it in a chair conceived by Florence Knoll. In 1945 she had designed the interiors of the Rockefeller family offices at Rockefeller Center. She looked for a small armchair for use as a side or pull-up chair. As she explains: "I knew exactly what I wanted even though it was one of the first office jobs I ever did. I wanted to have upholstery on the arms of the chair, more for a sense of luxury, rather than just having open wood arms like some chairs." Unable to find a suitable chair, she designed an upholstered armchair for the Rockefeller project; it was introduced by Knoll as a standard production item as the Model 43 (fig. 13).[25]

With the full cooperation of Florence Knoll, Saarinen adapted her Model 43 design to his reinforced-plastic chair family. Looking back, she recalled: "There's a big difference between what I did for the Rockefellers and what Eero did later. It was a similar form, except he did his using a bent material, so Eero's had more curves. Of course, he was working with materials that allowed that, and I was just using a very basic formed wood frame because that was all that was available then."[26]

The industrial designer Niels Diffrient, who was a student at Cranbrook from 1948 until 1952, worked with Saarinen on his furniture designs. "Eero had gotten his patent on the Womb chair as a segment of a warped cone. He persisted with that on the 71 chair; he just transferred the approach with a wrap-around back . . . in a simpler contour" (fig. 14).[27]

Saarinen's Model 71 armchair was introduced in 1950 and went on to become Knoll's most significant piece of furniture in its mass appeal for use in corporate interiors. Years later, Eames described the 71 armchair as "a very good chair. The balance was good. I think it was the best functional piece he did." The chair was used extensively in Saarinen's General Motors Technical Center and also in the interiors done by Florence Knoll for Saarinen's CBS Building in New York. She defines the chair's significance for Knoll as "the first real event in using one of Eero's designs in a big commercial establishment."[28]

Saarinen's 70 Series chairs played a critically important role in establishing Knoll Associates as a leading design company manufacturing products for the largest corporate interior projects. Saarinen's innovative use of reinforced plastic in his furniture made the American furniture industry a new center for technological expression. In the materials revolution in furniture design that followed, Charles and Ray Eames were recognized as leaders with their plastic seating. Saarinen's inventive use of technology was to be exceeded by his artistry in his next set of designs for Knoll.

THE PEDESTAL SERIES

In November 1954 Hans Knoll sent Saarinen a letter stating, "The prospect of having you work on a [new] furniture program after the first of the year is most encouraging and promising." Saarinen wrote back immediately,

Fig. 12 (opposite, top) Page from patent application for Knoll Womb chair, 1951

Fig. 13 (opposite, middle) Florence Knoll, Model 43 chair, 1945

Fig. 14 (opposite, bottom) Eero Saarinen, Knoll Model 71 chair prototype, 1949

Fig. 15 (above) Eero Saarinen, Knoll Pedestal chair models, 1955–56

saying: "I am really very enthusiastic about the whole idea. . . . I have been working evenings and have a whole wall full of sketches. I have come up with an idea that I think will wipe Herman Miller off the map!"[29] (Herman Miller Inc. was a main competitor of Knoll Associates at the time and remains so to this day.)

The idea, as Saarinen presented it to his office colleagues, was a one-legged chair. He later explained the rationale for a single-leg chair this way: "I wanted to make the chair all one thing again. All the great furniture from the past . . . has always been a structural total. With our excitement over plastic and plywood shells, we grew away from this structural total." Saarinen imagined a chair with a single leg made of a single material.[30]

But he found that the plastic material that allowed sculptural, compound molded forms was not strong enough for the support structure of a one-legged chair. The single-leg concept, however, was essential; it was Saarinen's solution to the "slum of legs" that he perceived as making for "an ugly, unrestful world." And so the base of Saarinen's "structural total" chair had to be made from metal. In 1958 he said, "I look forward to the day when the plastic industry has advanced to the point where the chair will be one material, as designed."[31]

As was Saarinen's custom, the final form of the chairs was developed using quarter-scale models. Don Petitt, the Knoll employee whom Hans Knoll lent to Saarinen for two years to develop this program, explained how the process worked: "I started out making little models, bending sheet metal and filling it with plastic. Eero used to give me an 8½ x 11 [inch] pencil drawing of a new chair. Sometimes I would do a little version of my own, but it was always his idea."[32]

Petitt's model making ran from June 1955 until the end of the year, and he saved all the models and photographed them, preserving the sequence of development of the shape of the Pedestal chair (fig. 15). They built full-size prototypes of the side chair in November 1955 and of the armchair in early 1956.[33]

Petitt and Saarinen visited Winner in Trenton with the models in October 1955. Production of the chairs did not begin until 1957, when they were shown at a special preview at Knoll's New York City showroom in May; the Pedestal collection was announced in a Knoll press release in September of that year. In March 1958 the full collection was presented to the public at a three-day event in the New York showroom (fig. 16).[34]

By this point Saarinen was being celebrated as one of America's leading architects, with a cover story in *Time* magazine in July 1956. His furniture was equally noteworthy. His innovative, prize-winning Museum of Modern Art furniture designs made with Charles Eames had shifted the center of international furniture design to America. His inventive uses of technology led the way in improvements in the form and production of twentieth-century modern furniture. His collaboration with his family friend Florence Knoll had played a significant role in establishing her furniture company,

Fig. 16 Eero Saarinen, Knoll Pedestal chairs and table, 1958

Knoll Associates, as a center for well-designed furniture for postwar corporate interiors.

Florence Knoll will frequently end a discussion of Saarinen's designs with a reminder that he was, after all, a sculptor. His Pedestal series for Knoll was just such a conclusion to his furniture design career: a reminder that as a sculptor, he always tilted the balance of art and technology in his innovative designs toward his artistry of form.

Notes

1. As related by Gunnar Birkerts in a speech delivered Aug. 12, 1995, published in *Saarinen Swanson Reunion Proceedings* (Bloomfield Hills, Mich.: Cranbrook, 2001), 38.

2. Eero Saarinen, *Eero Saarinen on His Work: A Selection of Buildings Dating from 1947 to 1964*, with statements by the architect, ed. Aline B. Saarinen (New Haven: Yale University Press, 1962), 6.

3. According to Ben af Schultén, design director at the Finnish furniture company Artek from 1964 to 2004: "The Greek revival style, like in the Klismos chair, was quite a common issue at that period. Gunnar Asplund in Sweden, Erik Bryggman in Turku [Finland] and certainly many others used it." Ben af Schultén, interview with the author, Helsinki, Finland, Sept. 22, 2005. Artek was founded in 1935 by Alvar Aalto, his wife, and two associates to oversee production and international distribution of his furniture designs; the Klismos chair is a light, elegant design that was developed by the ancient Greeks and became a standard, usually having four curving splayed legs and a narrow concave back supported by the rear legs. Aino and Alvar Aalto had designed such a chair in 1924 for their Häme Student Society Rooms interior.

4. In 1933 two important exhibitions brought international attention to Aalto's furniture: the Milan Triennial and a commercial show at Fortnum and Mason department store in London. Florence Knoll Bassett recalls meeting Aalto at Hvitträsk during one of her summer visits before her departure from Cranbrook in 1939 for architecture school in London. She relates, "Aalto had just come back from London and he was the one who suggested I study there, at the Architectural Association." Florence Knoll Bassett, telephone interview with the author, July 8, 2005.

5. Eero Saarinen and Charles Eames also collaborated on molded-plywood seating designs for the interiors of the Crow Island school designed by Saarinen, Swanson, and Saarinen beginning in February 1938.

6. Museum of Modern Art, *Project in Home Furnishings* report, June 24, 1940.

7. Numerous references in the literature of modern-era design substantiate Aalto's importance, the most notable of which is by Christopher Wilk: "Although many types of plywood furniture existed before Alvar Aalto turned to the material around 1929, his

designs became so well known and influential that they largely eclipsed other contemporary experiments with laminated wood. Much plywood furniture was produced during the 1920s, though neither as influential nor as aesthetically or technically innovative as Aalto's." Christopher Wilk, *Bent Wood and Metal Furniture: 1850–1946* (New York: American Federation of the Arts, 1987), 147. In 1932 Aalto and Korhonen had developed their molding techniques in a way that enabled plywood to be curved in three dimensions through the use of weights and formed molds. Korhonen was only successful enough with this new method to produce a handful of prototype compound-molded chairs, which were exhibited at a Nordic building exhibition in Helsinki that year. Problems with the supply of appropriate quality materials made mass production impossible; the chair was never put into production. Jukka Korhonen, interview with the author, Sept. 19, 2005.

8. Don Albinson, interview with the author, Coopersburg, Pa., May 26, 2005. The Haskell Manufacturing Company, which had been founded by Henry Haskell and his partners in 1917, made compound molded plywood canoes. Although there is no record of a patent on Haskell's plywood molding method, he was given credit for the technical innovation that made it possible to successfully mold plywood in three dimensions. A 1917 article in the journal *Hardwood Record* reports: "The making of the new [Haskell] canoe is the direct result of the discovery by Mr Haskell of a formula for a glue which is absolutely impervious to water." Haskell Manufacturing's boat production ceased in 1922; an aviation company acquired the rights to the molding process and the product that Haskell named Haskelite, forming a new company called the Haskelite Corporation.

9. Albinson interview. The names of the chairs are the titles Saarinen and Eames used on the drawings they submitted to the competition; Museum of Modern Art Archives, New York. In addition to the three chairs, they also submitted entries for a sectional sofa and a system of unit storage or case goods.

10. Gordon Bruce, telephone interview with the author, New Milford, Conn., May 25, 2005.

11. The Haskelite Corporation molded the shells, which were upholstered and assembled by the Heywood-Wakefield Company in Gardner, Massachusetts; wood legs were attached with a device patented by Heywood-Wakefield, Jan. 9, 1942, U.S. patent number 2343077.

12. Albinson interview. Saarinen had learned of a process called cyclebond, which the Chrysler Corporation had developed just before World War II for bonding brake linings to brake shoes and avoiding the use of rivets, which required holes in the braking surface, thereby reducing the braking effect.

13. Peter Blake, "S. and E.," *Interior Design*, July 1994, 28, 29.

14. In 1955 Hans Knoll died in a car accident; in 1958 Florence Knoll married Harry Hood Bassett. For clarity, Florence Knoll Bassett is referred to throughout this essay as Florence Knoll, the name she used through the introduction of the Pedestal series.

15. Saarinen, *Eero Saarinen on His Work*, 68.

16. Florence Knoll Bassett interview.

17. Florence Knoll Bassett, letter to the author, Aug. 13, 2005.

18. Florence Knoll Bassett interview.

19. Ibid.; Saarinen, *Eero Saarinen on His Work*, 68.

20. Eero Saarinen, letter to Irwin Miller, July 14, 1949, Eero Saarinen Papers, Manuscripts and Archives, Yale University; Eric Larrabee and Massimo Vignelli, *Knoll Design* (New York: Harry N. Abrams, 1981), 56; Charles Eames, undated interview with Ricky Wurman, Knoll International archives, East Greenville, Pa.

21. U.S. patent 2541835, applied for Dec. 4, 1948, granted Feb. 13, 1951.

22. Architectural drawing copies, done by Niels Diffrient, from his private collection.

23. Eero Saarinen to Astrid Sampe, letter 2 (undated, ca. 1949), box 1, folder 5, Astrid Sampe Collection of Eero Saarinen Correspondence, Cranbrook Archives.

24. U.S. patent 2606601, applied for Dec. 14, 1948, granted Aug. 12, 1952.

25. Florence Knoll Bassett, telephone interview with the author, July 22, 2005.

26. Ibid.

27. Niels Diffrient, interview with the author, Ridgefield, Conn., July 14, 2004.

28. Eames interview; Florence Knoll, quoted in Larrabee and Vignelli, *Knoll Design*, 56.

29. Hans Knoll, letter to Eero Saarinen, Nov. 15, 1954, Eero Saarinen Papers, Yale University; Eero Saarinen, letter to Hans Knoll, Nov. 22, 1954, Eero Saarinen Papers, Yale University. Peter Blake, an architecture critic and friend of Hans and Florence ("Shu") Knoll recalled: "There really was no one else in the US, with the possible exception of Herman Miller Inc., who was trying to manufacture well-designed modern furniture in a consistent way. Hans and Shu led the way." Peter Blake, *No Place Like Utopia* (New York: Norton, 1993), 172.

30. Saarinen, *Eero Saarinen on His Work*, 68.

31. Ibid.

32. Don Petitt, undated interview with Gail Hannah and Albert Pfeiffer, Knoll International archives. Hans Knoll asked Petitt, who was employed by Knoll Associates, to work for Eero Saarinen in his Bloomfield Hills office; he was a Saarinen employee from June 1955 until March 1957.

33. Don Petitt, letter to Eero Saarinen, Aug. 18, 1960, Eero Saarinen Papers, Yale University.

34. Prototypes of two side chairs, two armchairs, a dining table, two coffee tables, and two side tables were shown at the May 1957 event. The collection was expanded over the years to include a stool, a four-star base for the armchair, and an increased range of tables in various sizes and top materials.

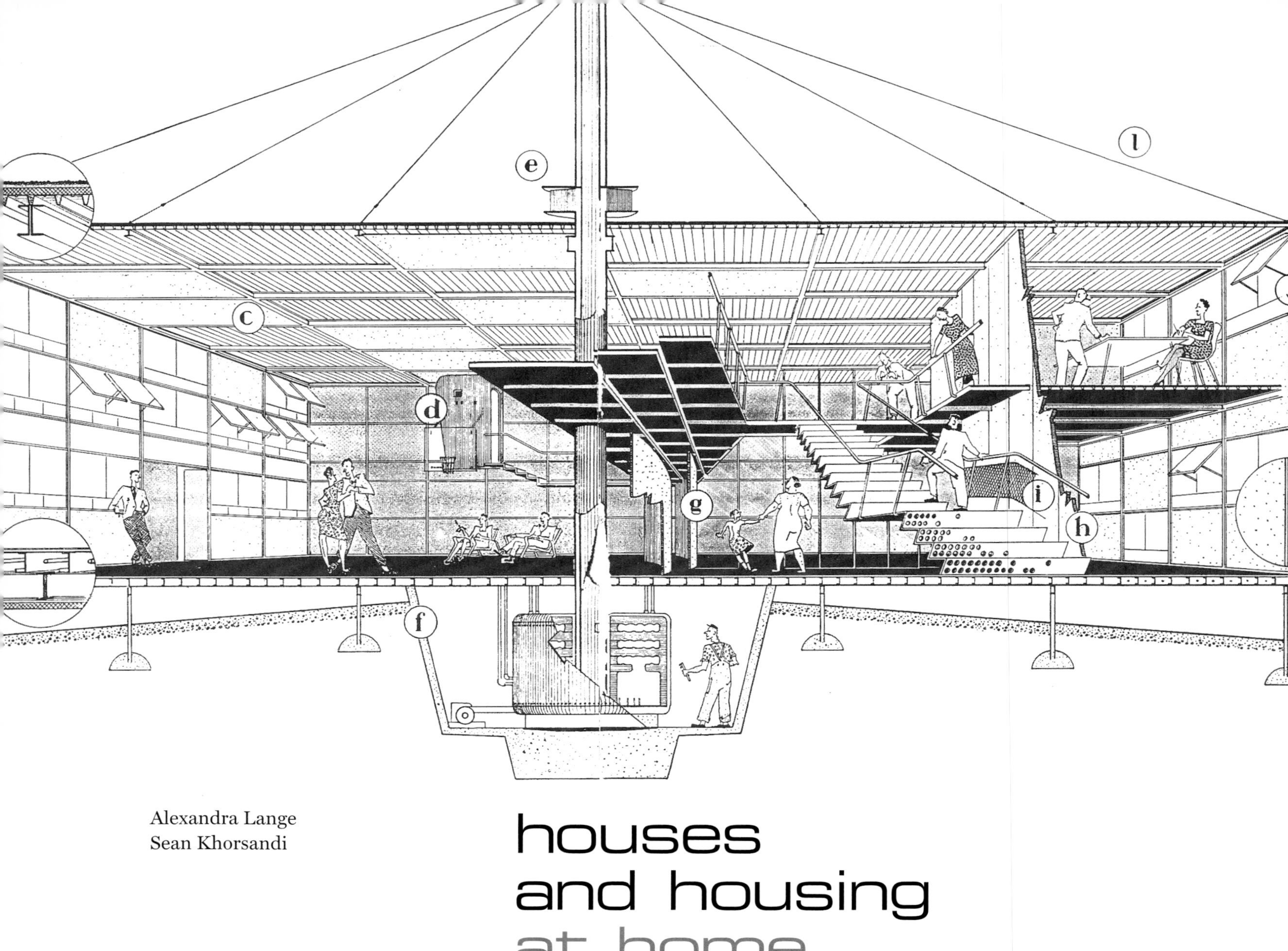

Alexandra Lange
Sean Khorsandi

houses and housing
at home with saarinen

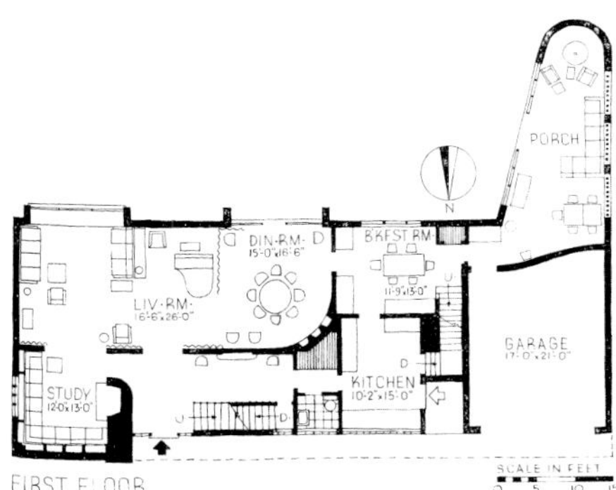

Fig. 1 Eliel and Eero Saarinen, Koebel House, Grosse Pointe Farms, Michigan, 1937–40, plan

Koebel House, Grosse Pointe Farms, Michigan, 1937–40
A Combined Living-Dining Room-Study Project, 1937
Bell House project, New Hope, Pennsylvania, 1941
Demountable Space Project, 1940
Wermuth House, Fort Wayne, Indiana, 1941–42
PAC (Pre-Assembled Components) Competition Entry, 1943

Was Eero Saarinen ever at home? His letters suggest not. After the family left Hvitträsk, Eliel, Loja, and Pipsan Saarinen settled in Michigan for good, while Eero went to Europe for sculpture training, then east to architecture school, after which he got married, got divorced, and got remarried, changing addresses on average once every three years. Even a cursory look at his biography suggests a restless soul. Saarinen was often silent—in response to criticism, he just puffed his pipe—but inside he seems always to have been working. It has long been said that Saarinen designed only one house, but new research reveals that he participated in the design of at least eighteen houses or housing projects (including his own renovations). Varied in style and clientele, the houses do seem to share the character of their creator—a neutral, even vernacular shell enclosing technically advanced, formally adventurous spaces for life and work. They also show an adolescent awkwardness—brick or aluminum? bar or square?—that is a far cry from the smooth luxuriousness of his best-known house, built for the Miller family in Columbus, Indiana.

In a speech he gave at the Schöner Wohnen congress in Munich the year before his death, Saarinen suggested that even he might be ready to settle down. He had picked a house site, "a densely wooded rocky side of a stream. This wild nature suggests an informal, dark, romantic structure."[1] But such a structure would not suit his taste, or his lifestyle, he explained. He glossed over the exterior, as he had in all of his domestic projects, and headed inside. He was inspired by the simplicity of Japanese houses, and he said,"I would solve the problem of furniture, with its inevitable 'slum of legs,' by eliminating it completely from the living room. Instead I would create a sunken area more or less in the middle of the living room, consisting of two large steps, carpeted like the rest of the room in neutral color." He admitted that such conversation pits had become fashionable to the point of cliché, but he noted that he had "more or less" invented the cliché twenty years earlier.[2] Besides the pit, little else would be needed other than end tables and some pedestals for sculpture.

The core of the house would be the work room, where his wife Aline would have her typewriter, and he his drafting table. Climate controlled, carpeted, and book-lined, this room would be freed from distractions by the use of a skylight, perhaps one "that ran around the perimeter of the room so that books were lightened by it by day and by artificial lights shining through it by night." Saarinen touched here on the elements that played a major part in all of his domestic designs, from the Koebel House of 1937–40 to the Miller House of 1953–57—the blank exterior and the built-in interior, the open-plan living area, the control of light, and the sculptural element. The custom-built house, he said, "is really coming back to the problem of total architecture."

The Koebel House was one of the first commissions for the firm of Eliel Saarinen and Eero Saarinen after the son graduated from Yale. The site was a large, flat corner lot in Grosse Pointe Farms, Michigan, and father and son designed a two-story, five-bedroom tan brick house (fig. 1). The house is rectangular in plan, except for a sun porch seemingly pulled from the southwest corner that ends in a graceful curve. In the roof above this rounded brick nub is a large oculus, which casts indirect light down the half-cylindrical brick wall, and foreshadows the circular skylights in Saarinen's chapels at Drake University and MIT. The canted wall of the porch faces a low, sinuous wall across the yard, bracketing the lawn.[3]

Inside the house, more curves create unusual openness and movement within the rigid plan. Living room, dining room, and music room are all one space, subdivided by sets of large windows and enclosed by a curving mahogany wall with sculpture niches. Loja and Pipsan Saarinen collaborated with Eliel and Eero on the interior design. Built-in seating created a sitting area by a large bay at one end, while at the other end of the room three concentric recessed circles in the ceiling located the dining table. This ceiling treatment, combined with the niches and the circular table, suggest a suburban variation on the Saarinens' own dining room at Cranbrook. The library is perhaps a tiny version of the work room Saarinen envisioned: built-in mahogany shelves, built-in L-shaped banquette, and a grid of square windows high on the wall and in the ceiling offering light and privacy. Unseen, incorporated into the walls, was an advanced electrical and sound system that could be controlled from Charles Koebel's bedside table.

Also in 1937, Saarinen was first published in *Architectural Forum*, which commissioned his design for "A Combined Living–Dining Room–Study."[4] This magazine project is very similar to the Koebel House parti of the same year, imagining the public areas of the home as one space divisible by material changes, curtains, and built-in seating. The project is more ostentatiously "modern" than the built house, with one wall of floor-to-ceiling glass and more emphasis on rearrangement and reuse of the furnishings for any event, from cocktails to "dinner for ten." In a set of unpublished photos, Saarinen plays with the miniature Alvar Aalto furniture, rearranging the pieces like objects in a display case as he would the sculpture he imagined for his own interior (fig. 2). The exterior of this project doesn't matter—*Forum* suggested it could be one unit in an apartment house, or a tiny glass house (well *avant la lettre*) with a roof terrace. This passing-over of the exterior would become a trope in Saarinen's domestic projects. He made them as plain as possible, while enriching the inside of the skin by building in banquettes, cupboards, shelves. The house he designed for his mother, Loja, in Bloomfield Hills, Michigan, in 1950 is

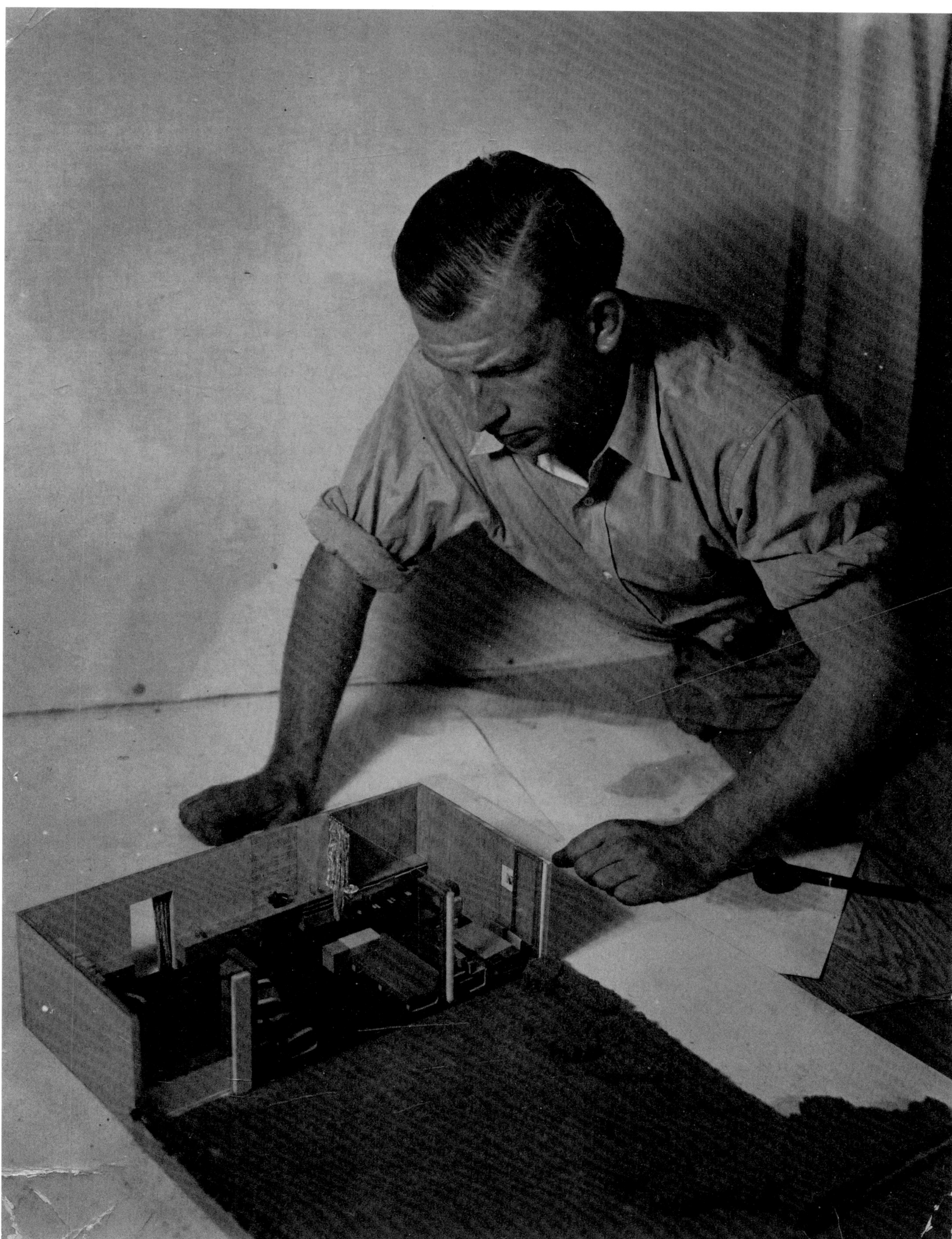

Fig. 2 Eero Saarinen with model of A Combined Living Room–Dining Room–Study, 1937

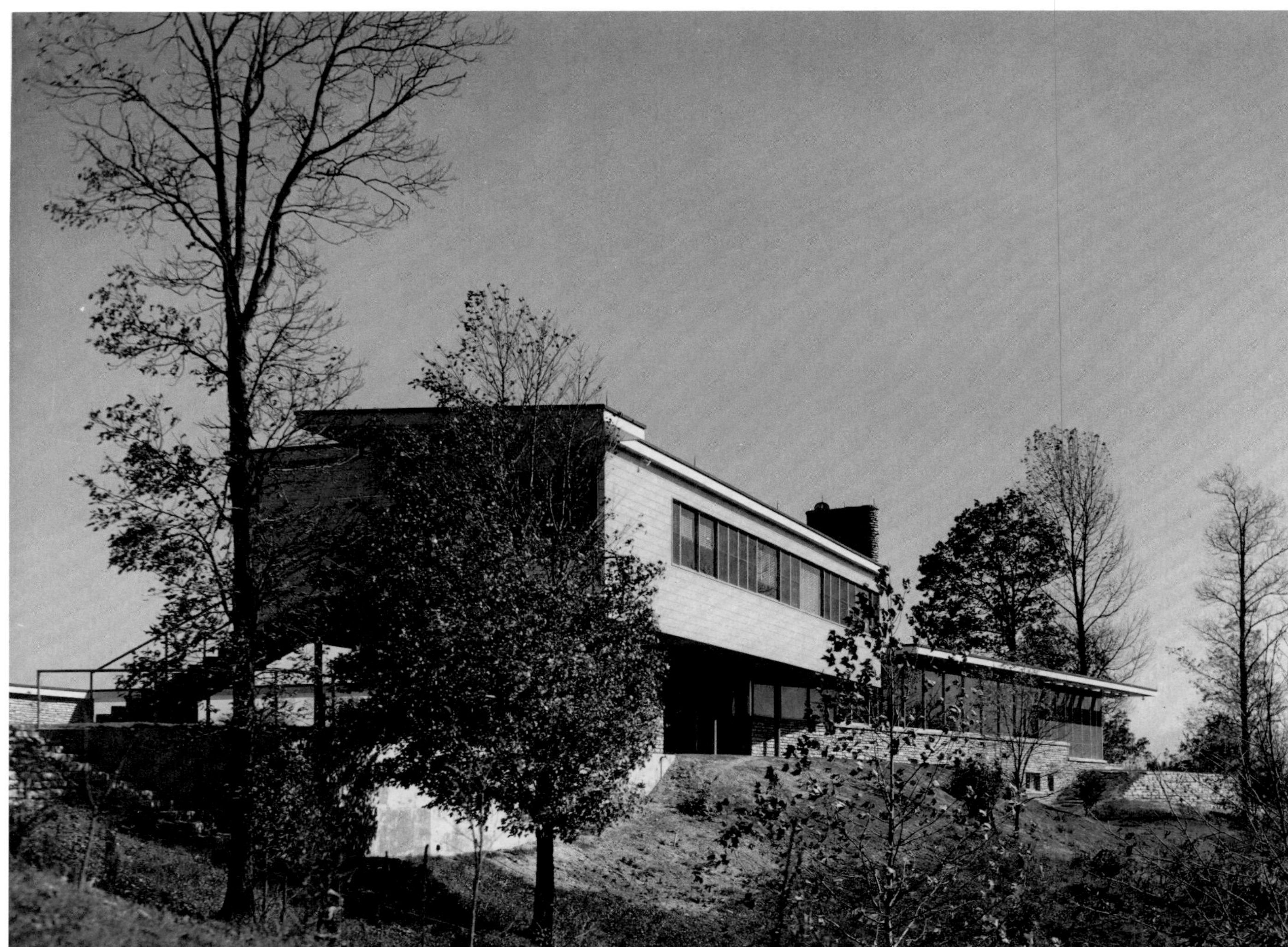

Fig. 3 Eliel and Eero Saarinen, Wermuth House, Fort Wayne, Indiana, 1941–42

not much more than this living room–dining room–study, with two bedrooms attached to one end, a kitchen and bath to the other, and sets of sliding glass doors on both sides.

Subsequent house designs by Eliel and Eero were, like Koebel, based on the rectangle: one long bar for public use, another for private activities, typically a series of tiny bedrooms off a long hall. But the partners began to pay more attention to site. The Wermuth House in Fort Wayne, Indiana, was commissioned by A. C. Wermuth, the contractor who built Cranbrook and the First Christian Church in Columbus (fig. 3). The Saarinens split the house into three parts: living, sleeping, and garage. The latter became an outbuilding, and the path to the front door deflected the public and private volumes away from each other. An undulating brick chimney rises high over the low house and the flat midwestern site, as purposefully vertical as the water tower at the General Motors Technical Center a decade later. The public volume is set in a bed of stone and has an overhang punched with openings straight out of Frank Lloyd Wright's Usonian houses. The back wall is lined with windows (the site overlooks a wooded ravine), which turn into screens at the far end. This room is also broken into three parts: from a low, stone-floored built-in seating area, one proceeds up two steps to a reception area with piano, and around the fireplace to a dining room. The bedrooms are located upstairs in a bar nonsensically raised on pilotis, or columns. Saarinen would make better use of this idea in his house for the Miller family in Ontario, Canada, in 1950–52. There the row of children's bedrooms shades a dining patio, connecting two single-story buildings that follow the V-shape of a natural bluff.

Had it been realized, the Bell House would have been a larger, more

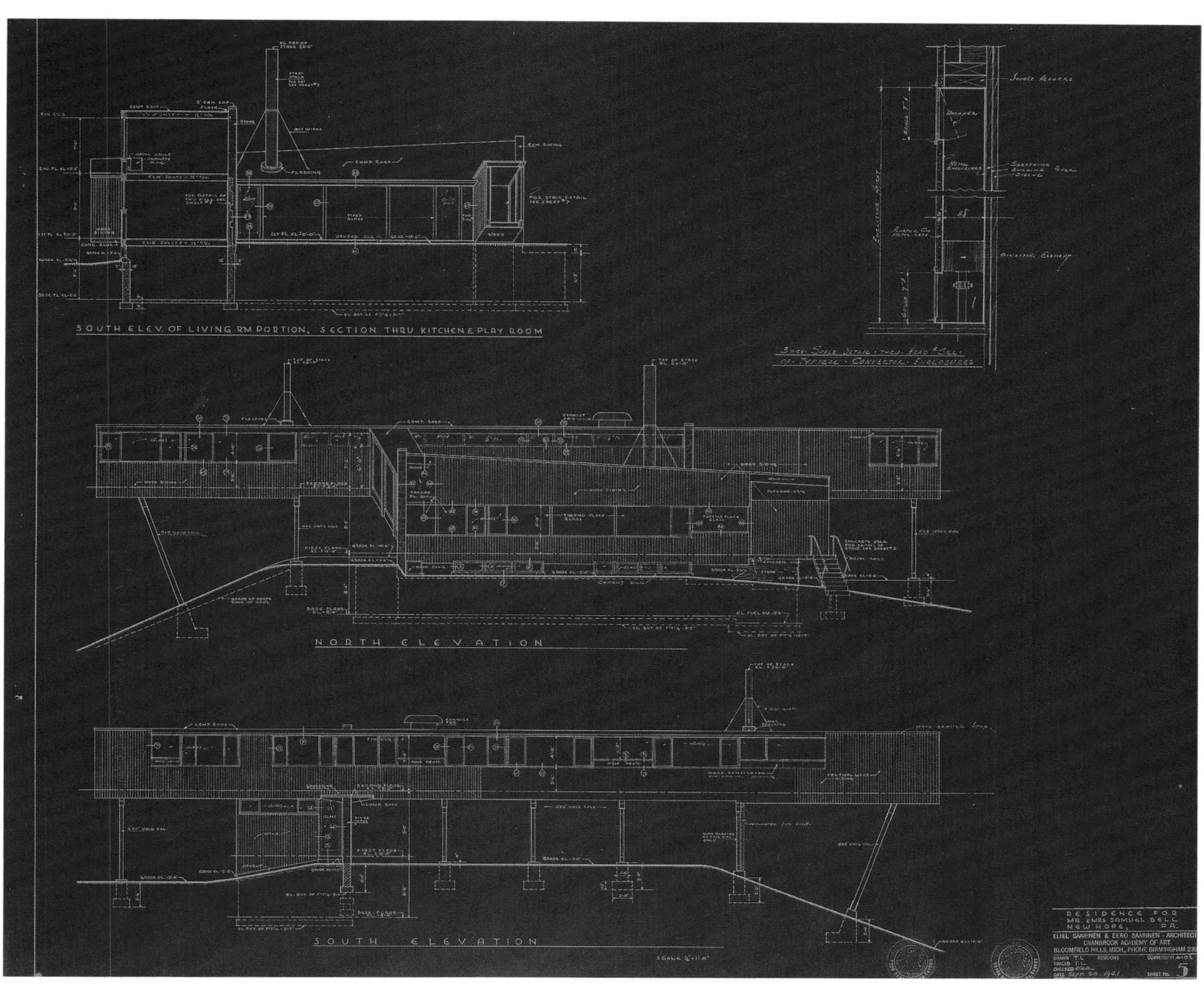

Fig. 4 Eero Saarinen, Bell House project, New Hope, Pennsylvania, 1941, construction drawing

elaborate version of the Wermuth parti: the house begins to break farther apart, its functionally differentiated rectangles connected by knuckles of stairs (fig. 4). As at the Wermuth House, Saarinen seems to have been uncertain about the cladding, covering sections in stone, aluminum, and wood. As with the other houses of the period, the living room has an open plan and extensive built-ins. For the first time, however, the fireplace becomes a freestanding sculptural element in the interior, as well as a vertical landmark on the exterior, that adds to the mechanical appearance of the whole.

That industrial language—a protective skin, an exterior frame—became more pronounced as Saarinen began to design houses and housing on his own. During the early 1940s, the firm worked on defense housing, designing curving rows of simply planned, inexpensively built units sometimes cleverly differentiated via cladding. During the war years architectural magazines sponsored a series of idea competitions, struggling with what might happen to housing in peacetime. *Arts and Architecture* (which would initiate the Case Study housing program in 1945) requested "Designs for Postwar Living" in 1942. When the results were published the following year, Saarinen won the competition with his then-partner and roommate Oliver Lundquist, proposing a house made of "pre-assembled components," or PACs (fig. 5). These components were made of resin-bonded plywood, formed to accommodate the "biological and mechanical functions"—sleeping, eating, bathing—into the walls of the house. The outside of the house is plain and rectilinear, the inside elaborately customizable and curvaceous. The main space, for socializing, is

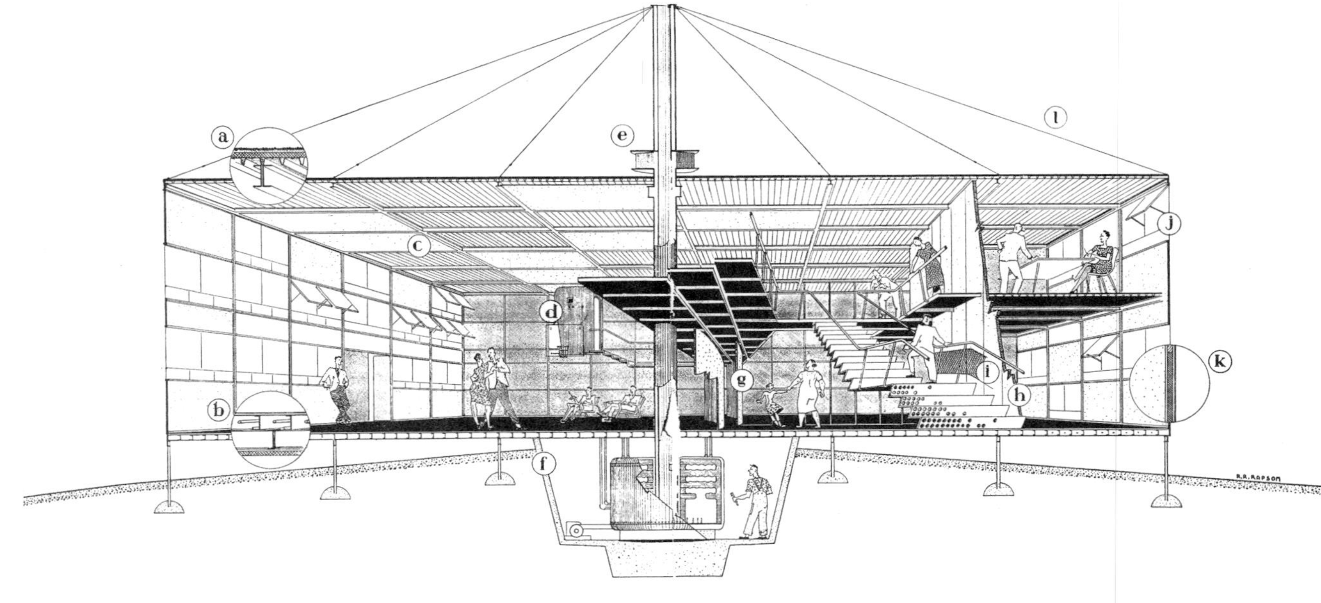

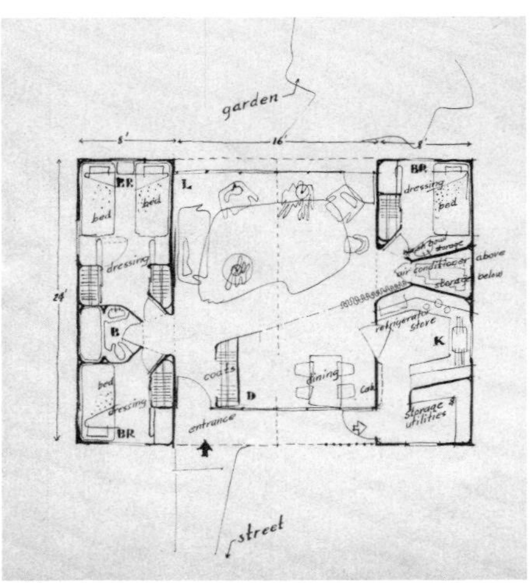

Fig. 5 Eero Saarinen and Oliver Lundquist, double PAC (Pre-Assembled Components) House, 1943

Fig. 6 (top) Eero Saarinen and Ralph Rapson, Demountable Space project, 1940, drawing by Ralph Rapson

centered on a freestanding fireplace and is broken up by a set of low stairs, along which a built-in banquette forms a seating area. The exterior, which already seemed like an afterthought in his built houses to date, is aggressively deemphasized: it becomes three plain sides and a glass front, masking the open space and the elaborate built-ins within.[5]

This project, especially when seen next to Saarinen's other experiment of three years earlier, the Demountable Space project, is a clear precursor to the design of Case Study House #9 (1945–49), for *Arts and Architecture*'s editor, John Entenza—banquette, steps, fireplace, and all. The Demountable Space was designed for a competition held by U.S. Gypsum to develop new uses for the company's wallboard products. Saarinen and Ralph Rapson's entry is an open-plan community center, intended to be part of a housing project, with steel-frame walls ready to be customized with panels or windows (fig. 6). The whole assembly was supported by a central structural mast, attached to building and ground with suspension cables.[6] If the PAC house suggests the Entenza interior, the Demountable Space suggests its structure: no mast, but a rooftop system of steel trusses, pin-wheeling around four centralized columns. The exterior walls were not load bearing, but filled in with vertical siding on three sides and windows on the fourth. *Architectural Forum* called it a "steel shelf with a view," an off-the-rack industrial structure with all its sensuality (curves turn up inside even the boxiest plans), the biological and the social, assigned inside.[7]

The house where Saarinen lived in Bloomfield Hills, Michigan, during the 1950s was an 1880 Victorian brick farmhouse on Vaughn Road, down the street from the offices of Eero Saarinen and Associates and close to the Cranbrook campus. Saarinen treated the Victorian structure, which was just the sort of architecture modernism rebelled against, as a mask. The only major intervention was a new stair hall, a vertical glass slot on the outside. Inside, he tore out historicizing elements and created a version of the serene, carpeted space he described in the Schöner Wohnen speech. A *Vogue* article, titled "A Modern Architect's Own House," shows Aline, Eero, and son Eames seated on the rug and in a Pedestal chair. A foam mattress served as a sofa until Saarinen designed one. In a room with floor-to-ceiling bookshelves, Aline and Eero worked opposite each other after Eames had gone to bed. In the article Eero said he was waiting to make his "architectural statement," making explicit the provisional nature of this living space, his previous residences, and his essays in housing to date.[8] By saying so, he showed that he was still working on the problem of home, experimenting behind a set of eminently reasonable facades.

Notes

1. Eero Saarinen, speech given at Schöner Wohnen congress, Munich, Germany, Oct. 24, 1960, Eero Saarinen Papers, Manuscripts and Archives, Yale University.

2. He was probably referring to the 1942–43 PAC Housing competition, in which his winning entry featured a set of curved, carpeted steps defining the living room. Saarinen had toyed with the idea of a Japanese living room before, in jest, when he wrote to William A. Hewitt, chairman of Deere and Company, that his boardroom ought to be without chairs; William A. Hewitt, "The Genesis of a Great Building—and of an Unusual Friendship," *AIA Journal* 66 (Aug. 1977), 36–37, 56.

3. "Four Bedrooms, Maid's Room," *Architectural Forum,* Aug. 1941, 112–13. Special thanks to James A. Kelly for providing information and a guided tour of the Koebel House. Kelly and Mariam C. Noland bought the house from the Koebel family in 1985, and have lovingly restored it to close to original condition.

4. "A Combined Living-Dining Room-Study," *Architectural Forum,* Oct. 1937, 303–5.

5. The PAC house, the Demountable Space, and the Unfolding House (1945) are discussed in Reinhold Martin, *The Organizational Complex: Architecture, Media, and Corporate Space* (Cambridge: MIT Press, 2003), 107–14. See also "Prize Winners," *Architectural Forum*, Sept. 1943, 88–89; "Demountable Space" advertisement, *Architectural Forum*, Mar. 1942, 50–53.

6. Buckminster Fuller used a similar structural system for his Dymaxion House, designed in the late 1920s but not built until 1945.

7. "Steel Shelf with a View," *Architectural Forum,* Sept. 1950, 97–99.

8. "A Modern Architect's Own House," *Vogue,* Apr. 1, 1960, 172–78.

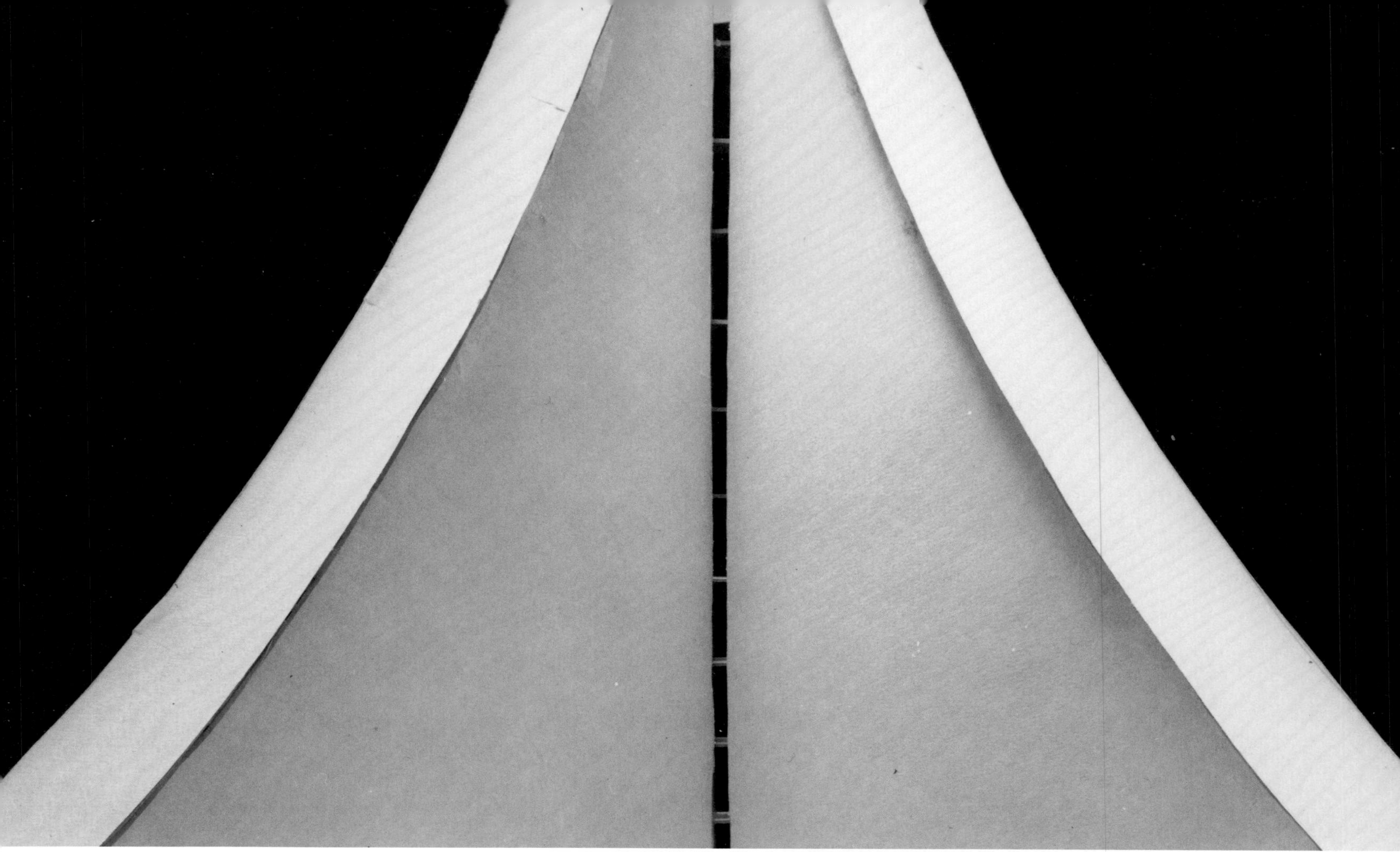

Jennifer Komar Olivarez

churches and chapels
a new kind of worship space

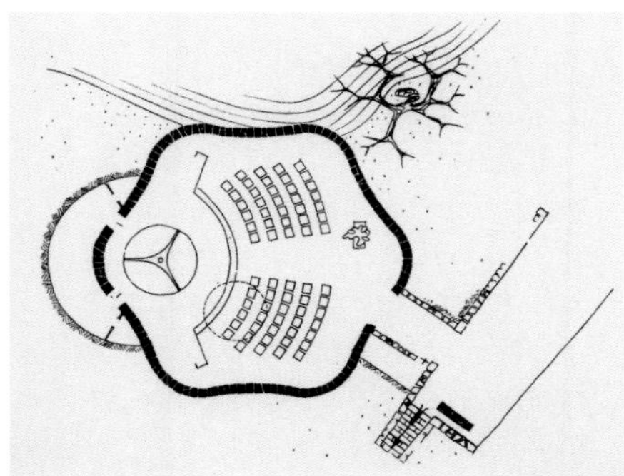

Fig. 1 Eero Saarinen and Associates, Brandeis University, chapel scheme, Waltham, Massachusetts, plan by Matthew Nowicki, 1949–50

Tabernacle Church of Christ, later First Christian Church, Columbus, Indiana, 1939–42
Christ Church Lutheran, Minneapolis, Minnesota, 1947–49
Kresge Chapel, MIT, Cambridge, Massachusetts, 1950–55
Prayer Chapel, Drake University, Des Moines, Iowa, 1952–56
Stephens College Chapel, Columbia, Missouri, 1953–56
Concordia Senior College Chapel, Fort Wayne, Indiana, 1953–58
North Christian Church, Columbus, Indiana, 1959–64

The modern movement in architecture during the early twentieth century and the concurrent liturgical revival resulted in new approaches to one of the most traditional building forms, the church. Along with his father, Eero Saarinen was not only a key part of this revolution in twentieth-century America but also influential in many ways. An examination of the plans, elevations, site plans, and contextualization of Eero's ecclesiastical structures, through a chronological study, reveals his influential rethinking of church architecture, a small but important part of his oeuvre.

The liturgical revival, begun in the late nineteenth century in Europe, led congregations and architects to explore a new approach to church design, beginning with the worshipful nature of its use. In 1938, the German architect Rudolf Schwarz wrote his influential treatise *The Church Incarnate*, in which he advised: "We must enter into the simple things at the source of the Christian life. We must begin anew and our new beginning must be genuine. The small congregation is given us today, the 'coming together of two or three,' the communion of the table, and certainly for us the Lord is in the midst of [them]. . . . Even when a new church is to be built, the simple ordering which we have just described remains. To us this is the great, simple, elemental form."[1]

To guide architects in rebuilding after the Second World War, the German Liturgical Commission in 1947 reinforced this liturgical approach, thus supporting its modern proponents, and as a result Schwarz and his German contemporary Dominikus Böhm led the way in postwar modern church design. In 1965, after Saarinen's death, the reform documents of the Second Vatican Council (Vatican II) allowed for significant changes in Catholic church design to reflect liturgical changes.

Architects found many concrete ways to apply this liturgical approach to modern church architecture. Most began with an open, honest structure, made possible by modern steel construction. By removing barriers between chancel and nave, and placing the pulpit to one side in favor of (or at least equal to) the altar or communion table, they deemphasized church hierarchy. Central-plan naves were ideal for situating the congregation equally and in close proximity to the communal celebration. Saarinen's central-plan churches and chapels prefigure the central-plan Catholic churches widely adopted in the United States in the mid-1960s.

Ludwig Mies van der Rohe said *The Church Incarnate* was "not only a great book on architecture, indeed, it is one of the truly great books," in his introduction to the 1958 English edition.[2] Although no specific reference to Schwarz or the liturgical revival has been found in the Saarinens' writings, in their ecclesiastical work the Saarinens certainly displayed an awareness of this new approach to church architecture.[3] They were always concerned with designing around the architectural program, so their organic approach fit in well with the liturgical revival. As well, their modern forms were a natural fit for this wholesale rethinking of the religious building.

TABERNACLE CHURCH OF CHRIST AND CHRIST CHURCH LUTHERAN

The Saarinens applied many of Schwarz's ideas about simplicity and intimacy to their two urban churches, Tabernacle Church of Christ (now First Christian Church) in Columbus, Indiana (1939–42), and Christ Church Lutheran in Minneapolis, Minnesota (1947–49). The resulting churches broke new ground for American ecclesiastical design. The architects began with a fairly traditional basilica plan, married it to a strong modern elevation, and made subtle but important changes to accommodate the Christian service. The congregation was eager to have a worship space that reflected their faith's "attempt to restore the simplicity of the church as described in the New Testament."[4] The Saarinens, understanding that "the function of the Chancel is asymmetrical in its nature," arranged the nave and chancel accordingly, with an off-center main aisle.[5] They placed the pulpit to the left, the choir to the right, and hid the immersion baptistery behind a screen at the back of the chancel. The overall feeling is open and uncluttered with the focus on the church service.

The elemental yet powerful elevation of the Tabernacle Church of Christ demonstrates the Saarinens' mastery of simple massing. They successfully juxtaposed a strong vertical form—a soaring rectangular tower—with a horizontal rectangle for the sanctuary wing, virtually creating the prototype for the "flat roofed" modern church with tower that would be adopted in variations throughout the country, especially after World War II, although most architects were unable to match Eliel and Eero's careful development of the plan and elevation.[6]

Seven years after the Tabernacle Church was completed, the Saarinens utilized a similar plan and massing for Christ Church Lutheran in Minneapolis. Christ Church has recently been linked with Böhm's celebrated St. Engelbert in Riehl, Germany (1930), an early circular-plan Catholic church with a nearly identical bell tower.[7] In the Minneapolis project, the congregation and its modest budget, along with further innovations by the architects, resulted in a plan and elevation that pushes the building subtly out of the rectangle. A study of the plan reveals a basically symmetrical nave, yet the walls of both the chancel and the rear chapel curve slightly (the latter is attached to the narthex to conserve space). The south aisle pews and the baptismal font project into a low wing adjacent to the main building mass. As well, the interior elevation eschews parallel planes and right angles in favor of a canted ceiling and angled north wall, all to improve acoustics and create drama with light reflections. At Christ Church, a hidden floor-to-ceiling window illuminates the altar as it does at Tabernacle Church of Christ.

These two churches, both built on city sites, reflect Eliel Saarinen's notable planning skills. At Tabernacle Church of Christ, the Saarinens elegantly resolved the housing of educational and social functions on the city-block-size lot by connecting the Bible School wing to the church by an elevated rectangle, allowing light to flow into the lower levels of the church and school wings. They added a terrace with a reflecting pool, an important unifying element preferred by Eliel for secular and ecclesiastical uses, and one that Eero would return to in later religious and secular projects. For Christ Church Lutheran, the Saarinens tailored the Columbus arrangement of opposing rectangular tower and sanctuary for the smaller site and congregation. They tied the new church to an existing building with an open arcade, creating an interior court area. In 1960, Eero designed a rectangular addition, including Sunday School, lounge, auditorium, and library, to replace the older building, therefore completing—yet not competing with—the firm's previous design.

KRESGE CHAPEL AT MIT

The nondenominational chapels that constituted most of Eero Saarinen's ecclesiastical architecture through the 1950s depart from the basilica church plans he developed with his father. Not tied to any particular religion, their open programs allowed Eero room for experimentation, resulting in some resonating structures. By nature, they are worship spaces distilled to their most elemental, and thus were executed in the spirit of the liturgical revival. The most celebrated is Kresge Chapel at the Massachusetts Institute of Technology in Cambridge, Massachusetts (1950–55), with its circular plan reminiscent of a windowless medieval tower.

Saarinen had first conceived the chapel as a rectangular steel-and-glass box recalling Mies's recently completed chapel for the Illinois Institute of Technology (1952). A letter from Eero to his Swedish friend Astrid Sampe, undated but probably from March 1952, accompanied by a sheet containing sketches of the chapel plan, elevation, perspective, and lighting detail, describes his recent arrival at the round chapel concept.[8]

Several influences may have been at work in Saarinen's rethinking of this now famous design. Significant here are Matthew Nowicki's chapel sketches for Brandeis University in Waltham, Massachusetts, prepared in collaboration with Eero in 1949–50 as part of an unrealized master campus plan. Nowicki (1910–1950) produced several different schemes for the chapel, from one with a cochlear "snail shell" entry into a round central section to a version consisting of a low dome punctuated with round skylights. Most notable is a Brandeis plan and interior perspective of the final scheme published in *American School and University* in 1951–52, and also shown in historic photos of Brandeis models: a chapel with undulating walls, with seating occupying the main interior area and an altar tucked to the back opposite the entrance (figs. 1, 2). A plan study for the MIT chapel dated 1953 shows great similarities between the two (including offset skylights), although Saarinen famously hid his undulating interior walls within a brick cylinder (fig. 3). This leads to one of two assumptions: either Saarinen was instrumental in the development of the Brandeis chapel, with Nowicki sketching his ideas, or (and this seems more likely) his MIT chapel was greatly influenced by the imaginative Brandeis sketches by Nowicki, a visionary architect and planner in his own right, who died before he could see a large body of work realized.[9]

Influential also for MIT is Eliel Saarinen's 1950 circular plan for a chapel for Stephens College in Columbia, Missouri, in elevation a monumental fluted cylinder with elements of a central plan. Eero knew that this project—his father's last—had been rejected by the client because it was "too big and too expensive."[10]

The MIT chapel sits across the plaza from Eero's low-domed Kresge Auditorium (1950–55). Both have been criticized since their completion for their adventurous forms and their apparent lack of dialogue. These two buildings were part of a larger commission, however. A site plan sketch in the Eero Saarinen Papers at Yale reveals that the chapel was part of a group of three buildings for the site, including the auditorium and an unbuilt student union, a rectilinear box at the edge of the plaza. As an arrangement of three forms on a plaza—the dome, the cylinder, and the rectangle—the concept has a sense of completeness not conveyed by the two built structures.

In addition, it seems that Saarinen's original landscape plan for the cylindrical chapel was meant to be evocative of a pastoral wooded setting, perhaps influenced by Gunnar Asplund's famously secluded Little Chapel of the Forest in Skogskyrkogården (Woodland Cemetery) outside Stockholm, from 1918. The MIT site plan including the student union shows an important role for landscaping on the plaza, with the chapel set in a dense grove of trees, while later models and renderings show the more abbreviated planting scheme that was carried out. Treeless on its west side, the chapel forgoes the seclusion of Saarinen's original intention, when he isolated the chapel in the trees, setting the rectangular student union as a foil for the domed auditorium. The chapel's moat, however, buffers the structure and provides reflective light into the chapel's interior.

DRAKE UNIVERSITY AND STEPHENS COLLEGE CHAPELS

Saarinen returned to the circular plan and cylindrical brick elevation of MIT for a small "meditation chapel" connected to the Bible School at Drake University in Des Moines, Iowa (1952–56). With the Drake and Stephens chapels, he moved the altar to the center of the structure, a dramatic step toward his central plan for North Christian Church in Columbus, Indiana, and a significant architectural realization of the liturgical revival. His "thrust-

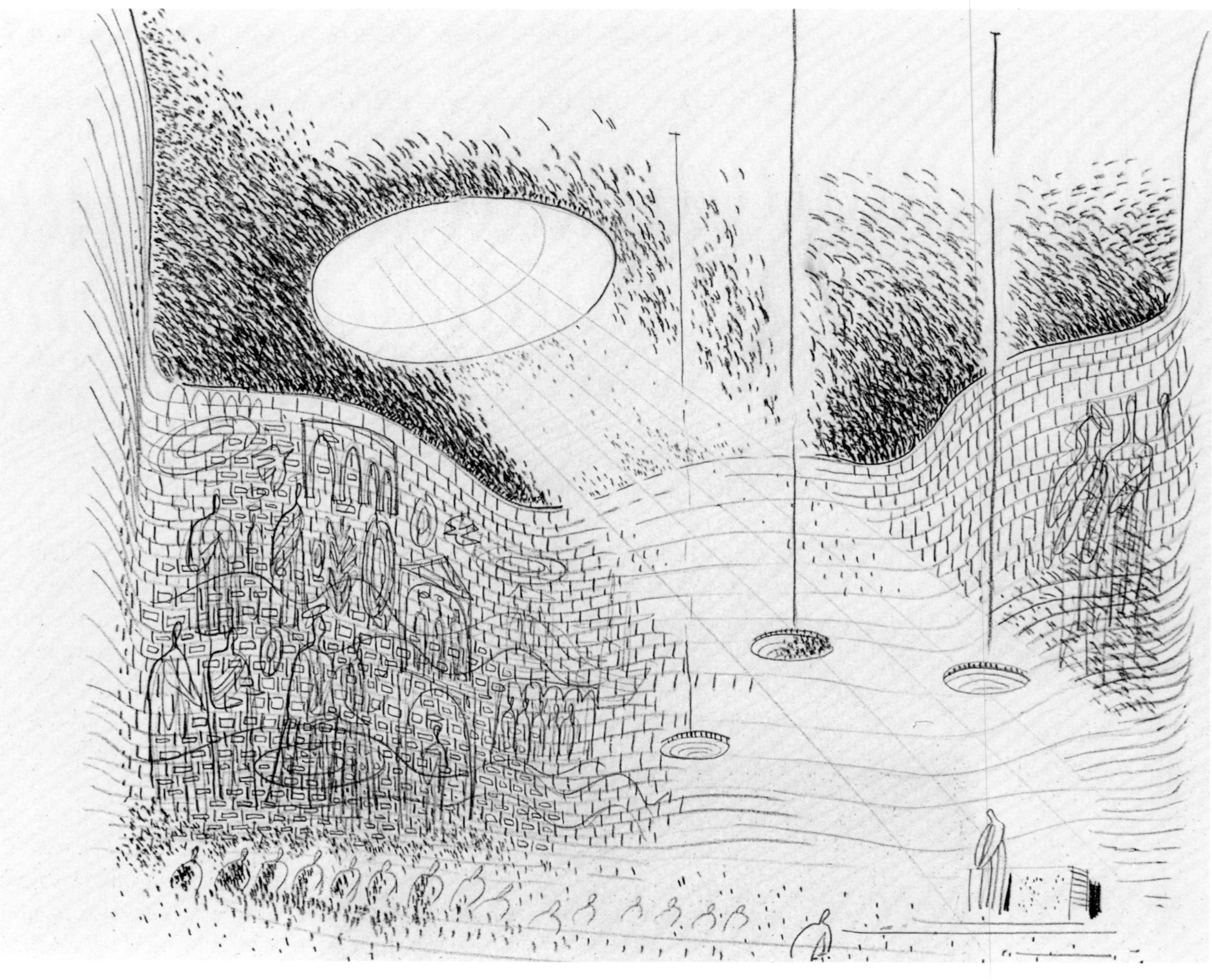

Fig. 2 (opposite) Eero Saarinen and Associates, Brandeis University, chapel, interior perspective by Matthew Nowicki, 1949–50

Fig. 3 Eero Saarinen and Associates, Kresge Chapel, Massachusetts Institute of Technology, Cambridge, Massachusetts, 1950–55, plan study by Merle Westlake

stage" approach to the Stephens College altar plan is also an example of the transfer of overtly theatrical qualities to Saarinen's later churches and chapels, particularly North Christian. His friend Ralph Rapson notably applied the "thrust-stage" at this same time for his Guthrie Theater in Minneapolis (1963).

At Drake and Stephens, Saarinen created his chapel designs in the context of earlier master plans that he and his father had developed. Ironically, when Stephens College tapped Eero to build its chapel in 1953 (it was completed in 1956), he turned away from Eliel's previous circular plan, preferring a square footprint with entrances in each of the four sides. The Drake and Stephens chapels are stark geometric volumes, though they tend to reflect the scale and vocabulary of the surrounding historic buildings (both brick and low-profile). The unbuilt Brandeis chapel was also envisioned as a windowless brick volume, though it was set in a more pastoral position at the edge of the wooded campus.

CONCORDIA COLLEGE CHAPEL

The straightforward liturgy of the Lutheran denomination guided the functional rectangular plan for Eero's chapel at Concordia Senior College, in Fort Wayne, Indiana (1953–58), yet the elevation—triangular, or A-frame—was dynamic and innovative. Saarinen designed the entire Concordia campus, and he intentionally gave the chapel's roof a steeper pitch than those of the secular buildings. Its profile is also emphasized by its central location at the edge of a man-made lake, an appropriate focus for a religious institution.

Eero was thinking of the A-frame solution for a church long before the Concordia commission. Letters he wrote to Florence Knoll, most likely from the 1930s, show three possible solutions to what he called an architectural "problem" for an unidentified "church competition."[11] He sketched three elevations for a sloping site, approached in each by ramps and stairs (fig. 4). The first sketch (A) owes much to the designs of churches by Saarinen and Saarinen, with its soaring bell tower adjoining a rectangular sanctuary, while the second (B) is the most innovative: an A-frame sanctuary with a separate, smaller tower. Coming nearly fifteen years before Concordia, this would be a very early imagining of the A-frame for modern religious architecture.[12]

The A-frame had great appeal to many congregations for its economy; its height eliminated the costly and now symbolic bell tower, and the two walls joining together eliminated the roof. Its dramatic modern form, symbolically reaching to the heavens, became popular through the 1960s, for both Protestant and Catholic congregations.

NORTH CHRISTIAN CHURCH

North Christian Church (begun in 1959 but not completed until 1964) is one of the most visionary American church designs of the twentieth century. In line with the tenets of the liturgical revival, Saarinen recognized that communion was an important act in the Christian service. He developed a hexagonal plan for the nave centered on the communion table, bringing the congregation close so that "everyone feels equal and joined together."[13] A famously successful contemporaneous application of this idea to secular architecture is the hexagon-plan Philharmonie in Berlin designed by Hans Scharoun in 1956 (completed in 1963) as a "container" for the musical activity within. At North Christian, Eero used the central plan and a theatrical approach to lighting to focus on the liturgy of the Christian service. He preserved the mystery of the service with an oculus dramatically illuminating the communion table, augmented only by subdued light at the perimeter of the seating area.

The many sketches and models Saarinen made to perfect the organic "building as spire" show him searching for drama and movement in ways he had not done with his previous churches and chapels, surely drawing on the forms and techniques of the TWA Terminal and Dulles International Airport (figs. 5, 6). Early form models show both triangular and square plans with

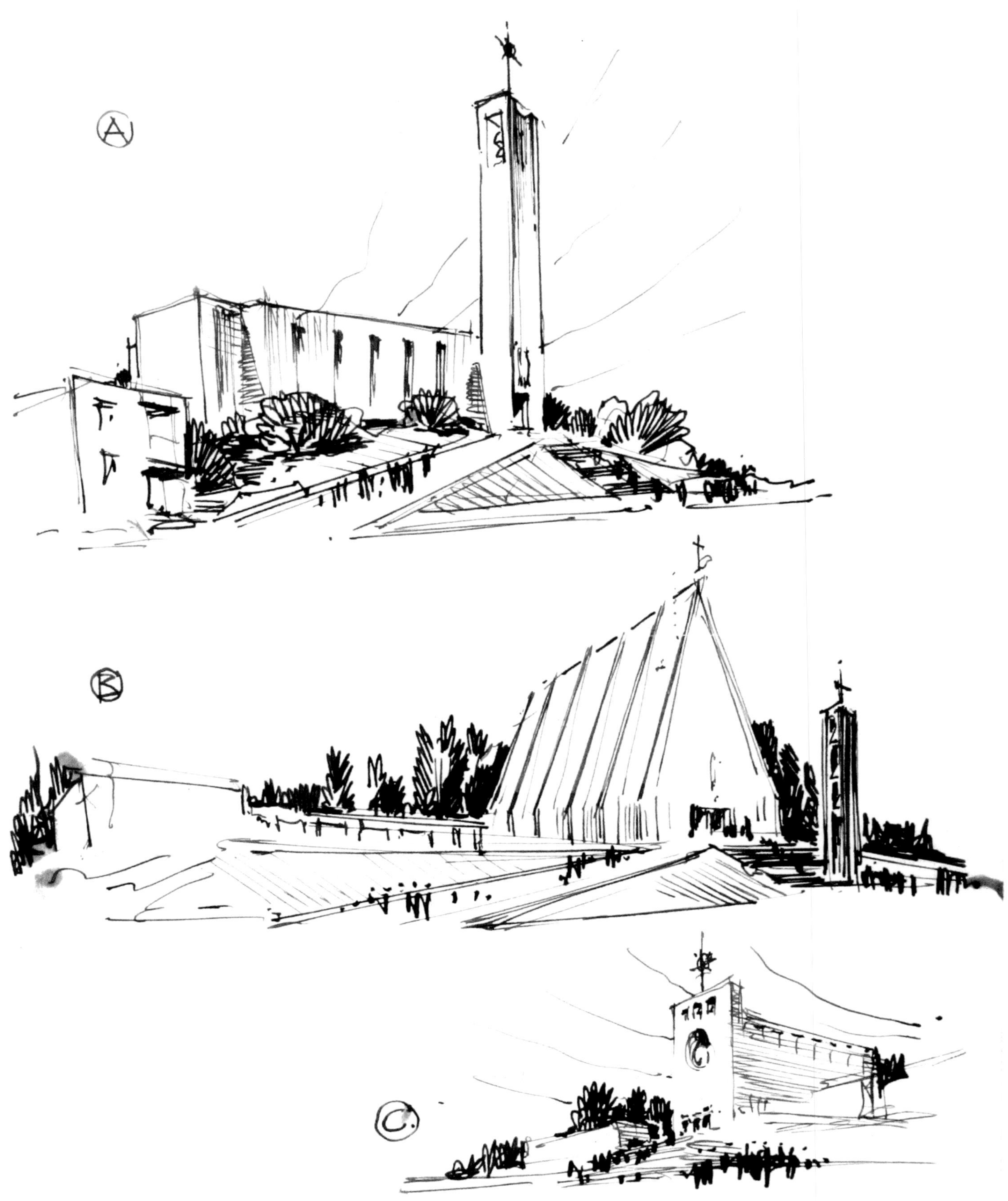

Fig. 4 Eero Saarinen, sketches of churches, from letter to Florence Knoll, ca. 1935

Fig. 5 (opposite, top) Eero Saarinen, North Christian Church, Columbus, Indiana, 1959–64, early elevation sketch 1959–61

Fig. 6 (opposite, bottom) Eero Saarinen, North Christian Church, early elevation sketch 1959–61

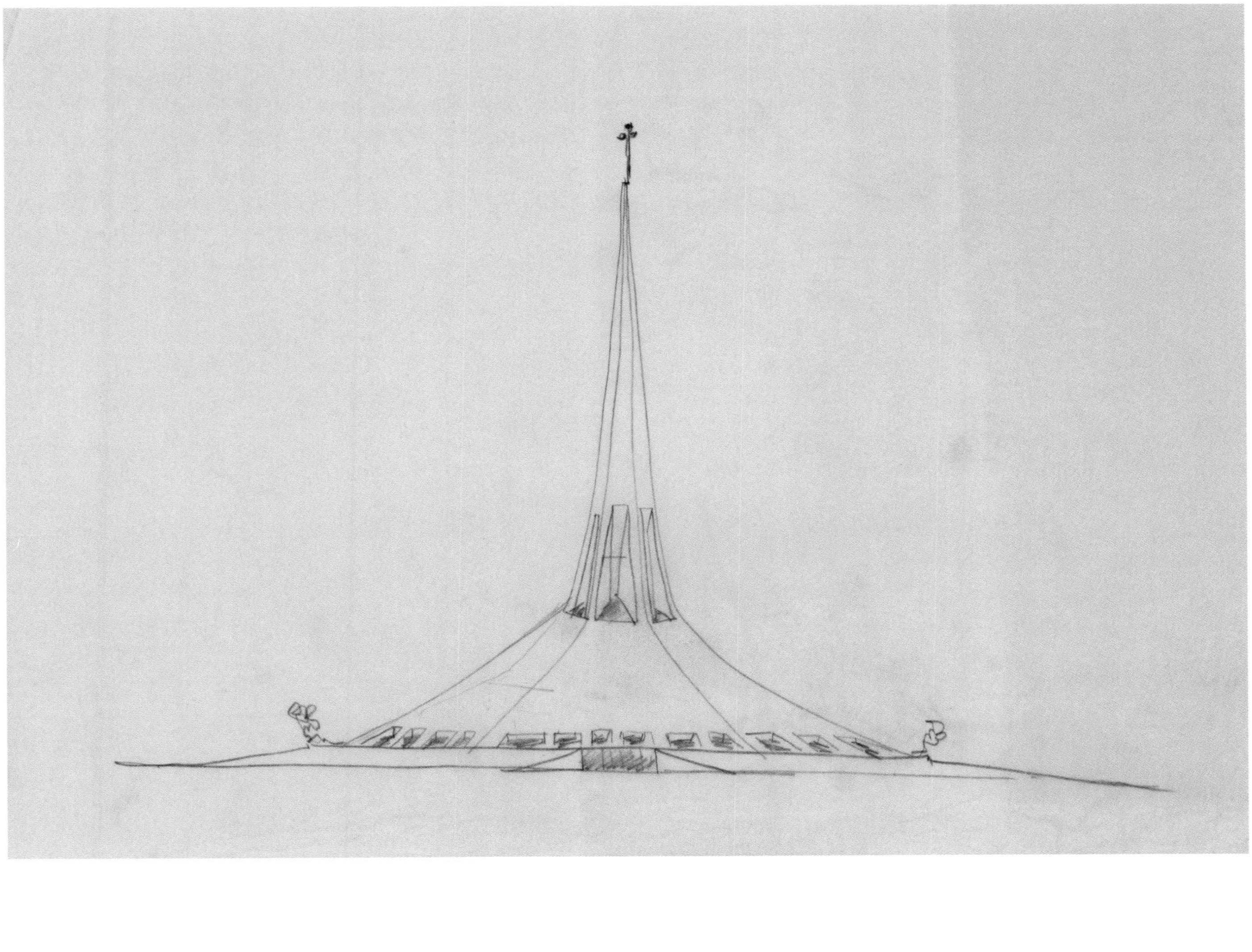

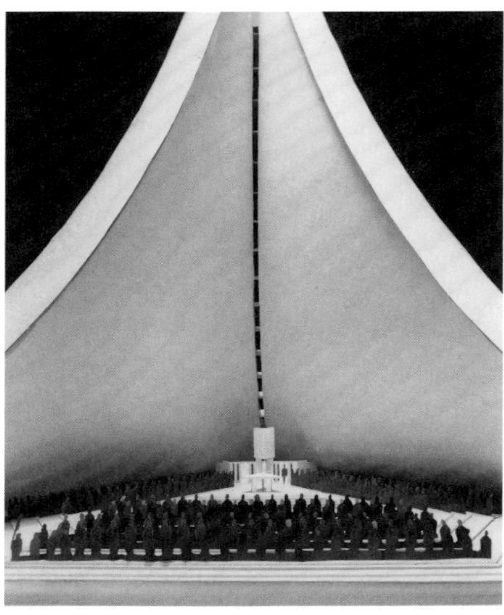

Fig. 7 Eero Saarinen and Associates, North Christian Church, early ceiling model

highly sculptural concave sides culminating in a spirelike point (fig. 7). He concluded early on that the flat lot needed an elevated form so that the church could be seen amid "the parked cars and the surrounding little ranch-type houses."[14] He was on the crest of a wave of American architects who made use of drama, new materials, and engineering advances to explore what has been called the "swooping" style for churches built in the 1960s. In particular Victor Lundy's exuberant design for the First Unitarian Church in Westport, Connecticut (1960), with its soaring sculptural roof and glass "spine" to let in natural light, is similar to Saarinen's early form models for North Christian.[15]

Eero carefully considered the site of the future North Christian Church when developing its design. Unlike the urban grids for the Tabernacle Church of Christ and Christ Church Lutheran, and the campus context of the chapels, North Christian's site was a flat, treeless lot in a residential district—almost a suburban location. Saarinen first thought of placing it in the center of a planned cemetery connected with the church, thinking this could be "a very beautiful thing."[16] He was perhaps again remembering Asplund's Little Chapel of the Forest, set amid flat grave markers. Both plan and model of North Christian show its footprint outlined by trees, perhaps again to evoke a wooded setting. An *Architectural Record* article from 1964 featuring the completed church supports this idea. It shows a proposed landscaping plan (presumably by Dan Kiley, listed as the landscape architect in the article) with an extremely dense nonlinear grouping of trees surrounding the church on all sides. Although this scheme was not carried out, the building's geometry is emphasized even further on its largely treeless site.

In December 1952, *Architectural Forum* predicted that among the innovators in church architecture at that time, including Frank Lloyd Wright, Bruce Goff, and Pietro Belluschi, "Only the Saarinen churches seem likely to develop a prototype even for the Saarinens themselves."[17] Although this statement was made before Eero's solo projects came to fruition, the influential qualities of father and son's churches remained in Eero's own work. The appeal of these structures, perhaps, was their crystallization of the ideas of the German liturgical revival: innovative elemental forms, carefully developed settings, and sensitivity to the specific liturgical needs of the congregations. The Saarinens' successful melding of these elements influenced American postwar ecclesiastical architecture for decades to come.

Notes

1. Rudolf Schwarz, *The Church Incarnate: The Sacred Function of Christian Architecture* (1938; first English edition, Chicago: H. Regnery, 1958), 35–36.

2. For a discussion of the liturgical movement and its context in architecture, see Edwin Heathcote and Iona Spens, *Church Builders* (West Sussex: Academy Editions, 1997).

3. Although it is not known whether either Saarinen had a copy of *The Church Incarnate* in his library, Eliel read German and thus would have had access to the 1938 German edition.

4. Albert Christ-Janer and Mary Mix Foley, *Modern Church Architecture: A Guide to the Form and Spirit of Twentieth-Century Religious Buildings* (New York: Dodge Book Dept., McGraw-Hill, 1962), 257.

5. "Tabernacle Church of Christ," *Architectural Forum*, Oct. 1942, 40.

6. See Ernest Born's design for a chapel for the Pacific School of Religion, "Campus Chapel," *Architectural Forum*, Dec. 1952, 102–5. The school later built an A-frame chapel.

7. Kathleen James-Chakraborty, "Dominikus Böhm in Amerika," in *Dominikus Böhm, 1880–1955*, ed. Wolfgang Voigt and Ingeborg Flagge (Tübingen: Wasmuth Verlag, 2005), 99. James-Chakraborty recognizes Böhm's and the Saarinens' shared modern philosophy that "abstract spaces infused with striking natural light can at their best foster a more meaningful communion with the divine than any degree of more obvious splendor." I am grateful to her for sharing the English version of her essay, in which she confirmed many of my own connections between the Saarinens and the liturgical revival in architecture. I also thank Paul Rogers for bringing this publication to my attention.

8. Eero Saarinen, letter to Astrid Sampe, n.d. but possibly from Mar. 14, 1952, per letter's envelope (translated from the Swedish), 1995-87, 1:5, Astrid Sampe Collection of Eero Saarinen Correspondence, Cranbrook Archives, Bloomfield Hills, Mich.

9. Original sketches for Brandeis are in the Eero Saarinen Collection, Cranbrook Archives. Some of Eero's earlier schemes for MIT are in "Saarinen Challenges the Rectangle," *Architectural Forum*, Jan. 1953, 130. Nowicki died in a plane crash in 1950 while at work on planning the city of Chandigarh, India.

10. Eero Saarinen, letter to Astrid Sampe, Mar. 12, 1953 (translated from the Swedish), Astrid Sampe Collection of Eero Saarinen Correspondence, Cranbrook Archives. Eliel's design was published in "Progress Preview: Chapel for a Women's College," *Progressive Architecture*, June 1951, 15–16. A photo of an interior rendering is in the Eero Saarinen Papers, Manuscripts and Archives, Yale University. The Saarinens created a master plan for Stephens College in 1945–47. See Albert Christ-Janer, *Eliel Saarinen: Finnish-American Architect and Educator* (1948; repr., Chicago: University of Chicago Press, 1979), 152.

11. Eero Saarinen, letters to Florence Knoll, n.d. (contained in folder dated 1935–36), Florence Knoll Bassett Papers, Archives of American Art, Smithsonian Institution.

12. Frank Lloyd Wright had drawn on the triangular form for his First Unitarian Church in Madison, Wisconsin, of 1947–51, yet his complex designs were difficult to imitate and thus have not had mainstream resonance in religious architecture.

13. Eero Saarinen, *Eero Saarinen on His Work: A Selection of Buildings Dating from 1947 to 1964*, with statements by the architect, ed. Aline B. Saarinen (New Haven: Yale University Press, 1962), 96.

14. Ibid.

15. Other examples of the "swooping" style include Skidmore, Owings, and Merrill's U.S. Air Force Academy Chapel, Colorado Springs, Colorado (1962); Wallace K. Harrison's First Presbyterian Church, Stamford, Connecticut (1958); and Warren Weber's First Congregational Church, Vancouver, Washington (1962).

16. Saarinen, *Eero Saarinen on His Work*, 96.

17. "Anarchy in Our Churches," *Architectural Forum*, Dec. 1952, 93.

Alexandra Lange

corporate headquarters saarinen in suburbia

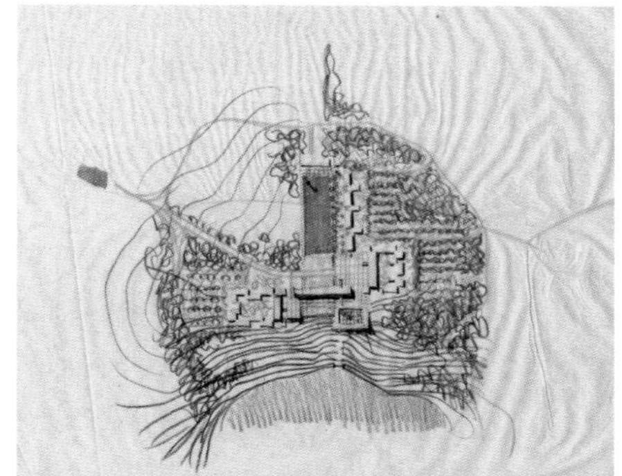

Fig. 1 Eero Saarinen and Associates, Time Inc. Headquarters project, Rye, New York, 1952, plan sketch

Time Inc. Headquarters Project, Rye, New York, 1952
IBM Thomas J. Watson Research Center, Yorktown Heights, New York, 1957–61
Deere and Company Administrative Center, Moline, Illinois, 1957–63

The first built phase of the General Motors Technical Center appeared in *Architectural Forum* in November 1951, and Eero Saarinen immediately saw the effect on his status, and on his commissions. "I have until recently had a reputation as being one of the best younger architects," Saarinen wrote in 1952. "The publication of the General Motors Technical Center put me about half way between that category and the category of being 'successful' with big business and industry (and also good)—Skidmore, Owings, and Merrill and Harrison [and Abramovitz] have been the two firms in this last category. Now if Time comes to us it really means that we will be thought of as the third firm on that plane."[1]

By "Time" Saarinen meant his latest—and then top secret—commission: a new headquarters for Time Inc., publisher of *Time, Life, Fortune*, and *Architectural Forum*, on a fifty-five-acre site in Rye, New York. Designs for this project surfaced among the Eero Saarinen Papers, which Kevin Roche gave to Yale's Manuscripts and Archives division in 2002, and they are published here for the first time (fig. 1).[2] The project shows Saarinen's approach to the corporate campus—a brand new typology—in the early stages of development, and includes formal concepts that were remixed into built campuses for Bell, Deere, and IBM. Saarinen may have created a "style for the job," but the company-specific symbolism in the corporate campuses was usually incorporated into the facades, while the plans are all variations on the same organizing principles. The essence of the corporate campus is, and was, its plan, and at Time, as at Deere and IBM, one can see Saarinen moving the corporate building block, the office module, away from conglomeration—the tower in the garden—and into the landscape. As architects began to carve plazas out of city blocks, so, in the suburbs, they cut holes in their horizontal skyscrapers, extended wings to civilize the countryside, and dropped parking structures into valleys, no one more dramatically than Saarinen. Saarinen's best corporate competitor in the 1950s and 1960s was his friend Gordon Bunshaft of Skidmore, Owings, and Merrill. Bunshaft's campuses maintain an urban vocabulary, and tend to resemble elegant Corbusian work-villas. Saarinen gave Time such an administrative villa, but he ultimately allowed his architecture to succumb to topography and, particularly at Deere, to the idiosyncrasies of corporate character.

Time's editor-in-chief Henry Luce had long been a supporter of modern architecture, and Saarinen was also lucky in terms of timing. Long on the drawing boards, the GM Tech Center was in construction before the bulk of the postwar building boom turned other chairmen's eyes toward the suburbs. After the outbreak of the Korean War, in a climate of fear of atomic bomb attacks on American cities, Time bought the Rye site as part of its "catastrophic planning," but also because the company was rapidly outgrowing its Rockefeller Center tower. The first major corporation to move out of New York City was General Foods, to White Plains in 1954. The insurance company Connecticut General, whose Bunshaft building is considered the first horizontal skyscraper, left downtown Hartford, Connecticut, in 1957. IBM began buying acreage in Westchester County in the mid-1950s, and finally moved its executives to Armonk in 1964. By 1976, thirty corporations had moved out, primarily to Westchester and neighboring Fairfield County, Connecticut. Articles on the moves often cited the need for greener pastures to recruit and retain employees. However, as sociologist William H. Whyte found, "of 38 corporations, 31 moved to a place close to the top man's home. Average distance: about eight miles."[3] Saarinen and Skidmore, Owings, and Merrill (SOM) became specialists in the new type of structure: a low-rise modernist building, often overlooking a water element, reached via a carefully landscaped drive, with parking dropped from view.[4] Although in the end it was not built, the Time Inc. campus would have been the first.

"Every director of a business corporation has a chance to make the next office building a little more beautiful, with a little more fun and joy in it, even if it adds 25 cents per square foot," said Luce in a speech on October 13, 1955. "We shall not have become true masters of our economy until we have taught it to serve also our ideals of beauty." His headquarters "cannot be in any skyscraper slab. . . . All we may require is an efficient (air-conditioned) anthill. But we can easily agree, I hope, that an anthill is *not* the *ideal*."[5] Luce's ideal included multiple low structures, with employee amenities both cultural (gallery, library, chapel) and physical (pool, gardens, tennis courts). Saarinen's designs include many of these facilities, but he began with a spatially based analysis of Time's corporate structure. His office prepared scale drawings of the hierarchy of each magazine, as well as the company's administration, and film and television departments (fig. 2). Saarinen translated the linear hierarchy of the masthead into square footage: each employee's name and title are boxed, and these boxes diminish in size as one heads from executive to assistant. Thick shaded lines that look like corridors link the boxes. One sees that each department of *Fortune*, for example, could be placed in its own pavilion, branching off the central executive suite. Saarinen also recognized that the whole company could be broken down into four equal parts: administration, *Time*, *Life*, and the remaining magazines and programs.

What I believe to be Saarinen's first plan for Time is solely based on this quadripartite division. This plan shows the company as a set of four low buildings pinwheeling out from a central square structure (fig. 3). The buildings form a rough swastika, each with a separate entrance (and

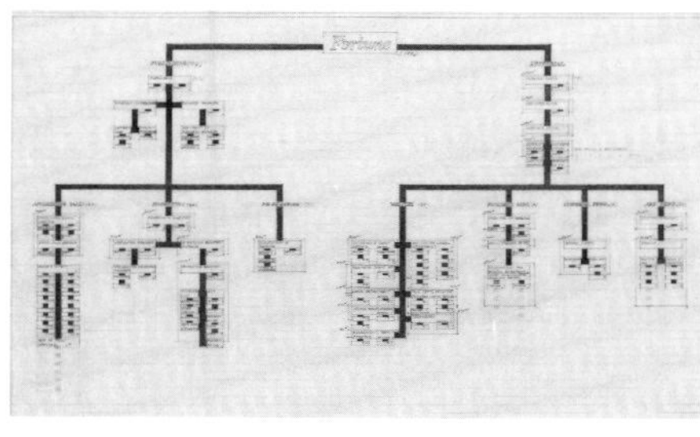

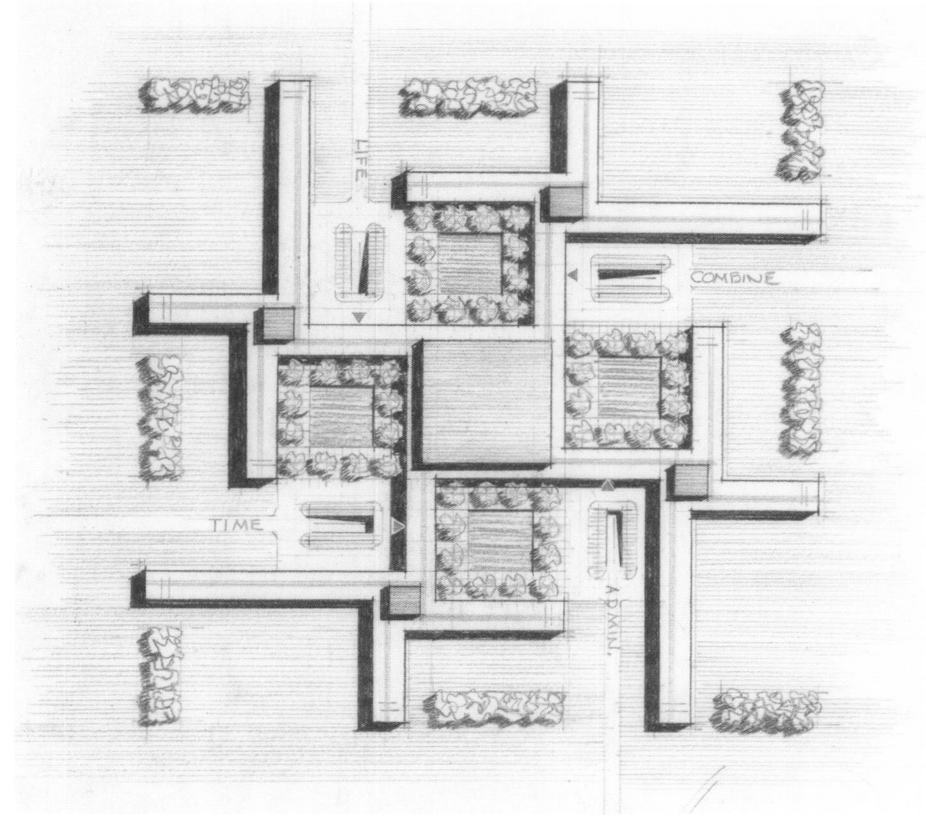

Fig. 2 Time Inc. Headquarters, programming diagram for *Fortune* magazine offices

Fig. 3 Time Inc. Headquarters, "pinwheel" plan

separate parking ramp) nestled inside one of the arms marked Time, Life, Admin., and Combine. One can imagine the slender arms lined with offices off a double-loaded corridor, while the central building seems ideally situated to hold Luce's desired amenities. No drawings of further development are extant, and it seems likely this plan, devised on a field of dots, ended with Saarinen's introduction to Luce's real site. Saarinen began here (and would again at Deere) with a tight geometric figure that was then broken down and settled into the site as planning progressed, taking the design from the general to the particular. What Saarinen kept from the pinwheel plan was the four-part harmony, and the idea, present at GM, of covering the entire site with an office-size grid. He was also bent, from the beginning, on giving every office a view.[6]

The bulk of the drawings concern a later and far more plausible scheme. The pinwheel has been spun out into its constituent parts and set out across a ridge overlooking a lake. A large rectangular pond, akin to the GM pond, is set perpendicular to the ridge, creating a second building axis. One would have encountered this complex not from the lakefront, as Saarinen planned at Bell, Deere, and IBM Yorktown, but from behind. A road through the sketched-in forest would have brought the visitor instead to a formal, even Italianate, piazza, with the pond on one's left and a view of the lake to the right, through the glazed base of the administration building, lofted on stilts. Only from the lake would this building stand out as the monumental centerpiece of the Time Inc. campus—at three stories. From the plaza, each division, housed in buildings of approximately the same size, would have been equally accessible (fig. 4). The only Saarinen project that also sets a building high on a ridge, rather than just below it, is the Milwaukee War Memorial (1952–57), a project originally designed as an urban arts campus, and initiated the same year.

Saarinen has broken up the long narrow arms of the pinwheel plan into sets of two-story office pavilions attached at the corners. This is a design idea that recurs at his next realized corporate installation, the IBM Manufacturing and Training Facility in Rochester, Minnesota (1956–58).

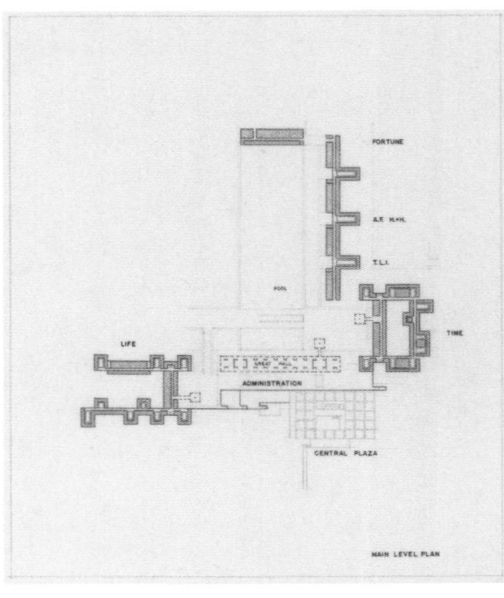

Fig. 4 Time Inc. Headquarters, plan of main level

There, larger office and manufacturing buildings touch at the corners (ideal for interior passage during the long northern winters), but also separate to leave spaces for interior landscaped courts. The plant was designed for outward expansion across the former farmland, and each new pavilion would have been paired with an equivalent open space. For Time, offices (on a five-foot module) are arranged along the outside edges of these pavilions, with views of either lake or pond. To keep the buildings low, the outer pavilions of the *Time* building are stepped down a story into the sloping ground toward the lake, a trick Saarinen would use at Yorktown. Even without labeled drawings, the organization of the corporation is instantly legible in plan.

Where it deviates from functionalism, and from reuse in subsequent work, is in its architectural language (fig. 5). John K. Jessup, the editor of Luce's essays, called it "a Moorish enclosure in upper Manhattan the size of Piazza San Marco in Venice."[7] Saarinen was an architect whose decorative streak typically exhibited itself in fields and planes of material—GM's glazed-brick end walls, or CBS's granite piers—or in commissions to friends like Harry Bertoia for large-scale sculpture. The modernist identified with Venice and with Islamic ornament is Edward Durell Stone, but his U.S. Embassy in New Delhi wasn't completed until 1958, and the Huntington Hartford Museum (also known as 2 Columbus Circle) until 1962. The concrete arches that hold up Time's administration building, along with the vaulted entrance canopies, could have been inspired by similar forms in domestic work by Philip Johnson (a close friend) from the early 1950s. The only similar shape in Saarinen's work is his Pedestal chair series, in development in the mid-1950s. Saarinen's architectural curves tended to occur in plan, as at IBM Yorktown, or as global structure, as at the Ingalls Hockey Rink or the TWA Terminal. The Time facades are flat, their flatness emphasized by the tic-tac-toe window pattern applied to all vertical surfaces. Saarinen would use jumpy up-down rhythms in his windows for the Oslo and London chancelleries, while his dormitory for the University of Pennsylvania also has windows sliced crisply out of the building fabric.[8] Perhaps Saarinen was trying to get as far from the facade language of GM as possible, to come up with one that was more urbane, more European, and more monumental. At the same time, those repetitive windows could be a nod to the information age—they resemble IBM's punched cards, to which Reinhold Martin has compared the modular office buildings of Saarinen, SOM, and others.[9] Eliot Noyes's IBM Aerospace Headquarters in Los Angeles (1964) features a similar pattern on its concrete, panelized facade.

Although Saarinen was excited about the client, he disliked the Time Inc. site. "I am absolutely queer about sites," Saarinen wrote in a letter in 1952; "clients have a way of thinking they are experts on this." He then described six projects in which he had lobbied for a site change, including "Time Inc.—I insisted on a new site (confidential) I think I will be successful." Among the drawings for Time are detailed examinations of the train schedules from New York to five alternate sites, including the former Untermeyer and Warburg estates in Westchester, and locations in Cos Cob, Connecticut, and Harrison and Dobbs Ferry, New York. A note at the bottom to reduce each drawing to eleven inches indicates that these were to be included in a presentation booklet.[10]

The plans show that Saarinen shared Luce's workplace ideal. Luce's employees, however, did not. They rebelled against the idea of moving out of town, because of the apparent impossibility of running a news organization from a country retreat. The company considered land just north of the United Nations, on the East River, and had Bunshaft develop an urban campus. In 1954, Saarinen was called back in to look at a 370-acre site in Media, Pennsylvania. But in the end, offered co-ownership by Rockefeller Center, Luce built an (air-conditioned) anthill on the

Fig. 5 Time Inc. Headquarters, rendering of plaza with administration building at right

Avenue of the Americas, designed by Harrison and Abramovitz and completed in 1959.[11]

IBM's director of design Noyes always identified IBM Rochester as the company's first important work of architecture. "Eero Saarinen appeared on the cover of *Time*," Noyes said in 1975. "To acquaint him with IBM, we asked him to lunch, and he was our man for the job."[12] IBM Rochester was just the beginning of fifteen years of international expansion for the company—150 plants, laboratories, and office buildings constructed between 1956 and 1971—in which Saarinen was one of the few architects asked back. After the completion of the Minnesota plant, Saarinen was immediately hired to design a set of laboratories for IBM's research department on 240 acres in Westchester. "We went down from Detroit and looked at it," remembers Saarinen's chief designer, Kevin Roche. "Eero as usual walked all over the place. The site as I recall had a slight curve in the landscape so that it sloped down." This curve would eventually become the generating factor for the building's design, a 1,090-foot arc that appears to cut an elegant, sharp-edged swath out of the grassy hillside. But before Saarinen settled on this still-unique form, he worked through a series of alternatives for IBM and two other exurban projects—Deere and Company, completed in 1963, and Bell Laboratories (1957–62). The site planning of Deere and IBM Yorktown, connected by the organization of building and parking into an existing sloped landscape, indicates a relationship to the Time project.[13]

An *Architectural Forum* article from February 1957 on "IBM's new corporate face" included Saarinen's early plan for the Yorktown site. The facilities are shown as a series of two- and three-story pavilions spreading out from a formal court, and set on a hill overlooking a man-made lake (fig. 6). The parallels to the Time project are fairly obvious, though the plan is looser and the footprint smaller. The offset pavilions are lightly attached, pairing solid with courtyard void, maximizing outside views, and creating both an overall grid and departmental foci. Study models of variations make the networked nature of this plan more apparent. One shows a web of Corbusian cross-shaped buildings stretching out from a central structure with a cutout courtyard (fig. 7). The other transforms the whole complex into a built hillside, layering labs like glacial deposits (and reminding one of Moshe Safdie's Habitat complex of 1967 in Montreal).[14]

Saarinen's next scheme was a single building, a symmetrical box with two cutout courtyards. Had this plan been accepted, IBM and Bell would have been twin research palaces with labs at the climate-controlled interior of the block. The structure flattens and dominates the topography, as the Time administration building might have done. At Time and IBM Rochester, Saarinen moved from a closed rectangular plan out into the landscape. In the Yorktown chronology, his first scheme is gridded and geometric in plan, but organic in architectural language, apparently growing out of ideas developed in Westchester and Minnesota. This second scheme seems closer to his rather generic starting points for other corporations.[15]

This design was also rejected, replaced in November 1957 by a curving plan close to the final product. Bell Labs "was a very logical, rectangular building," Roche says, and on a nearly flat site. "And how do you apply that to this curved site?" Saarinen did not fight the hill but molded his building along its ridge, gaining an extra floor in front, and thereby complying with local zoning. "We decided to do a series of rectangles like that," Roche explains, outlining on a tabletop a sequence of spokes radiating out across the slope. These spokes were sandwiches of labs flanking a utility spine, or offices flanking a storage wall, all on a four-by-six-foot grid. "Then you would have this curved walkway which would have a spectacular view of the descending landscape." In this description, one can see the link between the first and last schemes: the building rearranges the pavilions into a curved line, linked by a curtain-walled catwalk rather than courts. The

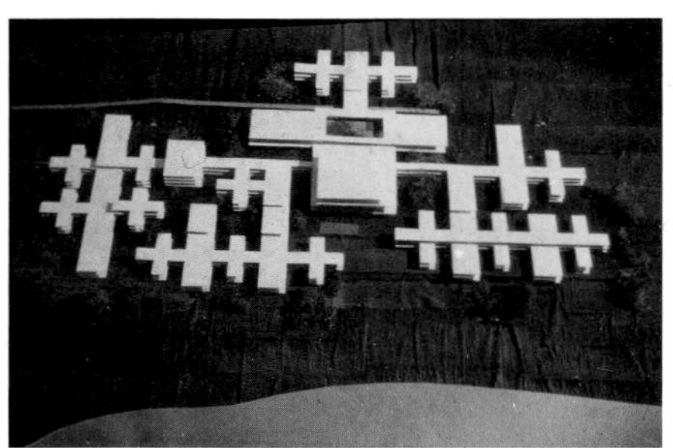

Fig. 6 Eero Saarinen, International Business Machines Thomas J. Watson Research Center, Yorktown Heights, New York, 1957–61, early sketch

Fig. 7 International Business Machines Thomas J. Watson Research Center, study model

landscape has become a view rather than an interactive environment, but the architects still thought of the scientists strolling thoughtfully between office, lab, cafeteria, and library. Saarinen wrote, "It has always seemed to me that many scientists in the research field are like university professors—tweedy, pipe-smoking men. In contrast to the efficient laboratories, we wanted to provide them with a more relaxed, 'tweedy,' out-doors sort of environment."[16]

John Deere arrived in Illinois in the late 1830s, and began making and repairing tools for the local farming community. The farmers' chief complaint was the difficulty of getting a cast-iron plow through the heavy, sticky prairie soil. In 1837, Deere happened upon a piece of steel, and he forged a plow from that smoother metal. Deere was soon producing a thousand plows a year. In 1847, he moved operations to Moline, where the Mississippi River provided inexpensive shipping. In 1948, William A. Hewitt married Patricia Deere Wiman, a great-great-granddaughter of John Deere. Hewitt was to be the company's last family chairman, but he was also the most urbane and best-connected chief executive in the company's history. In 1955, Hewitt decided to move the company's headquarters out of its nineteenth-century office building in downtown Moline. He wanted a new building, utilizing the latest technology, in order to symbolize Deere's powerful new products and expanding market share. Despite Moline's small size, he wanted a suburban corporate campus like those of his Harvard Business School peers.[17]

While an undergraduate at Berkeley, Hewitt had been friends with Robert S. McNamara. By the mid-1950s, McNamara was a director of Ford and had just built a new headquarters for the Automobile Division designed by Welton Becket. When Hewitt began looking for an architect, McNamara sent him a box of two dozen architects' prospectuses. Hewitt also sought advice from the industrial designer Henry Dreyfuss, a consultant since 1937. Dreyfuss recommended Saarinen and sent along five recent issues of *Architectural Forum*. "Now I am going to stick my neck way out and ask you to look particularly at the July 1955 issue showing the MIT Auditorium. This is by far the most extreme building he has done. Yet I think something like it would be a wonderful way in which to show farm implements. The very openness (with fine greenery outside) suggests the purpose of your product." Although Saarinen's showcase for Deere's farm implements does not look like MIT's Kresge Auditorium in Cambridge, Massachusetts (1950–55), Dreyfuss's stress on openness and greenery corresponds to Saarinen's ultimate design.[18]

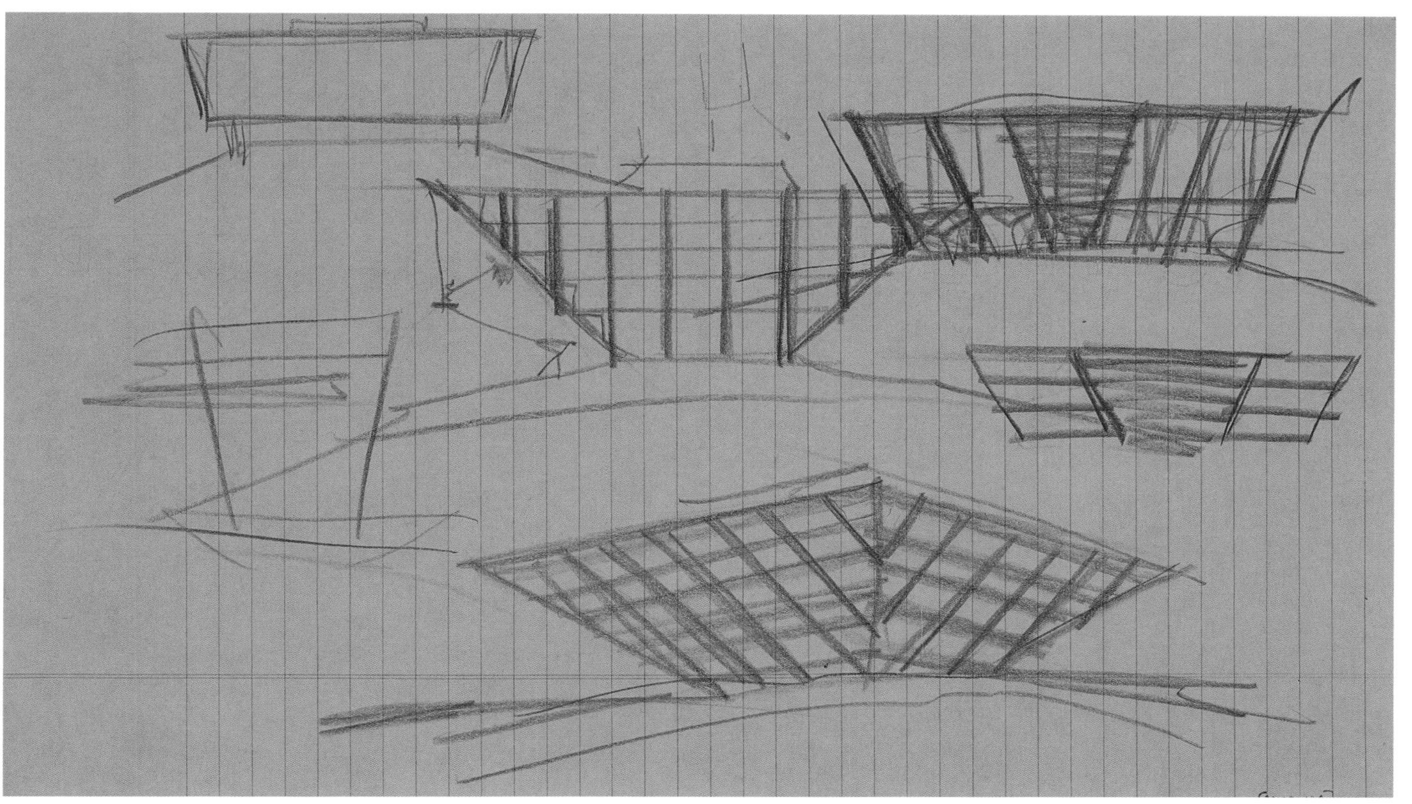

Fig. 8 Eero Saarinen, Deere and Company Administrative Center, Moline, Illinois, 1957–63, early sketches

After Dreyfuss's letter, Hewitt invited Saarinen to Moline. Hewitt took the architect to four potential sites, all hilly and wooded. They borrowed a utility truck with a telescoping tower so they could look over the tops of the smaller trees. Saarinen made his first presentation to Deere in January 1958. He showed a single building on the company's site, a concrete ziggurat with a 360-degree view over the valley (fig. 8).[19] The building was an inverted pyramid stepping out to a height of four or five stories around an open, skylit center. Offices wrapped in tiers around the outside of the ziggurat. The tractor display space was to be the entire first floor, which was glazed between the concrete supports. This scheme strongly resembles Saarinen's Breueresque design for Milwaukee. It also has the rigidity of the early schemes for both Time and IBM: boxy single-building plans divorced from geography. Hewitt asked for something rugged and exurban, and Saarinen's thoughts turned to concrete and visible structure.

Hewitt didn't like this scheme, and he pointed out various impracticalities to Saarinen. Hewitt said Saarinen had no response, merely puffed his pipe. Then, according to the architect's associate Warren Platner, Hewitt invited Saarinen down into the ravine. "He said, 'There's this little stream going through so there . . . could be a pond. . . . Why couldn't we have a headquarters building that's in the forest?'"[20] Six weeks later, Hewitt was shown a scheme close to the final product: at right, the single-story display pavilion and auditorium; at center, the seven-story administrative offices and cafeteria; and at left, a never-built research and development center, all strung together with an enclosed walkway, framed in Cor-Ten steel, and spanning the site's depths. Its height was now reserved for parking: a lot was sketched in where the ziggurat once stood. As at IBM Yorktown, the curve of the landscape broke down the box and became the dominant organizing principle. Saarinen planned both sites in descending order, rejecting the idea of a hilltop villa and ceding that land to parking, but at Deere, perhaps uniquely, he sunk the top-heavy structure into the land.

Although the Deere buildings nestle into the contour, they also convey a sense of movement. This effect derives from the strong horizontals of the steel louvers, and the additional horizontal of the "flying bridges." These walkways thrust visitors across the display pavilion, over the ravine, and into the core of the administrative center. Seen head on, as a string, the buildings do seem to be fording the lake and managing the hills with the ease of a Deere-engineered product. The symbolism latent in Saarinen's other corporate work—the metal-and-glass skin for GM's automobiles, the fieldstone for IBM's professors—becomes explicit here, where the building holds tractors and is as rugged as a tractor, and the Cor-Ten steel blends with the very trees the steel plow uprooted. Circulation emphasizes the integration of the building with the terrain. The building flows downhill from the parking lot, inverting the typical higher-is-better pattern of the urban office tower. The executive floor is below the flying bridge that is the major communication axis, and the lowest floor—the executive dining room—is the most spectacular. When one exits the elevator, walls of figured marble funnel the eye toward the water lapping at the ribbon window, framing the work of landscape architects Sasaki, Walker, and Associates.

Saarinen's ziggurat scheme included the suggestion of a formal garden, and initially the Cor-Ten building also had a rectilinear pool. But the architect returned from Japan and wiped that scheme away, ordered drawings placing all the existing trees, and developed a landscape plan in sympathy with the natural contour. The pool became two irregular ponds. Hideo Sasaki and Saarinen lofted balloons to simulate the entry sequence sight lines. One first sees the building across the lake, but then the road curves right, hiding its bulk and forcing one to enter the building perpendicular to the facade. At IBM Yorktown, one also gets this frontal view, and is then swept around to the hidden parking lots in back. At Time, cars were funneled underground.[21]

Only the thirty acres immediately adjacent to the buildings were intended to look finished; the rest was to be left "as is." Once Deere introduced lawn tractors for consumers, however, the hills became an irresistible demonstration zone. Though the urbanized architects privileged a natural look (however engineered), the company reasserted its products' power over the landscape. Today, the lawns are the lushly fertilized green of the Deere logo. Landscape architecture historian Louise A. Mozingo read the Deere grounds as having a dual role: naturalizing the building and providing a new community center. To merge interior and exterior, Saarinen needed the Cor-Ten to blend with the trees, and to finish the building's stark interiors with framed foliage. It was to be not an alien, urban presence, but a masterfully sited tree house. Meanwhile, public access to the grounds and display pavilion naturalize the building as a local amenity.[22]

Looking at Time, IBM, and Deere in chronological order, one sees Saarinen perfecting the idea of the natural corporate campus, a complex unique to both its client and its setting. All of these projects began with research, and Saarinen's first schemes tend to reflect the results of those studies. But from these boxy beginnings, he began to incorporate the landscape. He was right to be "absolutely queer about sites" because those sites ultimately make the buildings. The modular offices travel up, down, or across the hills so that each employee has a view, and one can perambulate on high-flying walkways. The plans represent the corporations' functions both to the outside world and to their employees, while the cladding develops as part of a larger revision of identity. If Saarinen and SOM created the typology, Saarinen clad those types with increasing appositeness. It was not enough to be imposing (in the style of Harrison and Abramovitz), nor was it enough to be up to date (like Skidmore, Owings, and Merrill). Saarinen's headquarters added narrative, both to the everyday approach, passing from highway to pastorale, and to the national profile, changing companies from generic names to symbolic places.

Notes

1. "General Motors Technical Center," *Architectural Forum*, Nov. 1951, 111–23; Eero Saarinen to Astrid Sampe, letter 2 (undated, probably 1952), box 1, folder 5, Astrid Sampe Correspondence, 1995-87, Cranbrook Archives, Bloomfield Hills, Mich., translated from the Swedish by Ann Gheorghiade, a volunteer at the archives.

2. Robert T. Elson, *The World of Time Inc.: The Intimate History of a Publishing Enterprise*, vol. 2, *1941–1960* (New York: Atheneum, 1973), 331; Eero Saarinen Papers, Manuscripts and Archives, Yale University. Several of the drawings are dated June 2, 1952, and an extensive space survey is dated Aug. 4, 1952. One schematic plan, dated Aug. 4, 1954, may correspond to a later Time project for a rural site in Pennsylvania, discussed later in this essay.

3. Elson, *The World of Time*, 331; William H. Whyte, *City: Rediscovering the Center* (New York: Doubleday, 1988), 284, 285. Whyte is best known for his studies of urban plazas, so it is appropriate, if ironic, that his research followed the corporations into the suburbs. The center of these relocations was Greenwich, Conn., where twelve chief executive officers lived in a circle four miles in diameter between the Burning Tree Country Club and the Fairfield Country Club. Luce had a weekend estate in Greenwich.

4. Louise A. Mozingo, "The Corporate Estate in the USA, 1954–1964: 'Thoroughly Modern in Concept, but . . . Down to Earth and Rugged,'" *Studies in the History of Gardens and Designed Landscapes* 20 (Jan.–Mar. 2000), 25.

5. Henry R. Luce, *The Ideas of Henry Luce*, ed. and with an introduction by John K. Jessup (New York: Atheneum, 1969), 272–73; Luce, quoted in Elson, *The World of Time*, 332.

6. Saarinen's plan for the J. Irwin Miller House, initiated in 1953, also began with a grid, translated into columns, and developed into a set of rooms that pinwheel around the central conversation pit.

7. Luce, *The Ideas of Henry Luce*, 262.

8. One of the facade studies for the London chancellery has a flattened pattern close to that of the Time Inc. buildings, but with all of the windows drawn the same size.

9. Reinhold Martin, *The Organizational Complex: Architecture, Media, and Corporate Space* (Cambridge: MIT Press, 2003), 159–60.

10. Eero Saarinen, letter to Astrid Sampe, June 28–29, 1952, box 1, folder 5, Astrid Sampe Correspondence, 1995-87, Cranbrook Archives. Commute times were around fifty minutes from the Rye site to Grand Central Station; the estates, in Greystone and White Plains, would have been slightly closer.

11. Elson, *The World of Time*, 332–33; Luce, *The Ideas of Henry Luce*, 262.

12. Edward F. Pierce, "The Brick and Mortar of IBM," *THINK*, Nov.–Dec. 1975, 31. Noyes and Saarinen had been acquainted since 1940, when Saarinen and Charles Eames won the Organic Design in Home Furnishings competition that Noyes had initiated as curator of industrial design at the Museum of Modern Art.

13. Thomas J. Watson, Jr., "Good Design Is Good Business," in *The Art of Design Management* (New York: Tiffany, 1975), 59; Kevin Roche, interview with the author, Hamden, Conn., Nov. 16, 2004. Martin analyzes the relationship between the interior planning of the laboratories at Bell and IBM Yorktown in *The Organizational Complex*, chapter 6.

14. "IBM's New Corporate Face," *Architectural Forum*, Feb. 1957, 110; slide collection, Eero Saarinen Papers, Yale University.

15. Copies of the presentation booklet are in the Eero Saarinen Papers, Yale University, and the Maurice Allen Papers, 1996-34, Cranbrook Archives. Maurice Allen worked for Saarinen from 1952 to 1962. Model photographs are also in the Eero Saarinen Papers, Yale University.

16. Roche interview; Eero Saarinen, "Statement on IBM (Thomas J. Watson Research Center) Yorktown, New York," Eero Saarinen Papers, Yale University.

17. "Deere and Co.," *Forbes*, June 15, 1966, off-print, Deere and Company Archives, Moline, Ill.

18. William A. Hewitt, "The Genesis of a Great Building—and of an Unusual Friendship," *AIA Journal*, Aug. 1977, 36; Henry Dreyfuss, letter to William A. Hewitt, Jan. 27, 1956, box 83424, folder D89008, Deere Archives.

19. Hewitt, "Genesis of a Great Building," 36. No plans or models of this scheme remain; this description is based on observers' accounts and a series of sketches by Saarinen in box 2, Jack Goldman Collection, 1995-46, Cranbrook Archives. Jack Goldman was employed by the Saarinen firm from 1955 to 1958.

20. Hewitt, "Genesis of a Great Building," 36; Warren Platner, interview with the author, New Haven, Conn., Nov. 6, 2003.

21. Paul Kennon, quoted in Toshio Nakamura, ed., "Eero Saarinen: An Appreciation," *A+U* Extra Edition, Apr. 1984, 235; Jory Johnson, *Modern Landscape Architecture: Redefining the Garden*, photography by Felice Frankel (New York: Abbeville, 1991), 32.

22. Mozingo, "The Corporate Estate," 39, 43–44; Johnson, *Modern Landscape Architecture*, 39.

Timo Tuomi

embassies and chancelleries
the necessity of unity

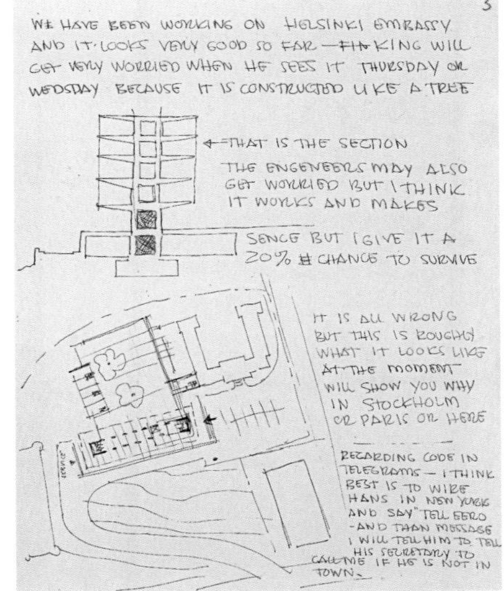

Fig. 1 Eero Saarinen, sketches of American Embassy Addition project, Helsinki, Finland, 1952–53, from letter to Astrid Sampe

American Embassy addition project, Helsinki, Finland, 1952–53
United States Chancellery Building, Oslo, Norway, 1955–59
United States Chancellery Building, London, England, 1955–60

"He will do so [design] with a free mind without being dictated by obsolete or sterile formulae or clichés, be they old or new; he will avoid being either bizarre or fashionable, yet he will not fear using new techniques or new materials should these constitute real advance in architectural thinking." This is how Pietro Belluschi, one of the first members of the Architectural Advisory Committee founded by the U.S. State Department's Office of Foreign Buildings Operations in 1954, described the kind of architect the committee was looking for to design embassy and chancellery buildings abroad that would support America's rapidly expanding presence on the global stage. In many ways Eero Saarinen fit the description perfectly, as is shown in the work he did for the Office of Foreign Buildings Operations.[1]

Saarinen designed three embassy and chancellery buildings in the 1950s. The first one was an unrealized addition to the American Embassy in Helsinki in 1952–53; the other two are chancelleries in Oslo (1955–59) and London (1955–60). All three reflect Saarinen's thoughts on the role of modern architecture in the postwar urban context—that is, the relation of the architecture of a single building to a larger urban entity. During the Helsinki project he began to express doubts about the suitability of using the sharp, rectangular Miesian vocabulary in an existing built environment. His United States Chancellery Building in Oslo shows how Saarinen abandoned the modernist ideal of a single, independent piece of architecture in favor of fitting the volume of his building into the surrounding urban structure, filling the triangular site with a triangular building. And in his London chancellery, against all expectations of the critics of the time, he designed a building that was totally contextual:

its size, massing, and materials all represent careful responses to the urban fabric. At the same time the three projects demonstrate how Saarinen developed his ideas about unity in architecture and how this basic ideal influenced his work in a way that was difficult for many contemporary critics to comprehend.

A fundamental change in the architectural policy of the U.S. embassy-building program after World War II brought about a construction boom in the 1950s. Before the war it had been customary for the United States either to buy suitable existing buildings for use as embassies and chancelleries or to erect new ones whose message of American democracy was expressed via interpretations of classical Greek temples or copies of American mansions. In Helsinki, for example, the embassy designed by Harrie T. Lindeberg in 1938 was modeled after Westover, a symmetrically proportioned red-brick plantation house in Virginia. But after the war, as Jane Loeffler describes in her book *The Architecture of Diplomacy: Building America's Embassies*, the State Department changed its building policy abroad as part of its cold war strategy. Classical models were now seen as outdated; they were also too evocative of the architecture of Germany and other totalitarian states of the recent past. Modern architecture was found to be the perfect new means to convey the values of democracy, openness, technical innovation, and progress. The new embassies the United States built in the 1950s contrasted strongly with the heavy neoclassical palaces that the Soviet Union continued to construct. In 1953 *Architectural Forum* ran a piece comparing the Soviet Union's new embassy in Helsinki and Saarinen's preliminary design for America's new embassy building there. After presenting more than ten new structures built abroad by the Office of Foreign Buildings Operations (FBO), the writer of the article concluded that the U.S. government had made American architecture a vehicle of cultural leadership.[2]

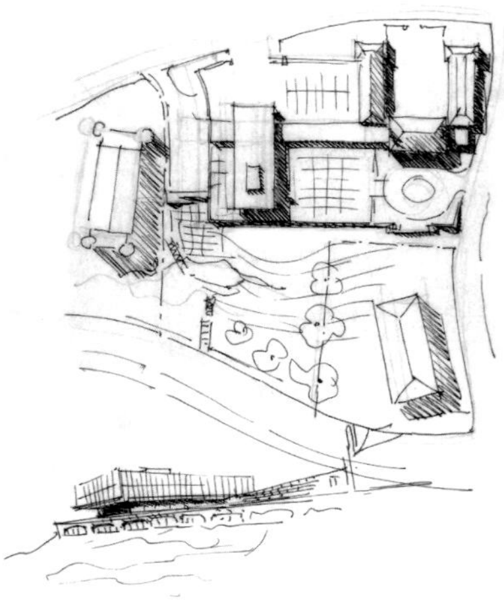

Fig. 2 Eero Saarinen, sketches of American Embassy Addition project, Helsinki, showing plan and perspective, from letter to Aline Louchheim, 1953

Another goal of the new policy was that buildings should not be pompous or ignorant of their surroundings. They were to take into account the cultural context, climate, and local architectural traditions and materials, in this way projecting sympathy with the host country while using modern architectural forms. This approach was also a critique of such American embassies as those designed by Harrison and Abramovitz in Rio de Janeiro and Havana (both in 1952), which were isolated modern creations that could have been placed anywhere, with no relation to the urban fabric.[3]

The FBO's Architectural Advisory Committee reviewed all of the U.S. government's architectural projects that were to be built abroad. The committee had a clear preference for younger, upcoming talent in choosing designers of the embassies. Paul Rudolph, for example, received his first embassy assignment, for Amman, Jordan, even though previously he had designed only a few private houses.[4]

Leland King, director of the FBO at the State Department, contacted Saarinen in 1952 about designing a new building as an addition to the American Embassy in Helsinki. In 1952–53 Saarinen made several studies for the project and was apparently excited by the possibility of building in his native country. The site, which sloped dramatically toward the sea, was occupied by the existing American planatation-style embassy building of 1938. A series of sketches in Saarinen's correspondence of the time illustrates the transformation of his views during the design process. A site plan published in *Architectural Forum* and a sketch in a letter to his friend the Swedish textile designer Astrid Sampe (fig. 1) demonstrate Saarinen's approach to the project according to a pure international modern ideal: the new building is situated at a slightly oblique angle to the old one, and there is no formal relationship between the two. All concentration has been directed to the creation of an individual architectural volume. The area in front of the old building is replaced by a parking lot, and a new front yard is positioned so

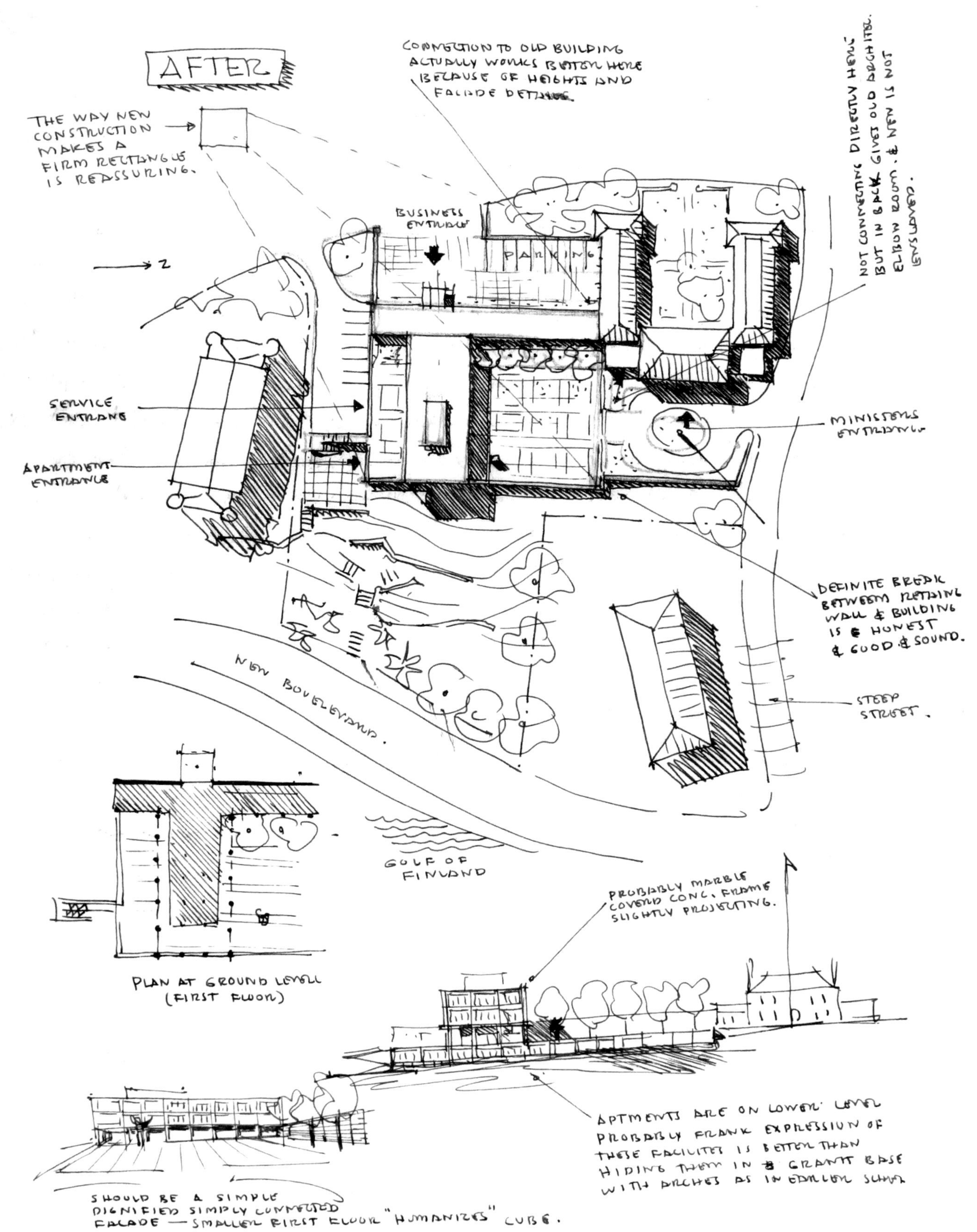
AFTER
THE WAY NEW CONSTRUCTION MAKES A FIRM RECTANGLE IS REASSURING.
CONNECTION TO OLD BUILDING ACTUALLY WORKS BETTER HERE BECAUSE OF HEIGHTS AND FACADE DETAILS
NOT CONNECTING DIRECTLY HERE BUT IN BACK GIVES OLD ARCHITEC. ELBOW ROOM. & NEW IS NOT ENSLAVED.
BUSINESS ENTRANCE
PARKING
SERVICE ENTRANCE
APARTMENT ENTRANCE
MINISTERS ENTRANCE
DEFINITE BREAK BETWEEN RETAINING WALL & BUILDING IS HONEST & GOOD & SOUND.
NEW BOULEVARD.
STEEP STREET.
GULF OF FINLAND
PLAN AT GROUND LEVEL (FIRST FLOOR)
PROBABLY MARBLE COVERED CONC. FRAME SLIGHTLY PROJECTING.
APTMENTS ARE ON LOWER LEVEL PROBABLY FRANK EXPRESSION OF THESE FACILITIES IS BETTER THAN HIDING THEM IN GRANIT BASE WITH ARCHES AS IN EARLIER SCHEME
SHOULD BE A SIMPLE DIGNIFIED SIMPLY CONNECTED FACADE — SMALLER FIRST FLOOR "HUMANIZES" CUBE.

Fig. 3 Eero Saarinen, sketches of American Embassy Addition project, Helsinki, showing plan and cross-section of site, from letter to Aline Louchheim, 1953

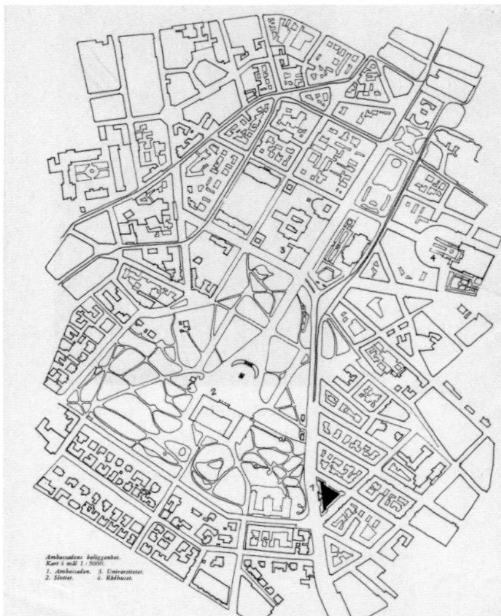

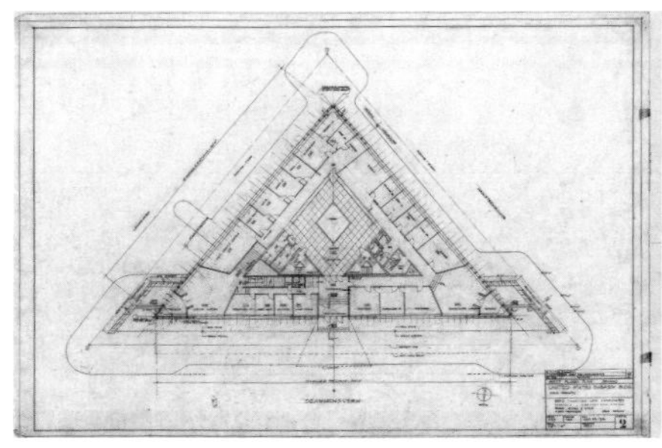

Fig. 4 Eero Saarinen and Associates, United States Chancellery Building, Oslo, Norway, 1955–59, site plan

Fig. 5 United States Chancellery Building, Oslo, main facade

Fig. 6 United States Chancellery Building, Oslo, plan

Fig. 7 (opposite) United States Chancellery Building, Oslo, central covered courtyard

that it mostly serves the new building, further diminishing the importance of the old embassy. Saarinen suggested a treelike structure for the new building, which he knew was daring and unlikely to be realized. He wrote: "[Leland] King will get very worried when he sees it Thursday or Wednesady [*sic*] because it is constructed like a tree. . . . The engineers may also get worried but I think it works and makes sense but I give it a 20% chance to survive." Saarinen even made playful references to the vast spruce forests of Finland in explaining his "Helsinki tree."[5]

Saarinen's first scheme for the Helsinki embassy was similar in character to Harrison and Abramovitz's new embassies for Rio de Janeiro and Havana, although Saarinen surely was aware of the criticism these buildings received for their complete ignorance of their physical and cultural contexts.[6] This response may or may not have influenced Saarinen to look elsewhere for a solution to his design problem. His sketches reveal that he was unsure how to proceed, but they also show him gradually starting to take the existing building into consideration and make the new structure part of an ensemble.[7] He turned his building around so that its short end faced the sea and positioned it at the same angle as the old embassy. The result, when seen from the main vantage point on the waterfront, was a balanced pair of volumes. He also equalized the hierarchy between the two buildings by connecting them with a low wing and giving both of them a front garden, by moving the parking area to the back of the wing. Thus the two structures stood side by side harmoniously, each with its own architectural identity.

With the placement of the new structure resolved, Saarinen could concentrate on the architecture of the addition. As he put it in a letter, "The thing to do now is to forget all this & focus on [the] exact architecture of the box." Saarinen was working at the time on the General Motors Technical Center in Warren, Michigan (1948–56), which was commonly acknowledged as a skillful interpretation of Miesian forms and ideals, but he employed other formal approaches in concurrent projects. In Helsinki he considered several strategies. His illustrated letters show a "before" view, where the new structure hovers above the waterfront, dominating the scene, and an "after" view, in which the building is given a role more equal to that of its surroundings (figs. 2, 3). Saarinen saw that the forms that were appropriate for a huge new industrial center on its own large plot of land were not universally applicable. As he wrote: "The hardest nut to crack right now for me in the office is the Finnish embassy facade treatment, the plan works basically, the elevations work but the facade system is difficult—so far it is just a Mies-like frame covered with marble. But I am not sure that is right next to the old—perhaps." Even if, in his sketches, the building still remained a box, as he called it, Saarinen started to move toward a more contextual design, suggesting that the new structure be covered with white marble since the entrance of the old building was also marble and the trim was white.[8]

Because of changes in the State Department that resulted in King's dismissal, Saarinen did not win the commission for the Helsinki embassy. In 1955, however, he was given the task of designing a building for another Nordic country, Norway. In Helsinki, the embassy was situated in a parklike area dotted with large villas, and Saarinen, therefore, did not have to address the problems of designing new architecture in a traditional urban context. In Oslo, by contrast, the site for the new United States Chancellery Building was a triangular lot in the city center along Drammensveien, a principal avenue, and opposite Slottsparken, the park where the royal palace is located. Before Saarinen was given the assignment, Ralph Rapson had made proposals for the same site in 1951, treating the building as a discrete mass that disregarded its surroundings. Saarinen's proposal aimed at something very different. In what he himself described as inevitable, he filled the triangular site with a triangular volume, adding the missing piece in the townscape (figs. 4, 5).

Fig. 8 Eero Saarinen (at left) with prefabricated facade units for United States Chancellery Building, Oslo

The chancellery was the same height as the buildings in the nearby blocks, and its front followed the streetline of its neighbors. It was only with the architecture of the building that Saarinen differentiated the chancellery from its surroundings.

Just as the chancellery's plan was triangular, many of the interior spaces were not right-angled, most notably the central covered courtyard, with its fountain and Roman travertine floor (figs. 6, 7). Even the elevators were diamond-shaped. Saarinen explained that the use of beige travertine, teak for the wall panels, and white-painted brick for the grills in the diamond-shaped courtyard was intended to give the space a feeling of warmth and enclosure, since Oslo was dark and cold for much of the year. The building shows how Saarinen tried in many ways to achieve a design where, in his own words, "inside or outside, the building sings with the same message."[9]

Saarinen's ideal also extended to the unity of structure and materials. He explained: "The precast façade is the most interesting and successful part of this building. Our attempt was to integrate the module, on which the offices are all based, with the structural system, so that one could conceive, all in one, a precast modular structural system with an integrated façade material." For the facade, Saarinen's office created a new material, precast concrete mixed with Norwegian pearl granite (fig. 8). The units were assembled in a way that gave the facade a three-dimensional checkered effect, which changed in degree as one walked around the building. Saarinen wrote that the building was in a sense a triangular Renaissance palace with rooms surrounding a court. This classical model was realized with progressive construction technologies, and the building itself was situated in the urban context in a classical manner, adding to the continuous street-wall composed of solid enclosed building masses.[10]

Saarinen repeatedly underlined his aim of creating a form based on one central idea, so that a building or environment would be a unified entity. He was able to move up and down the scale of forms, from an urban environment to an ashtray, and to see forms in relation to one another, to "always look at the next larger thing," according to his father's principles. Saarinen was familiar with analogies between different scales of architecture, between house and city. In the fifteenth century Leon Battista Alberti had noted that "the city is like some large house, and the house is in turn like some small city." Not only were the individual house and the city seen by planners and architects through the centuries as similar, but the analogy was extended to different parts of the house and different parts of the city. Camillo Sitte formulated his own version, with which both Eero and Eliel were surely familiar: "The forum is for the whole city what the atrium represents in a single-family dwelling: it is the well-appointed and richly furnished main hall." Eliel had underlined Sitte's continuing relevance to contemporary town planning in his book *The City, Its Growth, Its Decay, Its Future* of 1943. And in combining modernist planning of the 1930s, examples from antiquity and the Middle Ages, and Sitte's ideals in his own architecture and planning, he strove to achieve a totality of design, which came naturally to the younger Saarinen as well. Eero returned to these analogies between the scale and space of an entire city and of a single building a few years later, when he criticized both the open planning ideals of modern town planning and interior design that favored limitless, flowing space. In a lecture in 1960 he said: "Today many of us have come back to much more 'closed' plans, where rooms are really rooms with four walls. I suspect that in the rethinking of the urban picture we might be coming to a similar conclusion—that we may want to place our buildings in such a manner that the result will be more orderly and legible space."[11]

Saarinen's third and last building for the FBO was the United States Chancellery Building in London. It was one of the most criticized of his designs, not least because of the great expectations placed on it by British architects and the public. The site was the entire west side of Grosvenor Square, one of the city's most famous garden squares. The London chancellery was considered of such importance by the FBO that for the first time it held a competition. Kevin Roche later remarked that the circumstances in London were such that whoever designed the new embassy would have run into problems. Since the FBO had no precedents for a competition, it considered many alternative approaches, such as choosing four outstanding senior and four junior architects, or eight architects from various "schools" of architecture, for a limited competition. Finally, in 1955, eight architects were invited to take part in the competition. The architectural outcome was predetermined by the choice of the competitors, since all were known for their modernist designs.[12]

All the invited architects visited the site at Grosvenor Square in the same year. Saarinen spent more time in London than the others, even taking his three-week honeymoon with Aline Louchheim there. As Spero Daltas, an architect who worked in Saarinen's office at the time, later recalled, Saarinen would cover the walls of his hotel suite and even mirrors with sketches for the competition (fig. 9). Saarinen recognized that the London chancellery was a significant project, and he invested considerable time and effort in winning it. As he did for all competitions, he carefully reviewed what had been done with similar building types before, what could be done, and what the other competitors might do. Many different basic concepts for the building were considered, and studies were made using a curved facade, a central motif with side pavilions, a front court facing the square, a building with a Colossal order, and brick as well as other exterior materials (figs. 10–13). The final solution was a unified, symmetrical volume with a tripartite elevation with a base, a central band of four floors, and a top. In the middle of the front facade was a large main entrance with a great seal over it, emphasizing the building's compositional symmetry and its alignment with the central axis of Grosvenor Square. The required competition perspective from Grosvenor Square was made to resemble, as Saarinen's office described it, an English watercolor.[13]

The FBO's Architectural Advisory Committee, which acted as the jury for the competition, had difficulties choosing the winner, but it finally agreed on Saarinen.[14] After the competition was over, the building program was changed to accommodate additional public spaces, which necessitated the addition of another floor below the main level. Saarinen was pleased by this change, since, he wrote, "with time the competition design started to look like Toulouse-Lautrec—with too short legs." For the exterior, Saarinen devised a solution in which precast frames on the facade were load bearing, and a horizontal, zigzagging "diagrid" transferred the load from the facade to the cruciform recessed columns below. As he described it: "The facade one sees is the bones of the building. The coupled columns (precast frames) on the upper floors carry all the weight (floors, etc.) down to the outer edge of the diagrid; this diagrid transfers the load horizontally to the first floor columns."[15]

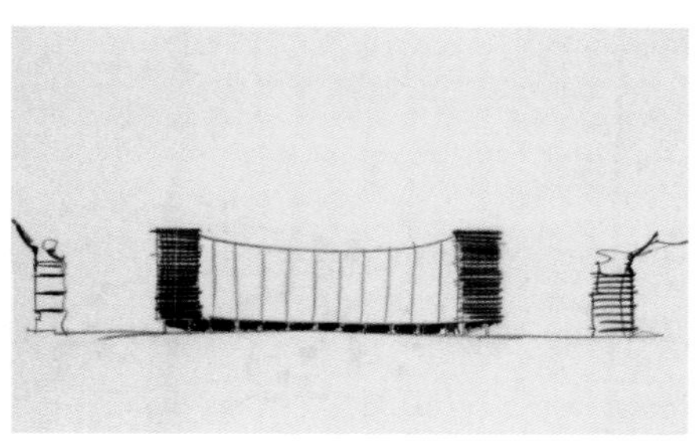

Fig. 9. Eero Saarinen, United States Chancellery Building, London, England, 1955–60, early sketches on restaurant placemat, 1955

Fig. 10 Eero Saarinen, United States Chancellery Building, London, facade study, 1956–57

In May 1956 Saarinen presented his new design (fig. 14). The final model for the State Department shows the sloping base of the building, which was thought to emphasize better the steps of the main entrance at the center of the facade. The load-bearing window frames were made more prominent than the non-load-bearing segments in between, so that the structural system would be both comprehensible and a part of the overall rhythm of the facade.

The Saarinen office had worked with a model of Grosvenor Square from the beginning of the competition. It showed not the existing buildings but rather the larger pseudo-Georgian blocks of flats that were going to be built there according to the new master plan commissioned by the Grosvenor Estate. This gave Saarinen the chance to emphasize the fact that his building was meant to fit into an environment of the future. He believed in what he called a good-neighbor policy in an urban environment, but only when the other buildings were permanent in nature. Saarinen noted that in the United States most of the permanent built environments were college campuses, and most of the country's big cities were going to be rebuilt in the near future.[16]

In 1957 the chancellery was already under construction when Saarinen suggested that the great seal intended for the main facade be replaced by a large

Fig. 11 (opposite) Eero Saarinen, United States Chancellery Building, London, facade studies, 1956–57

Fig. 12 Eero Saarinen, United States Chancellery Building, London, plan and perspective of an early scheme, 1956–57

Fig. 13 Eero Saarinen, United States Chancellery Building, London, facade study, 1956–57

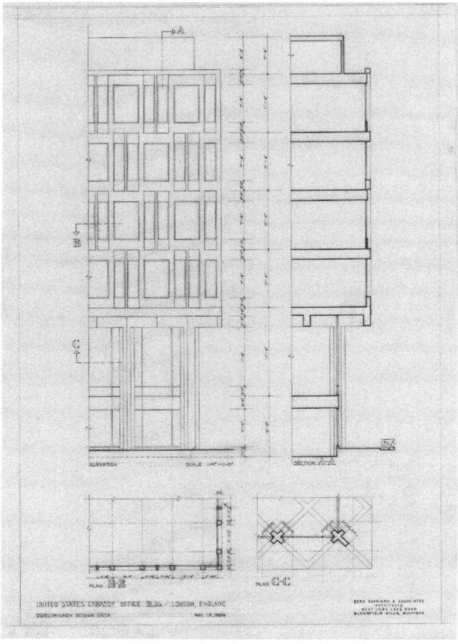

Fig. 14 Eero Saarinen and Associates, United States Chancellery Building, London, elevation, section, and plan of corner

sculpture of an eagle positioned on top of the cornice. That year Saarinen had become a member of the FBO's Architectural Advisory Committee, and in a unique committee meeting on February 24, 1958, he demonstrated his ability to convince others of his ideas while playing two conflicting roles at the same time. The minutes of the meeting state: "The meeting retired to the FBO conference room on the fourth floor where Architect Saarinen had erected a facade of the London office building. Mr. Saarinen gave an interesting talk, using colored slides to illustrate the use of the eagle throughout American history, and leading to his proposal to incorporate a heroic-sized eagle as the focal point on the facade of the London office building. At the psychological moment the facade was uncovered and the Panel was given the opportunity to study the size, design, texture and material of the eagle and its relation to the facade. It was unanimously agreed that the architect's presentation of his views was excellent." The sculptor Theodore Roszak had made seven studies of a large eagle, and finally a version with the bird's wings spread in a horizontal position was chosen. Because of its size and symbolic implications, the sculpture became one of the most controversial aspects of the building (fig. 15).[17]

Even before it was finished the London chancellery was criticized by British architects. In a discussion after a talk Saarinen gave at the Architectural Association in London in June 1957, one participant observed that he saw in the design an attempt by an American architect to create a historically sensitive design in a centuries-old urban context with which he was unfamiliar.[18] In London the FBO's policy of building architecture that respected the culture of the host country did not satisfy the critics. The chancellery was the first major American building erected in the center of London after the war and it was expected to be a showcase of the latest modern architecture. In addition, Saarinen's new designs in the United States were known, at least through publications, so expectations were high. When the London project was revealed to be a classically proportioned building, the disappointment overshadowed its structural innovations and thoroughly worked-out details in the entrance, lobby, and library interiors and furniture.

The building was also accused of being both falsely monumental and overly decorative, "monumental in bulk, frilly in detail," as Reyner Banham put it (figs. 16, 17). Several features contributed to the building's unwelcome monumentality: it was symmetrical, its main floor was slightly raised on a sloping base, which gave it a fortified effect, and it did not fill the whole site but left the two corners of the square open. Fello Atkinson compared the building to Greek temples: it was visible from all sides, it was slightly elevated above its surroundings, and after the new trees on Grosvenor Square had grown it would be like a temple in a grove. The hostility toward classical monumentality in postwar Europe was partly the outcome of the recent experience with totalitarian states, as Peter Smithson formulated: "Now monuments are out of favour in Europe, for obvious reasons, and there is some puzzlement why America—the idea of which we admire without reservation—should have produced these things."[19]

Even if classical monumentality was unthinkable after the war, modern architecture had to cope with the fact that, as Sigfried Giedion wrote, "people desire buildings that represent their social, ceremonial, and community life. They want these buildings to be more than functional fulfillment." The participants at a symposium on monumentality organized in London by the *Architectural Review* in 1948 were nearly unanimous in thinking that a new kind of monumentality could be formulated by taking examples from the "usable past" and combining them with new urban designs, thus eliminating the need for individual monumental structures. In this way the concept of monumentality was transformed to support the aims of modernist architecture and town planning. As Walter Gropius noted at the symposium: "The old monument was the symbol for a static conception of the world, now overruled by a new one of relativity through changing energies. I believe, therefore, that the equivalent for monumental expression is developing in the direction of a

Fig. 15 Claude de Forest, satirical cartoon showing U.S. Chancellery being carried off by Theodore Roszak's eagle sculpture

Fig. 16 United States Chancellery Building viewed from Grosvenor Square

Fig. 17 United States Chancellery Building, London, main level

new physical pattern for a higher form of civic life, a pattern characterized by flexibility for continuous growth and change."[20]

With this kind of eloquence the idea of monument and monumentality was detached from the historical monument and the individual building and applied instead to groups of buildings and other urban entities, which would also allow for change in the future. Understandably, the historical examples most often cited in this period were buildings and structures from different periods; the Piazza del Popolo in Rome or the Piazza San Marco in Venice were the "usable past" for the modernists. Saarinen, too, saw the same piazzas as a source of new urban solutions. He wrote: "I would like to go to Rome—or to Italy in general. There I like to study their public squares. I would like to sit a whole day on Piazza San Marco, and do the same to all the piazzas in Rome."[21]

Against the background of "New Monumentality," as formulated by Gropius and others as groups of buildings without a definite permanent character or formal unity, it was easy to criticize Saarinen's London chancellery. In addition, the great mass of the building and the detailing of the exterior grille were enough to give some leading critics the false impression that there was no unity between structure and form, in the sense that the modernist principle of honesty of expression would have demanded. J. M. Richards, the critic of the *Times*, wrote: "Each facade is skillfully designed to create an intricate pattern of Georgian-shaped windows; it is also most skillfully put together by an ingenious system of invisible masonry jointing. But this richly modeled effect has little to do with the underlying bones of the building. Only at first-floor level are the bones allowed to reveal themselves. . . . [I]f elsewhere the structure had been allowed to create its own medium of expression, the dignity and monumental presence that has clearly been aimed at might have been achieved." Richards failed to see that the structure did indeed form its own medium of expression and that, as Saarinen wrote to Richards, "the facade one sees is the bones of the building."[22]

Both Richards and Saarinen believed in honesty of expression, but in different ways. Saarinen explained in several of his speeches that the three fundamental tools for achieving a new architecture were functional integrity, honest structural expression, and awareness of one's own time. To these principles, which were shared by most modernist architects, he added three more: the building's ability to express purpose and meaning; a concern with a building's relation to its environment; and the importance of carrying a concept to its conclusion.[23] With these added guidelines he could rationalize the diversity of his designs, the respect he paid to existing urban environments, and the practice of using one basic idea in a building and carrying it through to the smallest detail.

Saarinen searched for solutions that would produce a better built environment, and each project was a step toward this goal. His honesty extended to his views on his own work; he could be critical of his designs, as when he said of the London chancellery, "In my own mind, the building is much better than the English think—but not quite as good as I wished it to be."[24] When Belluschi talked about designing "with a free mind without being dictated by obsolete or sterile formulae or clichés, be they old or new," he was unknowingly describing Saarinen's approach to the built environment. Saarinen showed in his embassy and chancelleries both unity of thought and unity of form, which resulted in technically progressive and contextual architecture. To create a good built environment, unity was a necessity.

Notes

1. Pietro Belluschi, memorandum to Nelson A. Kenworthy, Jan. 27, 1954, Miscellaneous Papers, Foreign Buildings Operations (hereafter FBO), Jane C. Loeffler Collection. I am grateful to Professor Loeffler for sharing her research material with me.

2. Jane C. Loeffler, *The Architecture of Diplomacy: Building America's Embassies* (New York: Princeton Architectural Press, 1998), 23, 24; "U.S. Architecture Abroad," *Architectural Forum*, Mar. 1953, 102. The design by Saarinen actually shows only a site plan, which makes it probable that there were no architectural drawings of the new building yet.

3. The criticism of the sameness of styles used in many embassies regardless of cultural context or climate is found in several FBO documents, for example, Nelson A. Kenworthy to Ralph T. Walker, Sept. 4, 1945, Miscellaneous Papers, FBO, Jane C. Loeffler Collection; and Minutes of the Fourth Meeting of the Foreign Buildings Architectural Advisory Committee, Dec. 3, 1954, Jane C. Loeffler Collection.

4. Loeffler, *Architecture of Diplomacy*, 11. Saarinen was a member of the committee in 1957–60, at the same time he was working on the chancelleries for Oslo and London. The possibility of a conflict of interest was resolved by the fact that he had been chosen for both projects before he became a committee member.

5. Eero Saarinen, letter to Astrid Sampe, Sept. 1, 1953, Astrid Sampe Collection of Eero Saarinen Correspondence, Cranbrook Archives, Bloomfield Hills, Mich.; Eero Saarinen, letter to Astrid Sampe, n.d., Astrid Sampe Collection of Eero Saarinen Correspondence, Cranbrook Archives. Saarinen referred constantly to the Helsinki project in his letters and even dreamed about it; Eero Saarinen, letter to Aline Louchheim, June 6 [no year, but most likely 1953], roll 2074, Aline Saarinen Papers, Archives of American Art, Washington, D.C.

6. See note 3, above. Most likely Saarinen heard about the criticism from various sources. Belluschi was a personal friend, and the contextual suitability of modernist architecture was widely discussed at the time.

7. Saarinen wrote: "Now I will tell you about the different thoughts on the [Helsinki] embassy. I am at the moment a bit confused about what is best." Eero Saarinen, letter to Aline Louchheim, n.d., roll 2074, Aline Saarinen Papers, Archives of American Art.

8. Ibid. The use of marble would most likely have resulted in great difficulties in the northern climate, as has been the case with Alvar Aalto's marble-clad buildings of the 1960s and '70s. It is worth noting that Saarinen was not by any means the only architect who considered the contextual suitability of his designs at the time. Even in the 1930s various Italian modernist architects freely used traditional motifs in their buildings; Dennis P. Doordan, *Building Modern Italy: Italian Architecture, 1914–1936* (New York: Princeton Architectural Press, 1988), 44. After World War II, Alvar Aalto and, to a lesser extent, Aarne Ervi, both of whom Saarinen knew well, became increasingly interested in the physical context of their designs.

9. Eero Saarinen, "Saarinen," *Perspecta* 7 (1961), 32.

10. Eero Saarinen, discussing the Oslo Chancellery Building in March 1959, in *Eero Saarinen on His Work: A Selection of Buildings Dating from 1947 to 1964*, with statements by the architect, ed. Aline B. Saarinen (New Haven: Yale University Press, 1962), 52.

11. Francoise Choay, *The Rule and the Model* (Cambridge: MIT Press, 1997), 74; George R. Collins and Christiane Craseman Collins, *Camillo Sitte: The Birth of Modern City Planning* (New York: Rizzoli, 1986), 146; Eliel Saarinen, *The City, Its Growth, Its Decay, Its Future* (1943; repr., Cambridge: MIT Press, 1965); Eero Saarinen, "Problems Facing Architecture," lecture delivered as part of Benjamin Franklin Lecture Series, University of Pennsylvania, Philadelphia, Dec. 8, 1960.

12. Kevin Roche, interviewed by Pekka Korvenmaa, Susanna Santala, and Timo Tuomi, Mar. 31, 2005. The other architects invited to compete were Edward Durell Stone; Hugh Stubbins; Yamasaki, Leinweber, and Associates;

Wurster, Bernardi, and Emmons; Anderson, Beckwith, and Haible; Ernest J. Kump; and José Luis Sert with Huson Jackson and Joseph Zalewski; Minutes of the Twentieth Meeting of the Foreign Buildings Architectural Advisory Committee, Sept. 14 and 15, 1955, Jane C. Loeffler Collection.

13. Marc Guberman, telephone interview with Spero Daltas, Aug. 11, 2004. Most of the large number of sketches and drawings of the different phases of the design are in the Glen Goldman Collection, Cranbrook Archives; Centre Canadien d'Architecture/ Canadian Centre for Architecture, Montreal; and the Eero Saarinen Papers, Manuscripts and Archives, Yale University. The Saarinen office afterward built up a portfolio with pictures of the various stages of design both before and after the competition; Eero Saarinen Papers, Yale University. Saarinen later remarked that some of his attempts to use the Colossal order on the facade were somewhat similar to Edward Durell Stone's competition entry—only better; Eero Saarinen Papers, Yale University.

14. Belluschi's wife, Marjorie, wrote: "The jury thought that both Stone's and Saarinen's entires were equally meritorious; and the one by Stone seemed to be the favorite. He [Pietro Belluschi] remembers voting for the Saarinen entry, but not with great enthusiasm." Marjorie Belluschi, letter to Jane Loeffler, Feb. 4, 1992, Jane C. Loeffler Collection.

15. Ibid.; Saarinen, *Eero Saarinen on His Work,* 48.

16. Saarinen, "Saarinen," 32.

17. Minutes of the Foreign Buildings Architectural Advisory Committee, July 26, 1957, Feb. 24, 1958, Jane C. Loeffler Collection.

18. Michael Brawne made this comment after Eero Saarinen's speech, "Function, Structure, Beauty," at the Architectural Association in London, Dec. 6, 1957. See "Eero Saarinen: Function, Structure, and Beauty—Discussion," *Architectural Association Journal,* July–Aug. 1957, 51.

19. Reyner Banham, cited in "Controversial Building in London," *Architectural Forum,* Mar. 1961, 84; Fello Atkinson, "U.S. Embassy Building, Grosvenor Square, London," *Architectural Review,* Apr. 1961, 257; Peter Smithson, cited in "Controversial Building in London," 81.

20. Sigfried Giedion, *Architecture, You and Me: The Diary of a Development* (Cambridge: Harvard University Press, 1958), 26–27; Walter Gropius, remarks in "In Search of a New Monumentality: A Symposium by Greogor Paulsson, Henry-Russell Hitchcock, William Holford, Sigfried Giedion, Walter Gropius, Lucio Costa, and Alfred Roth," *Architectural Review,* Mar. 1948, 127. The term "usable past" is employed and discussed in Riitta Nikula, "The City in the Writings of Alvar Aalto," *Alvar Aalto in Seven Buildings* (Helsinki: Museum of Finnish Architecture, 1999), 152; Robert Wojtowicz, *Lewis Mumford and American Modernism: Eutopian Theories for Architecture and Urban Planning* (Cambridge: Cambridge University Press, 1996), 45–50; and Van Wyck Brooks, "On Creating a Usable Past," *Dial* 64 (1918), 337–41.

21. Eero Saarinen, letter to Astrid Sampe, n.d., probably 1948–49, Astrid Sampe Collection of Eero Saarinen Correspondence, Cranbrook Archives.

22. J. M. Richards, "From the Architectural Correspondent of the London Times," *The Times* (London), Oct. 29, 1960; Eero Saarinen, letter to J. M. Richards, Apr. 11, 1960, Eero Saarinen Papers, Yale University.

23. Eero Saarinen, Dickinson College Arts Award Address, Carlisle, Pa., Dec. 1, 1959, Eero Saarinen Papers, Yale University, manuscript published in this volume.

24. Saarinen, *Eero Saarinen on His Work,* 48.

Susanna Santala

airports
building for the jet age

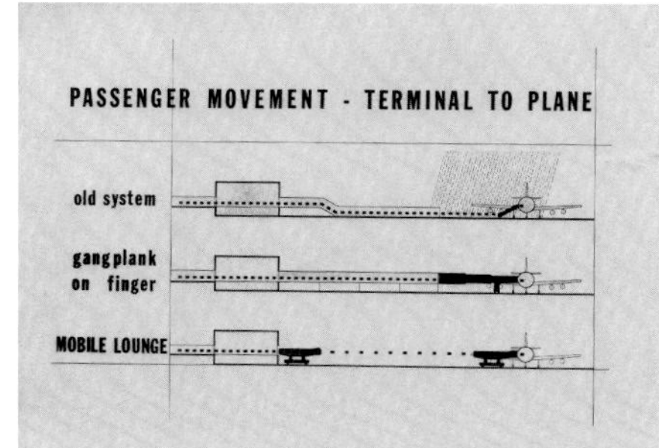

Fig. 1 Eero Saarinen and Associates, diagram showing passenger movement from terminal to plane

Trans World Airlines Terminal, New York, New York, 1956–62
Dulles International Airport, Chantilly, Virginia, 1958–63
Athens Airport, Athens, Greece, 1960–69

"We in the office spend so much time traveling, that we know only too well the physical comforts required by today's travelers. Using materials and structural systems appropriate to this century of flight, we have tried to make a building which is functional, comfortable and dramatic." Although Eero Saarinen wrote these lines about the TWA Terminal, the sentiment applies to all three of the airports he designed. His revolutionary terminals, planned in collaboration with the engineering firm led by Othmar H. Ammann and Charles S. Whitney, combined functional solutions with aesthetic expression appropriate to the dawning jet age. All three incorporated technologies and planning ideas that the Saarinen office derived from research on existing airports. Dulles, the first airport specifically built to serve jet aircraft, presented a design problem that was unique at the time. Yet its upturned concrete roof continued the search, begun with TWA, to express the excitement of flight. The Athens Airport proposed a solution for a modern facility set against the backdrop of classical Greek architecture. While TWA embodied the image of its corporate client, Dulles and Athens each represented the nations to which they served as international gateways.[1]

TWA: DRAMA AND FUNCTION

In an era of postwar prosperity and advances in aerospace expertise, airports were a frequent commission for second-generation modernists. These designers challenged the tropes of interwar modernism, achieving a new heterogeneity of form. Their questioning of the canon and genealogy of modern architecture as defined by the first-generation modern architects and historians reflected profound political, economic, and social changes, as well as contradictory aims of the era. Experiments with new uses for concrete, combined with advances in engineering, opened new options for form. The curving concrete shells and expressive structure of Saarinen's TWA Terminal became a central recurring example in the discourse on new possibilities in construction.[2]

For TWA, its first airport commission, the Saarinen office approached the design problem rationally, by conducting a number of studies. Employees timed enplaning, deplaning, and baggage claims at existing international airports in Philadelphia, San Francisco, Baltimore, Dallas, Chicago, and several European cities. The firm's research followed planning guidelines issued by the International Air Transport Association for evaluating adequacy of service for a given population, economic base, and distance from other communities. Special attention was paid to passenger comfort and the specifics of airplane plans, and the architects consulted both the National Airport Plan and Civil Aeronautics Administration (CAA) guidelines. This data, once collected and analyzed, served as the programming basis for all three airport projects.[3] Roger Johnson, who worked in the office at the time, recalled:

> At the time TWA started, commercial jet aircraft was still a thing of the future. They weren't operational and there wasn't anyone available in the Detroit area that we knew of to review the requirements for these planes of the future. New air terminals were few and far between. Almost nothing had been published on the subject. Eero asked me to do some research on air terminal[s]. I went to a number of libraries and checked out architectural journals. Very slim pickings.[4]

As airports, and airplanes, were still in a state of rapid development, Saarinen privileged flexibility and expansion in his planning. During the five previous decades of aviation, airports had developed from hangars to multiplex structures of terminal buildings connected to gates by long fingers—the concourses, concessions, and waiting areas (fig. 1). Within these structures, space had to be provided for ticketing, baggage, airline administration, and passenger comfort. Most postwar airports followed this decentralized model, but there was a growing interest in centralizing operations. TWA's operations at New York International Airport (popularly known as Idlewild at the time, later renamed John F. Kennedy International) were to be located in a single-airline terminal within a unit (or decentralized) airport structure, while at Dulles and Athens one terminal was to serve several airlines. The advantages of a unit terminal, like TWA, were fast check-in and shorter distances from the entrance to the gates, each situated in a spoke radiating from a central waiting lounge. Although such terminals functioned well when used by one airline, they had limited expansion possibilities within the airport. Other disadvantages included having to change terminals when changing airlines, and distanced communication with airport management. However, the single-airline terminals did not need to offer space to management entities like the Port Authority.[5]

TWA's striking structure derives from this singular purpose, and from Saarinen's careful research into creating efficient pathways from curb to plane. The curving concrete vaults shelter a main lobby with an information desk, a ticket counter, and a large flight information board. Several bars, restaurants, and lounge areas named after TWA destinations were situated on a mezzanine overlooking the lobby. Passengers moved from their cars under a canopy and proceeded directly into the lobby, where departures and arrivals were separated into different functional areas. The interior design paid special attention to the flow of baggage handling and the naturally circular movement pattern of passengers. Whenever possible, Saarinen was interested in mechanizing the movement of people and goods. Moving sidewalks were to run down the concourse tube and baggage carousels were to be automated, but these plans were never realized. Ultimately, Saarinen planned everything from the building to its ashtrays, creating a uniform environment with shells, wings, and curves at a multitude of interrelated scales. As such, this micro-world of travelers can be read as Saarinen's adaptation of the concept of the total work of art to the activities of the jet age. It became a corporate mark for the airline, proposing

TWA as the vehicle to unexplored worlds, and dominated the company's subsequent advertising. The complicated structure, arrived at through work on models, deepened Saarinen's devotion to this method of design development, while its form attracted attention, increased Saarinen's fame, and provoked criticism from an array of modernists.[6]

DULLES: GATEWAY TO THE CAPITAL

The volume of air travel multiplied after World War II as military innovations, and specifically the jet engine, revolutionized flight. Cold war fears of nuclear attacks on cities accelerated the movement of populations to the American suburbs. Exurban locations allowed airports room to grow but ultimately created connection problems between airport and city. Even in the 1950s, Washington National Airport, located only three and a half miles from the Capitol, suffered from numerous problems because of its location in the city. Noise from the new jet engines also made it imperative to locate airports outside urban centers. Washington National's shortcomings forced the successor agency of the CAA, the Federal Aviation Agency (FAA), to plan and construct Dulles International Airport. After the FAA conducted several studies on time and distance factors, a location about twenty-five miles west of the city, in Chantilly, Virginia, was selected.[7]

Building on its research for TWA, the Saarinen office extensively studied the future needs of the jet-dominated airport. At TWA the firm had been solving the needs of a single airline, but at Dulles it had to create a multicarrier terminal as well as lay out runways, maintenance facilities, and a control tower. Contemporary articles and design manuals suggested that airport design should be based on the number of operations—daily takeoffs and landings—anticipated for the present and future. Peak-hour traffic dictated the size of the terminal (and specifics, from the number of ticket counters to seats per square foot). Studies on wind and weather helped the office determine the best location for the airfield, and led to the design of two parallel north–south runways and two supplementary southeast–northwest runways (only one was built).[8] The manuals strongly suggested designing for expansion to accommodate new aircraft with faster speeds and larger turning radii. At Dulles, taxiways run parallel to the main runways and several turnouts were provided for different-size aircraft. The air control tower was placed at the location from which the airfield could best be monitored. Other facilities—aprons, airmail and cargo buildings—were also placed on the airfield. These one-story buildings were rectangular and clad in enameled aluminum, and their plainness reflected their hierarchical relation to the terminal. They formed a maintenance area separate from zones for the circulation of passengers and traffic, making operations more efficient and legible. Both physically and verbally, the airport had to communicate with air carriers and ground transportation, with the airfield and the local community.[9]

Saarinen saw Dulles as a threefold design problem: it was to express the optimism of the jet age, to be a gateway to the nation, and to relate to the federal architecture of Washington, D.C. It was of utmost importance that the airport represent the United States as the leading democratic, economic, political, and military power during the cold war. Saarinen's choice of materials was intended to relate his modern architecture to the neoclassicism of the National Mall. His use of limestone-aggregate concrete, the modernized columns on the terminal facade, the monumental scale, and the minimal structural form all relate the airport to the city's federal classicism. But rather than simply support a lintel, the columns of Dulles lean outward, counteracting the pull of cables and penetrating the suspended roof. The structure is active, inclining upward to the sky. Glass panels, which curve between the columns, suggest an openness rare in federal buildings.[10]

Viewed from a distance, the terminal structure hovers over the rural landscape, resembling a distant gateway. Saarinen paid particular attention to the access road to the airport. As with many of his suburban corporate campus projects, he and landscape architect Dan Kiley choreographed the views of the building and the visitor experience at multiple scales: a straight road leads to a generous ellipse, whose curve mimics that of the pedestrian access ramp. The terminal is located on the ellipse. In designing the building's entrance, Saarinen faced two problems: the difficulty of articulating the entry to a modern, repetitive structure (a problem that recurs in Saarinen's work), and that of providing graceful access to a building where the approach began via automobile and was completed on foot. The latter challenge was encapsulated by Kevin Roche, one of the office members who worked on the project: unfortunately, "you could not drive into the building." The problem was partly solved by the use of the ellipse, and the clarity of the terminal plan at the point of entry: passengers arriving in their automobiles enjoyed the magnificent views of the terminal; on reaching the terminal front, they walked through the entrance and arrived directly at the ticketing kiosk. Something of the sublimity of entering a grand, federal-style building or even an ancient Roman temple was maintained.[11]

The Dulles terminal had two floors: one for departing passengers, ticketing, and concessions, the other for arriving passengers, baggage claim, and ground transportation (fig. 2). Saarinen's real innovation at Dulles was the employment of new transport vehicles called mobile lounges, which were a sort of giant luxury bus carrying as many as ninety people from the terminal to their plane. Departing passengers proceeded from the ramp through ticketing to the runway side, which was fitted with gates for boarding the mobile lounge that would take them to the plane. Situating concessions and ticketing in the central space allowed free passenger circulation on the enplaning floor. Arriving passengers were transported to the terminal by the mobile lounges, whereupon they descended to the ground floor to claim their luggage and proceeded to surface transportation on a separate deplaning ramp, or walked along another ramp to the parking area. A south finger connecting the terminal to the air control tower had space for clubs, exhibitions, and private lounges.

The mobile lounges were a revolutionary approach to airport movement, and designing Dulles around them allowed Saarinen to do away with the usual multitude of finger gates found at most terminals. This pioneering connection between the terminal and the aircraft was inspired by the introduction of bus systems in several European airports. But buses required that passengers use stairs and transfer to the plane on the airfield, whereas the mobile lounge allowed same-level loading at both the terminal and the aircraft, which avoided exposing passengers to the weather and airfield hazards (figs. 3, 4). The mobile lounge could be loaded from both ends, and its height was adjustable to match that of the terminal as well as different airplanes. It was operated by a driver and had simple, buslike mechanics (fig. 5).

For the airport's management, the mobile lounge allowed operational flexibility by separating aircraft operations from passenger facilities. Passengers could be concentrated in one terminal. The mobile lounge could serve different-size aircraft from one gate. Because all airplanes were loaded with mobile lounges, the location of the aircraft did not matter much. Most were parked in two rows of aprons close to the runways so that taxiing (and the related cost of fuel) was minimized. The aircraft could be serviced in the same location as boarding, making it possible to load passengers on one side while mechanics attended to the plane on the other. Saarinen thought the concept was so promising that he hired his friends Charles and Ray Eames to create a film, *The Expanding Airport*, to sell the office's rationale for the lounges to the FAA. Although the federal government accepted the Saarinen office's argument, airlines were reluctant to adopt this system. The initial cost of the mobile lounges, which were developed by the Chrysler Corporation, was simply a burden to the airlines, which did not benefit from the reduction in construction costs resulting from the elimination of fingers.[12]

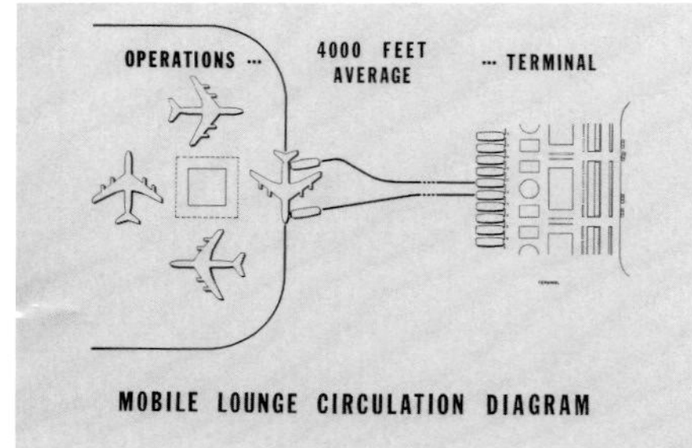

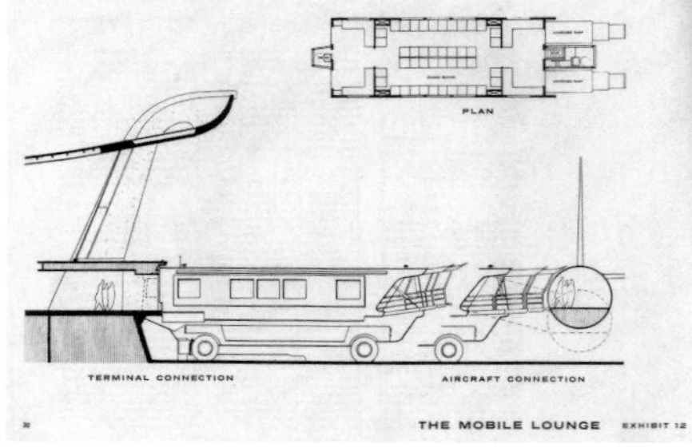

Fig. 2 Eero Saarinen and Associates, Dulles International Airport, Chantilly, Virginia, 1958–63, aerial exploded rendering

Fig. 3 Dulles International Airport, mobile lounge circulation diagram

Fig. 4 Dulles International Airport, diagram illustrating docking of mobile lounge

Fig. 5 Dulles International Airport, unsuccessful first attempt to dock mobile lounge to plane

ATHENS: CLASSICAL MODERN

Like Dulles, Athens Airport serves as the international gateway to a nation's capital. However, the warm climate and building site on the shore of the Mediterranean, where a rocky landscape descended directly from the terminal location, were quite distinct from the Dulles site and thus posed a different design problem from the start. Saarinen proposed a cantilevered structure that contrasted with the landscape but expressed continuity with the classical tradition. The use of Pentelic-marble-aggregate concrete, along with marble floors and desks, further linked the terminal project to local building materials. The broad, symmetrical layout takes a sedate and less skeletal approach to structure than at Dulles (fig. 6).

The Greek authorities rejected Saarinen's initial design, and it underwent several changes as it evolved toward a more open and modern form.[13] Even though the Saarinen office provided the city of Athens with a master plan, Athens Airport was really an extension of an existing national and military airfield. The access road from the city followed a curve, allowing varied views as one approached the airport, as at Dulles. Yet Athens officials were concerned not with gridlock but with delays caused by the pedestrians and animal carts that crowded the rural roads. The terminal building was composed of two rectangular forms, with a long box with a heavy cornice cantilevered above a modern peristyle hall. The four-sided concrete columns supporting the cantilever flowered out in a form reminiscent of a propeller. The main terminal, located in the lower volume, handled ticketing, passport controls, customs, and baggage claims in functionally separated areas. Monumental stairs led passengers from the ground level to ticketing and the transit hall, separating them from spectators who could observe the runway from a mezzanine observation deck or the restaurant in the cantilevered volume.

In the first scheme for Athens, a bus system carried passengers to "islands" between the runways, discrete waiting areas served by concessions, and surrounded by several gates. In the final scheme, open-air fingers replaced the bus system, a low-tech solution achievable in a mild climate, with landscaped terraces edged by low walls, pools, and flowers. Deplaning passengers entered the terminal at its corners from the open walkways, passed through passport

Fig. 6 Eero Saarinen and Associates, Athens Airport, Athens, Greece, 1960–69, model viewed from the rear

control and customs, claimed their luggage, and left the terminal for ground transportation. Athens Airport served essentially as a mediator between the automobile and the aircraft. By the 1950s, airports had developed into inconvenient, mazelike structures that functioned poorly. Saarinen approached the design problem rationally, aiming to make the airport a machine for mass transit.[14]

Airports embodied what Reyner Banham called the Second Machine Age, an era when smaller machines became available to households and aviation revolutionized the concepts of distance and speed. At a time when the public still marveled at the beauty of aircraft and was fascinated by flight, flying became affordable for a growing number of people. Its luxury diminished, but airlines still marketed air travel with sexy images of upper-class adventure. Travelers were ready to conquer the world on transatlantic flights, and it became commonplace to fly to business meetings across the continent (as Saarinen had been doing for years).[15]

All three of Saarinen's airports sought answers for the specific needs of the client and the location, and they offered those clients designs that were appropriate for the century of flight. Each had an innovative structural form following Saarinen's three principles of modern architecture: functional integrity, structural clarity, and appropriateness to the time.[16] All proposed innovative solutions, functioned as monumental symbols, and gave form to the jet age.

But airports are constantly undergoing change. Developments in aviation have imposed new requirements on existing structures. Although Saarinen anticipated these needs, his plans to accommodate future operations have been followed only sparingly. Yet in the twenty-first century, when most people no longer consider air travel a glamorous adventure and instead find it more of an inconvenience, cruising around Dulles in a mobile lounge offers a taste of the thrill that was once associated with postwar aviation. Passengers still marvel at the architecture of TWA and Dulles, architecture that expresses the past drama of a now commonplace activity.

Notes

1. "New TWA Terminal to Feature Unique Saarinen Design," press release issued by TWA, Nov. 13, 1957, 1, Eero Saarinen Papers, Manuscripts and Archives, Yale University.

2. The Lambert St. Louis Airport was designed by Helmuth, Yamasaki, and Leinweber in 1951–61. Skidmore, Owings, and Merrill and I. M. Pei constructed terminal buildings at Idlewild (JFK) Airport in New York (1957–71), and C. F. Murphy designed Chicago's O'Hare International Airport (1962). Philadelphia's new airport (1953) by Carroll, Grisdale, and Van Allen attracted attention, and many European airports, including Schiphol Airport in Amsterdam, Orly Airport in Paris, and Heathrow International Airport in London, were studied for the design of postwar American airports. Eero Saarinen's office collected data on all these designs, and they were extensively discussed in architectural magazines and planning manuals of the time; Eero Saarinen Papers, Yale University. See Alastair Gordon, *Naked Airport: A Cultural History of the World's Most Revolutionary Structure* (New York: Metropolitan Books, Henry Holt, 2004); David Pascoe, *Airspaces* (London: Reaktion, 2001); Hugh Pearman, *Airports: A Century of Architecture* (New York: Abrams, 2004); and John Zukowsky, ed., *Building for Air Travel: Architecture and Design for Commercial Aviation* (Chicago: The Art Institute of Chicago and Prestel-Verlag, 1996).

Panayotis Tournikiotis has identified three different discourses of modernism: operative first-generation discourse (Sigfried Giedion, Nikolaus Pevsner), derogative second-generation discourse (Reyner Banham, Manfredo Tafuri), and objective discourse (Henry-Russell Hitchcock); Panayotis Tournikiotis, *The Historiography of Modern Architecture* (Cambridge: MIT Press, 1999). In my view, these were followed by the operative discourse of postmodernism (Charles Jencks). Other attempts to rationalize the discourse and analyze the shifting meaning of such concepts as function, style, and modernism have been proposed by Adrian Forty and Hilde Heynen; Adrian Forty, *Words and Buildings: A Vocabulary of Modern Architecture* (London: Thames and Hudson, 2000), and Hilde Heynen, *Architecture and Modernity: A Critique*, 2nd printing (Cambridge: MIT Press, 1999).

3. International Air Transport Association (IATA), *Airport Buildings and Aprons: A Reference Document of Principles and Guidance Material for Use by Those Concerned with the Planning of Airport Buildings and Aprons*, July 1956, 1–35; "Twentieth-Century Building Type: Airport Terminal Buildings," *Progressive Architecture*, May 1953, 72–73.

The material collected in the Saarinen office's studies was organized into case study files and then analyzed and presented as diagrams and statistics for the client. Many of the firm's new and innovative technological solutions were based on these studies; Eero Saarinen Papers, Yale University.

Kevin Roche remembers that Saarinen always got on the plane at the last minute, not wanting to waste any time. Time spent traveling to business meetings made him extremely aware of the inconvenience of air travel; in letters to his wife, Aline (often written on board an airplane), he criticized bad airport management. Kevin Roche, interview with the author, New Haven, Conn., Mar. 31, 2005; Aline Saarinen Papers, Archives of American Art, Washington, D.C.

4. Cranbrook Archives, Bloomfield Hills, Mich., box 1, folder 22, correspondence, Roger Johnson, Apr. 1995–Apr. 1999, 1–2.

5. U.S. Department of Commerce, Civil Aeronautics Administration, *Airport Terminal Buildings* (Washington, D.C., Apr. 1953), 11–18; "Jet Airports: Passenger Terminal Building Design Principles," *Architectural Record*, Mar. 1960, 168–70; "Twentieth-Century Building Type," 70, 87–88.

6. "New TWA Terminal to Feature Unique Saarinen Design"; "Trans World Flight Center's Four Restaurant Facilities Reflect International Theme," press release issued by TWA, May 10, 1961, Eero Saarinen Papers, Yale University.

Balthazar Korab photographed the TWA model under different lighting conditions, using mirrors to study the effects of the curved inner space. Interviews with Raymond Bean, Cesar Pelli, and James Smith illuminate this working method; Cranbrook Archives, Saarinen/Swanson Reunion Records, 2001-14, box 1, folder 5, correspondence, Raymond Bean, May 1999, 1; Cranbrook Archives, Saarinen/Swanson Reunion Records, 2001-14, box 1, folder 33, correspondence, Cesar Pelli, Apr. 1995–Oct. 2001; Cranbrook Archives, Saarinen/Swanson Reunion Records, 2001-14, box 3, Cranbrook reunion transcript 1995, 1–3; Cranbrook Archives, Design in America Papers, 2002-16, James Smith speaks with John Gerard, Apr. 8, 1982, 5–8; Balthazar Korab, interview with the author, Detroit, Mich., Nov. 11, 2004.

7. *The Airport and Its Neighbors: The Report of the President's Airport Commission* (Washington, D.C., May 16, 1952); Adone C. Pietrasanta, "Aircraft Noise and Building Design," *Noise Control* 3 (Mar. 1957), 11–18, 88; Federal Aviation Agency, *Dulles International Airport Master Plan Report: Prepared for the Federal Aviation Agency, Washington, D.C., Issued August 15, 1964, by Ammann and Whitney, Eero Saarinen, Burns and McDonnell and Ellery Husted, Architect-Engineers for Dulles International Airport, Chantilly, Virginia*; Keller Easterling, *Organization Space: Landscapes, Highways, and Houses in America* (Cambridge: MIT Press, 1999); "Twentieth-Century Building Type," 78.

Toward the end of the 1950s the aerospace industry produced such new aircraft as the Boeing 707, Douglas DC-8, Convair 880/990, Comet IV, Bristol 200, and Caravelle. Most new jets had four engines, flew at up to 500 miles per hour at 39,000 feet, and were able to carry 80 to 165 passengers. High-octane fuels, radar, new radio-communications stations for air traffic control, new centralized data processing, and regulations also made aviation safer and more efficient and established new groups of aviation professionals. In 1958 the FAA was established to regulate and advance aviation; Roger E. Bilsten, *Flight in America: From the Wrights to the Astronauts* (Baltimore: Johns Hopkins University Press, 1984), 167–245; *Federal Aviation Agency's First Annual Report to the President and the Congress* (Washington, D.C., 1959).

8. IATA, *Airport Buildings and Aprons*, 37–47; "Jet Airports," 167–82; *Progressive Architecture*, May 1958, 69–136. Runway patterns dictated the location of airport terminals. Variously oriented runways provided for safe landings without crosswinds in different conditions. Faster landing speeds, tricycle and crosswind landing gear, and higher wind loads lessened the crosswind effect and allowed airports to have one main runway with a supplementary one oriented in a second direction. "Twentieth-Century Building Type," 78–80.

9. The Saarinen office collected brochures on the aerospace industry's future innovations and data on aircraft. Technical drawings for aircraft were copied and used for architectural planning (taxiing, turnouts, and so on). The design of Dulles followed design-manual guidelines but could not anticipate the rapid development of jet aircraft using shorter runways. See the collection of brochures and documents in the Eero Saarinen Papers, Yale University; International Air Transport Association (IATA), *Apron Requirements for Turbine-Powered Aircraft: A Reference Document of Principles and Guidance Material for Use by Those Concerned with Airport Planning*, Jan. 1958, 1–57; FAA, *Dulles International Airport Master Plan Report*; "Twentieth-Century Building Type," 80–81.

10. FAA, *Dulles International Airport Master Plan Report*.

11. Roche interview.

12. *FAA News: The Mobile Lounge Fact Sheet*, undated, 4; Eero Saarinen Papers, Yale University; "Twentieth-Century Building Type," 74; FAA, *Dulles International Airport Master Plan Report*; "Jet Airports," 170–71, 179–80.

13. The changes in design can be followed in the correspondence between local authorities and the Saarinen and Ammann and Whitney offices; Eero Saarinen Papers, Yale University.

14. "Terminal Building for Athens Airport (Greece)," presentation booklet by Ammann and Whitney, Engineers, Eero Saarinen and Associates, Architects for Terminal Building, and Charles Landrum, Airport Consultant for Terminal Building; Eero Saarinen Papers, Yale University.

15. Reyner Banham, *Theory and Design in the First Machine Age*, 2nd ed. (New York: Praeger, 1970; orig. pub. 1960), 329–30; Bilsten, *Flight in America*, 176–78, 233–38.

16. Eero Saarinen, "The Changing Philosophy of Architecture," draft of a speech given at the American Institute of Architects, 86th Convention, June 1954; Eero Saarinen Papers, Yale University.

Alan J. Plattus

campus plans context and community

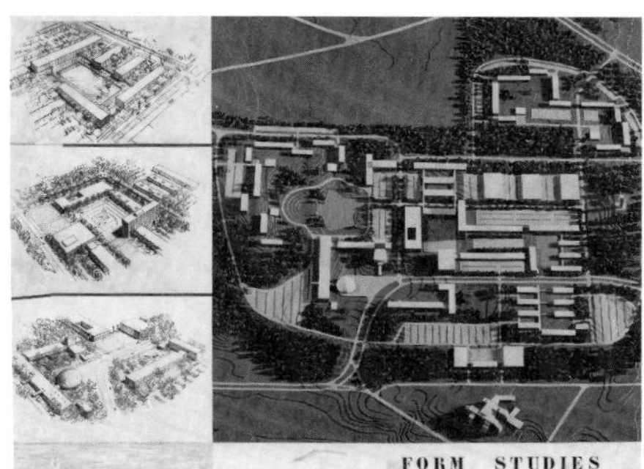

Fig. 1 Eero Saarinen and Associates, University of Michigan North Campus plan, Ann Arbor, Michigan, 1951–56, form studies

Brandeis University, Waltham, Massachusetts, 1949–52
University of Chicago, Chicago, Illinois, 1955–60
Concordia Senior College, Fort Wayne, Indiana, 1953–58
Emma Hartman Noyes House, Vassar College, Poughkeepsie, New York, 1954–58
Samuel F. B. Morse and Ezra Stiles Colleges, Yale University,
New Haven, Connecticut, 1958–62

In the late 1950s, at the height of his career and fame as the architect of iconic public and corporate structures, Eero Saarinen was invited to address the president and board of regents of the University of Michigan on the subject of campus planning. In 1951 he had been hired to prepare a master plan for a new campus expansion project, the North Campus, of that institution, a commission that Saarinen clearly saw as an important opportunity in his home state, and even as potentially exemplary of fundamental principles of group planning (fig. 1). Saarinen eventually resigned his position as master planner for the North Campus, after attempting to coordinate the work of five other firms on the central area of that campus, while himself designing and building only the peripheral group of the music school. In the wake of that experience, he chose to speak to his audience and former clients at Michigan on what he called the "dilemmas"—but what he really framed as the "failures"—of contemporary campus planning. This discussion would quickly become a striking indictment of the inability of contemporary architects to produce satisfying environments larger than a single building:

On the architectural side of the ledger, the picture is a very sorry one. The range between the good and the bad architect is far greater than, for instance, the range between the good and the bad dentist. The dentist plays on a narrow keyboard, the architect a broad one. Therefore there is the utmost importance to seek the good architect. Even some of the best architects have made terrible mistakes in relating buildings to each other on a campus plan.

. . . We have to remember that we're at a time in architecture when there is no formalistic discipline upon architecture such as there was in times when architects built Colonial or Gothic, Classical or Renaissance. To give an example—at the University of Chicago, one of the small courts is an all Gothic court built of Indiana limestone, but actually the buildings around the court were built in the '20s by four of the leading architects of that time, and the court is completely unified and beautiful, because all these architects had the predominant regimentation of Gothic, and they all agreed on and therefore lived within that. Today you could not build a court with four different architects building on each side of that court—you could build it but it would look like hell, because there is no dominant discipline that all can agree on. We have just that problem at Lincoln Center today, and it is my conviction that Lincoln Center would end up better if it had been done by just one firm.

. . . You have the problem with the architectural profession—their terrible weakness in understanding an overall problem of a total environment. Their minds are set on their own little building—they do not consider its relation in scale and mass and material to the neighboring buildings.

Well, the end result is that the campuses that I'm familiar with are all going to get spoiled. This is the situation. It seems like a hopeless one, if one aims higher than just a hodge podge. This is why I have resigned from campus planning at Michigan and many other places.[1]

Here, perhaps not surprisingly, given the fact that this talk was basically private and was to remain unpublished, Saarinen offered a far more frank and personal account of the evolution and motivation of themes familiar from his published article "Campus Planning," which appeared in the November 1960 issue of *Architectural Record*. But it was essentially the same line of argument that Saarinen summarized in the published article by referring to his father's famous admonition to "always look at the next larger thing."[2] In the Michigan speech this takes the form of an explicit and vehement plea to go beyond functionalism to what Saarinen insisted on calling a "total environment." Having surveyed the usual practical issues, he stated:

These are the ordinary, accepted and proven reasons for a campus plan. These are economical, logical reasons, the kind that the logical business mind can easily understand. In addition to this, we also hope to achieve a total beautiful environment that [has] unity and order. We are trying to achieve a beautiful 20th century environment that has significance in our lives—not just a hodge podge of buildings. Just to be absolutely sure that we're talking about the same thing, when we're talking about total unity and environment, I would like to cite some examples out of the past and present. There are: Oxford and Cambridge in England; Thomas Jefferson's University of Virginia; the pseudo Gothic environment[s] of Yale and Princeton—all of these have real unity that we should not disregard; my father's Cranbrook institutions; and—not a university—but an example of total unity of environment is also General Motors Technical Center, which we built. In all these groupings of buildings around courts, total unity of environment and total expression was achieved.[3]

Aside from being a fairly precocious expression of the sort of nostalgia for a more easily described and regulated stylistic contextualism and attention to precedent that was beginning to emerge in collegiate architecture at the time, and would take a much more explicit and widespread form in the 1970s, this speech also clearly represents an extraordinary instance of architectural auto-critique, even confession. The suggestion is that Saarinen himself remained somehow fundamentally unsatisfied by precisely those aspects of his—and his contemporaries'—work that would loom largest in architectural criticism and eventually in history as well, and harbored a largely unrequited longing for the unity of context and expression of community represented by his father's designs at Cranbrook and the other examples he cites.[4]

If nothing else, this is a remarkably candid statement on the part of an architect not only whose star was rising in most quarters but who had established himself as one of the most trusted architectural advisers to the best and brightest (and most powerful) individuals of his time—and nowhere more than in the hallowed halls of academia. In his talk at Michigan, Saarinen pointed out, accurately (but then crossed out—in modesty?), that "I've had quite a bit of experience, possibly more than anybody else today, with different universities on their master plans. At different times I worked with Antioch College, Stephens College, Drake University, Brandeis University, University of Michigan, M.I.T., Vassar College, University of Chicago and Yale University on the problem of the master plan as well as various buildings, and I've come to see certain common patterns and a common set of mistakes which prevent us from achieving the goal we set out to do."[5] Indeed, no architect emerged from the war years better situated to benefit from the spectacular postwar boom in college expansion and construction than Saarinen. After all, his father's first major commission after his move to the United States—and probably the opportunity that kept him there—was for the design of a new school campus in Bloomfield Hills, Michigan, that was to become the nucleus of the larger Cranbrook campus. For one of Europe's leading urbanists, and masters of "total" design in an era untroubled by his son's "dilemmas," this was an appropriate introduction to the opportunities and limitations of American urbanism.

In 1922, the year of Eliel Saarinen's brilliant and influential runner-up entry in the Chicago Tribune competition, and the year before the elder Saarinen moved, along with his thirteen-year-old son, Eero, to the United States, Werner Hegemann published a telling catalogue of American achievements in the field of "civic art." In a chapter titled "The Grouping of Buildings in America," Hegemann (and his co-author, Elbert Peets) illustrated American world's fairs, hospital complexes, and civic centers, but the most space is given, quite appropriately, to "educational groupings": mainly university campus plans. This important tradition has now been more fully discussed by Paul Turner and others, but Hegemann already saw its salient characteristics and, perhaps most important, recognized that it was within the limited field of the campus, at least as much as in the plans of the great fairs, that the principles of urban design that he espoused and promoted had been most seriously explored and comprehensively realized.[6] After all, the larger territory of city and suburb in the burgeoning American urban landscape was still (and perhaps remains) the home turf of laissez-faire capitalism, not of the sort of carefully cultivated—and extravagantly endowed—image of traditional community that so many colleges, in the years after the Civil War, developed in explicit distinction from the industrial metropolis. This phenomenon, combined with the incredible proliferation of academic institutions of all kinds and their explosive growth even before the boom that fueled Eero's career, stood in conspicuous contrast to the still relatively few ancient and elite European equivalents.

Europe, of course, had already witnessed the inspirational example of several generations of comprehensive urban design in response to the rapid urbanization of the nineteenth century: major capitals such as Paris, Vienna, and Barcelona in the 1850s and 1860s, and then after the turn of the century in provincial centers like Budapest, Ljubljana, and Helsinki. The elder Saarinen had helped lead the way in the last city, and as talented a designer of individual buildings as he was, his greatest achievements prior to his emigration were arguably the exquisitely rendered plans for Munkkiniemi-Haaga and Greater Helsinki, among other urban centers. It was then natural for Eliel, newly arrived in the United States and experiencing the normal reaction of European modern architects to the American city—simultaneous exhilaration and horror—to continue in the same vein, putting forward ambitious, unbuilt schemes for the Chicago lakefront in 1923 and the Detroit riverfront in 1924.

These monumental proposals, worthy successors to those of Daniel Burnham and Charles McKim, found no advocates or patrons at the scale of the city as a whole, so it was with the commission for the Cranbrook School for

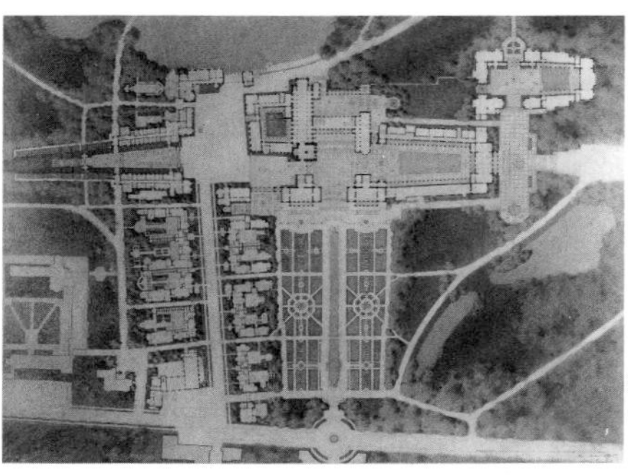

Fig. 2 Eliel Saarinen, Cranbrook Academy of Art, 1925, aerial perspective

Boys in the mid-1920s, to be built on private land in the Detroit suburbs, that Eliel's practice in America really took off. The Cranbrook School was the first component of what was to become, under Eliel's direction and later with Eero's collaboration, one of the most impressive "educational groupings" of the twentieth century. It is, however, quite important to note the differences between the boys' school, a brilliant but typologically and compositionally conventional essay in academic courtyard planning, and Eliel's original master plan for the Cranbrook Academy of Art of 1925 (fig. 2) and its subsequent development. While the boys' school, perhaps a belated swan song for Scandinavian national romanticism of the sort exemplified by Ragnar Östberg's Stockholm City Hall (1924), displays an original interpretation of both classical and Gothic decorative elements, it also bears comparison with its more literal collegiate Gothic contemporaries, such as Ralph Adams Cram's Graduate College at Princeton (1910) and James Gamble Rogers's Harkness Memorial Quadrangle at Yale (1917–21).[7]

The Cranbrook Academy of Art's plan is, however, something else altogether. While retaining both the armature of an axially organized Beaux-Arts composition and plenty of the picturesque play of towers and vistas, nooks and crannies that make the boys' school charming, it also exhibits a much looser, more open, and potentially more dynamic composition, which might even seem to parallel the mainly unbuilt compositional experiments of European modernists, such as Le Corbusier, Hannes Meyer, or the Russian constructivists, in the 1920s. Indeed, the notoriously influential compositional tour-de-force of Le Corbusier's entry in the 1927 League of Nations competition, which Eliel Saarinen entered as well, shows up again much more explicitly in some of Eliel and Eero's campus plans of the 1930s and 1940s, such as their entry to the competition for the Art Center at Wheaton College in Norton, Massachusetts, in 1938, as well as in the submissions of others, including Richard Neutra and Percival Goodman. All were clearly influenced by the layered planes, offset axes, and functional expression of Le Corbusier's scheme for the league.[8]

In the case of the art academy plan, however, the more relevant comparison is to an even more familiar, but perhaps less expected, urban design paradigm, the Piazza San Marco in Venice, with its gentle, almost imperceptible, forced perspective, its brilliant orchestration and punctuation of movement and vistas, and its dramatic mastery of spatial sequence. Less expected, perhaps, given the almost total absence of direct references in the plan as built over the years, but in the 1925 master plan one meets quite clear allusions at every turn. This comes as no surprise to anyone who has read Eliel Saarinen's 1943 book, *The City*, where the Piazza San Marco is given pride of place in a discussion of the medieval city that adumbrates much of what his, and apparently Eero's, campus planning and urban design projects sought to realize.[9] Nor, perhaps, should it be surprising to find a pencil drawing on yellow trace in the Eero Saarinen Papers at Yale of a partial but unmistakable plan of the piazza. This devotion to the iconic image of the Piazza San Marco, and much of the art of sequence and vista that characterizes Eliel's work and the best of Eero's campus designs, are traceable to the critical figure of Camillo Sitte, whose 1889 book, *City Planning According to Artistic Principles*, is central to Eliel's chapter on civic rehabilitation, as it was to both Hegemann and even Le Corbusier, before the latter proclaimed his rejection of Sitte's approach as "the pack donkey's way." It is Sitte's account of the Piazza San Marco—which he described as "the loveliest spot in the whole wide world"—that should be understood as the *locus classicus* for all of the above, if not for much more of modern urbanism than is usually recognized.[10]

Thus it is that the compositional strategies of the Piazza San Marco, mediated by Eliel's work at Cranbrook, became almost a signature theme in the campus planning work that Eero undertook as he began his career, first in collaboration with his father and then on his own. Their entry in the 1938

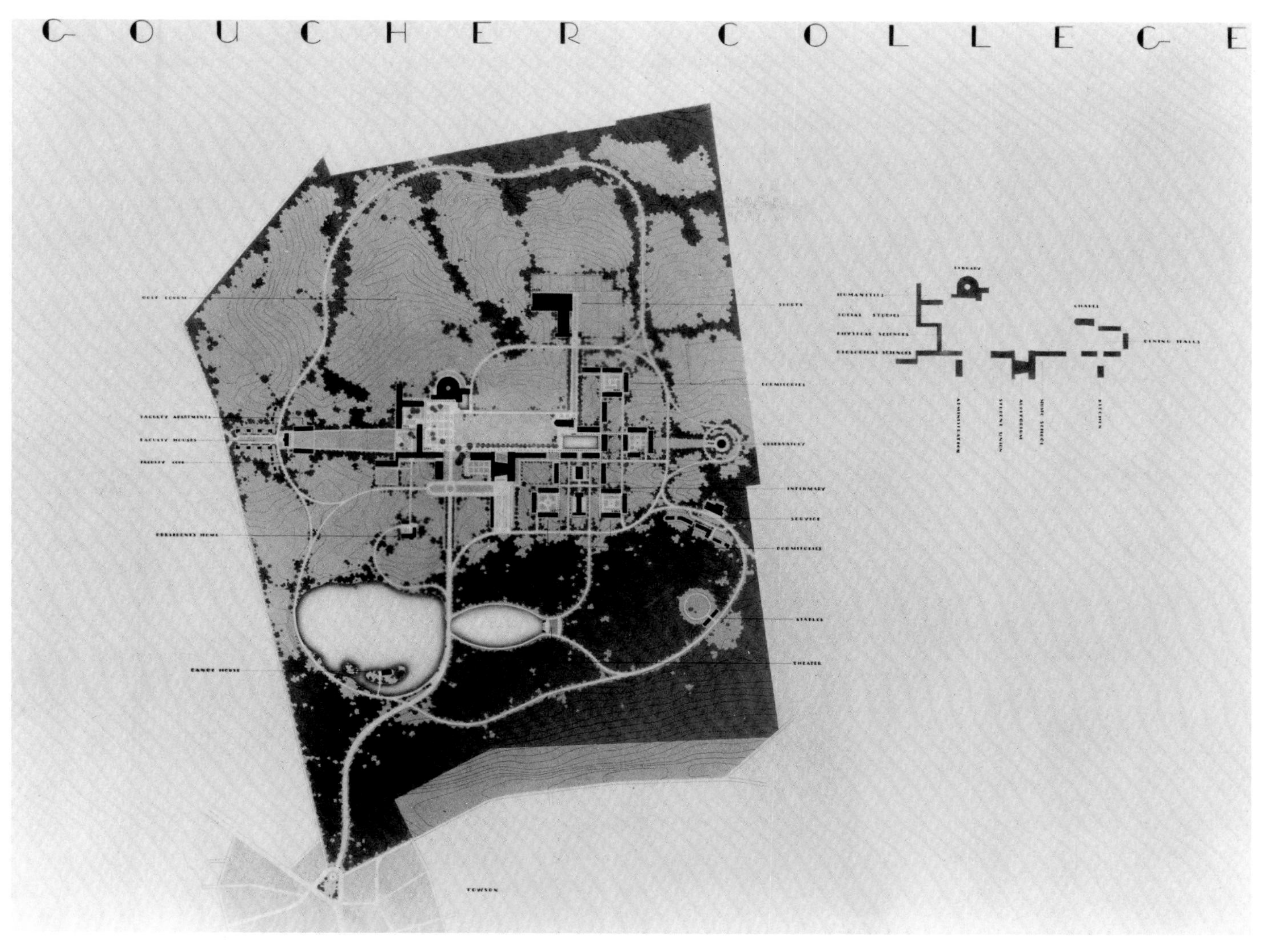

Fig. 3 Eliel and Eero Saarinen, Goucher College campus plan, Towson, Maryland, 1938, competition entry

competition for a master plan for Goucher College in Towson, Maryland, is almost pure Cranbrook in its overall composition, but symptomatically modernist at the level of individual buildings and the joints—or lack thereof—between them (fig. 3).[11] The 1945–47 campus plan for Drake University in Des Moines, Iowa, credited to Saarinen, Swanson, and Saarinen (largely unrealized, although here as in so many other cases Eero would later build a few fairly disappointing individual buildings and groups), deploys a rather attenuated but still recognizable variation on the San Marco theme to structure the main axis and cross axis of the campus, and then repeats it several times, almost mechanistically, at smaller scale to organize the dormitory groups (fig. 4). The 1945–47 plan for Stephens College in Columbia, Missouri, also credited to Saarinen, Swanson, and Saarinen, where Eero would later build a chapel that anticipated the North Christian Church in Columbus, Indiana, has some quite similar large compositional moves, but squared up and stiffened, almost to the point of rigor mortis.

Far freer and much more open and generous in every respect is Eero's first mainly independent campus plan, developed in 1949–52 for the recently founded Brandeis University in Waltham, Massachusetts. While quite recognizable elements and local groupings of buildings around piazza-like spaces remain, the overall plan is very fresh in its landscape-oriented, suburban, even literally picturesque grouping of educational structures and dormitories around a large central open space with no dominant axes (fig. 5). The aerial perspective gives a particularly strong sense of the campus as almost a clearing in the woods, harking back to such poignant images of early settlement on the North American continent as Peter Gordon's famous 1734 depiction of Savannah, or a wonderfully evocative 1839 view of the founding of Dartmouth College suggesting not only a recently cleared wilderness but also the sort

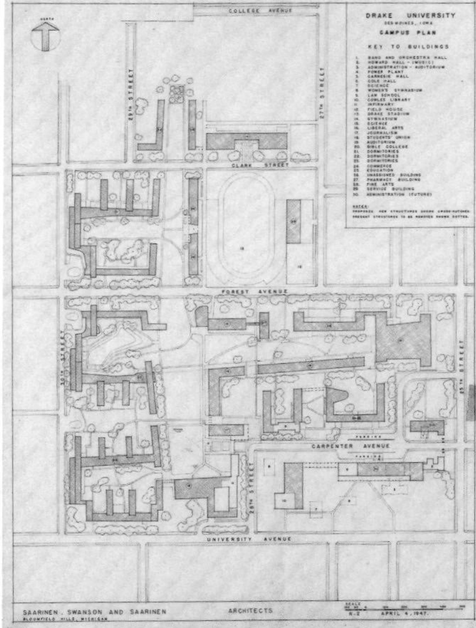

Fig. 4 Saarinen, Swanson, and Saarinen, Drake University campus plan, Des Moines, Iowa, 1945–47

Fig. 5 Eero Saarinen and Associates, Brandeis University campus plan, Waltham, Massachusetts, 1949–52, aerial perspective

of elemental academic community of teacher and pupils that had been conventionalized as early as 1465, in a manuscript image portraying William of Wykeham, the founder of New College, Oxford, England, lecturing to assembled fellows and students against the backdrop of what was arguably the first collegiate quadrangle.[12]

These iconic references would perhaps be a bit of a stretch, were it not for the survival of an extraordinary drawing prepared by Matthew Nowicki, the brilliant young architect then in Saarinen's office, already known for his Dorten Arena in Raleigh, North Carolina (1953). He would become famous for his contributions to the design of Chandigarh, before his tragic death in a plane crash in 1950. Nowicki's sketch is the culminating image of a suite of perspectives illustrating not just the projected architecture and interiors but also the life of the Brandeis campus at all scales, from that of the individual dorm room to the campus as a whole (figs. 6, 7). Unlike the other drawings, the one conspicuously labeled "The Idea of a University" (referencing John Henry Newman's famous book of 1854, *The Idea of a University*, in which the university is described as a gathering of strangers from many places in one place) is allegorical (fig. 8). A rather surreal landscape of vaguely fortified medieval buildings, elements of a garden, and free-floating paving patterns is inhabited by highly stylized academic aliens, who are apparently focused on a teacher figure mounted on a dais and sheltered by a baldachin. Nowicki seems to have assembled these drawings in a manuscript, perhaps intended for publication, and collectively they make a strong argument that Saarinen and his associates were clearly and tendentiously connecting their formal experiments in campus planning directly to the social and educational theme of community in a way more often associated with Louis Kahn's institutional work in the 1960s. In any case, it is not at all the theme that has come most readily to mind for critics of Saarinen's work.[13]

After such an ambitious and idealistic master plan, it is disappointing to find—and surely was disappointing for Saarinen and his associates—that his built work at Brandeis was limited to a seemingly nondescript dormitory and dining-hall group. Yet there is important revelation even in that rather bland ensemble, which was, after all, conceived not as a stand-alone tour de force, of the sort that one would later associate with Saarinen, but rather as a hierarchically situated component of the largely spatial and social organism of the campus. As such, although it may seem strange to attribute these intentions to Saarinen, it is fundamentally to be understood as *fabric*, rather than figure or monument. Indeed, the more one surveys the broader field of Saarinen's campus work—the ambitious master plans, and the more or less peripheral projects, often dormitories, that usually issue from the planning process—the clearer it becomes that Saarinen had a somewhat surprising sense of decorum about the role that individual buildings play in the shaping of the larger environment and community. In retrospect this observation is confirmed by a document such as the Michigan talk, but at the height of his career relatively little attention was paid to the many dormitory projects at places like Antioch, Brandeis, Concordia, the University of Chicago, the University of Pennsylvania, and Vassar. They were not very inspiring buildings in their own right, especially in light of what was being featured in the architectural media at the time by Saarinen and others. Not until Yale's Morse and Stiles Colleges did critics focus on this particular building type, and then for completely different reasons that are only peripherally related to the exemplary status of these projects—whatever their relative quality—in the context of Saarinen's campus planning work, which is of course how he would have seen them. In fact, two of his best known highly figurative (and therefore more characteristic, according to conventional accounts of his work) campus buildings, the Kresge Auditorium and Chapel at MIT in Cambridge, Massachusetts, were intended by Saarinen to be seen against the backdrop of an entourage of framing buildings, which would play the role of a more generic fabric still lacking in the newer parts of the MIT

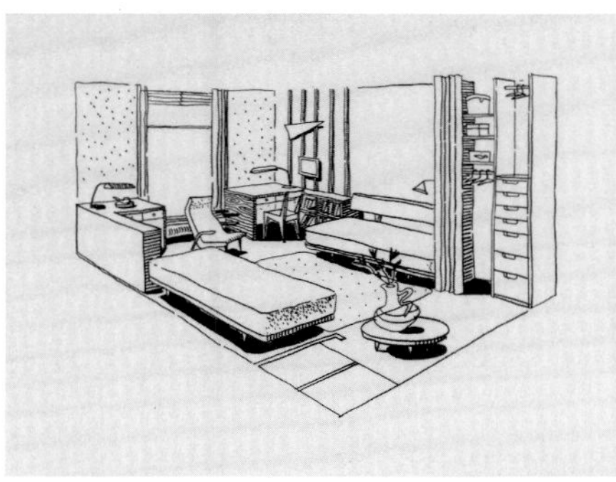

Fig. 6 Eero Saarinen and Associates, Brandeis University, perspective of a dormitory room by Matthew Nowicki

Fig. 7 Eero Saarinen and Associates, Brandeis University, Ridgewood Quadrangle Dormitories, 1949–50, perspective of lecture hall by Matthew Nowicki

Fig. 8 (right) Eero Saarinen and Associates, "The Idea of a University," rendering for Brandeis University project by Matthew Nowicki

campus. Even, or perhaps especially, the Yale colleges are, as I discuss below, to be more fully understood if they are viewed in relation to Saarinen's numerous college residential projects, which in effect led up to this rather more notorious version of the type.

A crucial intermediate step along this trajectory is the work that Saarinen and his firm did over at least half a decade at the University of Chicago. Beginning in 1955 Saarinen developed a series of analyses, master plans, area plans, and more detailed projects situated in the regular grid of Chicago's South Side, while evolving variations on the basic theme of the university's original collegiate Gothic quads. The boldest and most original planning move was the creation of two blocks on the southern edge of the great open swath of the Midway and the attempt to appropriate the Midway itself as a new central mall for the campus, as opposed to the edge—or rift—that it remains to this day despite Saarinen's efforts. Neither of the groups actually realized by Saarinen, a women's dormitory complex and the law school (figs. 9, 10) on the south side of the Midway, is likely to find a place among Saarinen's greatest hits—the law school being superficially similar to but not nearly as successful as Paul Rudolph's contemporaneous efforts at Wellesley College in Wellesley, Massachusetts—but the planning strategies and experience of working with the collegiate Gothic courtyards as context, and the invention of a new kind of campus space through the rereading of existing patterns, anticipate both the achievements and shortcomings of the Yale colleges. The methodology developed at Brandeis of studying interior and exterior spaces and their uses, as a nested hierarchy of social and educational experience, from the individual dormitory unit to the seminar room, social spaces, and lecture halls, to the campus as a whole, is developed even further at Chicago, but in a style distinctly more like advertising and in a manner quite a bit closer to the corporate boardroom than one finds in the more allusive, even somewhat spiritual, communitarian mode of the Brandeis drawings.

All of these projects are, both literally and figuratively, miles away from Saarinen's work at Concordia Senior College in Fort Wayne, Indiana, executed between 1953 and 1958 (fig. 11). At what was essentially a Lutheran seminary, Saarinen deployed and discussed some fairly direct references to Italian hill towns and northern European and alpine villages, although unlike at Yale, where such references were obvious enough to provoke considerable controversy, at Concordia the casual observer is not likely to think immediately of San Gimignano or Aichbühl.[14] Ironically, Concordia, where for once Saarinen had the opportunity to design an entire campus and all its buildings as the kind of "total environment" whose difficulty he lamented in his Michigan talk, is one of the least convincing renditions of his aspirations, more like a summer camp or state park for suburbanites than the sort of timeless, organic

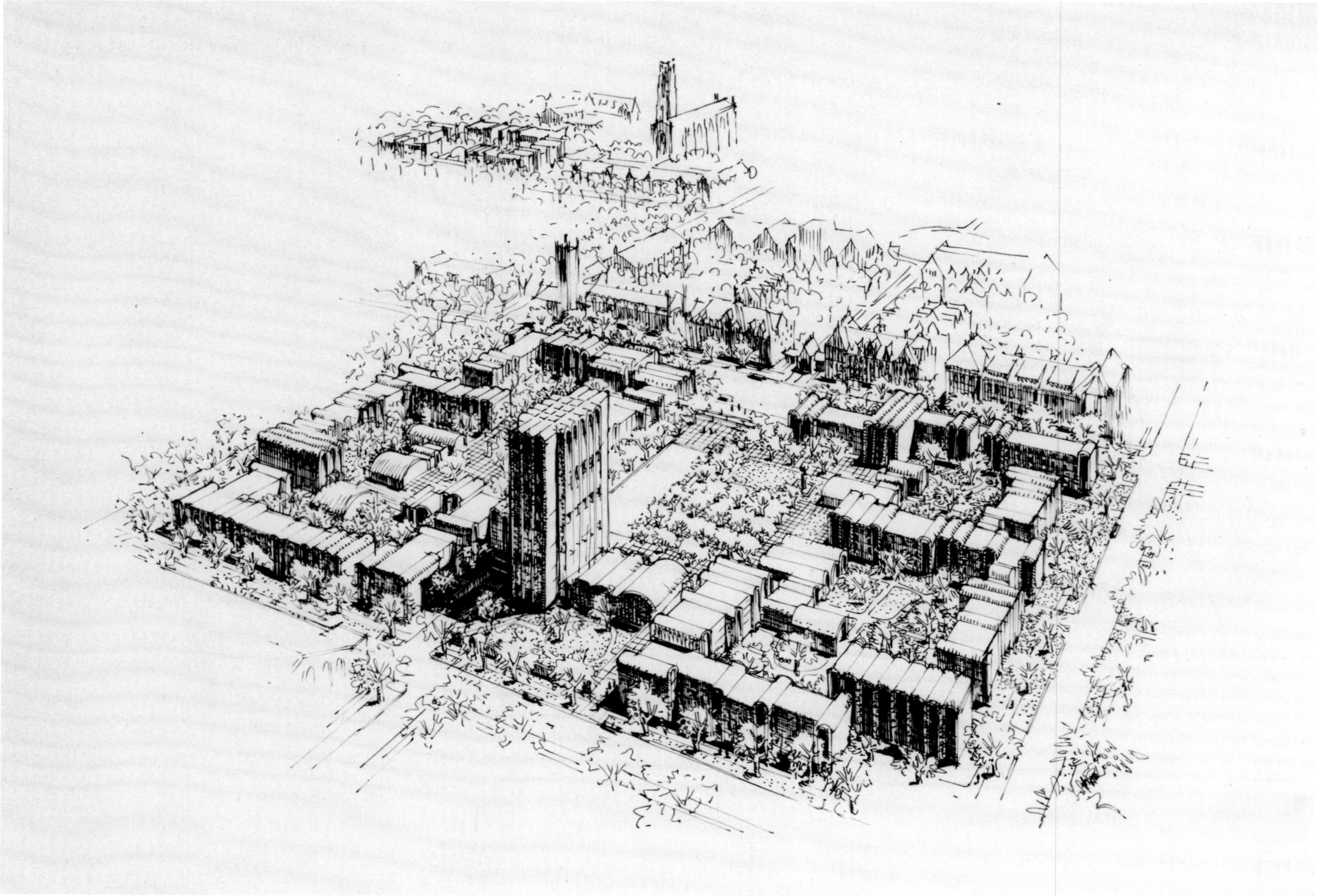

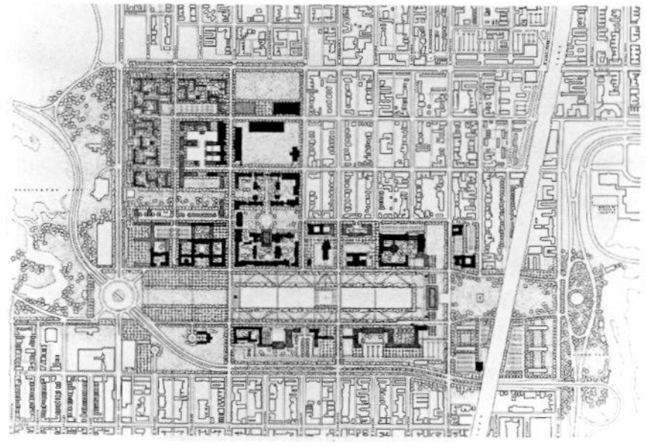

Fig. 9 University of Chicago master plan, aerial rendering of proposed residential quadrangle, 1955–60

Fig. 10 Eero Saarinen and Associates, University of Chicago master plan, 1955

community to which his references alluded. And yet, how different from most of its contemporaries, the continuous mat buildings and megastructures that represented international state-of-the-art campus planning in the late 1950s and early 1960s. Compared with the European campus projects of Candilis, Josic, and Woods, such as the Berlin Free University or the project for Bochum University or, in the United States, Walter Netsch's Chicago Circle, Concordia seems both touchingly naive for the architect of General Motors and IBM, and more an anticipation of later projects, like Charles Moore's Kresge College, or for that matter Saarinen's own roughly contemporary work at Yale, where the imagery of a traditional town is adapted and deployed as both representation of and hopeful framework for a sense of cloistered community in the midst of the mass corporate suburban anomie of the postwar landscape.

The Yale colleges are, for better and for worse, the culmination of this extended meditation on the campus as an enclave of traditional community, but in the same year that Saarinen finished his work at Concordia and began his work at Yale, he also completed a relatively neglected project that seems to form a more direct bridge to both the form and function of the Yale colleges: the Emma Hartman Noyes House at Vassar College in Poughkeepsie, New York. An early site plan in the Saarinen Papers at Yale shows the role he envisioned for this particular piece of campus fabric, mediating between the older, more formally organized areas of the campus; the freer, rather chaotic smattering of buildings that came later; and ultimately the landscape itself (fig. 12). In this respect, the hemicycle Saarinen envisioned, of which only one quadrant was built, merits comparison with its obvious precedent, John Wood the Younger's Royal Crescent in Bath, England, of 1767.[15] But it also, at least at the most literal level, anticipates the most ambitious version of Saarinen's residential college project at Yale.

Working at Yale was not just another collegiate commission for Saarinen,

Fig. 11 Eero Saarinen and Associates, Concordia Senior College, Fort Wayne, Indiana, 1953–58, model

nor even an example of his continued ascent through the corporate and institutional hierarchy, but also a return to the place where he had studied architecture in the early 1930s—sent there, in fact, by his father, whose letters to Dean Everett Meeks requesting his son's admission as a special student survive in the Yale School of Architecture files, along with Eero's transcripts. It should be remembered that Yale was at this time in the midst of its greatest building boom, fueled in large part by the construction of the residential colleges, a system to which Yale had been able to convert in spectacular architectural style thanks to a gift from Edward Harkness in the late 1920s. When Saarinen arrived in 1931, Harkness Quadrangle was being converted into Saybrook and Branford Colleges, and five other new residential colleges in both collegiate Gothic and Georgian style were under way, to be opened in 1933, at the beginning of Saarinen's final year at Yale. The principal project architect for the Yale colleges in the office of James Gamble Rogers, Otto Faelten, was teaching in the department of architecture, and Saarinen had him as a critic in 1932–33. Not surprisingly, one of the problems he assigned to his students was "A College of a University." Saarinen submitted his project on January 23, 1933, and also apparently did a sketch problem for a college master's house. Neither of these designs seems to have survived, but one does not need them to be reasonably certain that Saarinen was thinking about the architecture of a collegiate community well before he began working at Yale in the mid-1950s. Even without his student projects at Yale, one would be on pretty firm ground suggesting that after Cranbrook, Yale would have to be the other primary breeding ground for Saarinen's observations and thoughts on campus planning and architecture.

Not that he stopped there. To date the Yale archives have yielded at least twenty drawings of comparative campus plans to scale, including all those mentioned in the Michigan talk, which exhibit "unity of environment," as well as others, notably Mies van der Rohe's IIT plan. Such drawings bear out the testimony of office associates that projects typically began with research. In the case of Yale we also have President A. Whitney Griswold's account of his urging the architect to visit Oxford University (as if Yale itself was not sufficiently ancient to serve as a source of inspiration), and Saarinen's rejoinder that he would add San Gimignano to the itinerary for good measure.[16] Now references to these sorts of direct historical precedents are usually produced as evidence for the prosecution in discussions of Saarinen's sentimentally picturesque planning and creeping historicism, of the sort that led Reyner Banham to utter his famous pronouncement about Yale being "a very sick place."[17] But for the moment at least, I am interested less in the proto-postmodernism of Saarinen's stylistic and material adventures, and more in their relation to his planning process—at Yale certainly but also at the colleges he had worked at previously—and to his self-critique before the Michigan regents.

Now that the Saarinen Papers are accessible at Yale, one can begin to see what has always been suggested—that is, the broad scope of Saarinen's planning work at Yale, but also well beyond, into the core of New Haven's downtown and neighborhoods. Saarinen's work at Yale took place at the height of New Haven's important and deeply problematic experiment with redevelopment. Saarinen was by no means the principal planner of, or even the public face of Yale's role in, urban redevelopment in New Haven. That role was already taken by Yale planning professor Maurice Rotival, a French planner steeped in prewar European modernism, who as early as 1941 had produced dramatically conceived and rendered plans for the comprehensive rebuilding of much of central New Haven, including systems of inner and outer ring roads. Nevertheless, Saarinen's work, fragmentary though the evidence may be, seems to be a clear testament to Yale's embrace of, and even complicity in, the grand schemes and their automobile-oriented ideology. Saarinen's fascinating area studies for each section of Yale's campus not only propose the restructuring of the university's historic fabric but are tied to thoroughly contemporary ideas about urban transportation,

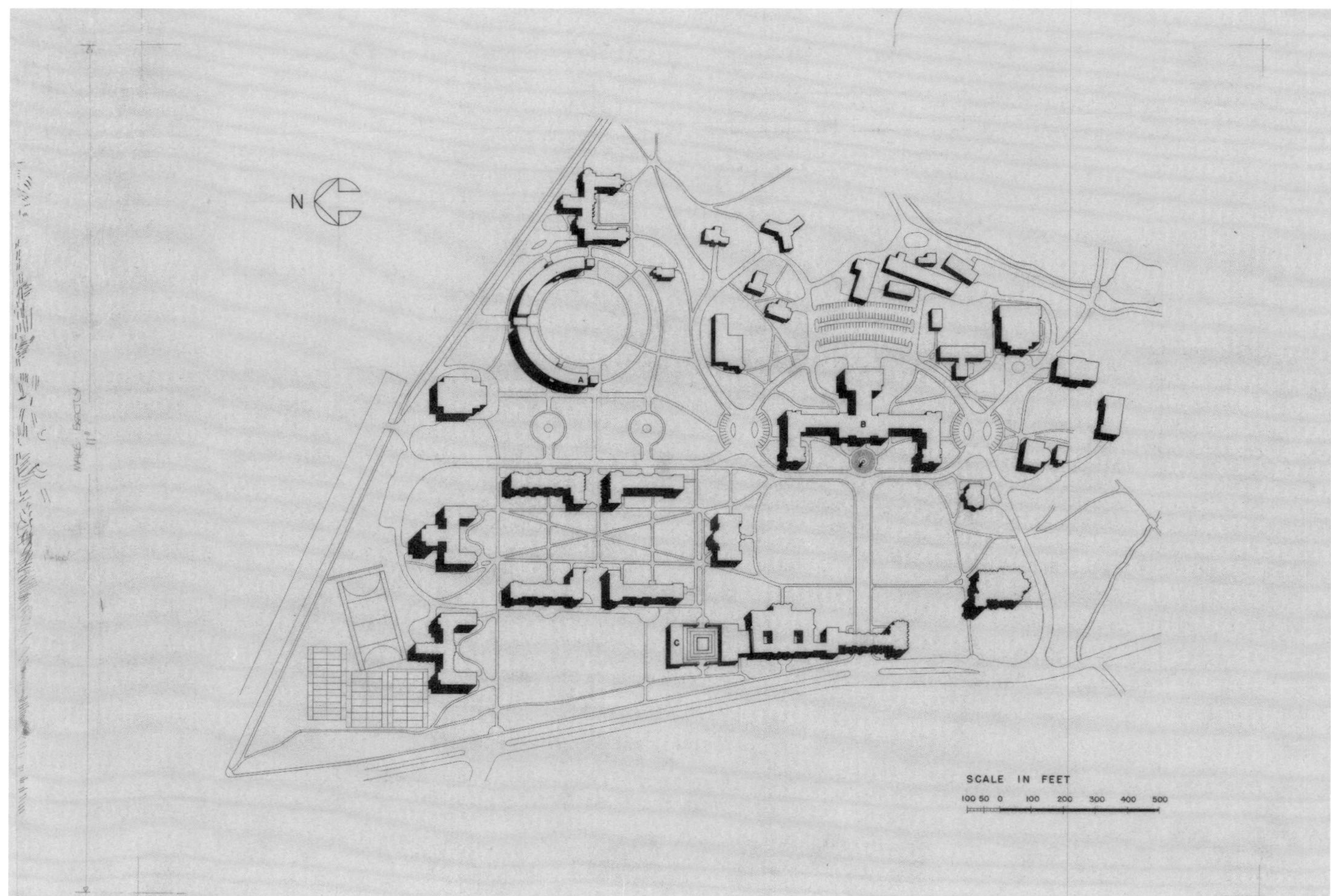

Fig. 12 Emma Hartman Noyes House, Vassar College, Poughkeepsie, New York, 1954–58, early site plan of college. Noyes House, with its curving footprint, is near center of plan.

including satellite parking structures of the sort New Haven was building, and an extensive inner ring-road system that would complement the larger-scale regional highway plans funded with federal dollars, while bypassing and further insulating the Yale campus. Many of the studies exhibit the potential contextual brilliance of some of Saarinen's planning work, as we have seen earlier in this essay, but others are as heavy-handed as some of the worst corporate and governmental complexes proposed by Saarinen and his contemporaries.

Proposals for completing the eastern end of the Cross Campus axis by rebuilding the block east of College Street, presented in a rather ominous rendering, and for the restructuring of Science Hill as something like a suburban shopping center or corporate office park, fall into the latter category. And while the early studies for Morse and Stiles Colleges seem to promise little more, they illustrate a gradual transformation to something altogether different and seemingly unprecedented in the work of Saarinen and his generation. Just when the unmistakable plan image of the thirteenth-century Piazza del Campo in Siena makes its appearance in the development of this project is unclear. But in the full-blown scheme (fig. 13) *three* college courtyards (loosely based on the scale and configuration of the adjacent Hall of Graduate Studies courtyard, which is deftly drawn into the figure-ground composition of the entire block) combine to shape a space facing the Payne Whitney Gymnasium and its tower, just as the Piazza del Campo faces and frames the Palazzo Pubblico and its iconic Torre Mangia. The paving pattern of this complex literally mimics that of the Campo. And although really unnecessary by now for confirmation, the smoking gun has turned up in the Yale archives in the form of a sketch plan of the Piazza del Campo, clearly labeled, drawn to scale on yellow tracing paper.

Interestingly, in the most ambitious of Saarinen's schemes for the colleges the principal approach to Payne Whitney would not have been the famously

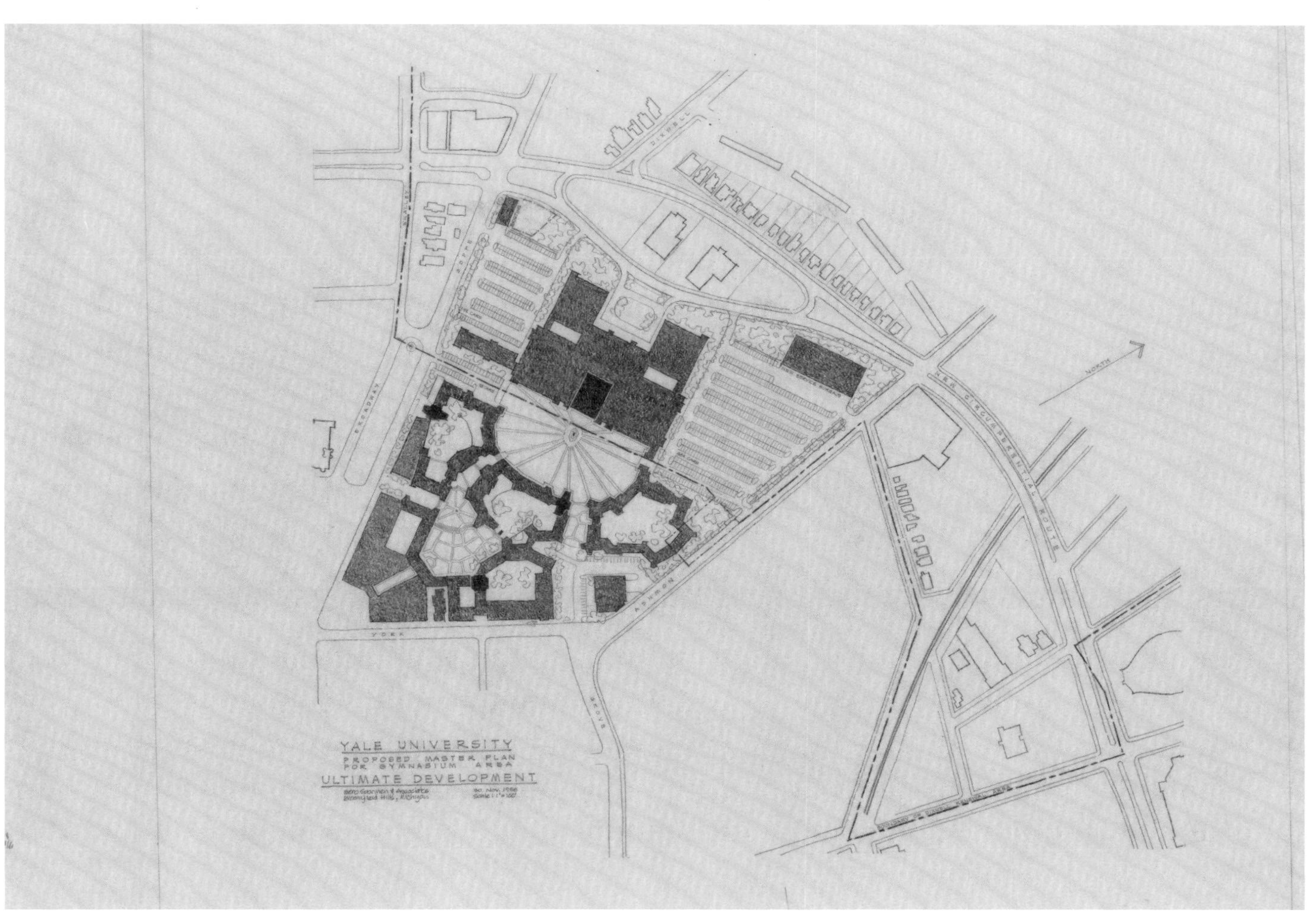

Fig. 13 Eero Saarinen and Associates, Samuel F. B. Morse and Ezra Stiles Colleges, Yale University, New Haven, Connecticut, 1958–62, site plan with third courtyard

picturesque midblock route up and down stairs between Morse and Stiles, but rather along Tower Parkway, a relatively new road laid out by John Russell Pope as he planned the gymnasium, the closure of which would have been made possible by Saarinen's ring-road bypass behind the gym. The third courtyard was, of course, not built, alas (its site is now occupied somewhat less convincingly by Herbert Newman's "Swing Dorm"), but a reminder of the priority of this approach remains in the brilliant alignment and conversation of towers along Tower Parkway (fig. 14). This, rather than the much more frequently photographed "hill-town" view of the Payne Whitney tower framed by the two colleges, is the real achievement of Saarinen's picturesque sensibility, interpolating the new tower of Morse College in between Rogers's Hall of Graduate Studies tower and Pope's massive gymnasium frontispiece. It is traceable not only to Saarinen's fairly conventional travel sketches of Italian hill towns—no match for Kahn's in power or perception—but also to his father's compositions at Cranbrook, and even more directly to the analyses of urban streets by his father's mentor, Sitte.

But for all the problematic brilliance of Saarinen's recuperation of the picturesque, it is the figure of the Campo that seems to lead us in new directions—and to preliminary conclusions—about the real significance of his campus planning work. One of the great public spaces of a period of civic efflorescence to which Saarinen and countless others have been recurrently attracted, the Campo and its urban entourage, including the Torre Mangia, also represent the ascendancy of the *comune* as a unified proposition over the separate identities of the individual noble families in their towered and fortified enclaves, and of the individual neighborhoods, the *contrade*, of Siena. At Yale these concepts come together in a neutral and regulated space for the good and honor of the entire city, and indeed Saarinen's exterior space between the colleges and the gym is just a sort of quasi-public arena, at the next larger scale and degree of commonality from individual cloistered

Fig. 14 Yale University, view west on Tower Parkway featuring towers of (left to right) Hall of Graduate Studies, Samuel F. B. Morse College, and Payne Whitney Gymnasium

college courtyards that Yale, for the most part, lacks. The Cross Campus is such a space, relative to Calhoun College and the two courts of Berkeley College, but Saarinen was able to invent the image and idea of an entirely new one, even if it replaced a public square formerly surrounded by New Haven's main high schools. Granted, it has little of the stern civic grandeur of Kahn's haunting rendition of the Campo, or of the institutional presence of the courtyard at Kahn's Salk Institute, but its aspiration, impressive enough at the time, was both to engage context and to create community within the one enclave of the American landscape where Saarinen and other architects have felt most comfortable and supported doing so—the college campus.

Notes

1. Eero Saarinen, address to the regents of the University of Michigan on campus planning, untitled, undated manuscript, Eero Saarinen Papers, Manuscripts and Archives, Yale University, 7–8.

2. Eero Saarinen, "Campus Planning: The Unique World of the University," *Architectural Record*, Nov. 1960, 123–30.

3. Saarinen, address on campus planning, 3.

4. For developments in the 1970s and the general history of American campus planning and architecture, see Paul Turner, *Campus: An American Planning Tradition* (Cambridge: MIT Press, 1984), chapter 7.

5. Saarinen, address on campus planning, 4. This paragraph, along with some marginal notes written by Saarinen, is crossed out in the manuscript.

6. Werner Hegemann and Elbert Peets, *The American Vitruvius: An Architect's Handbook of Civic Art* (New York: Architectural Book Publishing, 1922), 110–31; Turner, *Campus*; Stefanos Polyzoides and Peter de Bretteville, "Eight California Campuses to 1945: An American Culture of Place-making," in *The New City 2: The American City* (Miami: University of Miami School of Architecture, 1994), 52–95.

7. For the history and architecture of the Cranbrook schools, see the comprehensive guide by Kathryn Bishop Eckert, *The Campus Guide: Cranbrook* (New York: Princeton Architectural Press, 2001), and David De Long, "Eliel Saarinen and the Cranbrook Tradition in Architecture and Urban Design," in *Design in America: The Cranbrook Vision, 1925–1950*, by Robert Judson Clark et al. (New York: Abrams, in association with the Detroit Institute of Arts and the Metropolitan Museum of Art, 1983), 47–89. See also Peter Papademetriou, "Coming of Age: Eero Saarinen and Modern American Architecture," *Perspecta* 21 (1984), 116–43.

8. For these and other competitions of the late 1930s, the entries to all of which display similar compositional preoccupations that might be described as the more or less successful hybridization of European modernist group planning of the 1920s with the American campus planning tradition, see James D. Kornwolf, ed., *Modernism in America, 1937–1941* (Williamsburg, Va.: Joseph and Margaret Muscarelle Museum of Art, College of William and Mary, 1985).

9. Eliel Saarinen, *The City, Its Growth, Its Decay, Its Future* (New York: Reinhold, 1943), 31–72. Interestingly, Eliel cites the Piazza San Marco as a successful example of "style combination," of the sort that Eero would come to regret in the case of modern campus architecture.

10. Ibid., 103–38; Hegemann and Peets, *The American Vitruvius*, 7–27; H. Allen Brooks, "Jeanneret and Sitte: Le Corbusier's Earliest Ideas on Urban Design," in *In Search of Modern Architecture: A Tribute to Henry-Russell Hitchcock*, ed. Helen Searing (Cambridge: MIT Press, 1982), 278–97; Camillo Sitte, *City Planning According to Artistic Principles*, trans. George R. Collins and Christiane Craseman Collins (New York: Random House, 1965), 58–59.

11. Cf. Kornwolf, *Modernism in America*, 69–123.

12. Turner, *Campus*, 8–10, 16–18.

13. I have found a reference to the Nowicki manuscript, entitled "A Foundation for Learning—Planning the Campus of Brandeis University," in the collection of his papers at North Carolina State University, although I have not examined it. These and other studies from the Saarinen office should be compared not only to Kahn's famous sketches entitled "The Room" and "The City" from 1971, but also the dorm room studies, as highly rhetorical representations of an ideal modern dwelling unit, should be compared to drawings such as Le Corbusier's 1922 sketch of a prototypical artist's studio unit. On Kahn's preoccupation with the idea of community, and on communitarian ideals in postwar America in general, see Sarah Williams Goldhagen, *Louis Kahn's Situated Modernism* (New Haven: Yale University Press, 2001).

14. "For a New College, an Old Village Silhouette," *Architectural Forum*, Dec. 1954, 132–37; and "A 'Village' Design for a College Campus," *Progressive Architecture*, Dec. 1958, 88–101.

15. And now, Machado and Silvetti's campus plan and dormitories at Princeton.

16. Jonathan Barnett, "The New Collegiate Architecture at Yale," *Architectural Record*, Apr. 1962, 129.

17. Banham, "The New Yale Colleges," *Architectural Forum*, Dec. 1962, 110. This issue is well covered in Turner, *Campus*, 294–97, and revisited from a more personal perspective in Vincent Scully, *Yale in New Haven: Architecture and Urbanism* (New Haven: Yale University Press, 2004), 309-12.

Compiled by
Eeva-Liisa Pelkonen
with the assistance of
Donald Albrecht
Marc Coir
Leslie S. Edwards
Rosamond Fletcher
Sean Khorsandi
Kevin Roche
Robert A. M. Stern

chronology

1910–21

Eero Saarinen born August 20, 1910, in Kirkkonummi, Finland. Family includes many architects and designers: father Eliel (1873–1950), with whom Eero shares a birth date, is a famous National Romantic architect, and mother Louise "Loja" Saarinen (née Gesellius; 1879–1968) is a textile designer and sculptor, as well as the sister of Eliel's business partner Herman Gesellius. Eero's sister, Eva-Lisa, or "Pipsan" (1905–1979), becomes a designer and interior decorator. The family is bilingual; Loja's family speaks Swedish, and Eliel's, Finnish.

Eero grows up at Hvitträsk, the studio and residence twenty-two miles west of Helsinki that Eliel and his two partners, Gesellius and Armas Lindgren, built for their families. There Eero meets many cultural luminaries, including the German art historian Julius Meier-Graefe, the editor of the influential magazine *Kunstblatt;* Russian writer Maxim Gorky; and Finnish composer Jean Sibelius.

Eero is educated by a Swedish-speaking governess, and his uncle Severi Saarinen tutors him in the Finnish language. Isolated from his peers, Eero spends a lot of time at his father's studio. Eliel will later tell stories about his son playing under his drafting table and drawing nudes as early as the age of ten. Like most boys, Eero is fascinated by adventure stories. He especially likes books about American Indians, such as those by James Fenimore Cooper, and tales of medieval knights, especially Sir Walter Scott's *Ivanhoe,* from which he copies battle scenes.

1922

Wins first place in a matchstick design contest sponsored by a Swedish newspaper. This competition, the first of many that Eero will participate in throughout his career, calls for a story illustrated with pictures made entirely of matches. For his tragic tale of a lady abandoned after two suitors are burned to death, which Eliel helps write, Eero is awarded 30 Swedish Kroner, or $8. The same week, Eliel receives word that he has won second place in the international competition to design a new tower for the *Chicago Tribune* newspaper headquarters and is awarded $20,000. The design is widely celebrated as the best entry, garnering praise from Chicago architect Louis Sullivan, who writes in the February 1923 issue of *Architectural Record* that the unrealized proposal "is not a lonely cry in the wilderness, it is a voice, resonant and rich, ringing amidst the wealth and joy of life."

1923

Encouraged by the critical acclaim his *Chicago Tribune* competition entry has generated, and discouraged by the lack of work in Finland during the early years of the country's independence from Russia, Eliel decides to use his prize money to move to the United States. He arrives in Chicago early in the year and is joined by his family later in the spring; they move to 1136 Maple Avenue in suburban Evanston. Eero enters the local junior high school in the fall, and Eliel starts work on a proposal for Chicago's lakefront. He also serves as a visiting professor of architectural design for one month in the department of architecture at the University of Michigan's College of Engineering in Ann Arbor, during which time he and his family live on campus in two rooms in the Michigan Union. In December, the Saarinens meet George Gough Booth, owner of the *Detroit News*, at a welcoming reception for Eliel.

1924

The Saarinens move to 8 Geddes Heights in Ann Arbor in early January, when Eliel accepts a semester-long visiting professorship at the University of Michigan. One of his students is Henry Scripps Booth, whose father, George, commissions Eliel to prepare a waterfront study for Detroit. The family returns to Hvitträsk for the summer, as they will most summers until the outbreak of World War II. In the fall Eliel accepts Booth's invitation to design an Academy of Art at Cranbrook, Booth's estate in Bloomfield Hills, Michigan. Eero enters ninth grade at Baldwin High School in nearby Birmingham.

1925

In the spring, Eliel presents a grand scheme for the Academy of Art with a model made by Loja and Eero. Eliel returns to Cranbrook in the fall as the consultant to Booth and J. Robert F. Swanson (1900–1981), both of whom had been Eliel's students at the University of Michigan. The Saarinen family moves to Booth's Cranbrook estate, living first in part of the rectory, and later in an old farmhouse formerly occupied by Italian laborers.

1926

Eero's block prints are published in his school's yearbook, *The Baldwinian;* others appear the following year. He wins first prize in a national soap sculpture competition by carving a Rodinesque figure out of a bar of Ivory soap, the competition's sponsor. The Cranbrook Architectural Office is formed, and Eliel is named head and chief architect. Eero works in the office to gain experience, as he will continue to do for many years. He enters the American Gas Association small house competition to design a six-room dwelling, and though he is only in his teens and has to obtain permission to enter, it is granted because of his experience with Eliel. In May, Pipsan, encountering parental opposition to her intended marriage to Robert Swanson, elopes with him to Toledo, Ohio. In June, the old farmhouse where the family has been living is demolished and they move to Lone Pine Road in Bloomfield Hills. Construction of the Cranbrook School for Boys begins.

Hvitträsk in snow

Eero Saarinen, nude drawing, ca. 1920

Eero with his prize-winning soap sculpture, 1926

1927

The Saarinen family continues to work together on the Cranbrook School for Boys: Pipsan stencils ceilings and Eero executes sculptural details, such as

Eero Saarinen, sculpture of kneeling woman made while a student at the Académie de la Grande Chaumière, Paris, 1929–30

Eero Saarinen, Page and Marquis Hall at Cranbrook School for Boys, watercolor, ca. 1930

Pewabic tiles for fireplaces and small decorative cranes, the symbol of Cranbrook, to be inset into the dining hall's chairs. The school, originally called Cranebrook, opens in September.

1928

The Saarinen House, then known as Academy Group Residence #1, is completed. Between 1928 and 1930 Eero designs furniture for the house, including Loja's dressing table in the master bedroom.

1929

In February, Eero graduates from Baldwin High School; he works in the Cranbrook Architectural Office until June, then summers at Hvitträsk. In September, he begins studying sculpture at the Académie de la Grande Chaumière in Paris.

1930

In May, completes his studies at the Académie. Returns to Michigan to assist his father in the Cranbrook Architectural Office for the rest of the year, designing furniture for Cranbrook's Kingswood School for Girls.

1931

On January 15, Eliel writes to Everett Victor Meeks, dean of the Yale School of Fine Arts and chairman of the department of architecture, requesting permission for Eero to study architecture for two or three years as a special student, without the intention of graduating. Meeks welcomes Eliel's "boy" in a letter dated January 31.

Eero continues work on the Kingswood furniture into the spring, then travels through Europe. Itinerary includes his first visit to Italy.

Eero begins his formal architectural education at the Yale School of Fine Arts on October 1. Meeks's statement in the bulletin defines the program's pedagogical agenda as follows: "The Department of Architecture emphasizes architectural design but gives enough training in engineering to enable a graduate to understand the structural needs of design and to cooperate intelligently with an architect-engineer." During his first semester, Eero takes "Introduction to Architecture" with Carroll L. V. Meeks. He also enrolls in courses on Greek and Roman architecture, descriptive geometry, and calculus.

As part of the general curriculum at Yale, students work through a sequence of projects issued by the Beaux Arts Institute of Design. Each year, finished drawings are sent to the institute in New York to be evaluated for awards in a national competition. Eero's first-year projects include a water tower, a police station, a memorial tunnel entrance, a residence for a college dean, a palace for an exiled monarch, a garden club building, a synagogue, a monumental clock, and a fine city residence, all of which receive medals.

Outside the classroom Saarinen joins the decorating committee of the Biennial Grand Ball, an event organized by art and drama students. Saarinen's classmate Donal McLaughlin (b. 1907) reminiscences: "The hall of antique sculpture was transformed into a circus. Eero was responsible for erecting a screen around the nude Venus de Milo, shielding her from the navel on down. Then, using his sculptor's knowledge, he sketched a full-sized trompe l'oeil of a dancer delicately poised on a thimble."

1932

In the spring, Eero studies elemental design with Shepherd Stevens and takes on freehand drawing, engineering mechanics, medieval architecture, and economics. In recognition of his extensive professional background and studies in Paris, Eero is now listed as a fourth-year degree student on track to graduate with a Bachelor of Fine Arts in Architecture in three years when he reenters Yale in September—a standard duration being four years. His design teachers include Otto Faelten, chief designer at James Gamble Rogers's office and chief

Florence Schust and Eliel Saarinen, photograph by Eero Saarinen, probably mid-1930s

Eero Saarinen, $1,000 bill, student project, November 1933

design critic in the department of architecture; he also studies Renaissance architecture with Carroll Meeks, and sculpture and decorative arts with Theodore Sizer. The calendar Saarinen kept of his activities suggests that this year he also started to work on a design for the competition for the 1940 Olympic stadium in Helsinki, although the Olympics are later canceled because of World War II. It is not known whether he submits a design.

Eliel Saarinen is appointed the first president and head of the architecture department of the newly founded Cranbrook Academy of Art.

Florence Schust (later Florence Knoll Bassett; b. 1917) enters the Kingswood School for Girls at Cranbrook for her junior and senior years, graduating in 1934. An orphan, she spends her vacations with the Saarinen family, joining them on several summer journeys to Finland. After graduating from Kingswood she enters the Cranbrook Academy of Art, first to study interior design and weaving, and later architecture. Although Loja's hopes that Florence will one day become her daughter-in-law are never realized, Florence and Eero's friendship develops into a productive professional relationship in the 1940s.

1933

At Yale, Eero starts the "Class B" and "Class A" exercises in the spring. Spends the summer working at Cranbrook. In the fall takes "Archeology Research" with the noted architect Raymond Hood, who had replaced Faelten as chief critic in February.

1934

Among the courses Eero takes during his final semester are "Drama 12" (scenic design taught by the noted Broadway stage designer Donald Oenslager), freehand drawing with Deane Keller, and steel and concrete construction with Theodore Crane. He also takes an elective, "Modern Social Conditions," as well as his examination for "Greek and Roman Architectural History," a course he had failed to complete until then. In June, receives a Bachelor of Fine Arts degree in Architecture from Yale University. His thesis project, "Stevens Institute of Technology," is supervised by Raymond Hood. By this time Eero has received an extraordinary number of national prizes from the Beaux Arts Institute of Design and earns the nickname "Second-medal Saarinen" at Yale. In addition, he receives the silver medal of the Société des Architectes Diplômés par le Gouvernement Français for his thesis project, and wins Yale's prestigious Charles Arthur and Margaret Ormrod Matcham Traveling Fellowship for European travel, an award totaling $1,000 paid in four installments, upon his regular submission of fifty measured drawings of buildings.

After graduation, Eero spends the summer in Helsinki working on the Helsinki Central Post Office and Telegraph competition, for which he wins third prize (his submission is featured in *Arkkitehti* magazine in November 1934). In October, he begins fellowship travels, setting sail on the *Conte de Savoia* to Naples with the Swedish sculptor Carl Milles. They drive from Naples to Sweden, and Eero writes Everett Meeks about their visits to Rome, Florence, San Remo, Milan, Munich, and Berlin. After leaving Milles in Sweden, Eero travels on his own to Sicily, where he visits Palermo, Monreale, Agrigento, Taormina, and Syracuse.

1935

Travels extensively this year. Returns to Italy early on and then goes to Egypt, visiting Luxor, Edfu, Dendera, Abudos, Cairo, and Port Said before traveling to Jerusalem, where he stays in a Franciscan monastery. Reports to Meeks about the types of drawings he is doing. Even though he knows his travel scholarship requires him to submit measured drawings, Saarinen, more intrigued by the atmospheric qualities of the sites, submits watercolors instead. Travels to Beirut, Baalbek, Damascus, Cyprus, Rhodes, Constantinople, and Athens; in August to Vienna and Budapest; in December to Oslo and Stockholm.

While in Rome in April, Saarinen receives a telegram from his father asking him to go to Finland and finish the plans for the renovation of the Swedish Theater in Helsinki, on which Eliel is collaborating with architect Jarl Eklund (1876–1962). (Eklund was married to Loja's sister, Margarethe Emilie Gesellius.) Eero arrives in Finland in May, and the final design drawings are completed that September. He lives with Amos Anderson, editor-in-chief of the leading Finnish-Swedish newspaper, *Hufvudstadsbladet*, and the chairman of the board of the Swedish Theater. Eero also collaborates with Eklund on the Forum commission, which calls for a commercial building with a restaurant and shops for a prominent site in the center of Helsinki.

1936

Eero works on a competition for a central distillery for Alko, the Finnish alcohol monopoly, for which Eliel is invited to participate along with Alvar Aalto, Erkki Huttunen, Bertel Liljequist, and Väinö Vähäkallio, all established Finnish modernists. Working toward a March deadline, he is assisted by two Yale colleagues, Robert Hearsey and William Jenney. The design's strip windows, flat roofs, and white walls bear witness to Eero's exposure to International Style modernism.

In the spring and summer Eero finishes design work on the Swedish Theater and by the fall has traveled to Stockholm, Copenhagen, Hamburg, Amsterdam, Hilversum, the Hague, and Bremen, studying mostly city planning and housing. He writes to Meeks, "Hilversum was especially interesting from both a sociological as well as an architectural viewpoint."

In August he returns to the United States and works at the Cranbrook Architectural Office. By this time, Robert Swanson, along with Finnish textile designer Marianne Strengell (1909–1993) and ceramist Maija Grotell (1899–1973)—both Cranbrook faculty members who will later collaborate with Eero on various projects—have joined the office. Because of the Great Depression, however, work in the Cranbrook office is slow, and in September Eero joins a group of Cranbrook graduates at the Flint Institute of Research and Planning. Under the direction of Edmund Bacon (1910–2005), later the city planner of Philadelphia, Eero is put in charge of the proposal for the Flint Cultural and Civic Center. The project coincides with the historic strikes at the General Motors Flint Plant and is never executed.

1937

In February, Eero applies to the Michigan State Board of Examiners for registration as an architect and throughout much of the year works at the Flint Planning Office. Collaborates on several projects with Eliel, including the Fenton Community Center in Fenton, Michigan, and the Negro Community House in Michigan, but also works on his own on the Spencer House, in Huntington Woods, Michigan, and "A Combined Living-Dining Room-Study," which is published in *Architectural Forum*. Concerns about Cranbrook's nonprofit status as an academic institution prompt Booth to suggest that Eliel relocate the office to nearby Birmingham. Lilian "Lily" Swann (1913–1995), Saarinen's future wife, enters Cranbrook Academy of Art in the fall. In December, Eero travels for about five weeks with Bernard Harrison, a Yale classmate, to the Yucatán peninsula and Mexico City, visiting Mayan and Aztec ruins.

1938

In the spring, at the invitation of Worthen Paxton (1905–1977), a Yale alumnus and a partner in the New York office of Norman Bel Geddes, Eero works in the Geddes office and participates in the design of the General Motors Pavilion for the 1939–40 New York World's Fair. Saarinen works as a draftsman for the Highways and Horizons exhibit, widely known as the Futurama, which presents a compelling model of an automobile-dominated suburbanized nation, viewed from above by visitors, who are moved along on a conveyer belt.

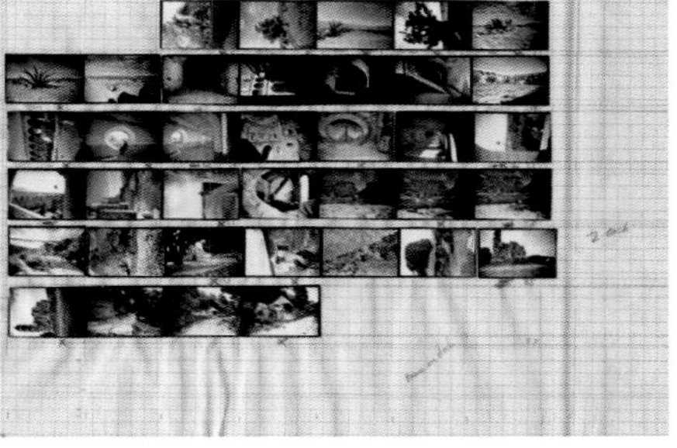

Eero Saarinen, watercolor made in Egypt, 1935

Eero Saarinen, watercolor made in Egypt, 1935

Eero Saarinen, strips from contact sheet of photographs taken in Mexico, 1937

Eero Saarinen, watercolor made in Mexico, 1937

While in New York, Eero independently enters a competition for an art center for Wheaton College, in Norton, Massachusetts. The competition is sponsored by *Architectural Forum* and the Museum of Modern Art, which will exhibit all the entries the following year. In the summer Eero participates in another competition, for a campus plan and college library for Goucher College in Towson, Maryland. Charles Eames (1907–1978), who had previously studied at Washington University in St. Louis and worked as an architect, enters Cranbrook to study with Eliel. In the fall, Eero works with his father on the Kleinhans Music Hall, in Buffalo, New York, and collaborates with Eames on furniture for the hall, the first of their several projects together.

Norman Bel Geddes, General Motors Pavilion, New York World's Fair, 1939

Charles Eames and Eero Saarinen with exhibition furniture for *Exhibition of the Work of the Academy Staff*, Cranbrook Pavilion, 1939

1939

A decisive year for Eero, who takes part in two important and well-publicized competitions that, along with the Wheaton and Goucher competitions, will play a major role in introducing modern architecture to the United States. In the winter, he wins first prize in a competition to design a festival theater and fine arts building to house the American National Theater at the College of William and Mary in Williamsburg, Virginia. It is not built, but his entry is exhibited at the New York World's Fair and the Museum of Modern Art and discussed in the *New Yorker* and *Time*. In the spring, Eero and Eliel win the two-stage competition for the Smithsonian Gallery of Art to be built on the Mall in Washington, D.C. Because entrants must be American citizens (Eliel and Eero are not), the design team includes Swanson, Eames, and Ralph Rapson (b. 1914). The building is not constructed.

At this time, Eero and Eliel also collaborate on the Tabernacle Church of Christ in Columbus, Indiana, which is constructed between 1941 and 1942. The project introduces Eero to J. Irwin Miller (1909–2005), later a noted industrialist and banker and member of the Yale Corporation. Miller will become Eero's most loyal client, commissioning four buildings in all, including two houses for his family.

On June 10, Eero marries Lilian Swann, the younger of two daughters of an established New York family, in Syosset, Long Island. Her father, Dr. Arthur W. Swann, had died when Lily was only two years old; her great-grandfather, Lucius Tuckerman, was a founder of the Metropolitan Museum of Art, and another great-grandfather, Theodore Sedgwick, was the president of the first New York World's Fair in 1853. Before studying sculpture with Carl Milles at Cranbrook, Lily attended the Chapin School and Hunter College in New York.

Eero joins the Cranbrook faculty in the fall and teaches city planning with his father until 1941. In December, *Exhibition of the Work of the Academy Staff* takes place at the Cranbrook Pavilion (now St. Dunstan's Guild Theatre); Eero and Eames are responsible for the installation design.

1940

With Eames, Eero participates in the Museum of Modern Art's Organic Design in Home Furnishings competition, winning two first-place awards for molded-plywood chairs and case goods. The jury consists of Marcel Breuer, Edgar Kaufmann, Jr., Eliot Noyes, Frank Parrish, and Edward Durell Stone. Joining Saarinen and Eames on the design team are Don Albinson, Harry Bertoia, and Ray Kaiser (later Ray Eames). In the fall the Kleinhans Music Hall opens.

Also this year, Eero becomes a U.S. citizen, a status for which he had applied in 1933. Lack of citizenship had limited his participation in national student competitions, such as the Paris Prize competition organized by the Beaux Arts Institute of Design. Despite his naturalization, the issue of Eero's nationality reemerges in 1959 when Representative R. Balton of Ohio objects to Saarinen, "a foreigner," designing the U.S. Chancellery Building in London.

1941

Eero participates with his father and brother-in-law in the design of several wartime housing projects, including the so-called Center Line Defense Housing

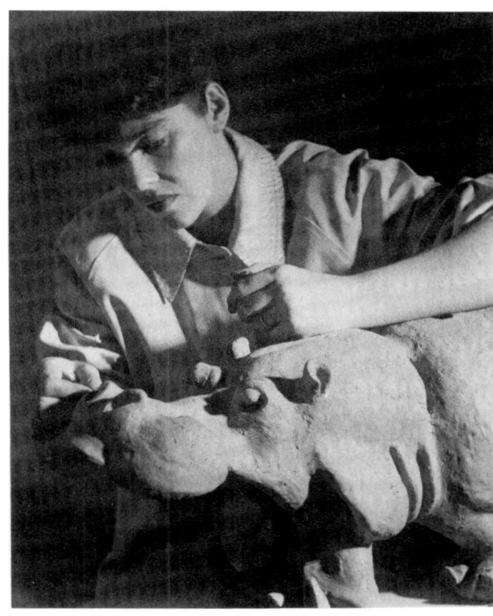

Lily Swann working on hippopotamus sculpture, part of Noah's Ark ensemble made for the Saarinens' Crow Island School, Winnetka, Illinois, ca. 1939

(later known as Kramer Homes Co-operative), a planned community in Center Line, Michigan. He is also appointed to the National Housing Office Board to advise on improving the appearance and livability of low-rent homes. Works on a house for Samuel Bell, an heir to the General Mills fortune and a Yale graduate who had gone on to study sculpture at Cranbrook, where he befriended Lily. Shortly before the end of the year, George Booth dismisses Eero from the faculty, claiming he has not committed adequate time to teaching and is too involved in his father's practice.

1942

Eero gives a speech at the National Authority of Housing Organization's Region V Conference on January 22 in Toledo, Ohio, titled "Architecture and Defense Housing," in which he addresses the technical, sociological, and psychological implications of the wartime housing intended for factory workers around airplane and other military plants, and cites Saarinen, Swanson, and Saarinen's Center Line and Walter Gropius and Marcel Breuer's New Kensington (Pennsylvania) defense housing project as exemplary. In late spring, Eero's Willow Run housing near Ypsilanti, Michigan, is featured in the Museum of Modern Art's exhibition *Wartime Housing: An Exhibition in Ten Scenes,* sponsored by the National Committee on the Housing Emergency and curated by Eliot Noyes. The show includes film footage accompanied by a soundtrack of President Roosevelt's speech on the war effort.

Eliel and Eero's Crow Island School is included in the Museum of Modern Art's book *What Is Modern Architecture?* the first volume of an introductory series on modern art.

The Saarinen, Swanson, and Saarinen office moves from the Wabeek Building in Birmingham to the old Circle School in Bloomfield Hills.

Eero enters military service, joining the Presentation Division of the Office of Strategic Services (OSS) in Washington, D.C. (the precursor to the Central Intelligence Agency), when Donal McLaughlin, a Yale-educated architect and friend who runs the unit, recruits him. Saarinen's first assignment is to provide illustrations for a manual on dismantling unexploded bombs, which will be distributed in England. Other assignments include designs for the Situation Room at the White House; a manpower study presented in illustrated form as "Army Personnel Control, Troop Basis and Accounting System" (dated July 4, 1944); and the design of an unrealized WAC recruiting tent, intended to be erected on the Mall in Washington, D.C. The scheme includes a plywood stand supporting a mirror for potential female recruits to view themselves wearing a uniform, which Eero devises with Edna Andrade (b. 1917), a textile designer in charge of the design of the uniforms. Others working at the OSS at the time include Oliver Lundquist (b. 1912), with whom Eero lives while in Washington. Eero continues working at the OSS full-time until 1944, then does pro bono work for the office after he returns to Bloomfield Hills.

On June 26, Eero and Lily's son, Eric, is born.

1943

With Oliver Lundquist, Eero wins the Designs for Postwar Living competition sponsored by *Arts and Architecture* magazine, which later publishes the entries. Jury members include Richard Neutra and Charles Eames; Eames, with his wife, Ray, is now living in Los Angeles. Using the PAC (Pre-Assembled Components) system, Saarinen and Lundquist's technically innovative design allows different-size components to be combined to create houses (and even motels) of various configurations and dimensions.

Eero opens a small branch of the Saarinen, Swanson, and Saarinen office in Washington, D.C., to do work for the National Capital Housing Authority. The Lincoln Heights project (1944–46) that emerges from the collaboration offers one-, two-, three-, and four-bedroom dwellings for returning veterans.

Florence Schust marries Hans Knoll (1914–1955), a son of a German furniture manufacturer. In 1945, Florence becomes the founder and head of the

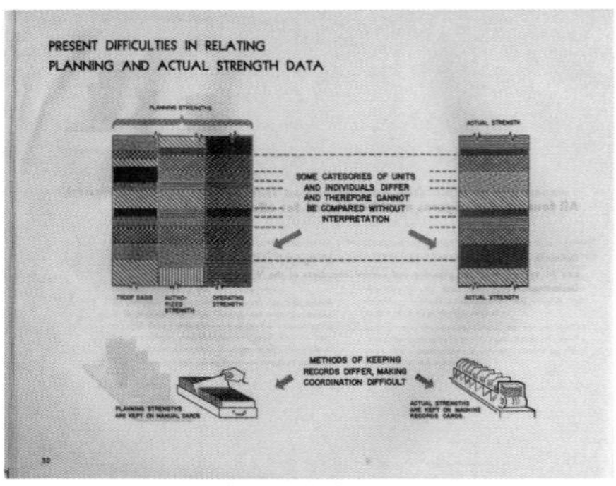

Eero Saarinen, page from "Army Personnel Control, Troop Basis and Accounting System," brochure produced for the OSS, 1944

Lily Swann Saarinen, drawing of herself, Eero, and their children, Susan and Eric, June 1946

Knoll Planning Unit, the interiors and space-planning arm of Hans G. Knoll Furniture Associates, spearheading the program "good design is good business." This marks the beginning of Eero and Florence's long collaboration in modern furniture design and manufacturing, starting with the Grasshopper chair, which is introduced in 1946.

Eliel's book *The City, Its Growth, Its Decay, Its Future* is published. In it he uses biological metaphors to argue that cities have become suffocating and unsafe, and advocates decentralization.

1944

Saarinen, Swanson, Saarinen's winning entry for the Smithsonian Gallery of Art competition, and Eliel and Eero's Crow Island School, are featured in the Museum of Modern Art's exhibition *Built in USA: 1932–1944,* which is intended to establish the basis for American architectural modernism twelve years after the museum's legendary *Modern Architecture: International Exhibition* in 1932. In the catalogue, the show's curator, Elizabeth Mock, states that the Smithsonian project exemplifies a new monumentality: "Democracy needs monuments, even though its requirements are not those of a dictatorship. There must be occasional buildings, which raise the everyday casualness of living to a higher and more ceremonial plane, buildings which give dignified and coherent form to that interdependence of the individual and the social group, which is of the very nature of our democracy. A building which comes close to this ideal is the project by Eliel and Eero Saarinen and J. Robert F. Swanson, which received the first prize in the 1939 competition for a Smithsonian Gallery of Art in Washington D.C."

For the first time, Eero and Eliel enter a competition separately, for a legislative palace in Quito, Ecuador, but neither scheme wins.

1945

On January 20, Eero and Lily's daughter, Susan, is born.

Also in January, *Arts and Architecture* magazine announces the Case Study House program. Eight architects and architectural teams are invited to create houses that fulfill "the specifications of a special living problem in the Southern California area." In addition to Eero and Charles Eames, the invitees are Thornton Abel, J. R. Davidson, Richard Neutra, Ralph Rapson, Whitney Smith, Spaulding and Rex, and Wurster and Bernardi. Charles and Eero's Case Study Houses #8, a residence for Charles and Ray, and #9, for the magazine's publisher, John Entenza, are showcased as winners in its December issue.

From February 21 until May 13, Eero and Charles and Ray Eames display their collaborative design for a wall storage unit, chairs, and benches as well as unit furniture in the Museum of Modern Art's exhibition *Integrated Building: Kitchen, Bath, and Storage.* The show circulates for three years after closing at MoMA.

At the same time, Eero works on several designs with his father and brother-in-law, including Birmingham National Bank; Birmingham High School; and the Lapeer Veterans Memorial project in Lapeer, Michigan.

Eliel is awarded the commission to design a new research center for General Motors outside Detroit.

1947

In September, Eero and his collaborators, which include his associate designer J. Henderson Barr (1909–2004), Alexander Girard (1907–1995), Dan Kiley (1912–2004), and Lily Swann Saarinen, are announced as one of the five teams of finalists chosen from a pool of 172 entries for the Jefferson National Expansion Memorial competition in St. Louis. On September 26, however, a telegram with this news is mistakenly sent to Eliel instead. Three days later, George Howe, the chairman of the jury, writes to Eero explaining the error; his

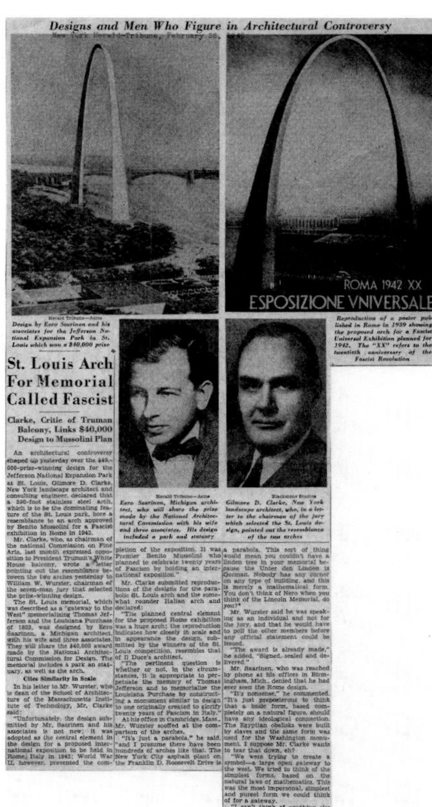

Designs and Men Who Figure in Architectural Controversy

Herald Tribune—Acme
Design by Eero Saarinen and his associates for the Jefferson National Expansion Park in St. Louis which won a $40,000 prize

Reproduction of a poster published in Rome in 1939 showing the proposed arch for a Fascist Universal Exhibition planned for 1942. The "XX" refers to the twentieth anniversary of the Fascist Revolution

Herald Tribune—Acme
Eero Saarinen, Michigan architect, who will share the prize made by the National Architectural Commission with his wife and three associates. His design included a park and statuary

Blackstone Studios
Gilmore D. Clarke, New York landscape architect, who, in a letter to the chairman of the jury which selected the St. Louis design, pointed out the resemblance of the two arches

St. Louis Arch For Memorial Called Fascist

Clarke, Critic of Truman Balcony, Links $40,000 Design to Mussolini Plan

An architectural controversy shaped up yesterday over the $40,000-prize-winning design for the Jefferson National Expansion Park at St. Louis. Gilmore D. Clarke, New York landscape architect and consulting engineer, declared that a 590-foot stainless steel arch, which is to be the dominating feature of the St. Louis park, bore a resemblance to an arch approved by Benito Mussolini for a Fascist exhibition in Rome in 1942.

Mr. Clarke, who, as chairman of the national Commission on Fine Arts, last month expressed opposition to President Truman's White House balcony, wrote a letter pointing out the resemblance between the two arches yesterday to William W. Wurster, chairman of the seven-man jury that selected the prize-winning design.

The St. Louis memorial, which was described as a "gateway to the West" memorializing Thomas Jefferson and the Louisiana Purchase of 1803, was designed by Eero Saarinen, a Michigan architect, with his wife and three associates. They will share the $40,000 award made by the National Architectural Commission for Design. The memorial includes a park an statuary, as well as the arch.

Cites Similarity in Scale

In his letter to Mr. Wurster, who is dean of the School of Architecture of the Massachusetts Institute of Technology, Mr. Clarke said:

"Unfortunately, the design submitted by Mr. Saarinen and his associates is not new; it was adopted as the central element in the design for a proposed international exposition to be held in Rome, Italy in 1942; World War II, however, prevented the completion of the exposition. It was Premier Benito Mussolini who planned to celebrate twenty years of Fascism by holding an international exposition."

Mr. Clarke submitted reproductions of the designs for the parabolic St. Louis arch and the somewhat rounder Italian arch and declared:

"The planned central element for the proposed Rome exhibition was a huge arch; the reproduction indicates how closely in scale and in appearance the design, submitted by the winners of the St. Louis competition, resembles that of Il Duce's architect.

"The pertinent question is whether or not, in the circumstances, it is appropriate to perpetuate the memory of Thomas Jefferson and to memorialize the Louisiana Purchase by constructing a monument similar in design to one originally created to glorify twenty years of Fascism in Italy."

At his office in Cambridge, Mass., Mr. Wurster scoffed at the comparison of the arches.

"It's just a parabola," he said, "and I presume there have been hundreds of arches like that. The New York City asphalt plant on the Franklin D. Roosevelt Drive is a parabola. This sort of thing would mean you couldn't have a linden tree in your memorial because the Unter den Linden is German. Nobody has any corner on any type of building, and this is merely a mathematical form. You don't think of Nero when you think of the Lincoln Memorial, do you?"

Mr. Wurster said he was speaking as an individual and not for the jury, and that he would have to poll the other members before any official statement could be issued.

"The award is already made," he added. "Signed, sealed and delivered."

Mr. Saarinen, who was reached by phone at his offices in Birmingham, Mich., denied that he had ever seen the Rome design.

"It's nonsense," he commented. "It's just preposterous to think that a basic form, based completely on a natural figure, should have any ideological connection. The Egyptian obelisks were built by slaves and the same form was used for the Washington monument. I suppose Mr. Clarke wants to tear that down, eh?

"We were trying to create a symbol—a large open gateway to the west. We tried to think of the simplest forms, based on the natural laws of mathematics. This was the most impersonal, simplest and purest form we could think of for a gateway.

"I can't think of anything else

"St. Louis Arch for Memorial Called Fascist," *New York Herald Tribune*, February 28, 1948

secretary had addressed the telegram to the first name on the office letterhead. Each team is awarded $10,000.

Joseph N. Lacy (1905–1997), a graduate of the University of Pennsylvania who had been recommended by Louis Kahn when Eero asked him to suggest candidates for the position of project manager for the GM Tech Center, joins the firm.

Eliel wins the Gold Medal of the American Institute of Architects (AIA). Long-brewing animosity between Eero and his brother-in-law, Robert Swanson, increases, which finally causes Swanson to leave the office and form Swanson and Saarinen with his wife, Pipsan. Eliel sides with Eero, and a rift in the family is created. Lily and Eero move to a relatively modest Victorian house on Vaughn Road in Bloomfield Hills.

1948

In February, Eero wins the Jefferson National Expansion Memorial competition. Almost immediately after the results are made public, Gilmore Clarke, a New York landscape architect and the chairman of the federal Commission of Fine Arts, writes to the jury that Eero's design is strikingly similar to a proposal for an arch designed by Adalberto Libera for the Fascist Universal Exhibition planned for 1942 in Italy. In its final form, Saarinen's design changed from a parabolic to a catenary arch. The popular press soon develops many nicknames for the structure, calling it the "world's largest gadget," a "stupendous hairpin," and a "stainless steel hitching post." The debate over the arch's imagery becomes an omen for the future; many of Saarinen's designs were controversial when first published.

Also in February Eero takes part in the Museum of Modern Art's symposium "What Is Happening to Modern Architecture?" stressing in his statement the importance of increased production and industrialized building techniques. The event is organized by Alfred H. Barr, Jr., and Henry-Russell Hitchcock as a response to Lewis Mumford's critique of International Style modernism, "Status Quo," which had been published in the October 11, 1947, issue of the *New Yorker*. Other panelists include the young art historian Vincent Scully (b. 1920) and the Polish-born architect Matthew Nowicki (1910–1950), who will later become one of Eero's collaborators.

In March and April, Yale invites Eero to serve as a visiting critic in its department of architecture. He declines, but accepts the invitation to serve on the University Council Committee on the Division of the Arts (1948–54) and help develop a modern arts curriculum for Yale. Saarinen's involvement with his alma mater soon expands to include seats on the Committee on the Yale Center for Fine Arts (1958–61); the University Council (1959–61); and the Architectural Advisory Committee for Yale's proposed science center (1960–61). Starting in the early 1950s, Eero's contributions to Yale also include master planning and building commissions, namely the David S. Ingalls Hockey Rink and the Morse and Stiles Colleges. Eero is also Yale's first choice to design the Art Gallery extension, but he declines the commission, claiming that he is too busy with General Motors; the project goes to Louis Kahn.

Eliel's *Search for Form* is published. The book is indicative of a growing interest in the formal rather than the functional and structural qualities of architecture, arguing that each culture expresses itself through a particular sense of form and that form also provides cultural continuity through time. Eliel's ideas about the migration of forms into new cultures support Eero's claim that the Gateway Arch is essentially free of ideological and cultural determinants.

In September, after the conclusion of a strike that had paralyzed GM from late 1946 to early 1947 and put the original 1945 design on hold, Eliel and Eero resume work on the General Motors Technical Center. The Saarinen office employs about ten people at this time.

Knoll Associates launches the Womb chair, which becomes an emblem of modern design in the popular media. On November 15, *Life* magazine publishes

Good Design exhibition window display at Merchandise Mart, Chicago, 1951

Model-building room at Eero Saarinen and Associates' Long Lake Road office, Bloomfield Hills, ca. 1953

an article titled "New Furniture: Top American Designers Make It Simple," which shows Eero sitting in the Womb chair. In contrast to the other furniture designers featured, such as Edward Wormley and Jens Risom, Eero and Charles Eames are described as being "more revolutionary" because they use industrial materials to produce strange shapes that are "nonetheless comfortable." The first of many in the magazine to feature Saarinen, the article is suggestive of publisher Henry Luce's strong support of modern art and architecture as an expression of the vitality of American society. Eero is frequently featured as one of the leading figures of postwar American modernism in Luce's magazines, which include *Time, Life, Fortune,* and *Architectural Forum.*

1949

In the spring, Eero serves as a visiting critic in advanced design at Yale, where Sven Markelius and Louis Kahn are also teaching. Yale's art program is changing radically from one based on a Beaux-Arts curriculum to one modeled after the Bauhaus, and this year Josef Albers leaves Black Mountain College to come to Yale.

At Eliel's invitation, Matthew Nowicki joins the Cranbrook faculty. He also does renderings for Eero's master plan and various buildings for Brandeis University in Waltham, Massachusetts.

In June, Yale confers upon Eero an Honorary Master of Arts degree, noting that he "has won a position of distinguished leadership in an ancient and honorable profession while still young enough to eclipse in the future his own achievements of the past and present."

The Saarinen family sells Hvitträsk.

1950

John Dinkeloo (1918–1981), a graduate of the University of Michigan, joins the Saarinen office in February, coming from the Chicago office of Skidmore, Owings, and Merrill. Kevin Roche (b. 1922), a young Irish architect who had arrived in the United States in 1948 after graduating from the National University of Ireland in 1945, joins the office in March after a brief tenure at IIT studying under Ludwig Mies van der Rohe and working with Harrison and Abramovitz on the United Nations Building in New York.

On June 30, Eliel, seventy-six, dies, and a memorial service is held on July 21 at Hvitträsk. His last completed work is Christ Church Lutheran in Minneapolis; the Detroit Civic Center (1943–51) is the last project on which Eero and Eliel collaborate. The firm is officially renamed Eero Saarinen and Associates and restructured. Joseph N. Lacy, who had joined the office in 1947, is made a partner in charge of the business side of the firm. Dinkeloo is put in charge of technical execution and research; Roche becomes Saarinen's right-hand man and, from 1954 onward, associate designer in charge of the design department. The office attracts young talent from around the country, including Robert Venturi (b. 1925), who works intermittently in the office until 1953. The firm, composed of about twelve people, is set up in an old schoolhouse just a few feet from the corner of Long Lake Road and Woodward Avenue in Bloomfield Hills. The same building houses Robert Swanson's office, despite the fact that the brothers-in-law are not on good terms.

Matthew Nowicki dies in a plane crash; in a letter, Eero subsequently declares the deceased architect to have been the third most significant influence (after his father and Charles Eames) on him, putting Mies van der Rohe fourth and Alvar Aalto fifth. He writes that these are "men whose appraisal but not necessarily agreement one would like to have."

1951

With the revival of the GM Tech Center project the office grows rapidly over the next few years. Notable presences at the firm during this time include the Finnish architect Olav Hammarström (1906–2002) and Glen Paulsen (b. 1917), both of whom had come to work for Eliel and Eero Saarinen in the late 1940s, as well as new arrivals Warren Platner (1919–2006) and Gunnar Birkerts (b. 1927).

Philip Johnson, chairman of the department of architecture and design at the Museum of Modern Art, selects Eero's furniture for the exhibition *Good Design,* which takes place in June at the Merchandise Mart in Chicago. Also featured is work by Benjamin Baldwin, Harry Bertoia, Charles and Ray Eames, Alexander Girard, Florence Knoll, Don Knorr, Jack Lenor Larsen, and Harry Weese, all Cranbrook alumni.

In the fall, Eero travels throughout Europe, meeting Max Bill, Sigfried Giedion, and Enrico Peressutti, one of the partners in the Milanese firm BBPR. Becomes president of the Detroit chapter of the American Institute of Architects and designs his father's memorial exhibition, which is installed at Cranbrook.

1952

Travels extensively this year, taking three trips—in February, late March to early April, and in August—to Paris, where he participates in the international competition to design the UNESCO headquarters. The design he submits on September 19 is eventually rejected and Saarinen is instead named a consultant to the international team of architects selected for the project: Marcel Breuer (U.S.), Bernard Zehrfuss (France), and Pier Luigi Nervi (Italy). Eero extends his spring trip to visit the Great Mosque in Cordoba, Spain, and the summer trip to visit Copenhagen, Stockholm, and Helsinki, where he has been commissioned to design an extension of the American Embassy. He travels to Europe again in December.

Saarinen is made a fellow of the American Institute of Architects (FAIA) at the AIA's national convention in New York in June. A frequent lecturer at AIA meetings, he gives the opening address, "Our Epoch of Architecture," at the Gulf States Region conference in Montgomery, Alabama, in October.

Marital problems between Eero and Lily become apparent as Eero pursues an intense work and travel schedule and Lily begins to feel increasingly isolated at home with their two children.

The Museum of Modern Art exhibition *Built in USA: Post-war Architecture,* curated by Henry-Russell Hitchcock and Arthur Drexler, opens in late spring. The show includes the three GM Tech Center buildings completed to date—Administration, Engineering, and Styling—and illustrates their placement around a large rectangular pool. The exhibition catalogue notes that the "repetitiousness of the vertical elements . . . exaggerated and suggest[ing] a façade turned out mechanically by the yard" is appropriate for an "architecture of increased industrial origin," while noting that the colorful bricks used on the exterior of the buildings help to "overcome the diffusion of architectural impact which results from the dispersal of buildings on a flat landscape."

1953

In late January, Aline B. Louchheim (1914–1972), associate art editor for the *New York Times,* visits Bloomfield Hills to interview Eero. A romance ensues between them. Louchheim's interview is published as "Now Saarinen the Son" in the April 26 issue of the *New York Times Magazine.* Born Aline Bernstein in New York, she is the daughter of two amateur painters—her father an investment banker by day—who encourage her artistic activities. She studied art and journalism at Vassar College, graduating in 1935, and received a master's degree in architectural history in 1941 from the Institute of Fine Arts at New York University. Her first job is as an art critic for *Art News.*

In February Eero travels alone to Paris, then to Des Moines (for Drake University), New York (for Time Inc.), Columbus, Indiana (for a potential new high school), Cambridge, Massachusetts (for MIT), and Ottawa, Canada (as a juror for a new art museum). He writes to Aline that he is tired of traveling, wishes his office were smaller, and fears he is becoming a mere administrator with no time to draw. The office now employs more than twenty-five people and jobs include MIT's Kresge Chapel and Auditorium, several projects

Saarinen with Frank Lloyd Wright, probably 1954

Knoll Associates advertisement for the Womb chair, 1955, graphic design by Herbert Matter

Coca-Cola advertisement with Haddon Sundblom's "Coca-Cola Santa Claus," 1958, featuring a Womb chair

for the University of Michigan, the American Embassy in Helsinki, and the Milwaukee War Memorial.

Later in the spring, Eero files for divorce from Lily and begins dividing his time between Bloomfield Hills and New York City to be with Aline. Stress leads to health problems and by the summer Eero has contracted mononucleosis. In the fall he is well enough to visit Fallingwater with Aline, where they are entertained by Edgar Kaufmann, Jr. Eero decides to take a two-week vacation to visit Charles and Ray Eames in California.

On November 20, takes part in a symposium, "Architectural Lettering," at Yale, where he meets the artist Gyorgy Kepes and lectures on the visual chaos in cities and the need to establish visual coherence using architecture and graphic design. Other symposium participants include sculptor J. H. Benson, architect Victor Gruen, Philip Johnson, Henry-Russell Hitchcock, and graphic designer Alvin Lustig.

Eero's firm receives First Honor Award in the AIA's National Awards Program for the Engineering Building at GM.

The office moves to new premises on Long Lake Road, Bloomfield Hills.

1954

On February 8, Eero marries Aline at her apartment in New York.

On May 27, Eero has dinner with Frank Lloyd Wright, about whom he had expressed mixed feelings in a letter to Aline in June 1953, in which he wrote: "In many ways we have come upon him from two opposite poles. . . . I have always had too little appreciation for him. I have recognized certain great contributions he made in his early career—contributions which most of modern architecture is partly based upon—but I have never liked his form." Eero does credit Wright for his ideas about landscape, organic unity, materials, and open, flowing space.

In June, delivers a lecture, "The Changing Philosophy of Architecture," at a meeting of the AIA Boston chapter, discussing the legacy of the modern masters and making suggestions for the future development of modern architecture.

Becomes a member of the National Institute of Arts and Letters and the National Academy of Design.

Cesar Pelli (b. 1926) joins Saarinen's firm, working first on a Time Inc. project for a site in Pennsylvania, for which they also join forces with Paul Rudolph (1918–1997), at that time an architect with a growing reputation based on a string of small houses in Florida. Rudolph works at the office on and off through July and August, more as a collaborator and an inspiration than as an employee.

1955

John Dinkeloo is made a partner in Saarinen's office.

David Powrie (b. 1930) joins the office in May, having previously worked for Oscar Niemeyer in Brazil. He becomes the job captain for the Ingalls Hockey Rink and the Deere Administrative Center, and remains with the firm and its successor, Kevin Roche John Dinkeloo and Associates, until 1993.

In June, the firm receives a commission to design the United States Chancellery Building in Oslo; between December and the following February it also participates in the competition to design the United States Chancellery in London. Aline, Eero, and office colleague Spero Daltas (b. 1920) travel to London in December for a prolonged visit to study the site. They stay for three weeks, longer than any other invited team.

Aline's article "Four Architects Helping to Change the Look of America" is published in the August 1955 issue of *Vogue*. It signals both the popular appeal of modern design and Eero's role as America's leading modernist. The piece also covers Gordon Bunshaft, Philip Johnson, and Ludwig Mies van der Rohe. Aline describes each of them, representing Eero as "a stocky man with a squarish face, receding sandy-colored hair, and intensely peering pale-blue

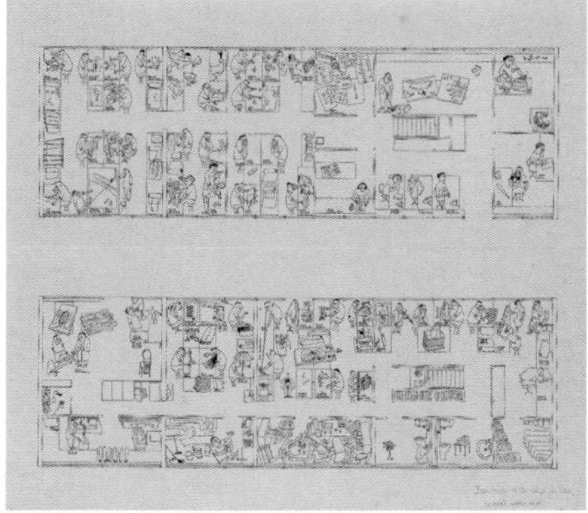

Claude de Forest, cartoon depicting people working at Saarinen office on Long Lake Road, ca. 1956

Eero Saarinen, drawing of Sydney Opera House competition entry by Jørn Utzon, inscribed "To the Hon. J. J. Cahill, Premier N.S.W., from Eero Saarinen," 1957

Eero Saarinen and Florence Knoll with Pedestal base, probably from Model 150 or 151 chair, 1957

Ticket from Saarinen's flight aboard the Boeing Dash 80, on June 21, 1958

eyes. Calm and deliberate, he seems even on first meeting a man of conviction and inner security. He has a delayed-action charm and a dead-pan, Charles Addams humor."

This year Eero wins several professional awards, including First Honor Award from the National Awards Program of the AIA for the restaurant at GM, as well as for the dining hall and dormitories at Drake University. The same projects win two of the four awards given by the AIA Detroit chapter.

GM commissions Saarinen to design a House of Tomorrow—an experimental project with a focus on technological experiments similar to the PAC house. It does not go into production.

Eero and Aline's son, Eames, is born on November 28.

1956

In February, Eero wins the London Chancellery competition. In May, the GM Tech Center is officially dedicated, with huge fanfare. GM's public relations department originally plans to have President Eisenhower launch an atomic bomb as part of the event, but the scheme is canceled.

Saarinen is commissioned to design the TWA Terminal at New York's Idlewild Airport. The office takes over a garage at the corner of Woodward Avenue and Long Lake Road to build large-scale models, which are later turned into a set of section cuts at different elevations. The firm grows to forty people, compromising the studiolike atmosphere it had sustained during the 1940s and early 1950s. J. Henderson Barr resigns in protest.

Eero becomes a consultant to the Secretary of the Air Force on the design of a new academy in Colorado Springs, Colorado. He is also a member of the selection committee for the new dean of Yale's School of Architecture, and contemplates taking the position himself, but decides he would rather wait ten years and continue producing his own work instead. The committee eventually selects Gibson Danes for the job.

The National Council of Churches selects MIT's Kresge Chapel as one of the best churches built in the previous twenty-five years; the chapel also receives the Grand Architectural Award of the Boston Arts Festival. The office wins *Progressive Architecture*'s First Honor Award in Education Category for Concordia Senior College.

The March issue of *Architectural Forum* includes "Three Critics Discuss MIT's New Buildings," with comments from European writers Bruno Zevi, J. M. Richards, and Sigfried Giedion that question Kresge Chapel's adherence to the modernist dogma of structural and functional integrity. The July 2 issue of *Time* magazine features Eero on its cover and, inside, Cranston Jones's article "Maturing Modern" celebrates him as a leading architect of his generation. Taken together, the two articles express a trend: Eero is disliked by many critics and historians, particularly those from Europe, but he is loved by his colleagues and the popular press.

1957

On January 2, Eero and Aline leave for Southeast Asia. They stop first in Indonesia, where President Sukarno asks Saarinen to consult on infrastructural issues and to design a stadium. After a brief vacation in Thailand and Cambodia, the couple arrives in Sydney, where Eero helps select the design for the city's new opera house. As the story goes, Saarinen arrives late to the deliberations and pulls Jørn Utzon's scheme out of the reject pile, saying, "Gentlemen, this is the first prize." Utzon is declared the winner of the competition on January 29. On the return trip the Saarinens stop in London.

On February 25, the exhibition *Buildings for Business and Government* opens at the Museum of Modern Art. The GM Tech Center, represented by a twenty-foot floor-to-ceiling section of glazed brick, is one of six buildings in the show that demonstrates how "clients are becoming patrons." Other examples include Mies's Seagram Building, SOM's U.S. Air Force Academy, and Edward Durell Stone's American Embassy in New Delhi.

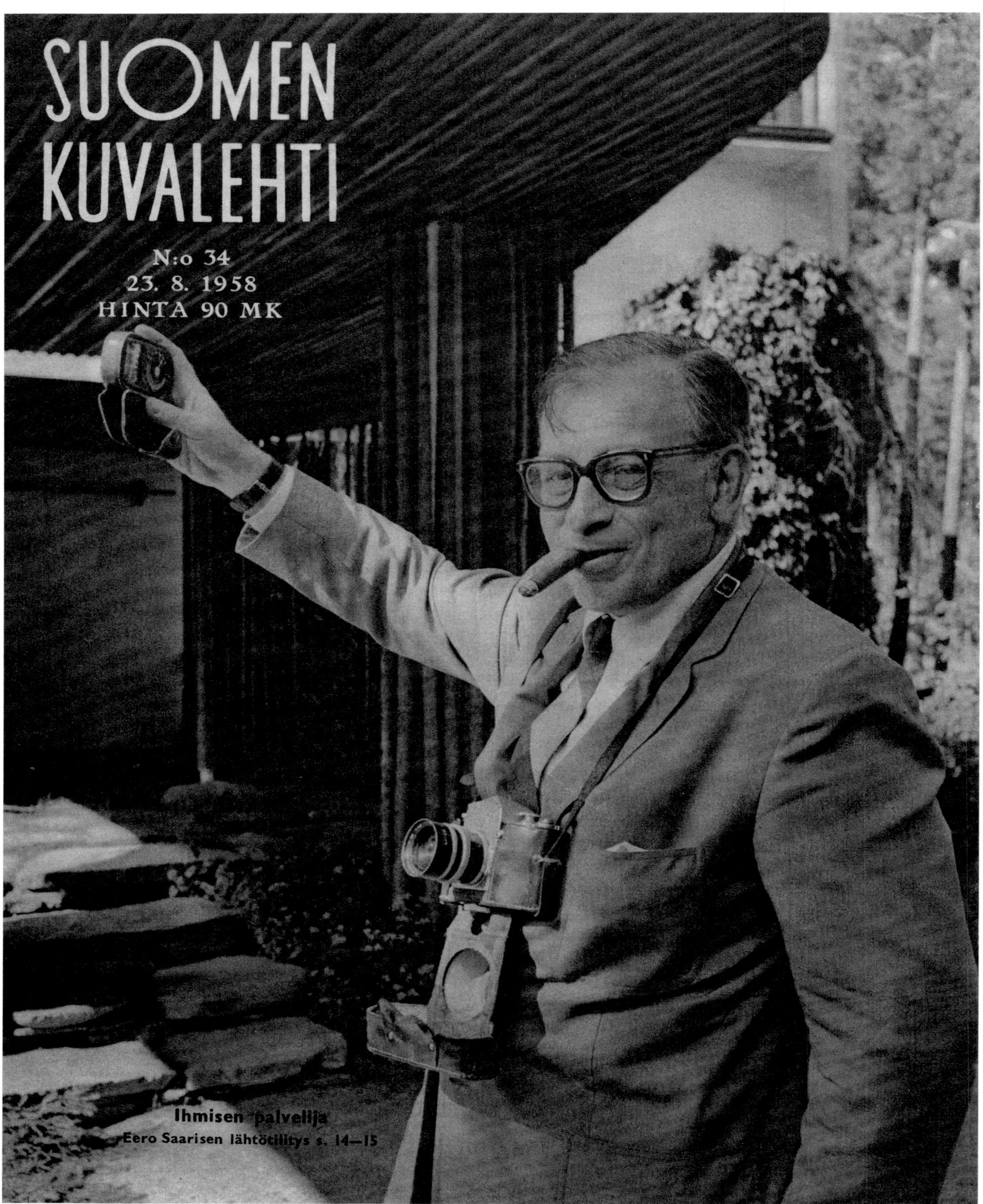

Cover of *Suomen Kuvalehti*, August 23, 1958, showing Eero at Villa Mairea, Noormarkku, Finland

The extended Saarinen family at Cranbrook, August 1958. Front row: Susan, Eero, Loja, Aline, and Eames; back row: Eric, Donald Louchheim, and Harry Allen Louchheim

Aline, Eero, and Eames Saarinen at their house on Vaughn Road, Bloomfield Hills, ca. late 1958

Aline, Eames, and Eero Saarinen photographed at home, October 1959, for "A Modern Architect's Own House," *Vogue*, April 1, 1960

In June, Saarinen lectures at the Architectural Association in London.

The office receives major corporate commissions, including IBM's Thomas J. Watson Research Center in Yorktown Heights, New York, the Deere and Company Administrative Center in Moline, Illinois, and the Bell Telephone Corporate Laboratories in Holmdel, New Jersey. The former Pontiac Cadillac showroom at 1300 North Woodward Avenue in Birmingham becomes the firm's new home, while the former office is used for building models. At this point the staff begins to grow even more rapidly, reaching one hundred workers in a few years.

John Dinkeloo, Anthony J. Lumsden (b. 1928), Warren Platner, and Kevin Roche consider launching their own firm when Platner receives a commission to design a factory for Sperry Gyroscope in Long Island, but the project does not proceed beyond the initial design stage. Dinkeloo, Lumsden, and Roche also submit four schemes to a competition to design the Reynolds Aluminum headquarters, which win four honorary mentions. Eero ultimately grows concerned that they will break away and dissuades the team from pursuing outside activities.

Edwin Gilbert's novel *Native Stone* is published. Modeled after Ayn Rand's *The Fountainhead,* it is the story of three young Yale-educated architects; Eero seems to be the inspiration for the pipe-smoking hero, Rafferty Bloom.

1958

In the beginning of the year Saarinen travels to Japan, where Kenzo Tange serves as his guide. During the trip he sees the Katsura Palace, which impresses him greatly. In a letter to William A. Hewitt, the CEO of John Deere, Saarinen writes: "We have just been working on models of the Executive Area [of Deere and Company Headquarters] and they show real promise of achieving interior of the same quality as Katsura." One can only speculate whether Saarinen saw Tange's Hiroshima Peace Center (1949–55), which bears a striking resemblance to Deere's final design, with its exposed concrete floor beams mimicking heavy timber construction.

In June, accompanied by Kevin Roche and a host of consultants for the Dulles International Airport project, to be built outside Washington, D.C., Saarinen travels to Seattle to visit the Boeing factory, where the group boards the Dash 80, prototype for the Boeing 707, for a flight around the city.

In August, Eero visits Finland with Aline, Susan, Eric, and Aline's sons, Donald (b. 1937) and Harry Allen (b. 1939). As Eero rarely traveled to Finland after the outbreak of World War II, this trip by the now world-famous son of one of Finland's great architects is a milestone media event. The Saarinens are hosted by Maire Gullichsen in Villa Mairea, her famous house designed by Alvar Aalto. The visit to Villa Mairea is featured in *Suomen Kuvalehti;* Eero is shown on the cover photographing the Aalto masterpiece, thus symbolically bringing together the two great contemporary Finnish architects. Apparently, Eero had always felt a sense of competition with Aalto, despite having considered him only the fifth-greatest influence on his own education. While in Finland, Eero also lectures about his work at Hvitträsk.

Aline publishes *The Proud Possessors,* which becomes a bestseller.

1959

On February 10, the exhibition *Architecture and Imagery: Four New Buildings,* co-curated by Arthur Drexler and Wilder Green, opens at the Museum of Modern Art. It includes drawings of Saarinen's TWA Terminal; Jørn Utzon's Opera House in Sydney, Australia; Harrison and Abramovitz's Presbyterian Church in Stamford, Connecticut; and Guillame Gillet's Notre-Dame de Royan, all making a case for broadening the formal language of modern architecture beyond the glass box.

June 8 marks the opening of the exhibition *Form Givers at Mid-Century,* organized by Cranston Jones and sponsored by *Time* magazine for the American Federation of Arts, at the Metropolitan Museum of Art in New York.

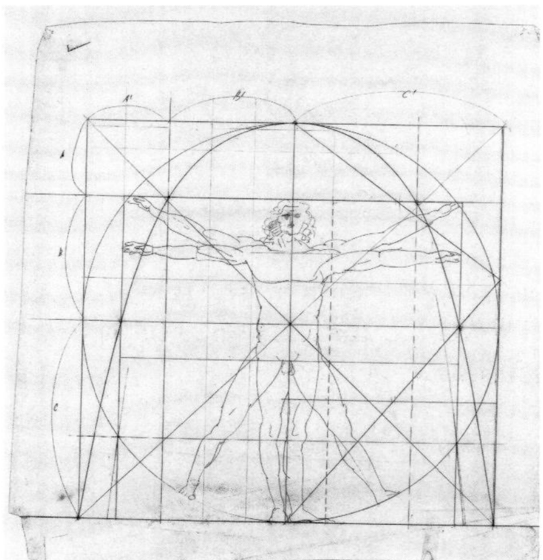

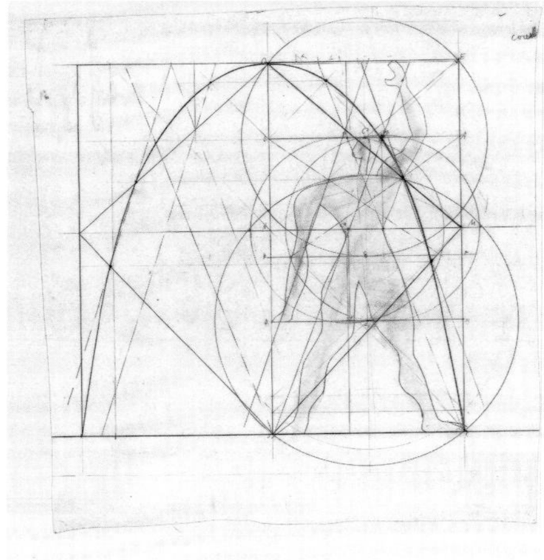

Eero and Eames Saarinen, drawing of car, ca. 1959

Eero Saarinen, Jefferson National Expansion Memorial, proportional studies of arch with Vitruvian man, ca. 1959

Eero Saarinen, Jefferson National Expansion Memorial, proportional studies of arch with Le Corbusier's Modulor man, ca. 1959

The show grows out of Jones's article "Maturing Modern" in *Time* and is based on the same thesis: that American architecture is now in the vanguard.

In June, ground is broken on the Gateway Arch in St. Louis.

Between September 17 and 23, Eero accompanies Aline to the World Conference of Art Critics in Brazil. On December 1, he receives the Dickinson College Arts Award and delivers one of his most important lectures, on what he calls the "six pillars of architecture." His office also receives First Honor Award in the AIA's Eleventh Annual Honor Awards Program for work on Concordia Senior College.

Harold Roth (b. 1934) joins the firm in December.

Eero decides to relocate the office to Hamden, a suburb of New Haven, Connecticut, and buys land in Guilford, outside New Haven, on which to build a house whose exterior will be made of reflective glass. Aline prefers to live in town, however, and the land is eventually sold to pay for a house in New Haven.

1960

In May, with Aline, Eero visits Athens, Greece, for meetings related to the design of the city's new airport. He takes a second trip to Europe in the fall, traveling to Italy and Greece, then to Munich to speak on October 24 at the Schöner Wohnen congress, where he talks about the house he hopes to build on the Guilford site. On December 8 he delivers a lecture, "Problems Facing Architecture," at the University of Pennsylvania.

Wins second prize in the World Health Organization competition in Geneva, Switzerland, the jury for which includes the Swedish modernist Sven Markelius. The first prize goes to Jean Tschumi.

Saarinen is elected a fellow of the American Academy of Arts and Letters.

1961

In January, Aline and Eero attend President John F. Kennedy's inauguration in Washington, D.C. The invitation reads: "During our forthcoming administration we hope to seek a productive relationship with our writers, artists, composers, philosophers, scientists and heads of cultural institutions. As a beginning, in recognition of their importance, may we extend you our most cordial invitation to attend the inaugural ceremonies in Washington on January 19 and 20."

In March, Eero attends the opening of *Form Givers at Mid-Century* at Cranbrook with Loja and Aline. In June and July attends a two-week seminar and workshop titled "R-17 Summer Seminar," held at the Cranbrook Academy of Art and co-organized by the Association of Collegiate Schools of Architecture. These would be Saarinen's last public appearances.

On August 21, Eero visits a doctor at the University of Michigan Hospital and is diagnosed with a brain tumor. On September 1, he undergoes surgery and dies of complications afterward.

Between September 6 and 12, Aline and Eames move to 10 St. Ronan Terrace in New Haven.

Saarinen's memorial service is held on September 9 in the Kresge Chapel at MIT. Leading figures in the worlds of art, architecture, and design attend, including Alfred H. Barr, Jr., Pietro Belluschi, Alexander Calder, Charles and Ray Eames, Alexander Girard, Louis Kahn, Dan Kiley, Jo Mielziner, and William Wurster. J. Irwin Miller reads from the Psalms and quotes Pericles, Elizabeth Barrett Browning, and Eero himself. In its October issue, *Progressive Architecture* notes that "Saarinen's death . . . is particularly tragic because it was the abrupt termination of a career that not only had accomplished much in a short span, but which also promised who knows what riches in years to come."

At the time of Saarinen's death, his office is in the midst of moving to Hamden, and nine major projects are under way. The TWA Terminal, Bell Labs, Dulles Airport, and Morse and Stiles Colleges are under construction and their interiors in design, while the Deere Administrative Center, the Athens Airport, North Christian Church, the Gateway Arch, and the CBS Building are

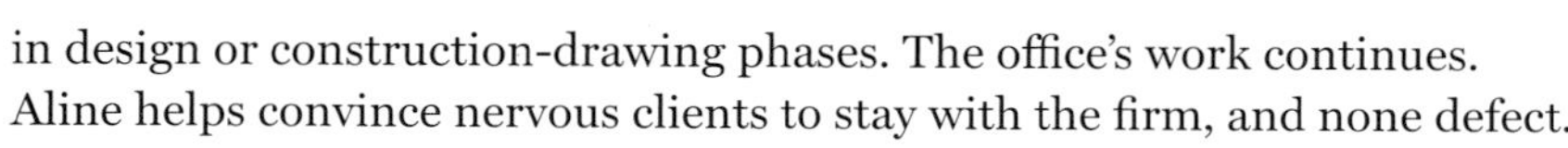

in design or construction-drawing phases. The office's work continues. Aline helps convince nervous clients to stay with the firm, and none defect.

1962

A book of Saarinen's writings, edited by Aline Saarinen and titled *Eero Saarinen on His Work: A Selection of Buildings Dating from 1947 to 1964,* is published. It consists of selected projects and extracts from Saarinen's articles, lectures, and interviews. Allan Temko's book *Eero Saarinen,* the first monograph on the architect, is also published.

The TWA Terminal is dedicated on May 28, as is Dulles International Airport on November 17–18.

Eero is posthumously awarded the AIA Gold Medal.

1963

On February 12, the first stainless-steel section of the Gateway Arch is put in place.

1964

In June, the Deere Administrative Center is dedicated with open-house festivities that span several days. Cesar Pelli leaves the firm to join DMJM (Daniel, Mann, Johnson, and Mendenhall) in Los Angeles as director of design.

1965

In October, the Gateway Arch, the final project by Eero to be completed, is finished.

Harold Roth leaves the firm to establish his own office.

1966

Joseph N. Lacy retires. The office is renamed Kevin Roche John Dinkeloo and Associates.

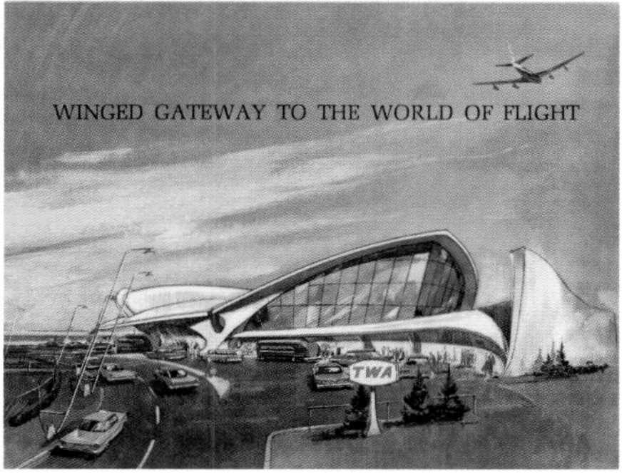

Aline Saarinen in Greece, probably the theater at Epidaurus, 1960

Eero Saarinen at the Temple of Segesta, Sicily, 1960

"Winged Gateway to the World of Flight," promotional brochure printed by TWA, 1962

ROMAN

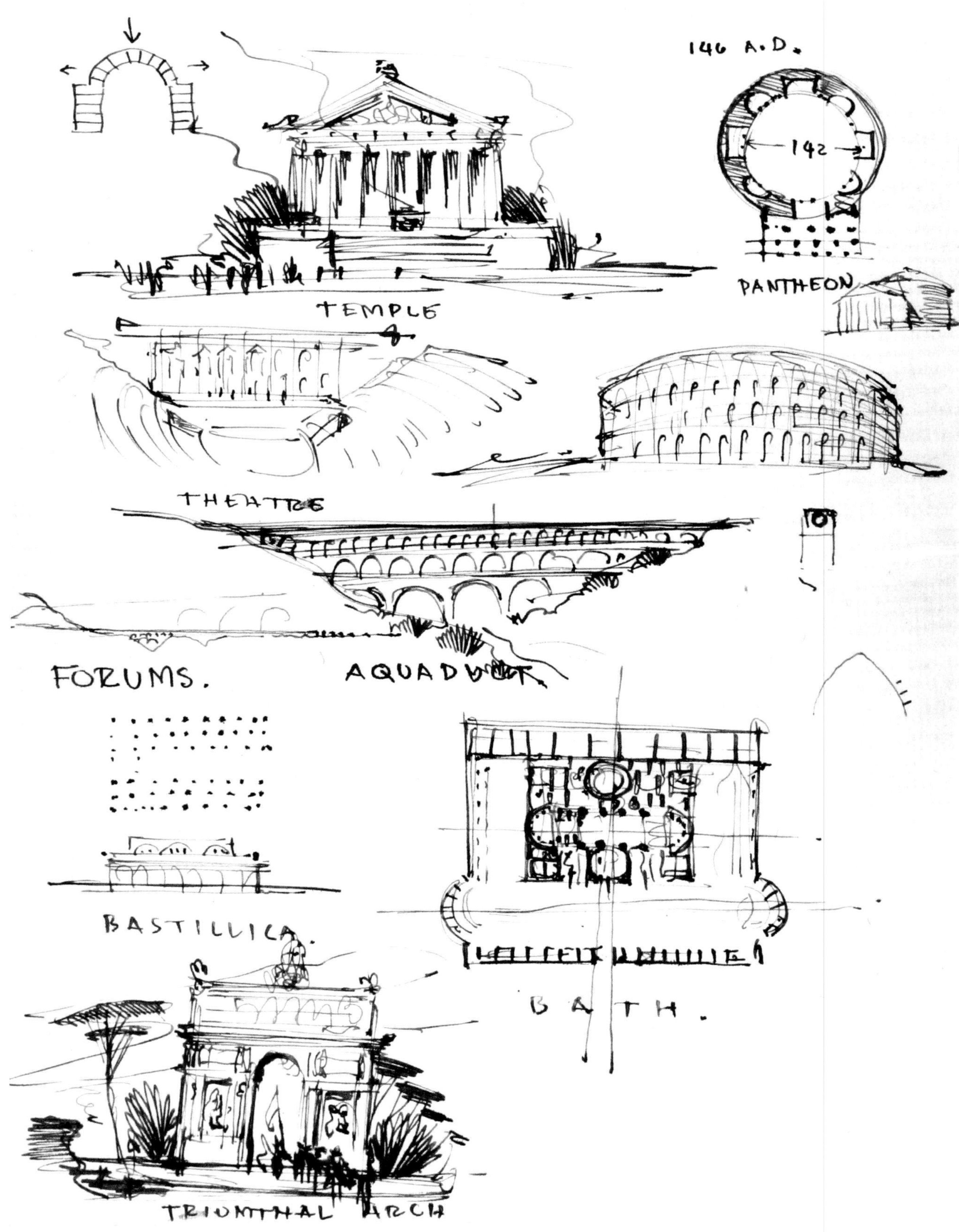

Eero Saarinen, sketches of Roman architecture, from letter to Florence Schust, ca. 1935

Edited by Eeva-Liisa Pelkonen

selected writings

When measured against his father, Eliel, the author of two significant books, *The City, Its Growth, Its Decay, Its Future* (1943) and *Search for Form: A Fundamental Approach to Art* (1948), Eero Saarinen can hardly be considered a major architectural writer. He did not produce a treatise or generate clear exegeses. He did, however, write numerous magazine articles and lectures and gave many interviews. These show that Saarinen was engaged with the architectural discourse of his time. The question of the current state and the future of modern architecture, particularly of American modern architecture, was the dominant topic. Like many other members of the second generation of modernists, such as Philip Johnson and Edward Durell Stone, Saarinen called for a richer and more flexible formal language than the one they had inherited from the modern masters.

The three previously unpublished texts featured here approach this issue from slightly different angles. The first piece, "Eero on 'Golden Proportions,'" written sometime during spring or summer 1953, takes up the discussion of the use of proportional systems both in historical as well as in modern architecture, a subject that dominated architectural debate during late 1940s and early 1950s. Saarinen criticizes the primacy given to any single system, calling for an architecture that would allow the structural, functional, and aesthetic aspects of a building to be taken into consideration. The perfect balance is, according to him, achieved by human "intuition."

The second text is a meditation on the genesis of what he refers to as "sculptural, curved shapes." Written later in the decade, around 1958–59, when Saarinen was in the process of designing and building some of his best-known works, such as the TWA Terminal and the Gateway Arch, it offers a glimpse of what such inclusiveness meant in practice. A detailed discussion traces how each project balances structural and aesthetic concerns. Here, too, human instinct serves as the ultimate measure.

Saarinen was named recipient of the Dickinson College Arts Award for 1959–60, and the third essay included here is an address he delivered to the college on December 1, 1959, elaborating on the state of modern architecture. (He used several paragraphs from this address more or less verbatim in an article published in *Perspecta* in 1961.) Perhaps the key text to his thinking, the lecture covers the major themes of his writings: the state of modern architecture, the legacy of the modern masters, the role of the second generation in general, the quest for communicative and expressive form, the role of new technologies, his concern with "total environment," and the notion that a building should be a "good neighbor." In what Saarinen terms the "six principles of modern architecture," he summarizes modernist dogma—that form should follow function, structure, and zeitgeist—and calls on architects to devote more attention to the effects and experiences that can be created by buildings and ensembles of buildings.

EERO ON "GOLDEN PROPORTIONS"

Undated and unpublished notes for a lecture written in spring or summer 1953. The essay's title was handwritten on the manuscript, probably by a secretary or perhaps by Saarinen's wife, Aline. It is not known whether Saarinen actually delivered the lecture, or where. The approximate date of its writing has been based on archival research.

Mr. Chairman, Ladies and Gentlemen:

I came here to argue against the properties applied through rules whether golden or divine; but after what we have heard from [José Luis] Sert and [Enrico] Peressutti, I wonder whether I am arguing on the right side of the fence. It would indeed be wonderful if one would, at some point in design, switch off one's visual sense of proportions and apply unfailing rules and regulations and be assured of a good result. No more worry about the shape of things—just leave it up to divine and indisputable laws.

I have just one reservation. Usually when something is made simpler and easier and candy-coated, it also has its negative side. Faust found this out; a hangover is the same kind of a phenomenon. The price we would pay if we became addicts of this game might be a very heavy price. Therefore, let us not jump into it too fast. Let's examine its past, when and how it worked, and if and how it applies to us.

It was born as a means of refinement during a time when the concept of Greek architecture was static. The book was full of rules by the time Rome became degenerate and fell. Then came the Barbarians, and all knowledge of rules was forgotten. During the Dark Ages that followed, new architecture sprang up unhampered by laws of proportions. The Romanesque and Gothic, the finest architecture that Western man has produced, was the result.

When we were in Milano and visited Peressutti and his partners [Gian Luigi Banfi, Lodovico Barbiano di Belgioioso, and Ernesto Rogers], we had the same argument as tonight about proportions. They showed us St. Ambrogio, which is one of the very finest places of early Romanesque. When we were looking at the slender, tall pilasters and the short squat columns, which are so typical of the Romanesque but against all the rules of the Romans, I said, "How can you argue for proportions? Here right in front of your nose, you have a wonderful example of an architecture that never could have been created had not the laws of proportions and the rules of applying this been completely forgotten." I never did get a straight answer.

The Romanesque and Gothic were periods of architecture, which embraced the whole keyboard of architecture. They set for themselves the problems of structure of material, proportions, mass space, texture, relation to sculpture, etc., and they solved their problem brilliantly. Chartres proved the result indisputably.

The Renaissance was another kind of period—great in many ways but perhaps a bit overrated architecturally, not because they did not solve their architectural problems well, but because their aims in architecture were limited. They were not able to create a form of their time. They borrowed Roman sub-assemblies and their main concern was how to use these in new ingenious and well-related ways. They ignored true structure, material, space, etc. To make architectural problems a little more interesting, they almost had to introduce the parlor game of proportions.

Our period is entirely different. Much more like the Romanesque and Gothic, we look upon the problems of architecture more broadly and more ambitiously. Whether or not we are masters enough to find a form has yet to be seen, but the ground rules are broad and ambitious. We are determined to solve as one integrated package a complicated formula which includes space, use, structure, material, texture, proportions, and last but not least, the spirit of our time. Therefore, we cannot allow one of these to be frozen by rules and regulations.

Throughout architectural history there always have been formative periods and static periods. Twelfth century France created Gothic; fifteenth century Florence created the Renaissance. During comparatively short periods, the ground rules of the whole style were set, the general direction of the form of their time was created. These were really creative periods. Then the following centuries refined and varied on the theme.

We are in one of those great periods right now. It began about 1900 and it may last for the rest of this century. The ground rules and the general direction have been set but there still is much to be done before the form of our time really emerges. During such a period we have to remain alert and flexible. New structural materials, new uses, a new spirit of our age. Yes, we are feeling new frontiers. This is not yet a period of refinement.

To distort our architecture to fit the [proportional and structural rules of the] Renaissance is fantastic. For anyone to want to dream up a new code for all of us is equally fantastic. Any proportion that might seem right to us today will surely be wrong tomorrow. I know it is a basic human trait to pigeonhole and make into systems everything around, but our period of architecture is too important for this. Intuition is the only safe guide we have to proportions today—let us not put an artificial governor on our intuition. Our intuition is a much finer apparatus. It can be compared to one of those IBM super mechanical brains filled with all the right information. It takes into account everything—the use, the structure, the material, the method, the spirit of our time, proportions, everything, and finally comes out with an answer. If we were to listen to the proportion boys, I suppose we would throw away the answer if it did not come out in round numbers.

All this stuff seems to emanate from one fountainhead—Corbu [Le Corbusier]. He is a great genius as an architect, but I have little use for his sideshow proportions. As an architect, he can be thought of as the Brunelleschi of our time; but what is he trying to do? Does he also want to be the Alberti and Palladio of our day? With Palladio the Renaissance ended.

No, I hope we can stop all this nonsense before it begins to confuse our larger aims and before it gets into our architectural schools and creates another confused generation like the Beaux Arts.

Undated and unpublished transcript from dictation, ca. 1958–59

GENERAL STATEMENT

about the sculptural, curved/shapes that we have been involved with, beginning with St. Louis, the water tower and dome at General Motors, MIT, Yale, TWA, and now the Washington International Airport

St. Louis:

The arch, in stainless steel, with a core of concrete. An absolutely pure shape where the compression line goes right through the center line of the structure directly to the ground. In other words, a perfect catenary. The absolutely simplest shape with the greatest impact and with a great deal of thought on its lasting qualities.

Then came the water tower at General Motors. The same stainless steel and recognizing that it is a piece of sculpture as well as a piece of structure. Recognizing that it is a piece of structure in plate with singular compound curve. After twenty different alternate designs we finally narrowed this down to this[,] which seemed like the most beautiful shape. It would have been easy to find a more rational shape of a purer structural shape because the flat sphere that rests on the three tubes has to be reinforced by an inside structure at the joints between tube and sphere, but after satisfying ourselves that the beauty of this shape was greater than any one which was made by a more visible structure, we had to decide on this. In other words, the water tower at General Motors is a departure from the completely rational. The cross ties at the bottom are however rational, although they could have had many different shapes. They help the bending moment in that all three tubes act as one where the bending moment is the greatest. Just as one thought of and learned a great deal about stainless steel as a cladding material in St. Louis, so one learned a great deal about its actual application at the water tank, but one also learned that the structural and rational cannot always take precedent when another form proves more beautiful. This is dangerous but I believe true.

About the same time came the MIT auditorium—the dome. There the belief was strongly in the structural rationalism of Mies, but applied to concrete and applied to a dome, and it can't help look different. The triangle is in a sense a pure shape in that it's 1/8th of a sphere and was carefully kept that way. The dome was kept as thin as possible and the edge beam was kept as small as possible.

The significance of the dome above and the shell which contains the passangers [*sic*] below seemed also to be of significance during the design period. Placing the whole building on a podium also seemed very important. In other words, the exact geometry of the parts of the exterior seemed very important. [Pier Luigi] Nervi criticized the fact that the forces at the three points do not come down in a spherical line but in a catenary line[,] [although he] was overweighed [*sic*] by the joy of getting the whole structure in to an absolute geometry. In retrospect one has to criticize this building. It looks like a half-inflated balloon. The windows bulging out, the round base, the narrow edge beam, and the complete spherical shape, I believe all contribute to that, and I do sympathize with Gideon's [*sic*] statement that this building looks earthbound. I do not sympathize with his statement that Hugh Stubbins' Berlin building [Congress Hall, 1957] is better because it is a bastard structure, but somewhere in between making a pure structure and an intentional flare to counteract the earthbound quality of the dome seems like a necessity. The complete geometry did not come off. The building also has been criticized for its lack of scale, or rather the comprehension of its scale. We were terribly careful when designing it not to molest the purity of the shape with any visible entrances. We learned a lot on that building. We learned that one cannot depend on geometry for the sake of geometry. We learned unfortunately that one doesn't have to come down within the compression line, we learned that the shell within does not play any conscious part of [on] the exterior. We also learned that glass is opaque, we also learned the need of concave to counterbalance convex forms. We also learned that some kind of flare on a building is needed, but we also learned some things about the technique of building. We found how to cover a concrete dome. We think. And then there was of course the reminder that a building has to have scale. But most of all, how does one counteract the earthbound quality of a dome?

Now, the General Motors Dome:
Soon after this Yama's [Minoru Yamasaki's] St. Louis airport domes came out. In some ways he did better[,] in some ways worse, but then his follow-through was miserable. You cannot place a series of domes on top of a loft building, even if you can tie them together within the floor. The General Motors Steel Dome worked much better. The wall around it avoiding the contact of the dome with the earth works well, and in a peculiar way this dome because of the wall around it and its shiny material I feel came off very well. The chief lesson we learned was not to cover a dome with aluminum, even if it's cheaper.

Now, the Yale Hockey Rink. (end of dictation)

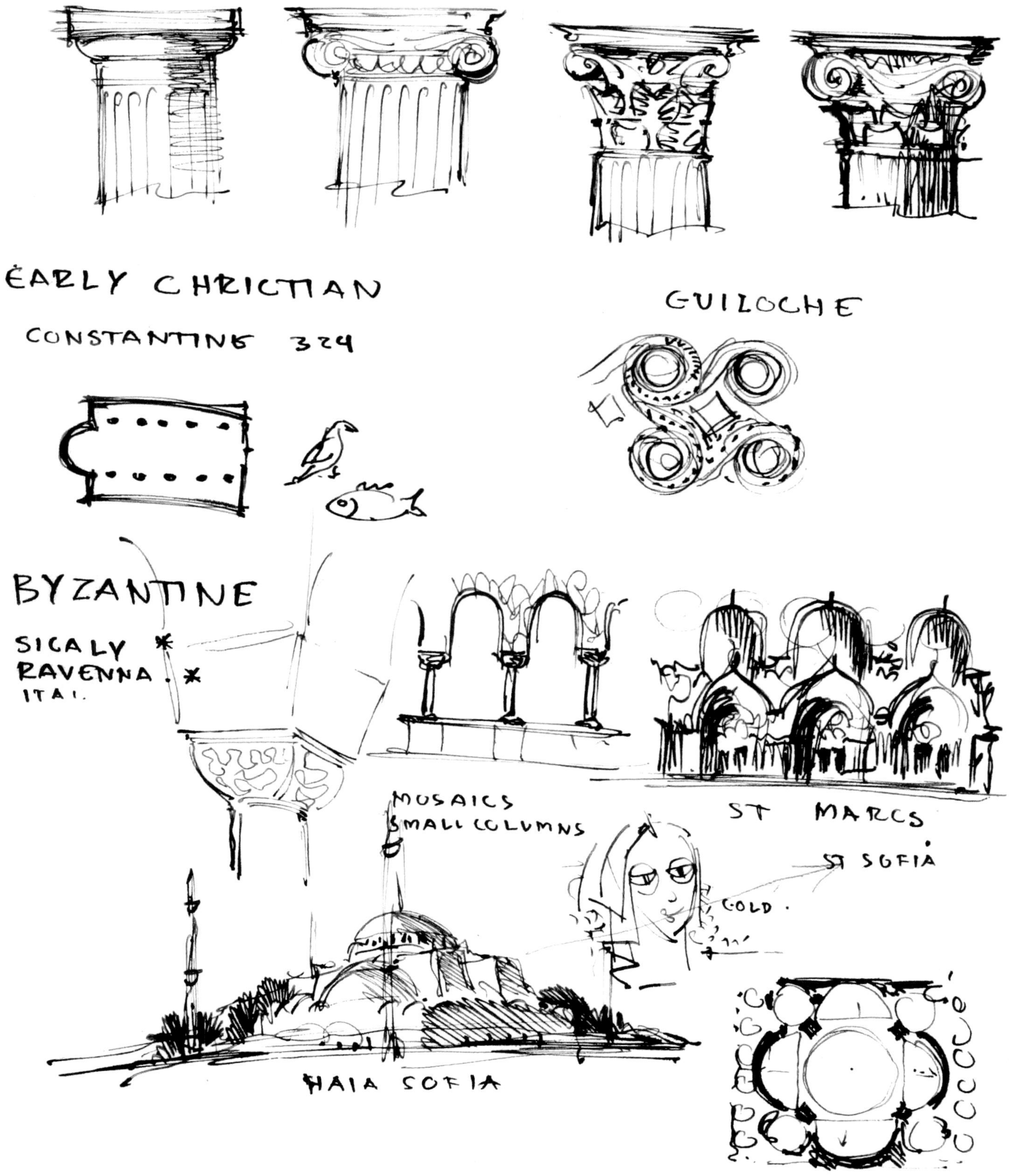

EARLY CHRICTIAN

CONSTANTINE 324

BYZANTINE

SICALY *
RAVENNA. *
ITAL.

MOSAICS
SMALL COLUMNS

ST MARCS

ST SOFIA

GOLD.

HAIA SOFIA

Eero Saarinen, sketches of early Christian and Byzantine architecture, from letter to Florence Schust, ca. 1935

Lecture delivered at Dickinson College, Carlisle, Pennsylvania, on December 1, 1959

DICKINSON COLLEGE ARTS AWARD ADDRESS

I thought I would ask three questions—the same kind of questions that I would ask a scientist or a doctor or a poet about his profession—and try to answer them straight.

They are: 1. What is architecture? 2. What is happening today in architecture? 3. What are you, Saarinen, trying to do?

What is architecture?

At the outset, let me explain that when I speak of "architecture" I am speaking of architecture as an art. We must recognize that most building today is very thoughtless and routine, done by architects who only possess the technique of producing plans and who look on architecture as pure business. But there is also architecture, and I like to think that is what is practiced by many of my colleagues and me, which is an art. Its driving force comes from its art characteristics. Unlike painting and sculpture, which have been at odds with society over the last 30 years, architecture has had to work with society and has succeeded. And also unlike painting and sculpture, where the individual works entirely alone, architecture involves many people. It is true that it all has to be siphoned through one mind, but there is always teamwork. Yes, architecture, as contrasted with building, is an art. And it is of such architecture that I speak.

Now, as to our question, what is architecture? The question has to be divided into two parts—what is its scope? and what is its purpose?

First, its scope:

I think of architecture as the total of man's man-made physical surroundings. The only thing I leave out is nature. You might say it is the man-made nature. Now this is not exactly the dictionary definition of architecture[,] which deals with the technique of building, but this is mine. It is the total of everything we have around us, starting from the largest city plan, includes the street we drive on and its telephone poles and signs, down to the building and house we work and live in and does not end until we consider the chair we sit in and the ash tray we dump our pipe in. It is time the architect practices only on a narrow segment of this wide keyboard, but that is just a matter of historical accident. The total scope of the job is much wider than what he has staked his claim on. So to the question, what is the scope of architecture? I would answer: It is man's total physical surroundings, outdoors and indoors.

Now, what is the purpose of architecture?

Here again, I would like to stake out the most ambitious claim. I think architecture is much more than its utilitarian meaning[,] which is to provide shelter for man's activities on earth. It is certainly all of that, but I believe that it has a much more fundamental role to play for man, almost a religious one. Man is on earth for a very short time and he is not quite sure what his purpose is. Religion gives him his primary purpose. The permanence and beauty and meaningfulness of his surroundings give him confidence and a sense of continuity. This I believe is a very important role that architecture plays beyond its purely functional utilitarian aspects. One senses this fulfillment in the great architecture of the past—the totality of the Gothic village with its central cathedral—the Greek, Roman, and Renaissance towns. Each civilization and culture has produced a total surrounding with an architecture which has come down to our day as its contribution to culture. We live in a period of accelerated transition where our surroundings have become total chaos; therefore, to live and believe we almost have to go around with our eyes closed. Because of this, it is difficult to comprehend and fathom what architecture (an architecture that includes our total surroundings) could or should be to us. Therefore, today architecture is far underestimated in importance. However, it is gaining strength. Much more interest and concern is showing itself for architecture today than we have shown in the very recent past. So, to answer the second part of our first question[,] which was, what is the purpose of architecture? I would answer: To shelter and embrace man's life on earth.

What is happening today in architecture?
Today there must seem a great confusion in architecture to the layman—different architects seem to be going off in different directions.

To explain and understand all this, it is necessary to go back historically and set the time and the place for the scene today.

The modern architectural movement began just before the turn of the century[,] paralleled to and caused in part by the industrial revolution. In itself it was like a revolution seeking to destroy all ties with the immediate "degenerate" past. Its leaders saw this new architecture eventually forming a new style of architecture, such as other cultures had formed styles—Greek, Romanesque, Gothic and Renaissance. It set out bravely. Because my father was one of the planners of this world movement, I remember from my early childhood in Finland the hopes and expectations and the almost religious dedication to this brave new world. The battle has gone through many phases.

First, the functional, where it was believed that a new architecture could be created just by following the needs, the program, and out of this came an oversimplification and the making of a catchword of Louis Sullivan's remark, "Form follows function." A remark far more profound and meaningful than is usually understood.

Then there were the corollary, almost moralistic, beliefs that great architecture could be created out of honesty toward structure and material.

The so-called "International Style" developed out of these beliefs.

The second phase began around the early 1940s when the emphasis shifted. Where once functionalism had been the front man—the thing architects depended on to make architecture—now it was structure that took first place. It was believed that architecture would automatically derive from the honest expression of structure. At this period, there was also increasing awareness of our time, of the new ideas, of the new science, above all of the new and exciting potentials of technology and industry for architecture.

To sum up, I would say that the three great principles of modern architecture had evolved, three fundamental tools for a new style: 1. Functional integrity. 2. Honest expression of structure. 3. Awareness of our time.

Tools alone do not make architecture. There must also be leadership to show the direction and thus the new architecture had its three great men—Frank Lloyd Wright, Le Corbusier and Mies van der Rohe.

Here I would like to interpret my theme to tell how I see their personal contributions. Frank Lloyd Wright's influence comes from another era; his forms do also. It is my prediction that he will influence the world of architecture more through his principles than his outward form. At the same time, one has to remember his great influence early in the century and realize that he will go down in history as one of the great giants of our time, just as Michelangelo did.

Le Corbusier, the genius, most versatile, like Leonardo da Vinci or Picasso, has not built much. But in sketches and indications he has opened up the most new worlds. He is the one who has given world architecture the most form.

Mies is the culmination of the Bauhaus style. Within a very limited vocabulary he has taken U.S. technology and simplified building into beautiful simplicity: Mies, "MR. LESS IS MORE."

These are the great leaders, especially Corbu and Mies, and these three made the great principles which together form our architecture. Mixed together, they make the broth which is modern architecture. In different parts of the world, the ingredients of the broth have different proportions. For instance, architecture in South America and Italy is primarily made up out of the fundamental principles plus Corbu. This forms a different product than that of the U.S.[,] which has primarily Mies, comparatively little Corbu,

Eero Saarinen, sketches of Romanesque architecture, from letter to Florence Schust, ca. 1935

and Frank Lloyd Wright as a spice. In the 40s and early 50s Mies was the overwhelming influence for the U.S. The followers of Mies codified his style into a very simple vocabulary of architecture which was to have universal application. American architecture had temporarily reached a comfortable simple plateau. It could have jelled into a style which could have become the style of our century with only refinements remaining to be done during the second half of the century.

Was this what the founders of the modern movement had dreamed about sixty years ago? No, it was not. The "style" that had developed was far too one sided a concept of architecture. Its vocabulary was much too narrow and it only recognized a few of its principles of architecture. It had been codified too quickly and too materialistically. This style saw the different problems of our day all fitting into the same glass and aluminum box—an airport, a skyscraper, a girls' dormitory—all looking the same. There was more to architecture than that. A startling thing happened. The leaders of the generation to follow refused to stop. We, I shall say, because it was my generation, felt that there must still be time for search. Many interesting things had not been explored. There were new and significant things to be done in structure.

The whole science of concrete thin shell construction was developing exciting new possibilities. There were new and unexplored materials. The most obvious of these is concrete and all the possibilities for prefabricating concrete that opened up a whole new form world to architecture. There were new things coming out of Europe from Corbu and his followers[,] where the wider vocabulary of the matter had not narrowed down the concept of the style but rather encouraged exploration. And, above all, the challenges of the great variety of problems to be solved seemed to indicate a greater variety of answers than such a "style" tolerated. The comfortable plateau was abandoned and a new era of exploration into the search for architectural principles and form began. This is where we are today.

As I said, today we have the second generation of architects. Never have the architects "had it so good." There is a great building boom. We can build at our hearts content. There is a greater recognition of architects than ever before. The second generation of leaders in architecture is a highly capable and talented group which views its mission in architecture with great idealism. They are now probing in many different directions and the vocabulary of modern architecture is being greatly expanded. Also, architecture has been returned to a more personal art. We respect each other's talent but we seldom agree on solutions. You should hear the terrible things we say about each other's architecture; I do not agree with some in this group who try to inject into their architecture a superficial feeling of delight and prettiness. Nor do I agree with some that hark back to pseudo-classical forms in their architecture. Nor do I agree with those who give the same character to a building, whether it is an embassy or a pill factory or a church. Nor do I agree with those who disregard the surroundings of their building. And these others do not agree with me on many issues. You can ask, is this just the usual backbiting between architects? No, I don't think so. I think there are some fundamental differences which I will try to answer in the next question.

What is Saarinen trying to do?

I am a child of my period just as everybody else is, and therefore I am enthusiastic about these same principles—function, structure, and being part of our time. And naturally, I feel the great debt that we owe to our three leaders: to Wright, not for his form, but for his concept of modern architecture; to Corbu for opening so many new doors and possibilities; and to Mies for his marvelous discipline.

The principle of respecting function is deeply embedded in me as it is in others of this period. But like others, I do not look to it to solve my architectural problems. Sometimes, however, the problem and the time are ripe for an entirely new functional approach to a problem, as for instance in the new

Washington jet airport, and at such moments function may become the overwhelming principle in directing the formula of design.

The principle of structure has moved in a curious way over this century from being "structural honesty" to "expression of structure" and finally to "structural expressionism." In my opinion, it is a potent and lasting principle, and I would never want to get very far away from it. Here, just as in the principle of function, the degree to which structure becomes expressive depends to a large extent on the problem. To express structure is not an end in itself; it is only when structure can contribute to the total and to the other principles that it becomes important. The Yale hockey rink and the TWA terminal are examples of this.

The third principle—the awareness of the thinking and the technology of our time—is for me an ever-present challenge. I want always to search out the new possibilities in new materials of our time and to give them their proper place in architectural design. I am not talking now glibly about colored plastic in decoration. I am talking about much more fundamental things such as concrete and pre-cast concrete, basic things whose possibilities in architecture have not yet been fully fathomed.

In short, I am dedicated to these three basic principles of modern architecture.

But I said I believed one essential quality of architecture, aside from pure shelter for man's activities, is its inspirational value to man. I also pointed out how this seems to be corroborated by historical examples, really the only measures we have. Therefore, it seems to me that these three are not necessarily the only pillars that one's work must rest on. The great architecture of the past did not rest on these pillars alone. There are other principles equally or more important, and now I wish to speak about those.

When I approach an architectural problem, I try to think out the real significance of the problem. What is the essence of the problem and how can the total structure capture that essence? How can the whole building convey emotionally the purpose and meaning of the building? Now it is true that not all problems have an essence or an inner meaning, but some do. The problem of a chapel is an obvious one. Imagine what Chartres Cathedral would look like if the Gothic master builders had not placed their main effort on the inner meaning and emotional impact of this building but instead concentrated their effort on making the plan work functionally. New problems created out of our technology, such as, specifically, the new jet airport for our nation's capital[,] which also should convey its purpose by its architectural expression. The excitement of travel and the stateliness of belonging to the federal capital should be conveyed. Another example of a problem is, for instance, a research center for a mass-production industry.

All these diverse architectural problems have an inner meaning that can be captured. The conveying in architecture of significant meaning is part of the inspirational purpose of architecture and, therefore, I believe, one of the fundamental principles of our art. And I would, therefore, add it as a fourth pillar.

Again going back to my overall concept of architecture, I see it as man's total physical surroundings. In a sense, architecture begins where nature stops. I see architecture not as the building alone but the building in relation to its surroundings. Now these can be anything from nature itself to other surrounding buildings. When we approach an architectural problem in this office, the first thing we do is build a model of the exact surroundings. This, as well as many visits to the site, gradually brings about a conviction about what should grow on the site. Among leaders in architecture, Frank Lloyd Wright did the most in finding a harmonious relationship between nature and architecture. He showed us how strongly, for instance, a dominant rocky nature can influence a building.

When it comes to man-made rocks, such as, for instance, the buildings on a college campus where the surrounding structures are permanent neighbors, I believe very strongly that the single building must be carefully

Eero Saarinen, sketches of Rococo and Romantic architecture, from letter to Florence Schust, ca. 1935

THE THIRD DIMENTIO-AN
INVENTION OF IMMORTAL SIGNIFICANCE.

Eero Saarinen, sketches of Swedish Theater alteration and expansion, Helsinki, Finland, 1935–36, from letter to Florence Schust, ca. 1935

related to the whole in the outdoor space it creates. In its mass and scale and material, it must become an enhancing element in the total environment. This does not mean that the building has to succumb to the total. Any architecture must hold its head high. I mean a way must be found for uniting the whole, because the total environment is more important than the single building. This, I believe, is a fundamental principle in architecture, which to a large degree has been ignored. It is understandable that this principle has not found much fertile ground to grow in because of the chaos which we call our cities, where almost every site has temporary neighbors. That is why I used the example of the university campus, almost the only permanent man-made environment we have. We have to remember, however, that we are on the eve of a period when our cities will be rebuilt. To rebuild our cities without great concern for this principle would be a crime. Some atrocious crimes have already been committed, crimes against older historical neighbors as well as crimes against 20th century bedfellows. The point I really want to bring forth here is that the surroundings of a building can shape its mass and form in a major way. The conviction that a building cannot be placed on a site, but that a building grows from its site, is a principle. This is the fifth pillar I would like to add.

I would like to return to the need and desire for architecture making a strong emotional impact on man. From early experience, where we built buildings that had a strong central idea which was not carried out in the continuing process of the design, I learned that impact can be pitifully diluted. Therefore, I have come to the conviction that once one embarks on a concept for a building, this concept has to be exaggerated and overstated and repeated in every part of its interior, so that wherever you are, inside or outside, the building sings with the same message. That is why, for instance, the interior of the TWA terminal had to be the way it is; that is why the interior of the new Yale colleges have to be just so. Now this seems to be a conviction and a principle which we try to carry out in all of our works: the principle of the total unity of a building. This, for my own work, I wish to add as the sixth pillar.

I have tried to show how the first fundamentals of modern architecture—function, structure and awareness of our time—were indeed important and timeless principles that mold modern architecture. But I have tried also to show that they are only part of the story. I believe that there are three other important and fundamental principles.

To repeat them again, they are: 1. The expression of the building; 2. The concern with total environment; 3. Carrying a concept to its ultimate conclusion.

In no way do I claim authorship for these added principles. They have been with architecture through the ages. They seem to me to be important, and they seem to me to be understated in much modern architecture today. Without the acceptance of these principles, I believe our architecture will stay an empty dance around the pages of the architectural magazines.

I believe that all six principles have to be included to create real architecture, and so I try to practice what I preach. The inclusion of the last three inevitably creates a diversity of solutions, and thereby the external form of my work varies greatly. But, inside of the solution of every problem there are six threads that hold it together, and these six threads, or pillars as I was calling them, join each building I have done to every other one. In fact, if it didn't sound too pompous, I would say that the common denominator in my work is the constant philosophy, the constant respect, for these six principles. So I think this is what Saarinen is trying to do.

I believe that our time and our culture will eventually come through and create an architecture worthy of itself. It will not necessarily be one architecture in the way we think of Gothic, and, parenthetically, we think falsely of Gothic when we think just of the architecture of the cathedrals, because that period had a very different wood architecture parallel to the stone vaulted buildings. Our society, with its diverse and complex problems, is vastly more complicated than the Gothic or the Renaissance period, and I can well imagine wide diversity remaining a characteristic of our architecture.

Kevin Roche and CBS chairman
William S. Paley, ca. 1962

Cesar Pelli
Kevin Roche
Harold Roth
Robert Venturi

appreciations by former collaborators
panel discussion

The following are extended excerpts from a panel discussion that was held at "Eero Saarinen: Formgiver of 'the American Century,'" a symposium held at the Yale University School of Architecture, April 2, 2005. The panelists were Cesar Pelli, Kevin Roche, Harold Roth, and Robert Venturi, all architects who worked at Eero Saarinen and Associates. The discussion was moderated by Robert A. M. Stern, dean of the Yale School of Architecture. Following the discussion, Dean Stern called for questions from the audience.

Robert Venturi

Because I have been invited to participate as one of Saarinen's friends and employees—and because I am an architect and not a historian or critic—may I start with an anecdote?

I first met Eero when I went to work in his office as a young architect. I was there for two and one-half years—from 1951 through the first half of 1953—at the suggestion of, and recommendation by, Louis Kahn. But after my first week I had decided it was not the place for me—I was not particularly/architecturally happy. But the evening of the day I had resigned, Warren Platner came to my apartment—very graciously—to ask me to stay on—and I did.

Why I did not feel totally at home—although my fellow workers, including John Dinkeloo and Kevin Roche, were very sympathetic—is complex. It was partly because I was working on the GM Technical Center, which was distinctly Miesian in its style, and in those days you were either a Mies guy or a Frank Lloyd Wright guy, and I was the latter (although now I am more a Miesian than a Wrightian). And it was not because I was pre-postmodern: Le Corbusier's Villa Savoye was my favorite building of the twentieth century, and it still is. Perhaps there was also what has been called Eero's eclecticism within his modernism—but then that's funny because my master's thesis of two years before was on the significance of context and its effect on architectural design—but then Eero's expressive variety did not derive from contextual accommodation. What did it derive from? Let me come back to that important issue—what could be called Saarinen's expressionistic eclecticism—in a moment.

Another issue involving differences between us: I was about to spend some time in Rome to study historical architecture at the American Academy—and this was weird at the time for a modern architect to do. And then there is—right at the end of my time with Saarinen, 1953—the Saarinen quotation which I found the other day: "The real environment that our time—our industrial revolution—has created you can see best of all outside of Detroit and Chicago. And you see litter and lettering; you can see hamburger stands, you can see gas stations, you can see car lots, and it is really a terrible mess." Granted, my, and [Venturi's longtime architectural partner] Denise Scott Brown's, acknowledgment of and interest in the pragmatic, everyday urban landscape and the relevance of pop culture did not evolve until some time later—but Eero's commitment to the ideology of pure modernist urbanism would be eternal. The stance of modernist architecture and urbanism was to remain revolutionary and not evolve as evolutionary. Above all, be original (but modern).

Vincent Scully's description of Saarinen's varied kinds of architecture is eloquent, as he has referred to "arbitrary eclecticism" and "impatient formalism"—and his use elsewhere of the word "spectacular" I find most appropriately descriptive.

In the end I might put it that Eero's work acknowledged and expressed, via its kind of baroque drama, complexity—complexity not *within* the projects but *among* the projects—and thereby did not and does not fully connect with our era, which is *mannerist*—where pure unity cannot happen—where exceptions have to be accommodated within conventions. So Saarinen distinctly was not—is not—mannerist.

And is it not ironical that the neo-modernism characteristic of today's architecture, which is spectacularly expressionistic via its forms rather than richly iconographic via its symbolism, can be said to represent a kind of Saarinen revival—or survival?

A few years ago I read in Anne Tyng's book containing Louis Kahn's letters to her [*Louis Kahn to Anne Tyng: The Rome Letters,* 1997] his mention of Eero's not entirely positive letter of recommendation for me for the Rome Prize fellowship—and recently a scholar accidentally found the letter in the archive of the academy [in Rome]—but that's all right—a recommendation of mine for him might have been ambivalent too.

Let me end by saying this ambiguity I've felt about Eero Saarinen's work—and he would have felt about mine—does not exist concerning Eliel Saarinen's work in Finland and at Cranbrook. I unambiguously love it. And then there is Eero's furniture, which I enormously admire, and have employed in our work. And then, despite my mixed feelings, I must proclaim my deep admiration of the St. Louis Arch—of its modern structure, monumental scale, and appropriate symbolism!

And then there is my favorite architect of the twentieth century—who is Finnish—who is Alvar Aalto!

Harold Roth

I was the baby of the office. Dee [Roth's wife] and I arrived in Birmingham, Michigan, in December of 1959, just in time for the office party at the Bloomfield Hunt Club. What a beginning. Though Ingalls Rink was under construction while I was a graduate student here [at Yale], Eero's work was rarely discussed on the fourth floor of the art gallery, where all four years of the architecture school camped out. Louis Kahn had his master studio on the second floor. Paul Schweikher had faded after a brief stay as chairman, and Paul Rudolph's presence was just beginning to be felt as studio critic during my last term. Corbu seemed to be the source of every student diagram. But a visit to the Kresge Auditorium and Chapel at MIT had a significant impact on me, though Vince [Scully]'s concern that the forms lacked integral entrances was overcome at Ingalls. Two years in the military, following Yale, allowed me time to mull over my list of the top ten American architects. On a meager lieutenant's salary, I put together a portfolio of work and sent it off to Eero, who had risen to the top of my list. A note from Kevin [Roche] shortly after said, "Come," and I replied, "I'll be there." The long drive from Galveston to Michigan was wonderful; it was our honeymoon. I had never been to Detroit, I had never met Eero, and fortunately I avoided the test to draw a horse, which I would have failed miserably.

With the Christmas party behind us, I plunged into the ongoing charette of Cesar [Pelli]'s team on Morse and Stiles. I was handed the two college libraries. The vocabulary for the project was well established. Watching [Costantino] Nivola endlessly sketch sand sculptures for the walls was fascinating. Following six months detailing interiors on Dulles, IBM Yorktown, and the visitors' center at the arch, Kevin asked me to head up the design of the CBS tower, which had just come into the office. It was the CBS Building that provided me the opportunity to work with Eero and observe his powerful instincts. Etched in my memory, I can still hear him calling me with his lilting Finnish accent in that cavernous, windowless space behind the Pontiac showroom. Early on I believe Eero imagined CBS as his first and only high-rise structure, not as a sculptural object but as an extrusion rising up through the ground. We tried some awful schemes with Paul Weidlinger, the structural engineer, looking at how the tower met the ground. It never went anywhere, but it provided Eero with more back-burner time while the project continued to be productive. At one point he expressed interest in the system of high-rise multiple elevator banks. We built a model of a generic elevator system with individual cabs sliding up and down, which he found fascinating. Major design decisions were made on CBS before Eero died, but detailing continued after the [firm's] move to Hamden [in 1961].

The office was not a place for fast-track projects. Though the hours were long, exploring schemes for each design issue seemed not to be a search for some theoretical ideal, but rather a serious interest in getting it right, whatever that might be. Eero was an architect of boundless creative energy. I recall several occasions during charettes when Eero and Aline in formal dress would stop in at the office past midnight to check on the work. He would always leave with his encouragement to keep working. Architecture was his world, and he provided us all with an extraordinary legacy.

Cesar Pelli

I worked with Eero Saarinen from 1954 until he died in 1961, and after his death I continued working on projects, particularly Stiles and Morse Colleges, which were in construction when Eero died. Through that time I was very fortunate; I was one of the few who worked very intimately with him on many, many one-on-one design sessions. Through those years, unquestionably, I developed enormous respect and affection for him, so that everything I say about him is very colored by this affection. On the other hand, because we worked so closely we were also very aware of the weakness in the design processes or in the thinking, so we are perhaps more severely critical about those very same projects.

We were working in Bloomfield Hills, which was truly an intellectual desert, so we were very isolated. We depended primarily on ourselves, and many deep bonds developed among those who worked in Eero's office. Bob [Venturi] mentioned that Eero had an uncanny sense for finding people with talent. I do not think that was quite as I would put it. Many of us just came there for all sorts of peculiar reasons, not necessarily very carefully selective. But he did have an uncanny eye both for finding who could contribute, who could help him achieve his goals and to encourage and to allow us to develop whatever talent we had. In some ways many of us made ourselves, or were made, in Eero's office. It is not that we were particularly special before going there. There must have been some talent there, but it was nurtured and allowed to grow in his office. As long as we all helped him achieve his goals, he was very generous with allowing us any search or exploration to design large pieces of projects. For example, the two beautiful staircases of [the] GM Tech Center were designed almost completely by

Kevin, but they were allowing Eero to have the right element in the right place, so he was perfectly happy to let us design large complex elements in his buildings. All of us did that. What I remember best are the pieces I designed, almost by myself: the supporting columns of TWA, which was a very difficult structure to resolve aesthetically. I worked very much alone but Eero came by regularly and OK'd my progress.

Why do you think there is so much interest today in Eero's work? I believe this is no doubt because there are changes in the way we see architecture today, as different as it was seen in the 1950s or 1960s when much criticism [of him] appeared. But this reconsideration of him only makes sense because of his buildings, because his buildings are still there and they are still wonderful. Very uneven, unquestionably—there are some extraordinarily great buildings and some very weak buildings. Eero was the first to recognize when his buildings did not come out the way he thought they should. But some of his buildings are still moving, truly works of art and architecture, and we have to deal with those. That is what forces us to think about Eero again. I agree with Bob Venturi that the St. Louis Arch is perhaps the most sublime of the things that Eero designed. Very interesting because the project was designed so early in his independent career. It took his competition entry many, many years to be fully designed and built, but it is still, I think, absolutely glorious in St. Louis. Unquestionably, there are other great projects like John Deere or the Dulles Airport, and the TWA Terminal, which are the ones that make us stop and say, "Who was this guy?"

Every project was a reason for a new exploration. Every project was different, the circumstances were different, the sites were different, the clients were different, the functions were different, the place was different, and that in his mind required another exploration. This was extraordinary for us, the young designers working with him, because each project was a whole new learning adventure, guided by Eero Saarinen. On his explorations, we were not necessarily guided by one vision, we were directed to do it better every time. He may not have known what better was, but he knew when better was achieved. And better was on many, many different levels—more beautiful, better built, better functioning, cheaper, all of those qualities very equally important in Eero's mind.

And I believe this is perhaps what I remember most. He was extremely vulnerable. Within the office, he never was a guru or an overall leader or [thought] that he knew what the answers were. He did not know what the answers were, and he asked us to help him find them, and we looked everywhere, under every rock around. And we would look again, again and again. We worked very hard, but we worked with a purpose, and those were wonderful years to be young in Bloomfield Hills.

Kevin Roche

Since there has been a slight autobiographical aspect to the other speakers, let me say how I got there. I came as a graduate student to IIT in 1948 after having applied to work with Le Corbusier, Alvar Aalto, Sven Markelius, and a few others. I had finally decided Mies was it, so I got to Chicago, stayed there for two semesters, decided I got the message, and that was enough.

The big project that was going on at that time was the United Nations, so I went to New York and I managed to get a job working at the United Nations on the site. In the course of things in New York, you tended to get laid off after a few months, and after about eight months or so I was laid off. I was out of work in New York in 1949 for about five months, completely broke, really completely broke. I had a cousin who was an aspiring movie actress in England, and she got a contract with MGM. I was really on the skids, and she arrived in New York with this MGM expense account. So we went on a tremendous binge for about a week. Somebody I had worked with at the United Nations had recommended me to Eero. Eero left a message that he would be at the Plaza Hotel on such and such a day, and could I come first thing in the morning for an interview. I was up all night the night before at the Stork Club and arrived at eight o'clock as Eero was getting up in his bedroom. He began to interview me, and I sat on the edge of the bed in the overcoat that I had been doing something else in all night. I sat on the edge of the bed, and Eero had a rather boring delivery, and I fell asleep, sound asleep. I woke up and he was still going on about something. The last place in the world I wanted to go was Detroit. I almost went to Scranton, Pennsylvania. In any case, Eero hired me, and in a few days I got on a train to Detroit and got a bus to Bloomfield Hills, which was an almost abandoned intersection of two roads in the heart of the executive residential area of General Motors.

There were about ten people in the office at that time, and the General Motors [project] was just really starting up. It was the spring of 1950. Eliel was still alive and he would come in occasionally to do things. Everything seemed to be going okay and Brandeis started up, and I was assigned to do a rendering of something at Brandeis, which I did. I wasn't a very good renderer, but I did it anyway. Eero hadn't seen it and he got on the overnight train to go to New York with this rendering he had not seen. The next day, he called the office and said, "Fire that guy." So I have the distinction of being the only guy ever fired by Eero. However, he relented, and I was not actually fired. It all settled down. We moved from that small building to a new office that Eero designed, across the street. Projects started to come in, and it was really extraordinarily exciting for a young man. Cesar said that Eero searched out people, and he did, people of talent, but it was really the only game in town. There was no place else you could go. You could go to SOM [Skidmore, Owings, and Merrill] in Chicago or SOM in New York. I. M. Pei had just started up; Louis Kahn was really not that well known. So Eero was really the only game in town in the early '50s. It became an extraordinary experience; it became a family, a community. As Cesar said, we were working in a basement, a figurative basement, surrounded by nothing in the cultural sense. So we were really very dependent on each other, and as the office grew we became more and more dependent. Eero was both a brother, a father figure, a mentor, and really a guiding light for all of us. Anybody who worked for Eero who is still around will have the same emotions as the four of us do today, because he was a truly extraordinary man and a great architect.

Now, as to the archeological dig that is going on at the moment. As with all archeological digs there is sometimes the tendency to take a few fragments and invent a civilization. We have to be careful that we do not do that. I am reminded of what St. Paul wrote to the Corinthians regarding the past: that when we look at the past we look through dark glasses, or as St. James put it, "through a glass darkly." So we have to be careful as we look back. We [have to make sure to] have both as much information as we can possibly get and that the interpretive nature is conditioned by the circumstances and culture of the period. I am sure that all that will in due course get settled out. One of the things that I hope comes out of it is not only the recognition of Eero again, very belatedly, forty years or more [after he died], but that people will go back and look at these buildings, and in a time and a world where everything that we see and hear is digested for us first, that they will go back with fresh eyes, look at these buildings, criticize them, enjoy them. While you may never have had the privilege of knowing this truly great human being, anybody who goes back and looks at these buildings will be able to see and recognize and appreciate this truly great architect.

Robert A. M. Stern calls for questions from the audience.

Diana Balmori
landscape architect

There has always been this enormous question about where Eero's forms were coming from. And because you have experienced this in terms of very specific projects in the office, I thought we could hear from you about this issue of the search for form on any one of your specific projects. Just take any one project that you worked on and say okay, why were we looking at these kinds of forms? Why were we going here? How many forms did we look at? You know, anything that has to do with the nitty gritty of facing the job.

Roche I think that the thing we should say at the outset is Eero never started with form, unlike some architects we know. He had an approach rather similar to a scientist or researcher of starting with trying to define what is the problem. In the exercise of trying to find what is the problem, he was absolutely relentless. In the case of the airplane thing, which we are all very familiar with—the stopwatch and timing, when planes take off and when they land, these kinds of things—he did the same thing when it was the colleges. For example, we visited many of the colleges. He would speak to the masters of the colleges at Harvard, Cornell, Princeton, and say what is it you are trying to achieve? What is it that the students want? He did this endless, endless research into everything before he even started thinking. There were a few occasions when he would arrive in the morning with a sketch; one of them was the airport in Athens, which was not featured in any of the things we have talked about in the last few days, and which was, in its own sense, a remarkable structure. But it was one of the few times that I remember where it arrived fully born right off. Otherwise, the process was very slow, very, very methodical, and very careful. By the time he got to thinking of the form, he already knew more about the subject than probably the people who had asked him to do the building in the first place. More about what was needed, more about the functional aspects, and he had thoroughly investigated also all of the other relationships, the urban design, the cultural environment, all of these things which one normally takes into account. The process is methodical, careful, exasperatingly slow at times, and thorough. I think one of the things that excited me about it was that, unlike the experience with Mies van der Rohe, where there was a religion and a way that you had to do it—there was a black and white that was either wrong or it was right—and mostly it was wrong with anybody else except Mies.

With Eero, there wasn't that. There wasn't a black or white, right or wrong, so evident at any point in time. What there was was this extraordinarily careful assembly of the information and research and facts. And for a young architect, that was very encouraging because you felt there was a process that you could follow and at the end of the process the form would emerge, something would emerge, and then you could begin to make judgments about the form and its place and use and all of that.

Venturi You and I are not agreeing. I think that the question relates less to programmatic efficiency or programmatic care and accommodation, or to making the building work well, which is extremely important, and more to stylistic expression. But I think there is the issue where we are interested now, very much, in acknowledging multiculturalism, and where thereby there can be many ways of expression that can connect with different cultures: there is not one universal culture anymore. But I don't think this is what Eero's eclectic expressionism was about. What worries me and worried me about Eero is—you could not call it multiculturalism because it was/is a little like every building being in a different costume—you are relating to the environment at a costume ball where someone goes as one thing and another person goes as another thing. It is a funny analogy, but that worries me, that there seemed to be no particular connection, that the expressionistic variety was not derived from what we would call multiculturalism now, but from a kind of arbitrary, stylistic, fashionable approach. That is being a little overly negative, but I think there is that problem. I am not putting this very well, because I did not understand it so well, and I still kind of don't get it. But I was worried at the time where at the same time in the office you are doing a building that looks like Mies and then you are doing a building that is this way and a building that is that way. So on the one hand I am saying, hey, complexity and contradiction are appropriate. But on the other hand, it was a kind of stylistic, costume-like approach. It could be argued that one would be concerned about that.

Roche I would like to answer that with two examples. One is General Motors Technical Center, which we spent a lot of time yesterday and today talking about, the influence of the IIT campus and Mies van der Rohe. Actually you have to remember that it was in Detroit where Albert Kahn had been building factories for sixty years, there was a culture of this kind of architecture which already had gone to Germany and come back via Mies to Chicago and back to Detroit in a more refined way. But that was a basic culture of design, pragmatic, straightforward, no nonsense, very, very direct. That was really an underlying and guiding principle in the development of General Motors Technical Center as far as the technical aspects of the architecture are concerned. Another example is one which, if you take the MIT auditorium, which is an entirely different-looking building from General Motors, and you again refer back to Mies, who had this famous photomontage of a factory building which was actually a contractor building, with the auditorium in it, which was an absolutely ludicrous idea in terms of making a working auditorium, but was symbolic of what Mies was saying, which says that you have a universal enclosure and in that all kinds of functions can take place. Eero, instead of taking a factory building, he took the emerging shell concrete construction and made a dome, which is not the typical form of the auditorium. Instead of an audience and the stage, he put everything into a form that was a completely original form for an auditorium. So at GM and at MIT you have two different-looking buildings, but they can come, in a sense, from the same philosophy, or the same directness of approach. So I would argue that Eero did not think in terms of fancy dress; he did not think in terms of a style for the job or a style for a particular thing. He thought more in terms of an evolution, and if it was appropriate to be contextual, he was contextual. If it was not appropriate to be contextual, he was not. It wasn't that he was putting a costume on it; it was the very nature of what he was designing.

Venturi But you can compare the MIT auditorium to the rink at Yale. You can say that a rink should be a generally functional building, and the way you normally span a rectangular-shaped space is that you make the big span go across the shorter part of the rectangle, not the long part of the rectangle. Now there are moments when you do things like that. If you are doing a cathedral which engages symbolism, you have an expressionistic opportunity to be not highly efficient. I do think there is a kind of dramatic quality to the athletic rink that is questionable.

Stern Clearly, you have yet to understand hockey at Yale.

Roche Let me respond to that too. The obvious thing is not to just go across the short dimension. You have to place these things in the moment of time. Fred Severud had just designed a cable structure for a cattle shed in North Carolina and Eero was very interested in the idea of the cable as a spanning beam. Now if you start with that, and you think in terms of covering the rectangle, if you put a single arch over the center the cable span is longer. If you put the arch in the long span, the cable span is shorter and makes more sense. So the form, you could argue, could . . .

Venturi It could be that the cable span isn't that sensible.

Pelli I think actually that Bob [Venturi] made an interesting point. I remember two of the projects: one was the elevation of the American embassy [in London]. He had covered a wall with alternative designs. Some of those that he would always like to do were versions of Renaissance palaces, including lions by the entrances because they helped him to organize his mind about what was the symbolic nature of this kind of building. There were really about thirty kinds of designs for the elevation, but he just pondered over those. None of them ended up in his final design. But those were very critical in his exploration. He was really exploring, and the reason he had all of those alternative choices of forms was just to see which one would fit best with the problem as he understood it with his interpretation of what modern design requires, of what the nature of the project was. So, it was not quite like what you said, Bob. I don't think it was being capricious. This was all being guided by his interpretation, his impression, of which one of his alternatives would best fit this specific project.

Roche If I could just add to what Cesar said. Eero was going though a whole series of studies to determine what was the appropriate federal expression, the expression of the federal government. The fact that [the U.S. Chancellery Building] was in a park in London and was going to prove to be disastrous in many ways, we kept talking about that and telling Eero that this is London, this is another world, and American federal expression is a dangerous thing in Grosvenor [Square]. That didn't make any difference to Eero. He was going through the same process of research, trying to establish what, in this case, was an appropriate expression for a federal building. Which he did succeed in doing with Dulles Airport where it was an entirely different thing.

Pelli Sometimes he felt he had indeed achieved it and other times, after the building was built, or sometimes even before, he felt, "no, I didn't get it."

Roche Eero had this great, wonderful characteristic of being completely human, so he did things that were not good and things that were good.

Roth In the case of CBS, we spent an enormous amount of time studying New York City zoning. This was Eero's first building in Manhattan, aside from Lincoln Center, which of course was an institutional building. And CBS being a commercial building, it was critical to understand the zoning. And fortunately it was at a time when the New York City zoning was undergoing a major rewrite. In fact, in the end, many of the provisions were rewritten to accommodate the CBS tower, which derived from the core size and the amount of office space, which was a very rational approach, studying the modules and what other office buildings had been successfully completed or were under way at the time. There was a huge amount of time devoted to an understanding of that before we really moved on to any of the architectural expression aspects of the project.

Roche This related back to his relationship with Gordon Bunshaft. He contacted Gordon to get advice on what you do in building a building in New York. Gordon brought in Ed Matthews, his business partner, who spent a lot of time with us, telling Eero what the possibilities were with the new zoning, which was just emerging at that moment in time. Again, this whole methodology of beginning at the beginning, finding what is possible, and then going from there. You might then go from that point to the structure, which was again to be realized in concrete. Because the cost of concrete was going down, it was emerging as a possible construction material for high-rise buildings. And CBS was, I think, the first high-rise building to be built entirely of concrete. Weidlinger was a brilliant engineer, but we have to remember this solid vertical was like Raymond Hood with the Daily News Building twenty or thirty years before that, or Rockefeller Center. So when Vince was criticizing it yesterday as being arbitrary, in fact you have him starting from precedent in all those buildings with the single vertical solid, the vertical glass, the vertical solid, et cetera. Again, this same thing of the research, the study, doing all of the preliminary work before, as Eero said, you get to the point where the building begins to become a building. And at that point, you make a number of different alternatives inside the constraints of the groundwork you have established, and then the design plan emerges.

Venturi

We had a different relationship with Gordon Bunshaft quite a few years later. It would have been a wonderful big project we were presenting to the Washington Fine Arts Commission when he referred to our design as "ugly and ordinary," and it didn't go ahead. We said at the time: well, considering the source, we are going to take that as a compliment, and that became the motto of our firm—"ugly and ordinary" instead of "heroic and original."

Kurt Forster
architectural historian

As I listen to the questions or what I believe in part is behind the questions—How do you arrive at this choice of shape? Where does this shape find its justifications?—I am reminded of [the] unspoken part of your otherwise incredibly illuminating answers, [and] one is that you explain a perfect process: you get down, you examine all the factors that could be thought to be at play, and you work through them. And then the answer stops because there is a leap, then all of a sudden this notion or idea appears and, of course, the idea that it may have historic precedent. Historians who should rethink it aren't making it more legitimate or less willful. In fact, it is precisely for having historic precedent that the willfulness shows its full power. There [is] something in this mind and in this procedure that is very illuminating. On the one hand, you study everything, you get really into the heart of the matter, and then comes this inexplicable leap; and once that leap has been made you become, not so much the prisoners of your earlier functions and analysis, but you become, if you are the prisoner, the prisoner of that choice that you have made. A similar leap occurs, but in the other direction, when, with the TWA building, it is effected. Proof of the wonderful capacity of the architect to work with clients, et cetera. And then, he wants time to rework it, rethink it, and do another leap.

Pelli

All architects have to make choices at some point or another. I think what Eero had was a very well developed methodology to get to the point where you can jump and also to test it afterwards with his intuition. Many times, he jumped and he didn't like it, and he went back and started again.

Roche

It is commonly called a creative process of genius.

Greg Lynn
architect

I am having a lot of difficulty evaluating the conversation. I would just throw out the problem that it is tough to be a genius without a discourse. And most of the architects that Saarinen has been put into relation to were known for their greatness in discourse before the greatness in building. So for Mies, my attraction to Mies is partially the buildings; it is actually more the discourse or my love of Villa Savoye as the greatest building in the twentieth century because it has all of Le Corbusier's five points of architecture. So I am wondering, was there discourse in the office that was guiding these decisions and these leaps, and even if there wasn't a discourse in the office, what were Saarinen's affections, let's say, for Mies in terms of the discourse, or was it more an affection just for the style of building and methods of construction and the materials?

Roche

Well, of course there was a discourse. You cannot get ten or fifteen or twenty or fifty hotshot architects in the room together and not have a discourse of some sort. Not that much of it made any difference to Eero; he had his own internal discourse. Occasionally some of it might rub off on him from us, but most of it was coming the other way.

Pelli

What is important in all of Eero's work, which always followed the discourse, is that he wanted his buildings to do everything. He wanted them to function fantastically, to be the most advanced technologically, to be gorgeous, to be very true to modernism. He wanted his buildings to come in on time, within the budget. He wanted the buildings to do absolutely everything, to fit in the context, to respect the surroundings, to be loved by the people who would use them, to be comfortable, and each one of those objectives was discussed, was balanced against the other; we all worked very hard. But he was extremely interested in exploring all the ramifications of architecture, of what building is.

Venturi I am the one guy who is somewhat negative here, but let's rather say I am ambivalent. I think you have to say that the variety in his work is stylistic. I cannot agree with people who talk about symbolism—an idea that was completely rejected in the '50s—and you wonder how did you get from the preliminary analyses referred to, to choose the style that it was to become. Maybe it is not right to use the word style, but I think there is such an irony that modernism rejected the idea of style but that Eero's modernism was stylistic—stylistically eclectic! Modernism engaged originally a reaction against eclectic styles. In the Victorian time when you got the same architect you could get different styles—Gothic, classical, whatever. It is sort of an irony that here this modernism was eclectic-stylistic. And I don't know how Eero went from the analyses mentioned to end up in his ultimate expressionistic stylistic expressions.

Stern I think something Kevin said earlier should be kept in mind. We must judge the work in terms of the time in which it was made. And modernism was being questioned by Saarinen, by Rudolph, by Johnson, by a host of other people; Americans as well as Europeans. It was being questioned for its absolute discourse, for its lack of connection to popular taste, for its lack of connection to place, et cetera. And I think that Saarinen's work, though it often didn't make people—both students and other professionals—happy because it was seemingly inconsistent in appearance, where Mies's was seemingly consistent in appearance (another myth, in reality), but part of that discourse, and I think many of the quotations that have come up so far in the symposium from the very scholarly talks, quotations from Saarinen's writings, a myth of which is he never wrote anything because he had nothing to say—not true—show you that he was grappling very much with the issues of context. Foreground buildings, background buildings, et cetera, and Alan Plattus makes this very, very clear. So I think it is unfair to say that he was not part of the discourse. And his discourse was maybe not waved on a flag because he did not have to do what young architects have to do which is to write a manifesto to get a little attention. He had it a little easier in the sense that he had an office behind him and his talent was given the way to express itself through that amazing competition leap, in particular, at the Jefferson Memorial.

Roche I think, just to reinforce that, also to remember the cultural and historic heritage that he had from his family and from his background and from his country. Those are all very significant elements in what made Eero's architecture.

(opposite, top) Saarinen examines United States Jefferson National Expansion Memorial model

(opposite, bottom) Saarinen and associates Kevin Roche (second from left) and Cesar Pelli (right) study model of Trans World Airlines Terminal

Trans World Airlines Terminal, waiting room

about the contributors

DONALD ALBRECHT
is an independent curator and is curator of architecture and design at the Museum of the City of New York. He has organized a number of exhibitions on twentieth-century American architecture and design, most notably *The Work of Charles and Ray Eames: A Legacy of Invention* for the Library of Congress and the Vitra Design Museum (1997), *Making Architecture: The Getty Center* (1997), and *The Opulent Eye of Alexander Girard* (2000).

MARK COIR
is the director of Cranbrook Archives and Cultural Properties. He has published books and organized exhibitions relating to the architecture of the Detroit area, such as the *Guide to Building Research in Detroit* (1978). In 1995 he organized the Saarinen/Swanson Office Reunion at Cranbrook and wrote a history of the Saarinen architecture office for the published proceedings of the reunion.

ROSAMOND FLETCHER
assists in coordinating exhibitions at the Center for Architecture, AIA New York chapter. She has taught architectural design and theory at Rhode Island School of Design and Georgia Institute of Technology. She is a graduate of the Yale School of Architecture's Master of Environmental Design program, for which she wrote a thesis titled "Negotiating the Interface: Communication and Collaboration in Building Technology, from Graphic Manuals to Software."

SANDY ISENSTADT
is an assistant professor in the department of art history at Yale University. He has written numerous articles on postwar reformulations of modernism, including those by Richard Neutra and José Luis Sert. In 2003 he co-curated *Picture This: Windows on the American Home,* a show at the National Building Museum, with Donald Albrecht. He is the author of *The Modern American House: Spaciousness and Middle-Class Identity* (2006).

SEAN KHORSANDI
is practicing architecture at Pei Cobb Freed and Partners in New York. He received his master's degree from the Yale School of Architecture.

ALEXANDRA LANGE
received her doctorate from the Institute of Fine Arts at New York University in 2005. Her dissertation was titled "Tower, Typewriter, and Trademark: Architects, Designers, and the Corporate Utopia, 1956–1964." Her articles and exhibition reviews have appeared in *Grey Room*, the *Journal of the Society of Architectural Historians*, *Metropolis*, *New York*, and the *New York Times*.

HÉLÈNE LIPSTADT
is a research affiliate in the History Theory Criticism Section at the Massachusetts Institute of Technology and a founding director of DOCOMOMO US. She edited *The Experimental Tradition: Essays on Competitions in Architecture* (1989) and has written many articles and essays on European and American modern architecture, including a text in *The Work of Charles and Ray Eames: A Legacy of Invention* (1997) and several studies of Eero Saarinen's Gateway Arch. She is presently preparing a book on the French sociologist Pierre Bourdieu and architecture for Pennsylvania State University Press.

BRIAN LUTZ
worked in the sales division at Knoll International in New York before moving to Helsinki, where he served as export director for Artek Oy AB. Now based in Pennsylvania, he is U.S. market manager for the Swedish furniture company Lammhults.

REINHOLD MARTIN
is an associate professor at the School of Architecture, Planning, and Preservation, Columbia University. He is the author of *The Organizational Complex: Architecture, Media, and Corporate Space* (2003). He is also a founding editor of *Grey Room* and a principal of Martin/Baxi Architects, based in New York.

THOMAS MELLINS
is curator of special exhibitions at the Museum of the City of New York. He has also organized exhibitions at the National Building Museum, Washington, D.C., and is the co-author of three books on the architecture and urbanism of New York City: with Robert A. M. Stern and Gregory F. Gilmartin, *New York 1930* (1987); with Robert A. M. Stern and David Fishman, *New York 1960* (1995); and with Robert A. M. Stern and David Fishman, *New York 1880* (1999).

WILL MILLER
is chairman and CEO of Irwin Financial Corporation of Columbus, Indiana. He serves on the boards of numerous nonprofit cultural organizations, including the National Building Museum and the John D. and Catherine T. MacArthur Foundation, and is a Fellow of the Yale Corporation.

CHRISTOPHER MONKHOUSE
is curator of architecture, design, decorative arts, craft, and sculpture at The Minneapolis Institute of Arts. His interest in midcentury American architecture and design led to organizing the exhibitions *Ralph Rapson: Sixty Years of Modern Design* (1999) and *Marcel Breuer in Minnesota* (2002). Before moving to Minneapolis he was the founding curator of the Heinz Architectural Center at the Carnegie Museum of Art.

JENNIFER KOMAR OLIVAREZ
is an associate curator at The Minneapolis Institute of Arts, where she has organized numerous installations and exhibitions on twentieth-century architecture and design, including *Ralph Rapson: Sixty Years of Modern Design* (1999) and *Marcel Breuer in Minnesota* (2002). She has published articles and essays on modern architecture and design.

EEVA-LIISA PELKONEN
is an assistant professor at the Yale School of Architecture, where she directs the Master of Environmental Design program. She is the author of *Achtung Architecture! Image and Phantasm in Contemporary Austrian Architecture* (English ed., 1996; German ed., 1997). Her second book, *Alvar Aalto: The Geopolitics of Architecture,* is forthcoming from Yale University Press.

ALAN J. PLATTUS
is a professor of architecture and urbanism at the Yale School of Architecture. He founded and directs the Yale Urban Design Workshop, a community design center engaged in projects all over the region.

MICHAEL REY
earned a master of architecture degree from the Yale School of Architecture in 2005. He currently works for Overland Partners Architects in San Antonio, Texas.

SUSANNA SANTALA
is a doctoral candidate in the department of art history at Helsinki University, where she is completing a dissertation on Eero Saarinen's airports. She also works as a curator of Kunsthalle Helsinki, Finland. She has curated exhibitions on contemporary art and design; edited exhibition catalogues, including *Seppo Renvall,* co-edited with Maija Tanninen-Mattila (2004); and published articles in such magazines as *Muoto, Arkkitehti,* and *Frame News.*

VINCENT SCULLY
is Sterling Professor Emeritus of the History of Art, Yale University, where he has taught since 1947. There are now two chaired professorships in his name at Yale. His books include *The Shingle Style* (1955); *Frank Lloyd Wright* (1960); *Louis I. Kahn* (1962); *The Earth, the Temple, and the Gods* (1962); *American Architecture and Urbanism* (1969); *The Shingle Style Today, or The Historian's Revenge* (1974); *Pueblo: Mountain, Village, Dance* (1975); *Architecture: The Natural and the Manmade* (1991); and *Modern Architecture and Other Essays,* edited by Neil Levine (2003). He was Jefferson Lecturer of the National Endowment for the Humanities in 1995 and the first recipient of the Vincent Scully Prize of the National Building Museum in 1999. In 2004 he received the National Medal of Arts, the United States' highest honor for artistic excellence.

TIMO TUOMI
is director of the research department at the Museum of Finnish Architecture. He has written on, and led research teams studying, postwar architecture, and has edited two books, *Aspects of the 1960s: Architecture as Social Activity and Art Form* (2000) and *Tapiola: Garden City, Life, and Architecture* (2003).

index

Page numbers in **boldface** type refer to the "Inventory of Buildings and Projects" in the Project Portfolio

photo credits

Every effort has been made to locate and acknowledge rights holders. We sincerely regret any errors or omissions.

Numbers indicate page number; t = top, b = bottom, l = left, c = center, r = right; parentheses indicate additional page; C = cover, B = back cover

© Wayne Andrews/Esto, 132r; Reprinted from *Architectural Forum*, 85 (March 1956), 232 (July 1949), 233b (March 1953), 259 (August 1941), 290t (March 1961); From the Collections of Arteaga Photos LTD, C (xvi); Reprinted from *Beaux Arts Institute of Design Bulletin*, 123r; © Ferenc Berko, 165l; © Boeing Management Company, 335b; Reprinted from *California Arts & Architecture* (August 1943), 264b (258); Collection Centre Canadien d'Architecture/Canadian Centre for Architecture, Montreal, Gift of David Graham Powrie, 221l, 273t, 273b, 293b, 294, 295t, 295b; Redrawn by Janice Carapelucci, 59l (based on as-built plan by Will Miller), 162l, 171b, 174l, 174r, 182t, 182b, 192r, 193r, 197r, 198r, 200b, 204b, 207r, 209bl, 213b, 216t, 216b, 219l; © CBS/Landov, 219c; © Chicago History Museum/Hedrich Blessing, 61r, 131c, 130t, 194b, 194r, 216l, 228 (222); Courtesy Christ Church Lutheran, 156r; © The Coca-Cola Company, 333b; © Avery Architectural & Fine Arts Library, Columbia University in the City of New York, 5b, 20 (12), 207l; © Cranbrook Archives, 14 (Saarinen Family Papers), 31l (Saarinen Family Papers), 31r, 32b (photo by George W. Hance), 33t, 33b (photo by Richard G. Askew), 34, 35 (photo by Richard G. Askew), 38, 39 (Marguerritte Kimball Papers), 40, 41 (Marianne Strengell Papers), 102 (photo by Richard G. Askew), 103 (Swanson Family Papers), 121r (photo by Mark Coir), 123l (Douglas Baker Papers), 125r (photo by Joseph Munroe), 126 (photo by Richard G. Askew), 127r (J. Robert F. Swanson and Pipsan Saarinen Swanson Papers), 127l (photo by Richard G. Askew), 128 (photo by Richard G. Askew), 129l (photo by Richard G. Askew), 129r (photo by Richard G. Askew), 131r (photo by Richard G. Askew), 131l (photo by Richard G. Askew), 133t (photo by Richard G. Askew), 133b (photo by Richard G. Askew), 134r (photo by Richard G. Askew), 134l (120) (photo by Richard G. Askew), 136l (photo by James Packard), 136t (photo by Richard G. Askew), 138l (photo by Richard G. Askew), 138r (photo by Richard G. Askew), 139l (Swanson Family Papers), 139r (photo by James Packard), 140l (photo by Richard G. Askew), 140r (photo by Richard G. Askew), 141r (photo by Joseph Munroe), 141l (photo by Richard Shirk), 145l (photo by Harvey Croze), 146r (photo by Harvey Croze), 147b (photo by Harvey Croze), 148l (photo by Harvey Croze), 156l (Swanson Family Papers), 166l (S. Glen Paulsen Papers), 166t (photo by Richard Shirk), 167l (photo by Richard Shirk), 169r (rendering by Chuck Bassett), 176 (photo by Richard Shirk), 179l (S. Glen Paulsen Papers), 180l (photo by Richard Shirk), 183 (S. Glen Paulsen Papers), 184b (photo by Richard Shirk), 209l (S. Glen Paulsen Papers), 249 (photo by Richard G. Askew), 250 (photo by Harvey Croze), 252 (photo by Harvey Croze), 253c (photo by Harvey Croze), 253b (photo by Harvey Croze), 256 (photo by Richard Shirk), 262 (photo by Richard G. Askew), 263, 270 (John Mesick Papers), 271 (drawn by Merle Westlake), 283 (Jack M. Goldman Papers), 287 (Astrid Sampe Papers), 293t (286) (Jack M. Goldman Papers), 297t (S. Glen Paulsen Papers), 313 (photo by Richard G. Askew), 316b (Maurice Allen Papers), 324b (Saarinen Family Papers), 328t (photo by Richard G. Askew), 328b (photo by Richard G. Askew), 329 (photo by Harvey Croze), 334t (Claude DeForest Papers; Courtesy Cranbrook Archives, 30 (photo by Chicago Press Bureau), 192l (photo by Fotograf Teigen); Collection of Cranbrook Art Museum, Bloomfield Hills, Mich. (CAM 1992.25), photograph by Balthazar Korab, © Cranbrook Art Museum/Balthazar Korab, 32t (28), 122; Collection of Cranbrook Art Museum, Bloomfield Hills, Mich., Gift of Mark Daigler (CAM 1986.6), Photograph by R. H. Hensleigh and Tim Thayer, 248t; Collection of Cranbrook Art Museum, Bloomfield Hills, Mich., Gift of Laurence S. Rockefeller (CAM 1986.35), Photograph by R. H. Hensleigh and Tim Thayer © Florence Knoll Bassett, 254c; Collection of Cranbrook Art Museum, Bloomfield Hills, Mich., Gift of Eliel Saarinen (CAM 1928.39), 312; © George Cserna, 206l, 206t, 206r; © 1983 The Detroit Institute of Arts, 247; © *The Detroit News*, 223; © 2006 Eames Office LLC (www.eamesoffice.com), 91, 106, 149; © Reynold Ferguson/*St. Louis Post-Dispatch*, 365t; © 2001 Robert Galbraith, 22–23; Evelyn Hofer/*Vogue* © 1960 Conde Nast Publications, Inc., 337b; Courtesy IBM Corporate Archives, 51; Courtesy Irwin Union Files, 61l; © Knoll, Inc., viii, 142r, 150, 155l, 155r, 185c, 186–87, 189l, 189r, 253t, 333c; © Balthazar Korab Ltd., 3b, 4, 18, 50t, 59r, 60, 90, 110 (98), 163, 164r, 168l, 175, 192b, 214l, 244 (10–11), 335b, 365b; © Balthazar Korab/Cranbrook Archives, 121l; © John Lane Studio, 190l, 190r; © *Los Angeles Herald Express*, 161r; Courtesy Brian Lutz, 248b; Courtesy Miller Family, 58t; © Will Miller, 63t, 64, 65, 66t, 66b; © Museum of Finnish Architecture, 124l, 124r, 124b; © The Museum of Modern Art/Licensed by SCALA/Art Resource, N.Y., 136b, 137; Courtesy of the National Gallery of Art, 24; Reprinted Courtesy of *New Haven Register*, 243, 245; © *New York Herald Tribune*, 331; Reprinted from *Pencil Points*, 144b; © Alan Plattus, 320; Reprinted with permission from *Progressive Architecture*, © Penton Media Inc., 84; © Ralph Rapson, FAIA, 133r, 138c, 141c, 264t (258); Printed by permission of the Norman Rockwell Family Agency © 1959 the Norman Rockwell Family Entities © 1959 SEPS: Licensed by Curtis Publishing Co., Indianapolis, Ind., All rights reserved, www.curtispublishing.com, 7; Courtesy of Michael D. Salazar, Pasadena, Calif., 326b; © J. Paul Getty Trust, used with permission, Julius

Shulman Photography Archive, Research Library of the Getty Research Institute, 148r, 180r, 181, 238; Courtesy of the Florence Knoll Bassett papers, 1932–2000, in the Archives of American Art, Smithsonian Institution, 125l, 272, 340, 345, 348, 351, 352; Courtesy of the Aline and Eero Saarinen papers, 1857–1972, in the Archives of American Art, Smithsonian Institution, 185l, 288, 289; © Ezra Stoller/Esto, B, 3t, 5t, 6, 16–17, 53b, 54 (44), 62, 63b (56), 80t, 88 (vi), 94b, 95, 96l, 107 (xii), 108, 113t, 164t, 164b, 179r, 182l, 190b, 196t, 197l (xi), 199l, 199r, 201b, 202–3, 204r, 209br, 210l, 210b, 210r, 239 (236), 332b, 366; © Ezra Stoller/Courtesy of *Vogue*, Conde Nast Publications, Inc., 237; Courtesy Mr. & Mrs. Ronald Saarinen Swanson, 29, 31t; © Suomen Kuvalehti (photo by J. Pohjakallio), 336; © 1951 Time Inc., 47t; © 1955 Time Inc., 47b; © 1956 Time Inc., 46; © 1959 Time Inc., 93b; © Abba Tor PE, 76, 77, 200r; Courtesy University of Pennsylvania, Architectural Archives, Collection Venturi, Scott Brown, and Associates, 178r; © Tony Vaccaro, 337c (322); © Lawrence S. Williams Inc. Collection, The Athenaeum of Philadelphia, 205l, 205r; Courtesy Eero Saarinen Collection, Manuscripts and Archives, Yale University, 2, 8 (photo by Bernice Clark), 19, 20, 21, 49, 50b, 52, 53t, 58b, 64b, 68, 70, 71t, 71b, 72l, 72r, 75t (354), 75b, 79, 80b, 89, 92 (photo by Fotograf Teigen), 93 (82) (photo by Fotograf Teigen), 94t, 94c, 96r, 99, 104, 105, 109, 111, 112 (photo by GM Photographic), 113b (reprinted from *Look* magazine), 130b, 131c, 132l (photo by Howard S. Abbitt, Jr.), 135l, 142l, 143t, 143b, 144l, 144t, 145c (photo by Dearborn-Massar), 145r (photo by Dearborn-Massar), 145b, 146l, 147l, 147t, 151, 152l (photo by Warren Reynolds, Infinity Inc.), 152r (photo by Warren Reynolds, Infinity Inc.), 153r (photo by Warren Reynolds, Infinity Inc.), 153l, 154, 156c, 157, 158t, 158b, 159, 160, 161l, 162r, 162b, 164l (photo by GM Photographic), 165r (photo by Fritz Kaeser, K2 Photography), 166b, 167r, 168r (photo by H. R. Oakman), 169l, 170, 171l, 171r, 172–73, 174l, 174r, 177, 178l (photo by Dan Page), 184t, 184r, 185r, 188, 189t, 191l (116–17), 191b, 191r, 193l, 194t, 195, 196b, 198l, 198t, 198b, 200l, 201t, 204l, 208 (photo by Cervin Robinson), 209r (i–ii) (photo by Cervin Robinson), 210c (photo by Harold Corsini), 211, 212l, 212c (photo by Dan Page), 212r (photo by C. T. Alburtis), 213t, 214r, 215, 217l, 217r, 219r, 220, 221r, 225, 226, 227, 231, 233t (230), 234t, 234b, 242, 251t (photo by Wurts Brothers), 251b, 254t (246), 254b, 255, 261, 267, 274 (266), 277, 279l, 279r, 281 (276), 282t, 282b, 290b, 290c (photo by Fotograf Teigen), 291 (photo by Fotograf Teigen), 292, 296, 297c, 297b, 301, 304c, 304b, 304t (300), 305, 306, 309, 314b (308), 314t , 315t, 315b, 315r, 316t, 317, 318, 319, 324t (photo by P. J. Bogelund), 325t, 326t, 327cb, 330t, 330b, 332t, 333t, 334b, 335 (photo by Scott Hyde), 336, 337t, 337c, 338t, 338c, 338b, 339t, 339c, 339b; Courtesy Yale University Art Gallery, Art Library, Transfer, Gift of Aline Saarinen, 324c, 325b, 327t, 327ct, 327b.